The World as a Company Town

World Anthropology

General Editor

SOL TAX

Patrons

CLAUDE LÉVI-STRAUSS
MARGARET MEAD
LAILA SHUKRY EL HAMAMSY
M. N. SRINIVAS

MOUTON PUBLISHERS · THE HAGUE · PARIS
DISTRIBUTED IN THE USA AND CANADA BY ALDINE, CHICAGO

The World as a Company Town

Multinational Corporations and Social Change

Editors

AHAMED IDRIS-SOVEN
ELIZABETH IDRIS-SOVEN
MARY K. VAUGHAN

MOUTON PUBLISHERS · THE HAGUE · PARIS

DISTRIBUTED IN THE USA AND CANADA BY ALDINE, CHICAGO

301.183
W 927

Distributed in the United States of America and Canada
by Aldine Publishing Company, Chicago, Illinois
ISBN 90–279–7610–4 (Mouton)
ISBN 0–202–90070–3 (Aldine)
Jacket photo by permission of ABC Press, Amsterdam
Jacket photo by Allen Bruce Zee
Indexes by Society of Indexers, Great Britain
Cover and jacket design by Jurriaan Schrofer
Phototypeset in V.I.P. Times by
Western Printing Services Ltd, Bristol
Printed in Great Britain

General Editor's Preface

Anthropology, born on the silver-spoon side of the colonial system, was colored by the biases and interests of its own background. *Anthropologists* were, however, self-selected for their interest in people on the other side, and sooner than others came to understand and to empathize with the poor, the powerless, the oppressed. We might have been more helpful to them had we devoted our talents also to understanding the rich and the powerful; but we were small in number and the tools which we developed were not then adapted to this difficult task. Only now — and perhaps demonstrated in the present book better than in any effort so far in anthropology — do we seem ready to study the changing power structure as it bears on the lives of the rapidly increasing numbers of poor. Probably we had to wait until we could be joined in the task by some of the victims of colonialism; and it may be more than symbolic that this book emerges from a worldwide congress of anthropologists which included a powerful representation from the "Third World."

Even leaving aside colonialism, anthropology — like most contemporary sciences — is a product of a single (European or Western) tradition. If we are to understand the species, our science needs substantial input from scholars who represent a variety of the world's cultures. It was a deliberate purpose of the IXth International Congress of Anthropological and Ethnological Sciences to provide impetus in this direction. The *World Anthropology* volumes, therefore, offer a first glimpse of a human science in which members from all societies have played an active role. Each of the books is designed to be self-contained; each is an attempt to update its particular sector of scientific knowledge and is written by specialists from all parts of the world. Each volume should be read and reviewed individually as a separate volume on its own given subject. The set as a whole will indicate what changes are in store for anthropology as scholars from the developing countries join in studying the species of which we are all a part.

The IXth Congress was planned from the beginning not only to include as many of the scholars from every part of the world as possible, but also with a view toward the eventual publication of the papers in high-quality volumes. At previous Congresses scholars were invited to bring papers which were then read out loud. They were necessarily limited in length; many were only summarized; there was little time for discussion; and the sparse discussion could only be in one language. The IXth Congress was an experiment aimed at changing this. Papers were written with the intention of exchanging them before the Congress, particularly in extensive pre-Congress sessions; they were not intended to be read aloud at the Congress, that time being devoted to discussions — discussions which were simultaneously and professionally translated into five languages. The method for eliciting the papers was structured to make as representative a sample as was allowable when scholarly creativity — hence self-selection — was critically important. Scholars were asked both to propose papers of their own and to suggest topics for sessions of the Congress which they might edit into volumes. All were then informed of the suggestions and encouraged to re-think their own papers and the topics. The process, therefore, was a continuous one of feedback and exchange and it has continued to be so even after the Congress. The some two thousand papers comprising *World Anthropology* certainly then offer a substantial sample of world anthropology. It has been said that anthropology is at a turning point; if this is so, these volumes will be the historical direction-markers.

As might have been foreseen in the first post-colonial generation, the large majority of the Congress papers (82 percent) are the work of scholars identified with the industrialized world which fathered our traditional discipline and the institution of the Congress itself: Eastern Europe (15 percent); Western Europe (16 percent); North America (47 percent); Japan, South Africa, Australia, and New Zealand (4 percent). Only 18 percent of the papers are from developing areas: Africa (4 percent); Asia-Oceania (9 percent); Latin America (5 percent). Aside from the substantial representation from the U.S.S.R. and the nations of Eastern Europe, a significant difference between this corpus of written material and that of other Congresses is the addition of the large proportion of contributions from Africa, Asia, and Latin America. "Only 18 percent" is two to four times as great a proportion as that of other Congresses; moreover, 18 percent of 2,000 papers is 360 papers, 10 times the number of "Third World" papers presented at previous Congresses. In fact, these 360 papers are more than the total of ALL papers published after the last International Congress of Anthropological and Ethnological Sciences which was held in the United States (Philadelphia, 1956).

The significance of the increase is not simply quantitative. The input of scholars from areas which have until recently been no more than subject matter for anthropology represents both feedback and also long-awaited theoretical contributions from the perspectives of very different cultural, social, and historical traditions. Many who attended the IXth Congress were convinced that anthropology would not be the same in the future. The fact that the next Congress (India, 1978) will be our first in the "Third World" may be symbolic of the change. Meanwhile, sober consideration of the present set of books will show how much, and just where and how, our discipline is being revolutionized.

Readers of this book will be interested in others in the series which show how modern anthropology treats the cultures of the world and problems of urbanization, migration, ethnicity, education, modernization, etc., — not to mention the politics of the profession itself.

Chicago, Illinois   SOL TAX
May 12, 1978

Table of Contents

Introduction

AHAMED IDRIS-SOVEN, ELIZABETH IDRIS-SOVEN, and
MARY K. VAUGHAN

This volume is the result of a panel on multinational corporations held at the IXth International Congress of Anthropological and Ethnological Sciences. There, anthropologists, economists, sociologists, historians, and community organizers discussed various aspects of the multinational corporation (MNC) and its importance as an area for investigation. From the panel emerged three major themes into which we have divided the material in this book.

In the first part, we discuss the MNC in a global context: its structure and impact on society and the ecosystem. In the second part, the MNC is considered within the context of social science research. In the final part, we include case studies linking the MNC to social change in different areas of the world and at different levels of sociopolitical organization, i.e., the tribal community and the peasant village, the plantation, the nation-state, and internationally.

Our treatment of the MNC and its impact on culture and people is far from exhaustive. Because research on the social impact of the MNC is in its beginning stages, analysis is often tentative and subject to discussion and revision. We seek to stimulate further research by presenting a broad perspective on MNC-related change.

The multinational corporation (MNC) is primarily a firm of North American, European, or Japanese origin engaged in manufacturing, agriculture, banking, finance, raw-material extraction, processing, and distribution in several countries. Between 1969 and 1973 alone, total foreign assets of U.S.-based MNC's rose from $108 billion to $165 billion. The MNC is involved in a process of global extension, rationalization, and integration, penetrating all available capital and consumer markets. It is predicted that by the year 2000, three hundred MNC's will account for 90 percent of world production and services (CIC Brief

1973: 3a). Because of actual and potential power over international production, the MNC challenges the autonomy of the individual nation-state, which finds itself a captive of the MNC and increasingly unable to cope with the problems that multinationals create: problems of inflation, unemployment, resource misutilization, and environmental destruction. The advance of the MNC depends on a delicate balance between capital-owning classes of individual nation-states and an emerging capitalist class.

The effect of MNC's on workers in advanced industrial countries is beginning to be felt. The MNC generates inflation by setting prices to cover the costs of expansion and expensive technology, by influencing the value of currency through speculation, and by forcing the expansion of the monetary supply through the accumulation and reinvestment of capital at ever-increasing rates. Appropriation of surplus value, use of automated production techniques, and the transfer of industrial jobs abroad aggravate a situation of chronic unemployment. In advanced capitalist countries, the attempt to correct a condition of under-consumption by consumer-debt financing, the creation of false needs through advertising, and military expenditures exert pressure on the monetary supply to expand. The consequence is a situation of spiralling prices, declining incomes, and growing unemployment.

Some inflationary factors that may seem unrelated to the MNC's are in fact closely associated with them. For instance, it is argued that increased demand for industrial raw materials such as oil and chemicals pushes prices up. Multinationals not only control the sources, processing, distribution, and hence the prices of these raw materials, but also determine how, where, and at what rate they will be used. That manufacturing today is based upon the ecologically destructive petrochemical industry is a case in point. As Anthony Wilden points out in his article on ecology, multinationals are engaged in a process of so misusing the world's natural resources that ecological problems are probably not soluble within the present system of production with its law of unabated growth for the sake of capital accumulation.

Wilden also begins to raise questions about the assumptions of Western thought and social science that prevent us from perceiving the depth of the ecosystem's crisis. Indeed, the system of production today represented by the MNC exercises a growing impact not only on our scientific conceptions but also on our culture and social relations. The ways in which the economy produces a proliferation of material goods, alters behavior patterns, encourages values such as competition and conspicuous consumption, fosters alienation, and depresses creativity have scarcely been analyzed, and yet such analyses are crucial if we are to cope with the crises ahead.

Although the entire complex of consumer culture is being transferred increasingly to the Third World through the symbols of Coca-Cola, Sony, and Colgate-Palmolive, to the Third World the MNC is not an entirely new institution. As George Beckford illustrates in his study of West Indian peasants and plantation workers, sugar corporations such as Tate and Lyle represent a system by which the Europeans have drained the Caribbean of its wealth since the sixteenth century. From 1492 onward the Third World served Europe as a source of raw materials, specie, agricultural products, and markets for manufactured goods. Capitalism for the Third World has meant depriving peoples of their traditional means of subsistence in order to create a class of laborers for the production of crops and minerals for export.

In South Africa, as Bernard Magubane explains in this volume, Europeans seized the major portion of land in "wars of conquest," forcing Africans onto inadequate marginal lands where they provided pools of cheap labor for the mines and more recently for urban industry. In colonial Latin America the Spaniards engaged in a similar process of expropriation, which metropolitan powers intensified in the late nineteenth century when their demand for plantation and mineral products increased.

Where further expropriation was impossible, the colonizer found other means of augmenting the labor supply. From China and India cheap labor was imported into Africa, Latin America, and the Caribbean. In the West Indies peasants were induced to work for plantations through the imposition of taxes and prohibitions against squatting. In many areas of the Third World at the end of the nineteenth century, the philosophy of European liberalism that emphasized the values of private property, work, and competition legitimized the breaking up of communities and taxation of the poor in order to "root out idleness and train them in the arts of civilization." The ideology of civilization through work, states Magubane, was merely "a smokescreen for the most sinister scheme of proletarianization."

Often Europeans allowed the traditional structure of indigenous society to remain superficially intact: they introduced only such changes as would allow for the appropriation of labor and other forms of wealth. Traditional authorities became a privileged class of property owners identifying with the colonizer. The chief in South Africa and the *curaca* or *cacique* in Latin America acted as both labor recruiter and policeman. He also acted as middleman, facilitating the peasantry's role as consumers of European-produced goods. As the contributors to this volume suggest, the peasant community exists in relation to the dominant European society. Concepts such as "dualism" or "pluralism," Gerrit Huizer and Bernard Magubane point out, are false concepts obscuring clear-cut relationships between community and society that must be analyzed if social change is to be understood.

Is anthropology, as John H. Bodley argues in this volume, no more than a product of European civilization designed to serve its aggressive ends? The real causes of ethnocide or "acculturation," Bodley suggests, are not the "inevitability of advancing civilization" but the direct result of economic, political, and ideological policies facilitating the exploitation of tribal resources for the benefit of industrial civilization. All too often anthropologists rationalize "a process of conquest in which a single technologically powerful culture type forces other, less-powerful cultures to comply with its wishes." Certain factors, Bodley points out, are involved in the ecological stability of indigenous communities. These include the land-man ratio, a world view making people a part of nature and not its conquerors, wealth-levelling devices, and local self-sufficiency that prevents forces from being applied to the local ecosystem that are unresponsive to changes in those systems. "When these and other stabilizing factors are weakened, the way is opened for perpetual relative deprivation [poverty] and rapid environmental deterioration." This process of underdevelopment has taken place throughout the Third World.

While some regions of the globe escaped resource depletion in the past because metropolitan centers lacked the technology to extend their domain to remote areas, today no part of the world is immune. As the Trans-Amazonia Highway barrels through the hunting grounds of tribal peoples, U.S. and European mining, oil, lumber, and agribusiness firms expropriate Indian land with full assistance from the Brazilian government. Should anthropologists accept this process as the "waning of the primitive world," asks Shelton Davis, or should they document the morbid social realities and assist in a campaign for Indian survival? Instead of gathering the "exotica of native myth," anthropologists might, he suggests, compile exact accounts of present tribal land systems to prepare legal briefs in defense of the Indians' rights. They might expose the role of the MNC's in the despoliation process. Such a task has been undertaken by one group, the Deltec Research Project, whose research on the Deltec Corporation is contained in this volume.

In recent years the MNC has intensified poverty in rural areas of the Third World. Priority given to industrialization often involves decapitalization of the countryside, stimulating the expulsion of thousands from the land. Puerto Rico is a classic example. When capitalization of agriculture occurs, it also tends to increase unemployment. Mechanization in the West Indies, noted by George Beckford, is a trend in export agriculture dominated by plantation corporations and, more recently, by U.S. agribusiness. In Mexico, where U.S. agribusiness dominates both export and domestic food production, small-scale farmers cannot compete nor can they find alternative employment on the mechanized farm.

Further, nonagricultural MNC's are bidding for land. Beckford notes that the penetration of mining, tourism, and "land development" corporations in the Caribbean reduces the amount of land available to the peasantry. This trend is further documented by Mina Davis Caulfield in her treatment of Grand Cayman island. In Western Samoa, Paul Shankman explains, a U.S. lumber firm has leased potential agricultural land at a time when population pressure requires more food production. The firm not only is cutting food production but also cannot provide jobs for those dispossessed of land.

A historical byproduct of foreign penetration and resource monopolization in rural areas has been the creation of a surplus labor force obliged to migrate in search of employment. In recent decades, rural migrants have swelled the ranks of the jobless in cities where machine-oriented MNC's cannot hire them. They subsist by doing marginal service-oriented work. In countries where the industrial revolution first took place, production developed by way of gradual substitution of new forms in factory organization and technique. Capital accumulated at the cost of marginalizing the Third World allowed for the sophistication of technology now transferred to the poor countries. Not only does the capital intensity of MNC technology offer relatively few jobs in areas of mounting unemployment, but also it creates even more unemployment by eliminating the more labor-intensive local firms. It may limit employment further when it fails to create backward and forward linkages in the economy. As Paul Shankman notes, decisions on inputs for production and their sources and on location of production and market destinations are made within the context of the global corporate economy rather than the context of the development needs of the nation in which the firm locates. Al Gedicks shows in his analysis of the U.S.-owned Chilean copper industry that Anaconda and Kennecott created neither backward linkages in utilizing local equipment or raw materials nor forward linkages in refining and fabricating copper in Chile.

In this volume, Steven W. Langdon challenges the myth of export-oriented development as a solution to growing unemployment. Because of the capital-intensive nature of import-substitution industrialization, it is often argued that a viable alternative lies in export-oriented development whereby the more labor-intensive firms in electronics, food processing, and textiles would move to the Third World to exploit cheap labor in the manufacture of a product to be exported to industrialized countries. In the case of Kenya, Langdon discovered that export-oriented firms tended toward capital-intensive production conforming to metropolitan product standards and technological levels and in keeping with the parent company's conviction that needed labor can and should be reduced to a minimum. Importing most of their inputs, these firms stifled the development of backward linkages in the national economy, while forward linkages were limited by the global production schemes of the companies. This particular line of development tends also to be unstable.

Without roots in the local economy, the MNC may transfer production elsewhere if headquarters strategy changes or local costs of production rise. Puerto Rico, whose early industrialization was based almost exclusively on the export-oriented, labor-intensive firm, is rapidly losing this source of employment to cheaper and more politically docile areas such as Haiti and the Dominican Republic.

In rare cases MNC penetration may generate a situation of temporary overemployment, as in the construction industry sparked by the mercurial tourist and tax-haven trades in Grand Cayman island, described by Mina Davis Caulfield. However, deepening unemployment is the trend in Third World countries. In Latin America the total number of unemployed rose from 2.9 million in 1950 to 8.8 million in 1965. While the labor force in agriculture dropped from 62.4 percent of the total in 1925 to 46.1 percent in 1965, the manufacturing sector employed almost exactly the same share of the population in 1965 as it did in 1925. The service sector — "a well-known catchall for disguised unemployment" — absorbed most of the increment in the labor force (Pompermayer 1973). The paucity of employment in Third World metropolitan areas has forced migration to European and North American industrial centers: Mexican and Puerto Rican workers man assembly lines at Zenith in Chicago; Dominicans, Colombians, and Haitians compete with Puerto Ricans and Afro-Americans to push racks in New York's garment district; West Indians drive London's buses; Turkish, Algerian, Spanish, and Portuguese workers crowd together in ramshackle Citröen dormitories in Paris suburbs. Uprooted from their cultures, often separated from their families, subject to discrimination, generally unprotected by labor unions, and harassed by immigration authorities, these people form a permanently migrating pool of surplus labor as well as cultural pockets divorced from the mainstream of society.

Because of the concern of U.S. policymakers to know the revolutionary potential of unemployed rural migrants in the Third World and of Third World minorities in the United States, most U.S. social scientists in their work among slum-dwellers have examined attitudes, expectations, and potential for politicization rather than documented the grim realities of urban slum life. Assuring us that the urban poor are not to be feared, most of these studies emphasize factors inhibiting politicization — such as perceptions of betterment over the rural situation and contentment with minor improvements. Although we do not doubt the weight of these factors, is this type of research a reflection of the class bias of social scientists? Is it, as Gedicks and Huizer suggest, a reflection of class distance, insensitivity, and biased research methods and techniques? How do social scientists explain the extensive politicization of Chilean slum-dwellers during Allende's regime, frequent urban land invasions in Mexico and Colombia, the proliferation of the community-control movement in the United States, and the recent development of caucuses and unions of migrant workers in the United States and Europe?

Why do we investigate the attitudes of the poor toward their situation when we might, as Magubane argues, investigate the role migrants play for the dominant class in keeping wages low and in dividing workers and inhibiting their ability to organize? Why not examine the tactics of the dominant society designed to prevent politicization — such as police repression, the fostering of racial antagonisms, the creation of co-optive, bureaucratic "community improvement" programs, and the system of formal education, which imposes models of the dominant culture, denigrates the poor, and dangles before them the distant possibility of mobility if they work hard and play by the rules of the society? Why not investigate *how* the migrants' attitudes are formed? For instance, in our panel discussion, Joe Collins of the Institute for Policy Studies referred to a study financed by the advertising firms of McCann-Erickson and J. Walter Thompson among slum-dwellers in Caracas. This study suggested that advertising has the effect of dampening class consciousness and creating the illusion that with "luck" the same goods are available to all.

Advertising is an extremely important area for study. Indeed, dependent development in the Third World involves the creation of false needs just as it does in the advanced industrialized nations. The criterion for the production of a particular commodity is not its utility but the possibility of selling it, which depends upon manipulating demand through creating wants. In moving to another country, the MNC prefers not to alter its product. Rather than concentrating research and development efforts on adjusting production to the requirements of the local economy, the MNC is more likely to research ways of making, for example, Colgate toothpaste more appealing to the Brazilian, Jamaican, or British people (Girling 1973a:50). Despite arguments that the MNC exports technology for the "provision of abundance," its technology is highly specific, attached to a given product, and not easily transferable to other sectors of the economy. Automobile technology, as David Barkin illustrates, is limited in its application. In capital-scarce countries the decision to produce family cars for a restricted market rather than mass public transportation and heavy machinery represents a critical misallocation of resources.

Anthropologists and other social scientists have too often assumed that the consumption of modern products such as transistor radios, televisions, machine-made clothing, and Pepsi-Cola in poverty-stricken areas is an indication of progress. On the contrary, the question to examine is the specific utility of a product in relation to other potential investments the country might undertake. Many of the modern goods foisted on peasants through the persistent colonial or neocolonial market apparatus are superfluous, while others can be frankly damaging. Collins suggested in our panel discussion that the elaboration of chemical-based inferior food by U.S. agribusiness has contributed to the decline of nutritional intake in countries such as Mexico. How many Mexicans are more likely to consume Hostess Twinkies and Pepsi-Cola than eggs today? In the case of Grand Cayman, Mina Davis Caulfield demonstrates how the process of penetration by MNC's has resulted in the destruction of local agriculture and fishing: the former protein-rich diet of the Caymanians has been replaced by imported canned food.

Despite pretensions of providing "abundance," the MNC probably contributes to increasing income inequality in the Third World. Development economists put forward a Keynesian argument to justify income inequality in early stages of growth: concentrated wealth will encourage investment for increased production and employment. This model does not consider the historical relationship between advanced industrial nations and poor countries. It does not account for profits repatriated by MNC's, the tendency of local elites to invest in MNC's outside their nations, and capital-intensive technology, which limits employment. Inequality worsens as the pools of jobless and underemployed grow, while their presence holds wages down. Those with steady work find restrictions against trade-union organization an obstacle to defending themselves against inflation, which the MNC generates in the cost of its imported technology, restricted production, and price-setting tactics.

Income inequality is perpetuated in dependent industrialization tied to local elites. While the Keynesian model assumes competition, monopoly of wealth and political power is characteristic of Third World countries (Girling 1973b:90). Economic opportunity is open to those with political power, whose interest in profit rather than development influences their growing association with the multinationals. That the dominant political-bureaucratic bourgeoisie stands to gain in influence and wealth through collaboration with the MNC's is shown by Steven Langdon in the case of Kenya. There, Associated Portland Cement Manufacturers of England and the U.S.-owned Continental Ore Company coveted the fluorspar deposits operated by a local Swahili entrepreneur. Through their contact with the Kenyan Government the foreign firms succeeded in stripping the local businessman of his claim and persuaded the government to establish a joint venture through which the political elite apparently sacrificed Kenyan control over a valuable mineral for their own particular gain. Langdon further illustrates how the political influences of MNC's with the local government, manifest in large concessions in finance, land, and taxes, banking and import-restriction exemptions, and generous profit-remittance allowances, place the local economy at the mercy of foreign corporations, who control markets, prices, the amount of national income retained, and the direction of its reinvestment.

It may be argued that distinctions must be made between political-bureaucratic elites in the less-industrialized Third World countries and elites with historically well-developed economic interests, such as those of the larger Latin American nations. However, the tendency of the latter toward partnership with the multinationals is well-documented here in the articles on Deltec, which explain the process through which foreign corporations gain control over the direction of investment, development, and resource utilization in countries such as Argentina and Brazil. This phenomenon has led Malori Pompermayer and William C. Smith to note that in the largest Latin American countries — Brazil, Mexico, and Argentina — the state increasingly represents a horizontal integration of the local industrial bourgeoisie, segments of the state bureaucracy and armed forces, and external bourgeoisies in the MNC's, foreign governments, and international agencies. National integration and internal transformation of the social structure become secondary considerations as society and economy are "reorganized around the axis of a restrictive industrialization model" accompanied by increasing income inequality and political demobilization, including repression of independent trade unions and political groups. The regulatory and administrative capacity of the state is modernized in planning, infrastructural development, and national security to facilitate the penetration of foreign business (Pompermayer and Smith 1973).

This process, which assumes an unequivocal partnership between national and foreign entrepreneurs, is not without contradictions. Some sectors of the national bourgeoisie in the Third World countries occasionally demonstrate effective if singular opposition to multinationals. Such was the case when an Argentine magistrate defeated Deltec's attempt to sabotage the Argentine meat industry, as explained in this volume. While such cases are more exceptional than general, national bourgeois governments in many countries have found in the natural wealth of their nations a new and exceedingly powerful weapon with which to bargain with metropolitan countries and MNC's. The Arab oil embargo of 1973 and the rise of the Organization of Petroleum Exporting Countries are important challenges to MNC monopolies over the valuable industrial minerals of the Third World. While this movement weakens the hegemony of the metropolitan countries and increases the cost of living in them, it remains to be seen how national bourgeois governments will reinvest their increased revenues. Will oil-rich countries invest in the genuine development of their own and other Third World nations, as Fidel Castro has urged, or will they continue to pour their funds into General Motors and Chase Manhattan Bank?

In this volume we discuss ways of coping with the problems created by multinationals. Bruce Vandervort, former assistant to the General Secretary of the International Union of Foodworkers, explains the strategy of the international labor movement in linking workers along industrial and MNC lines to confront industry as an international working class. He gives instances of international strike solidarity and the activities of global industrial workers' councils in coordinating actions against the companies.

Al Gedicks, on the other hand, in his analysis of the Chilean copper industry, argues that the state can serve as a vehicle for redressing the critical imbalances that MNC's create. Nationalization of the copper industry under the Unidad Popular government of Salvador Allende was designed to integrate the copper industry with national industrial development and employment needs. Many of the problems created by multinationals seem beyond the scope of traditional trade unions. As George Beckford emphasizes, trade unions in the West Indies have played a key role in protecting plantation workers' wages and jobs and in achieving national independence in coalition with political parties, but they cannot as trade unions solve the mounting crisis of unemployment. Because dependent development involves critical resource misallocation, the state is probably one of the only institutions capable of repairing this misallocation.

It is within this context that movements of national liberation in the Third World, based upon the participation of workers and peasants and committed to meeting their needs, are perhaps the most critical counterforce in the world today. At the moment, national liberation movements in Latin America, Africa, and Asia demonstrate far less confusion on the crucial issues of survival and human well-being than do distinctly bourgeois states of the Third World or those of us in the industrialized world, who are, as technical and production workers, frustrated and confused in our attempts to cope with runaway inflation, structural unemployment, uncontrolled technology, consumer ideology, and the rude unmasking of the undemocratic practices of our so-called democracies. Most of us vaguely understand that the very survival of the world ecosystem is likely not to be guaranteed within the present structure of economic relations with its law of insatiable growth. Most of us find our ability to grapple with these issues paralyzed by our programmed isolation, our sense of helplessness, and our political inexperience. But the objective situation — which is in fact a question of human survival — demands our fullest attention, energy, and commitment at all levels — in trade unions, in political parties and organizations, and in consumer and community-action groups. Any form of action, however, must be based upon a clear analysis of realities, to which this volume may contribute in a preliminary way.

REFERENCES

CIC BRIEF
1973 *An examination of the multinational corporation.* New York Corporate Information Center.

GIRLING, ROBERT
1973a "Dependency, technology and development," in *Structures of dependency.* Edited by Frank Bonilla and Robert Girling. Palo Alto: Stanford University Press.
1973b "Dependency and persistent income inequality," in *Structures of dependency.* Edited by Frank Bonilla and Robert Girling. Palo Alto: Stanford University Press.

POMPERMAYER, MALORI
1973 "Dependency and unemployment: some issues,' in *Structures of dependency.* Edited by Frank Bonilla and Robert Girling. Palo Alto: Stanford University Press.

POMPERMAYER, M., W. C. SMITH
1973 "The state in dependent societies: preliminary notes," in *Structures of dependency.* Edited by Frank Bonilla and Robert Girling. Palo Alto: Stanford University Press.

SECTION ONE

The Multinational Corporation in a Global Context

Multinational Corporations: The World as a Company Town

Movements of international capital have changed significantly in the last twenty years. Scholars have had a difficult time keeping up with the changes as old models prove inadequate to incorporate new data. The international economy has had an impact on the lives of ordinary Americans in a baffling and disturbing way. The purpose of this paper is to define some of the changes that have taken place. In the following analysis, I am indebted to the work of Charles Levinson, general secretary of the International Chemical Workers, whose book, *Capital, inflation and the multinationals* (1972), helped my understanding of the influence of the multinational corporation (MNC) on our lives as citizens of the United States. In this article, I have combined material from many sources — especially from business periodicals and journals. In broad outlines, I have relied upon Levinson except in areas in which I find his treatment weak. For instance, he is concerned almost exclusively with the most advanced sector of capitalism — the most heavily capitalized, largest global industries (oil, petrochemicals, electronics and metallurgy) and workers within them. For him, the struggle of the future is one between management and labor in the most advanced sector of the most advanced countries. For most of the world, this is not the struggle. Levinson is almost entirely silent on the problems of multinational corporate penetration of the Third World.

It is his analysis of the "heart" of the advanced industrial world that is informative, for Levinson addresses himself to questions that Americans face every day as they ask why economist politicians have been unable to alleviate the problems of rising prices and unemployment. Fiscal, monetary, and income policies have not solved the problems of the economy for masses of Americans. These policies have been based on assumptions of Keynesian economics, which reflect an earlier industrial experience.

According to Keynesian theory, reduced demand for goods and services through wage controls will lower prices while allowing for increased profits for increasing investment in expanding industrial capacity, which in turn will increase the level of employment and the volume of goods and services. As the cures have not worked, the assumptions must be questioned. Prices rise, unemployment deepens, and industrial capacity has not significantly expanded.

According to Levinson, the cause for failure is the refusal to recognize a major structural change which he locates in the emergence of the MNC (Levinson 1972:30–31). The MNC does not primarily invest in expanding domestic industrial capacity for increased employment. Its investment is in technology for labor displacement and in foreign ventures that fail to augment industrial capacity and hence the level of employment in this country. Unprecedented amounts of capital are required for this form of investment. To meet investment needs, companies must raise their prices despite falling demand. The crucial issue here is cash flow, or a firm's retained earnings plus depreciation after wages, dividends, and taxes have been deducted. Financing investment requires increasing cash flow, obtained through raising prices through introducing labor-saving technology and through global rationalization and integration, which involves penetrating all available capital and consumer markets, producing in cheap labor areas, and exporting to high-priced ones. It also requires the manipulation of accounts to allow the corporation to escape paying taxes in high-tax countries.

The MNC is not an exclusively American phenomenon although the United States introduced it. Of the top ten MNC's, eight are U.S.-based, and two are Anglo-Dutch. Of the top one hundred corporations, sixty-three are U.S.-based, twenty-nine are European, and eight are Japanese (*Tribune de Genève* 1972). The MNC comprises only one sector of the U.S. economy, but it is the dynamic sector principally engaged in oil, chemicals, plastics, electronics, and metal, especially in the automotive industry. In the United States at the present time, fewer than 200 of 200,000 firms possess more than 60 percent of the nation's capital (Levinson 1972:40). According to *Fortune*, the nation's 500 leading industrial firms account for 65 percent of sales and 79 percent of profits and employment of all U.S. enterprises (*Fortune* 1974:231). Raymond Vernon estimates that 187 firms account for 80 percent of U.S. foreign investment and more than half the volume of U.S. manufactured exports. Company mergers and the concomitant rise of the multiproductive, multi-industrial multinational giant are increasing at a rapid rate. In 1968, there were 40,000 mergers in the United States; the rate of mergers rose by 72 percent in 1969 and 80 percent in 1970. The largest companies have access to or control the nation's money supply through their integration with banks and with each other and through their penetration of the world's economy. As Levinson points out, the huge sums of capital required to enter this exclusive group assure protected positions to just a few firms. According to Harold Perlmutter of the Wharton School of Finance, within the next decade 300 supergiants — U.S., European, and Japanese — will dominate business, producing more than half the world's industrial output (Tyler 1972:2).

Through growing joint ventures, financial links, and other forms of interpenetration, the largest companies are closely bound up with one another and so administer prices. According to Levinson, more than 80 percent of consumer prices in the United States are administered by agreements between these companies (Levinson 1972:214). They compete not through prices but through advertising, discounts, product quality and differentiation, and global integration of production and distribution — all of which require vast amounts of investment capital in research and development (R and D) and extension. The fastest-growing sector of the economy in terms of productivity, the lowest in relative labor costs, the MNC's are in a better position to lower prices than the marginal, labor-intensive sector. On the contrary, they jointly increase prices in order to increase their retained earnings for further investment. While the giants will control more than 80 percent of corporate assets in this country in 1985, they will employ only one-tenth of the labor force (Levinson 1972:84). Their capital investment is not for increasing industrial capacity and jobs at home but for global concentration, rationalization, and integration.

It is the purpose of this paper to examine the two major components of capital investment — research and development and foreign investment — in order to understand some of the repercussions this investment has on workers and consumers in the United States and abroad. Investment for R and D absorbs the greater part of capital investment — more than 65 percent, according to Levinson (Levinson 1972:63). R and D serves two purposes: technological innovation for labor displacement and the development of new product lines, which in themselves may be labor-displacing, e.g. electronic office equipment.[1] Through military contracts, U.S. taxpayers have financed a large part of R and D for private industry. An examination of the contracts awarded to General Electric, Honeywell, Westinghouse, and others for development of the air war in Indochina would indicate the use of new electronic and chemical devices for peace-time application — notwithstanding the firms' eagerness to use public funds for destructive purposes. While two-thirds of private industry's R and D expenditures were financed by the government in 1963, the figure is considerably less today — thus increasing the capital investment

[1] For a good discussion of the origins of the technological revolution see Magdoff (1969). For the best analysis of the impact of technological change on the structure of the labor force in the United States, see Braverman (1974).

needs of leading corporations and hence the upward pressure on consumer prices.

In terms of automation through technology, the United Nations estimates that more than 80 percent of gross national product (GNP) growth in industrialized countries as a whole is the result of technological innovation (Levinson 1972:51). In the United States and Sweden, the countries with the highest wages, labor contributes only 10 percent to GNP. By the year 2000, seven out of ten workers in the advanced industrial countries will be in the service sector: only three will be in production. In 1960, the reverse was the case (Levinson 1972:62). To name but one of the labor savers in the last few years, the flat-glass industry has been rationalized by an automated process system that requires the labor of only thirty-six workers. In contrast to vastly reduced labor costs, the new process cost $500 million in R and D alone. In the 1960's, computers invaded capital-intensive industry in data processing, scientific research, handling of payrolls, inventories, and orders, and in setting gauges and adjusting valves in oil refineries and steel mills. Completely automated computer control systems operate in oil and some chemical refining (Levinson 1972:47–48).

Automation in recent years has affected both white- and blue-collar workers. Ford Motor Company President Lee Iaccoca sees automation of assembly-line production as the challenge of the 1970's. International Business Machines' strategy involves a reduction of domestic employment at several levels in the years ahead. The electronic data-processing point-of-sales terminal — an elaborate cash register that cost $18 million to develop — can save users such as Sears and Jewel Food Stores, Inc., as much as 1 percent in gross sales through better management and inventory control and through cutting the number of clerical workers. Honeywell's Alpha 3000 Control Center will take the place of three engineers and five security officers for Kemper Insurance of Long Grove, Illinois, according to whom the direct labor savings alone will pay for the system in about three years (*Business Week* 1973d:53–54; *Wall Street Journal* 1972b; *Fortune* 1973:26).

According to Louis B. Knecht, executive vice-president of the Communications Workers of America, Bell Telephone has cut its work force by almost half since 1950. As Knecht points out, automation not only implies job loss but boredom and skill-downgrading for remaining workers as they watch computers tend their machines. What happens, he asks, to the machinist who used to work a machine for a week that now produces the same product in fifteen minutes without the "interference" of human hands? Does he watch the lights and push the buttons or does he cut out with severance pay (Knecht 1972:18)?

Automation cuts costs and the uncertainty caused by labor action. It is also a necessary step in competition. Partly in order to compete with the

Japanese, the U.S. steel industry reduced its labor force from 495,000 in 1965 to 367,000 in 1972 (*Business Week* 1972b:82). In the highly competitive brewery industry, Schlitz plants in Memphis and Winston-Salem each produce 4,400,000 barrels annually with only 483 workers, while the much smaller Falstaff plant has 1,800 workers in St. Louis producing 4,100,000 barrels annually. The Schlitz barrel costs $1.08 to produce while the Falstaff barrel costs $4.39. This phenomenon has two repercussions for workers. It allows Schlitz to ship beer from Winston-Salem to Brooklyn so that it can shut down its more labor-intensive Brooklyn plant. Secondly, it has forced the best-run breweries in recent years to automate so that one or two workers control all operations from a central panel (*Fortune* 1972:176).

The major development of the 1970's, writes Levinson, will be the computerization of machine operations with computer-directed tools taking over the machinery process, controlling conveyors, warehouse systems, and assembling (Levinson 1972:49). One glimpse of the new type of factory is the Pope and Talbott plant in Oakridge, Oregon, a completely computerized sawmill that will process wood chips for shipment to Japan (*Wall Street Journal* 1972b). This new kind of factory, to be built here and in other countries, will aggravate the problems of unemployment here and abroad.

The other crucial factor of capital investment that cuts and limits the expansion of productive capacity at home is foreign investment. Foreign investment quite obviously takes capital funds out of the country. Richard J. Barber, former counsel for the U.S. Senate Anti-Trust Committee, has stated that between 1958 and 1968, U.S. manufacturing increased its overseas capacity by 471 percent versus 71 percent at home. The problem is aggravated by foreign investment for imports or re-imports (parts sent abroad for assembling and then re-imported into the United States). Foreign investment directly reduces jobs in the United States when the product formerly manufactured here for export is now manufactured abroad and when U.S. corporations set up subsidiaries or contract foreign firms for importation of products they once manufactured in the United States.

According to Levinson (1972:68), U.S. foreign investment at the moment represents 12 percent of total U.S. private investment. If 12 percent of investment goes abroad and 65 percent is for labor-displacing technology, noncapacity and nonemployment investment represents three-quarters of the total. If Levinson's judgment is exaggerated, it describes a growing trend. Foreign investment should rise to 20 percent of total investment by the end of the decade, while GNP should increase by only 3 to 5 percent. The process of reduced growth at home and increased expenditure abroad is self-generating and will exercise increasing pressure on the world's monetary reserves insofar as an increasing portion of productive investment consists of capital raised in one country and sent to another (Levinson 1972:88–89). Evidence of such critical pressure is the dollar crisis, caused by $286 billion floating around the world and generated by U.S. capital exports.

The United States had $70 billion invested abroad in 1969; by the end of 1971, this figure had risen to more than $90 billion. Altogether, U.S. foreign direct spending, reinvestment of profits, and portfolio investment is over $120 billion. Thirty-two leading U.S. firms had more than half their net earnings outside the United States in 1970 — among them, Exxon, IBM, National Cash Register, Woolworth, Squibb, and Upjohn (Adam 1971:362). By the end of the decade over 35 percent of the West's non-U.S. production could be accounted for by U.S. subsidiaries and U.S.-associated firms (Levinson 1972:20). As Ludwell Denny wrote, "We are not without cunning. We shall not make Britain's mistake. Too wise to govern the world, we shall simply own it (Levinson 1972:91)."

Much has been said of the balance-of-payments and trade problems (excess of imports over exports), which in fact are caused by MNC's. The sales by U.S. firms overseas are more than five times the value of U.S. exports — a reversal of classical trends — and the proportion is increasing. Although exports of capital equipment and intermediate products generated by U.S. subsidiaries abroad have a disproportionate and negative impact on the Third World countries which import them, exports in the classical sense of physical exports figure less and less in the present economic equation. Hungarian economist Gy Adam estimates that U.S. firms produce six times as much overseas as they export from the United States (Adam 1972:309–310). As Levinson points out, it is management and capital that cross borders now. The new role of U.S. firms is to "industrialize" the distribution of credit on a global scale: "They will be concerned with the creation, distribution, and raising the profitability of capital" (Levinson 1972:133).

According to Gus Tyler writing in *The American Federationist* (1972:2), insofar as U.S. workers are concerned, the United States is engaged in a process of exchanging profits for jobs. The number of workers unemployed because of imports, now estimated to number one million, will continue to grow. In 1968, the U.S. Department of Commerce estimated that 14 percent of U.S. imports came from U.S. subsidiaries. For instance, practically all radios, tape recorders, casettes, and a growing number of TV's produced by U.S. corporations are imported. The Department of Commerce figure does not include imports from U.S. joint ventures, licensing arrangements, or foreign companies in which U.S. firms hold part interest. For example, Dodge Colts are made by Mitsubishi, in which Chrysler has a 15 percent interest.

Imports are fostered by U.S. corporations and banks. Major U.S. banks connected with the domestic steel industry heavily financed the development of Japanese steel, which undercut employment in the United States. When the U.S. textile industry objected to Japanese competition, three U.S. firms (Burlington Industries, J.P. Stevens, and Clark Schwebel Fiberglass) moved into the Japanese market in joint ventures with domestic firms. The corporation prospers as U.S. workers lose their jobs. Ford Motor Company's lagging negotiations with Toyo Kogyo alarmed the Japanese auto industry, for if Ford, the only major U.S. auto company without an interest in the Japanese car industry could reach an agreement with the Japanese firm, there would be no quota on Japanese car imports to the U.S. (Pacific Rim Project 1970:170). In view of such corporate collusion, U.S. labor's "Buy America" campaign appears wholly inadequate.

In analyzing the balance of trade and payments problems, we should note the changing nature of foreign investment. The earlier pattern of importing raw materials and exporting a finished product was one on which U.S. prosperity was based. Where the major portion of U.S. foreign investment prior to 1945 was in raw materials and primary industries, today the thrust is in manufacturing. The process of manufacturing abroad began after World War II with U.S. investment in Japan and Europe. As these countries quickly imitated U.S. product lines and technology, they set up tariff barriers against the import of U.S. manufactured goods and so forced U.S. firms to extend their manufacturing base within the countries themselves. To circumvent tariff barriers of the European Economic Community, U.S. investment in Europe increased by 500 percent between 1959 and 1969. The process of U.S. foreign investment has led Japanese and European firms into multinational investment so that, for example, in the U.S. alone in 1971, 700 manufacturing firms were partly or wholly owned by 500 foreign firms. With the recent dollar devaluation making U.S. firms "cheap" and the prices of imports into the U.S. "high," there has been a rush of foreign direct investment highlighted by British American Tobacco's acquisition of Kohl supermarkets, J. Lyons and Company's purchase of Squibb's beverage operations, and acquisitions by St. Gobain and Nestlés. To take advantage of the growing U.S. market for "luxury" products, Moet Hennessy, the prestigious French champagne maker, has launched an $8 million project in California's Napa Valley. To guard against further revaluations of the yen, which make Japanese imports expensive in relation to U.S. goods, and to avoid the possibility of an imposition of quotas on their exports, the Japanese are heavily investing in petrochemicals and electronics in the United States. They are willing to pay higher wages to preserve their biggest export market. However, like their American counterparts, they emphasize cutting labor costs. Their firms will be capital-intensive while they will try to exploit cheap labor by establishing plants in the southwest and in Puerto Rico.

Multinationalism means concentration and interpenetration within a rich-man's club of the largest and wealthiest U.S., European, and Japanese corporations and banks. The institution of the MNC is currently the joint venture between corporations of different national origin and between MNC's and national firms, banks, and governments. The joint venture is a means by which a firm preserves and enhances its competitive edge in the international market. The simplest joint venture is a marketing arrangement whereby a foreign firm penetrates a market via a domestic firm. For instance, Canon of Tokyo markets Microform Data Systems, Inc., products in Japan and the Pacific basin. Telecor, Inc., is the exclusive distributor in eleven western states and Alaska for Panasonic products of the Matshushita Electric Corporation. The initial marketing arrangement may proceed to the manufacturing stage. Thus Gillette entered a joint venture with Kaneblo, Ltd., of Osaka to make and sell toiletries in Japan.

In the Third World, the joint venture between MNC's and local governments and/or local firms draws upon local capital in a capital-scarce world and assures access to markets and raw materials while acting as a hedge against possible nationalization. Du Pont, which formerly avoided joint ventures with local parties, has entered two such arrangements in Mexico — one with the Banco de Comercio to modernize and expand a titanium dioxide plant and another in conjunction with the state financial development corporation and several private Mexican firms to build hydrofluoric acid facilities (*Business Week* 1973b:95).

Joint ventures *between* multinationals pool their marketing, technological talents, and capital in an increasingly competitive world. British Petroleum's acquisition of 54 percent of the stock of Standard Oil of Ohio will give Sohio access to BP's supplies of foreign crude oil and will give BP access to Sohio's domestic market. To pool capital for R and D in atomic energy, Gulf and Royal Dutch/Shell have entered a joint venture that will allow Shell to cash in on Gulf's Energy and Environmental System Company while giving Gulf the assistance of Shell's international marketing network (*Business Week* 1973c:36). In order to pool capital for exorbitant R and D expenditures and to penetrate the European market, United Aircraft and General Electric have each entered joint ventures with European firms to develop a new line of jet engines for commercial aircraft (*Business Week* 1973c:36). In order to compete with IBM, which has 56 percent of the European computer market, Siemens, CII of France, and Philips of Holland have integrated their computer operations in a single company, Unidata. Allis Chalmers and Fiat merged their construction operations worldwide, while the full merger between the British tire company, Dunlop, and the Italian giant, Pirelli, in order to survive in the face of U.S. competition, is well-known. Related to this pooling of huge amounts of capital is the creation of international consortia for the development of industry, infrastructure, or natural resources in Third World countries. Occidental Petroleum, Tokyo Gas Company, and El Paso Natural Gas, for example, plan to develop Siberia's natural gas resources (*Wall Street Journal* 1973). Such consortia have long been typical of the oil industry in exploration, ownership of wells and pipelines, etc.

Multinational banking follows the multinational firm. First National City Corporation has almost 300 branches or affiliations in sixty nations. Bank of America has branches and affiliations in eighty countries. Chase Manhattan, which outstrips Citicorp in international extension, was one of the first U.S. banks in Saigon and is the first to have a correspondent relationship with the People's Republic of China. International banking is truly international with no loyalties to the nation-state or nation of origin. It distinctly favors the largest corporations linked with the largest banks. Orion, Ltd., an international banking consortium put together by Chase Manhattan and involving the Royal Bank of Canada, National Westminster Bank, Ltd., of London, Westdeutsche Landesbank Giron-zentrale, Credito Italiano S.P.A., and Mitsubishi Bank, Ltd., is a new tool for doing international business on a huge scale. With access to the multi-currency resources of parent banks, it can, according to its creators, guarantee enormous, quick, and anonymous financing to the client who wants none of the publicity connected with syndicate financing. Pooling the global contacts, investments, and expertise of its members, it can potentially control whole blocks of world industry (*Wall Street Journal* 1973d).

As an unofficial rich-man's club, multinational corporations and banks penetrate Third World countries for reasons of their own. In a process of establishing global power and rationalization, the multinational cor-poration seeks to (1) assemble and produce parts, components, and final products at least cost, i.e., in cheap labor and supply areas; (2) to sell in the highest-priced markets, i.e., the industrialized countries; (3) to gain footholds in the capital and consumer markets of every country and every region with a view to absorbing available capital and servicing existing and potential local markets; and (4) to globalize operations in such a way as to avoid tax burdens in any single country.

There are two expansions of international capital to the Third World: one concerns capital-intensive industries and the other marginal, labor-intensive operations. The expansion of the U.S. auto industry in South-east Asia illustrates both cases as the capital-intensive industry exports its labor-intensive process abroad. Ford's plans for Southeast Asia call for the production of engines in South Korea, engine blocks in Thailand, electric motors and plastic components in Singapore, axles and trans-missions in Indonesia, steering wheels in Malaysia, and stamping in the Philippines. Final vehicle assembly will take place in locations throughout the region for export both within the region and outside it (the China market is one under consideration). GM has similar plans. The companies anticipate protection from a common market of the countries involved which will create multilateral tariff preferences for vehicle parts imported from within the group and steep tariffs on imports from outside the group.

At the present time, Ford Fieras are assembled in the Philippines while their power-train components are imported from Britain. Other parts are locally produced by Ford and other manufacturers. The company will increase the share of locally and regionally produced parts to reduce the costs of importing parts from high-wage countries. The company can then exploit cheap labor and supply sources while practicing economies of scale within the region. National entrepreneurs will benefit through joint ventures whereby the foreign company buys into existing local assembly and manufacturing plants and retail enterprises. Local owners then become dependent on the foreigner for patents, parts, models, production processes, shipping arrangements, and intercompany, cross-country trade arrangements. For the MNC, this type of venture represents a double hedge against nationalization: it effects a partnership with the local bourgeoisie while it prevents any single country from producing a whole automobile on its own.

GM and Ford envision the production of a standardized Asian vehicle: a small, doorless, four-wheel utility vehicle for transport of cargo and people. However, higher-priced cars and trucks will also be produced for export, while parts and components can likewise be shipped out of the area for assembly.[2] Scientific managers view global standardization of parts, components, and models as a means of cutting costs while boosting profits. Standardization is likewise important in resisting labor demands. Strikes can be ignored when production can be transferred elsewhere.

The auto industry is not alone in global rationalization, which is a general pattern among multinationals. Global rationalization has incalculable advantages in increasing cash flow through dodging taxes, which is accomplished through manipulation of accounts or transfer pricing. Through nonrepatriation of profits and profit transfers to tax havens like Liechtenstein, Bermuda, Curaçao, Panama, Switzerland, and the Virgin Islands, a company avoids paying taxes in high-tax countries. In addition, the global institution operating hand in hand with branch banks draws local capital into its coffers and is able to manipulate international currency markets to its own advantage. Whole sections of MNC management are devoted to manipulating currency markets and changing exchange rates. The purpose of this financial apparatus is to control as

---

[2]   Data on the auto industry is from Pacific Rim Project 1972b: 147–149.

much capital as possible and to reproduce it as efficiently and profitably as possible.

The second movement in foreign manufacturing predominates in the still labor-intensive industries, which export the runaway shop. Labor estimates that more than 700,000 jobs have been lost in the last five years as companies move their assembly operations abroad. Runaway plants are generally established by industries in which labor costs are relatively high and economies of scale are not great: canned and frozen fruits and vegetables, textiles, clothing, leather, furniture and wood products, simple machine tools, sewing machines, components and spare parts, electrical parts and assemblies (Adam 1971:352). Thus far the home firm has transferred usually only a part of production: technological and capital-intensive operations remain at home while the labor-intensive work of assembling is exported. However, as labor and material costs rise and it becomes expensive to renovate plant and equipment, the trend is to expand the actual manufacture of parts to the foreign country as the sole supplier of the U.S. market (Adam 1971:352).

Thus far major recipients of U.S. runaways have been Puerto Rico, Mexico, and Southeast Asia. Northern Mexico's Border Industrialization Project involves 257 U.S. firms employing over 41,000 workers largely in textiles and electronics. The fastest-growing sector of Mexican industry, the region exports more than $500 million a year in merchandise to the United States (*Business Week* 1973b:97, *Visión* 1972:44). U.S. parts and components are shipped over the border where Mexican workers who assemble them for thirty cents an hour replace U.S. workers who once did the job at $2.50 an hour. Warwick Electronics, for example, cut out 2,000 jobs in Illinois and Arkansas to move to Mexico.

Whole Southeast Asian countries have built their economies around the runaway shop. In Singapore, the most spectacular example, electronics is the fastest-growing industry. U.S., European, and Japanese companies have established subsidiaries there not only to assemble but to produce a variety of products from semiconductors, integrated circuits, and transistors to consumer electronics goods and highly specialized electrical machinery.[3] Like other Southeast Asian countries, Singapore promises generous tax conditions and a docile, controlled labor force. Companies are tax-exempt for five years, and their profits are taxed at a 4 percent rate. Low wages are government-enforced, sick pay and sick leave are severely restricted, and management are able to hire and fire virtually at will. Most electronics workers are young women between the ages of sixteen and twenty. Although they are educated, they receive among the lowest wages in Singapore — a dollar a day. As one businessman noted, "If I had been assigned to write the labor ordinances of

[3]   Data on Singapore is from Pacific Rim Project 1972c.

Singapore, I couldn't have done a better job for my company or any other." Such a situation characterizes most authoritarian regimes in Southeast Asia.

Offering generous tax rebates, favorable foreign exchange and trade conditions, and other benefits to foreign capital is typical of these governments. The new trend is to create export-processing zones (EPZ's) similar to Mexico's Border Industrialization Project. The EPZ's are designed for ventures in the manufacturing, processing, and assembling of export products composed of imported components and raw materials (Adam 1971:353–354). They are intended to supply world and regional markets. EPZ's are enclaves in which foreigners live like an occupying army, exploiting coolie labor drawn from the distant ranks of Southeast Asia's unemployed. Governments build the plants, which foreigners rent at low cost. Wholly owned foreign enterprises are completely tax exempt for five years and pay only 50 percent of normal taxes for the next five. Wholesale trading is permitted within the zone while there are few if any restrictions on exports and imports. The foreigner invests relatively little and can move out at will. South Korea, the Philippines, Taiwan, Thailand, and even Mauritius have EPZ's. Zenith, RCA, Admiral, and Philco-Ford have shifted their monochrome and color TV production to Taiwan's EPZ.

Puerto Rico is the model for the EPZ and proof of its fragility as a basis for economic growth. Operation Bootstrap, initiated just after World War II and considered a model in the first U.S. foreign aid program of Point Four, invited U.S. industry with seventeen-year tax exemptions, government-constructed, low-rent facilities, no export duties, and cheap labor. It attracted textile and other marginal industries, many of which went bankrupt within a short time. The Puerto Rican textile industry soon found itself undercut by the Philippine and Japanese textile industries just as the Hong Kong textile industry is today being undercut by plants in Macao. It is characteristic of runaway shops to keep on running away to cheaper areas. Often a single MNC will undermine its production in one area by creating a subsidiary in another. Thus, Burlington Industries' Japanese plants undercut its plants in Puerto Rico. With an increase in prices and labor costs in Puerto Rico, the industries that come to the island these days are no longer labor-intensive ones but the capital-intensive petrochemical and pharmaceutical industries, which employ relatively few workers in a heavily populated country. Up to a point, Puerto Rico was able to avoid social tension because of the migration of surplus labor to the United States (over one-third of Puerto Rico's people have migrated to the United States). However, today Puerto Rico faces a deepening socioeconomic crisis characterized by soaring unemployment which shows no signs of abating.

Puerto Rico, Mexico, and Southeast Asia are not the only recipients of the runaway shop. Haiti, Jamaica, and the Dominican Republic have a growing share. Goodyear makes shoes in Guatemala, Sears makes them in Spain, and Weyenberg Shoe Manufacturers of Milwaukee have a plant in Northern Ireland that exports its entire output to the United States. North American corporations are now flocking to Ireland to take advantage of cheap labor, cash grants for plant construction, and tax exemptions for products which can then be exported to Common Market countries (*Business Week* 1973a:34). Southern Europe is the site of runaways from high-cost northern Europe. Dutch textiles are made in Hungary and Romania for export to the United States; Swedish furniture is made in Poland, finished in Sweden, and then exported. The Japanese make extensive use of Southeast Asia for the production and assembling of electronic components and textiles for import to Japan and export to the United States and Europe.

This, then, is the decade of the MNC. In the 1970's, the MNC will have three-quarters of its production and sales outside the home country. According to Levinson, the greatest capital gap in history is opening in the United States as corporations will need 60 percent more capital between 1971 and 1975 than they needed in the previous five years (Levinson 1972:189). As the international competition for funds intensifies, only the biggest corporations integrated with the largest banks will survive. To increase the profitability of capital, cash-flow managers will cut costs by producing in cheap-labor areas and by manipulating accounts to avoid taxes and to profit from changes in exchange rates. They will further reduce the labor content of their production to increase profitability. A vicious circle ensues when expensive investment for automation to reduce labor costs increases cash-flow needs — and thus prices — while cash flow is in turn poured into more automation to further reduce labor costs. As sales fall off, instead of cutting prices to bolster sales and restore income, the loss of income is compensated through upward price adjustments jointly administered. Prices are determined by cash-flow needs, not by demand. For example, in 1970, GM reported its worst sales in two decades, and a ten-week strike resulted in what the company claimed was a 65 percent fall in net earnings. Nonetheless, GM forecast a rise in capital spending of a record $1.1 billion, 25 percent of which was earmarked for overseas. GM did not intend to tap its stockholders or banks for funds, but to obtain them through upward price adjustments (Levinson 1972: 217–218).

U.S. workers and consumers will pay higher prices and higher taxes. They will pay higher taxes to cover increasing unemployment and welfare rolls. They will pay higher prices and taxes to clean up the environment the corporations have destroyed. They will pay for the rising costs of health, education, and care of the aged. They will pay the taxes the corporations do not pay as they relocate their profits in tax havens.

According to labor economists cited by Levinson, U.S. workers need a 9 percent pay raise just to keep ahead of a 5 percent inflation and to keep up with average productivity increases. For annual incomes of $6,000 to $9,000, the 9 percent increase would boost real income by only 5 or 6 percent because one-third would go for taxes. To achieve the 9 percent necessary in real terms, the increase would have to be 12 to 15 percent in contrast to the 5.5 percent limit imposed by the Nixon wage-control board.

In addition to falling wages, the U.S. worker will be threatened with job loss. While automation could be the ultimate in human freedom — and in some socialist countries, it is used for humane and social purposes — for the Western world, profits and growth are the sole concern. The firm automates with no thought for the worker it dismisses or might otherwise employ or for the quality or utility of the product it produces. In cases of job loss through automation and export, there are no humane or rational provisions for retraining, relocation, or re-employment. Supplementary unemployment benefits programs affect workers only temporarily laid off — not the victims of automation or job export. The "adjustment assistance" of the Trade Expansion Act of 1962, affecting workers who lose their jobs due to imports, is likewise temporary (Knecht 1972:19). Many of the workers affected are women or members of minority groups for whom most trade unions offer little protection. Where will these workers with educational advantages structured out of their lives find jobs?

The MNC has no national loyalties. It moves over the globe for profit and growth. In an effort to steer the company away from an exclusively "U.S. point of view," Union Carbide recently reorganized, dividing its operations along product and geographical lines (*Business Week* 1973e:91). Such provincialism was apparently damaging its competitive position. The Dutch giant, Philips, recently regrouped for global sourcing: it switched from the old pattern of a network of factories in a single country producing a broad range of goods for local consumption to a network of global plants, each specializing in a single product line for several foreign markets. This plan will double production while cutting costs by 25 percent. A tightly centralized structure, the new organization will discourage integration with national economies and direct management's attention to the central headquarters, where the world's resources will be allocated, production sites determined, investment priorities selected, and markets chosen (*Business Week* 1973a:64–67).

According to Gy Adam and American economist Stephen Hymer, the future structure of world capitalism will be one in which labor-intensive operations are carried out in the hinterland and sophisticated technological operations, research and development, marketing, distribution, and management are concentrated in the already industrialized countries

(Adam 1972:313; Hymer 1972:114). If the transfer of production abroad signified a real transfer of income to the world's poor, the issues here might be complex. But throughout the world, present trends promise a redistribution of income from working people to fewer and fewer, wealthier and wealthier people. This process seems clear in the United States: it also seems clear when one examines the impact of the MNC on the Third World.

While foreign control over natural resources remains characteristic of Third World dependence on metropolitan capital, post-1945 foreign investment in the Third World has been most dynamic in the manufacturing sector — a phenomenon that has increased both dependence and poverty in Third World countries. Since 1945, foreign investment in Latin America, for instance, has virtually denationalized the "national bourgeoisie." Between 1932 and 1945, when links between the industrialized nations and Latin America were weakened by the Depression and World War II, a native entrepreneurial class emerged through import-substitution in manufacturing. Eventually import-substitution reached a point where it "required" the import of heavy capital goods and machinery, duly supplied by the United States. When Latin American nations were unable to pay for these expensive imports with the meager foreign exchange they earned from primary exports, the International Monetary Fund and the U.S. Export-Import Bank lent them money on terms facilitating the penetration of foreign capital. Tight credit restrictions eliminated many national entrepreneurs while the IMF insisted on the dismantling of restrictions on foreign investment.[4] Through joint ventures, licensing, patents, acquisition of stock in local industry and banking, and the creation of subsidiaries, foreign corporations bought into and in many cases bought out the national bourgeoisie. For instance, 33 percent of recent U.S. investment in Colombia and 36 percent in Mexico have been used to buy up existing local firms (*Wall Street Journal* 1972a).

The MNC attempts to orient Latin American development toward its own global interests. The MNC has financed its investment by monopolizing local savings and capital through buying shares in local banks and establishing branch banks where law permits. In this process, it has outcompeted local industry for access to capital. An estimated 80 to 83 percent of the capital of foreign firms in Latin America is of local accumulation. In Brazil, foreigners control 38 percent of the resources of domestic credit institutions (Serra 1973:127). Prior to the Peruvian military coup, U.S. banks had been rapidly purchasing Peruvian banks to the point that only one remained under national control (Quijano 1971:26). Deltec International, a giant North American financial net-

---

[4]   The impact of IMF policies on Latin America is discussed in Payer (1971:37–49).

work, functions almost exclusively to draw Latin American capital into U.S. ventures.

The outflow of capital from Latin America exceeds all capital inflows from private and public sources (Viero-Schmidt 1973:25). More than 60 percent of Latin America's foreign exchange, which could be used to further internal development, is absorbed in repatriation of profits, the importation of machinery, parts, and intermediary products, the payment for patents and licenses, and debt and service payments to foreign creditors. Further, 10 percent and a rising share of Latin American foreign exchange is absorbed by food imports, which have increased with disinvestment in the domestic agricultural sector and concentration instead on commercial export agriculture (Johnson 1972:78). Latin America's trade deficit with the United States has grown from $49 million in 1960 to $897 million in 1970.

This balance-of-payments problem has been aggravated by multinational corporate hegemony over world markets. As Latin American countries watched the prices for their primary exports decline in relation to manufactured goods' prices, the industrialized countries refused to accept Latin American manufactured exports. The patents extended by MNC's to Latin America were usually tied to the import of expensive equipment and carried with them clauses forbidding exports of the finished product as U.S. firms sought to maintain their monopolies over international markets. With the spread of global sourcing by the MNC, Latin American countries, like Southeast Asian nations, are now exporting more manufactured articles to metropolitan centers, but these generally come from foreign-controlled plants: the nature of the product, its destination, its price, and its quantity are determined not by the country which produces it but by the MNC which owns it.

Income from manufactured exports does not begin to cover the expense of equipment and intermediate goods the MNC charges to Latin America. MNC's cleverly manipulated local export-import laws and financial legislation at the expense of the country's trade balance. The Argentine General Tax Revenue Authority (DGI) estimates that such manipulation has aggravated the trade deficit in Argentina. Between 1967 and 1969, the DGI claims the average increase in new industrial exports was $36 million a year, while imports of intermediary products increased by an average of $95 million a year (International Metalworkers' Federation 1972:5). The DGI concludes that such maneuvers stimulate "the activities of productive sectors with their headquarters outside the country to the disadvantage of the integration of the industrial life of the country itself and of the public treasury."

Having access to capital, possessing technology and management expertise, practicing economies of scale, and monopolizing international markets, the MNC overwhelms the local entrepreneur who must join forces with it or disappear. For instance, Goodyear's control of the Guatemalan shoe industry, by nature of the firm's ability to control whole national markets and production systems, eliminated dozens of small shoe manufacturers and the jobs these more labor-intensive firms provided. Further, the MNC introduces capital-intensive machinery and forces surviving local entrepreneurs to adopt it, thus aggravating the unemployment problem.

Latin America's unemployment problem is the consequence of dependence. Reduction in the death rate has contributed to a burgeoning population. An antiquated and unequal land-tenure system coupled with multinational corporate penetration of large-scale agriculture has increased population pressures on the land, impoverishing marginal peasants, swelling the ranks of the landless proletariat, and encouraging rural-to-urban migration. According to a report by the United Nations Economic Commission on Latin America, the number of jobless in Latin America in 1969 was 23 million out of a labor force of 83 million, i.e., one-quarter of the labor force was unemployed. Development economists have long argued that the importation of capital-intensive machinery could not relieve Latin America's unemployment problem. Insofar as the foreign firm eliminates the more labor-intensive local producer or forces him to adopt new technology, it exacerbates the unemployment problem even further. Despite industrialization, the number employed in manufacturing in Latin America has not significantly increased. From 1925 to 1967, the share of industrial output in the total gross internal product of the region rose from 11 percent to 23 percent, but the percentage of the labor force in industry remained a steady 14 percent, while actually declining in Chile, Colombia, and Peru between 1965 and 1970.

An ECLA study of the chemical industry in Latin America estimates that a concentrated chemical industry serving the 20 republics would generate no more than 10,000 jobs. In the absence of regional integration, the five largest producer countries could create 24,600 jobs. These figures must be put in the context of a labor force expanding by two million a year in the 1960's. The Venezuelan oil industry, while accounting for 86 percent of the country's foreign investment, 90 percent of its export earnings, and 63 percent of its revenues, employs only 1.1 percent of its labor force. The Rockefeller Creole Petroleum Company, through the introduction of computers, nearly halved its employment from 9,000 in 1957 to 5,000 in 1967 while increasing production. Reynolds Aluminum convinced the Venezuelan government to invest millions in the most modern aluminum factory on the continent — so modern it employs 600 people (International Metal Workers' Federation 1972:7). Nor does it seem feasible that the labor-intensive runaway plant can absorb significant numbers of the unemployed. These shops use machinery which is still relatively capital-intensive, while the employment they offer is usually temporary and always undependable.

As many economists have pointed out, "economic development" controlled by the MNC represents a serious misutilization of national resources in relation to national needs. Instead of concentrating on the development of mass transportation systems, infrastructural investment favors the expansion of firms producing one-family cars. Instead of producing agricultural machinery for small farmers who might be organized in cooperatives or collectives, industry produces such inputs for large-scale agribusiness, which is increasingly dominated by the MNC. The product mix of advanced capitalism in the metropolitan center is usually transferred unaltered to Third World countries so that a whole array of consumer goods of dubious utility — from electric toothbrushes to pills for psychosomatic diseases — is dumped upon the Third World market. People are made to want these goods through advertising, also dominated by MNC's and articulated through the now ubiquitous radio and TV media, which are also increasingly controlled by foreign corporations. Sale of these products depends to a large extent upon an expansion of consumer credit, so that in Brazil, for example, the debt level of middle-income groups and the best-paid sector of the working class rose by almost 50 percent between the military coup of 1964 and 1973 (Serra 1973:106).

"Development" in Latin America is based upon a redistribution of income upward. In Mexico in 1950, the richest 10 percent of the population took 49 percent of national income; in 1969 they absorbed 51 percent. In 1950, the poorest 40 percent of the population received 14 percent of national income; by 1969, their share had dropped to 8 percent (International Metalworkers' Federation 1972:3). It is estimated that the Brazilian "economic miracle" has resulted in a relative and even absolute decline in living standards for 85 percent of the population and an improvement of only 1 percent (Serra 1973:81). Brazilian workers' real wages have declined so radically that the legal salary reverted to its post-World War II subsistence level (Serra 1973:81). Between 1958 and 1969, the real earnings of heads of families in São Paulo decreased by 39.2 percent. Reductions in state subsidies for health, education, and welfare have added to upward redistribution of income. School dropouts have increased by more than 50 percent since 1964, while infant mortality in São Paulo rose from 62.9 deaths per 1,000 births in 1960 to 83.8 in 1969.

In order for dependent capitalism to continue in Latin America, an increasingly authoritarian and repressive state must function in favor of the national and foreign bourgeoisie. It is no coincidence that most of Latin America lives today under military dictatorship, the installation of which has been facilitated by the U.S. government. In most countries, the labor movement is tightly controlled by the state and/or compromised by its collaboration with the state, employers, and the U.S. American Institute for Free Labor Development, which has consistently engaged in union-splitting and strike-breaking throughout Latin America. Although North American social scientists have tried to prove that the swelling marginal populations of the continent — especially those in urban slums — are not inclined to protest their increasingly untenable lot, political movements within the *barriadas* and *colonias* have in fact surged in recent years in Mexico, Venezuela, and Peru — to say nothing of Chile — and have elicited from the state increasing police and military repression. Peasant land invasions and student protests have provoked a similar response.

It is likely that in the short run, authoritarianism will also be the response of metropolitan governments to the social and economic crises brought on by the MNC's. In European countries with strong social-democratic movements, the trend toward the elimination of democratic forms will probably be strongly contested. In the United States, which lacks such a tradition in its labor movement and where ideological domination favoring corporate enterprise and discouraging social questioning holds profound sway through the media, schools, and political system, the move toward an anti-democratic solution may be smoother. Production for profit rather than human needs is not in the long run a viable or humane solution to societal development. The question remains whether or not the military and ideological power at the disposal of MNC's is capable of defending their model of world order against a more rational and creative solution.

REFERENCES

ADAM, GY
  1971 New trends in international business. Worldwide sourcing and dedomiciling. *Acta Œconomica* 7(3–4).
  1972 Some implications and concomitants of worldwide sourcing. *Acta Œconomica* 8(2–3).
BARNETT, RICHARD J., RONALD E. MULLER
  1974 *Global reach: the power of the multinational corporations*. New York: Simon and Schuster.
BRAVERMAN, HARRY
  1974 *Labor and monopoly capital*. New York: Monthly Review Press.
Business Week
  1972a November 4.
  1972b December 9.
  1972c December 23.
  1973a January 13.
  1973b April 28.
  1973c June 9.

1973d July 1.
1973e July 14.
1973f July 28.

Fortune
1972   November
1974   May

HYMER, STEPHEN
1970   "International trade and uneven development," in *Economics and world order*. Edited by Jagdish Bhagwati, 113–140. New York: Macmillan.

INTERNATIONAL METALWORKERS' FEDERATION
1972   "Report to 2nd regional conference of metal, mechanical, and metal mining workers of Latin America and the Caribbean." Buenos Aires.

JOHNSON, DALE
1972   "Dependence and the international system," in *Dependence and underdevelopment*. Edited by James Cockcroft, Andre Gunder Frank, and Dale Johnson, 71–114. New York: Doubleday.

KNECHT, LOUIS B.
1972   The worker in the age of communications. *The American Federationist* 79(7): 16–22.

LEVINSON, CHARLES
1972   *Capital, inflation and the multinationals*. New York: Macmillan.

MAGDOFF, HARRY
1969   *The age of imperialism*. New York: Monthly Review Press.

MAYER, LAWRENCE A.
1973   The clouded prospect for corporate profits. *Fortune* (May) 183–187.

PACIFIC RIM PROJECT
1970   *Pacific Imperialism Notebook* 3(3).
1972a   *Pacific Imperialism Notebook* 3(3).
1972b   *Pacific Imperialism Notebook* 3(5).
1972c   *Pacific Imperialism Notebook* 3(7).

PAYER, CHERYL
1971   The IMF and the perpetuation of dependence. *Monthly Review* 23(4): 37–49.

QUIJANO, ANIBAL
1971   Nationalism and capitalism in Peru: a study in neoimperialism. *Monthly Review* 23(3).

SERRA, J.
1973   "The Brazilian economic miracle," in *Latin America: from dependence to revolution*. Edited by James Petras. New York: John Wiley and Sons.

Tribune de Genève
1972   July 24.

TYLER, GUS
1972   The multinationals: a global menace. *The American Federationist*. 79(7): 1–7.

VIERO-SCHMIDT, BENICIO
1973   "Dependency and the multinational corporation," in *Structures of dependency*. Edited by Frank Bonilla and Robert Girling, 17–33. Palo Alto: Stanford University Institute of Political Studies.

Visión
1970   40(5) March 11.

Wall Street Journal
   1972a August 28.
   1972b November 20.
   1973a April 18.
   1973b April 20.
   1973c May 23.
   1973d May 25.
   1973e July 13.
   1973f July 17.
   1973g August 7.
   1973h August 9.

The Blocked Path: International Labor and the Multinationals

BRUCE VANDERVORT

In what follows, discussion will be limited to two main items: a presentation of the international trade-union bodies that aspire to represent workers in their struggles against multinational companies (MNC's) and an analysis of their capacity to do so. In both areas, attention will be focused on the international trade secretariats (ITS), which have laid the most extensive claims to a leadership role in those struggles. It should be made clear at the outset that what is being assessed here is the *potential* of the ITS and kindred international trade-union organizations to build a countervailing force to multinational corporate power. As we shall see, in no case can it be said that this potential has yet been realized.

A HISTORICAL PREFACE

Transnational capitalism is at least as old as the seventeenth century "commercial revolution," which spawned the joint-stock company and with it the first real multinational enterprises, in finance, plantation agriculture, and shipping.[1] The eighteenth- and nineteenth-century industrial and bourgeois political revolutions in Europe and America made inevitable the "globalization" of manufacturing and mining, as national markets proved unable to absorb new levels of production and

Bruce Vandervort, a former graduate student in European labor history at the University of Wisconsin, was employed in Geneva as a journalist and researcher by the International Union of Food and Allied Workers' Associations (IUF) (1972–1975) and as assistant to the general secretary of the International Federation of Building and Wood Workers (IFBWW) (1975–1976). The views expressed in this article are his own and do not necessarily reflect those of his previous employers.

[1]   For North American examples, see Wilkins (1970).

cash flow; imperial forays into Africa, Asia, and Latin America and ventures into the more-developed nations on the rim of the industrialized world (the Balkans, Russia, Spain) provided the needed outlets. Meanwhile, within the "First World" itself, cartels to rationalize international competition began to appear, in meatpacking[2] and metalworking,[3] for example. These transnational pacts were the precursors of the more sophisticated world market "carve-ups" that, since the 1920's, have characterized international business.[4]

The first international clashes between capital and labor, however, took place before the dominance of the older, commercial sector had given way to manufacturing and extractive interests. Thus, the First International (or International Workingmen's Association), founded in 1864 to curb the international flow of labor during strikes, took aim at employers in the luxury export trades who were involved in disputes with skilled artisans. And the creation of the International Transport Workers' Federation (ITF), in London in 1900, was inspired by a massive "waterside" strike in the United Kingdom in 1889 against the big British shippers and their ancient monopoly over dockers' and seamen's wages and working conditions.[5]

Interestingly, the first significant resistance to the more modern forms of transnational enterprise came from the nascent unions of the colonial world. In India, for example, a widespread campaign in 1905–1908 to protect local textile production against the implantation of British-owned mills was spearheaded by the unions of Bombay and Calcutta, led by the revolutionary nationalist L. Tilak (Tahmankar 1956). Further, the Mexican Revolution of 1910 was preceded by major strikes against U.S.-owned mining and textile firms.[6]

These were, however, localized, uncoordinated actions. Efforts toward building an international trade-union movement capable of facing up to the new "captains of industry" before World War I (and later) were hampered by both external and internal constraints. To begin with, most national unions were too preoccupied with securing basic workers' rights to give adequate attention to international matters. Besides, serious

[2]   Competition between U.K.- and U.S.-based meatpackers operating in Argentina was regulated by a 1912 agreement (Treviño 1972).
[3]   Pre-1914 trends toward establishment of a Franco-German steel cartel were documented by the French revolutionary syndicalist militant Alphonse Merrheim (1913). This work is all the more remarkable in that its author was forced to leave school at age ten to take a job in a metalworking factory.
[4]   A good example of this phenomenon is the 1925 agreement (still in force) between AT&T and ITT, whereby the former agreed not to compete with ITT abroad in exchange for a free hand on the U.S. market (Sampson 1974:25).
[5]   The ITF was not, however, the first international trade secretariat. The International Metalworkers' Federation (IMF), for example, was founded in Zurich in 1893.
[6]   Flores Magón, who died in Leavenworth prison in Kansas in 1921, was a major figure in the 1906 strikes that effectively launched the Mexican Revolution (Ferrúa 1971).

ideological differences arose. Thus, an International Secretariat of National Trade Union Centers (1901–1913) collapsed in a prophetic split between the social democratic Northern European unions and their "Latin" counterparts, who subscribed to revolutionary syndicalist principles. Basic to this dispute was the contention of the Northerners that such questions as anti-militarism and the general strike were political and thus had no place in international trade-union discussions; rather, they were the province of the parties that made up the Second (socialist) International (1889–). Challenges to that position, and to the statist conceptions that underlay it, were only beginning to make inroads — though with considerable force, even in the European and North American bastions of reformist unionism — when war came.[7] Therefore, it was within the Second International and its component socialist parties that the major pre-1914 debates on transnational capitalism — e.g., its role in imperialism and its potential for starting wars — took place.[8]

The pre-World War I cracks in labor's front against international capitalism widened to fissures in the interwar years. In the belligerent countries, the general discrediting of the social democratic parties and union leadership, due to their support for the war, plus the attraction of the 1917 Bolshevik Revolution, led to a postwar radicalization of the industrial working class. The Second International split, with its more revolutionary elements; rallied to Lenin's call for a Third (Communist) International (1920–1944). On the trade-union side, the social democrats founded the International Federation of Trade Unions (IFTU) (1919–1945), while the Comintern sponsored the formation of a Red International of Labor Unions (RILU) (1921–1935). Simultaneously, there was a second proliferation of ITS, grouping workers by craft or industry in the manner of the ITF. These last, while enjoying some ideological and structural autonomy from the IFTU, generally followed its lead in matters of international trade-union policy (relations with the RILU, anti-fascist activities, etc.).[9]

It was this disparate array of international labor bodies, fragmented ideologically and structurally, that would aspire to represent workers in their fight against the growth of transnational capitalism in the interwar period and, with some changes in nomenclature, down to the present time. Thus, despite the dissolution of the RILU in 1935 (to facilitate

---

[7] The most complete account of the growth of an "international revolutionary syndicalist" movement on the eve of World War I is in Gras (1971).

[8] The debate within the pre-World War I socialist community provoked a spate of theoretical studies of lasting importance on capitalism and imperialism: Lenin's *Imperialism* (1966) and Rosa Luxemburg's *The accumulation of capital* (1951), among others.

[9] The International Union of Food and Allied Workers' Associations (IUF), founded in 1920 in Zürich, was one of the ITS that departed to some extent from IFTU ideological directives during this era. Thus, the Soviet Federation of Food and Drink Workers' Unions was an IUF affiliate from 1923 to 1929 (United States Department of Labor 1959:3).

popular frontism) and the Comintern in 1944 (to strengthen Allied unity), the two organizations persist in altered form: today's World Federation of Trade Unions (WFTU), founded in 1945, is a logical continuation of the RILU, while the periodic conferences of Communist parties, such as the June 1976 gathering in the German Democratic Republic, perform a function similar to that of the old Third International. In the social democratic camp, the Second International stumbles on under a new name (Socialist International), the IFTU has been succeeded by the International Confederation of Free Trade Unions (ICFTU), founded in 1949, and the several ITS continue to operate more or less on their original lines. However, as we shall note, the ITS no longer exercise their former monopoly on international organization by craft/industrial branch, being forced to share the field with parallel bodies set up by the Communist and Christian international trade-union confederations.[10]

DIVISIONS OF LABOR

The two main structural divisions within international trade unionism are rooted in distinct (and sometimes opposed) historical conceptions of labor organization. Thus, the international trade-union confederations exist primarily to give national trade-union centers some kind of coordinated presence before national governments and international bodies: e.g., the Organization for Economic Cooperation and Development (OECD) and the various UN agencies, particularly the International Labor Organization (ILO). The three groupings of international professional associations, on the other hand, are structured along craft/industrial lines.

The three existing trade-union confederations are: (1) the social democratic International Confederation of Free Trade Unions (ICFTU) in Brussels; (2) the ex-Christian World Confederation of Labor (WCL) also in Brussels; and (3) the Communist World Federation of Trade Unions (WFTU), in Prague.

In terms of membership (not all dues-paying), the WFTU is the largest of the three, claiming some 151 million members in 46 affiliated unions in 39 countries and in its 11 professional associations (ICFTU 1973b). (Separate figures for the two types of organizations are not available.) The ICFTU, meanwhile, lists 118 affiliated unions in 88 countries with a total membership (all dues-paying) of 51.8 million (ICFTU 1975), while the

---

[10]   An International Confederation of Christian Trade Unions (ICCTU), composed of Catholic workers' organizations, was founded in 1921. After World War II it absorbed certain Protestant unions and then de-confessionalized itself, becoming the World Confederation of Labor (WCL).

WCL claims slightly more than 4 million members (not all dues-paying) in 65 affiliated unions in 60 countries (WCL 1973). In terms of geographical spread, however, the ICFTU is in the forefront. More than 95 percent of the WFTU's members are in the state capitalist (Communist) bloc, with no fewer than 98 million of them coming from Soviet affiliates (ICFTU 1973a). The WCL, while claiming to be the only international trade-union movement with real presence in the Third World, has very little membership in those areas: 3 million of its members are from European affiliates — principally of Belgium, Holland, and France — with one-fourth of the rest coming from Canada (WCL 1973).

The WFTU's already limited impact outside Eastern Europe seems in danger of even further decline. Traditionally, its only real clout in the capitalist bloc has been in the French CGT and the Italian CGIL. But at the 1973 WFTU Congress the CGIL had its status within the confederation changed from "affiliate" to "associate," the better to pursue its program of trade-union unity in Italy. Further, the WFTU's influence in Latin America, largely confined to the Chilean CUTch, the Peruvian CGTP, and the Uruguayan CNT, has been eroded as a result of military coups in those countries.[11] The WCL's position is even more precarious. Edmond Maire, general secretary of the French CFDT, astounded delegates to the confederation's 1973 congress by calling upon the WCL to disband and rally to the ICFTU. And, on January 1, 1976, the Catholic national center in the Netherlands merged with the socialist center, an ICFTU affiliate.

There are also three groups of international professional associations: (1) the seventeen ITS, which work more or less closely with the ICFTU but are not directly tied to it; (2) the twelve international trade federations (ITF), which are organically linked to the WCL; (3) the eleven trade-union internationals (TUI), which are appendages of the WFTU.

The first international professional associations, the ITS, were established to coordinate international trade-union activity at craft/industry level (chemicals, civil service, construction, metalworking, teaching, textiles, etc.). As such, they have often viewed themselves as more legitimate spokesmen of labor at international levels than the successive international trade-union confederations. In the 1920's, for example, certain ITS demanded that the IFTU be based on trade groupings rather than national trade-union centers.[12] This conflict eased in the 1930's, as the threat of fascism fostered greater international labor solidarity, and

[11] The Chilean CUTch-in-exile, whose executive is evenly (and scrupulously) divided between communist and socialist militants, now enjoys the support of both the ICFTU and the WFTU.
[12] This view, discussed in ITS circles since at least 1922, was officially put forward by the International Transport Workers' Federation (ITF) in 1927 but was rejected. It was turned down again by a 1932 ITS Conference, only to be taken up again by a special ITS–IFTU conference ten years later (U.S. Department of Labor 1959:34).

dissipated altogether in the Cold War era, as lines between the Communist and "free world" labor movements hardened once again. From the 1950's to roughly 1969, most ITS operated under the umbrella of the ICFTU, then closely tied to U.S. foreign-policy positions through the predominance within it of the AFL-CIO. With the AFL-CIO's departure in 1969 and the subsequent drift of the ICFTU, some ITS were able to reassert their independence. This trend was recognized in a 1973 pact between the ICFTU and the ITS that spelled out a clear division of labor on MNC questions. Henceforth, the ITS would handle direct industrial action (boycotts, solidarity campaigns), while the ICFTU would confine itself to representing international trade-union views on MNC questions before national and intergovernmental bodies (International Union of Food and Allied Workers' Associations 1973:9).

The WCL's ITF and the WFTU's TUI, created by their respective international trade-union confederations as parallel organizations to the ICFTU's ITS, have seldom engaged in meaningful industrial activity. The ITF, which had only 1.4 million dues-paying members in 1972, are in any case too small to have much impact. (WCL fusion with the ICFTU, expected in the near future, would probably lead to a merger of the ITF and the ITS.) The TUI, meanwhile, suffer from the same limitations as their parent organization, the WFTU. Almost all of their members are employed in the state capitalist bloc, where strikes and other historical forms-of industrial action are forbidden and organization along industrial or company lines is purely formal. Even where they have membership outside Eastern Europe (the Arab states, France, Italy), the TUI are ineffectual, since they bow to Communist party control of affiliated national unions. The Western Communist parties — the French party is the classic example of this — have traditionally viewed unions as captive voting blocs and have tried to subordinate industrial action to national or international political considerations (popular fronts, détente, etc.).

GLOBALIZATION OF ENTERPRISE: LABOR'S STRATEGIC RESPONSE

In the Capitalist and Mixed Economies

Though the Western trade-union movement has been concerned with the implications of the rise of the multinationals for some time, it is safe to say that a countervailing strategy has only begun to emerge in the last decade. The slowness of Western labor's response is in large measure due to the deadening effect of at least three decades of subservience to national governments and reformist electoral parties. The current disarray of governments in various parts of the world — the electoral stalemates in

Belgium, Denmark, Italy, the Netherlands, and Sweden, the "Watergate" crisis and its aftermath in the United States, the Lockheed and related scandals in Japan — should thus have had a liberating effect on national trade-union movements. Even conservative union leaders should by now have concluded that the nation-state is either woefully ineffective in protecting workers' interests against multinational sprawl or, as is often the case, a simple tool of business. There is some evidence that the message is beginning to sink in, e.g., the recent flurry of international trade-union conferences and work groups on multinational questions, world company councils, and attempts at international solidarity actions during collective bargaining or strikes.

The ultimate purpose of all this activity is, however, unclear. Will its aim be to create a simple countervailing force to international capital — in other words, to try to do for ongoing society what its governments cannot or will not do, i.e., "regulate" the "excesses" of the multinationals — as Professor David Blake suggests (1973:179–205)? Or to lay the bases for a new, genuinely international working-class movement, as various European left-wing observers — André Gorz (1966), Walter Kendall (Kendall and Marx 1971), Ernst Piehl (1974) — have hoped? At this juncture, the most optimistic assessment of opinion within the international trade-union movement is that served up by Charles Levinson, general secretary of the International Federation of Chemical and General Workers' Unions (ICF).

Ex-Chancellor [Ludwig] Erhard, the so-called father of the so-called "German economic miracle," once declared: . . . "the economy determines the fate of man." Unionists agree with Dr Erhard, strangely enough and perhaps for the first time, and further reason that if the economy is man's fate, it is man's democratic right to participate directly in deciding his fate. That is the common inspiration: to transform a purely formal, political democracy into a full and substantive social democracy which extends to where the majority of people spend the most precious, healthiest years of their lives — in factories and offices (1972:204).

Some readers will have noted with alarm that Levinson speaks of achieving "social democracy." However, it should be recalled that, like other social movements, social democracy has undergone a certain evolution over time. Under pressure from the trade unions, to which they are closely linked, and left-wing elements within their own ranks (the Jusos in the Federal Republic of Germany, for instance), the social democratic parties of the Benelux countries, the Federal Republic of Germany, and the Scandinavian states have moved beyond a policy of simply protecting the workers' slice of the economic pie to one of backing substantial worker participation in enterprise management.

That there are, however, serious limits to social democratic schemes for workers' "participation" is revealed in legislation on the subject recently enacted in the Federal Republic of Germany. The March 1976 bill, the result of six years of horse-trading among the country's three major parties, purports to give workers "equal representation" on the supervisory boards of all companies with more than 2,000 employees (including MNC's). The catches are that the "labor" side is defined so as to include one middle-level manager and that, in case of a deadlock, the board chairman, usually a stockholders' representative, is entitled to a second, tie-breaking vote. Thus, management will have a voting edge in all important matters to come before the boards (future investment plans, rationalization schemes, etc.) (*International Herald Tribune* 1976).

Though there are some immediate benefits to be gained from pursuing this strategy of "advanced social democracy" — better health and safety laws, equal pay for work of equal value, greater access to company financial information — it is unlikely that attaining them, in the present piecemeal fashion at least, will give international labor the clout to check the growing power of the multinationals. In short, it remains a *localized*, *defensive* strategy. What seems necessary is to push beyond the limited possibilities of generalized national or regional action and thus away from the still-too-close reliance on electoral parties and governments and into confrontation on the global, company plane.

Realizing this, a growing number of Western trade unions view "advanced social democratic" demands as a sort of "minimum program" designed to open breaches in the global capitalist system that can be widened until "participation" gives way to *autogestion* or "workers' self-management." While proponents of this process can be found in many unions (including those of the Second and Third Worlds), its leading advocates are in the French CFDT, certain Italian industrial federations, and the Yugoslav trade-union confederation.[13] It was the CFDT (900,000 members in 1976) for example, that engineered the celebrated Lip watch factory "work-in" of June–August 1973, during which the employees made watches without management supervision, sold them at cost, and paid themselves out of the proceeds (Vandervort 1974). An equally important thrust toward *autogestion* was the April 1974 collective agreement between the Italian Metalworkers' Federation and the Fiat conglomerate. Some of the major points were:

(1) The union and Fiat will jointly decide how the company's investment capital will be allocated over the next two years.

(2) In all new Fiat plants priority will be given to building buses, not individual passenger cars.

---

[13]   On the Italian experience, see R. Aglieta *et al*. (1972) and *Autogestion et socialisme* (1974). While the best introductory study in English on Yugoslav *autogestion* is probably Broekmeyer (1970), several interesting papers on the subject were presented to the second international conference on workers' self-management (Ithaca, N.Y., 1975) (see note 15 below), e.g., Byrd (1975).

(3) Wherever the firm puts up new plants, it must provide crèches and public transportation for workers (Padovani 1974:34).[14]

A historical note: the movement for *autogestion* is as old as trade unionism itself. Once mainly associated with artisan cooperative ventures, it took on full-blown revolutionary proportions in the early part of the present century when it was espoused by, among others, the anarcho-syndicalist majorities in Argentine and Spanish labor, the revolutionary syndicalist French CGT, the IWW in Australia, Chile, Mexico, South Africa, and the United States, and the "workers' councils" (Soviets) in the Soviet Union and elsewhere. However, implemented only briefly in Republican Spain during the Civil War, and derailed by the growth of state power as a result of two world wars and the advent of fascism and Stalinism, it only really surfaced again in the 1960's, explosively, in the May–June events of 1968 in France. This revival should not, however, be seen as confined to Europe. There are suggestions of an urge toward *autogestion* in the 1972 Lordstown auto strikes in the United States (Aronowitz 1973:21–50)[15] and in the struggle of rank-and-file unions in Argentina against Peronist repression in March 1974 and following the military takeover in April 1976.[16]

In the Centrally-Planned Economies

The most important thing to note about the attitude of the world communist trade-union movement toward the multinationals is that, whereas the more progressive Western unions tend to view state political power as the servant of multinational interests, the WFTU conception is the inverse. Thus the global expansion of International Telephone and Telegraph is seen as the disguised spread of U.S. or Western state imperialism, not the growth of an autonomous entity with an inherent dynamic and

[14] For the background of this important breakthrough,see Lanzardo (1974).
[15] In 1974, a group called People for Self-Management was formed in the United States. Sponsored by the Cornell University industrial relations school and largely campus-based, the group has hosted two international conferences on workers' self-management, one at Cambridge, Mass. (January 13–14, 1974) and another at Ithaca, N.Y. (June 6–8, 1975). People for Self-Management publishes a *Newsletter* at P.O. Box 802, Ithaca, N.Y. 14850.
[16] I want to insist here on the importance of the concept of *autogestion* in Latin American labor history. A good recent example is the worker-run EFCSA meatpacking plant, which operated from 1958 to 1968 in the Cerro working-class quarter of Montevideo. Though the experiment was brought to an early demise by state-business repression, it has provided an important incentive for meat workers' unions throughout Latin America. The Argentine Meat Industry Workers' Union, which has been demanding workers' control of all *frigoríficos* in the country since at least 1971, came part of the way towards its goal with the achievement of co-determination of three of Argentina's packinghouse complexes in the autumn of 1973 (Vandervort 1974). For workers'-control experiments in the Chilean public sector under Popular Unity government, see Jeanneret (1975).

economic and political interests of its own. This notion is perfectly plaus-ible, since the parties that dominate the WFTU and its TUI (principally the Communist party of the Soviet Union) exist primarily to wield national or regional political power. Therefore, communist trade-union leaders continue to argue that the demands of labor are best met by the "workers' state" and that the privileged instruments for international action against capitalism should remain the concerted efforts of the various local Communist parties and the global shield of the Soviet Union.

Toward the end of the 1960's, there was reason to hope that, with the general discrediting of Stalinism, a resurgence of trade-union militancy in the state capitalist bloc would force a more independent outlook on the WFTU. That hope faded in 1968. The Soviet invasion of Czechoslovakia was intended to wreck not only Dubcek's "socialism with a human face" but also a budding rank-and-file labor movement in Eastern Europe. As such it was at least a partial success. Despite successive and widespread strikes against government attempts to raise food prices, in 1970 and 1976, it would appear that the party bureaucracy in Poland still has the strength to contain trade-union dissidence. Further, a rightward shift within the Hungarian Communist party has apparently succeeded in curbing an incipient workers' control movement in that country (Bimbi 1973; Haraszti 1976). Outside Eastern Europe, the dilatory role played by the French CGT during May–June 1968 and the militarization of the Cuban labor force by the Castro regime provide further proof of the damaging effect of "substitutionism" on the working-class movement.[17]

The continued unwillingness or inability of the communist-dominated unions to secure real power for workers at plant, company, or industrial level today constitutes a threat, not only to those workers, but also to workers in all countries. ICF general secretary Charles Levinson has devoted more than fifty pages of his *International trade unionism* to a listing of Western-based firms that either have invested in the state capitalist bloc or are engaged in "co-production" schemes with state companies in those countries. He further argues that:

such industrial interpenetration will influence the policy and positions of unions in the direction of expanding contacts, discussions and cooperation with the Eastern unions for a number of reasons: not the least to talk with [them] about their social-ist governments' dumping of low-priced goods on our markets and the transfer of capitalist enterprises to the East to exploit lower labour costs, both of which practices posed a threat to our workers and our unions (Levinson 1972:142–143).

For the moment, the "dialogue" that Levinson considers so imperative would have to be conducted at the level of rhetorical abstractions, as an

[17]   A useful source on the militarization of Cuban labor is Mesa-Lago (1974). More recent developments are summed up in Dolgoff (1976).

Italian trade-union delegation found out on a trip to Moscow in early 1974.

Taking Fiat as an example, an Italian trade union delegation in Moscow recently asked . . . how Soviet workers would react if they were asked for solidarity action if there were a strike in a western country within the same multinational. [It] was given the answer, "This is a political question and trade unions in the USSR are not involved in politics" (International Metalworkers' Federation 1974:1).

Some changes may be forthcoming, however. Though the present situation is bleak, there is still a chance that the Eastern European unions can win a greater measure of autonomy from the party apparatus. Much will depend on their response to the economic crisis now beginning to hit the Eastern bloc, which will inevitably result in appeals for wage restraint and lower levels of consumption. The state capitalist regimes' desire to apply Western capital-intensive technology to production could also spark militancy, as automation exacerbates an already serious problem of underemployment. However, it seems likely that the surest impetus for change will come from outside. Should the Western European Communist parties' "declarations of independence" from Soviet control and claims of support for "pluralism" in national politics have a liberating impact on the trade-union organizations associated with them — and this seems plausible, especially in Italy — vibrations might encourage similar initiatives in Eastern Europe. Increasing contacts with Western trade unionists could also play a positive role in this regard, assuming that the two sides can establish sufficient autonomy in their relationships to move beyond formal, high-level exchanges of views.[18]

THE FUTURE: ROADBLOCKS AND DIVERSIONS

Having briefly examined the framework of the international labor movement as it relates to the fight against multinational company power, we may now ask the question: Does this movement (and here we will be speaking mainly of the Western international trade-union structure, especially the ITS) have the capacity to lead the struggle of working people against the multinationals? While it is probably too early to give a categorical response, it seems clear that international labor is beset with ideological and structural problems that make doubtful its ability to pursue even the moderate "advanced social democratic" program referred to earlier. (Since most of the following analysis of these problems

---

[18] Since 1974, representatives of ICFTU- and WFTU-affiliated unions have met annually to "exchange views" on common problems. Given the rigidity on both sides, the meetings have been largely *pro forma* affairs.

is based on the observations and opinions of the author, little in the way of formal documentation will be provided.)

Operational and Structural Problems

Neither the ICFTU nor the several ITS taken as a body now possess the structural coherence needed to lead workers' resistance to transnational capitalism. In part this is due to the normal ebb and flow of interest in international affairs on the part of their constituencies: during the present world economic crisis many national unions have reduced international commitments (including dues) in order to deal with pressing local problems (government income policies, unemployment). But even in the best of times the Western international labor movement is hard put to offer a united front to international capital. The ITS, being structured along craft/industry lines, face the inherent problem of jurisdictional disputes, sometimes of an exasperating complexity. A good example is the forest-products industry, where two ITS, the International Federation of Building and Wood Workers (IFBWW) and the International Federation of Plantation, Agricultural and Allied Workers (IFPAAW), compete for membership, while paper-mill workers' unions are affiliated with the chemical workers' international (ICF). Further, the IFBWW, which has jurisdiction for the construction industry, does not as a rule affiliate cement-workers' unions, which are claimed by the ICF.

The upshot of this situation — and other examples could be given — is that the ITS and their affiliates often lack the necessary data and the degree of consensus on strategy and tactics to wage an effective joint struggle against MNC's, an increasing number of which benefit from centralized management and vertical linkage. In the end the ITS, unless they abandon their narrow craft/sectoral orientations, will lose whatever capacity they still have to *anticipate* events; they will continue simply to *respond* to them.

Some will object that the main reason for the international trade-union movement's failure to form a solid front against the multinationals is a disparity of resources among its component organizations. There is some truth in this. Some ITS have sizable budgets and therefore can carry out extensive organizational and research tasks; others can barely meet office expenses. For some ITS, however, the financial argument serves as an alibi for inaction. Content to function as letterboxes or as agencies for "trade-union tourism," they have been unable to communicate a sense of urgency in the battle against the multinationals.

To the extent that these operational and structural difficulties stem from administrative inefficiency, corruption, or personal feuds among ITS general secretaries, they can be overcome. It will be harder to grapple with problems that spring from the very nature of contemporary Western trade unionism: its archaic divisions along professional lines, its bureaucratic structure,[19] and, as will be spelled out in more detail later, its lack of autonomy in relations with its "social partners," the state and the corporations.

Ideological Problems: Class Struggle vs. Welfare System

Perhaps the most significant political development of this century has been the ability of state bureaucracies to integrate potentially fractious groups — particularly the working class — into the ongoing capitalist (or state capitalist) system. In most countries, the autonomy of workers' organizations has been whittled down to manageable proportions. Its demands confined to "bread and butter" issues, its means of securing them restricted to collective bargaining and lobbying, its political dimensions frozen in (at best) a reformist cast, Western trade unionism is nearly at the end of its historical rope.

The downhill slide of the Western trade-union movement began with its definitive abandonment of the concept of class struggle in the Cold War era and its subsequent swallowing of the dogma of welfare statism. As a result most Western unions today accept the principle that improvements in wages and working conditions should be tied to overall economic "growth," i.e., to the profitability of capitalist enterprise. Hence, the subjection of workers to a classic panoply of profit-guarding schemes: compulsory arbitration, income policies, no-strike agreements, productivity packages, etc. Beyond the bargaining table the identification of workers' interests with those of the company and/or state has led to a general alignment of trade unions with the foreign policies of their respective nations (or regional blocs).This sentiment, though most blatant in the AFL-CIO's support for U.S. government policies in Asia and Latin America, has parallels in other national trade unions and in the labor internationals as well. Thus the "regional chauvinism" of unions in the European Economic Community bloc, which manifests itself in such aberrations as calls for the creation of "European multinationals" to compete with Japanese- or U.S.-based firms. Thus the refusal of Swedish trade-unionists to believe that their version of social democracy is not infinitely reproducible in such diverse settings as East Africa, India, or Portugal. Thus, most importantly, the all-too-numerous cases of uncritical support by ITS for Western-bloc foreign-policy positions (even when, as we shall see, some of them have been discarded by the governments themselves).

[19] "Marie Martin" (pseudonym) sees this development as "inevitable" (Martin 1976).

To those who have worked for ITS, it should be clear that most of them, like too many of their affiliated unions, have been slow to cast off the rigidities of the Cold War period. While some of these attitudes, such as pessimism about the motives behind "détente," can be justified, others are simply discredited.

One of the cardinal tenets of ITS faith is support for the Israeli state. ITS general secretaries routinely send telegrams of solidarity to Israeli affiliates in the event of hijackings or *fedayeen* raids, without prior authorization from their management or executive committees or consultation with other affiliated unions.[20] Needless to say, no condolences are addressed to the victims of Israeli raids — on Palestinian refugee camps in Lebanon, for example. Because of this knee-jerk backing for Israel, the ITS have had virtually no impact on the Arab trade-union world (save for unions in fringe countries such as Tunisia, Lebanon, and Morocco) and have had some difficulties in relations with affiliated unions in Africa.

Equally unfortunate has been the backing of some ITS for U.S.-government policies in Latin America. Knowing the AFL-CIO's distaste for the late Popular Unity government and the national trade-union center, CUTch, in Chile, most ITS have been sparing in financial or verbal support for the CUTch-in-exile, despite a considerable ICFTU commitment to its cause.[21] At least one ITS has worked actively against the CUTch.[22] At a June 1976 meeting the executive committee of IFPAAW voted to admit into membership a Chilean farm workers' organization of Christian-Democratic extraction although aware that such action contravenes ICFTU and general ITS policy. (It is accepted in international trade-union circles that any union allowed to operate in

---

[20]   On one occasion known to me, a statement of support from an ITS was directly solicited by an Israeli government official on mission in Geneva. The general secretary of the ITS in question handed the text to the official in the afternoon of the day the request was made.

[21]   Certain national centers affiliated with the ICTFU have been particularly steadfast in support of the CUTch. The German DGB is especially dogged in protesting against persecution of Chilean trade-union militants and has helped to resettle Chilean workers and their families. The Swedish LO has been successful in securing the release of Chilean unionists from the junta's prisons and getting them work permits and jobs in Sweden.

[22]   In late 1975 the Northern Californian Chile Coalition (NCCC) charged five ITS — the International Federation of Commercial, Clerical and Technical Workers (FIET), the International Federation of Free Teachers' Unions (IFFTU), the International Federation of Petroleum and Chemical Workers (IFPCW), the International Transport Workers' Federation (ITF), and the Post, Telephone and Telegraph International (PTTI) — with helping to undermine the Popular Unity government in Chile. It was alleged that, in collaboration with the U.S. government-business-labor organization, the American Institute for Free Labor Development (AIFLD), they subsidized the series of strikes that helped "de-stabilize" the Allende government. See NCCC (n.d.).

Some erstwhile supporters of Chilean labor err more through neglect than malice. Thus, a financial contribution from a Danish affiliate to the International Federation of Building and Wood Workers (IFBWW), intended to help worker victims of the Pinochet regime, lay untouched in the IFBWW coffers from late 1973 until early 1976.

contemporary Chile is bogus by definition and that to accept one of them into affiliation only serves to legitimize the Pinochet regime.)

While other examples of the ideological confusion of the ITS and their affiliated organizations could be detailed (e.g., their silence concerning charges that European member unions had funnelled CIA money to the Portuguese socialist party in the fall of 1975; their general refusal to take seriously Third World governments' and unions' demands for a "new world economic and social order"; and their tendency to scoff at the revolutionary programs of French and Italian unions), it should already be evident that this sort of backing for the domestic and foreign policies of Western-bloc governments is a weak base for pursuit of an active campaign against MNC power; for, however damaging such stances are in their own right, they are doubly harmful to the international trade-union movement in that they undermine its credibility as the leader of working-class resistance to the multinationals. Thus, to take but one example, progressive Latin American trade unionists find it hard to accept ITS credentials in this regard when some of their number are accused of complicity in the "de-stabilization" of the Popular Unity government in Chile, the main beneficiaries of which were multinational firms such as Anaconda Copper.

CONCLUSION

There is no easy way out of this dilemma. Some would argue that these are basically "generational" problems, that solutions will be forthcoming with the passing of the old, Cold War trade-union leadership. While a more youthful look might have some beneficial effects, it is unlikely to produce startling changes; for the problems the international trade-union movement faces are structural: its unwieldy mode of organization, its often symbiotic relationship to state and intergovernmental bodies, and its too-frequent espousal of the principles of "business unionism." Such deep-rooted problems are not susceptible to cosmetic jobs; they must be sorted out within the trade-union movement itself, in debates that permit the full participation of the rank-and-file, which pays the dues.

REFERENCES

AGLIETA, R., *et al.*
    1972 *Révolution dans l'enterprise: le mouvement des délégués ouvriers en Italie*. Paris: Editions Ouvrières.
ARONOWITZ, STANLEY
    1973 *False promises: the shaping of American working class consciousness*. New York: McGraw-Hill.

Autogestion et Socialisme
1974   Mouvements ouvriers de gestion et d'action directe en Italie. *Autogestion et Socialisme* 26–27.

BIMBI, GUIDO
1973   "Il Salario a Csepel." *Unitá*. December 5.

BLAKE, DAVID
1973   International labor and the regulation of multinational corporations: proposals and prospects. *San Diego Law Review* II(1) November.

BROEKMEYER, M. J., editor
1970   *Yugoslav workers' self-management*. Dordrecht: D. Riedel.

BYRD, R.
1975   "A participating strategy for nation building in the Third World: the case of Yugoslavia." Paper presented at Second International Conference on Workers' Self-Management. Ithaca, N.Y.

DOLGOFF, SAM
1976   Structures of power in Cuba. *Interrogations* 7:47–66.

FERRÚA, PIETRO
1971   Ricardo Flores Magón en la Revolucción Mexicana. *Reconstruir* 72.

GORZ, ANDRÉ
1966   *Strategy for labor: a radical proposal*. Boston: Beacon.

GRAS, CHRISTIAN
1971   *Alfred Rosmer et le mouvement révolutionnaire international*. Paris: Maspero.

HARASZTI, MIKLOS
1976   *Salaire aux pièces: ouvrier dans un pays de l'Est*. Paris: Seuil.

INTERNATIONAL CONFEDERATION OF FREE TRADE UNIONS
1973a *Information on communist-controlled trade-union organizations*. Circular 55. August 10.
1973b *WFTU Varna Congress*. Circular 103. December 27.
1975   "Report on activities of the Confederation." Paper presented at the eleventh World Congress in Mexico. Brussels.

International Herald Tribune
1976   'Worker participation in West Germany." March 23.

INTERNATIONAL METALWORKERS' FEDERATION
1974   *News* (12) March.

INTERNATIONAL UNION OF FOOD AND ALLIED WORKERS' ASSOCIATIONS
1973   *News Bulletin* 5–6.

JEANNERET, J.
1975   "Structure of participation in the Chilean quasi-labor-managed sector." Paper presented at second international conference on workers' self-management, Ithaca. N.Y.

KENDALL, W., E. MARX
1971   *Unions in Europe: a guide to organized labour in the Six*. Center for Contemporary European Studies. Sussex: University of Sussex.

LANZARDO, LILIANA
1974   "Luttes spontanées et organisation — notes sur les luttes de la Fiat 1968–1973." *Autogestion et Socialisme* 26–27.

Le Monde
1976   July 21.

LENIN, VLADIMIR ILICH
1966   *Imperialism, the highest stage of capitalism; a popular outline*. Moscow. Progress Publishers.

LEVINSON, CHARLES
1972   *International trade unionism.*
LUXEMBURG, ROSA
1951   *The accumulation of capital.* Translated by Agnes Schwerzschild. New Haven. Yale University Press.
MARTIN, MARIE [pseud.]
1976   "L'inevitable bureaucratie du syndicalisme international." *Interrogations* 7:31–47.
MERRHEIM, ALPHONSE
1913   *La Metallurgie. Son origine et sa développement. Les forces matrices.* Paris: Fédération des métaux.
MESA-LAGO, CARMELO
1974   *Cuba in the 1970's.* Albuquerque: University of New Mexico.
NORTHERN CALIFORNIA CHILE COALITION
n.d.   "The AIFLD, International trade secretariats and fascism in Chile: an open letter to the labor movement." Berkeley, Calif.: Northern Californian Chile Coalition.
PADOVANI, MARCELLE
1974   "L'Empire Fiat ébranle." *Nouvel Observateur* 488.
PIEHL, ERNST
1974   *Multinationale Konzerne und internationale Gewerkschaftsbewegung* Frankfurt am Main: Europaische Verlaganstalt.
SAMPSON, ANTHONY
1974   *The sovereign state of ITT: the secret history of ITT.* London: Coronet.
TAHMANKAR, D.V.
1956   *Lokamanya Tilak, father of Indian unrest and maker of modern India.* London: n.p.
TREVIÑO, PEPÉ
1972   *La carne podrida: el caso Swift-Deltec.* Buenos Aires: Peño Lilla.
UNITED STATES DEPARTMENT OF LABOR
1959   *The International Union of Food and Drink Workers' Associations.* Washington: United States Government Printing Office.
VANDERVORT, BRUCE
1973   "The factory is where the workers are: the Lip affair." *Liberty* (October).
1974   "Deltec and the great Argentine beef steal." *Community Action on Latin America Newsletter* 3(5).
WILKINS, MIRA
1970   *The emergence of multinational enterprises: American business abroad from the colonial era to 1914.* Cambridge, Mass.: Harvard University Press.
WORLD CONFEDERATION OF LABOR
1973   "Budget 1974." Draft prepared for XVIII Congress of the World Confederation of Labor, Evian-les-Bains, France.

The Multinational Corporation as a Stage in the Development of Capitalism

DELTEC RESEARCH PROJECT

INTRODUCTION

The multinational corporation (MNC) is a qualitatively new structural phenomenon in world capitalism. Industrialized Western countries, including the United States, are themselves subject to the forces of disequilibrium that the MNC can cause in the Third World, such as technological displacement, inflation, currency fluctuations, trade deficits, and capital outflows that lead to such well-known phenomena as rising unemployment, increasing prices, currency devaluations, and falling real wages.

Neither can MNC's be thought of as one nation-state's economy in competition with another's. In the 1960's J.J. Servan-Schreiber (1968) saw MNC's as a means of U.S. takeover of the European economy. In the 1970's there is a growing trend of U.S. economic thought that views MNC's as enabling Europe and Japan to out-compete the United States. However, both these perspectives miss the point that MNC's are independent of any single nation-state. The very nature of their global organization and strategy causes them to have no allegiance to any country. MNC's should not be simply viewed as super-monopolies. Although it is true that MNC's may have monopoly control of markets and production with a concurrent reduction in competition, they also have global control over the direction of scientific research, the technological applications of that research, and the diffusion of knowledge. The impact of this control over scientific research and the diffusion of knowledge on social institu-

The members of the Deltec Research Project are Ahamed Idris-Soven, Anne Lonigro, Colleen Reeks, Terence Turner, and several who must remain anonymous. They would like to give special thanks to the North American Congress on Latin America for its help in collecting primary sources.

tions and culture raises the MNC to a new level of significance not yet clearly understood.

Any inquiry into the activities of MNC's should be interdisciplinary because MNC's affect the political, social, and economic institutions of industrial and Third World countries. Furthermore, the meaning of post-industrial capitalism in a global context may best be understood through in-depth examination of single corporations. Aggregative studies that depend heavily on statistical information tend to have difficulty in defining the cultural and political impact of MNC's. It is hoped that through in-depth studies of many single corporations the distortion of social and political institutions by post-industrial capitalism may be defined, and meaningful, purposeful action taken by human beings to counteract such distortion.

In view of this the Deltec Research Project was formed along interdisciplinary lines for the study of a single MNC — Deltec International Limited (hereafter called Deltec). The remainder of this paper will be primarily concerned with Deltec's activities in Latin America, where it does most of its business, and wherever possible draws conclusions that fit into a theoretical framework of multinational corporate strategy.

Deltec is one of the largest and most important MNC's operating in Latin America. Deltec was organized at the end of World War II by Clarence Dauphinot, who began his career by selling frying pans and Old Crow whiskey in the provinces of Brazil. By 1972 Deltec had become one of the largest merchant banking companies in Latin America, having issued a total of more than $1.3 billion in loans and discounts. Deltec has been associated from its inception with the Deutsche Bank and Chase Manhattan.

Deltec's business falls into three areas of activity: international merchant banking, food distribution, and real estate development. At the same time it should be recognized that Deltec's principal activity is locating capital for expansion of its financial sector. For example, although at one time Deltec owned substantial industrial properties in Los Angeles and Australia, these properties were acquired only with the aim of selling them at a profit in order to generate capital. According to Deltec's 1973 annual report: "The combination of Deltec and IPL [a global meat-processing industry] took place in 1969. The following year the Company [Deltec] began a program of selling all industrial assets. The sales in 1973 resulted in extraordinary gains . . ." of more than $47 million.

However, Deltec remains one of the world's major distributors of basic food commodities, especially meat. There is reason to believe that Deltec's pattern of investment, similar to that of other MNC's engaged in food commodities, may be responsible for the long-term decline of employment in the U.S. meat-packing industry and for the maintenance of the high food-price structure. More about this will be explained later.

Deltec first came to the attention of the Deltec research group through one of its members, Terence Turner, an anthropologist doing field research among several Indian tribes in northern Brazil. It was while acquiring land for beef-cattle raising in northern Brazil that Deltec, through its then subsidiary, Swift International, became involved in the expropriation of the tribal lands belonging to the Indians that Turner was studying. In the process of our research it was found that Deltec has by no means limited its incursions to Brazil or Latin America, as Deltec's 1973 annual report cynically points out:

> In international banking, we see enormous opportunity in Southeast Asia, where the combination of ancient culture and a dedication to work with a new receptivity to outside ideas is likely to produce in short order a whole series of economic miracles. . . . In the economic sphere, the impact of nationalism is almost uniformly destructive, and we deplore it.

It is our hope that interdisciplinary research projects of the type represented by the Deltec Research Project may be used by international labor unions and other politically active organizations as a tool to demonstrate the common interest of working-class people in Third World countries and industrialized nations as well as indigenous peoples in changing the present economic system dominated by MNC's to one more directly interested in human welfare.

THE MULTINATIONAL CORPORATION AS A STAGE IN THE DEVELOPMENT OF CAPITALISM

The MNC, a new stage in the development of capitalism, has as its dynamic essence the object of control over markets and production processes. Although the MNC existed more than one hundred years ago, it was not a general feature of capitalist economy as it is today. One object of this section is to explain why the MNC has become a general feature of the capitalist economy. The basic requirements of capitalism, growth and profitability, intimately influence each other. That is to say, increases in growth lead to increasing profitability and vice versa. This leads in the direction of ever-increasing control.

A second object of this section is to explain why growth and profitability, through the structure of the MNC, have come to play such central roles in maintaining the existence of the capitalist economy. Finally, we suggest that Marx's theory of the fundamental contradiction of capital indicates a limit to the growth of capital.

Many of the arguments used in the following framework were advanced primarily by Karl Marx and Paul M. Sweezy, a contemporary

Marxist. It should be kept in mind that the framework is abstract and is intended to point up the essential relationships of the capitalist economic system. It may not, therefore, explain every peculiarity of capitalism.

The capitalist enters into the following social relation between money and commodities: $M-C-M'$. The capitalist begins with a certain quantity of money, or capital (M), and buys with it factors of production (C) such as labor, raw materials, and machinery. The raw materials are then transformed by labor into final products, which the capitalist sells in the market for a quantity of money (M') greater than the initial investment (M). It is apparent from the above outline of capital circulation that the entire process would be pointless for the capitalist unless the quantity of money at the end of the process becomes larger than the quantity of money the capitalist had at the beginning. That is, $M' - M = \triangle M$ must be positive (Sweezy 1942:139). According to Karl Marx, "the expansion of value, which is the objective basis or mainspring of the circulation $M-C-M'$, becomes his subjective aim, and it is only insofar as the appropriation of ever more and more wealth in the abstract becomes the sole motive of his operations, that he functions as a capitalist" (Sweezy 1942:80).

Capitalism is production for profit. The capitalist's passion for wealth is not a mere idiosyncracy but rather a function of his special position in the social relations of production. By means of the control of wealth the capitalist and the corporate bureaucracy can maintain control over other people and over the organization of social relations itself. It is by means of profit that this control can be extended.

The expansion of value $(\triangle M$ positive) is derived from surplus value. Surplus value is that quantity of wealth that is produced by labor above the subsistence needs of labor but extracted and realized by the capitalist when he sells "his" product. For example, suppose labor works eight hours daily and the time necessary for labor to produce its subsistence needs (food, housing, clothing, etc.) is four hours; then the remainder of the working day is spent by labor in producing surplus value; that is, value produced above the subsistence needs of labor. In this example we made the assumption that labor is paid in wages only that amount necessary for it to acquire its means of subsistence; that is, the amount necessary for labor to sustain itself in order to keep the system running. Although it is possible for labor to receive wages above its needs of subsistence, it should be evident that labor could never receive wages equal to the value of the commodities it produced (i.e., wages sufficient for labor to purchase all of the commodities it produced) for then there would be no profit (equivalent to surplus value) for the capitalist and the system would fall apart.

Thus surplus value is a deduction (Marx used "expropriation") from the wealth produced by labor. It is the source of all the wealth of the capitalist and the only vehicle by which he can accumulate wealth. But the absolute size of the extracted surplus value is not a measure sufficient enough for the capitalist to gauge how efficiently he is using his money. For example, if capitalist A invests $100 and gets back $110, he has extracted $10 of surplus value ($110-100=10$). His rate of profit would be $100 \div 10 = 10$ percent. On the other hand if capitalist B invests $1,000 and gets back $1,010, his rate of profit is then $1,010 - 1,000 = 10$, $\frac{10}{1000} = 1$ percent.

Obviously capitalist A, by extracting more surplus value for every dollar invested, is using his money more efficiently. In a competitive economy capital used more efficiently would tend to absorb capital used less efficiently, hence the tendency toward centralization and the maintenance of the highest rate of profit possible. The goal of all capitalists is to maximize profitability (rate of profit) by maximizing the rate of surplus value extracted. This, however, is a model of a perfect competitive system that no longer exists. The dynamic of present-day monopolies is more complex and will be discussed later.

The main methods by which the capitalist can increase the rate of surplus value deducted from labor's production is by (1) lowering wages, (2) extending the working day, and (3) increasing the productivity of labor.

Methods 1 and 2 are especially applicable to MNC's and will be discussed later. The most general and pervasive trend of modern capitalism has been the effort to increase the productivity of labor.

It will be recalled that capitalism entails a dynamic process of expansion of money that can be accomplished only through continuously throwing money back into the system. More than that, capitalists must throw more money back into the system than they started with, that is, they must invest part or all of the surplus value appropriated from labor plus the initial money they started with. This increase in investment produces still more surplus value, which at the end of the process enables still another increase in investment. "This is the process known as the accumulation of capital; it constitutes the driving force of capitalist development" (Sweezy 1942:80).

According to Marx, "the development of capitalist production makes it constantly necessary to keep increasing the amount of capital laid out in a given industrial undertaking, and competition makes the imminent laws of capitalist production to be felt by each individual capitalist as external coercive laws. It compels him to keep constantly extending his capital, in order to preserve it, but extend it he cannot except by means of progressive accumulation" (Sweezy 1942:81).

Capital accumulation leads to expanded production. In other words, it enables the capitalist to buy more raw materials, machinery, and labor. This increased demand for labor tends to cause a rise in wages. But at the same time a rise in the value of labor causes a *decrease* in the rate of surplus value. This explains the trend toward increasing mechanization or, put in another way, the trend toward increasing the productivity of labor. The use of machines enables less labor to produce the same or a larger amount of goods. The demand for labor is thus decreased and hence a decrease in wages results. The rate of surplus value and profitability is maintained or increased. For example, in the production scheme used earlier, labor worked four hours for itself and four hours for surplus value. Now with increased mechanization labor need only work two hours for its needs of subsistence while six hours are spent in producing surplus value.[1] Thus accumulation enables and requires capitalists to squeeze out of labor higher rates of surplus value and profits. But at the same time this constitutes the fundamental contradiction of capitalism.

Marx states this fundamental contradiction as follows:

The creation of . . . surplus value is the object of the direct process of production. As soon as the available quantity of surplus value has been materialized in commodities, surplus value has been produced. . . . Now comes the second act of the process. The entire mass of commodities . . . must be sold. . . . The conditions of direct exploitation and those of the realization of surplus value are not identical. They are separated logically as well as by time and space. The first are only limited by the productive power of society, the last by the consuming power of society. This last-named power is not determined by either the absolute productive power or by the absolute consuming power, but by the consuming power based on antagonistic conditions of distribution, which reduces the consumption of the great mass of the population to a variable minimum within more or less narrow limits. The consuming power is further restricted by the tendency to accumulate, the greed for an expansion of capital and a production of surplus value on an enlarged scale. . . . This internal contradiction seeks to balance itself by the expansion of the outlying fields of production. But to an extent that the productive power develops, it finds itself at variance with the narrow basis on which the condition of consumption rests. On this self-contradictory basis it is no contradiction at all that there should be an excess of capital simultaneously with an excess of population. For while a combination of these two would indeed increase the mass of the produced surplus value, it would at the same time intensify the contradiction between the conditions under which this surplus value is produced and those under which it is realized (Sweezy 1942:175–176).

This fundamental contradiction flows from the objectives of capitalism itself: the expansion of exchange value and the ever-increasing accumulation of capital "without any reference to the consumption which alone can give it meaning" (Sweezy 1942:175). In order for capital to accumu-

---

[1] Sweezy (1942) indicates in Chapter 6 *"The falling tendency of the rate of profit"* that Marx assumed a constant rate of surplus value (S') with increasing organic composition of capital (q). But Sweezy goes on to show that S' may increase or decrease with increasing q. In another volume, *Monopoly Capital*, Baran and Sweezy demonstrate that S' does increase with increasing q in a monopoly economy.

late and exchange value to expand, labor must be paid wages less than that necessary to buy back all that it produces. Hence, in a capitalist economy there exists the tendency toward underconsumption relative to supply. Sweezy gives formal proof of the tendency toward underconsumption by showing that "the ratio of the rate of growth of consumption to the rate of growth of means of production declines . . . [while] the ratio of the rate of growth in the output of goods to the rate of growth of means of production remains constant" (Sweezy 1942:180–183).

It should be noted here that the tendency toward underconsumption is not merely a problem of maldistribution; that is, it cannot be corrected by an equitable distribution of wealth under capitalist production. A redistribution of wealth from capital to labor would decrease the profitability and rate of accumulation of capital. Moreover, the capitalist class would lose control over the working class. In other words, the primary conditions of capitalist development would be destroyed.

Economic crises and/or stagnation result from the tendency toward underconsumption. But underconsumption is a tendency that may be deferred to some future time because of several counteracting factors. These factors are primarily the increasing global growth of capital, debt-financing, and waste.

Growth of capital investment yields an increase in effective demand (buying power) because there is a separation in time between the construction of means of production and final output of goods. That is, wages are paid to labor for the building of factories and machinery and the extraction of raw materials that do not yet enter into consumption. These wages are then used to consume the oversupply of goods produced by previously constructed means of production. But when the goods from newly constructed industry enter the market the oversupply of goods relative to effective demand would increase unless capital investment increases yet again.

Up to this point we have assumed a competitive economic structure, but we must stress that the present structure of capitalism is dominated by monopolies and oligopolies and all trends indicate that capital is becoming more concentrated and centralized.

Recall in our previous discussion of rates of profit that companies having higher profit rates tend to absorb those having lower profit rates. The centralization process is hastened by the credit system, which tends to put capital in the hands of capitalists having higher profitability and higher accumulation rates. The natural development of this process over time has resulted in a relatively noncompetitive economic structure characterized by monopolies and MNC's. Monopolies have the ability to restrict growth of supply and maintain an inflated price structure within a given industry. This tendency of monopoly to restrict growth of industry causes an overwhelming tendency to stagnation. This brings us to the role of government as a counteracting factor. Government, however, cannot counteract the sources of the problem: the very existence of monopolies and MNC's, which are natural structural developments of contemporary capitalism.

The major effects of stagnation are massive unemployment and underconsumption, which government can temporarily relieve by engaging in debt-financing (deficit spending). Government borrows money (at an interest rate) from capitalists in order to pay other capitalists to build certain industries. Part of this money is used to employ workers, who increase effective demand throughout the economy. In the United States the military industry is the primary channel for deficit spending. This is a good choice from the point of view of enhancing effective demand since the products of the military industry do not enter into the consumer market; hence there is no oversupply problem from this sector. It should be noted too that products of the military sector, composed of all major monopolies, do not compete with the other products of these monopolies.

In terms of consumption the government is in the business of creating waste. Sweezy has estimated that in 1970, 25.6 percent of the U.S. labor force was employed in the military industry. "For comparison, the highest unemployment rate ever recorded was 24.9 percent at the depth of the depression in 1933" (Sweezy 1972:3). But government debt financing introduces contradictions of its own. The rate of U.S. government borrowing ($495 billion cumulative debt in 1974) is accelerating and interest is accumulating faster (United Nations 1972:653). In spite of the talk of shutting off the money pumps, government finds that it must keep them going at full speed just to keep the economy running at the stagnation level. Hence today we discover the phenomenon of simultaneous stagnation and inflation. It should be pointed out that it is the working class who must pay back the money that government borrowed — with interest. But it is not only government borrowing that bolsters employment and sagging demand. Between 1965 and 1973 commercial bank loans more than doubled, consumer installment credit increased by 253 percent, and remortgages of homes — that is, money used for purposes other than acquiring homes — increased by 600 percent (*Monthly Review* 1974:9). The working class is clearly going bankrupt.

All the above "cures" act to expand the monetary supply. Within a monopoly economy the rate of price increase must at least equal the rate of increase in the money supply just to maintain profit rates. These price increases and inflation lead to further centralization because under inflationary conditions monopolies have an advantage over non-monopoly corporations: they can successfully raise prices and restrict supply *simultaneously*, while nonmonopoly corporations must follow the supply/demand curve. It should be no surprise then that *Fortune* magazine reported in 1974 that the top 500 corporations accumulated more wealth and made higher profits than ever before in history. We need only mention here that unutilized productive capacity has been steadily increasing throughout the period 1965–1973 and presently hovers at around 25 percent (*Monthly Review* 1974:9).

It should be apparent from the preceding analysis that the techniques of deficit spending and consumer borrowing act to mask or to forestall but in no way to resolve the fundamental contradiction of capital. It may be said that the "cures" only exacerbate the problem and accelerate the process of capital accumulation.

We now shift our point of view when we discuss the development of MNC's. We noted earlier that the monopoly does not invest all of its increasing cash flows in expanding its own production. To do that would destroy the artificially high monopoly price structure. Therefore monopoly capital must spread into other industries and countries. Along this line 46 percent of MNC investment is in the acquisition of already existing corporations abroad. An additional percentage of investment is in expansion of distribution and sales networks, a minor part of investment being used in the actual construction of new plants (*CIC Brief* 1973:3b). Aside from providing investment opportunities for MNC's, the Third World additionally reinforces MNC cash flow. MNC's tap approximately 50 percent of savings in Third World countries, and "development" typically proceeds through loans to Third World governments which effectively determines government behavior toward MNC's (*CIC Brief* 1973:3c). But "the problem of *deficiency* of effective demand does not arise here, for government investment is large in relation to the productive potential which is very low despite abundance of labor. As a result the situation is characterized by inflationary pressures on a scarce supply of necessities rather than by inadequate effective demand, even though disguised and also open unemployment is in existence. . . . The central problem here is at whose expense the country is to be developed. If inflationary pressures on scarce supplies of necessities (especially food) persist, it is broad poverty-stricken masses of the population that bear the burden of high investment" (Kalecki 1971:76–77).

By absorbing Third World industry into the MNC network and by placing local bourgeoisie in management and subordinate ownership positions, the MNC is fostering development of an international capitalist class. Within this multinational framework the corporation has relatively little allegiance to its base country. The MNC profits from currency crises and different inflation rates in different countries by playing one country off another — even the United States. In addition, MNC's can take advantage of the lower wage rates and longer working hours of labor in Third World countries — an opportunity closed to the corporation operating exclusively in an industrialized country.

In this context the well-being of any one nation-state is subordinate to the well-being of the MNC operating in a global environment. "The modern giant corporation has a profound need to *dominate* and *control* all the conditions and variables which affect its viability" (Sweezy 1972:21). That is, it acts to ensure the perpetuation of its existence beyond that of any single industry or nation-state, even of the industrial world.

The MNC, by absorbing Third World economies into its structure, is making these countries face the same contradictions as advanced capitalist countries. For example, although MNC's are investing in Third World nations, there is a net capital outflow of 264 percent (*CIC Brief* 1973:3b). From this it follows that although foreign investment as a mode for the absorption of surplus capital may have been attractive initially, this cannot be entirely true today because Third World foreign investment is generating surplus capital at a rate 2.6 times greater than in the industrial countries. In this context we note the development of a worldwide "monopoly-capitalistic culture."

MNC's are currently engaged in the expansion of a global system of distribution and sales. One strategy of this expansion involves the creation of needs in people for those products produced by high-technology industries. In Third World countries MNC sales generally remain limited to local elites and the middle sector (i.e., government employees, the Army, and corporate technocrats). The advertising industry plays a critical role in the generation of high-consumption markets and, at the same time, because of the unproductive nature of advertising, it also serves to absorb surplus. Furthermore, the sales effort commands the nature of production itself; it demands that products undergo annual superficial cosmetic changes in order to increase saleability, rather than utility. This command over production further absorbs surplus and the resulting amount of wasted human effort, capital, and resources cannot begin to be estimated in a global context. However, the auto industry, one of the largest global industries, suggests the dimensions of this waste: it has been estimated that if no auto model changes had been made beginning in 1949 the consumer price today would be about $700 per car (Baran and Sweezy 1966:135–138). Waste, with all its social and ecological destructiveness, is the price of growth under capitalism. The only alternative to growth that capitalism offers is depression.

In Third World countries where there is a pressing need for basic foodstuffs such as grains and cereals, MNC's are instead producing processed foods of low nutritional content; instead of developing basic infrastructure such as mass transportation, the MNC produces high-profit-yielding cars catering to a very narrow market.

Up to this point the analysis has proceeded at a fairly high level of abstraction, which enabled us to understand the fundamental relationships and processes of capitalist development. In our case study of

Deltec we find corporate behavior patterns that at times appear quite irrational. However, by keeping the previous framework in mind, this seemingly irrational behavior becomes quite rational within the paradoxes of capitalism.

THE SEARCH FOR CAPITAL

Deltec International Limited is a primarily a sales network. Deltec was established by a consortium of U.S. and West German banks (principally the Rockefeller Chase Manhattan bank) (Vandervort n.d.:1). Deltec is mainly in the business of funneling North American and European capital, in the form of loans, into Third World countries, especially in Latin America. In other words, Deltec acts as a financial intermediary between lending and borrowing institutions. This capital is lent to Third World governments, subsidiaries of European, North American, and Japanese corporations, and locally owned corporations. Third World governments in turn use these loans to support and expand their military (Brazil borrowed DM 40,000,000 in 1969 for military housing), to lend to other MNC's for corporate expansion, and for locally owned corporate expansion. The flow of loan capital through Deltec increased almost 1,000 percent from 1963 to 1973, when it made loans totaling nearly a half-billion dollars (Deltec International Limited 1972:8, 1973:9). In return for its services Deltec makes a profit rate as high as 10 percent (*Columbia Journal of World Business* 1969:56).

Deltec has expanded its own equity base and cash flow by setting up mutual funds, particularly in Brazil. The behavior patterns of local elites must be changed to facilitate the conversion of savings into shares, and this often entails a form of manipulation that is Deltec's main strength.

For example, in 1966 Deltec and Companhia Brasileiro de Investimentos (CBI) were involved in a stock scandal that shook Brazil's financial structure. CBI distributed a stock issue of $20,000,000 for Dominium, a Brazilian coffee company originally capitalized at only $9,000,000. The stock issue was directed mainly to small investors in order to ensure Dominium's continued control. In order to make the shares attractive to investors, a fixed interest rate of 36 percent per annum was guaranteed. This was in flagrant violation of Brazilian financial practice. On May 6, 1968, Dominium declared bankruptcy, in part caused by its inability to pay the 36 percent interest rate. Dominium owed $12,000,000 to 45,000 investors and 40 financial institutions. The president of Brazil ordered a full investigation to determine "the civil and criminal responsibilities of those involved." The eventual outcome was that Dominium was declared a national patrimony, that is, a firm so vital to the national interest that the government would subsidize it. The government's investigation stopped short of publicly involving Deltec, although our research has revealed that Deltec had considerably more than a passive role in this affair (Deltec Research Project, this volume).

In order to complete its plan of global integration, Deltec has allied itself with Nikko Securities, Japan's second-largest investment banker. A prime reason for this alliance, which will considerably aid the flow of Japanese capital, was pointed out by the financial journal *Business Latin America*: "As Japanese manufacturing firms mushroom in major Latin American countries, Japanese financial interests are following their lead with selective buying into the area's key institutions." It further noted that "use of the Japanese capital market was recently illustrated by the extension of loans worth $300 million by the Bank of Japan to IBM World Trade Corp. . . . The Japanese government is giving special encouragement to this type of financial arrangement, particularly for projects in developing nations, to sop up some of its huge foreign [dollar] reserves surplus" (*Business Latin America* 1972:250).

One reason for the intense interest in Latin America is the existence of large pools of cheap labor, an interest that can best be illustrated by the Brazilian "economic miracle." While the Brazilian GNP has been growing at annual leaps of 10 percent since 1968, the real minimum wage has dropped by 35 percent. Union activity is stringently regulated by the government and wage increases can only be achieved by collective wage claims to the government's Labor Tribunals. But ". . . it is common practice for companies to sack the least-skilled workers, rehiring them after the wage award at the lowest wage authorized by the wage tribunals" (Cardoso 1973:10). In fact, only 10 percent of urban workers received "real income increases generated by the Brazilian economy" (Cardoso 1973:10). As pointed out earlier, it is the MNC that can take advantage of wage differentials existing between countries; hence there should be no surprise that investments in the Third World have 264 percent higher profit rates than in the industrial nations. MNC's do not merely take advantage of these differentials passively. On the contrary, through the establishment of political alliances, MNC's actively participate in the creation of those conditions conducive to exploitation.

For example, among the members of the council of administration of Companhia City de Desenvolvimento, a Deltec Brazilian subsidiary, were Senator Irinen Bornhausen — ex-governor of the state of Santa Catarina; Professor Lucas Nogueira Garcez — ex-governor of the state of São Paulo; and Ambassador Juracy Montenegro Magalhaes — Ex-Minister of Foreign Relations and ex-governor of the state of Bahia. An Argentine Deltec subsidiary, Swift de la Plata, had on the Board of Directors Adelbert Krieger Vasena — Minister of Finance of Argentina, and Pedro and Antonio Lanusse — brothers of the former Argentine President Lanusse.

In terms of capital accumulation the political involvement of MNC's has had immediate payoffs. Again, the "economic miracle" of Brazil will be used for illustration. In 1970 the Brazilian government instituted the Program of Social Integration (PSI), which was designed to benefit workers. The program operates by imposing a small income tax on all companies in the country and placing this money in a PSI bank account in which all workers have a share. At the same time these payments can be deducted from total corporate income tax. "By June 30, 1972, over 740 m. cruzeiros had been collected and this money was used for the benefit of the companies themselves: Cruzeiros 423 m. went to finance industrial production, 82 m. on trade, 85 m. on service sector companies and 179 m. to the capital market" (Cardoso 1973:10). Workers who cashed their share in 1972 received an average of only 20 cruzeiros. In 1971 the government showed its interest in agrarian reform when it organized Proterra — Program for Redistribution and Incentive to Agro-Industries in the North and Northeast. Instead of financing small local farmers, the low-interest money was lent to big businesses (Cardoso 1973:10). Hence it is not difficult to imagine where the rising stream of migrants that fill Brazil's shantytowns comes from.

Deltec described its intentions of taking advantage of these government benefits in 1971:

The long-term thrust of Deltec's ranching activities will center around the exciting potential of the Amazon Valley. Deltec and King Ranch own 176,000 acres of virgin land in the state of Para. It is our belief that this area will, in the future, become one of the most important producers of animal protein in the world. The accessibility of this region is rapidly improving with Brazil's ambitious Amazonian highway development. . . . Financial and investment incentives being granted by the Brazilian government have rapidly accelerated the development to the region and Deltec with its project is in the forefront of a large number of investors who are entering this region . . . (Deltec International Limited 1971:24).

But, in order to qualify for government loans and incentives the land must be officially classified as "cleared" of Indians (Indigena Report 1974:13). The labor used to build and operate these ranches is procured through labor brokers who gather workers from small villages and take them into the jungle (Cardoso 1973:11). The Indians living on this land are either killed, put in concentration camps, or "integrated" into the national economy (Indigena Report 1974:13). Although Deltec benefited from these "clearing" operations, there is no evidence that Deltec participated in them.

In spite of the rate at which the Brazilian people are being exploited,

Table 1. Public debt in Brazil

	1964	1965	1966	1967	1968	1969
Domestic: long-term (thousand million cruzeiros)	152.1	169.7	1,116.6	3,153.8	3,777.7	4,856.9
Domestic: short-term (thousand million cruzeiros)	857.7	2,244.8	2,971.2	3,553.0	5,181.3	5,147.1
Foreign dollars (millions)	11.1	9.1	7.1	5.4	—	—

Source: United Nations statistical yearbook 1971 1972:655

Brazil, like all other Third World nations that choose this path of development, is rapidly going into debt.

Clarence Dauphinot, Jr., chairman of Deltec's Board, pointed out that "One of the critical current problems is that an increasingly larger portion of new loans must be designated to service old loans" (*Columbia Journal of World Business* 1969:58). Yet, paradoxically, it is Deltec that benefits from these loans and gauges its success from the volume of loans it makes. But Dauphinot understands this contradiction, and in order to make a profit his company is taking advantage of it. "What it comes down to is this," Dauphinot says. "The Latin American countries in one way or another must export in larger volume than they ever have before. They must continue to sell their commodities and raw materials abroad, but they must also intensify their efforts to sell their new industrial products in the major markets of the world" (*Columbia Journal of World Business* 1969:58).

In order to accomplish this effort Deltec has inserted itself into the middle through the creation of a worldwide distribution and sales network. The pattern of Deltec's investments reveal that it generally avoids direct ownership of productive facilities, which are subject to nationalization and labor unrest, but instead makes these productive facilities dependent on Deltec's sales network. Deltec's multinational structure allows it to remain independent of any single nation-state's production or market. As Dauphinot explains: "When one country shuts off, we hope others will remain open. Last May France had its strikes; and in late November a run on the franc. We have to sit out these events and be flexible enough to concentrate our sales efforts elsewhere — Germany, Switzerland, Spain. Fortunately, the markets do not all bust up at the same time. We have to remain extremely flexible these days" (*Columbia Journal of World Business* 1969:57). How Deltec manages to remain flexible in order to achieve domination and control will be the subject of the next section.

THE STRUGGLE TO CONTROL

The primary objective of the MNC is the maintenance of its existence. In order to realize this the MNC must gain control over as many of the variables that affect its existence as possible. Occasionally this means engaging in relatively unprofitable ventures in the short term if this will assure increased profitability in the long term. The need for control is a result of the modern corporate structure itself, that is, a monopoly structure that requires control over supply and market conditions. The rationale for the development of monopoly has been pointed out in the first section. The MNC is a monopoly corporation that finds, because of its surplus capital, a need to diversify both geographically and in terms of production. At the same time the MNC finds that it must extend its monopoly control over as many sources of production and as many markets as possible. The source of this pressure comes not only, nor primarily, from competing MNC's, but from the structural nature of the corporation itself, the degree of its accumulation and concentration.

One way in which the MNC extends its control is by integrating capitalists of a country into its structure through selling them loans and minority shares and giving them managerial positions. Once the MNC has established a dependent economic relationship, the state, as the extension of the local bourgeoisie, will grant the MNC such economic concessions as tax shelters, investment credits, and subsidies.

Because MNC's are occasionally confronted with unforeseen political circumstances, many have developed a structure that is flexible and relatively unharmed by such situations. The fundamental requirements for such flexibility are sources of production in several geographic areas and a finance structure enabling monetary assets to be rapidly shifted out of the crisis-ridden country to one where capitalist economic institutions are protected by the government. Deltec's president, Dauphinot, clearly describes the ideal conditions for the successful operation of his business: "What we are looking for in any country is relative stability in the foreseeable future. If the trend is such that we think the institutions of the Western world are in danger of being destroyed, then we cannot operate where that is happening or threatened. The particular government in power does not matter; nor does it really concern us who is the head of the government — as long as the basic institutions of the nation's political and economic life are not disturbed. We could not function in Venezuela under Perez Jiminez nor in Brazil under President Goulart. But once these gentlemen departed and the disrupted institutions revived, we were back in business" (*Columbia Journal of World Business* 1969:57).

The political allegiance of the state to the MNC is particularly important since it assures it of stable working conditions. Many MNC's look favorably upon military dictatorships, and in some instances have even helped install them. The best labor movement for the MNC is one that is totally controlled by the state.

The state-controlled labor unions of Brazil have been mentioned in the previous section. The case of the Uruguayan meat industry is particularly instructive for it demonstrates the power of the MNC even in the face of a strong labor movement. In 1959 Swift and Armour, two of the largest MNC's in the meat industry, were thrown out of Uruguay over a series of scandals. Shortly thereafter the meat industry was nationalized and put under workers' control. But in 1969, when Deltec acquired International Packers Limited, it constructed plants in the interior of Uruguay, where it could obtain cheap, indigenous, unorganized labor. This effectively crippled the labor movement, for when cattle was diverted from labor-controlled plants to Deltec's own plants, the former plants were forced to shut down (Yglesias 1971:3). The ability of many MNC's to shift production from one country to another demands that they constantly cultivate the friendship of local elites and government officials and win their allegiance to the goals of the corporation. In this way they can be assured of a country receptive to their capital in the event it becomes impossible to operate in another country. For example, in order to coerce the Argentine government into granting economic concessions to Deltec, Deltec paralyzed the vital Argentine meat industry by shutting down its plants there and shifting production to Brazil. At the time Deltec was shifting production to Brazil, Antonio Delfin Neto, finance minister of Brazil, biased taxation against domestic ranchers and packers to favor the large foreign corporations. Furthermore, Francisco Cavalcanti, who during his tenure as agrarian reform chief had proven himself to be a friend of MNC's, was installed as minister of agriculture (Vandervort n.d.:3).

The preceding example may be viewed as a strategy that may be used by MNC's in general to exploit divisions within the capitalist class of developing countries. That such divisions exist has been indicated by numerous empirical studies by both neoclassical establishment economists and Marxist economists. When an MNC enters a developing economy it typically purchases already existing means of production rather than constructing new ones. Although local capitalists often sell these means of production to MNC's willingly, they may as a class feel they are losing control over their economy to foreign corporations. As a consequence of MNC penetration a conflict is created between those local capitalists who have been integrated into the MNC corporate structure and those who would resist the influx of foreign capital.

To alleviate such intraclass conflict there is evidence that MNC's are moving in the direction of a new organizational form of control, one that is confirmed by the Deltec case study. This new organizational structure affirms local majority ownership of an MNC's subsidiary and rejects majority parent ownership. Rather, the MNC exerts its control at the points of finance, distribution, and marketing. Production decisions at the local level become subservient to the distribution and marketing apparatus that the MNC controls. For example, when Deltec purchased meat-production plants in a number of countries, the output of these facilities consisted of 20 percent processed meat and 80 percent fresh meat. Within four years Deltec had restructured these plants to produce 80 percent processed meats, which could only be sold through its distribution network. These plants were then sold back to local capitalists but remained dependent on the distribution network. In addition, trademarks and such technological innovations as the Cryovac process of packaging meats create entry barriers not easily overcome by local capitalists.

Above all Deltec binds these capitalists to its structure by its ability to make loans in return for production outputs. In this way overt conflict with local capitalists and threats of nationalization are avoided. Although hierarchical relationships definitely exist within the capitalist class on the infrastructural level, these remain covert and unrecognized because legal title of ownership continues to be viewed by local capitalists as a decisive instrument of control.

CONCLUSION

The capitalist structure of Third World countries is dependent on the financial structure of MNC's. More often than not local capitalists benefit from this dependency. MNC's must maintain this dependent relationship for their existence: it is essential as a mode for increasing profitability and cash flow and essential as an outlet for accumulated capital.

The great mobility of large blocks of capital controlled by the financial arm of the MNC is the fundamental factor in the MNC's ability to control the relationships between itself and the economies in which it operates. It is the potential power of large quantities of liquid capital that is decisive, making it possible to out-compete locally controlled firms through temporary price wars, to establish larger, more integrated firms on the same soil, to deprive local firms of foreign markets, and above all to deprive these firms of capital. This potential, which need not be realized, induces local capitalists to become absorbed by the multinational corporate structure and prevents them from leaving it.

The MNC is dominant in this pattern of social relations in spite of the legal title of ownership of a subsidiary that may be held by local capitalists. The juridical form of ownership of the means of production no longer has the meaning attributed to it by traditional capitalist and Marxist theory. The control of large quantities of capital brings into being a qualitative change in the meaning of ownership and control that need not have juridical form. It is control of capital in the abstract that means everything.

REFERENCES

BARAN, P.A., P.M. SWEEZY
    1966   *Monopoly capital*. New York. Monthly Review Press.
Business Latin America
    1972   "Japanese financial move into Latin America." *Business Latin America* August 10.
CARDOSO, HENRIQUE
    1973   "Workers share in Brazilian economic miracle." International Union of Food and Allied Workers' Associations *News Bulletin* 43(11–12).
Columbia Journal of World Business
    1969   Entrepreneur, middleman, builder in the world of investment: an interview with Clarence Dauphinot, Jr. *Columbia Journal of World Business* 4(1).
Corporate Information Center Brief
    1973   "An examination of the multinational corporation." Corporate Information Center.
DELTEC INTERNATIONAL LIMITED
    1971   *Deltec country area reports*
    1972   *Annual report*
    1973   *Annual report*
Fortune
    1974   The Fortune directory of the 500 largest industrial corporations. *Fortune* 89(5).
INDIGENA REPORT
    1974   Riding over the Indians. *Brazilian Information Bulletin* (12).
KALECKI, MICHAEL
    1971   Theories of growth in different social systems. *Monthly Review* October.
Monthly Review
    1974   Keynesian chickens come home to roost. *Monthly Review* April.
SERVAN-SCHREIBER, J.J.
    1968   *The American challenge*. New York: Atheneum.
SWEEZY, PAUL M.
    1942   *The theory of capitalist development*. New York: Oxford University Press.
    1972   On the theory of monopoly capital. *Monthly Review* April.
UNITED NATIONS
    1972   *United Nations statistical yearbook: 1971*. Washington, D.C.: United Nations Printing Office.
VANDERVORT, BRUCE
    n.d.   "Deltec International: outflanking the nationalists." Unpublished.
YGLESIAS, E.
    1971   Testimony by Uruguayan delegate in *International Food Workers Union Conference Report 1971*.

Ecology and Ideology

ANTHONY WILDEN

THE ECOSYSTEMIC PERSPECTIVE

Most people are acquainted with ecology and with the "environmental crisis" — some to the point of being sick and tired of it. And yet, in spite of ten years of publicity about it, in spite of the daily newspaper reports about it, what is actually happening is not well understood. On the one hand, a number of ecologists predict our imminent extinction — which of course nobody can believe. On the other, people write, read, and talk of such matters as air and water pollution as if they were analogous to a rising crime rate accompanying rising population. But the crime rate under more or less normal social conditions always refers to a more or less fixed percentage of the population. The population of "criminals" is controlled to a major extent by the same factors as those controlling the population as a whole (with due allowance for special cases of social disruption, e.g., the rise in hard-drug addiction stemming from the Indochina War). Unlike air and water pollution, the crime rate is not necessarily *accumulative*.

Accumulated air and water pollution are, however, still no more than symptoms of underlying processes, and it is these processes we need to understand. At the risk of explaining to some readers what they already know, I begin with a summary of the *kinds* of processes involved in ecosystemic relationships.

What I am seeking to show is that the current "problematic of the future" is not an "ecological" crisis in the usual sense of the term, but a crisis in the *economic* organization of the global ecosystem. Since economics concerns the fundamental kind of relationship between people in a given economic system — as well as their relationship to "nature" (which is in any case a social category) — the economic crisis becomes an unprecedented kind of *social* and *political* crisis. The "problem of the environment" reveals itself to be an ideological smoke screen. Just as the phrase "the Negro problem" projected the psychological and economic fact of white racism onto the very people it exploited and oppressed, the phrase "the environmental crisis" projects the responsibility for the crisis away from its actual source. It implies that the natural environment is the problem, rather than its exploitation by industrial capitalism.

This ideological process of projection occurs at every level in the social ecosystem. It is complemented by the idea that man- and womankind are responsible for the crisis — i.e., "human nature" — whereas what is in fact involved is the historically determined exploitation by capitalism of everything it chooses to define as the *environment* of capital: nature, other classes, other races, the Third World.

The "ecological" danger to the future results from an ideology of the benefits of economic growth, which is a covert metaphor for the systemic and objective necessities of capital accumulation. The exponential and super-exponential increases in population, in pollution, and in the exhaustion of the nonrenewable matter-energy reserves of the planet are not the result of Western "ethics" or "ways of thought." The Western epistemology, as I have sought to show in detail elsewhere (Wilden 1973), is derived from socioeconomic organization, and not the other way around.

Naturally, our ideology — based on the myth of "free and equal" and "autonomous" individuals in "open" and symmetrical competition in a free marketplace of commodities and ideas — says the opposite. Nevertheless, this myth of the abstract individual should not deter us from trying to analyze what is happening to real people in the real world, especially once we realize that it is our own survival that is at stake.

Since ecosystemic processes are interlinked — increased population increases the use of energy which increases pollution, for instance — it is not possible to talk of these processes in the traditional linear terms of cause and effect. Whereas we have been trained and educated to think in a language of causality which says that "like causes produce like effects," the ecosystemic perspective requires us to think in a different vocabulary. For example, in the biosphere (the life-support systems of the planet), seemingly insignificant causes can produce enormous and unexpected effects, because very small disturbances in the complicated system of natural relationships may undergo amplification as they are transmitted throughout the system.

Changes in one part of the system may also have effects on other parts that do not at first sight seem to be very closely connected with the area in which the changes first occurred. Our failure to see the connections is part and parcel of the way we have been trained to think of cause and effect. We have inherited our doctrine of causality and our metaphors of change from classical physics. But the relations between the inorganic particles and forces studied by classical physics are of a different type of complexity from those involved in the relations between organisms.

What is significant is that one of the basic tenets of the ecosystemic perspective, the *multiplication of causes by their effects*, applies in all biological and social systems. For example, a relatively small withdrawal of affection and/or lack of sensory stimulation in the first year of the life of a human child becomes amplified into relatively large psychological and developmental changes throughout the child's later life. Some of these changes, like ecological changes, prove to be irreversible.

The ecosystemic perspective involves radical changes in our way of thinking about *all* kinds of relationships. But changes in thinking are useless without radical changes in ways of behaving. Such changes in behavior, however, are not in general possible for the single individual. Our individual behavior is linked to sets of values, on the one hand, and to socioeconomic organization on the other; our "individual" values are, within certain clearly defined limits, the values of of our culture. Consequently, any valid ecosystemic perspective must necessarily seek to locate the real source of the problem in cultural and economic values, not in "individual" values. It seeks change in the socioeconomic sphere, not simply in the individual.

As Paul Sears said in 1964, the questioning of what he called "growth for the sake of growth" by ecology makes ecology a subversive science: so subversive in fact that it generates problems of almost intolerable difficulty, shaking the values of our culture — and the values of the various countercultures — to their foundations. To take the simplest example: population stabilization through birth control is one thing for the relatively affluent white majority in the United States. It is quite another matter for the racial minorities in that country, many of whose members see no possibility of significantly affecting the economic and social discrimination of the white majority against them except through an increase in their numbers.

The solution to this sort of problem depends upon the introduction of the idea of *context*. The context of white values may call for a stabilization of population growth. The context of the minorities calls for population increase. It is not possible to apply the same set of values, in the abstract, to both populations. A contextual approach — but one which is undoubtedly unacceptable to the white majority — would call for a *decrease* in the white population matched by an *increase* in the minority population. Population stabilization would then be achieved by altering the present ethnic ratios, not by a general limitation on growth which seeks to maintain those ratios at their present levels.

What is of further concern is that there presently exists no detailed scientific theory adequate to deal with the complexity of ecosystemic processes and relations. For example, nobody has any idea what, whether, or how the *relationship* between DDT and PCB compounds found in animal tissue may involve combined long-range effects that are more harmful than the effects of either compound alone. It is difficult enough to deal scientifically with the cumulative effects of a single chemical of this type in complex food-chains (e.g., plankton→little fish→big fish→birds and humans), much less two. An ecologist will deal in detail with one part of a complex cycle, or with one aspect of the ecological damage occurring in it. But he is unable, for practical and theoretical reasons, to deal adequately with a whole set of other interdependent and interrelated factors — some of which he hasn't heard of yet anyway.

The principal reason for this difficulty is that ecological systems are *open* systems (open to some "environment" or other, including their own "parts," and to many levels of the general environment), whereas the vast and sophisticated theoretical armory of "hard" science and scientific method (notably physics) is founded on the study of *closed* systems (or of systems defined as closed by the methodological requirements of experimentation). We may well wonder, therefore, what may be the combined effects of the increasing amounts of two of the most persistent of synthetic chemicals found in mother's milk, DDT and PCB — and be even more concerned to know what it means to discover that white-tailed eagles in Sweden contain not only DDT and PCB, but also another particularly persistent set of toxins: mercury compounds.

My point in speaking of the relatively simple possible interactions between these three groups of pollutant compounds is that the inability of present theory to deal properly with these and other much more complex ecological interactions means that *every ecological statement we read about is inherently and necessarily much more conservative in its estimates and predictions than the probable future state of the reality it is describing*.

This conservatism of the most "radical" ecology is a matter that exists entirely apart from the fact that science is inherently conservative, and resistant to fundamental changes in its theoretical base. It is also quite apart from the fact that scientists, because of their privileged status by class and caste, are, as a group, conservative people — whatever their discipline. They are conservative in the "liberal" sense of those who consciously or unconsciously draw their fundamental beliefs from the middle-class ideology of the seventeenth and eighteenth centuries, rather than from a critical understanding of contemporary or historical reality.

A. N. Whitehead once said that Western civilization is still living on the intellectual capital accumulated in the seventeenth century. He also said that the culture that cannot break through the framework of its own concepts is doomed. This is, after all, the period of the capitalist revolution, of the fundamental reorganization of social relations resulting from a historically novel type of commodity production. The technical and technological innovation represented by capitalist social organization was accompanied by two allied events: (1) the invention of the abstract, autonomous individual and the atomization of social relations through a quantitative and one-dimensional principle of social "performance" (currently represented, in particular, by the IQ test); (2) the invention of the Newtonian-Cartesian scientific method based on mechanics, closed systems, a new atomism, and linear causality, as well as on three basic, nonecosystemic principles: that no effect can be greater than its cause (the "scientific" basis of Descartes' ontological argument for the existence of God), that like causes produce like effects, and that action and reaction are equal and opposite (symmetry).

I cannot go into the complex historical process of these changes in detail. It is enough to say that (1) it is precisely at this period that "nature" became defined by science, by ideology, and by economic relationships as an *object* of control, exploitation, and domination; (2) at the same time, the development of capitalism was being financed through the designation of the nonwhite world as a similar environment for the system to exploit (capitalist development resulted from the violent *de-development* of the civilizations that we now call "undeveloped" as if it were their natural or genetic condition); (3) the physicists' model of atoms and closed systems related by self-regulating internal forces was immediately imported into biology, psychology, and the social sciences, *where it still remains* (e.g., Freud, Parsons, Lévi-Strauss, Piaget); (4) the same model was also imported into political theory (the U.S. constitution) and became the foundation of modern left- and right-wing liberalism. Liberalism is based on the idea of free and equal social atoms in one-dimensional and symmetrical relations of separable and individual responsibility for their own situation. (Compare the genetic argument for the "inferiority" of women. Given the real relations of oppression and exploitation in our society, it became necessary to show that some atoms were less equal than others, e.g., also the slaves and the current politics of human genetics.); (5) the same model naturally turned up in economic theory seeking to justify social relations under capitalism, e.g., the myth of free enterprise, the mechanics of "equilibrium dynamics" in the work of Alfred Marshall, and current game theory.

In a word, science, ideology, and economics all became united around a conception of the individual *and the organism* (cf. Freud, Claude Bernard, Piaget) as isolated systems, governed like billiard balls by "forces" ("instincts" in psychology and ethology), all on the same plane of being, all separate from their environment(s) and from the various levels of the general environment. Organism, atom, and person became ontologically and ideologically equivalent — and explained by overt or covert mechanical metaphors. The "free" individual was in fact — and still is — a metaphor of her or his status as a commodity in the marketplace, measured against the linear yardstick of money or a similar "general equivalent." The accompanying ideology sought to homogenize and digitalize the individual, just as the factory system devalued the qualitative aspect of human labor (human creativity) and made it both abstract and quantitative (cf. again the IQ test), making the laborer the equivalent of an interchangeable machine part in a social system conceived of as a production line.

What is significant is that none of these basic conceptions or values have changed significantly over the last two hundred years. (Note, for instance, that both relativity and indeterminacy reinforce the closed-system basis, as well as the idea that not only are all atoms equal, but that all *standpoints of interpretation* are also equal.) The liberalism of the university and society remains based on these notions (in spite of certain inconsistencies). The academic notion of the "free marketplace of ideas" not only reflects the fact that knowledge itself had become a commodity by the nineteenth century, but also implies that ideas themselves are atoms. Hence the hostility of academia toward explicitly systemic interpretations of social reality (the systemic liberal ideology is preferred to remain unconscious). As Garry Wills points out in his *Nixon agonistes*, the liberal ideology is based on the self-regulation of the market — Adam Smith's "hidden hand" — in spite of the fact that if unregulated free competition actually existed, capitalism would have fallen into stagnation and collapse long ago.

In a word, this whole complex of ideas and realities militates against the kind of ecosystemic understanding — with an open commitment to the ideology of long-range survival — that is essential if we are to have a human future. At this point, we can identify several aspects of the ecosystemic perspective that are in general excluded both by liberalism and by the energy-entity epistemology of modern science. (Using a "systemic" vocabulary is not, one notes, the same as understanding it or its implications. One often finds it simply overlaid on a basically Newtonian model.)

These aspects may be summarized as follows: (1) the multiplication or amplification of causes through feedback processes; (2) the transmission of events in one part of the whole system into unexpected events in its other parts; (3) the recognition of organic and social complexity and the inadequacy of present methods of explaining it in detail; (4) the necessity for a properly contextual analysis of the values and behavior of any given system; (5) recognition that open systems are goal-seeking and involve levels of communication and control; (6) the distinction between energy-entity explanation and communicational-relational explanation; (7) the assumption that all behavior is communication; (8) recognition that the distinction between "organism" or "system" and "environment" is not a boundary equivalent to a barrier, but a locus of communication and exchange; (9) the problem of dealing with relations between relations (i.e., between systems, environments, and ecosystems); (10) the distinction between long-range and short-range effects, e.g., the transformation of adaptivity into counteradaptivity over time; (11) the protective and stabilizing nature of redundancy in such systems and the instability of efficiency; (12) the understanding that what survives in nature is not the fittest individual, but the fittest ecosystem, i.e. that what must survive above all is not the "entity" but the *relation* between system and environment; (13) the distinction between causality and constraint, between "determinism" and relative semiotic freedom; (14) the recognition that levels of communication and control can be distinguished by their logical typing, and that these relations can be reversed in human ecosystems.

This is a rather programmatic list, I'm afraid, and I shall not be able to deal with all these questions in a short paper. But it serves to indicate what is usually unrecognized in the traditional epistemology and ideology, neither of which can be properly applied to the kind of human and biological reality that is our primary concern here.

One final point of major importance: if open systems seek goals, then they involve *values*, which are hierarchically ordered. Consequently, the epistemology and the science of such systems is primarily and overtly qualitative, or should be.

ENVIRONMENTAL "IMPACT": LINEAR CAUSALITY AND FEEDBACK

Significantly enough, the U.S federal government now requires environmental impact statements for all major projects in the country. But the very term "impact" reveals the traditional dependence on a mechanical conception of linear causality that simply does not apply to ecosystemic relationships. (From acquaintance with the "environmental guidelines" being set up by one major federal agency, I can assure the reader that the term "impact" is a precise metaphor of the underlying mechanical model.)

In any ecosystem or any level of the overall ecosystem, interventions (impacts) result in reciprocal feedbacks. But the kind of causality involved in organic and social ecosystems means that this feedback is in no way comparable to the cause and effect relationship implied in the mechanistic term "impact," e.g., the impact and rebound of a rubber ball.

The momentum of the ball is absorbed or dissipated by impact with a soft medium and is largely reflected by a hard one. In any case, the ball returns with less momentum or force than it began with, and in so doing, it follows predictable paths. The feedback from a disturbance induced in a biosocial ecosystem is quite different. It is not primarily a sort of reflected or deflected and predictable force. Because the system is goal-seeking, reproducible, and adaptive, and because both matter-energy and informational relationships are involved, ecosystemic feedback may appear as totally new and unexpected disruptions — or *kinds* of disruption — elsewhere in the system, or at another level in the system, as the ecosystem seeks to adapt itself to the original disturbance.

This is especially the case when the difference between short-term and long-term effects in ecosystems means that the major feedback is delayed. In fact it is much more likely to be delayed than immediate, because of the capacity of ecosystems temporarily to make up for their losses by, e.g., increased reproduction or longer-term mutations, and so on.

Part of the reason for this is that impacts on ecosystems do not just leave scars behind, like scratches on rock, or craters on the moon. They also affect the future behavior of the system, and restrict or enlarge the scope or the kind of its future possibilities. In mechanics, the effects of causes do not result in adaptations, nor do they change the rules or laws governing the possible activities of the system. But an ecosystemic disruption may well change the ecosystem's rules of behavior, as it were, or the constraints on its rules.

In natural and social ecosystems, disruptions are not necessarily or primarily received as the impact of matter or the transformation of energy, but also and more importantly as *messages*. The kind of adaptations that come about as the system and its subsystems seek to "obey" their goals are thus directly comparable to the way "errors" or "noise" in the transmission of an order between human beings might change one instruction into another one. (The basic analogy, of course, is with the genetic instructions contained in the DNA molecule, which can get jumbled up or wrongly punctuated and produce mutations.)

At some point, then, given sufficiently high short-term disruption or sufficiently continuous long-term disruption, the subsystems or the ecosystem will adapt by mutating or evolving into new systems.

In a social ecosystem, we call such mutations "revolutions" — as when the factory system fundamentally and irreversibly changed the face of the relations between capital and labor — which, in the nineteenth century, at least, was fine for the business level of the social ecosystem but appalling for the factory workers.

In ecosystems, then, causes do not necessarily have specific, or single, or visible, or predictable, or isolated effects. Moreover, given that such systems are goal-seeking and reproducible, the feedbacks may not simply be displaced, transformed, or delayed. They may be, and very often are, amplified before they return to other parts or levels of the system or to their original source. Here they reappear as new causes of other effects, or as new constraints on the possibilities of the system or the source.

This is in part the result of the fact that such systems involve *levels* of communication and control. A small input at the right level in the system will be multiplied and accelerated by the system's information-processing capabilities. This is an aspect of what most clearly distinguishes biosocial ecosystems from mechanical or purely matter-energy systems, i.e., the way they employ information to control their behavior and organization, to trigger and time energy output, and to govern the disposition of the matter-energy available to the system.

For example, a relatively small adjustment to the bank discount rate or the allowable tax-depreciation rate in an economy undergoing recession will usually have large effects. In recession, investment in the capital-goods circuit (plant, labor, and materials) controls the behavior of the consumer-goods circuit (with feedback between them, of course). Government action making capital easier to get or cheaper to use encourages investment in capital goods and in new labor, which reduces unemployment and increases production. Increased production increases total incomes, which increases consumption, which increases production and decreases unemployment further, and so on. At least this is the case until rising real wages and the tendency of production to overshoot possible consumption, along with other factors, begin to reduce the rate of profit and make outlets for capital investment scarcer or less attractive at the very moment when industry is beginning to overproduce. In a given national system, the result is another recession, with too little money chasing too many consumer goods.

This is a classic case of the impossibility of applying a linear causal model to an ecosystem. The government action in, say, making money cheaper at a given point in a recession cannot be properly called a "cause" at all. It is rather a change in the *constraints* controlling the behavior of the system. The government's action is not a force driving the system to change, because the system is not an entity that can be pushed or pulled around (like a billiard ball), but rather a set of relations. The government's action involves a change in informational constraint. There are many goal-seeking subsystems (corporations) in the economic ecosystem who are placed in a more favorable potential profit position by the government action. Consequently, a large number will freely follow their own judgment and (yet) be induced to invest. Some will act in order to get the jump on their competitors. Others, if they are monopolies, for example, will be provided with necessary outlets for accumulated investment capital. Each corporation will have acted not because it was caused to do so, but because the *degree of freedom* for it to follow certain courses was raised (or the constraint on its possible courses of action was lowered).

We might carelessly say that the government's action had an impact on the economy, but that is an ingrained habit of speech, not a scientific statement. The term "impact" itself is a metaphor of the kind of linear relation of causality between self-subsistent entities (involving, e.g., momentum, mass, inertia, gravity) described by the Newtonian mechanics on which physics was first founded. What happens to a causal impact — say between two billiard balls — in a mechanical system? The impact has a certain effect (e.g., cue ball strikes eight ball), but the fundamental operation is one of the dissipation of one kind of energy into the mechanical environment by its transformation into another kind, usually in the form of unusable heat ("bound" energy, energy no longer capable of work).

This process involves a one-way, irreversible, and nonretransformable transformation of energy. The change in the discount rate is quite different. Since it involves information, it is itself reversible and retransformable. It is multidimensional (affecting some parts of the economic system, e.g., banks, differently from others) and (at least) two-way: it feeds back as an effect on both government revenues and political stability, for example, besides its effects on the accumulation of capital.

But there is a significant difference in the definition of the reversibility and transformation of the *systems* involved (as distinct from that of what changed their disposition). Other matters being equal, *time* and *place* have no significance for the two-dimensional billiard-ball system (which has no internal source of energy and seeks no goals in its behavior). The application of the same force will always — i.e., with a very high statistical probability — produce the same result, so that its application in the opposite direction will always return the system to its original state.

This is not the case for the multidimensional economic system, nor for any biosocial ecosystem. Such systems have an essential relation to both time and place, and no transformation of the system is ever truly reversible. The same input at different times will not have the same results, except in very general terms (e.g., the economy is "expanding" or "contracting"). The placing of the input at different levels of communication in the system will also have different results, as may its placing in different subsystems within the whole. Moreover, the way ecosystems use information to control their organization, development, and reproduction means that a given input may eventually come to affect *itself*, something that is impossible in a linear, mechanical system.

In an unlimited environment these differences between the two types of system and inputs may not be more than theoretically significant. Moreover, so long as the environment is *believed* to be unlimited, like Newtonian space — i.e., so long as people believe that unlimited future transformations and expansions are possible — then the theoretical difference will *not in general be perceived or recognized at all*. In consequence, people will tend to model the second, highly complex ecosystemic relation on the first, the mechanical relation, which is more simple, more immediate, and more "visible."

Only when the whole system begins to approach its own limits will the enormous differences in the practical effects of this theoretical difference begin to be generally recognized — by which time, of course, it may well be too late to do anything about them.

IDEOLOGY OF GROWTH AND LIMITS TO GROWTH

Most economists, of whatever political persuasion, are aware that industrial and "post-industrial" capitalism (state or private) depends on growth for its own immediate (short-range) survival. The apologists for capitalism know perfectly well that the system itself is inherently unstable unless it can continue to expand: growth for the sake of growth masks the reality of growth for the sake of *stability*.

Now, however, since the publication of the report of the President's Commission on Population Growth and the American Future, with that of *The Ecologist*'s "Blueprint for Survival," and especially with the publication of the Club of Rome's *Limits to growth*, our consciousness of the dangers of growth and accumulation for their own sakes — i.e., the growth of capital for the sake of capital — continues to increase, if in varying degrees.

The M.I.T. research team who wrote *Limits to growth* use a cybernetic and systemic world model as the basis for computer simulations of the future development of the global socioeconomic system. They insert into the simulation various factors and combinations of factors, e.g., population growth, capital growth, available land for agriculture, pollution, reserves of nonrenewable resources, and so on. They find that even under the best of circumstances and no matter how the various inputs are combined, the continued economic development of our present system will result — at the very least — in the inevitable exhaustion of our natural resources over the next one hundred years.

The publication of this book raised a storm of opposition. Opponents of *Limits to growth* are in fact hard put to know what to do with it. They tend either to attack its scientific validity on the basis of their own conception of science and validity, or to continue to place their faith on unknown technological changes which, it is hoped, will provide solutions. Since the "science" of these opponents depends precisely on the anti-ecological foundations of Western science in general (its tendency to view systems in isolation from each other), the arguments they use are already suspect *theoretically*. We do not even have to consider the *ideological* position of the opponents to the thesis of *Limits to growth* (although it remains true that their theory and their ideology are indissolubly linked).

As for those who place their faith in technology to solve, e.g., the problem of energy resources, one has only to point out that it has been the amplification of technological innovations, linked to growth, which is primarily responsible for our present danger. Because of technological "advances," the amount of energy consumed by every member of the population of some industrialized countries is up to 500 times greater than that consumed by each member of the populations of the developing countries (*Los Angeles Times* 1970). Technological increase (e.g., the invention of the steam engine) tends to increase technological increases (e.g., the factory system) and consequently to increase the "energy-index" of the individual human beings involved. It is precisely the irreplaceable loss of available free energy (fuel, raw materials) that concerns the Club of Rome. Faith in technology goes hand in hand with faith in growth — and no amount of faith in new (but as yet unknown) technological innovations as such provides any *rational* way of approaching the problem, if only because even if such innovations are really possible, they may nevertheless come too late.

The fact is that both belief in the benefits of growth and faith in efficiency through technology have historically performed the same ideological function. Growth — in the capitalist sense of increased production, increased capital investment, and expanding markets — has traditionally been used by the apologists for our economic system to excuse economic inequality in the distribution of incomes. Any suggestion of limiting growth thus puts the entire fabric of their argument in question. The argument has traditionally run as follows: economic expansion and continued development of technology are the only true roads to economic justice. As production and sales rise, the economic divergence between the incomes of the affluent and poor will necessarily tend to decrease. As the rich get richer, the poor will get richer also.

The proponents of this theory have conveniently ignored the fact that growth under capitalism has historically created greater and greater economic distance between the "haves" and the "have nots." Their illusions about increased economic justice have always depended on an explicit or implicit isolation of part of the economic system from its total context. Thus, before the publication of Michael Harrington's *The other America* in the early sixties the official line of the apologists for the American system was that economic expansion had made poverty negligible in the United States.

French apologists for the economics of neocolonialism in Africa use similar arguments. They have made much of the "economic miracle" of the Ivory Coast, for example. They have conveniently forgotten that recent increased per capita income in that country is unevenly distributed between the white capitalists and their local *compradores*, on the one hand, and the local (especially rural) population on the other (Vignes

1972). They have also neglected the size and the effects of the exportation of profits back to the industrialized countries, to say nothing of the wholesale destruction of the forests of the Ivory Coast by European lumber companies.

This last feature of European exploitation of the Ivory Coast is particularly significant. It is estimated that the exploitation of the forests will result in their effective disappearance in eight or ten years. Lumber exports represent about 20 percent of all exports, a figure that happens to be equivalent to almost the entire surplus of exports over imports in the trade of the Ivory Coast. Thus, Jacques Vignes can go on to point out that in this respect, the current economic "prosperity" of the country can be said to depend almost entirely on the destruction of its limited forest reserves.

In fact, the "economic miracle" of the Ivory Coast — a country now busy seeking trade and contact with South Africa through French intermediaries — is characteristic of the economic dilemma of most of the ex-colonies in Africa: economic growth through European exploitation of natural and human resources, *without* any accompanying real economic development of the country. This example reinforces the necessity of contextual explanations of the system-environment relations involved. The only properly critical scientific judgments that can be made about the economics of the Ivory Coast must include its situation as a (biosocial) environment for Western industrial exploitation. The French economic planners create an unscientific and invalid model of an economic miracle by concealing the total set of relationships involved. They treat the Ivory Coast as if it were an isolated, *self*-regulating *system*, whereas it is in fact an *environment* regulated by the external control of white industrialists over the form and character of its supposed development. In this sense, the Ivory Coast is defined by the industrial countries, on the model of "mastery over nature by mankind," as a "nature" for "mankind" to pillage in the quest of capital profits.

From the moment that the ideology of growth can no longer be used, like the Christian idea of heaven, as a means to justify present economic inequality through promises of future blessedness, then all the values of Western society are put on trial. And as increasingly large numbers of people become conscious of how the ideology of growth has been used against them, the old excuses — how colonialism provides jobs in "underdeveloped countries" and does all sorts of other good things, for example — begin to reveal their exploitative basis.

The authors of *Limits to growth* conclude from their projections that, even assuming an optimistic range of technological benefits, if our present system continues without radical changes, the *"behavior mode of the world system is exponential growth of population and capital, followed by collapse"* (Meadows *et al.* 1972:142). What is therefore essential to *any* stable model of the world ecosystem is that both population growth and capital growth be stabilized.

The authors' estimates are thoroughly conservative. In spite of this, the attacks of their opponents tend to be wearisomely specious, and often thoroughly vicious (e.g., Beckerman 1972). We are in effect witnessing a replay of what happened when Rachel Carson's *Silent spring* blew the whistle on insecticides and herbicides in 1962.

Limits is conservative not simply because the authors leave wide margins for error, for future discoveries of new energy and other resources, for future utilization of marginal farmland in food production, and so on. The estimates are conservative, first, because the global model used is extremely "coarse," and consequently totally unable to deal with apparently minor factors that could eventually reach a stage analogous to a "critical mass," with disastrous consequences (e.g., human genetic damage resulting from long-term, low levels of exposure to chemical or radioactive pollutants). Second, past experience makes it almost certain that there already exist environmental hazards to human beings and to the human future that have not yet been discovered or that are not yet understood. It is indeed much more probable that unknown hazards exist than it is that as yet unknown technological innovations will be able to deal with the problems we already know about. Third, the past records of international bodies, governments, industry, regulatory agencies, and the scientific establishment have invariably been dictated by the short-range economic interests of the wealthy, and not by consideration for the long-range welfare of ordinary people (viz., black-lung disease in American coal mines, for which the taxpayers now subsidize the mine owners through a federal health program).

More important, however, is the conservative effect of the most serious deficiency of the authors' world model, the deficiency their opponents have seized on to generate a smoke screen of "expertise" and to mount a campaign of vilification. The fact is that there is no properly adequate mathematics for such a complex set of interactions as they are describing.

In the first place, an open system with multiple and interdependent variables is inherently unpredictable except along extremely broad lines. Consequently, the economists who oppose the theses of *Limits to growth* are reduced to saying that the authors' economics are faulty, i.e., as faulty as their own. But since the question involved is that of human survival, and not that of the fate of an academic paper at an economists' colloquium, if the opponents cannot prove that the theses of the Club of Rome are false, *by means of a more adequate world model*, then their arguments lack any properly scientific basis. (Note that the predictions of *Limits to growth* cannot be *proved* to be true; they can only *become* true.)

Second, the model is weakest in its attempts to deal with the interactions of relations with relations. It is presumably logically impossible — and it is certainly scientifically impossible — to correlate the interrelations of, say, PCB in animal tissue, nitrate contamination of ground water by fertilizer, rising ambient water temperatures resulting from thermal pollution, increased carbon dioxide in the atmosphere, and DDT-resistant insects. There may well be no chemical or physical relationship between insects and carbon dioxide, but there is inevitably at least one place where such apparently isolated phenomena *are* related (in unpredictable ways); in human society, in the *social ecosystem*. And even where there are physical relationships — as in the relation between water availability, water pollution, and land use for food — the authors of *Limits to growth* may not have any way of linking them mathematically. In any case, the world model they use does not include many more than a hundred major feedback links, and the authors are explicit about its inability to take into account other amplifying feedbacks. It does not deal with feedback relations between nations, for example, and the only explicitly social factor in their model is birth control. But these inadequacies are not of the type to produce an overstated case. Because of all the missing connections, and all the missing connections between connections — and especially the missing connection between the exponentially decreasing "quality of life" and political consciousness — predictions based on such a simple model must necessarily *understate* the probable future state of the global ecosystem.

The theoretical base of the world model used by the authors of *Limits* is based on the physical and biological relationships of matter, forces, and energy. It generally leaves out of account the fact that it is *information* flow that, by *organizing* the patterns and the disposition of matter-energy in the biosphere and the sociosphere, links the whole biosocial ecosystem together. Because of this relation between information, organization, and matter-energy, every single set of parameters and variables used in the various submodels outlined in *Limits to growth* involves a political question. DDT and PCB's, for example, are not simply spread in the biosphere by biochemical laws and as a result of inexorable or unavoidable human "needs." DDT (spread by design) and PCB's (spread by accident) are technical instruments of the capitalist mode of production, and capital is neither matter nor energy. Like labor, capital *controls* organization, and whatever controls organization in bioeconomic open systems is not energy but information.

Thus the inherent weakness of *Limits to growth* — the weakness suggesting that our future is even more radically in question than *Limits* implies — is that the desired state of global "equilibrium" is described mainly in the terms of energy relationships. These relationships are purely quantitative, and their theoretical base does not provide adequate ways to deal with the *qualitative* economic changes that are on the one hand necessary and on the other, inevitable. In a word, *Limits to growth*, like Keynesian economics, still speaks from *within* a historically determined mode of production — capitalism — and not yet adequately *about* that mode of production.

Nevertheless — and this is the truly radical content of the study — the analysis put forward by the Club of Rome shows that the contradictions inherent in the continued growth of capital for the sake of capital (rather than for the sake of human beings) are truly paradoxical. Logically, this means that capitalism views itself as a closed energy system operating in an infinite environment (much like a diesel generating plant supplied with unlimited resources of cooling water, spare parts, and fuel), whereas in fact it is an open communications system in a finite environment.

Paradoxes involve situations where, if you take one side of the question, you are then forced logically to take the other side, and so on, without limit, e.g., am I telling the truth when I say: "I am lying"? The paradox involved is that if capitalism is to survive, it can neither *obey* nor *disobey* its own organizational imperative: growth. Whereas purely *contradictory* relationships in both logical and ecological systems can in principle continue indefinitely, paradoxical relations — double binds — in ongoing systems sooner or later move the system to a point where it can continue to survive only by a radical change to a new level of organization, one where the particular paradox is no longer in effect, because the rules of communication controlling it no longer operate.

If this is indeed the case, then zero economic growth can never be maintained in terms of the quantitative limits on the use and organization of matter and energy proposed by the Club of Rome's report. The reason for this is simply that under the present rules of production and consumption, such a state would still be subject to the one inexorable "iron law" of capital: unlimited accumulation and expansion. Under the capitalist relations of production, zero growth cannot be maintained by the straightforward recycling of capital proposed by *Limits to growth*, because for capital to be in equilibrium is the end of capital as we know it. For the moment it can be said that, in any properly human terms, it is capital itself, as it is presently distributed, that is in fact the most fundamental form of unrecyclable waste in the global ecosystem: waste of matter-energy, waste of human beings, waste of the creative potential (labor power) of women and men.

So long as *quantitative* labor power (purchasable by money) circulates as a commodity in the social ecosystem, no human solutions to the ecological crisis will be possible. We have in effect to discover a way of circulating between each other the *qualitative* component of labor power: the creative aspect of the human ability to organize and "in-form" matter and energy and relations. This is the aspect of labor power expressed when we give form, i.e., organization, to an amorphous lump of clay on a potter's wheel to produce a vase, for example. The same organizing power was at the roots of human evolution, at the time when we collectively evolved from the simple levels of group organization found among gregarious animals to complex forms of social organization. These are the forms expressed in systems of kinship and rules of marriage; in the production of forms of economic surplus — going beyond immediate needs — that can be exchanged as links between individuals and groups; in the organization of the exchange and communication of words, knowledge, and symbols; in the development of a division of labor going beyond the purely biological division of labor.

In other words, we cannot expect to understand or overcome the social crisis represented by the ecological crisis unless we understand the actual — but hidden — functions of both capital and labor in our economic system. We have to understand that whereas *all* forms of labor as such — "skilled" and "unskilled," "manual" and "intellectual," individual and collective — are commodities that are bought and sold in the marketplace, *labor power* — the qualitative and creative component — is not a commodity in the usual sense (although it can be, and is, effectively reduced to one by the power of capital to expropriate and control it).

It is this aspect that makes each of us not an abstract individual — not an economic abstraction exchanging human value for monetary exchange value, not a commodity in the economic machinery worth a specific, competitively defined, quantity of dollars per hour to a part of the system over which we have no control — but a *qualitatively differentiated* individual, inseparable from our dependence on complex and undefinable sets of nonexploitative communications and exchanges with our fellow human beings.

In a society based on the circulation of creativity and the true recognition of human difference, the economic abstraction represented by the so-called free and equal autonomous individual — representing the freedom and equality of one commodity among so many other commodities — would disappear. In such a society, class, race, and sexual exploitation could no longer exist — for in matters of creative power, as distinct from ability to perform in a rigid economic system of caste and class, all human beings are truly equal. Equal because there is no way to measure the loving of a child against the building of a dam or the writing of a book, no way to sell human sensitivity in the market, no way to quantify the imagination of a working-class or ghetto child against the "educational performance" of her or his middle-class counterpart — and in a rational society, of course, no need to do so.

Such is the only truly *realistic* approach to the ecological crisis.

THE REAL QUESTION

The real question our species faces as a result of the historical economic development of Western society over the past two hundred years is not, and never has been, "man's struggle to live with himself" — a metaphor favored in one form or another by both reactionary conservationists, liberal "environmentalists," and idealistic pseudorealists of all ages (and the subtitle of a recent book on the "environmental" crisis). The real question is that of man- and womankind's struggle to live with capitalist expropriation.

The real question is therefore much more simple and much more frightening. The biosphere has already imposed biophysical limits on growth that we shall inevitably reach no matter what happens. Consequently, we have a simple choice between an ordered sociopolitical solution and outright chaos.

We must therefore ask ourselves: *are socioeconomic limits on growth possible without socioeconomic revolution, and is revolution possible without limits on growth*?

And what is the potential of *violence* in this necessary qualitative economic change? It is significant that, although our socioeconomic system is founded on the institutionalization and rationalization of every form of violence, violence is not regarded as an economic category by the apologists for state and private capitalism, nor by the social democratic or liberal "socialists" and "communists" of the West, nor by the upper-middle-class leaders in power in Third World countries — those who speak of an African or Peruvian socialism, for example, which in almost every respect is a simple transformation of the exploitative-expansionist values of white Western capitalism. It is clear that the classic "socialist" solution to the question of revolutionary change — insofar as it has invariably been based on the idea of the unlimited abundance of goods — has always been a totally inadequate one. In fact, because of the global universalization of the values of a particular culture and economic system on which it is based, it bears a positively reactionary potential.

Like the liberal conception of racial integration, and like the universalist and abstract preconceptions of the social democrat criticized by Sartre in his *Anti-Semite and Jew*, the socialist recognizes "man" in the abstract to the detriment of women and men in particular and in particular cultures. The reactionary potential of the "socialist" solution (e.g., Michael Harrington in the U.S., the Communist party in France) is the result of its middle-class (and usually elitist and intellectualist) conceptions of social progress and human needs. Its reactionary character derives directly from its conception of the world on the basis of a one-dimensional universalization of progress and need. Although it is clear that the Chinese experience teaches us something quite different about possible futures, the Western socialist seems in general to remain trapped inside the bourgeois ideology of our society. He is the mirror image of what he believes he is exposing. Like some aspects of women's liberation and much black militancy, traditional socialism simply tends to push the values of that ideology, and of its economic base, to their limit, but without ever going beyond them, without adequately communicating about them.

The socialist consequently tends to view the ecological crisis as an upcoming disaster rather than as an opportunity. He fails to see its truly revolutionary potential because he has always failed to see what the values of Western industrial capitalism really represent, *as a limit* on future possibilities. The opportunity we have is no longer a simple question of moral or political choice between multiple alternatives. The opportunity to return technology to the service of the human ecosystem and to expropriate capital's control over it (and us) has at last become the only truly "self-serving" choice. The fact that many socialists do not see the ecological crisis in this way reveals their implicit identification with the capitalist conception of individualism and with the accompanying capitalist values of growth for the sake of growth. Yet it is perfectly clear that as long as capitalism could historically pursue its unlimited growth, the social inequality and the expropriation of human labor power on which it is based could not be overcome. The contradiction between capital and labor is so weighted on the side of capital — because capital controls the flow of *information* and the *organization* of our system — that there is no reason to suppose that, under the conditions of continued expansion, it can ever be transcended.

The economic revolution that is essential to our human survival cannot under any conceivable circumstances be a simple *linear* development proceeding out of the rules controlling the organization of the capitalist system. It cannot under any human circumstances result from the reformist strategy that seeks to make capitalist reality (the reduction of human relations to relations between commodities) conform to its accompanying ideology (freedom, equality, individual rights, and so on). There is no way of reforming the system from within the system, for the simple reason that the ideals of the ideology are every bit as anti-human, and every bit as alienating, as the socioeconomic relations it seeks to justify. In order to go beyond the capitalist revolution, we have eventually to make a break, to achieve a quantum jump to a new level of social organization, *however presently inconceivable such a new level may be*. As the predictions of the ecologists surely tell us, it is the controlling economic values that must be changed if we are not simply to run out of time, space, and energy. Clearly, unless we revolutionize the revolution — and by whatever means are necessary — capitalism will have been the death of us.

CAPITAL AND ZERO GROWTH

Many people are concerned about the human future — to say nothing of the present — find themselves explicitly or implicitly in an "anti-capitalist" or "anti-Western" position. Unfortunately, this position is most often a purely ideological stance — sometimes even revealing an unconscious identity with the mythical ethic of free enterprise under early capitalism — and not very often based on an adequate critical analysis of the deep structures of socioeconomic organization in our society. Ideas have an important role to play in change, but the finest set of ideas can have no effect unless the economic constraints on the system are also changing. If, for example, Keynesian economic theory had not been necessary to save capitalism from its own inherent instability — necessary in the sense that it codified and explained what people in the world of politics and business were already doing — it is unlikely that we would ever have heard of Keynes.

Consequently, it is worth remarking on a few of the significant characteristics of capitalism in order to correct the deficiency of the purely ideological approaches to futuristics, and at the same time to show that the economic conditions for radical change are indeed being produced by the logic of capitalism itself.

Given the grotesque misunderstanding of Marx prevalent in academic circles, and the self-serving misreadings of what he was trying to say, it is still very difficult to find people who have *read* him in any really useful way. Thus, in what follows I have deliberately avoided basing the argument on the labor theory of value (the in fact self-evident idea that only human labor can expand the value of raw materials so as to produce commodities, including the machines used in manufacture) so as to avoid the possibility of the argument being sidetracked into an irrelevant discussion about "value" and "price."

In spite of similarities with other exploitative social systems, modern capitalism involves specific and unique characteristics.

Briefly put, any division of labor in any society results in processes of exchange within it. The division of labor may be the result of biological differences in the process of natural reproduction; the result of myth, ritual, education, and kinship rules in the reproduction of ideology (tradition) and concrete social organization; or the result of specialization in economic activities (cooking, hunting, crafts, and so on). At this level, the means of production and reproduction are in general controlled collectively or individually. In a monetary economy of simple commodity production, the individual producers control their means of production and sell one commodity in order to buy another they need, e.g., one sells clothing to buy food, and another sells food to buy tools, and so on.

The system of exchange in such a system is governed by the necessity of circulation, as in all communications systems, but here the circulation of commodities is controlled by naturally and socially defined real needs. The commodities therefore circulate in terms of their *use value* (or utility) in the system as a whole. They are exchanged on the basis of their *qualitative* differences from each other. One sells in order to buy. Both the concrete social function of such exchange, as a system, and the individual's subjective consciousness of what is involved are therefore closely connected.

Under capitalism, however, the use value of commodities is totally subjected to their *exchange value*. The capitalist does not sell in order to buy, he buys in order to sell — and he sells for profit.

Simply put, the class of capitalists — a complex and nonhomogeneous set of people in whom capital is "embodied" — enter the market with money. Money is used to buy two essential commodities necessary to capitalist production: the total "means of production" represented by (1) the labor power of the worker as a commodity (wages and costs, called variable capital), and (2) the required capital goods (raw materials, machinery, and so on, called constant or fixed capital, or manufacturing assets).

The capitalist mode of production organizes labor power and machinery so as to produce other commodities out of raw materials. The expanded (exchange) value represented in these commodities is then "realized" (i.e., extracted) on the market in the form of more money. This money is then available for *consumption* by the capitalist in various ways, but also, and more important, for reinvestment in a further quantity of constant and variable capital. Until it is so invested, the money remains as money. When it is invested in new capital goods, it becomes new industrial capital, which is the most important kind of capital. Thus there is a fundamental distinction between the *accumulation of money* and the *accumulation of capital*. Unfortunately, we usually confuse the two, forgetting, for example, that workers' savings are almost entirely deferred consumption, whereas the savings of the capitalist class are a form of hoarding (refusal to invest).

Remembering the distinction between money and capital, we can see why Marx calls this productive process "unlimited." Money — in the sense of what can be converted into capital through accumulation (investment in plants and machinery) — is the beginning and the end of the process. The relation commodity-money-commodity, based on use value (selling to buy), becomes converted to: money-commodity-money (capital), based on exchange value (buying to sell).

Capital governs the circulation of commodities in order that it may be expanded. The *qualitative* differences in the various use values represented by commodities and labor power are consequently reduced to *quantitative* differences ("price"). Commodities serve therefore in the main as the *instruments* of the expansion of capital, their use value being a mere secondary characteristic. Hence the well-known tendency for capitalism to produce more and more essentially useless goods under a system of planned obsolescence, and to rely on advertising and other means to make such goods "needed."

The expanded value realized in the market by the capitalist is never simply that required to replace worn out or depreciated or outmoded capital equipment, for the accumulation of capital is not like simple interest on money. Nor, as it turns out, is it like compound interest (exponential increase). Because of the logic of expansion involved in capitalism, capital accumulation always tends toward super-exponential increases (increases in the *rate* of accumulation). This is the case even though capitalism is prevented by its own logic from actually realizing this kind of increase in any given industry, country, or market (i.e., in any *relatively closed* system).

By "capitalist," of course, we refer to the system as a whole, not to a particular person or to a particular group. And "capital" refers both to power over organization (the organization of organization) represented by capital and to the means to exercise that power. In the wide sense, then, "capital" refers not to a thing, but to a system of relations organized by power. Since its rules of relation and rules of production are based entirely on exchange value for profit under competition, then objectively the capitalist mode of production is a system of the expansion of exchange value *which the "capitalist" does not control*. An analogy might be made between the capitalist and individual speaker of a (restricted) language (an example used by Marx). His freedom to communicate and exchange is a semiotic freedom governed by the different levels of constraint in the system. But he does not control these constraints. They are systemic: embodied in the system as a whole, and not in individuals or groups as such.

Certainly the "human nature" of some capitalist or other has nothing to do with the workings of advanced capitalism. It is perhaps not even true to say that capital is based mainly on the maximization of profit as such. More fundamental to the workings of the system is the fact that, as all economists recognize, the accumulation of capital within a given system is a positive feedback process with its own, built-in, negative feedback controls. Economists will say that there is a tendency for the rate of profit to fall as capital accumulates. Consequently, in order to protect the system of accumulation *itself*, new outlets for investment capital must constantly be found. The system must expand if it is to remain viable in its own terms. This positive-negative feedback relation may certainly be referred to by such terms as the necessity for the "maximization of (the *rate* of) profit." But what is more fundamentally involved is the necessity of protecting profitability itself, the necessity to protect the continuing *possibility of profit*. This is the sense in which economists agree that capitalism must expand to ensure its own stability.

Along with this oscillating instability, which results from the tendency toward underconsumption (overproduction, recession), capitalism also tends toward a *disproportionality* between capital goods and consumer goods. The production of capital goods (the locus of accumulation) always tends to increase at a faster rate than that of consumer goods.

What makes the system even more unstable and even more dependent on expansion is the fact that there is not simply *one* kind of capital or *one* kind of industrial production involved, but many. These different types of capital remain in competition with each other. If a given monopoly restricts investment in its own area for example, then other free capital will seek out less restricted areas, e.g., retailing, or new industries, such as recently happened with the electronics industry. Thus, at every level, the capitalist system *promotes* its own *uneven* development, creating new depressed areas and industries within its own sphere (e.g., railroads).

It might be expected that the system would "learn" to avoid such disruptive cycles by greater foresight. Historically, this has never happened, because of the constant appearance of new markets for capital, especially just as the system begins to recover from recession, e.g., World War II.

These new markets include: (1) geographical extension (into non-capitalist areas or into less advanced areas of capitalism, e.g., the American invasion of both the Third World and Europe); (2) new industries resulting from technological advances (e.g., integrated circuits, pollution control); (3) realignments or bankruptcies of domestic and international competitors; (4) government defense spending; (5) other government programs, including anti-poverty projects, freeways, and so on; and (6) population growth.

The export of capital is an especially important factor. It reduces the amount of spare capital seeking investment in the home country, which would normally put pressure on the labor market and drive up the cost of labor, tending to bring about a crisis. But workers are not in general free to move from one area of the world to another; wage rates are never equalized globally. Thus the export of capital has the effect of maintaining the domestic rate of profit as well as providing high profits from low wage costs abroad. A high rate of profit at home may also assist the corporation in underselling its foreign competitors abroad, if necessary, by "dumping" (with or without government assistance through subsidies). Moreover, the raw materials controlled by exported capital in the Third World do not simply provide an essential source of *supply*, but also an essential source of *profit*. With wages low and profits high in the Third World, the corporation is protected from the dangers of underconsumption (it has greater freedom to control prices, for example) and doubly protected from this effect of overaccumulation because of the vast possibilities for new investment in industrialization in such countries.

I hope the preceding schematic outline of capitalist expansionism has made it clear why the two major feedbacks in the model proposal by *Limits to growth* — population growth and capital growth — are not of the same level of importance. The authors of *Limits* place these two feedbacks in a *symmetrical* relationship, but it is clear that they are not of the same logical type. We can express this difference very simply. Although exponential population growth is probably undesirable, population could continue to grow for some considerable time under a system of production *not* based on the production of commodities for the sake of capital accumulation. *But under no circumstances can capital accumulation continue its super-exponential growth for very much longer.*

It would seem that there are in essence only two related possibilities: capital will run up against its own *internal* barriers to continued accumulation as its previously "unlimited" human and natural environment manifests its finitude: or the growth of capital will be more directly stopped by the *external* effects of a finite natural environment — or both.

What is clear is that the accumulation of capital is the controlling factor in the world crisis. It is of course impossible to say how imminent is the impending chaos projected by *Limits to growth*: the authors suggest that we have perhaps less than one hundred years at the present rate of growth, but the symptoms of the final crisis will necessarily appear well before that time. The consequence is that we have only a very limited period in which to consider what (political) action must be taken, for the nature of exponential growth is to pass the point of no return before we are fully aware of it.

The authors' "ideal" program for a stable world system makes the question of limits on time very clear. They list the following ideal policies, designed to achieve a global system with reasonable per capita industrial output and long-term stability. Except for (2) policies were to be introduced *beginning in 1975*:

(1) The stabilization of population by equalizing the birth and death rate;

(2) The stabilization of industrial capital by equalizing the depreciation and the investment rate, beginning in 1990;

(3) The reduction of the consumption of natural resources to one-fourth of the 1970 level per unit of industrial output;

(4) The shifting of economic preferences in society away from material goods toward services, such as education;

(5) The reduction of pollution per unit of industrial output to one-fourth of its 1970 level;

(6) The diversion of capital to food production (even if "uneconomic") with the goal of providing food for all people and overcoming traditional inequalities in distribution;

(7) The diversion of a part of agricultural capital toward soil enrichment and preservation to avoid soil erosion and depletion;

(8) An increase in the lifetime of industrial capital (capital goods) to counteract the low final level of capital stock (constant capital) resulting from the first seven policies.

These conditions are projected to hold population close to present levels, with more than twice as much food per person as the average in 1970. Average per capita industrial output would be considerably higher than present levels, services per capita would triple. Total average income (industrial output, food, and services) would be about $1,800 per capita (half the present U.S. average, equal to the present European average, and three times the present world average of $600).

Of course, this particular stable state is technically impossible, since the two major factors in the positive feedback loops, capital growth and population growth, cannot possibly be stabilized as quickly as the policy suggestions require. Nevertheless, the more realistic — i.e., technically realizable — policies put forward by *Limits to growth* still depend on the same set of factors.

The basic factors are policies (2), (4), and (8). Policy (2) requires the end of the "expanded reproduction" of capital (accumulation), in other words an end to the continued profitability of capital. Policy (4) cuts into the trend toward increased productivity and automation, especially in the capital-intensive production processes of heavy industry. Policy (8) not only reinforces policy (2), but also militates against continuing technological improvements in production (which have the effect of outmoding present capital investment and requiring its replacement).

Policy (4) has the further effect of shifting labor power away from the productive process of major industry toward economic activities (services) whose historical increase appears to have been dependent on increased production and productivity in industry. It is not clear how we can have the one without the other.

This whole question requires a far more profound analysis than I can undertake here. But it is surely clear that the suggested policies call in effect for an end to the capitalist and state-capitalist modes of production. With the exception of a moderation in population growth — and even that in itself constitutes a problem for continued capital accumulation — none of these policies are realizable under any form of capitalism. The objections of the critics of *Limits to growth* consequently make more sense than hitherto. What they are principally objecting to, whether they know it or not, is the fact that *Limits to growth* is a call to revolution, a call for the overthrow of the capitalist system if humanity is to survive.

The result of it all is not despondency but hope. We are no longer faced by the simple (moral) choice of whether or not to take political action against an iniquitous system (on whatever grounds and of whatever type). If we have consciousness, we no longer have such (moralistic) liberty. Nor can we simply wait around for the "inevitable" overcoming of capitalism — since in the absence of radical political change, that overcoming means chaos.

Political action and political preparation thus become a completely *necessary* form of class consciousness — no longer a question of moral arguments and short-range survival — completely necessary in order for it to become possible for *humanity* itself to take charge of a potential ecological-economic crisis and possible state of chaos the like of which the world has never seen.

REFERENCES

BATESON, GREGORY
  1972   *Steps to an ecology of mind*. New York: Ballantine.
BECKERMAN,
  1972   Article in *London Times*. May 31.
Los Angeles Times
  1970   Article in *Los Angeles Times*. June 21.
MANDEL, ERNEST
  1962   *Marxist economic theory*. London: Merlin.
MEADOWS, D.H., D.L. MEADOWS, J. PANDERS, W.W. BEHRENS III
  1972   *Limits to growth*. New York: Universe Books.
VIGNES, JACQUES
  1972   Article in *AfricAsia*. January 10.
WILDEN, ANTHONY
  1972   *System and structure: essays in communication and exchange*. London: Tavistock Publications.
  1973   *Ecology and ideology: the structure of domination in Western society*. London: Tavistock Publications.

Financial Colonies: Inflation, Recession, Debt, and the Multinational Corporation

GREGORY A. PALAST

> A factory
> has also another aspect, which we call the
>   financial aspect
> It gives people the power to buy (wages, dividends
> which are power to buy) but it is also the cause
>   of prices
> or values, financial, I mean financial values
> It pays workers, and pays *for* material.
> What it pays in wages and dividends
> stays fluid, as power to buy, and this power is
>   less,
> per forza, damn blast your intellex, is less
> than the total payments made by the factory
> (as wages, dividends AND payments for raw
>   material
> bank charges, etcetera)
> and all, that is the whole, that is the total
> of these is added into the total of prices
> caused by that factory, any damn factory
> and there is and must be therefore a clog
> and the power to purchase can never
> (under the present system) catch up with
> prices at large,
> and the light became so bright and so blindin'
> in this layer of paradise
> that the mind of man was bewildered.
>   EzRA Pound, "Canto XXXVIII"

SPAIN ON $5 A DAY

This is no tourist rate. Five dollars is the average daily wage in Spain's factories. And it's falling, as wages have fallen in almost the entire

This article was financed by the affection of Elizabeth and Ahamed Idris-Soven, Harriet Cooper, Susan Hamovitch — and Anne Joelle Lonigro.

Western world. It is not that workers are paid fewer pesetas or dollars — they have actually increased. But the increases are unreal. *Real* wages, figured in purchasing power, are declining (United Nations 1974:533,539,600). The difference between wages real and unreal is *inflation*, the rise in prices.

There exists the illusion that inflation comes from nowhere or that it is a market quirk, a momentary disequilibrium, or a mistake of government. No visible connection can be made to the corporations. It often even appears that business shares the burdens and sorrows of inflation with the working person. "You want to know who's really getting hurt by this inflation?" asked the chairman of the President's Council of Economic Advisers. "The brokers," he answered (*New York Times* 1974b). But there *is* a connection — complex, indirect, not readily visible. *Finance*, the corporate system of capital creation and circulation, links the corporation to inflation — and to recession.

Inflation is a financial process — the heating up of demand not so much for goods but for money itself. When finance, originated to provide funds to facilitate production, begins instead to entangle production, recession results, with crippling effects on wages, employment, and national and international development. While other articles in this volume concentrate on multinational production as it directly affects the employees' welfare and culture, this article concerns itself with the not-so-direct effects of the financial operations of the multinationals on the economy as a whole. This scrutiny of the financial dimension of the international corporation does not necessarily supplant, but rather supplements, other theories of economic crises.

Within the multinational corporation (MNC) Western finance and Third World production meet. There is more to be had in the Third World than low-wage labor and cheap resources. From Third World wage earners and their governments the multinationals extract cheap capital while providing costly capital in meager amounts to these nations. Such biased circulation has always been the stock-in-trade of colonial imperialism. Traditionally, the "Mother Country" took exclusive rights to raw materials purchased cheaply and sold back to the colonies as expensive finished goods. In like manner the MNC absorbs financial resources that are cycled back as "finished," only having been stamped with the Mother Corporation's logo trademark.

This bias, the very heart of the system of capital financing, breeds inflation and recession. Denied access to their own capital, and impoverished by the direct and indirect costs of indebtedness to the multinationals, the Third World is denied the means or benefits of development. The implications are severe even beyond the Third World as huge private and public debt at high interest rates, unutilized capacity, unemployment, and inflation — all generated by the need to supply and subsidize credit for the corporations — attack wages in the industrial "first" world.

THE CIRCLES OF FINANCE

To understand the increasingly financial character of international industrial capital, we can compare its financial operations to that of the traditional financial institution, the bank, and its manner of obtaining and controlling wealth. When you hand your money to a bank, you can expect it back along with a gratuity — interest. Likewise, those other financial institutions, insurance companies, pay out nearly as much in claims as they receive in premiums. Then where do Bank of America and Allstate make their money?

Suppose I were to give you a billion dollars to hold on to, and someone else asked you to hold on to his billion just as I demand mine back. Then another person asked you to hold on to his billion dollars just as the second person asked for his back. As this process of deposit and withdrawal continues, although you will always owe one billion dollars (a liability), you will also always be receiving one billion dollars (an asset). At no time are you left without a billion dollars, dollars that are yours to consume or invest. Although your balance sheet here shows no *profits* (unless your investments make a profit), your *wealth* is substantial. The present actual total of such circulating assets for the financial corporations of the United States stands at $2.5 trillion (*Survey of Current Business* 1974c:8), having doubled in seven years. As in banking, what has become important to owners of industrial corporations is the amount of money coursing *through* these corporations.

The profitability of the MNC rests, in part, on its financial growth. This concern for financial growth eclipses even the concern for profit.

Furthermore, the circulation must *accelerate*. Returning to the banking example, while the nature of double-entry bookkeeping insures that assets equate with liabilities, it is still clear that an acceleration of the flow is needed to maintain a secure margin of inflows to outflows. If you are given not $1.0 billion but $1.1 billion while I demand my $1 billion back, you will be holding a net of $100 million. But when the $1.1 billion is demanded back, you will have to expand your operations, picking up not $1.1 million but a $1.2 billion deposit to maintain that net difference of $100 million. In the words of the manager of the Singapore office of the First National Bank of Chicago, "It's not nice that we're able to do business here, it's a necessity" (*New York Times* 1974a). By 1967, 264 foreign branches of U.S. banks had contributed $9.1 billion to U.S. parent assets.

Capitalization of Capital

Having shown the reason for financial growth and revealed its circulating form, we now move to the mechanics of how it is done — and the specific attractions of the Third World. Banks seek deposits; in like manner the industrial corporation seeks not only capital sources but also the conditions that will allow the corporation to actually *generate* the funds it will circulate. The bank-like process by which industrial capital attracts more capital to itself is *capitalization*. *Equity* and *debt* are the two circulating components of capitalization from external sources.

The monopoly of the circulation of capital is the essential financial goal of the MNC; the business of finance is the capturing of investment capital for resale at a higher price. In the circle of debt, as we shall see, corporations borrow money from the Third World at low interest rates, lending it back to the Third World at high interest rates. The equity circle, involving the ownership of industry, is a bit more complicated. Just as a bank takes in deposits the international corporations draw in Third World money for stock and other investments in the multinationals. Foreign deposits in New York total $105 billion (*Survey of Current Business* 1974d:2–5), foreign holdings of stocks and bonds total no less than $85 billion plus an additional $22 billion in "direct" investments, and foreign holdings of U.S. government and commercial short-term debt amount to $114 billion (Aliber 1973; *Wall Street Journal* 1975j). Just as the banks pay low interest on the money they borrow from the Third World and lend it back at a high rate, so multinational industrial corporations take in investment capital from the Third World on which they pay a low yield — and return this money as "direct investment," as foreign subsidiary operations. For this returning capital, too, the multinationals charge a high monopoly price, usually termed high profits. That price, rather than being paid as high interest, is paid by low wages.

EQUITY. Equity represents ownership in an enterprise. The Third World's equity capital is captured by the MNC directly in one of several ways: by the Third World investors' purchase in New York of the stock of the parent corporation or the stock of the multinational's subsidiary in the Third World; by acquisition mergers of Third World companies into multinational firms; and by joint ventures with Third World governments.

The sale of stock equity provides cheap capital for the corporation. For multinationals dividend payments tend to run at less than 5 percent of the market value of the stock — the most speculative corporations, such as McDonald's, pay no dividend at all — while the price of that share of stock ranges, with few exceptions, far above the book value of the share of assets that stock represents, and about eight times the corporation's profits. Of these profits only about 30 percent will be paid out to share-holders, the corporation retaining the remainder.

The purchase of multinational stock represents only one side of the equity ownership cycle; part of the cycle is completed by the multi-national's purchases of equity in the Third World. It is central to any consideration of the benefits of foreign investment that nearly 40 percent of U.S. capital expansions abroad go to acquiring existing Third World operations (*Fortune* 1975:210–211). While its own stock sells at a mul-tiple of its book value, the multinational purchases Third World oper-ations at break-up value or less; the net investment is often zero or negative. The takeover may not even have to be paid for with cash — through a *merger* transaction the multinational merely prints up stock certificates to "buy" the equity of the other firm. Using this merger technique, the assets of International Telephone and Telegraph leaped from $1.8 billion in 1964 to $10.7 billion in 1974. As ITT acquired more corporations, the more capable it became of making acquisitions by capitalizing the assets of each new subsidiary for other purchases. ITT stock accepted by local entrepreneurs was so overpriced that its purchase in 1964 would have resulted in a 4 percent loss by 1975 (*Barron's* 1975).

Third World investors will sell their own local ownership interests at a low price to buy shares of the multinational at a high price for fear of competing with international firms for financing, sales, and supplies, and for the opportunity to reap new profits with reduced risk. By conferring on its acquired subsidiaries the parent corporation's capitalizing powers, the financial value of the subsidiary must rise by the mere acquisition itself, thus jacking up the wealth of both taker and taken. Companies with low credit ratings and low price/earnings ratios can suddenly multiply every dollar of profit with seventeen dollars of capitalization once the Xerox name is stamped on their stationery. Third World firms suddenly have available to them hard-to-obtain dollar-currency capital. New membership in an internationally diversified oligopoly reduces risks in sales, supply, and finance markets, providing safety for holders of multi-national equities. The sale of a local company to an international one affords some immunity from political control: although Chile could expropriate a mine, it could not expropriate shares of Anaconda. To the above list are added peculiar advantages of multinational operation such as tax minimization.

By studying a recent acquisition we can understand how the multi-national absorbs capital cheaply. In April 1975, Texas-based Tesoro Petroleum purchased Commonwealth Oil Refining Corporation (Corco), the largest employer in Puerto Rico, by paying $14.50 per share for 38 percent of Corco's common stock, the book value of Corco's assets well exceeded $14.50 per share, and Corco's president Norman Keith let it be known that the value of the corporation to Tesoro was twice as much, or about $800 million, about $28 per share. Later, Tesoro will probably swap its shares for the remainder of Corco's. The results of the transaction: Tesoro ends up with the capital in Corco at a net cost to Tesoro of about negative $200 million; the wealth of the Puerto Rican owners of Corco has risen by about $200 million. The reason why Corco's owners could be said to have sold cheaply is that they sold their interest at less than its value to Tesoro and the rate of return on their equity will decline. The percentage rate of return on Corco's equity will decline not because its cash profits will decline but because the value of the equity has risen.

Multinationals acquire Third World equity capital not only through acquisitions but through the direct sale of parent and subsidiary stock and other securities. Through the purchases of multinational securities Third World wealth holders seek to diversify their portfolios so as to avoid the greater risks of investing in a volatile small local market. For this protection from risk, they are willing to pay an extraordinarily high price for the multinational's stock.

It is claimed that MNC's benefit the Third World by providing much-needed investment capital, but as a result of this attraction of local capital to the multinational, the multinationals can absorb foreign capital far in excess of what they provide. For example, Tesoro may now choose to capitalize its new wealth in Corco's assets by removing the wealth from Puerto Rico.

As a result of their ability to attract capital, multinationals remove more investment capital than they provide. U.S. Department of Commerce figures for a sample of MNC's and their majority-owned affiliates indicate the ability of multinationals to draw funds from foreign sources. Between 1966 and 1972, U.S.-based parent corporations provided only 26 percent of their foreign subsidiaries' external financing (only 7 percent for Latin American subsidiaries). The remainder of the finance capital was supplied by local sources. External funds borrowed from the multinationals' own sources abroad totaled only $1.8 billion while other foreign sources provided $20.2 billion to the multinationals' subsidiaries. The reinvestment of profits accounted for only 8 percent of total subsidiary financing (*Survey of Current Business* 1975:32,37). If we look at the total flow of monetary capital across borders, we find that, as of 1973, for every dollar of U.S. assets abroad, seventy-two cents has been provided by investors *from* abroad investing in the United States, up from forty-eight cents in 1966 (*Survey of Current Business* 1974d:16). In addition, for every dollar of U.S. assets held abroad, the average U.S. corporate subsidiary sells $2.48 in securities in their foreign markets (*Survey of Current Business* 1974b:29).

The latest (1973) Commerce Department figures repeat the theme that MNC's provide little, if any, of their own funds for their investments outside the United States, drawing instead upon foreign capital. Direct investment outflows in 1973 from the coffers of U.S. parent corporations to their foreign operations came to $4.9 billion. This investment was more than offset by (1) the sale abroad of $2.5 billion in parent corporate securities (*Survey of Current Business* 1974e:27); (2) the sale of another $9.1 billion in U.S. corporate securities to foreigners in the New York market; (3) the repatriation to the United States of $9.4 billion of total subsidiary profits of $17.4 billion; and (4) a $12.9 billion rise in the value of U.S. multinational investments abroad, 13 percent. A $25.5 billion rise in U.S. assets abroad (to a total of $226 billion) coincided with a total investment of only $13 billion (*Survey of Current Business* 1974d: 4–6,28). We can conclude that U.S. multinationals provide, on net, a *negative* sum of capital to the nations into which they are expanding their operations: multinationals' investments merely return a portion of the investment capital that originated in those host countries. For their net investment of less than zero dollars, the multinationals reap yearly earnings and yearly gains in the value of their assets abroad. Capital-starved Third World nations have become capital exporters, to the extent that 55 percent of all U.S. corporate capitalization for foreign *and* domestic operations is financed — and financed cheaply — from foreign sources, up from 27 percent in 1955 (*Business Week* 1974). With Third World equity cheaply absorbed by the multinationals, equity financing needed for development must be cajoled back from these same corporations with costly blandishments.

With local capital absorbed by multinationals, Third World governments are often backed into so-called joint ventures, as in the case of Mexican copper development in which resource ownership is divided with Litton Industries, not out of a need for technical assistance, but a need for Litton's sources of capital, which are denied the Mexican government. Mexico will provide the ore, the technology, the labor, and the pesos for labor's wages. What Litton provides is basically its name on the securities.

DEBT. Money never stops. It must pass continually from one hand to another. There is not a single class of debtors in the world of multinational finance nor a unique class of creditors; both working and capital classes provide credit to each other and receive it back as debt — though the costs of the debts and the effects of providing credit set the working class and capital class on two sides of a widening chasm. For example, while the MNC receives three-quarters of the capital needed for new investment from local sources, the remaining financing that they provide may represent only paper unsecured loans to the subsidiary to disguise later remittances of profits to the parent corporation as loan payments (a tax shield).

The taking in and giving out of credit, as the greater part of the corporations' bank-like operation, strengthens corporate profitability. High debt capitalization, within bounds, in and of itself is a measure of corporate wealth; its extension, *leverage*, strengthens a corporation's fiscal powers and profile. Oppositely, for wage-earners and governments, debt undermines purchasing power, in the long run boding increased chances of insolvency, risks for which creditors must be compensated. Thus the very nature of borrowing for the corporation as opposed to the nature of borrowing for labor and governments gives rise to the difference in the costs of credit for each.

In the debt circle the colonial trade relationship is most evident. Government development agencies of the Third World commonly borrow capital through costly bond issues and then lend the money right back to the multinationals. Recently Puerto Rico and Chile borrowed money (issued bonds) from a subsidiary of ITT, Hartford Insurance (the buyer of the bonds). Chile and Puerto Rico then used this money to capitalize ITT utilities in their nations (*Wall Street Journal* 1975e:1975f). Capital recirculation is usually more indirect though not less costly to Third World nations and no less of a bargain to corporations. The five major bond issues during the week of this writing exemplify the difference in the cost of credit to Third World governments as opposed to the cost to MNC's (*Wall Street Journal* 1975b). Mobil Alaska Pipeline Company (a subsidiary of Mobil Oil), Commonwealth Edison, and First Boston Corporation (a bank holding company), will have to pay 8.45 percent, 8.7 percent and 8 percent interest respectively to obtain money, whereas bonds floated simultaneously by the government of Mexico will cost that nation 10 percent; the Government of Puerto Rico's bonds will cost Puerto Rico an equivalent $13\frac{1}{2}$ percent (the value to corporate holders of their 9.14 percent coupons exempt from all local and U.S. taxes). By borrowing money from Mexico at 8 percent and selling it back to Mexico at 10 percent, First Boston Bank turns an immediate 25 percent profit; using the same maneuver on the Puerto Rican debt, First Boston will turn a 69 percent profit (including their tax advantage).

Through their superior capitalization powers, multinational financiers control access to the capital markets. (Underwriters' brokerage commissions for selling unrated bonds such as Mexico's run about 1.4 per cent as compared to 0.7 percent for the AAA-rated multinationals [Robichek and Coleman 1967:479]). Underwriting banks buy the debt securities, which they will resell. The immediate rise in the open-market price of Third World government debt securities and the fall in the price of multinational corporate securities imply that underwriters have systematically underpriced Third World bonds (by $1\frac{1}{2}$ percent for Mexico, $2\frac{1}{2}$ percent for Puerto Rico) while overpricing corporate bonds (1 percent to 6 percent).

Public Debt

To understand how the corporations have colonized the debt-credit circle we must understand the peculiar functions of debt in the relationship between public and corporate treasuries.

The rise of the owners' share of production income must finally cut into labor's ability to consume that production. The surplus, the unconsumed products, reduces the need for more production, reducing the need for labor, which leads to layoffs and wage reductions. This, in turn, further erodes labor's purchasing power. Increasing surpluses result in recession and, ultimately, depression. Any time production outpaces wages, recession can be temporarily averted if laborers borrow to consume the stockpiling inventories. The American working person is presently suffering his or her first decline in hourly wages and family wealth since World War II, while personal debt has risen, between 1971 and 1974, from 18.55 percent of income to 20.48 percent (Willis 1974). As the payments on such debt reduce purchasing power in the long run, the debt must continually increase. Unlike corporations, which borrow from strength, wage-earners borrow from weakness, and weakened by the borrowing (including ever-higher interest charges to compensate for the risk of their default) soon strain the limits of personal debt. The *fiscal*, or Keynesian, mechanism of financed deficit spending transfers the debt burden from individual to government, the latter having a somewhat more extended period of solvency by way of its powers to tax and print money.

Through publicly financed government expenditures, labor indirectly employs itself. Those so employed must only produce waste — such as military hardware — lest their production add to the surplus problem. Welfare administration, subsidized featherbedding in industry and agriculture, excess civil-service patronage, armed forces personnel in excess of one million, and employment in nonsecurity military industries yield about twenty-six million Americans who work without producing usable goods or services (Kelso and Hetter 1967:141–143). As Mexican production in the early 1970's outpaced wages by 30 percent, government-owned Petroleos Mexicanos became as much a make-work as a make-oil program.

Even if the recession ends, the increase of debt, although inflationary, cannot be avoided, for the government must cover expiring debt with new debt or its insolvency will appear. D. Ranson of the U.S. Department of the Treasury, privately figured the true national debt (having eschewed the official figure of $474 billion). He found present commitments of our federal government alone, inclusive of civil service, military retirement, and social security, to exceed $4.2 trillion while our reserve source of payment is presently around $60 billion (Laffer 1974).

MATHEMENON

Where does the money come from — the money for equity and debt credit circulating between bank, corporation, and public treasury? Unlike your money, which is "made" if you work for a living, these other moneys are *born*. When nations need it, they print it. When bankers need it, they write checks against that circulating stream that resides only temporarily and fractionally in the bank vault. The study of the inflationary effects of credit creation, *Mathemenon*, reveals the sources of inflation and names the beneficiaries and the injured.

The Mechanism

The method by which the credit supply expands, as recognized by most economists, is as follows: a state treasury may print and sell debt issues to commercial banks and investors. The nation's central bank may then buy up these issues from the commercial banks — with money it has literally printed for the purchase.

But a one billion dollar purchase by the central bank does not raise the economy's money supply by a mere one billion dollars. Given that a bank will follow a U.S. requirement that it hold onto one-fifth of the funds deposited with it, any bank can invest 80¢ of each dollar of this new money it receives. Another bank, receiving that 80¢ from a deposit made by the corporation invested in, will then lend out 80 percent of the 80¢, or 64¢. The economy's money supply by this time has increased by the original $1 plus 80¢ plus 64¢, or $2.44. A third bank will extend a corporate credit for 80 percent of that 64¢, or 51.2¢ — and likewise to a fourth and fifth bank until that one billion dollar purchase by the central bank has mushroomed into a *five* billion dollar increase in the total money supply — the process termed *credit creation*.

The Effect

When more credit money is loaded into the economy while production remains the same, each dollar is worth less — the process called *inflation*. As dollars represent nothing more than a share of the economy, their increase reduces the value of each dollar-share proportionately. Based on Irving Fisher's Quantity Equation,

$$\text{Prices} = \frac{\text{Money Credit Supply}}{\text{Consumable Goods Produced}} \times \text{Velocity.}$$

(Velocity is, roughly, the number of times a dollar changes hands in a year.) Given the same amount of consumable production (and no change in velocity), prices, on the average, will increase by 10 percent for each 10 percent rise in the credit supply.

Corporate Mathemenon

We now move beyond the restricted concept that only governments' central banks may increase the credit money supply. (The government's role will be discussed in more detail in the section on fiscal policy following.) The concept of the process of credit expansion must incorporate the financial operations of the nonbank corporations, which are, after all, the ultimate recipients of investment credit. Credit is a product created instantaneously by its demand. Because it is the corporations that demand credit, it is the corporations that call credit into being. *If corporations capitalize in excess of the needs of production, the excess credit will generate price inflation.* Another way to view the cause of inflation consistent with the Equation is that the more money there is in the system, the higher the price will be paid for goods. The significance is that workers' wages compete with capital's profits and interest earnings for goods and services. By creating credit for themselves, capitalists bid up prices and gain a greater share of real goods as wages stay unchanged. The more credit capitalists generate, the lower the purchasing power of wages. The following sections show how corporations generate inflationary credit.

EXTERNAL FINANCING REVISITED. While Standard Oil of Indiana earned a record $0.97 billion in 1974 (*Fortune* 1975: 210–211), it raised its dividend a paltry ten cents per share. One-half billion dollars of earnings were retained (Moody's 1975:2327) not out of the need for expansion of oil refining capacity but to lure yet more capitalization. When a corporation decides to increase the total dividend payment the dividend per share will seldom rise. Rather, the corporation will seek to sell more stock, keeping the dividend per share constant. In 1974, Standard doubled the number of shares of common stock outstanding with a 100 percent *stock* dividend. An additional $250 million in debentures (debts) of Indiana Standard and its multinational subsidiary, Amoco International Finance, were paid off — not with cash out of profits but with more common stock (value: about $285 million) (*Chicago Sun-Times* 1974b) so as not to reduce capitalization. The long-run effect of redeeming the debentures is *increased* debt capitalization. Corporations can sell about three dollars of debt for every two dollars of equity which will eventually allow for the sale of more than $400 million in additional debt issues. Just as its profits were not used productively, the additional capitalization of this, the sixth-largest oil company, was used not to expand production but rather in an attempt to take over Occidental Petroleum, ninth-largest in the industry. The credit newly created for the capitalization of Indiana Standard continues to circulate. These dollars created for capitalization compete with wages for the existing amount of goods and services in the economy, thereby bidding up all prices.

DEPRECIATION: SELF-FINANCING. Depreciation is listed on a corporation's income statement as an expense. It is not an expense, but rather a *cash inflow*, that part of a corporation's sales revenue set aside each year by the corporation to represent the return of the capital provided by its investors. Using loan terminology, depreciation is the repayment of principle, while earnings, "profits," are the return *on* that principle.

Depreciation is cash that can be spent or capitalized. Together, depreciation and earnings constitute a corporation's cash inflow (Vaughan, this volume).

Clearly, a corporation can hide profits by charging itself excessively for depreciation. The amount a corporation charges itself for depreciation is limited only by the boldness of its accountants and the regulations of government. The basic rule is that a fair charge for depreciation equals the deterioration of plant and equipment. If a plant worth $100 million is expected to last fifty years, depreciation should be approximately $2 million each year. Nevertheless, accountants for the multinationals tend to use *accelerated* depreciation by which as much as 50 percent of a plant's value is depreciated in a single year. By this method profits equal to 19 percent of total corporate sales revenues are hidden or about twice the average corporation's declared profits (*Survey of Current Business* 1974b:19).

According to development economics as expressed by Walt Rostow's influential Stages of Growth theory, the growth of depreciation as a percentage of national production is required for development in a capitalist economy. This merely suggests that a greater share of national wealth should go into the pockets of corporate investors. This increase in depreciation, representing no increase in consumable goods, drives up prices. In 1973 the cash flow (combined depreciation and retained earnings) of U.S. MNC's increased by 26 percent, well above their increase in production (*Wall Street Journal* 1974a).

FINANCING OF ACQUISITIONS AND OTHER NONPRODUCTIVE INVESTMENTS. While the rate of expansion of plant and equipment assets of multinational foreign subsidiaries has remained relatively constant over the years, the rate of growth of financial assets has doubled (Polakoff 1970:366). When financiers extend credit without an offsetting rise in production, prices must rise.

In the previous section, it was mentioned that when the Tesoro and Corco companies merged, the new wealth for equity holders of the two companies, about $400 million, seemed to appear through accounting magic from nowhere. In fact, however, the full sum came from the pockets of wage-earners. The rise in the wealth of stockholders of Tesoro and Corco was accomplished without production; Corco claimed its operations remained virtually unchanged (*Barron's* 1975). E.F. Hutton led other finance houses in extending new credit to Tesoro, with Corco used as collateral. Without an offsetting rise in production, such new, financially gained wealth, when capitalized and spent, bids up all prices in the economy. Labor shares in the inflation caused by nonproductive investments, but not in the gains, as such investments need not reach labor as wages. The cost of inflation from this merger is shared among the workers of Puerto Rico and the U.S. mainland.

Other capitalized investments that reduce production while creating credit include:

Acquisitions of competitors, distributors, or suppliers and any other purchase that seeks monopoly restraint of production; e.g., Exxon purchased Libyan oil reserves for the purpose of keeping much of this oil off the market (Vernon 1974).

Restraint of technology. For example, IBM and Xerox, in leasing rather than selling their machines, retain ownership of their products and therefore have a vested interest in suppressing development of new technology that would make their machines unexpectedly obsolete. Kaiser Industries, a major aluminium producer, has little desire to use a simplified method of aluminum processing now available because that could lead to the greater independence of Kaiser's Third World bauxite suppliers who would themselves use the simpler process rather than sell the bauxite to Kaiser. These corporations use large research, development, and engineering budgets to monopolize the ownership of patent technology and scientific talent to prevent a major advance in technology that could threaten their present market position.

Technology that replaces labor but does not increase production. The credit created from Commonwealth Edison's bond issue will be used to switch company operations from labor-intensive coal plants to automated nuclear power plants.

Capitalization of real estate. Adding no consumable good to the economy, the capitalization of increases in land and property values can be inflationary.

THE TIME FACTOR IN CAPITALIZATION. Finance allows funds to be generated at a rate faster than if these funds were an inseparable part of the production cycle. For example, the earnings from a future operation are presold, prematurely financed, and committed to other investments while the operation is still just a gleam in management's eye. The Mobil Alaska Pipeline debt issue has raised $300 million although expenditures are years off. In the meantime, the money will subsidize Mobil Oil's acquisition of Marcor (Container Corporation and Montgomery Ward). This premature creation of credit prior to its productive employment inflates prices. In the Quantity Equation, premature financing and other forms of accelerated capitalization may be expressed as an increase in "velocity," roughly the number of times a dollar changes hands during a year. By speeding up their cash flow, corporations effectively create credit, which may be inflationary.

Mathemenon, Financial Circles, and the Third World

By combining knowledge of credit creation discussed in this section with knowledge of the circular pattern of control of credit internationally, as discussed in the first section, we find that the *quality* of money that goes into the Third World is inferior to the quality of money going out. We find that involvement of the credit-creating powers of state treasuries and central banks adds a special dimension to already lopsided circulation. Thus, "One central point of each experience [of Caribbean nations] was the very close association between granting domestic credit and the loss of their foreign reserves" (Clivey 1972:44).

Third World governments swell the supply of credit to attract investment. Credit is supplied not only to directly finance development projects (through loans or joint ownership) but to indirectly finance capitalization of industry by printing money for distribution to investors by local banks. Credit is additionally expanded to attempt, as we shall later see, to hold down interest rates. Unfortunately, when printed local currency is lent to a foreign corporation, the corporation does not draw the credit in that currency. Rather, only the nation's reserves of foreign exchange (the currency of industrial nations, usually dollars) is withdrawn in gold or goods. For example, in the first year of its operations, the Central Bank of Guyana extended credit worth $11 million in hopes of luring foreign investors who would add to the Guyanan funds with their own hard-currency capital. The bank was surprised to find that its hard-currency reserves soon declined by $11 million after foreign investment had been procured (Clivey 1972:44–45). Foreign investors, it seems, had removed all the hard-currency capital provided by the government bank. Guyana had, on balance, provided 100 percent of the foreigners' investment capital out of its own resources. In the process, MNC's gained perpetual ownership and the profits thereof in Guyanan industry. Guyana's labor constructs and operates the multinationals' factories for wages paid in local currency that had to have come from their central bank in the first place. On net, the MNC's have invested nothing in the way of dollar capital.

To much of the Third World, multinational investment is trademark and patent licenses, stock certificates (from merger acquisitions), debt and equity cash locally raised, funds from foreign central banks, and depreciation. What goes out are goods or hard foreign currency. Other figures also lead us to believe that what multinationals put into economies by way of their investments is qualitatively different from what they take out. While taking out real goods and labor value, they do not invest hard cash. Since 40 percent of all new multinational investment in foreign subsidiaries comes from foreign cash flow (depreciation and retained earnings) and two dollars of earnings are withdrawn for every dollar of this investment (*Survey of Current Business* 1974e:1–24), we can conclude that multinational investment abroad increasingly consists of depreciation and less and less the hard cash of earnings. The "investment" of depreciation adds nothing to the nation's reserves of foreign exchange.

A Third World nation's reserve of foreign exchange is one indicator of its share of the ownership of world production. The international purchasing power of its currency (and thus the purchasing power of wages) partially rests on the ratio of the supply of that currency to its foreign exchange reserves. The expansion of local credit with resultant foreign exchange drainage in effect devalues the nation's currency relative to other lands, spurring an inflation of prices as the base of consumable goods is effectively contracted. Continually undermined, Third World currencies have lost their liquidity, i.e., are no longer negotiable for either the products of other nations or the products of multinational subsidiaries within their borders. As a result the industrial nations have gained *seigniorage* rights over the Third World: the exclusive power to create international trading currency and credit. The corporations of the United States and to a lesser extent the European industrial states have been able to buy foreign products simply by creating credit — with the bonus to the United States of exporting inflationary dollars. Likewise, Third World currencies are no longer accepted as payment for their mounting international debts.

As the need for dollar currency rises, the cost of obtaining those dollars rises. Dollars are obtained not only through borrowing, in which the high cost appears as high interest rates to be paid out of hard currency reserves, but also through the export of goods and resources: the high cost of these dollars appears as the low cost of the goods sold. For example, Mexico sells oil through oil firms to the U.S. market for 54 cents a gallon though it could sell that oil to its own people for twenty-one pesos, or $1.75. But because those pesos are not dollars and therefore cannot pay the government's debts to U.S. banks, the Mexican government must sell to the oil companies at this two-thirds discount to obtain dollars.

Unable to obtain financing for their own development, Third World nations must seek out foreign corporations to develop their industries. For financing development projects by their direct investment, the multinationals add an implicit finance charge that rises as the nation is more financially pressed. This implicit financial charge by multinational nonbank corporations takes a form other than the payment of high interest, the form of low wages.

We must remember that the capital has been provided to the multinationals by the Third World peoples themselves. Therefore, the multinationals monopolize the credit market by first absorbing all local investment capital and then returning this credit at a monopoly price. By absorbing a nation's capital, a corporation may absorb a nation's labor and resources.

The dollar chase is a major motive behind worker migration, as some nations — notably Mexico, Algeria, and Italy — must export their laborers to the United States or Germany in hopes they will send home their hard-currency paychecks.

As the export industries established by the multinationals have begun to concentrate on manufacturing, additional labor is wasted on boosting the dollar balance of payments rather than used for internal development or consumption.

FISCAL FOLLIES

After public debt-spending, credit expansion is the major arm of government anti-depression policy. A simple inversion of this anti-depression program — attempted credit contraction — serves as the government's main weapon against inflation. Such policies encompass both camps of capitalist economics, the Fiscalists, identified with John Maynard Keynes, and the Monetarists, whose leading spokesman is Milton Friedman. To reverse recession or depression, both camps would raise capital investment through credit expansion and thereby, they reason, production and employment. By a similar light they have determined that to halt price inflation it is necessary that production, investment, and employment (or wages) be decreased, the decrease to be accomplished by credit contraction. Policy for Third World development is merely the extension of anti-depression policy that is rooted in the belief that growth requires expanding investment of monetary capital.

Now-dominant fiscal policy also hinges on the assumption that an increase in the currency supply will lower interest rates permanently, which should lure capital holders to borrow and invest inactive money — although the incumbent money-supply expansion admittedly could cause inflation. Oppositely, inflation calls for credit contraction to force up interest rates and induce capitalists to pull their money out of circulation altogether (termed *dis*investment).

Interest Rates and Capital Investment

The spectacular failure of fiscal policy to reverse recession, stem inflation, or stimulate growth derives from ignorance of the historical role of interest rates in the apparatus of capital financing. Capital circulates; it does not move in and out of investment markets. Interest rates solely determine the distribution of investments such that the rates of return are equalized and maximized, but the aggregate *amount* of capital circulating is not affected by interest rates. Corporations and wealth-holders whose investments do not earn a profit at least equal to the going interest rate will lend to those who can earn a higher rate of return, lending directly through their purchases of stocks or bonds or lending indirectly through their bank deposits. Since the object is the maintenance of capital's share of the income flow, protection of the profitability of production capital requires that the basic formula by which the interest earnings and borrowing charges are determined in the financial markets and banks reflect exactly and only the *expected* rate of *coming* inflation:

Interest = Profitability of (New) Capital + Expected Inflation (Aliber 1973).

Interest charges on the average must equal the return on investment added to the expected amount of inflation over the period of the loan such that *real* interest (stated interest minus inflation) will not significantly fluctuate. As long as the real interest rate does not fluctuate, fiscal changes in the stated interest rate cannot affect the aggregate amount of capital investment.

The basic motivation of fiscal anti-recession and development policies is the stimulation of inactive capital into investment. But capital is never sleepy. Continually circulating, it never needs to be awakened: capital cannot pass out of the capital markets and is therefore always totally invested by way of bonds, stocks, or bank loans and deposits. As for fiscal anti-inflationary policy — until the day that banks pay interest on deposits they neither intend to invest nor loan, i.e., that banks won't circulate, *capital demand will not be slowed by high interest rates*. The very week the prime rate hit a record 11.45 percent, the Federal Reserve Bank of New York recorded an increase in the area's business loans of $551 million (*Chicago Sun-Times* 1974a). One must also question whether banks would invest or lend greater or lesser sums when the change in interest rates does not necessarily change the *spread* between the interest the banks pay for money coming in and that received for money going out.

Credit Creation and Interest Rates

Not only is the effect on investment due to interest rate changes in doubt but also the very manner in which fiscalists have tried to manipulate interest rates. Fiscal planners insist that a larger money supply keeps interest low and "tight" money keeps interest high, although the total supply of currency does not directly figure into the formula (above) for determining interest. A government-precipitated increase in the money supply does, in fact, immediately lower interest rates as the markets flood with government debt securities. But the lowering of interest rates is as misleading as it is short-lived, for this rain of bonds turns into a monetary cloudburst when multiplied by credit creation. The inflated money supply leads to price inflation, which leads to a jump in interest rates to reflect that inflation. By ignorance of both the financial role of interest rates and the relation of interest rates to credit creation, governments' fiscal reactions frustrate their own ends, often furthering the inflation they seek to subdue and raising interest rates they seek to lower.

Governments and Credit Creation

The problem of governments' fiscal activity exacerbating inflation and recession is not a technical slapstick requiring only a new routine. Though we have shown the mechanics of government involvement in the credit-creating process, the realpolitik of international financial markets dictates the aggregate supply of credit. *A government cannot of its own volition increase the money supply of a nation or of the world*. Unable to determine the flow of credit, governments cannot determine the rate of inflation. This is the ultimate frustration of both fiscal and monetary policy and the hopes of a political reform of the marketplace. Although monetarist policy does not involve manipulation of interest rates as does fiscal policy, it too falters as it postulates absolute control of the credit supply's increase or shrinkage by the hand of the central bank: that the central bank can order a decrease in the money supply by 10 percent that will automatically decrease the gross national product by a like 10 percent. A public treasury or central bank cannot restrict the supply of money in the face of present demand for money as long as credit substitutes for money are available. As for credit expansion policy, a central bank can print all the bonds, bills, and currency it desires, but their infusion into the economy cannot occur without a present demand for those funds.

Corporations are the central components of credit demand. If these corporations do not desire additional currency, it cannot enter the economy. Conversely, if the government or central bank refuses to supply capitalists with liquidity, the banks will manufacture credit-money as needed. A government cannot strictly enforce restrictions on credit creation, first because such restrictions implicitly require banks to take in (and pay interest on) money they cannot loan, a condition which, if adhered to, would destroy a bank's profitability, and second because national fiscal restrictions cannot affect international corporations, which can transfer funds across borders. Even if a central bank chooses to restrict the supply of currency, a rising demand for capital can still be met by banks creating their own credit. This could be accomplished by a corporation issuing bonds or stock; the bank borrows to purchase these securities, using the securities themselves as collateral for the credit. From December 1972 through July 1974, when the Federal Reserve Bank tried to maintain tight money by increasing the official money supply by only 9 percent, bank credit exploded by 23 percent (*Survey of Current Business* 1974e:S,17,20). By forcing governments and central banks into the role of creators of liquidity, some of the debt and interest burdens of capitalizing business have been passed on to the taxpayer.

Interest Rates, Wages, and Inflation

Interest rates reflect the rate of price inflation so that the purchasing power of finance capital (monetary assets) will rise in value to maintain parity with the value of real capital (physical assets). As inflation climbs, real capital assets rise in money value; however, the real wealth represented by a factory — its potential to produce — is unchanged by product price fluctuations and thus must rise in dollar value by the amount of inflation (land appreciates similarly). The prices charged for goods held in inventory are marked up with inflation (the rise in prices *is* inflation, by definition). Monetary assets that represent these real assets, or are liens against them, must then also rise in money value with inflation. The bond purchaser, bank, or other capital creditor is protected against rising prices by an equal rise in interest income. Capital debtors are reimbursed for these higher interest charges as they borrow for investments rising in value with inflation. Thus, the capital speculator —

debtor or creditor — literally does not care how high interest rates climb.

But for wage earners who do not borrow to purchase real or monetary capital assets, the stated interest rate is the *cost of money* for consumer expenses such as mortgage debt and installment buying. Since consumer debtors must compete for financing with capital speculators, they must pay the same inflation premium — even though their means of payment (wages) has not risen automatically as it has risen for the capitalists, the sellers of goods. While the net transfer of money among capitalizers due to high interest rates is nil, the net transfer of money from consumer debtor to creditor runs, in the United States, to $200 billion annually (Keyserling 1974). While *stated* U.S. interest rates, the cost of money to consumers, stood at 9 percent by 1974, a postwar high, the real interest rate, the cost of money to capitalizers, was actually a negative 4 percent. Stated interest in Brazil consistently is more than 20 percent (United Nations 1974:618). The consumer is doubly charged for inflation — the inflated interest charges are tagged on to the already inflated product prices. The working person bears the entire brunt of inflation.

Interest and Multinational Investment

The MNC's are as much financial rationalizers as they are production rationalizers. The geography and nature of their investments are determined as much by the costs and availability of capital and capital markets as the cost and availability of labor and sales markets.

Because the interest rate in a country reflects that country's rate of price inflation, the difference between the interest rates of two countries must equal the difference between their inflation rates. If the inflation rate in Argentina is 10 percent greater than in the United States, then the interest rate on Argentine pesos should also be 10 percent higher than on the U.S. dollar. If dollar interest is 10 percent, then Argentine interest should be 20 percent. If Argentine interest exceeds 20 percent, that is, if the premium paid for capital is too high, the multinational will borrow from the dollar markets and invest in Argentina, i.e., "lend" to their foreign subsidiary. Conversely, if Argentina's interest rates are forced below 20 percent, then cheap pesos will be borrowed in Buenos Aires and invested locally in real assets or shifted abroad where higher real interest returns can be had on other currencies. The latter possibility, open only to the multinationals, causes disinvestment, opposite the aims and expectations of fiscal low-interest policy. These parities have been thrown out of whack with the aid of monetary authorities attempting to raise or lower interest rates to variously attract capital or cap inflation — assisted by multinationals that, eyeing riskless financial windfalls, move their money with the cycles of the political economy.

The fiscal competition between nations attracts the most advanced of the multinationals such as Deltec. They are mere holding companies whose volatile capital rapidly moves in and out of industries and nations — and out of production itself — having three investment routes for playing off aberrations within and between different nations: direct investment (industry creation), indirect investment (securities portfolio), and banking (withdrawal to the position of financial intermediary). Some industrial firms merge with financial companies to take advantage of such opportunities: ITT taking on Hartford Insurance, Tenneco taking and leaving the Bank of Houston.

Argentina provides an example of such maneuvering. Like many in the Third World, the Argentine government artifically reduced interest rates through accelerated credit creation. In some years, the inflation-discounted real rates were negative (Pazos 1972:18; Villanueva 1970:355–360). At such a time a corporation such as Deltec could borrow in Argentina and invest in its own industries their equity in other companies in their portfolio (which removes financial support for local operators). The money supply, inflated to hold down interest, eventually drove up both prices *and*, thereby, stated interest rates. Real interest also began to rise, reflecting lenders' fears of the instability of the economy and the extraordinary riskiness of the currency as a means of debt repayment. With a jump in Argentine interest, Deltec could switch to its banking and brokerage function, i.e., lending money and buying bonds. Low-interest financing, subsidized by the public through inflation and ostensibly provided for manufacturing, winds up financing non-productive financial operations.

The failure of either a credit expansion or credit contraction policy in one year usually sets off a mad scramble to reverse the policy the following year. This institutionalizes the disparities to the greater profit of the multinationals.

Inflation, Devaluation, and Interest Rates

The exchange rate (or exchange ratio) of currencies reflects solely their relative purchasing power. Devaluation of a nation's currency occurs when the price inflation of that nation exceeds that of another. As earlier stated, the purchasing power of a currency in the global market is additionally affected by its holdings of hard currencies, which must also then affect rates of exchange. Often, the international corporation is described as passively taking advantage of official interest-rate policies, but the fact is that multinational operations create the very conditions that allow them to loot public funds. As the multinational pulls from a nation purchasing power in the form of goods and hard currencies, the purchasing power of local currency declines. Once the exit of hard currency and the weakening of the economy makes its appearance, speculators unload all their local currency, speeding up the outflow of hard currency reserves until the government, in fear of insolvency, devalues its currency — which upvalues the currency to which the speculators ran. One European subsidiary of a multinational bank has a computer wired to lights and buzzers that go off when conditions signal imminent official currency intervention.

SOMETHING THEY CALL THE LIQUIDITY CRISIS

The Third World's problems do not originate with their fiscal policies, for the contradiction in policy goals and methods are only the manifestation of the underlying contradiction between the goal of development and the method for achieving development: increased monetary capital investment.

Poor nations may choose to "competitively" devalue their currency beyond what their price inflation calls for in order to lure foreign capital by artifically cheapening local labor and goods. This process costs, for the amount of local currency that can be traded or capitalized on each dollar has increased, causing credit denominated in the local currency to expand, leading to inflation. Further devaluation is required to maintain the bargain rate of real interest for foreign capital — while stated interest (for the consumer) mounts apace with the inflation. Inflation, credit creation, and devaluation (competitive or forced) race each other until the whole thing bursts, as it did for Brazil in 1967 when the cruzeiros that working people held were called in and replaced with the *new* cruzeiro. The new cruzeiros cost 1,000 old ones, and the cycle of Mathemenon was given a fresh start (World Bank 1967:22).

Uruguay ran to the International Monetary Fund for a line of supporting credit when it tripled its money supply, keeping the interest rate down to 15 percent for business and inflation at more than 100 percent (United Nations 1974:547). The IMF imposed a devaluation to be followed by Uruguay's commitment of its hard currency to support the new exchange level at any cost (Couriel and Lichtenszten 1966:69,169–189). (Support means buying back a nation's own currency with hard currency.) By imposing this crossed policy of devaluation and upvaluation, the IMF appeared more like an agent of Uruguay's creditors and capital debtors than an agent of development. This is not an accusation of IMF duplicity but a singling out of the contradictions in the notion that development requires corporate investment. Uruguay is forced to accept the contradictory policy goals of (1) providing ready, cheap capital (accomplished by devaluation) and (2) maintaining the value of that capital once it is in investors' hands (accomplished by supporting the currency).

Currencies that are forever prostrate suffer exceptional penalties in the finance markets. Beyond the loss of currency seigniorage rights, the notoriously weak currency loses its capacity to be capitalized. Italians must pay an implicit excise fee to Liquigas for meat the company raises and exports from Brazil because Liquigas finds it cannot capitalize the stream of earned lire at the same ratio as dollar or Swiss franc income. Those foreign debts that cannot be paid for with hard currency must be paid for in goods (and labor). The resulting unchanged credit supply causes economy-wide price inflation — besides such phenomena as Argentina's meatless Mondays. In international hard times, certain goods take on the aspect of reserve currency: "There's more leverage [capitalization] in food than in finance," says Chairman Clarence Dauphinot of multinational Deltec. This is bad news for people who would prefer eating their food to leveraging their food, because such devaluation of their currency results in a rise in food prices.

In the International Debt Circle

Let us take Argentina as an example of Third World financing. When the peso rapidly declined to its limits, Argentina backed it by exporting all the beef the market would accept. Argentina — squeezed out of the capital from its own credit markets by foreign corporations — eventually turned, as all other Third World countries must, to foreign markets to scrounge the capital to back its currency. Argentina is presently in the Eurodollar market to the tune of $800 million.

The greater the woes of a country's economy, the costlier foreign capital becomes. Surfacing again in our study is the catch-22 of development finance: for market nations, strong economies are needed to obtain and hold capital; yet at the same time capital is a requisite for a strong economy. What has resulted is the "tiering" of interest rates, the Third World nations paying a premium charge (for being poor) above the interbank rates and the prime rate paid by the multinationals. *The Wall Street Journal* reports that "foreign borrowers are expected to seek a record sum here [in New York] this year, although all will be forced to pay higher than comparable domestic issuers..." (*Wall Street Journal* 1975b). This week's major corporate borrowers, First Boston, Mobil (Oil) Alaska Pipeline, and Com Ed, will pay 8 percent, 8.45 percent and 8.7 percent respectively against Mexico's 10 percent. Multinational haven South Korea, which is seeking $200 million to cover looming balance-of-payments deficits that the loan would not even meet, was hard pressed to find a bank to manage the debt sale though it was willing to pay

29 percent above the Eurodollar interbank rate (and devalue the Korean wan to boot) (*Wall Street Journal* 1975a).

In addition to the explicit interest charge, South Korea, like most Third World nations, is in no position to demand competitive bidding from its underwriters. Underwriting charges by banks organized into single consortia average double the competitive charge (Kessel 1971).

The excessive interest charged to the poorer nations crops up in insurance rates. Insurance companies are financial institutions, paying claims on premiums just as banks pay interest on deposits. The ratio of claims paid to premiums received yields an implicit interest rate return on investing in insurance. U.S. insurance companies pay out an average $1.05 in claims and costs to obtain for every $1 in premiums obtained in the United States, an effective interest of 4 percent, while foreign claims paid out amount to only 80 cents for every foreign dollar paid in. U.S. insurance companies thus pay a *negative* 27 percent on their foreign accounts, or, viewed another way, earn a 32 percent profit even before they invest their cash flow.

The credit obtainable by the Third World for necessary imports is the most costly — so-called suppliers' credits, installment credit provided directly by the multinationals, which by 1965 accounted for more than one-seventh of total Third World debt; for nine nations, over 80 percent of their debt to foreigners was in the form of suppliers' credits (these include Mexico, Spain, Cambodia, Greece). While explicit interest runs about 100 percent higher than alternate forms of development financing, corporate overcharges on the principal cost of the purchases put the actual interest charges 400 percent higher. Suppliers' credits have risen to 56 percent of the total private financing to private parties in the Third World. A World Bank report notes that most of these credits are used for establishing monopoly industries. Though Third World governments commonly guarantee these credits, the industrial governments also subsidize such schemes to bolster their exports — one-third of England's exports are so involved — though the savings are not passed on to the Third World (Work Bank 1967:12,19–20,(V)4–6). For example, the U.S. government's Export-Import Bank records a $56.3 million loan to Zaire at 8 percent to pay Flour Corporation of Idaho for a mining project. The Ex-Im Bank also guarantees the matching loan from Chase Manhattan Bank for which Zaire is charged 10.8 percent. Looking closer, this is the financial equivalent of a $112.6 million loan *to Chase Manhattan* at 8 percent, which they will then charge to the Zairis at 9.4 percent. Chase Manhattan reaps an extraordinary 17 percent profit (selling money at 9.4 percent that it bought at 8 percent) while Flour Corporation acquires a cheap line of capital purchased with foreign and domestic public funds.

The Short/Long Squeeze

The shakier a nation's economy, the more unpredictable will be its currency and credit, moving creditors to require that they be paid back in shorter time. To obtain its loan, South Korea, besides taking "certain measures" required by Morgan Guaranty bank, had the repayment period of its loan cut down from seven years to five. First Boston Corporation will have seven years and Com Ed and Mobil Oil will have thirty years each to pay back their loans, while Mexico will have only five years.

The cutting edge is that the majority of the Third World's borrowings cover payments on previous borrowings that had failed to shore up capital drainage. While we saw how Standard Oil of Indiana smoothly "rolled over" $250 million of short-term debt into long-term, Third World nations were fighting to cover long-term debt payments with short-term loans (which means leaning even more heavily on suppliers' credits). Short-term interest is usually below that of bonds of longer maturity. But as short-term issues by the Third World indicate risk, the premiums have remained as high or higher than their older long-term debts. This has been quite a boon to international financiers as older lower-interest long-term debt is covered with high-interest short-term borrowing, a system known in the neighborhood as loan sharking: Mexico's new 10 percent debt will cover payments on an 8 percent debt maturing in 1997.

The recent crisis has sent average short-term interest rates reeling upward by 91 percent from May 1972 to December 1974, while interest rates paid by the MNC's for new long-term bond borrowings increased by only 20 percent. At times during the period, the average *absolute* interest rate on stable short-term securities actually exceeded the long-term corporate rate by as much as 58 percent (*Financial Weekly* 1974).

Crisis

Though the direct and indirect costs of capital formation are inequitably "shared" between corporations and the wage-earners and their government, this does not constitute the Crisis. The Crisis is the inability of those countries that need credit most to obtain credit, or at least to obtain credit at a price that does not enslave their economies. Finance keeps the benefits of any development from the people who build and operate these industries. Due to financial exigencies, foreign investment in production and technology does not meet people's need for employment and basic consumption. To answer why Third World incomes have grown haltingly and then declined — Third World production dropped from a fifth of the world's total to a sixth during the Decade of Development (United Nations 1974:11) — we must first ask why credit cannot get to those who need it from those who have it, why it is costlier and costlier to get, and why once gotten capital cannot be kept or often cannot be used productively.

Let us look more closely at Mexico's indebtedness. The length of the repayment period is significant. If all of Mexico's debts were to be amortized (amortization is the annual payment of principal) over five years, annual debt service payments would amount to 20 percent of the total debt payment of principal plus 10 percent interest for a yearly total outlay equaling 30 percent of the outstanding debt. (By contrast, Mobil Oil, with its thirty-year payback terms, would pay only 3.3 percent of the principal of its total indebtedness plus interest at 8.45 percent, a total outlay of only 11.75 percent.) Mexico's 30 percent debt-service burden, three times that of the corporation, portends crisis. If Mexico must pay 30 percent on a total outstanding debt of $1 billion, its $80 million borrowing the week of this writing will not even provide for a net inflow of capital. All of Mexico's borrowing will go solely to cover other debts. Further, projecting a total year's borrowing of $500 million, the sum of *spendable* credit left to Mexico will be only $50 million — after making payments on both the original debt ($300 million) and on the new $500 million debt (interest $50 million, principal $100 million). Although Mexico's creditors will only be putting up $50 million in new net capital, Mexico will have to pay them interest on a loan technically ten times that amount, $500 million, the full face value of the new loan. Therefore, while stated interest on the new loan runs 10 percent, the *effective* interest on the $50 million borrowed for expenditures is 100 percent. With borrowings increasingly committed to covering other borrowings, to obtain that net $50 million for expenditures five years from now (given no change in credit terms), Mexico will have to raise its total debt to over $6 billion.

Effective interest skyrockets not only when stated interest increases but as the total debt burden increases, as repayment periods are shortened, and as the amount of total borrowings is restricted. Public financial crises result inevitably from the system of capital financing itself, because any increase in public borrowing reduces its credit worthiness. This forces on the public agencies the whole panoply of worsened credit terms which, as we see by the Mexico example, require still greater indebtedness. Already by 1964, 40 percent of the Third World's debts had maturities of five years or less. The growth of Third World debt has outstripped the growth in production fivefold over the past decade (Avramovich 1964:110,113,162; United Nations 1974:28). Debt service has increased at a rate three times the rate of the increase in debt. The Third World invites foreign ownership of labor and material resources not out of hopes of a mutually beneficial partnership for development but solely to meet their payments to other foreigners, to finance old foreign obligations with new ones. Put another way, Third World peoples must pay dearly for the use of purchasing power. The contradiction is that attempts to lure more dollar investment or to refinance foreign debt must eventually, given the costs, result in a more excessive withdrawal of foreign exchange. According to the Organization for Economic Cooperation and Development (OECD), the gap between the Third World's foreign exchange needed and foreign exchange received widened during the 1960's by $20 billion annually. When debt goes to cover debt, precious little capital is left for development. Economist N. S. Lichtenszten of Uruguay determined that the amount of capital and savings available for development financing after foreign interest payments has dropped from 16.2 percent of gross national production to 12.8 percent (Couriel and Lichtenszten 1966:128).

Problems become crises when problems feed on themselves and the only available solutions damage rather than alleviate. High interest charges on borrowing, the rolling over of long-term debt with short-term, increased external borrowing to make up for declining dollar reserves, and increased treasury subsidies to foreign capitalizers all erode the credit position of the Third World nations, which requires creditors to again raise interest charges and shorten credit terms. This forces greater external borrowing, which bleeds dollar reserves. Fiscal and monetary reactions — ever-accelerating credit creation to maintain lower real interest rates or to entice capital into production, competitive devaluations, or tax subsidies — are but financially fatiguing shadow-boxing, creating not productive investment but price inflation that further undermines the nations' liquidity positions. Greater investment means greater investment returns. Their exit and the exit of capitalized funds gotten cheaply by the multinationals reduces the credit worthiness of the economy, especially when a financial expansion exceeds the expansion of production. Whether or not these profits are carted back to New York, they reduce the wage share of national income, especially when financial capital accumulation provokes price inflation.

Contrary to the popular theory of a "business cycle," the theory that postulates that price inflation will offset recession and that recession reduces inflation — in other words, that the market corrects itself — price inflation and recession can give rise to each other and can make each other more severe. With price inflation, the purchasing power of wages declines. Industrialists, unable to sell their goods to wage-earners, reduce production and create unemployment. Here we see that inflation can cause recession. Furthermore, there is no particular reason to believe that the corporate demand for credit will be reduced by recession, although the corporate *need* for credit is certainly less. General Motors, facing in early 1975 its second greatest postwar decline in sales, floated a record-size bond issue for an industrial corporation ($600 million). If the demand for credit is not reduced as the production of consumable goods declines, such a recession could only *raise* prices.

Squeezed Out: The Competition for Capital

The Third World's lack of capital makes it harder for the Third World to obtain capital. Thus poverty impoverishes. The credit position of the Third World erodes with the erosion of its economy. Under these circumstances, to continue to attract capital to develop its industries the Third World must put on its pants while running downhill.

But Third World peoples have not been denied access to capital by their poverty alone. Neither do the evident risks of their insolvency fully account for the stringent terms and usurious charges on the capital they do manage to scrounge. In spite of the explosive worldwide expansion of dollar credit, many economists and development authorities analyze the problem as a lack of available "liquidity" — not questioning where the burgeoning credit has gone. As money must circulate, the great credit explosion should have afforded the Third World some inexpensive financing — that is, if there were not, sitting at the top of the circle of finance, MNC's to compete for that liquidity and bid up its price.

The race for liquidity has a peculiarly grotesque nature: the competition itself strengthens one contestant and debilitates the other. Just as for consumers, for state treasuries (which usually spend rather than invest), the stated interest rate is the cost of capital, while for the corporation, real interest (stated interest less inflation) is the significant cost of borrowing. For the government as for the wage-earner, debt itself reduces long-term purchasing power while raising the risk of insolvency. On the other hand, a corporation's borrowings extend its stock of capital which should only improve the company's profitability and hence improve its credit position. Standard Oil's capitalization of its $250 million debt improved its chances of obtaining still further credit whereas South Korea's debt exhausted its credit arm. Since high stated interest negatively affects only the public borrower, the stated rate for the public (government and consumers) will always remain above the *stated* corporate rate. The spread in *stated* rates compensates the keeper of liquidity, who cannot lend money to consumers and governments at the same price as to capitalists because the public's income, unlike that of the capitalists, does not automatically increase with inflation. The worse inflation becomes, the wider the spread between the interest rates paid by the corporations and those paid by the public.

Third World nations cannot hope to compete for credit with MNC's, even for the financial wealth generated within their own nations. International corporations offer international diversification as protection against risk, control of the flow of resources through vertically integrated monopolies, and extraordinary financial profits. The multinational conglomerates absorb credit for mergers and takeovers, acquisitions returning more than their costs in a very short time. The Third World has little to offer investors, the bulk of their borrowings being used to cover other debts, support their currencies, import scarce resources, or subsidize corporations.

Multinational monopolies offer some shelter to the investor against recession. The 500 largest industrial corporations, in the face of world recession, posted aggregate increases in profit earnings by 13 percent, in assets by 13 percent, and in sales by 25 percent (*Fortune* 1975: 210–211). The rise in sales and the 4.7 percent decline in real output suggests immediately that the monopolists need not produce to profit but can maintain price increases by reducing supplies. Laborers, state treasuries, small businessmen, and state-owned industries stand as a buffer between the multinationals and the earnings erosion that would come of depressed consumer purchasing power. Unemployment maintains profit margins; private and public debt maintain sales. The consumer and small businessman give up their liquidity to the multinationals in hard times: the difference in interest rates charged to top A-rated borrowers and B-rated borrowers (on the Moody's scale) doubled in the three years, 1972 to 1975. The smattering of government-owned enterprises in the Third World suffers a disproportionate burden of the swings in demand for a product. For example, during the major declines in demand for copper since 1960, the state-owned mines of Zaire, Chile, and Zambia reduced their output by three times as much as that by Anaconda and Kennecott (*Wall Street Journal* 1974d).

Having so far considered the time terms and interest charges of the various borrowings of this one week (of February 20, 1975), we should now look at the absolute amounts garnered by the competing bond issuers: for Mexico and Puerto Rico, $80 million and $50 million respectively; for First Boston (bank), Commonwealth Edison, and Mobil (Oil) Alaska Pipeline Corporations, $100 million, $125 million, and $300 million respectively. The large difference in the gross borrowings exhibits the competitive superiority of multinationals over Third World governments in the credit market. (These three corporations took 70 percent of the total funds going to new listed bonds.) We must look beyond gross totals to determine if the credit *needs* of each borrower have been met. The sums borrowed by the Third World governments are clearly insufficient, covering only 4 percent of Mexico's 1974 international deficit and 5 percent of Puerto Rico's (*Wall Street Journal* 1975a; United Nations 1974). On the other side the credit needs of the MNC's are more than satisfied. Viewed from the standpoint of the entire economy, the corporations' borrowings are either excessive or wholly unnecessary: Commonwealth Edison, presently underutilizing its capacity and facing a decline in consumer demand, does not need these funds for expansion (the funds will go instead for wasteful automation). Mobil, by having radically reduced production in its abundant Saudi Arabian reserves, indicates that it has no need for a pipeline from Alaska. The pipeline itself, which will terminate on the U.S. West Coast, an energy surplus area, would be economically unfeasible if not for massive subsidies from the federal government and local public-utility commissions. First Boston seeks through its bond issue additional finance banking capital although there is little need for capital investment with world recession and 12 percent of the production facilities in the United States idle (*Wall Street Journal* 1975d).

Mexico and Puerto Rico are among the few lucky Third World governments that still retain some — although precarious — liquidity in the New York market, while others are banished to markets with creditors more expensive and less stable. In the early 1970's, a plethora of five-year notes to cover the fifteen-year debts of some Third World nations was underwritten by European branches of Japanese banks, creditors who could not be counted on to renew these notes. This cast further doubt on these nations' long-term solvency, reducing their liquidity with other creditors. As it happened, by mid-1974, the Japanese Eurobanks all but closed their doors.

Some Third World nations fare worse. While the system is glutted with inflationary amounts of monetary capital — capital created in part by the Third World — many of these nations go begging. Said an executive of a London branch of a U.S. bank, "We just slammed the door" (*Wall Street Journal* 1975i). Industrial nations now fighting for their own survival can no longer supply development funds to the last-resort multilateral agencies. The Inter-American Development Bank (BID) has barely won a temporary extension of its existence. Unable to stay on the capital treadmill, entire economies have gone into bankruptcy — *rescheduling* in the parlance of the international bankers — including Ghana, Chile, Liberia, Turkey, and more than twice each for Argentina and Brazil. With the exception of Turkey's rescheduling by the OECD, the bankrupts were turned over to the "Clubs" by the IMF. The Paris Club, the Hague Club, and others, European bank consortia, act as the international collection agencies that take control of the insolvent nation's fiscal and spending policies, guaranteeing its debts to any MNC's and establishing the ground rules for new investment (World Bank 1967: 21–23).

With usury has no man a good house made
of stone.

POUND, "Canto LI"

Two hundred thousand peasants who
have deserted their "conucos" and the
plantations now live under the bridges in
golden Caracas, or along gullies or upon
the hillsides above the city, in ironically
named "ranchoes," shacks made of packing
boxes, discarded tin sheet, wall board, and
burlap. . .

O'CONNOR (1963)

CONSEQUENCES OF THE MONOPOLY OF FINANCE

Ironically, the Third World nations do not lack financial wealth, only the
ability to retain control of their wealth. MNC's can out-compete Third
World nations for the credit and wealth for investment created within
their own borders. To obtain credit, then, the Third World is forced to
buy back from these corporations the capital that was theirs in the first
place — and is forced to pay a monopoly price for that capital. The
consequences of this monopoly of finance capital by the MNC's is world
inflation and recession, the impoverishment of the Third World, and the
frustration of its development.

*World Inflation, Recession and the Monopoly of Financial Circulation:
The Case of Oil*

The monopoly control of the international creation and flow of dollars by
MNC's and banks both inflates the price of oil, inflating the price of all
commodities worldwide, and depresses oil production, leading to world
recession. The pattern in oil may apply to the production of other
resources as well.

Until recently the Arab oil states have been used as the repository of
the inflationary excess of U.S. dollars in the world money market, credit
created especially to obtain this oil. Unfortunately there were just so
many paper dollars the Arabs could take in before the dollars were
recognized as just so much paper. With total circulation reaching $600
billion by 1980 (one-third of the total resource transfer between nations),
the excessive amount of dollar credit created for the capitalization of the
oil corporations' purchases in the Middle East seriously undermines the
value of the dollars. Neither can these so-called petrodollars be placed
profitably enough to cover the losses due to inflation-induced devaluation of the dollars. While other Third World nations pay premium
interest to the banks on their borrowings, oil-exporting states must take a
cut in the interest they receive of nearly 35 percent under the Eurodollar
interbank rates when placed in those banks in short-term accounts. This

knot in the system of finance makes it more worthwhile for oil-exporting nations to "bank" their oil in the ground and hope for oil prices to rise in parity with the inflation of other commodities, rather than sell their oil and bank the dollar earnings.

For this reason Saudi Arabia has limited production to eight and a half million barrels of oil a day instead of the twenty million it could produce, and Kuwait has limited production to two million instead of a possible six. Still, concedes Chase Manhattan President Willard Butcher, the surplus of oil dollars that cannot be productively handled will reach $53 billion within four years (W. Butcher, personal communication). This credit surplus, combined with depressed world production due to oil's financially created scarcity and high price, must further undercut the value of the dollar receipts, forcing further reductions in oil production to maintain the real value of oil income. The restricted production of oil has depressed all industries throughout the Western and Third Worlds. In the face of a decline in the demand for oil created by this depression and in hopes of ballooning prices, the multinational oil consortia, on whom distribution depends and whose interests coincide with neither the world's need for oil nor the oil nations' need for income, have reduced production below already low ceilings. The international oil companies, combined as Aramco, refused in 1975 to pump more than 6.5 million barrels a day in their Saudi Arabian concessions, though the Saudis authorized production of 8.5 million. With or without their assent, output for Venezuela, Abu Dhabi, and Kuwait was reduced by 30 percent, 66 percent, and 24 percent, respectively, in 1975. By April 1975, production in oil-exporting nations declined to 19 percent below production during the period of an official export boycott at the end of 1973 (*Wall Street Journal* 1975g).

Underlying both finance and development, or underdevelopment, is production, but the mechanics of their relationship are determined by the MNC. Historically, financial processes were tools by which capitalized wealth sought to extend production and productivity. Now the system is inverted: the production process has become the means for seeking capitalized wealth's maximum financial extension. When finance chokes, production chokes, as production has now been subsumed under finance. While oil nations reduce exports because their monetary assets cannot be profitably used, other nations go begging for both oil and capital.

First Boston Bancorp named itself a major underwriter of its own 8 percent bond issue. For its 10 percent bond issue, the government of Mexico named as one of its main underwriters — First Boston Bancorp. Herein a tale is told. By merely switching its income into Mexican bonds — selling money at 10 percent bought at 8 percent — First Boston can net an immediate 25 percent profit plus commissions on both ends of the deal. The bonds, as monetary assets, may still be invested. World poverty can be a major source of enrichment for those who control the uses of purchasing power. According to the U.S. Department of Commerce:

Foreign petroleum-importing countries financed much of the extraordinary rise in the cost of their petroleum imports by large borrowings from U.S. banks (especially in the first half of the year). . . . Some of these countries' payments to petroleum-exporting countries, were, in turn, invested directly in the United States by the members of the Organization of Petroleum Exporting Countries (OPEC). Some were invested by OPEC members in Euromarket banks. *And those banks then* channelled the funds to the United States. These funds were attracted by high U.S. interest rates (*Survey of Current Business* 1977e:23, emphasis added).

By lowering the interest paid to the oil-producing nations by two percentage points while charging an extra two percentage points to oil-consuming nations, banks such as First Boston can earn 80 percent returns. This profit has been taken by intercepting the oil nations' liquidity and controlling the resale of their oil. When the oil-consuming nations purchase their oil from corporations, the funds eventually return to the oil-producing nations as royalties, the corporations having taken *their* profit for transferring the oil — and the cycle begins anew. The banks have cashed in on a crisis of need in energy. Their monopoly control of the transfer of financial liquidity between oil producers and consumers depresses oil production and raises the price of both oil and credit until consumers are no longer able to finance all their oil and other needs.

Behind the Decline of the Dollar

The interception and control of financial liquidity by multinational enterprises has threatened the development of the West, a crisis expressed as the decline of the dollar. In the case of oil we saw how the excessive creation of dollar credit undercut the dollar's value. Brobdingnagian sums of dollar credit sent out of the United States eventually recirculated, the quantities returning exceeding those going out. While in 1973, $20 billion left the United States for the Middle East, $32 billion returned in profits, interest, and cheap investment capital (*Survey of Current Business* 1974a:40–42,56). The repercussions of the declining value of the dollar go beyond rising prices within the United States: the dollar, the very instrument of international liquidity and trade, was fast becoming unliquid, curtailing all production, driving up interest rates, and inflating prices in currencies back by the dollar.

Claiming the dollar to be "inconvertible" or "overvalued," most economists and policymakers sought to pin the blame for economic woes on the dollar bill rather than on the economic system that undermined the dollar's purchasing power. The world's financial officials have signed a succession of permanent agreements on exchange rates, none of which has proved either permanent or agreeable. Attempts to bolster the dollar failed because in the end the dollar is merely a share of national and world production, the U.S. dollar only as good as the U.S. and world economies. Crisis did not result from the sheer amount of, or method of denominating, the dollar; crisis resulted from the *use* of the dollar (and the peso and the pound), or, more correctly, the failure to use the dollar productively. When the 1971 U.S. balance of payments showed a net outflow of $10 billion, dollar holdings by overseas institutions rose by $27 billion (Bell 1973:18–31), from which we can conclude that much of the U.S. payments deficit is the simple switch of corporations' dollar holdings to operations outside U.S. borders. The Eurodollar market (the name for dollar-credit creation outside the United States) has grown in one decade from $10 billion to $360 billion, about $175 billion being cross-deposits between banks. With dollar-credit creation expanding while U.S. production declines, the dollar must weaken. Financiers have not abandoned the dollar but have abandoned the dollar's U.S. production base; they have abandoned the United States.

Underdevelopment and the Monopoly of Finance

As a result of their being denied sufficient capital credit and the exorbitant charges paid for any capital obtained, Third World nations remain undeveloped, their working peoples facing lower wages and higher unemployment than ever. In addition they are increasingly dependent on multinational financiers.

In determining the international purchasing power of a currency and its allied interest rates, particular weight is given to the size of national reserves of hard currencies as well as to other factors bearing on the future creditability of the currency and solvency of the economy such as the public debt, the growth of capital assets, and the growth of export industries (for obtaining hard currency) and import trade dependencies. This puts the MNC in an enviable position. In the tight fist of the multinationals are the precious dollars of capital investment. The price of multinational hard-currency capital grows dearer, not reflecting the nations' desires for development but their fear of defaulting on international debts. Once the multinational has been lured by the availability of cheap capital, fattened tax subsidies, and high-interest liens on wages, authorities soon find that the resultant repatriation of capitalization, profits, and interest soon exceeds the capital invested. The 1973 withdrawal of U.S. multinationals' recorded profits from abroad exceeded reinvestment by about $9 billion annually (*Survey of Current Business* 1974:16). The financial stranglehold of the MNC's on the Third World tightens as these corporations absorb the credit available within the Third World itself. Even during the Decade of Development, 1957 to 1967, the foreign assets of MNC's grew by $61 billion, though the multinationals' investments totaled only $20 billion (Polakoff 1970:362,365,547).

Puerto Rico, for example, must import most of its investment capital, resorting to government advertisements in the *Wall Street Journal*: "With an unemployment rate at 12 percent, the people of Puerto Rico are anxious to work" (*Wall Street Journal* 1974e). With an increase in the import of investment capital has come an increase in Puerto Rico's unemployment to 18 percent. This is linked to the increase in the *export* of capital, which exceeds capital imports by more than a billion dollars annually. Underdevelopment is an unalterable aspect of the system of finance because the *sole* business of finance is the monopoly of financial wealth: absorbing capital cheaply to resell at a higher price. The cases of Venezuela, Mexico, and India provide us with clear examples of underdevelopment caused by the corporate monopoly of finance capital.

Venezuela cannot use the $10 billion in 1974 oil revenues to finance its own work force even though 30 percent of its work force (*Wall Street Journal* 1974c) lack full-time employment. A flood of funds into Venezuela's capital markets would result in both price inflation and currency depreciation (since financiers are refusing to use new funds for local production) and also the loss of the capital as firms siphon it off for foreign investment. (The funds presently sit in short-term low-yield accounts in New York banks.) Venezuela has been forced to reduce oil production by 30 percent, to one million barrels a day, due to a combination of world recession, its inability to usefully employ its oil earnings, and its dependence on foreign firms for marketing and capitalization of oil operations.

Earlier we observed how Mexico, to obtain capital financing for development of its copper industry, had to share ownership of the industry and its resources with multinational Litton Industries. For Mexico's state-owned petroleum company to pay its foreign creditors — who charge Petrolios Mexicanos 24 percent more than they charge Mobil Oil — Mexico must export 70,000 barrels of oil a day. The Mexican government, to obtain foreign exchange to cover its foreign obligations, has encouraged the forced migration of 7,000,000 of its workers to the United States. It is evident here that "development financing" is a contradictory term, for development does not require a paper abstraction called capital; development requires only labor, labor to extract and convert resources, to construct and operate machinery. Little development is possible for Mexico when the means of development — labor and resources — must be exported to purchase capital.

Financial capitalization would be productive if it were provided to those who need it most for basic consumption, which would also stimulate employment. The basic shortcoming of the system of finance is that those who need the capital most are least likely to receive it. The marketplace does not respond to need; it is, rather, regulated by *demand*, which is solely the expression of purchasing power. For example, "the shortage of food in India is not actually a shortage of food, . . . nor is it one of food producing potential. It is rather a shortage of purchasing power on the part of the developing countries" (Goldsmith 1971). Put succinctly by the U.S. ambassador to the World Food Conference, "The food is there, the financing isn't." Starving children who have no liquidity have no demand for food.

Finance and Development: The Relationship of Capital to Labor

The underdevelopment of Third World nations is but the aggregate appearance of the underdevelopment of the working peoples of those nations. We can understand the underdevelopment of nations by examining the basic relationship of labor to capital.

Laborers cannot transfer their production directly to other laborers. All production must be passed through the capital corporations, as capital monopolizes ownership of the physical means of production, labor-power, tools, and products, placing the corporation in a position not unlike that of an imperial state to its colonies. The MNC's have extended their colonial hold on the transfer of goods to the transfer of value (monetary wealth), which can be routed between *and within* nations of laborers only in the form of finance capital and only by way of the established circles of equity and debt. The control of the international flow of production capital by financial intermediaries jeopardizes the efficient transfer of resources between nations in need. In 1974 the West faced a 12 percent decline in steel production, while insolvent Italian railroads faced rail shortages (*Wall Street Journal* 1975g). Financiers would not allow unemployed U.S. steelworkers to provide rails to Italian railroadmen. "I wouldn't lend to the Italian railroads unless I were tied to the tracks," suggested an American Euromarket banker (*Wall Street Journal* 1974b). In this way labor suffers under-development. If nations find they can obtain financing only by way of the MNC's, this is only the extension of the exclusive right of capital to organize and utilize labor.

Only in their ability to divide labor-power from the laborer and expropriate it can wealth accrue to capital holders, for all wealth must and can only come from production, and all production must and can only come from labor. As is the case with the profits of industrial capital, financial wealth has only this one source — the wealth created by laborers, though financial and industrial profits are obtained in different manners.

For industrial capital the single capital corporation pays a wage less than the value of the product, the difference being profits and interest for the corporation and its capital creditors. Financial wealth is also supplemented by created capital liquidity, which does not come out of wages as the profits of industrial capital. Nevertheless, this created liquidity buys the products of labor just as wages do; in this manner, looking from the point of view of the economy as a whole, the capital class takes labor's wages indirectly through financially induced inflation (and concomitant high-cost debt), diminishing the purchasing power of wages of the entire working class.

Inflation (and crisis) reduces wages rather than capital because labor cannot financially extend its liquidity: labor cannot "labor-ize" as capital capitalizes. This is because there is no labor equity as there is capital equity to leverage: a laborer does not own the product of his own labor. As long as laborers continue to sell their labor-power and as long as purchasing power can be created and controlled in the abstract (finance), a monopoly on the ownership of abstract labor-power and purchasing power is inevitable; and therefore underdevelopment is inevitable.

In a finance economy, where the wages of laborers are exclusively paid for by debt or equity capitalization, the gains of economic expansion are already sold to the holders of the capital. (The "investment" of labor does not provide perpetual returns after it is expended, as does capital.) Thus, an increase in gross national product, the commonly accepted definition of development, may not at all signify development for the subnation of laborers. Foreign bureaucrats and social liberals still insist that the importation of multinational capital will raise labor productivity and therefore raise the market's demand for labor, driving up wages. However, the division of productivity between capital profits and labor wages is determined by a social relationship that the markets merely reflect. As labor-power is alienated from the laborers, their wage reflects less and less their productivity, allowing for expropriation of production gains, witness the Miracle of Brazil. While since 1964 the gross national product has doubled in real terms, by 1967 the real base wage declined by 16 percent, followed by five years in which the wage gains of industrial workers reflected only half the rise in labor productivity. For all workers of the Western world and the Third World, the monopoly of capital financing has meant that real wages represent a shrinking share of what they produce. According to United Nations statistics, in manufacturing, Latin Americans receive in wages but one-fourth of the value added by their labor, Africans and Asians one-fifth; the factory worker in the United States receives one-third, but that is declining (United Nations 1974:199–210).

SUMMARY

Third World laborers and their governments — as all laborers and governments — provide cheap and abundant capital to international corporations either directly through the wealth embodied in their labor, through their debt payments, or indirectly through the investments of Third World capitalists. Conversely, Third World laborers and their governments must obtain the credit and investment capital they need from the MNC's, capital for which they must pay a high price. We can conclude then that the Third World laborers buy back, at a high price, capital resources that were their own in the first place. The direct cost of this uneven circulation is borne by labor in low wages, by high interest charges on public and private debt, and by high taxes. The systematic consequences of capital financing are (1) price inflation, the decline in real wages and (2) recession, the decline in production, employment and development.

Governments' fiscal and monetary policies are unable to counteract effectively inflation or recession. The system of multinational finance affords capital some protection from inflation and recession. At the same time, inflation and recession allow multinationals to outcompete Third World nations for the investment capital in the Third World, increasing the dependence of the Third World on multinational capital.

As a consequence of the monopoly of finance capital, those who most need capital are least likely to obtain it (and may even lose the capital they have). This financial relationship between the Third World economies and the international corporation is merely the extension of the relationship of capital to labor. The economic problems of Third World nations and working peoples compound each other. Recession and inflation result in a greater drain of capital, higher finance charges, deeper recession, and accelerating inflation.

As Walter Wriston, chairman of Citicorp, puts it, "The significant realities are still invisible: they are the distortions and long-range disasters that cannot be instantly observed — and so are neglected" (*Wall Street Journal* 1975d).

REFERENCES

ALIBER, R.
   1973   *The international money game.* New York: Basic Books.
AVRAMOVICH, D., *et al.*
   1964   *Economic growth and external debt.* Baltimore: Johns Hopkins Press.
Barron's
   1975   *Barron's.* April 28.

BARTHE, D.
1971 *La inflacion en la república Argentina: consideraciones sobre la manera de corregir el proceso inflacionário.* Buenos Aires.
BELL, G.
1973 *The eurodollar market and the international finance system.* New York: John Wiley and Sons.
Business Week
1974 *Business Week.* October 12.
Chicago Sun-Times
1974a *Chicago Sun-Times.* June 28.
1974b *Chicago Sun-Times.* October 28.
CHOWN, V.
1968 *International bond markets in the '60s.* New York: Praeger.
CILINGIROGLU, A.
1969 *Manufacture of heavy electrical equipment in developing countries.* Baltimore: Johns Hopkins Press.
CLIVEY, T.
1972 *The structure, performance and prospects of central banking in the Caribbean.* Jamaica: University of the West Indies.
COUNCIL OF CORPORATIONS OF FOREIGN BONDHOLDERS
1972 *99th annual report.* London: Council of Corporations of Foreign Bondholders.
COURIEL, A., N.S. LICHTENSZTEN
1966 *El FMI y la crisis economica nacional.* Montevideo: Fundación de Universitaria.
Financial Weekly
1974 *Financial Weekly.* December 30.
Fortune
1975 *Fortune.* May.
FRIEDMAN, M.
1972 *The eurodollar market: some principles.* Chicago: University of Chicago Press.
GOLDSMITH, S.
1971 The world food crisis. *Journal of Public Health* (8).
HAAN, R.
1971 *SDR's and development: an inquiry into the monetary aspects of a link between SDR's and developmental finance.* Sweden: H.E. Stenfert, Kroese, N. V.
INTERNATIONAL BANK FOR RECONSTRUCTION AND DEVELOPMENT
1967 *Suppliers' credits from industrialized to developing countries.* Washington, D.C.: International Bank for Reconstruction and Development.
KELSO, L., P. HETTER
1969 *The 2-factor theory: the economics of reality.* New York: Random House.
KESSEL, R.
1971 Underpricing of new issues of debt by underwriters. *Journal of Political Economy* (3).
KEYSERLING, LEON
1974 *Chicago Sun-Times.* June 5.
KOOT, R.
1969 *Wage determination and the role of wages in the inflationary process: a study of Chile and Mexico.* Philadelphia: University of Pennsylvania Press.

LAFFER, A.
1974 "The international undress." Unpublished manuscript.

LITVAK, I., C. MAULE
1970 *Foreign investment: the experience of host countries.* New York: Praeger.

MASON, R.
1967 *An analysis of benefit from U.S. direct foreign investment in less developed areas.* Palo Alto: Stanford University Press.

New York Times, The
1974a *The New York Times.* June 24.
1974b *The New York Times.* October 11.

PAZOS, F.
1972 *Chronic inflation in Latin America.* New York: Praeger.

POLAKOFF, M., *et al.*
1970 *Financial institutions and markets.* Boston: Houghton Mifflin.

ROBICHEK, A., A. COLEMAN
1967 *Management of financial institutions.* Hinsdale, Ill.: Dryden Press.

SHEEHAN, D.
1971 *Projective economics.* Darkwoods, Calif.: Tenure Press.

SORTER, G.
1970 "Principles of accounting." Unpublished manuscript. University of Chicago Graduate School of Business.

Survey of Current Business
1974a *Survey of Current Business.* March.
1974b *Survey of Current Business.* May.
1974c *Survey of Current Business.* June.
1974d *Survey of Current Business.* August.
1974e *Survey of Current Business.* December.
1975 *Survey of Current Business.* July.

UNITED NATIONS DEPARTMENT OF ECONOMIC AND SOCIAL AFFAIRS
1967 *Exports credits and developing finance.* New York: United Nations Printing Office.

UNITED NATIONS DEPARTMENT OF SOCIAL AND ECONOMIC AFFAIRS
1974 *1973 statistical yearbook.* New York: United Nations Printing Office.

VERNON, RAYMOND
1974 Unpublished lecture. Chicago: University of Chicago.

VILLANUEVA, P.
1970 *Conference on inflation and growth in Latin America.* Edited by W. Baer and I. Kerstenetzky. New Haven: Yale University Press.

Wall Street Journal, The
1974a *The Wall Street Journal.* May 28.
1974b Janssen, Richard, "Eurojitters: fears about the stability of banking system in West are spreading." *The Wall Street Journal.* p. 21. July 26.
1974c Martin, Everett, "Embarrassment of riches: Venezuelans ponder how to best spend $10 billion windfall from oil resources." *The Wall Street Journal.* August 12. Page 22.
1974d *The Wall Street Journal.* October 30.
1974e *The Wall Street Journal.* December 12.
1975a Pearlstine, Norman and Seth Lipsky, "Fund drive: South Korea learns it's getting harder to borrow nowadays." *The Wall Street Journal.* February 14. Pages 1 and 21.

1975b "Bond markets: offerings of foreign debt in US surge; Montreal and Mexico seek $50 million each." Page 36, February 19.
"$125,000,000 Commonwealth Edison Company first mortgage bonds." Page 29.
"$300,000,000 Mobil Alaska Pipeline Company 8.45% guaranteed debentures." Page 33. February 20.
"$100,000,000 First National Boston Corporation 8% notes." Page 21. February 21. *The Wall Street Journal.*
1975c "Notable and quotable." Page 18. *The Wall Street Journal.* February 19.
1975d Malabre, Alfred, "Prices abroad: inflation rates ease in many foreign lands as economies decline." Page 1. *The Wall Street Journal.* February 19.
1975e "$75,000,000 Puerto Rico telephone authority revenue bonds." Page 21. *The Wall Street Journal.* April 21.
1975f "$53,446,152.60 guaranteed promisory notes, Corporacion de Fomento de Produccion." Page 27. *The Wall Street Journal.* April 23.
1975g Stabler, Charles, "Estimates of petrodollar surplus are cut." Page 4. *The Wall Street Journal.* May 23.
1975h "US bankers seen more choosey in 1975 on foreign lending." *The Wall Street Journal.* Page 11. July 21.
1975i *Wall Street Journal.* July 30.
1975j *Wall Street Journal.* October 29.
1976a "Steel output rose 2.3% in week ended January 4." Page 36. *The Wall Street Journal.* January 6.
WILLIS, R.
1974 *Barron's.* August 26.

SECTION TWO

The Multinational Corporation and the Social Scientist

Applied Research on the Multinational Corporation: A Symposium at the IXth International Congress of Anthropological and Ethnological Sciences

AHAMED IDRIS-SOVEN, Chairperson.
DAVID BARKIN, BERNARDO BERDICHEWSKY, JOSEPH COLLINS, AL GEDICKS, GERRIT HUIZER, AND MARY KAY VAUGHAN, participants

Gerrit Huizer: Rather than presenting a formal paper I would like to speak about the reasons this session has been organized. Through very simple applied anthropological work in rural areas of the developing countries, I, like many of my colleagues, came to discover the need to tackle an issue as seemingly distant from peasants as multinational corporations. You see these corporations here in Chicago and could not imagine anything further away from the lives of peasants. Yet, if you look closely at rural life you will discover, as I did by trial and error, that it is impossible to work with what are normally considered anthropological tools without considering the MNC. Most anthropologists work at local community levels. Applied anthropologists, who are working to induce change and development, particularly find themselves at some stage involved in contradictions and conflicts obstructing projects for change. Many prefer to leave it at that, but some go beyond the immediate situation to investigate the roots of conflicts: for instance, conflicts between peasants and landlords, or between peasants and merchants.

In their investigation they find that the communities in which they work are parts of a whole system that includes both centers and a periphery: the villages are the periphery while the towns and cities act as centers of exploitation where all, or almost all, of the benefits produced by the peasants in the villages go. But if you look still more carefully you can see that even at the regional level, socioeconomic relations are part of a larger national system. In several countries at least, the social structure stands against real change. You cannot bring about change at the local level without bringing about changes in this national social structure.

In the rural areas, for instance, both the land-tenure system and the

The symposium took place September 15, 1973, in Chicago, Illinois. The following is from the revised proceedings, including both presentations and discussion.

commercial system deeply exploit the local communities. Having worked in the field of community development, I have come to the conclusion that most community projects, for example, land reform projects do not get off the ground without strong peasant organization to support them. Looking at this problem pragmatically, as I have for many years as an applied anthropologist and as an official of the United Nations, I saw that the peasant organizations attempting to defend the interests of the people we sympathize with are faced by tremendous odds. The odds favor the local landlords, who are supported by a whole system of repression prevailing in the developing countries.

I have had several personal experiences that indicated to me the extent to which a national system of repression forms part of a much broader international system, of which the MNC is the outstanding expression. That is, the national system of repression forms part of an international capitalist system that dominates the world. I found this, for instance, when I was working in Peru studying cases where peasants had gotten into trouble with the authorities. The military repressed the peasants with napalm and other deadly weapons. At the same time a high official of the Peruvian army was nominated to the board of directors of Philips Peruana, a Dutch-owned company in Peru. I was shocked by this tie-in between the repressive force of the army and international commercial interests in Peru. It was a symbol of a much more complicated relationship that anthropologists ought to examine.

There is a need for a different kind, a more profound and realistic kind, of research that goes beyond the village level to broader areas, which in the end lead back to our own countries. The operations of these MNC's are not very well known. How they really function has yet to be studied and determined. But the interesting thing is that when you study them and their effects on the community you research abroad, you then come back to your own country, where the same corporations create problems very similar to those they create in developing countries. For instance, the farmers in the area around the university where I teach in the east of Holland suffer from the same kinds of repression from the Unilever Company as the peasants in Ghana where Unilever is one of the most powerful forces — some people say it is even stronger than the Ghanaian government. When you see these links, you can draw conclusions about another step that anthropologists can make in their research — namely, going from research into action. If one sees that in one's own society people suffer from the same problems as do people in the developing countries, one may conclude that action in our own countries might help the people who suffer from exploitation, ethnocide, and all the other problems besetting the Third World.

As regards the ways in which this action should be brought about, we can at times learn from the experiences in organization and mobilization of Third World peoples. The case I have described in my paper on Cuba is exemplary. The Cuban peasants did not start off to make a revolution. They started to defend their most basic right to their land, which was threatened by U.S. plantation corporations. They were kicked off their lands; their houses were burned; they were forced to flee into the mountains. Pursuing every possible legal path, they went to the courts, and failing there they resorted to acts of civil disobedience — that is, they invaded lands they thought they could reclaim. When this failed too, they turned to violence to defend their lives and to get what they wanted. They overthrew the system and they created something new. Perhaps a similar strategy could be used in our countries. It is very difficult to talk about socialism and revolution to people who have been brainwashed in the other direction for over twenty-five years. But when one starts to organize people around the very issues of exploitation that they face daily, then, like the peasants of Cuba or Mexico or anywhere else, they will learn from experience what it means to confront the immense powers of MNC's. It is hoped in the process of struggle, little by little, they will radicalize enough to see change in the overall system as one of their main purposes.

My reasoning then for studying MNC's is to understand their impact on the lives of people and what most effectively can be done to counteract them. I might propose to anthropologists from several countries comparative studies of the operations of these companies. We should be able to build up a system of intercommunication so that all can share and benefit from the information gathered. I am sure, for instance, that in Holland we can benefit tremendously from the struggle in the Third World and that they too can benefit from our struggle.

Al Gedicks: The starting point for the research being conducted by Community Action on Latin America (CALA), a Wisconsin-based research/action group that I work with, is the belief that an understanding of power relationships on a community, national, and international level is an essential prerequisite for communities to exert some influence over the decisions that affect their lives, as Gerrit said. While it may seem incongruous for a group whose primary concern is with Latin America to be investigating multinational corporations in northern Wisconsin, an understanding of the operations of U.S. Steel in the Great Lakes region is impossible apart from an understanding of its operations in, for instance, Brazil and Venezuela, just as an examination of the Anaconda and Kennecott Copper companies in Chile is essential for understanding the recent Kennecott move into Wisconsin following Chile's nationalization of these companies in 1971.

Since the late nineteenth century, the Upper Great Lakes region — encompassing the northern areas of Michigan, Wisconsin, and Minnesota

— has been a major producer of iron ore for America's steel mills. This region fired U.S. furnaces with the best and cheapest ores that were the foundation of J.P. Morgan's empire of steel. To maintain this empire, however, J.P. Morgan's U.S. Steel Corporation, the Hanna Mining Company, and others also had to control potentially competitive sources of iron ore around the globe.

Within the basic context of growth and profitability, U.S. Steel and Hanna Mining Company, at the end of World War II, decided to phase out a substantial portion of their Great Lakes operations and increase their investment in potentially competitive source areas as Brazil, Venezuela, Canada, and Australia. Because of the dominant position of these MNC's within the Great Lakes regional economy, their investment decisions ended the Great Lakes iron boom and threw the entire region into a severe economic depression. Today approximately 1.3 million people live in the fifty-three counties of the Upper Great Lakes region. Unemployment rates are typically double and triple the national average. About 30 percent of all families in the region earn less than $3,000 yearly, making this one of the most depressed areas in the country.

Both the University of Wisconsin (with grants from the Ford Foundation and the Office of Economic Opportunity) and a research-action group, CALA, for which I conduct research, have been investigating the Upper Great Lakes region. The definition of the problem, the perspective employed in analyzing the problem, and the manner in which the research is used are very different in the two series of investigations. The way in which social problems come to be defined has important implications for the ability of social scientists to illuminate the underlying determinants of the social formation at hand and thus to propose solutions that get to the root causes of the problems.

In the series of studies carried out by the University of Wisconsin's rural sociology department, the focus of study was on how various communities in northern Wisconsin related to the problems of economic depression: low income, high unemployment, poor housing, inadequate health care, and poor educational facilities. While the authors of the studies do not make explicit the paradigm of social-scientific research they employ (which dictates the kind of data they gather), the focus of the studies is very clearly not toward understanding the causes of economic depression. Rather, the studies are interested in how people react to their desperate situation. This focus points to the class bias inherent in the type of research conducted by sociologists employed by institutions of the ruling class to report on the activities and attitudes of America's poor. Who wants to know about the problems of the poor in northern Wisconsin? The poor people of northern Wisconsin know what their problems are. But the people entrusted with maintaining the maldistribution of wealth in this society do not. Knowledge of these problems is essential, however, for those who stand at the heights of the political economy if they are to make sure that dissident elements in the population are kept in check and that the system favorable to themselves continues to function smoothly.

Once the problem has been defined in this manner, the relevant unit of analysis becomes the particular community about which certain kinds of information are desired. There is no investigation of the way in which the community relates to the regional, state, national, and international structure that has clearly determined the situation of economic depression: there is no investigation of the cause of poverty. Nor are the residents of northern Wisconsin ever likely to see the monographs published by University of Wisconsin researchers. This is not surprising in view of the fact that the studies were not undertaken to help people understand their social situation in the first place. The studies were carried out by those who have been entrusted — albeit quite unconsciously — with the function of reporting on the movements of the subject population: their attitudes toward their situation, toward social change, toward community action, etc. In the words of one such study: "It is hoped that the study will provide information that will enable federal, state, and county program planners and developers to better formulate working solutions to the socioeconomic ills of the area." Presumably the poor of northern Wisconsin will have to wait patiently until those with knowledge and power decide to do something about their problems. Meanwhile, the researchers have provided scientific sanction for a fatalistic posture toward the facts of economic depression in the area. Now that the research has been completed, the power structure is relatively more powerful and knowledgeable, while the subject population remains as ignorant and impotent as before.

There are approximately 170 socioeconomic studies of northern Wisconsin, but not a single one systematically investigates any one of the handful of steel corporations that have had such a strong influence on the pattern of development and decline in the region. The conspicuous absence of social scientific studies of these centers of corporate power and the resulting inability of academic social science to make any significant statements about the political economy of this area or its patterns of development are eloquent testimony to the bankruptcy of traditional social-science methodologies.

The focus of CALA's research, on the other hand, is twofold. Our first concern is with the phenomenon of economic depression — why and how the area came to be depressed. Our second concern is with the future of mining development in Wisconsin, which is coming to assume significance in the light of the Chilean nationalization and the resulting restructuring of the international copper industry, with heavy emphasis on the development of U.S. domestic copper reserves. Kennecott Copper has purchased more than 2,600 acres near Ladysmith, Wisconsin, and plans to develop an open-pit mine there. Kennecott is but one of approximately forty companies carring out exploratory operations in the region. John Rigg of the U.S. Department of the Interior predicts that northern Wisconsin and northeastern Minnesota will be the largest copper- and nickel-producing regions in the U.S. by the year 2000.

Neither of these research concerns can be dealt with apart from an analysis of the MNC in its global context as an entity operating in a number of nations to maximize profits not of its individual units on a nation-by-nation basis, but of the corporate economy as a whole. In multiplying opportunities to buy cheap and sell dear, a closely coordinated corporate policy often involves playing one source of raw materials off against another, one nation's workers against another's, and so on. The experience of Chile with Kennecott and Anaconda is most enlightening on this point. The basic conflict that emerges from the Chilean experience is the conflict between the corporate economies of Kennecott and Anaconda and the national economy of Chile. The major decisions about the pace and direction of Chilean national development were dictated by the corporate officials of Kennecott in New York, who were unaccountable to the Chilean body politic.

When the steel companies in the Upper Great Lakes regions began to phase out a portion of their operations there, they increased their investments elsewhere — in Brazil, Venezuela, Canada, and Australia. The fact that this move set in motion a serious economic recession in the Upper Great Lakes area was of little concern to the corporate directors of U.S. Steel or Hanna Mining Company. That was simply one of the unchallenged prerogatives of the MNC.

The same story can be repeated for Anaconda and Kennecott. During the eight-month 1967–1968 U.S. copper strike, these companies were able to withstand a drop in U.S. ore production of one half thanks to the continued availability of ore from their Chilean operations. In July 1971, as the Chilean government nationalized Anaconda and Kennecott properties, Anaconda tried to pass off its losses to workers at its brass plant in Kenosha, Wisconsin. Anaconda told the workers that promised pay raises would not be given due to its losses in Chile. After much protest by the local union, the company reversed its position and granted the pay increases. But Iris Kwek, an employee at Anaconda's brass plant in Detroit who had stayed with the company for thirty years because of its pension plan, was not so lucky. Anaconda eliminated her job as part of its economy program. Many other Anaconda employees also lost their jobs and pension rights following the Chilean nationalization. All of these instances involve a series of power relationships between a specific corporation and the communities in which it operates. One of the critical variables in the maintenance of these unequal power relations is that those directly affected lack knowledge of the operations of the multi-nationals.

Because the Upper Great Lakes region once generated vast wealth, the question that needs to be answered is not how people react to the problem of economic depression, but where all the wealth of the region has gone. What are the underlying power relationships that ensured this transfer of wealth? How can alternative mechanisms operate to benefit the economy of these communities today?

CALA's research perspective is that of those who look at society from the bottom up. They see all the wealth that has been taken out of the area to finance the growth of an industrialized society that has left the local people behind. It is also the perspective of those early immigrants who participated in the militant, socialist labor struggles on the iron ranges in the early 1920's. Social science either ignores this history of exploitation and struggle or treats it as a pathology. In the series of studies conducted by the University of Wisconsin, repeated reference is made to the area's "social and economic lag," a term that enables the researchers to disguise their optimistic, liberal evaluation of the facts of uneven development of capitalist society. The term also serves to obscure the power relationships that still dominate the area.

In the entire length of the fifty-four mile Gogebic iron belt in Wisconsin and Michigan there is not one acre of land that is not held by one of the giant steel corporations — U.S. Steel, Hanna, Jones and Laughlin, and Inland Steel. Most of this land was granted to the corporations by county boards with the understanding that the area would be developed. No such development has taken place. While the steel companies have phased out mining operations in the area, they still retain ninety-nine-year leases on the land, which contains large known iron-ore reserves. A large corporation like Jones and Laughlin pays only $6,000 in taxes each year on its lease while unemployed citizens of the area pay rising property taxes. For many of these properties the valuation of the surface rights has not changed since 1930. In the face of overwhelming sentiment in the area for the development of the deposits, the steel companies have urged the communities to be patient. When market conditions are favorable, the people are told, consideration will be given to developing the deposits. The State of Wisconsin Attorney General's office investigated the possibility of breaking the leases but concluded that the contracts are "airtight."

In the face of these conditions the only recourse for large numbers of people has been out-migration. With each exodus the possibilities of organized groups pressuring the state and federal government diminish. This virtually forced movement of the rural population to the cities has been amply documented by the University of Wisconsin researchers without mention of any of the power relationships underlying the movement. Instead, the researchers refer to the movement as "a pattern of adjustment to the general imbalance of resources in the area, as well as to the influence of changes in other parts of the state."

While the steel companies pursue a "wait and see" strategy with regard to their holdings in the area, state and local planners with the help of social scientists propose the development of tourism as a partial solution to the area's problems. From the point of view of the steel companies this solution is ideal, as it provides them with the revenue from their land holdings without requiring their sale. Meanwhile, social-science researchers dutifully perform the role of pacification agents in the area until the steel companies decide to return to exploit their remaining sources of ore.

When the University of Wisconsin researchers interviewed individual residents in northern Wisconsin they found that each one was resigned to the condition of economic depression. On the basis of these interviews they also concluded that these people as a whole were resigned to the existing conditions. What they failed to consider was the possibility that if all these people were brought together to talk about their shared frustrations and powerlessness they might cease to feel frustrated and powerless. If people were actually brought together to discuss their problems they might begin to see the social character of their oppression and begin to formulate collective solutions to their problems. André Gorz cites a number of cases where the circulation of results of social-scientific research on the attitudes of workers in factories has been followed by violent outbreaks and spontaneous strikes. Once workers discussed things among themselves they found out that they felt alike and that they could do something about their social situation. But it is precisely the social character of oppression that social science obscures. It is almost too much to expect social science to start helping people understand how they can exert more control over the institutions that affect their lives. At the very least it would require social scientists who place more value on publishing easily understood articles in newspapers than on publishing esoteric articles in professional journals.

Ahamed Idris-Soven: Speaking for the Deltec Research Project, I would like to explain the reasons why we selected Deltec as the focus of our research and what we hoped to accomplish. Our research was initially undertaken as a collective project by some of the members of the Chicago chapter of ARPA (Anthropologists for Radical Political Action). This group felt that the most meaningful form of "political action" open to them as anthropologists would be to employ their professional skills (including research techniques, linguistic skills, access to relatively inaccessible sources of information, and a command of various bodies of social-science theory) both to further the general understanding of the contemporary capitalist political economy and to be of practical use to groups lacking such research skills and resources by placing at their disposal knowledge and analysis of aspects of the capitalist political-economic system bearing specifically on them. The group felt particularly committed to an effort to relate in this way to exploited groups within our own community (Chicago), as well as to the struggle to defend and assist groups that could be considered more conventional subjects of anthropological concern, such as the indigenous societies, peasants, and workers of Third World countries. It was desired, if at all possible, to combine these goals within a single project. This, we felt, would serve as a practical demonstration of the fundamental continuity of general research and specific political relevance, at a time when some radical social scientists were asserting the incompatibility of the two and, therefore, the need to abandon the former for the sake of the latter. We also hoped by this means to help bring home to members of the various groups affected or touched upon by our research their common interest in the struggle against the exploitative institutions or phenomena that formed the subject of our research.

Deltec International Limited, a multinational corporation, first came to the attention of one member of the research group in the context of his research on the contemporary plight of the native peoples of Brazil (the case of the purchase of the Urubu-Kaapor reserve by Swift, then a part of Deltec, reported above). From this research it was evident that the Deltec operation was a case in point of the brutal expropriation of Amazonian Indian groups by Brazilian and foreign-based private enterprise. By the same token Deltec became a prime target for action by groups actively opposing such exploitation, particularly sectors of the North American Indian movement that have concerned themselves with these problems. This information has been communicated to various concerned groups and publicized in numerous conferences and publications.

At the same time, through contacts with other researchers working on multinational corporate economic penetration and domination of Latin America, this member of the group also learned that Deltec represented an unusually interesting and as yet poorly understood type of MNC. From these indications it seemed likely that an investigation of Deltec could make a contribution of general value to the understanding of MNC's and their evolving strategies for domination of Third World economies.

Deltec's involvement in the meat business also made it potentially relevant to an important local (Chicago) issue: namely, the decline of employment in the meat-cutting and packinghouse industry, once among Chicago's major sources of employment. Deltec's operations in the stimulation of production and international distribution of processed meat products clearly fitted into the larger picture of technical developments and the export of productive operations through which U.S.

capitalists have sought to circumvent higher-paid and more effectively organized U.S. workers in the meat trades and exploit the lower-paid labor available in countries such as Brazil and Argentina. The head-quarters of the Amalgamated Meat Cutters and Butcher Workmen of North America is in Chicago, and the possibility of making a useful input into the union's research program was the clinching factor that made the Deltec project seem capable of fulfilling all of the major goals set forth at the beginning of this section. Immediately following the initial decision to undertake research on Deltec, members of the group visited the research department of the union to discuss the project. The purpose of this initial contact was to find out if the union felt the proposed research was potentially useful, and if so to seek cooperation and assistance from the union's research department. The union's research staff reacted posi-tively to the proposed project and gave valuable advice and assistance, particularly in the initial stages of the research. We hope that the final report of the project will be of use to the union in helping to clarify some of the political and economic considerations underlying the recent development of the production in Third World and certain Eastern European countries of processed meat products and the expansion of international trade in these products. Processed meat products, inci-dentally, have constituted the fastest-growing and most profitable part of the world meat business in recent years and are currently being imported in significant quantities into the United States. Such imports constitute a potential target of union pressure for government regulation. At the very least a broader awareness of the strategic considerations relating to the exploitation and dominance of Third World economies by the MNC's involved in the current boom in the international trade in processed meat products should help to clarify specific issues in which the union has interests in common with other groups. These include the Third World workers and indigenous societies being exploited and expropriated by the corporations in question, as well as groups in the United States working in their behalf.

It should be made clear that although the Deltec research group began as an ARPA project, its members from the outset have been for the most part nonanthropologists. None of the members of the research collective had had much prior training or experience in corporation research, let alone multinational-corporation research, nor any professional back-ground in economics or international economic relations. Insofar as our research represents a contribution to the general understanding of the strategies of MNC's in the Third World, and insofar as it is at the same time able to make some contribution to the struggle of U.S. workers and of the native peoples, workers, and national liberation movements of the countries in which Deltec operates, it may serve to demonstrate that small groups of politically committed researchers, organized within the context of academic institutions or professional associations, and with no more specific qualifications than generalized research skills, the necessary languages, and a willingness to work, can at least begin to bridge the gap between academic research and the practical needs of oppressed groups in their struggles against the international capitalist system.

Mary Kay Vaughan: I want to say something about trade unionism, especially as Ahamed referred optimistically to the prospect of working with U.S. unions around the issue of multinationals. I worked for the international trade-union movement and am sympathetic toward unions, but I want to play devil's advocate here in suggesting that European and North American trade unions may collaborate with multinationals in the exploitation of Third World workers.

In part because the U.S. trade-union movement has lived off the exploitation of the rest of the world, it is somewhat provincial. In its provincialism it ignores and is ignorant of the rest of the world. It is well known that in the international sphere the U.S. labor movement has been far from progressive. The foreign policy of the AFL-CIO, under the leadership of the anti-Communist Jay Lovestone, has been destructive of militant workers' movements throughout the world. The AFL-CIO has collaborated with U.S. multinationals and the U.S. government in neutralizing trade unions in Latin America. For instance, if Exxon of Uruguay has a tough union on its hands, it has only to pick up the phone to call the local AFL-CIO representative, who will come in to split the union and co-opt leadership. At the moment we are aware of the U.S. labor movement's assistance to the U.S. government in training white-collar workers in Chile to oppose the trade-union movement, which solidly supports the democratically elected government of Salvador Allende.

This is not to suggest that U.S. workers and all U.S. trade unions are in agreement with George Meany and Jay Lovestone. However, there are objective circumstances that may lead people to believe that the interests of U.S. and Third World workers conflict. The multinational hurts U.S. workers in its generation of inflation, in the taxes that workers must pay to replace the taxes the corporations do not pay, in health hazards, etc., but perhaps the largest problem the MNC poses for U.S. workers is job loss through automation and export of work. Because the MNC is governed by the law of profit maximization and sees labor costs as a hindrance to increased earnings, it is engaged in a rapid process of automation at home. Because it aims at extending its global structure it also moves abroad to manufacture what was once manufactured and exported from the United States. Furthermore, certain MNC's in labor-intensive industries like textiles and electronics go abroad in search of cheap labor. They move to Southeast Asia, Mexico, and the Caribbean to assemble products once assembled here, then reimport the finished goods into the

United States. European MNC's use southern Europe in the same way.
The phenomenon of the international runaway shop has alarmed the U.S.
trade-union movement. At present the AFL-CIO is backing the Burke-
Hartke Bill before Congress to protect the jobs of U.S. workers by
limiting U.S. overseas investment. It seems naive to ask the U.S. Congress, which is strongly influenced by multinationals, to limit overseas
investment upon which the future of a corporation depends. In trying to
limit the establishment of subsidiaries abroad, the Burke-Hartke Bill has
the arrogance to tell Mexicans or Puerto Ricans, "No, you can't have this
shop in your country because it will deprive Americans of jobs." The bill's
position overlooks the structural connection between high employment
and wealth in the industrialized world and unemployment and poverty in
the Third World. It seeks to maintain a position of privilege detrimental
to the Third World. In the short run at least it appears to express a conflict
of interest between workers of the industrialized world and the masses of
the Third World.

In its approach to the MNC the U.S. labor movement tends to be
short-sighted in its "economist" approach. I might illustrate the problem
with reference to a recent case in Puerto Rico. U.S. industry moved to
Puerto Rico because it was offered a number of profit-yielding benefits
among which were low wages. For years, management, the Puerto Rican
government, and the U.S. government fought the application of U.S.
minimum-wage standards to Puerto Rico on the grounds that if the
minimum applied, factories would move elsewhere, leaving Puerto
Ricans unemployed. Several years ago the Amalgamated Meatcutters
sent a dynamic representative to Puerto Rico who immediately took issue
with the disparity in minimum wages between mainland and Puerto Rican
workers. Criticizing the U.S.-dominated labor movement there for con-
doning this system, he claimed that any trade unionist who justified low
wages was not a trade unionist. He set about negotiating for parity in the
minimum wage for mainland and Puerto Rican workers. Just recently the
U.S. government, which exercises ultimate control over its Puerto Rican
colony, approved the principle of parity. Immediately following this
victory the governments of Barbados and the Dominican Republic wrote
to U.S. industries in Puerto Rico urging them to relocate in their countries
where wages were lower and workers more docile. Within the present
system of economics, the runaway shop keeps running away from one
cheap labor area to another. There is nothing wrong in fighting for higher
wages in particular areas, but the shortsightedness of a policy that limits
itself to struggle at the local or even national level is self-defeating. The
most international and farsighted institution in the world today is the
MNC: for workers to contest it, they must recognize that their class is
international, too.

Three international trade-union secretariats (ITS) that bring together workers in different branches of industry are in the process of formulating a policy for confronting the multinational. The ITS's involved are the International Metalworkers Federation, with considerable impetus from the United Auto Workers of the United States, the International Food Workers, and the International Chemical Workers Federation, whose general secretary, Charles Levinson, is the author of two books on multinationals and trade unions. To deal with the multinational, the ITS's have established global councils for each industry and for each multi-national; for instance, there is a global council of electrical workers, which involves workers from G.E., Westinghouse, Philips, Honeywell, Siemens, etc., and there is also a global council for W.R. Grace and Company, which includes both food and petrochemical workers. Global councils aim at coordination of collective bargaining in such a way that each national trade union can obtain the maximum from the bargaining process. They also seek to persuade MNC headquarters to divulge investment plans so that workers can keep abreast of company movements from one area or region to another. One of their primary functions is to gather and disseminate information on the MNC's to member unions throughout the world, thereby assisting weaker unions that cannot afford the expense of research. If interests can be harmonized between Third World and "First World" workers it would probably be within the context of the global council.

One of the most effective areas of trade-union solidarity to date has been international strike support. It is not possible to strike successfully at Ford in Detroit without the support of Ford workers in Germany and England. Because of the increasing trend toward standardization of parts and models, production can be transferred from one country to another with a flick of the Telex. In such a way the company can ward off strikers' demands for an unlimited period of time. For the last several years no major auto-workers' gains have been made without the assistance of workers internationally.

I see several problems involved here. First, most rank and file workers are not aware of the international aspects of their struggle. It is primarily an affair for the upper levels of the trade-union bureaucracy, which meets periodically in Geneva and other places. In many countries trade-union leadership has been co-opted and is conservative in its approach to capital. Such leadership might inhibit the development of a creative program to confront the MNC or otherwise cripple the effectiveness of international trade-union action. In some countries trade unions are not even permitted to function; in such situations the MNC has a free hand. Crucial also is the fact that the international movement itself is divided politically between the Communist WFTU, the "free" trade unions, and the Christian movement, with little hope for effective unity in the near future.

Further, trade unions have traditionally engaged in defensive holding actions to protect the immediate self-interest of workers — for instance, in the areas of wages and job security. To date this defensive reaction appears to benefit workers of the advanced industrialized countries at the expense of workers in the developing countries — in part because the greater strength of unions in advanced industrial nations gives them an advantage. International trade-union actions have tended to center on the problem of job loss through automation, rationalization, or job export to the Third World. One is tempted to see in this policy the already-referred-to contradictions between the demands of European and North American unions that companies not go abroad and the needs of Third World workers for employment.

Finally there is the dilemma that the MNC itself creates for Third World workers. It contributes to the underdevelopment of the Third World. It eliminates the jobs that less efficient national production provides while the capital-intensive nature of much of its own production fails to generate adequate employment. We must remember that although technology in the capitalist world has served the interests of profit and thus has aimed at job elimination, it developed gradually in consonance with other industrial needs such as the extension of markets and trade routes. For the industrial world it probably created more jobs than it eliminated in the early and middle stages of development; insofar as it created a labor surplus, that surplus found outlets in migration to underdeveloped areas. On the other hand the most highly developed, job-saving technology of the industrialized world now invades the Third World to create unemployment and increasing marginalization of the population. Despite a half-century of industrialization and urbanization, only 14 percent of Latin America's labor force is engaged in manufacturing. This 14 percent constitutes a labor aristocracy — a privileged sector of workers that some observers have included in the middle class. International trade unionism organizes this sector of Latin America's workers. It must be asked if they are part of the problem or part of the solution. Multinational-corporation workers in Third World countries gain additional privileges in the form of the assistance they receive from trade unions of the industrialized world in strike support, research data, and international seminars and conferences. Do these workers identify with the model of dependent development based on the multinational corporation, or does the labor aristocracy see itself as a vanguard for the dispossessed of the nation? The current situation in Chile seems to indicate two possible paths, two different answers to this question. Miners who worked for the leading multinationals in Chile constituted something of a labor aristocracy; in the Unidad Popular government they have proved to be more interested in wage increases than in building socialism in their country — perhaps because of their long history of economist trade unionism. Other workers in Chile, however, have seen themselves as a vanguard in building an alternative system based upon national and majority interest. Such a larger societal vision beyond the immediate plant situation would seem necessary given the problems of mass unemployment, resource misuse, and skewed industrialization that the MNC creates.

A further dilemma of workers organizing relates to the problem of migration. MNC-related development in Latin America, for instance, has generated a mass exodus from the countryside, either because emphasis on industrialization decapitalizes agriculture or because the penetration of U.S. agribusiness eliminates small farmers. Unable to find steady or remunerative employment in the cities, in-migrants form a cheap labor pool that keeps wages down and makes unionization difficult. For instance, U.S. owners of the labor-intensive electronics and textile runaways in northern Mexico post hiring notices throughout rural Mexico to draw a surplus of labor, which will hold wages down and forestall unionization along the border. The ultimate in metropolitan migration for workers in northern Latin America is the United States. Ninety-seven percent of immigrants to the United States are Latin American. Long regarded by the U.S. labor movement as a threat to the high wages of U.S. workers, the migrants — legal and illegal — are, along with blacks and women, inadequately protected by trade unions. Obliged to accept the worst jobs, they are without employment security or the possibility of skill acquisition and advancement. Theirs are the first jobs to be automated or exported back to Latin America. Subject to racial discrimination in housing and education as well as work, Latins and blacks not surprisingly organize along ethnic, community, and interclass lines rather than as workers. Given the bureaucraticization and discrimination of the U.S. trade-union movement, the rise of rank-and-file groups such as the General Brotherhood of Immigrant Workers, who demand honest and militant union leadership, is a positive step. More steps of the same kind are needed if trade unions are to creatively confront the problems created by the MNC.

Joseph Collins: I am not an anthropologist by professsional training, although I believe I share some interests with anthropologists. I accepted the invitation to this world meeting of anthropologists in order to speak to some of these common interests as they relate to my studies of global (or "multinational") corporations. More importantly, I wish to indicate where in this juncture of interests I have so often felt the lack of anthropological research. To paraphrase my opening sentence, I believe I *should* share some interests with *more* anthropologists. Naturally I have also come prepared to be surprised: perhaps there is much anthropological work related to global corporations in underdeveloped countries of which I have simply been ignorant.

For the past three years I have been working as a member of a team (interdisciplinary, yet lacking an anthropologist) researching the significance of global corporations.[1] Throughout our work we have sought to understand the phenomenon of the global corporation (or global corporate system). Most directly we have sought to document the impact on the lives of people — the inhabitants of both underdeveloped and industrialized countries: workers, managers, consumers, and others. We have concluded that the managers of the global corporations are not simply manufacturers and vendors of particular consumer products but that they are in a profound sense managers of social change. In a real sense their chief product is not crackers, computers, and Chevrolets but a planetary culture of capitalist production and consumption. Attempting to manage the earth as a single unit, these "executives" are in our time making a bid for power — more power than most sovereign governments of the world — to determine where people will live, what work, if any, they will do, what they will eat, drink, and wear, what sorts of knowledge schools and universities will encourage, and what kind of society their children will inherit. Global corporations were active long before anyone in universities took note of them. The head of one global corporation, John Powers of Pfizer, likes to point out that "practice is ahead of theory." First to study the global corporation were the leading business schools — not surprising, given their relationship to big business. Then came some economists and eventually a few political scientists. Still there are virtually no anthropologists studying the global corporation despite its impact on humankind and society.

The specific focus of this forum is "multinational" corporations in the underdeveloped countries. A major part of our research has concentrated on the impact of the global corporations on the people in underdeveloped countries. Here I am not going to discuss much of our findings. Allow me to make only a few points. Against the backdrop of deteriorating living standards of the bottom half of the populations of underdeveloped countries, we have investigated the structural, institutionalized sources of the power of the global corporations. We have examined the often cited and generally presumed contributions of the global corporations: capital, technology, employment, development, etc. We have documented how these presumed contributions are in reality largely mythical and indeed often perversely false. All of this — it is important to emphasize — has been with a working research principle of examining the *normal* business practices of the global corporations, "business doing its thing," as Jacques Maisonrouge, chief manager of IBM World Trade, has claimed. We have not allowed ourselves to be

[1] The result of this research is Barnet and Miller 1974.

sidetracked into thinking of intervention only in terms of the notorious ITT Chile memoranda.

Rather than to discuss further our findings, let me reiterate that I have come here to speak of the several key areas in our research in almost two dozen underdeveloped countries where we have looked for and have not found relevant work of anthropologists. We were often surprised and disappointed that anthropologists seemed uninterested in giving insight into humankind and human culture in the context of global corporations and underdeveloped countries.

When I speak of global corporations and the underdeveloped world I am not thinking of mining corporations that go to a country to dig a hole in the ground and haul a mineral back "home." For the global corporation, "home" is everywhere (or, if you prefer, nowhere). A global corporation in a basic way takes the underdeveloped country seriously. For the global corporation, an underdeveloped country is frequently a production center (part of the "Global Factory") and always a market (part of the "Global Shopping Center"). The global corporation is in the business of shaping values, mores, habits — in short, culture.

There is much work for anthropologists to do toward understanding the impact of the global corporation on the workers — the culture of work, if you will — in an underdeveloped country. For instance, in Mexico I was interested in researching major U.S.-based agribusiness corporations such as Del Monte. I had hoped to find some anthropologists who had studied, among other things, what it meant in the lives of peasants to change to contract farming for the processing factories of Del Monte.

Anthropologists should similarly find a rich field to explore in the global corporation's efforts to create consumption values that create the demand for those particular items to be found in the global corporation's "basket of goods." Almost totally wide-open is the field of advertising in underdeveloped countries. Very much lacking are studies of the impact of advertising on the "marginal" population — the values shaped, the fantasies provoked, the dreams packaged. In looking throughout Latin America for such studies we were able to find only some early ones by an anthropologist at the Central University in Caracas. Her research was paid for by J. Walter Thompson and McCann-Erickson, two of the largest U.S.-based global advertising agencies operating in the underdeveloped world. Among other things, she finds that these *marginales* seem to be losing a perception of class difference through the influence of advertising. She told me, "They think there are, to be sure, rich and poor, but that all have access to the same consumer goods. For them, it is a matter of luck whether they have the money to buy the things they hear and see advertised. They always think their luck might change." Anthropologists interested in the development of language would find interesting her work on the impact of commercial jingles and advertising slogans on the speech — and, indeed, mental habits — of these poor. She is also studying the impact of advertising on values in relation to family, sex, love, prestige, race, and leisure.

Anthropologists should be professionally able to contribute many insights (for instance, in the area of identities and loyalties) to one overall crucial question that must be asked of global corporations in underdeveloped countries, namely, what are the long-range social (and, therefore, political) effects of advertising on people who earn less than $200 per year?

Another general area in which I sought anthropological research and could find virtually none is that of the impact of the global food corporations on dietary patterns. George Orwell once hypothesized: "Changes in diet are more important than changes of dynasty or even of religion." We found nutritional (calorie-protein) data indicating that in absolute terms the diet of the bottom 40 percent of the population of countries such as Mexico is deteriorating. A growing number of nutritionists are analyzing "commerciogenic" malnutrition. But what are the anthropological aspects of the "intervention" of ITT's Pan Bimbo (Wonder Bread) in a rural tortilla-eating family?

Again, here I have mentioned only a few broad areas of possible anthropological research on the impact of global corporations in the underdeveloped world. There are undoubtedly others that will come to mind for many of you, but these at least are areas where we repeatedly sought in vain the collaborative work of professional anthropologists.

Finally, such research should naturally be the task of Third World anthropologists in their own countries. But is it also not fitting that anthropologists of the dominant countries — the headquarters countries of the global corporations — contribute *with* their professional discipline and *to* their professional discipline by studying the penetration of global corporations in the cultures of underdeveloped countries?

David Barkin: I have some remarks to make in trying to wind this up. We err in calling these corporations multinational. This is a mystification that the companies themselves imposed on us. They are not multinational in any sense except that they operate in many countries. Basically they are controlled in one, two, or three countries. It seems more appropriate to understand and label them as "transnational" corporations (TNC's). "Transnational" suggests that one octopus extends many tentacles in different directions rather than that several decision-making centers in various parts of the world come together. There is only one center, and in most cases this center is only about a thousand miles from here [Chicago]: New York.

One of the things we've been trying to do here is to understand how academics can use their knowledge of transnationals in a constructive way. The transnational corporation has affected virtually every aspect of life in virtually every country of the world — even in those in which it is not present. I suspect that this is apparent to people at this Congress, although to listen to the papers we'd never believe that they had thought about it. It is not only a question of relations of production, trade-union movements, or capital flows — although the TNC's own more dollars in foreign countries than the U.S. government owns in the United States — but rather, it is a social and cultural thing that affects every aspect of our lives. It affects the way we go to work and the kinds of jobs we can find. It is reorganizing society in a spatial sense, in a cultural sense, in every sense of the term. The way we deal with our friends is influenced by Coca-Cola and General Motors. I, as an economist, and other academics somehow miss the point because we've been educated wrongly. We've been educated to believe that money is the proper way to establish social relations. Money has social significance in our society because it is a control over people; it is power. The power concentrated in the 178 decision-making centers representing the most important TNC's is translated into a cultural phenomenon shaping our lives in a total sense. For instance they decide what we can buy. We can't buy what they don't produce. Our education is based on models that assume that there is independent consumer choice, that people have free will and the independent ability to make decisions that we must respect when the decisions they make are between a Lincoln Continental and a Cadillac; i.e., very minimal decisions. I would suggest that we have to ask whether the nature of the freedom now available to us is in fact freedom at all. Technology, the way things are produced, determines our physical environment.

It likewise determines that there are not enough jobs available. There is a global unemployment crisis. Robert MacNamara, head of the World Bank, answers this crisis with the solution of birth control. The World Bank has embarked on an important birth-control program that is a further indication of the ways in which transnationals affect our lives. I am not against family planning or allowing people to make decisions about their own lives, but birth control as it is peddled by the transnationals via the World Bank is not the same as allowing people to make decisions affecting their own lives.

Birth control is a popular program of the international banking institutions and U.S. Agency for International Development; they encourage sterilization, they promote contraceptive devices, and develop new techniques for mass communication that might effectively carry the message of birth control to the hordes of uneducated people who know no better. They do this, they explain, because exploding populations make it more difficult to solve the employment problem and also further exacerbate the unequal income distribution in developing countries. They argue that with fewer children being born, less would have to be invested in education, medical care, and other social services, and more jobs could be created.

This line of reasoning is deceptive, to say the least. Unemployment will not end when population growth slows down; unemployment is an integral part of the present system in which TNC's increase production through mechanized and automated procedures and in which people without jobs are used as a threat to discipline potentially rebellious workers.

It is instructive that in societies that have successfully begun the transformation to socialism, like China and Cuba, the huge unemployment problem has rapidly improved. Jobs were found for all the people and efforts have been made to ensure that women and elderly people who previously were not working could join in to help solve pressing social problems. In Cuba the unemployment problem was rapidly transformed into a labor shortage during the years of rapid sugar production. In many socialist countries, the birth rates have declined, not as a result of vacuous preaching by self-serving "authorities" but rather as a result of the rapidly changing conditions in which the majority of the people live.

I have difficulty thinking of any aspect of our lives that the transnational does not invade. I will limit myself to briefly discussing the automobile. The transfer of automobile production from the industrialized world to the Third World throws Third World countries into a quandary. For example, three years ago in Chile, economists were asking the question, "How can we rationalize automobile production?" A group of economists and technicians got together and determined they would throw out all the companies and open an international competition to get an efficiently produced automobile. It never occurred in a serious political sense to those at the decision-making level that there was only one way to rationalize automobile production in Chile, and that was to end it. It does not make sense for a country on the verge of starvation because of inherited structural problems to produce automobiles when it could be mass-producing public transportation in a basic redesigning of society.

The automobile is an incredible instrument. If you have automobiles you can build Shakey's pizza parlors and McDonald's hamburger stands. If you build these things, you ruin the downtown cafés and destroy the basis for urban agglomerations in which people interact with one another. We have seen this process in the United States and in other cities around the world. We know something here about the changes in our social patterns brought about by the automobile culture — for instance in the proliferation of "passion pits" at our drive-in movies. The automobile has ramifications for the structure and efficiency of our hospital service. It has contributed enormously to our pollution problem. I will not elaborate further on this, but I would suggest that the decision to produce certain products is very important. But in most parts of the world it is the decision of a minority group with vested interests in the production of specific kinds of goods and the perpetuation of a certain consumer life-style.

Because of the extent and influence of the transnational, we obviously have a fantastic subject for study. The *Wall Street Journal* seemingly has its staff working on the transnationals. The U.S. Department of Commerce has been investigating the phenomenon for some time now and the U.S. Congress has set up a subcommittee on multinationals. They are becoming a popular area of investigation. I would suggest that just studying them is not enough; the problem is to begin to ask questions not only about their structure but about alternatives. These alternatives cannot be phrased in terms of laws controlling the corporations. There is no way to control them. There is no way to deal with them on their own terms. They will win. We must think about other possibilities. We can't resolve social problems like unemployment and poverty without going to a different level of understanding and looking for alternatives based on new models of social relationships.

(From the Floor): I have been listening, hoping to hear something that didn't come out — something on which anthropologists including myself are for the most part woefully inadequate. That is the question of international finance. We've been hearing about multinational or transnational or global corporations as if all they do is make things. The real problem is the finance that supports them and that they in turn support, i.e., the international banks and insurance companies. The products of corporations are practical symbols that people work with and that affect us most thoroughly and most completely, but the real TNC, or MNC, is the bank or insurance company like Lloyds of London or Metropolitan Life, which have been respectably transnational for years. Although I don't know much about this, it seems to me it ought to be mentioned.

A. Idris-Soven: You're absolutely right. When I discussed Deltec, I didn't go deeply into its involvement in international finance, but that is exactly what it is — a financial institution. In fact, for Deltec, production is merely a method it uses to increase cash flow for its finance operations. For example, Deltec typically buys already existing factories in Third World countries and, a short time later, sells them for a huge profit. Deltec usually buys ailing corporations that, when they become Deltec subsidiaries, immediately jump in value by virtue of the name alone. Thus the same corporation, with not much change, can be sold for a profit. This strategy, known as "asset stripping," is increasingly coming into use by many, if not all, MNC's.

D. Barkin: There's another point that has to be made here. You make a distinction between finance and industrial capital. One of the things transnationals do is eliminate the distinction completely.

(From the Floor):   Some of them just open banks of their own. Sears Roebuck, for instance, developed a bank of its own because that's what it needs. Dow Chemical has the seventh-largest bank in Switzerland.

D. Barkin: It's really important to understand that in the period of the expansion of capital, finance capital has engulfed industrial capital in many areas. Finance capital is important but does not move independently of industrial capital, however, and at the present moment there is much literature attempting to determine how industrial and financial conglomerates interact, arguing the one or the other is more influential. This is not the place to enter into this dispute — rather, I refer you to the Union of Radical Political Economists where more information on this debate can be obtained.

(From the Floor):   Can you go into greater detail on how we can actually combat the trend of multinational corporations? You laid out the details of what they are doing, but what do you think can be done in terms of affirmative action?

M.K. Vaughan: It will probably be multifaceted. I think people have a lot to say about this. I know a lot of people in this room who are into different kinds of actions relating to MNC's. In the United States, MNC's will probably be hit from all sides. For instance, the consumer movement will grow in militancy. While it can be argued that consumer protest in itself will not create a true alternative to the present mode of production, it is nonetheless a legitimate expression of protest against a phenomenon of advanced capitalism — absorption of the surplus in the production of useless and shoddy goods.

A. Gedicks: Let me make another comment on that. There is no one strategy, of course, especially when you are dealing with a global phenomenon. However, one of the things that social scientists in general should be aware of is that in relations between corporations and the community, the monopoly the corporation has on knowledge about the workings of industry is a very important dimension of power relations. If you look at the history of Chilean relations with the copper corporations, you note the evolution of the government's position on the companies in proportion to its knowledge of the workings of the industry. The bargaining position evolved, from a stand demanding greater benefits from the industry, to a realization that, given the workings of the industry and the corporation, there was no other possible way to make copper serve Chile than through nationalization of the companies. The potential value of knowledge can also be illustrated in the case of Papua-New Guinea. There an international copper research project in which I am participating is using information we collected on the copper industry to help the New Guinea government bargain with Kennecott Copper Corporation. Six months ago, New Guinea was willing to take a 10 percent share on the profit while guaranteeing Kennecott very liberal depletion allowances, tax breaks, and the like. Now the New Guinea government has turned around completely and is demanding 50 percent of the profit as a starting measure. It is also demanding that Kennecott invest in local productive activities that would have some beneficial effect on the New Guinea economy. The whole power relationship between the country and the corporation changes partially on the basis of knowledge about the workings of the corporation. Social scientists clearly have the expertise and resources available to them to gather this sort of information.

B. Berdichewsky: We have heard a lot of interesting things here, but really they are not new. What is new is that transnational corporations are more sophisticated today than they were in the past and that they are somehow more openly viewed by their own people than they have been. I would say that almost everyone today has said two or three sentences about Chile. When I was a student at the university in Chile many years ago, we knew everything about those corporations in copper and saltpeter mining. We used to give a name to those corporations. We used to call them imperialists. I think that name is quite good. We didn't invent the name. That name came out of the discussion of workers in Europe at the beginning of this century. People like Rosa Luxemburg, Lenin, and others really made the first analyses of these corporations. Certainly the problem now is much bigger than it was in their time, because, as David Barkin said, now transnational corporations are everywhere. One interesting thing I might say on the basis of our experience in Chile is that while as a student I might have known what was needed for Chile, today what is needed in Chile is known by the common people of our country. After the scandal with ITT most people understood what a big corporation is. Nationalization of the copper mines in Chile — one response of our people to the TNC's — was an act of tremendous popularity among the people. Everybody — every part on the Chilean political scene from right to the far left — voted for nationalization. It was the only decision Salvador Allende made that was completely unanimous. The scandal with ITT helped to create that unanimity. As the problem of transnational corporations becomes clearer for everyone, social scientists must understand it. Social science is knowledge and knowledge is power — power that could really help to understand society and to change it. We also need to understand what David Barkin has pointed out — the tremendous impact of TNC's on cultures throughout the world, on every facet of human life that we as anthropologists usually call culture. If we are studying human culture, why not study the tremendous impact of TNC's on it? I don't think many anthropologists are studying this problem. Second, the example that Ahamed gave of the Brazilian Indians is very good. It is not new, because the rubber industry in Brazil at the beginning of the century also resulted in the death of many Indians. As anthropologists we should study the direct impact of TNC's on Indian communities and other communities.

(From the Floor): I have a question and comment together. I have no background on TNC's. I was doing migration studies in Turkey — a problem that very much involved the question of employment. I was impressed with a number of things. One is the important role of economists in decision-making and the role of planning commissions in the developing world. Economists can be centralists — overtly nonideological — or they may be radical leftist economists, but they all seem to agree that you need capital-intensive development. You need machinery, you have got to industrialize. I found no questioning of this idea. I was wondering about the assumption, as it seems to me, that capital-intensive development encourages the influx of TNC's and the kind of industrial structure that they represent.

(From the Floor): Capital-intensive industrialization is the assumption of development economics that legitimizes economic growth through TNC's. Most professionals are trained in this theory of development. In graduate school I took a course in anthropological economics and we used Walt Rostow for our theory of development.

(From the Floor): Much of the criticism of development economics comes not from economists but from other scholars who often cannot offer the same level of expertise to enact the alternative solutions they suggest. Often economists in positions of power will criticize the existing theories of development, then implement them unwittingly because alternatives are not that clear to them.

(From the Floor): One area of crucial importance to the Third World that we have not yet discussed is the transfer of development technology. For the Third World to have access to this technology, which is becoming an increasingly large percentage of European and U.S. exports, what are the conditions, terms, and risks involved in purchasing this technology? I

think this classic problem of diffusion of knowledge should provide an entire new field of study for anthropologists.

M.K. Vaughan: The transfer of technology is one of the biggest dilemmas for developing countries. As I understand it, the Chileans have preferred joint ventures rather than nationalization in many of their capital-intensive industries, as they were dependent upon foreigners for both technology and management. Western technology can severely distort development in Third World countries, not only because it causes unemployment but because the expense of its importation aggravates balance-of-payments problems and pushes the prices of consumer goods up to inflationary levels. Western technology has been introduced primarily to increase profits, not to fulfill human needs. While the Russians and the Chinese are today very interested in adopting Western technology, they will probably be careful in adopting it to serve social needs rather than those of profit.

(From the Floor): Part of the complexity of the issue is that our technology carries with it an ideology and a consumer-oriented cultural bias. It creates needs — needs usually associated with the materialist-oriented U.S. middle class. This is certainly an important area for anthropologists to study.

(From the Floor): Someone mentioned that TNC's were primarily controlled from New York City. I am wondering if it is still useful to think of separate economic power loci in the United States, Western Europe, and Japan. Is the transnational network centered overwhelmingly and unquestionably in New York City or are there other significant independent centers throughout the world?

(From the Floor): I think it's important to understand that New York City is still the center for the American environment. You don't have to go 2,000 miles away to understand where imperialist decisions are made. Clearly that is the case with certain industries such as agribusiness and electronics. You could deal with other parts of the United States and other centers of power. Finance capital — if that distinction is still to be made — is still focused in New York City.

M.K. Vaughan: I find the tendency to see the United States as *the* imperialist power myopic and even chauvinistic. While New York City is a transnational center, capital is rapidly becoming internationalized. We might note the trend toward the joint venture among North American, European, Japanese, and even state capitalist — or socialist — capital. Westinghouse, for example, wants the Russians to joint-bid with them to build a power generator for the Grand Coulee Dam. Of importance also is the internationalization of banking. Not only does this movement involve the establishment of U.S. branch banks throughout the world but the development of supranational consortia such as Orion, Ltd., a venture involving Chase Manhattan, Royal Bank of Canada, National Westminster Bank, Ltd, of London, Westdeutsche Landesbank Gironzentrale, Credito Italiano, and Mitsubishi Bank, Ltd. In the internationalization process we should note increasing foreign investment in the United States. According to Charles Levinson, by 1975 a quarter of the U.S. GNP will be produced by foreign firms in the United States. The recent dollar devaluation encouraged a flood of Japanese and European investment here. As devaluation made imports such as Volkswagens more expensive in relation to U.S. goods, foreign companies moved to manufacture here to preserve their markets. Increasingly the TNC appears to be an entity above national loyalties whose decisions are made within the context of the corporation's own global economy and frontiers.

(From the Floor):   Maybe it would be useful to separate the question of ownership from the question of control. We all know that majority stock ownership is not necessary to control a corporation. If, as anthropologists, we are talking about people who consciously manipulate patterns of symbolic structure, whom do we look for in terms of this kind of manipulation? Who is controlling?

M.K. Vaughan: There are various theories put forward. Many believe that only a handful of men are responsible for all major corporate decisions. I think there can be little doubt that this is a stage of monopoly capitalism in which relatively few firms and banks dominate production. I believe this monopolization is more important than the probability that a majority of the firms and banks would be United States in origin.

(From the Floor):   I think the question is really directed toward the central concept: is there indeed international competition? Or is it becoming a process of interpenetration and mutual accommodation?

M.K. Vaughan: Mutual accommodation and interpenetration are not exclusive of competition within an oligopolistic framework. The select few who compete within a rich-man's club understand the rules of their game and the necessity of accommodation from time to time. For instance, in order to compete with IBM in Europe, Siemens, CII of France, and Philips of Holland have integrated computer operations. The point, I believe, is that competition takes place above the level of the nation-state. Capitalism today will not destroy itself through international trade wars although competition gives rise to contradictions that, for example, Third World nations can exploit to their advantage.

(From the Floor):   I think there is a difference of opinion between Mary Kay and myself. When you look at this accommodation, I think it's important to see where the money is going when finance and industrial capital have been brought together from our own imperialist country. As I look at Japan — and I have done research on Chicago firms in Japan — I can point to instance after instance where it's a joint venture, to be sure with a bank headquartered in the Philippines or Singapore, with British capital participating and so on, but the Chicago firms have been able to penetrate the very tightly controlled Japanese industrial sectors, purchasing up to 7 percent of stock in major Japanese finance houses and industrial firms. The same is true of U.S. TNC's in Europe. Accommodation occurs but U.S. companies have much more say-so in terms of capital put into those ventures than European, Russian, or Japanese firms.

(From the Floor):   There is a question of the nation-state. It was asserted in one of the meetings the other day that despite other competitors, the nation-state still must be considered the main locus of power. Obviously, your position on the TNC is in conflict with this theory. To what extent do U.S.-based TNC's identify themselves with the United States?

M.K. Vaughan: This is a tricky question and the subject of much debate, but I believe we are witnessing the recession of the nation-state as the major locus of power. Marxists would argue that the nation-state serves the interests of capital; today the nation-state, even in the most advanced industrial countries, is seen as a hindrance to capital. The foreign policy and international policing apparatus of the U.S. government is certainly still of vital assistance to TNC's in providing a climate of so-called political stability in which the firms can produce, but when the nation-state interferes with the operation of capital — for instance, in its tax laws — the TNC will bypass it. The situation is more startling in Third World countries where TNC's behave without regard of national needs — for instance, draining a country of its natural wealth with no consideration for using that wealth to build local industry, or constructing a polluting petrochemical complex that employs few people in job-desperate countries. Although Third World states attempt to negotiate with the TNC to their own advantage, as in the cases of Chile and Peru today, the trend in nonsocialist Third World countries is toward TNC dominance of the state apparatus that supplies both capital and infrastructure for TNC penetration.

(From the Floor):   I think it would be a mistake to forget that these corporations do not exist alone. There is a class base for TNC's. We used to call these people imperialists. The bourgeoisie is still the fundamental enemy of the people of the world. That has not changed. Corporations do not exist apart from the bourgeoisie. We're not talking about power-mad corporate monsters that exist separate from the bourgeoisie. There seems to be some tendency here to think that they are in some fashion separate from this particular social class. Is that your position? That they are as classless as they are nationless?

A. Idris-Soven: Absolutely not. The bourgeoisie own and control the TNC's. What we are witnessing in this case is the internationalization of this capital-owning class. They should not be seen as faceless, all-powerful models of efficiency and production without beneficiaries and decision-makers. We wish to stress the newness of their global structure and their ability to distort cultures throughout the world. We believe it is important to understand the structure in order to understand the distortions.

(From the Floor):   When Nixon defends the TNC's, as he has done with a special task force to publicize their positive role in the U.S. economy, he clearly does not conceive of the corporations as you do. He does not view them as fundamentally different from the old imperialist corporations. The argument about the newness of TNC's seems to depend on the idea that managers no longer see themselves as bound by national loyalties — that they put nationalism behind them. Is Nixon naive? Does he not realize where his power is coming from? Is he still using the old categories? Or does he have some other game going?

A. Idris-Soven: This is the dilemma of a capitalist nation-state. Nixon is bound to defend the interests of the TNC even when those interests are in contradiction to the needs of the U.S. people.

(From the Floor):   It would be good if we had case studies of instances where MNC's worked for interests demonstrably not in the nation's interests.

M.K. Vaughan: International runaway plants are not in the interests of U.S. workers who lose their jobs. The TNC causes unemployment at this and other levels. The dollar crisis was in part precipitated by U.S. TNC's as they transferred vast reserves of dollars to other currencies. The U.S. balance-of-payments problem is aggravated by U.S. corporations like Zenith and Chrysler manufacturing products overseas and reimporting them into the U.S.

A. Gedicks: It's easy to confuse the global outlook of a corporation with the class base of a corporation — and class has always been international. There is also a tendency to assume the MNC's are something entirely new. That is certainly not the case with mining corporations, which have had a global outlook from their very inception. Corporations exploiting raw materials could not exist in an environment in which they did not keep as much of the world as possible under their own control in order to keep other people out. Control over every possible source of a mineral is necessary, as a surplus of it could depress the entire world price structure.

(From the Floor):   I'd like to talk about the Canadian situation. There is quite a bit of work being done now in investigating Canada as a branch-plant economy. People have been looking at how Canada is kept in the role of a primary producer instead of being able to do its own manufacturing. One thing that appears to be developing is the realization that if you want to accomplish anything you have to go into political action. You have to have the kind of socialist alternative that is international in scope and not limited to national solutions. If the MNC is indeed a real phenomenon, then you would need an international socialist movement to confront it. This is one of the things we have not got at present. The Communists, Maoists, and so on are each building separate power blocs. If anthropologists and other professionals are going to do anything about the TNC they are going to have to get into politics.

G. Huizer: Is there any group in Canada that works along these lines?

(From the Floor):   Groups are presently beginning. For example, the New Democratic Party, the CCG. We are building groups that attempt to investigate and publish information on the control of each industry. We hope we will begin to make links with groups in other parts of the world to build a more global socialism.

M.K. Vaughan: International socialism seems the logical answer. The logical place to begin would be with the international working class. What is your opinion, Gerrit, of the work being done in the international trade-union movement? I know you have quite a bit of contact with trade unionists.

G. Huizer: What the international federations of metal, food, and chemical workers have been doing is excellent. I am not sure, however, that they are clear on what they are heading for. They are tackling the MNC's in struggles over wage issues, but I think none of them has a clear view toward an international socialist society. These questions were discussed at a meeting in April 1972 in Santiago, Chile, which included the abovementioned trade unions as well as radical unions of Christian orientation and trade unions from the socialist countries. There was no basic agreement on the idea of working toward change in the system as a whole beyond the limited struggles for wage increases and improvement in working conditions. I know that some of the leaders of these organizations recognize the problem, but their programs are still not oriented toward changing the system. I think as long as this is the case, the struggle is going to be difficult. Most probably the corporations will let them have their wage increases in order to appease the trade-union movement; the corporation prefers this to a struggle for a complete change in the system.

Another development that may be more interesting is the issue of nationalization in Europe. Nationalization has of course occurred in Egypt, Tanzania, Chile, Cuba, etc., but we tend to view it as a strange happening that could not possibly occur in our own countries. But the British Labor Party is currently considering the nationalization of twenty-five of the largest companies in the country — a nationalization that would bring these companies under some kind of state control. They have a decent chance to win the next election since Heath's government has performed so badly. In France, if the leftist parties — the Communists, Radicals, and Socialists — get together and win the next election, nationalization may be seriously considered there also. It is difficult to foresee how nationalization will affect TNC's, but I think it is a serious possibility.

(From the Floor):   Nationalization has been criticized by some people as a move to forestall revolutionary movements. In those cases it is just a form of state ownership where power remains in the hands of the corporations and is simply managed and guaranteed by the state, which becomes a partner of the corporation.

G. Huizer: That is indeed quite a danger. In Italy, for example, there are a number of state companies that are no different from privately owned companies. One of the most essential differences in socialized production is worker participation in the management of companies. But I think it is difficult to foresee an ideal system that solves all these problems at the same time. Perhaps we have to proceed step by step — first nationalization, then worker control. In Chile it seems to proceed the other way around at the moment. Workers take over plants and the government is forced to nationalize them. One of the things that may come out of the discussion here is a comparative study of nationalizations in different countries. People in our countries are very frightened when they hear the word "nationalization" — especially in the United States. But there are countries that have nationalized industry very successfully. A study that has been prepared for this Congress on cooperatives, collectives, and co-participation in nationalized industries is exactly about the case of Chile. These cases should be studied and explained in simple language so that everyone can become acquainted with these possibilities — so that people will stop thinking of these things as impossibilities. I think that would be an important role for the anthropologist.

(From the Floor):   Could you speak more about alternatives and steps that can be taken? What occurred at the workshop, where people talked about models of control and industrial process?[2]

G. Huizer: Unfortunately the person who was to present the paper on Chile was not here to discuss it. What was discussed in the panel on worker control was the Bolivian case, where the mines were nationalized about twenty years ago. For a variety of reasons the Bolivian nationalization has not been a success. The imperialist forces regained power in Bolivia and now are in control in a very sad way — at the cost of many lives and with many people in jail.

With regard to the possibilities for action, the political nature of anthropological research will be more thoroughly discussed tomorrow in the session on the politics of anthropology.[3] Anthropology now supports the existing structure. An increasing number of anthropologists today feel the need to go beyond research to become involved in community action focusing on certain companies to awaken the people to the damages these companies have done. Many feel the need to explain to people that the effect of the company is not an absolute fate — that people in developing countries have been able to confront the MNC, to take control of their own fate, through nationalization for instance. We realize that we have work to do in our own countries — for instance, we can stop a company from investing in areas clearly dangerous to people in the surrounding communities. There are several cases we can point to where people who live around factories have been mobilized to combat the MNC, just as peasants in Cuba were mobilized locally when their lands were taken from them or their situation was rendered difficult by the intrusion of sugar companies and landlords. In the same way and very modestly (not mentioning revolution or socialism) it can be clearly shown how these companies damage the environment, cause pollution, or influence employment in very drastic ways; and gradually people may become alarmed and start taking action — through the courts or even in some cases by occupying factories. The more these actions are taken and the more they are explained to people in terms of the need for control over these companies, the more the idea that a socialist solution is the only

[2] The papers of this workshop appear in the volume *Popular participation in social change* of this series.
[3] See also the volume *The politics of anthropology* of this series.

solution will come to people's minds. In our countries we have for twenty-five years been made to fear and belittle socialism by the media and press, which these companies control. Today these companies are doing such negative things throughout the world that it is again possible to start thinking the other way around.

We must combine research with political action in our own countries as has been done in the developing countries. We must find ways of communicating this information to people. I think anthropologists should not only learn to communicate with the people they study abroad, but we ourselves should learn to communicate with our own people. Most of us are as alienated from our neighbors and working-class people as the anthropologist who goes to Tanzania, Nigeria, or Bolivia is from the people he or she studies. We should start to overcome this through, for instance, doing a more profound professional job. I think this would be better anthropology than I have been hearing at the Congress.

REFERENCE

BARNET, R.J., R.E. MILLER
1974   Global reach: the power of the multinational corporations. New York: Simon and Schuster.

Anthropology and Multinational Power: Some Ethical Considerations on Social Research in the Underdeveloped Countries

GERRIT A. HUIZER

THE ETHICAL QUESTION

It would be interesting to study why, in the last few years, the ethical implications of Western sociological and anthropological research in underdeveloped countries have received increasing attention. Particularly in the United States, where the debate on ethics started, anthropology has developed rapidly since World War II (particularly as to the number of people involved). It might be that the "Establishment," which financed this relatively innocent ivory tower, in the end wanted something in return, research to serve the maintenance of the Establishment, including counter-insurgency research.

Although in Western countries a subservient anthropology formerly existed at Royal Institutes for Colonies or Tropics, this was so self-evident in those days that it did not arouse debate on professional ethics. The unexpectedly strong resistance of Vietnamese peasants to U.S. domination, which resulted in an escalation of the Vietnam War, has helped to bring the issue of subservience of anthropology acutely to the foreground. To understand and cope with the resistance, anthropological studies were used in psychological warfare. More and more anthropologists discovered that their work was (mis)used for such purposes. One could almost say that in addition to food and some history-making revolutions, we are at least partly indebted to the peasantry for this new ethical concern; and also to students and some younger anthropologists in our own countries who drew attention to the involvement of anthropologists in the Vietnam War at meetings of the American Anthropological Association. However, it is doubtful whether the students would ever have gained sufficient attention if the resistance movement in Indochina had not been so unexpectedly strong — or, for that matter, if the Latin

Americans had not made such a fuss about the Camelot project in Chile (Horowitz 1967).

Anyway, it is becoming increasingly clear that the ivory tower of social science is also a mere pawn in the chess game of vested interests and powers. In the service of whom and of what does anthropology really function? What is its purpose? What is its usefulness?

WHY RESEARCH?

The way in which social research projects are frequently initiated should be analyzed briefly to help answer this question. Generally the social research workers themselves propose the problems they want to study. For some reason, frequently irrational and sentimental, they are interested in some specific, more or less exotic, country, area, or ethnic group. They read about it, gain insight and possibly go there for some time. Their interest increases and they apply for funds from some foundations or from their universities for an investigation of certain aspects, chosen by themselves, of the lives of those in whom they happen to be interested. The projects should appear to be a contribution to science and give more insight and knowledge to the specialists, who already know a great deal about the subject. These specialists judge the research projects; if they are accepted, the research can start. It all looks rather detached and one could speak indeed of hobbyism. It seems as if the most immediate purpose of each research project is to satisfy the rather arbitrary curiosity (or urge for knowledge) of the social researcher. The satisfaction of this urge, according to the rules of the game of scientific effort and the passing on of the knowledge gained to others, determines the career and promotion of the research workers.

If they play things correctly, they eventually get highly lucrative posts as professors. There are some common characteristics with the system of private enterprise. In the freedom of research (and choice of subject), the problems of society are not the main concern or even reckoned with. Predominant are the desires of the research worker or — for that matter — the entrepreneur: more knowledge or more profits (economic power). Is this a sufficiently ethical or social justification?

KNOWLEDGE IS POWER

A question that easily arises in this context is whether there is a relationship between knowledge and power. The popular saying, "knowledge is power," suggests that there may be something more behind the gathering of knowledge than mere satisfaction of curiosity and other urges of the research worker. Can the research and the research worker be used? During the years that I worked with the United Nations in Latin America I knew several social-research workers with peasant societies as a hobby who were highly surprised and sometimes even indignant when, in 1967, the *New York Times* (following *Ramparts*) published lists of researchers and foundations that were directly or indirectly financed by the CIA, particularly when they found their own name or that of their sponsor. Some were honestly unaware of this possibility and went through a crisis of conscience.

The interests of those who supply research funds have hardly been subject to scientific investigation, although more has been done in this respect in the United States than in Europe. That scientific research policies have something to do with power and politics will no longer be denied. What exactly scientific research policy has to do with politics should now be taken from the field of ethical speculation and concretely investigated. It is interesting to know, for example, that the Council for Pure Scientific Research in the Netherlands includes three official representatives of multinational enterprises (Unilever, AKZO, and Philips). In addition, several professors, members of the Council, are consultants to such enterprises. How "pure" is "pure science"? How are decisions about financial allocations made?

An example of research into interests behind scientific research and related activities in Latin America is the work that has been going on for more than five years by the North American Congress on Latin America (NACLA). A group of young social scientists of various disciplines with very few resources is studying and publishing material about the influence of the United States in Latin America. Their publications contain a great deal of material about the "influence structures of economic and political elites," a subject only very recently investigated in the Netherlands and Germany (Mokken and Stockman 1971; Koubek, *et al.* 1972).

In 1970 NACLA published the *NACLA research methodology guide*, which indicates how the power structure can be most fruitfully investigated. In 1977 the booklet *Subliminal warfare: the role of Latin American studies* was issued. It described the relationship between the industrial-military complex and the scholarly centers for Latin American studies.

As regards Asia, a similar group working in the United States issues the *Bulletin of concerned Asian scholars* (1971). This bulletin has dedicated a special issue to analyzing and publicizing the operations of the Center for Vietnamese Studies at Southern Illinois University as part of the Vietnam War effort.

Regarding the role of social research that serves U.S. interests in Africa, the Africa Research Group published a report in 1970, *African studies in America: the extended family (a tribal analysis of U.S. Africanists:*

who they are; why to fight them), with a wealth of material including a short case-study of a refusal to publish research data on American financial interests in Africa by several scholarly journals, including *Human organization* and *Economic development and cultural change* (African Research Group 1970).

It is clear that concerned scholars in the United States are far ahead of those in Europe. I wonder how many ethically concerned European research workers even know the material of their American colleagues and in how many university libraries it is available. An even bigger question is how many European research workers pose themselves serious questions regarding the background of their own grants or regarding subsidizing as such or, the scientific research policy and its background.

THE INTERESTS OF THOSE TO BE INVESTIGATED

If little attention has been given to the interests behind scientific social research, even less is given to the interests of the people who are being investigated. The interests or needs of the objects of research are at the most seen as an interesting aspect of the subject. That the research could possibly serve the interests of the people investigated or even remedy their distress hardly occurs to most social scientists. Such a thing might occur by chance, but generally any interference with the realities under investigation is seen as disturbing or dangerous for the scientific quality of the research.

The Ethical Code of the American Society of Applied Anthropology, written before 1940, emphasized that it was not desirable that anthropologists participate in the change processes of the groups they study. Only during World War II was there considerable deviation from this view, but after the war the old point of view predominated again. This point of view was, as Richard Adams noted (1967), determined by the *laissez-faire* ideology.

If we examine the conditions of exploitation and poverty in which many of the people studied by anthropologists live, it appears just — at least according to common-sense human ethics — to disqualify the laissez-faire type of research, which does not care about the awkward conditions of its object, as asocial, not to say simply immoral.

IS SNOOPING ALLOWED?

The Dutch anthropologist Andre Köbben remarked in a paper (1971) on the relationship between ethics and anthropology that it happens that social researchers are refused admittance because people do not want the "snooper" (and this is what he is basically) to be around, since there are too many things that they prefer remain undiscovered.

With this remark Köbben poses implicitly the ethical problem at times put forward by distrustful peasants or slum dwellers. Instead of the term "snooper" one could also use a term from psychopathology: "voyeur." The ethical dilemma that arises is: should this be allowed at all?

During my twelve-year period in various so-called developing countries, I was confronted several times very concretely with this dilemma. For example: at an agricultural extension meeting in western Sicily the participating peasants bluntly refused to meet any longer when Danilo Dolci, chief of the regional research and development project of which these meetings were part, wanted to tape-record our session. Their argument was: we don't want him to make another book or article showing the whole world how backward and stupid we are. In former years Dolci had widely publicized the backwardness and poverty of western Sicily, as a result of which the project had been initiated. Another example: in an area of Coquimbo province in Chile, peasants were reticent or even hostile toward some Chilean sociologists (guided by an Englishman from the United Nations) until the local leaders had been convinced that the research would be useful in relation to the land reform needed in the area (Huizer 1972: chapter 2).

In order to really understand the problem of snooping we should on the one hand try to see it through the eyes of peasants in a developing country; on the other hand, we could try to imagine a similar situation in which people from the outside world come to investigate *us*. How would we react if an anthropologist from China came to investigate the internal policies of our anthropology or social-research institute, posing questions regarding how decisions are made concerning the program, the research being done, the nomination of professors or assistants, the ranking of staff members, etc. One can imagine, knowing the secrecy that is maintained about such petty rivalries and grudges in our institutes, that snoopers would not be too welcome, maybe even bluntly unwelcome. Are the patronage systems and factional strife in village communities abroad not basically more important to the people involved than is the management of our institute to us? Not to mention such a loaded subject as internal power struggle. I specifically took the example of a Chinese researcher since Köbben in his paper frowned on certain restrictions encountered in China by the Swedish researcher/journalist Jan Myrdal. I can imagine that investigators from China would not be allowed at all into our Western countries. Our understanding of the sensibilities of people in the Third World would increase if we would be more realistic about our own, and we would — consequently — become more modest in our role as snooper in developing countries. Basically, it is surprising that we are allowed there at all.

Ethically one could focus the whole dilemma more sharply and ask where anthropologists find the courage to go snooping in countries where their compatriots in the past and in the present have brought under-development and exploitation. In earlier years and even today some anthropologists have served the colonial regimes or their inheritors and have been well paid for their services. But apart from that, are the inter-esting books that result from the snooping — from the point of view of the people in the underdeveloped countries — not just another way of exploitation: authors trying to become famous and (eventually) well-to-do at the cost of their ignorance? It is a somewhat demagogical question but not completely misplaced, and in any case it is a question that the objects of research sometimes pose. What do they benefit from the dissertations, articles, books, etc., written in a language foreign to them and hidden in academic libraries?

One could probably say that the fact that so many snoopers are still allowed and even kindly received by people in underdeveloped countries is often a consequence of the "culture of repression" in which these people still live.[1] They are accustomed to submit to all that comes from above or from outside, although they may show some resistance, e.g., in giving incorrect answers or by saying what they think outsiders want to hear. Perhaps the fact that peasants and slum dwellers in some countries start to show more open reluctance towards snoopers is a sign of their emancipation and their increasing sense of dignity and resistance against the culture of repression. Maybe anthropologists who are really con-cerned with those whom they want to study and who value highly con-scientization and emancipation of the people should be glad of signs of distrust or resistance shown toward them by their objects.[2]

WHEN CAN SNOOPING BE JUSTIFIED?

Although on the whole it appears difficult to justify the usual forms of snooping by Western social researchers in underdeveloped countries, there may be some reasons that would make certain forms of social research not only acceptable but even desirable. In my opinion these reasons are related to the serving function of the research. At present

[1]   The concept "culture of repression" was developed by Holmberg (1966).
[2]   I am aware that the terms "conscientization" and "emancipation" can easily lead to confusion. They imply a value judgment on what is good for human beings. Conscientization is a term introduced by the Brazilian educator Paolo Freire indicating the raising of people's consciousness about their own generally repressed situation (Freire 1970). The term emancipation as I use it here is best explained by Wertheim (1974).

most *laissez-faire* research serves mainly the academic careers of persons in the highly developed countries, not to mention the research that directly serves the maintenance of the established order and Western interests. Very few cases are known of social research in underdeveloped countries that serve more or less directly the interests of those who are the object of the research, such as peasants, slum dwellers, a minority group, or women (that forgotten group). Of course, one can argue that it is impossible for us to determine what serves the interests of people in underdeveloped countries. This difficulty can be overcome if we try seriously to identify with their way of living and thinking and — together with them — focus on those elements that are important for con- scientization and emancipation.

When speaking about people in underdeveloped countries, a clear distinction should be made between those who are generally the object of investigation, the poor strata of society, and those who are powerful in those countries. It is increasingly clear that the latter category, although they also accuse the Western social scientists of academic colonialism, are often themselves parasites on the majority of their compatriots. The term *internal colonialism* has been introduced in Latin America to indicate this problem.[3] Often the influential groups in underdeveloped countries are more or less direct accomplices of Western interests.

Generally it is not difficult to observe or discover the situation of exploitation or repression in which the majority of people in under- developed countries live, a thing that is important for the ethical position-finding of the Western researcher. Is it not ethically reprehen- sible to remain neutral when you see that there are victims, not only in the statistics of infant mortality and undernourishment but also in the little- known statistics of assassinated peasant- and trade-union leaders, of a situation for which you, as a Westerner, are also responsible?

SELF-EDUCATION OF THE RESEARCHER

One of the most important and highly needed ways to gain knowledge about human beings in our own and other societies is to gain self- knowledge and to recognize our own feelings, desires, grievances, and reactions in those we are studying. Phenomenological methods, iden- tification, empathy, and *Einfühlung* are the professsional terms for this way of gaining knowledge. It could also be simply called solidarity. Try to see the reality of the other persons through their own eyes: including hunger, repression, exploitation, resentment, resistance, and other

---

[3]   The term *internal colonialism* was introduced particularly by the Mexican sociologists Pablo Gonzalez Casanova and Rodolfo Stavenhagen. See for example, Stavenhagen (1970).

phenomena that exist on a large scale in countries where anthropologists prefer to do their research. The effort to understand such phenomena through empathy would contribute considerably to the self-education of many social scientists. It is surprising how much middle-class intellectuals can learn as human beings and gain in common sense by living in and effectively sharing the life of a village or a slum area (or a factory, for that matter).[4]

The benefits of such efforts would become even greater if the researchers would act according to the new understanding they are gaining and would effectively try to support the people they are living with in overcoming their awkward conditions. "Participant observation" may naturally lead to "participant intervention."[5] It can even become full commitment to the emancipatory effort in which those people are or may become involved, the role of "militant cum observer."[6] Thus the laissez-faire anthropology can become "liberation anthropology" (Frank 1969: chapter 7).

THE SCIENTIFIC VALUE OF ACTIVE COMMITMENT

A common objection raised against active involvement of social scientists in the processes or situations they are studying is that this approach distorts the research results and diminishes their scientific value. Against this objection I would argue, from some of my own field experience, that the opposite seems to be the case. Active involvement in the life of the people among whom one is working not only may bring some benefits to those people but also quite valuable scientific insights, at times even insights that are more scientific (or simply truer) than the insights gained through mere observation, snooping, or pure research. Objectivity, as claimed by pure researchers, is not so much a question of detachment from what one studies but rather the distance or detachment that researchers can take from themselves and their personal and cultural biases while they are in the field or writing their observations.

The kind of objectivity generally striven for by social researchers in all kinds of situations, not putting themselves into the game and remaining emotionally aloof or outside at all costs, seems an illusion. It is one of the forms of alienation from which many people in our Western societies seem to suffer. It is also a bad thing for gaining true and relevant scientific

---

[4]   I am speaking here from my own trials and errors described in articles in literary reviews in the Netherlands and in Huizer (1965).
[5]   See Huizer (1965) for a discussion of these research methods. The term *participant intervention* was introduced by Allan Holmberg when describing the well-known Vicos experiment in Peru.
[6]   This term comes from Stavenhagen (1971).

insights. Time and again we see how anthropology remains a Western intellectual effort and therefore subjective. Some classic examples of biased and typically Western research are some of the works of Charles Erasmus, George Foster, and Edward Banfield.[7] The way in which Erasmus and Banfield discuss — or conspicuously neglect — the socialist- or communist-oriented actions of peasants in the areas they studied (northern Mexico and southern Italy respectively), indicates clearly their own political bias and determines to a large extent how their work served the Establishment to which they belonged (Huizer 1972: chapter 3).

The tragic thing is that the research of these and numerous other scholars contains some unscientific and simply wrong conclusions, which create a great deal of misunderstanding about the outlook and attitudes of the poor peasants in the world. The persistency with which such misunderstandings of the peasants and their potential for change of society remain in vogue can probably be explained by the detached and static way in which the peasant population is generally approached by anthropologists. To me it seems that this approach is part of the bias that scientific research cannot coincide with active participation in the change processes that occur in some peasant societies. From my own experience I would say that active involvement in the change processes in peasant societies, and participation in various experiments or occurrences, tends to give a clearer understanding of the potential of peasants for change than mere *laissez-faire* participant observation (Huizer 1972: chapter 2).

It seems that in addition to being — one hopes — helpful to the emancipation or conscientization of the people in underdeveloped countries,[8] and of oneself, active involvement can even serve the cause of science as such.

REORIENTATION OF RESEARCH TOWARD THE OVERALL POWER STRUCTURE

One aspect of the self-education that may follow from active involvement and consequently a deeper understanding of the problems of people in underdeveloped countries has considerable bearing on the whole issue of the ethics of snooping, presently under discussion. The understanding one gets of the obstacles faced by the people and the culture of repression or internal colonialism of which these obstacles are merely an expression

---

[7]   For a critique of some of the theoretical conceptions used by these three social scientists, see Huizer (1972: chapter 3), which is an elaboration of Huizer (1970), and the answers of Erasmus and Foster in the same issue.

[8]   For a discussion of various ways in which social scientists can concretely serve the emancipation or liberation of the people in the underdeveloped countries see Stavenhagen (1971); Frank (1969); and Fals Borda (1972).

gives one almost automatically a better insight into the power structure prevalent in the underdeveloped countries. It is then only a continuation of the line that shows the involvement of our own highly developed countries in the maintenance of this structure. This latter insight may increase the sense of responsibility of Western social scientists for the state of affairs in their home countries, as it relates to that of the people abroad whom they are studying and with whom they sympathize.

As a Dutchman, it is easy to see such links when studying, e.g., peasant settlements in Venezuela in the neighborhood of Maracaibo. The villages contrast strikingly with the neat "concentration camps" of bungalows of the foreign personnel of the oil companies, such as Royal Dutch Shell (*Podium* 1969). Widely publicized figures of profits give further perspective (Shell made three billion Dutch guilders in 1971, of which one-third accrues to Dutch shareholders, more than the whole Netherlands Foreign Aid Program).

The only relevant ethical consequences to be drawn from this knowledge about the interdependence of developed and underdeveloped countries is to get a better understanding of (and eventually control over?) the power elite at home on which the power elite in the underdeveloped countries partly depends. Snooping may thus find another justification if it concerns itself with the power structure that ties the home countries of the researchers to that of their interests. This seems to be a field particularly suited for investigation by ethically concerned social scientists — a field that has been until now too conspicuously neglected.

Richard Adams indicated that the neglect of studying the power structure abroad, in Latin America, found its reason in the ethocentric bias of the Euro-American tradition and is

related to the fact that the very strangeness of the phenomenon has led interpreters to regard it as inexplicable or irrational and as characteristic of a structure that is thought to be immature or underdeveloped. . . . It would not be an exaggeration to say that the entire internal structure of the upper sector is a series of relationships established and altered by virtue of a constant concern for gaining and using power (Adams 1967: 25–26).

But why then are the mature and highly developed power structures of our rich countries not taken into account? Was this mere naïveté (or a middle-class-centric bias, to paraphrase Adams), were social researchers guilty of some kind of self-censorship (to avoid "touchy subjects"), or was it a question of overall scientific research policy (channeling of funds)? As regards the latter point, conscientious social scientists who want to probe into the power structure, which, in the end, also dominates their own lives, may well find that the Establishment at home as well as in the country of study will no longer collaborate with them in the pursuit of knowledge. Freedom of scientific research, however, is as yet sufficiently guaranteed in our countries to make an investigation of the overall power structure, particularly the multinational corporations, feasible for those who are willing to gain such needed knowledge even when they do not get ample funds from established sources. The NACLA effort, mentioned above, is an example. So is the book that reveals for the first time in a systematic way at least some of the most striking aspects of Dutch power in the Third World.[9] If the results of such research are fed back to those in the underdeveloped countries who, for reasons of struggle for emancipation, are interested in them, snooping may become an ethically highly justifiable effort.

Moreover, participation in such efforts can give to scientific research the excitement of detective work in addition to the satisfaction of ethically justified commitment. One wonders why so many social scientists are still following the rule of remaining outsiders to the change processes of the societies they study, whether their own or others. Have not some of the greatest breakthroughs of social science been brought about by Marx and Freud, scholars who were both in a very practical way related to their field of study and who consciously merged theory with practice? This cannot be valid only for the greatest of the social scientists. The time seems to have come when social scientists should leave their ivory tower, as many of them did during World War II[10] in order to contribute to the rescue of the occupied countries. Problems in the underdeveloped countries appear of similar magnitude to those faced by the highly developed countries in those years. The only way to prevent social research, particularly abroad, from remaining asocial, is to strive for a merger of theory and practice at the service of those who are subjected.

REFERENCES

ADAMS, RICHARD N.
1967   *Ethics and the social anthropologist in Latin America.* No. 47 Offprint Series. Institute of Latin American Studies. Austin: University of Texas.
AFRICAN RESEARCH GROUP
1970   *African studies in America: the extended family (a tribal analysis of U.S. Africanists: who they are; why to fight them).* Cambridge, Mass.
Bulletin of Concerned Asian Scholars
1971   February.

[9] See Paërl (1971). This book is the result of the efforts of many volunteers coordinated by Eric Paërl. In Freiburg, West Germany, a group called Informations Zentrum Dritte Welt is producing similar fact-finding studies, e.g., about German investments in Brazil. See also Grosche and Lehmann-Richter (1970).
[10] See also Köbben (1971), who expressed his thankfulness to the U.S. anthropologists who "involved" themselves in the liberation struggle of *those* days.

FALS BORDA, ORLANDO
1972   *Causa popular, ciencia popular. Una metodologia del conocimiento a través de la acción.* Bogotá: Rosca.

FRANK, ANDRÉ GUNDER
1969   *Latin America: underdevelopment or revolution.* New York: Monthly Review Press.

FREIRE, PAOLO
1970   *Pedagogy of the oppressed.* New York: Herder and Herder.

GROSCHE, G., R. LEHMANN-RICHTER
1970   *Die Gewinne aus deutschen Direktinvestitionen in Entwicklungsländer.* Bochum: Institut für Entwicklungsforschung und Entwicklungspolitik der Ruhr-Universität.

HOLMBERG, ALLAN R.
1966   *Some relationship between psychobiological deprivation and culture change in the Andes.* Cornell American Year Conference. Mimeographed.

HOROWITZ, IRVING LOUIS, editor
1967   *The rise and fall of Project Camelot: studies in the relationship between science and practical politics.* Cambridge, Mass.: M.I.T. Press.

HUIZER, GERRIT A.
1965   Evaluating community development at the grassroots: some observations on methodology. *America Indigena* 25(3).
1970   Resistance to change and radical peasant mobilization: Foster and Erasmus reconsidered. *Human Organization* 29(4).
1972   *The revolutionary potential of peasants in Latin America.* Lexington, Mass.: Heath Lexington Books.

KÖBBEN, A.
1971   *Sociale Wetenschappen en Ethiek.* Mimeographed.

KOUBEK, NORBERT, et al.
1972   *Wirtschaftliche Konzentration und gesellschaftlich Machtverteilung in der Bundesrepublik Deutschland.* Serie "Aus Politik und Zeitgeschichte." Bonn: Bundeszentrale für politische Bildung.

MOKKEN, R. J., F.N. STOCKMAN
1971   *Invloedstrukturen van politieke en economische elites in Nederland.* Mimeographed.

NORTH AMERICAN CONGRESS ON LATIN AMERICA
1970   *NACLA research and methodology guide.* New York and Berkeley.
1971   *Subliminal warfare — the role of Latin American studies.* New York and Berkeley.

PAËRL, ERIC
1971   *Nederlandse macht in de derde wereld.* Amsterdam: Van Gennep.

PODIUM
1969   *Podium* (3).

STAVENHAGEN, RODOLFO
1971   Decolonizing applied social sciences. *Human Organization* 30(4): 333ff.

VELIZ, CLAUDIO, editor
1967   *The politics of conformity in Latin America.* London and New York: Oxford University Press.

WERTHEIM, W.F.
1974   *Evolution and revolution.* London: Penguin Books.

WOLF, ERIC, J.G. JORGENSON
1970   Anthropology on the warpath in Thailand. *New York Review of Books.* November 19.
1970   "Classes, colonialism and acculturation," in *Masses in Latin America.* Edited by Irving Horowitz. New York: Oxford University Press.

Alternatives to Ethnocide: Human Zoos, Living Museums, and Real People

JOHN H. BODLEY

The problem of ethnocide, or the forced modification of one culture by another, has again become a topic for anthropological concern. This concern is reflected in recent resolutions by anthropology organizations, the revival of the International Work Group for Indigenous Affairs and the attention ethnocide will receive at the IXth International Congress of Anthropological and Ethnological Sciences. While this new concern is distinctly more humanitarian than the frequently expressed concern for the loss of valuable data or "urgent anthropology," any search for alternatives to ethnocide will be hampered if it fails to consider the question from a viewpoint wider than that of industrial civilization. Significant alternatives might be disregarded if anthropologists do not recognize the bias in their own profession which, as some have recently acknowledged (Lévi-Strauss 1966:126; Gjessing 1968:399), is itself a product of industrial civilization and designed to serve its ends. In an effort to overcome some of this bias and as a stimulus for further discussion, this paper will briefly survey the general anthropological view of ethnocide, attempt to present it in larger perspective, and finally discuss "cultural autonomy" as a radical solution to specific ethnocide problems.

ETHNOCIDE, ACCULTURATION, AND MODERNIZATION

The current use of the term "ethnocide" represents a belated but explicit recognition of the frequently destructive aspects of culture modification policies. Earlier terms such as *acculturation* (Redfield *et al.* 1936) and

This investigation was supported in part by funds provided by the Graduate School Research Funds from the National Science Foundation Institutional Grant through Washington State University.

culture contact were widely used to cover all culture-modification phenomena during the period when anthropologists were most frequently employed by colonial governments and were unanimously taking an ethically neutral position on their work. These terms served to legitimize culture modification as a topic for scientific study and at the same time obscured both the unpleasant side effects of "change" and the actual causal factors involved, while the very neutrality of the terms reinforced a stand of scientific detachment. Enormous research effort has been devoted to acculturation but most anthropologists still scrupulously avoid any sort of value judgment on any aspect of cultural change. During the post-colonial period anthropologists have largely replaced *acculturation* with such terms as *modernization* and *economic development* which, when applied to tribal peoples, refer to essentially the same phenomena, but again continue to obscure many of the realities of the change situation. Steward (1967:16, 20–21) for example, called modernization a value-neutral term, and felt that the causal factors involved were still "not well conceptualized."

STATE ETHNOCIDE POLICIES AND ANTHROPOLOGY

Professing humanitarian motives and concern for progress, industrial states have always assumed that tribal areas must ultimately be fully assimilated or integrated with the national polity and economy at whatever cost to the peoples involved. This fundamental assumption seems to underlie all official state policies toward tribal cultures which are designed to extend administrative control over tribal areas, promote economic development, create national loyalties, and to modify or eliminate any cultural patterns considered as obstacles to these objectives. Expansive modern states have never questioned the ultimate rightness and inevitability of these policies, even though they must often be carried out in the face of obvious resistance. However, such policies are explicitly ethnocentric and must be considered ethnocide whenever they are opposed by tribal peoples. As participants in industrial civilization, anthropologists have directly supported such policies by attempting to reconcile the natives to the "inevitable" loss of their cultures and even by working to speed the process of their destruction. There has also been a clear tendency for anthropologists to disregard their own admonitions concerning ethnocentrism, cultural relativism, and the fundamental right of different life-styles to coexist, and to develop theoretical concepts and arguments that mask the realities of ethnocide.

ANTHROPOLOGICAL ETHNOCENTRISM AND CULTURAL RELATIVITY

Along with other members of industrial civilizations, many anthropologists have often taken the ethnocentric position that tribal cultures must be drastically modified because of their assumed inadequacies. At the same time anthropologists have long recognized the dangers of ethnocentrism, and urged that cultures be evaluated only in their own terms. This conflict places many anthropologists in a moral dilemma which is resolved by assuming an ethically "neutral" position, which has only recently come under attack (Berreman [1968] and Gjessing [1968] for example), or by rejecting cultural relativism as "romanticism." Goodenough (1963:62) considers romanticism to be an over-identification with exotic peoples, or a "private compulsion" that is really ethnocentrism in reverse. Barnett (1956:59–60) calls it a "quixotic fixation," and "emotional investment" which sometimes makes anthropologists object to "tampering with native life and evokes nostalgic laments over its passing." While Murdock (1965:146) dismisses cultural relativism as simply unscientific "sentimental nonsense," many anthropologists consider it a positive hindrance to their profession. Foster (1962:263) complains that "Anthropologists are indoctrinated to see the good in all cultures" and sometimes suffer "nostalgia over vanishing primitives." He advises that applied anthropologists not hesitate in making judgments "on the relative merits of the ways of life of other people" (1969:136), and declares (1962:263) that some cultures may be in such bad shape that "a major cultural overhaul for them would be the best possible thing in the world." Mead (1961:367) has also warned anthropologists against "romanticism" and called cultural relativism an "overstatement." She declares "no forebodings about the effect of destroying old customs" (1961:19–20).

Redfield explicitly proclaims his ethnocentrism as a justification for cultural modification. He finds modern civilization "more decent and humane" (1953:163) than primitive cultures and feels that in view of our more humane standard a cultural-relativist position will be difficult to maintain. After all, Redfield asks, what modern nation could permit its tribal peoples to carry on such inhumane practices as headhunting and cannibalism? According to Redfield, anthropologists were greatly relieved when the United Nations statement on human rights did not follow a strictly relativist position, thereby leaving nations free to suppress "disgusting" native customs. Unfortunately for tribal peoples, this "more humane standard" has been applied in a variety of ways even by other anthropologists to justify the abolition of various cultural traits. Elwin (1959:250–251), for example, would interfere with customs that were "clearly and unnecessarily impoverishing the people," while ideally,

British colonial policy would only allow customs to exist if "compatible with justice, humanity and good government" (Lindley 1926:375). In many areas the "standard" has been stretched to its logical extreme, as for example in Australian New Guinea where:

The political autonomy, economic habits, religious practices, and sexual customs of organized native groups, in so far as they threaten European control or offend Western notions or morality, must be abandoned (Reed 1943:xvii).

Tribal cultures have been variously described by anthropologists as "backward" and "retarded" (Kroeber 1948), or simply "inferior" (Pitt-Rivers 1927:17), while the not-uncommon belief that tribal peoples are "sick" or mentally incompetent also finds support in the anthropological literature. Kroeber, for example, states:

When the sane and well in one culture believe what only the most ignorant, warped, and insane believe in another, there would seem to be some warrant for rating the first culture lower and the second higher (Kroeber 1948:298).

Other anthropologists (Arensberg and Niehoff 1964:4–6) refer to economic "underdevelopment" as a "sickness," speak of the "medicine of social change" and compare change agents to brain surgeons. Tribal economic systems are criticized more severely than virtually any other aspect of tribal culture. In spite of abundant evidence to the contrary, many anthropologists still feel that tribal economies are so unproductive and technologically inadequate that they are barely able to support life. Levin and Potapov (1964:488–499) called the hunting and fishing economies of Siberia "a very poor support for life," and others have emphasized the assumed "precariousness" of tribal economies (Nash 1966:22) or the "ever-present threat of starvation" (Dalton 1971:27). One anthropologist even speaks of raising a tribal economy "up to the subsistence level" (Elwin 1959:76).

THE INEVITABILITY ARGUMENT

Perhaps the strongest bias with which anthropologists view ethnocide is the familiar assumption that it is natural, inevitable, and probably even beneficial. This position seems to be almost unanimously accepted by anthropologists today and presents a serious obstacle to any real search for alternatives to ethnocide. Anthropological pronouncements on the "inevitable fate" of "primitive" cultures are virtually indistinguishable from similar statements made over the years by political leaders, development experts, and missionaries. We are told by anthropologists, for example, that the disappearance of traditional tribal life "simply seems to be an inevitable process" (Berndt 1963:394), or that "changes can not be prevented" (Elkin 1946). Some speak of tribal disruption as the "inevitable logic of events" (Manndorff 1967:530), "facts of life" (Huff 1967:480), or "destiny" (Hoernle 1934).

The forced modification of tribal cultures is still justified by anthropologists as a case of "survival of the fittest" in which maladapted cultures, those "out of harmony with the modern setting" (Keesing and Keesing 1941:259), or possessing a "life style which flies in the face of world trends" (Cunnison 1967:9), must either be changed or eliminated. This argument basically does not differ from the characteristic views of colonial writers who called tribal peoples "feeble survivals of an obsolete world" (Merivale 1861:510), who were "doomed to elimination" (Maunier 1949:716), and who must either "perish, or be amalgamated" (Merivale 1861:510). The same opinion is expressed by a recent writer on economic development: "Perhaps entire societies will lack survival value and vanish before the onslaught of industrialization" (Goulet 1971:266). Pitt-Rivers represents a British functionalist who supported this view. He spoke (1927:2) of the "rigid and ruthless process of selection" which operated in the culture contact situation and favored "higher" cultures over "lower." More recent anthropologists continue to support this view, as for example Ribeiro (1967:115–116) who tells us that Brazilian Indian cultures "represent obsolescences in modern Brazil"; they are "anachronisms . . . whose coexistence with an ever more homogeneous industrial civilization is not feasible." While the American applied anthropologists Arensberg and Niehoff (1964:58) merely assure us that "people of different cultures are always in competition" and that superior technologies always conquer, modern evolutionary anthropologists following Leslie White's lead have elaborated "The Law of Cultural Dominance" to account for the "inevitable" disappearance of tribal cultures:

> . . . that cultural system which more effectively exploits the energy resources of a given environment will tend to spread in that environment at the expense of less effective systems (Kaplan 1960:75).

Most anthropologists still probably agree with Elwin (1959:59–60) that they do not want to stop the "clock of progress," and feel strongly that traditional cultures must make way for progressive evolutionary trends toward world cultural homogeneity which are considered to be "natural and necessary trends in human progress" (Ribeiro 1970).

There can be no disagreement with the fact that historically the expansion of industrial civilization has been at the expense of less-powerful cultures, and it can be granted that tribal cultures are not at the same level of evolutionary complexity and energy consumption as industrial civilization, but we need not agree that therefore *all* cultures must inevitably follow these trends or even that it is beneficial that they do so. Progressive trends certainly occur in biological evolution without the loss of simpler forms, and likewise simpler cultures may not be "predestined" to extinction merely because they can be modified at will by an evolutionarily more "advanced" culture. The inevitability argument may well have become a self-fulfilling prophecy which has prevented serious consideration of alternatives to tribal extermination.

ETHNOCIDE AS RESOURCE EXPLOITATION

If examined in perspective, the disappearance of tribal cultures over much of the world in the past 150 years can be seen as the direct result of government policies designed to facilitate the exploitation of tribal resources for the benefit of industrial civilization. When viewed in this manner, rather than in terms of ethnocentric appeals to "inevitable progress" or evolutionary trends, the immediate causes of ethnocide become more apparent and possible alternatives become more realistic.

A wide comparative view of the official tribal policies of socialist, capitalist, and newly independent nations will show that more efficient exploitation of tribal resources has always been a prime concern of governments. In this regard, "tribal resources" must be interpreted to include not only tribal land, minerals, and other natural resources, but also tribal peoples themselves who have been considered valuable "human resources" for cheap labor, markets, military manpower, tax-paying citizens, religious converts, and material for research projects and museums. Government concern for more efficient tribal exploitation can be seen first of all in official policies which have promoted "uncontrolled frontiers" where private citizens were permitted to harvest tribal resources without legal restrictions and at little government expense. When this process met tribal resistance, governments resorted to military force and extended administrative control over formerly independent tribal regions so that resource exploitation could continue through legal means and at greater rates. "Administration," whether by "direct" or "indirect" rule, destroyed tribal sociopolitical autonomy and brought further measures that undermined their economic independence. Once under political control, tribal peoples were taxed and "educated" to create "new needs" and thereby encouraged to participate further in the national economy. More direct measures included official decrees requiring labor or the planting of cash crops, and the creation of "native reserves" designed to be inadequate to support the traditional economy. More recent measures are usually called "economic development" and involve many more forms of direct force and subtle persuasion to reach the same goals.

The critical significance of these policies is that they create conditions under which a tribal life-style can no longer be a viable alternative for those wishing to pursue it. On the contrary, in the absence of government policies to promote the exploitation of tribal resources, there is abundant evidence that tribal cultures can maintain contacts with other cultures on their own terms and still retain their own viability. There are many examples of cultures that have been in continuous communication with "higher" cultures, and merely borrowed selectively from them.

These facts must be emphasized because many anthropologists and development experts still argue from the ethnocentric position that mere *contact* with a "superior" culture will cause tribal societies to reject their own cultures voluntarily. Then, assuming that it would not be possible to maintain any people in *total* isolation, ethnocide could therefore never be prevented.

According to this "demonstration effects" view, all people share our desire for material wealth and "prosperity" and have different cultures only because they have not yet been exposed to industrial civilization. The availability of the "better life" results in the "self-destruction" of traditional cultures, and "ethnocide" in the usual sense would therefore rarely occur at all. This position is clear in the writings of many development anthropologists (e.g., Foster 1969; Goodenough 1963; Arensberg and Niehoff 1964; Dalton 1971), and is represented in the following statements:

... men in every culture harbor unexpressed wishes to have more in order to be more. Once it becomes evident to them that it is possible to desire more, they will, by and large, want more ... (Goulet 1971:76).

The structure of traditional village society becomes undermined because its traditional functions become displaced once superior economic and technological alternatives become available (Dalton 1971:29).

These arguments serve as rationalization for what is still essentially a process of "conquest" in which a single technologically powerful culture type forces other less-powerful cultures to comply with its wishes.

ETHNOCIDE, ECOCIDE, AND RELATIVE DEPRIVATION

Ethnocide resulting directly in large-scale depopulation would not normally be defended as acceptable culture-change policy today, but other long-range consequences of cultural modification which cannot always be foreseen but which may be fully as serious are still being disregarded. Attempts to prevent ethnocide continue to be opposed as the romanticizing of traditional culture and undue emphasis on the detrimental effects of cultural modification. We are told that "sentimental considerations must not be allowed to become an obstacle in the path of progress of indigenous peoples" (Métraux 1953:884), and cautioned against placing "undue stress" (Reed 1943:258) on the disintegrating effects of change. However, we are also warned that people should not suffer too much, or pay too high a price for progress, while it is frequently admitted that "progress" may not even make people "happy." It is felt that they must at least be made to think that, whatever the cost, progress will be desirable. As a recent government report from Papua-New Guinea, stated:

... there remains the task of awakening in the people such a desire for progress that they will be prepared to pay the price of major social change (Australia n.d.: 3).

Promoters of cultural modification evidently consider themselves competent to evaluate whether or not change will be worth the unknown "costs" that it is certain to involve, but it now seems particularly urgent to reassess the "price" of cultural modification in view of recent concern for overpopulation, resource depletion, and environmental deterioration. At the same time, economists warn that world development goals may well be unrealizable or may benefit only a small segment of any population (Ward et al. 1971). Anthropologists have long realized many of these problems, but have failed to take them seriously. Now it may not be considered too cynical or romantic to suggest that very often tribal peoples have been forced to accept unreachable goals, whose pursuit may in the long run bring more hardship than those goals originally promised to alleviate.

Tribal peoples have been quick to recognize the price of "progress," but have been powerless to do anything about it. In 1948 the Maya villagers of Chan Kom complained to Redfield (1962) over the shortening of their swidden cycles, which they realized was the direct result of population increase due to new health measures. They also complained that the new roads made them poor because of unfulfilled new "needs." Population pressure on Tikopia in the thirties prompted the Tikopians to suggest to Firth that infanticide be legalized (Keesing and Keesing 1941:64–65). Some tribal writers have recently observed that environmental pollution may eventually invalidate treaties containing such phrases as "as long as the grass shall grow."

Ecological stability may well prove to be the most costly price tribal peoples will pay for cultural "progress." While no one would argue that all tribal cultures were in complete harmony with their environments, it must be acknowledged that tribal cultures are generally characterized by distinctive features which are notably absent from industrial civilization and which contribute to ecological stability. Among these features are: (1) a world view that makes man part of nature in contrast to the view that he must conquer nature (Meggers 1971:1–2; White 1966); (2) a "limited good" concept (Foster 1969:83) which kept wants from going unfulfilled and prevented relative deprivation; (3) wealth-leveling devices, which in combination with a "limited good" concept lead to "no-growth" economies; and (4) local self-sufficiency, which as Rappaport (1971) and Meggers (1971:151–152) point out, prevents forces from being applied in local ecosystems which will be unresponsive to changes in those systems. As might be expected, all of these features are considered "obstacles to progress" by applied anthropologists and are slated for drastic modification. When these and other stabilizing factors are weakened, the way is opened for perpetual relative deprivation (i.e., "poverty") and rapid environmental deterioration. As wants and population increase, the resource base dwindles and people soon discover that the new goals that have been forced upon them remain just out of reach and are becoming progressively more difficult to reach. They are then told that they must abandon even more of their culture and that they have "no choice but to go forward with technology" as Redfield told the people of Chan Kom (1962). We should not be surprised that tribal peoples often feel angry and frustrated over the results of culture modification, and that as one observer from New Guinea has recently pointed out: "Inevitably they blame the purveyors of industrial civilization for their troubles" (Distroff 1971:39–40).

THE INTEGRATION ALTERNATIVE

Over the past 150 years modern nations have consistently advocated the incorporation of tribal peoples into state political systems, and what may be called an "integration" policy is the only alternative to ethnocide that has ever been generally acceptable to anthropologists. This approach calls for the transformation of independent tribal populations into ethnic minorities within a nation, the goal being to institute "progressive" change, which ideally would be freely chosen by the population. In fact, the actual wishes of the people involved are completely immaterial. Integration policies usually anticipate the eventual loss of ethnic distinctions and in practice often merge imperceptibly into assimilation policies. Clearly this approach does not reject the necessity for cultural modification, and to the extent that coercion is involved it would condone partial ethnocide while leaving open the possibility of any ultimate retention of ethnic identity. In effect, "integration" as an official state cultural-modification policy is not a real alternative to ethnocide at all, in spite of its wide acceptance and long history.

Since the early nineteenth century native peoples have generally been treated as "wards" of the state to be protected and gradually "improved" (i.e., integrated) by their guardians regardless of their possible wishes. For example, when British humanists became alarmed over the extermination of native populations in the wake of colonization, the 1836 House of Commons Select Committee on Aborigines was called upon to recommend ways to "promote the spread of civilization" and the "voluntary reception" of Christianity among tribal peoples with "justice and protection of their rights" (British Parliamentary Papers 1836:iii). The possibility that the natives might not desire "civilization" was apparently never seriously considered. Most individual nations took similar positions on their respective "native problems" and various international organizations have supported them. One of the earliest international statements of this type occurs in the *General Act* of the Berlin Africa Conference of 1884–1885 which calls on the fifteen signatory powers to support organizations designed for educating the natives "and bringing home to them the blessings of civilization." The Brussels Act of 1892, in article 2, called on the powers "to raise them [African tribal peoples] to civilization and bring about the extinction of barbarous customs." Similar views are expressed in the 1919 League of Nations Covenant (article 22) which gave "advanced nations" responsibility for "peoples not yet able to stand by themselves under the strenuous conditions of the modern world," thereby placing many tribal peoples officially under "tutelage" as "a sacred trust of civilization." Under the 1945 United Nations Charter, many of these same tribal peoples were identified as "peoples who have not yet attained a full measure of self-government" and their "advancement" was to be promoted by their guardians by "constructive measures of development" (Articles 73 and 76 United Nations Charter).

When discussing possible alternatives to ethnocide anthropologists usually set total *isolation* and no change on one side and complete *assimilation* on the other as the unacceptable extremes, and then support *integration* as a moderate middle position and the only rational alternative. Isolation is vigorously rejected as immoral and impossible, while assimilation is considered undesirable only if hurried too fast, and is expected to be the probable outcome of change in the long run. The middle course of integration has been in anthropological favor since at least the turn of the century when "indirect rule" began to be advocated as scientifically sound administrative policy. By 1929 Malinowski (1929:3) felt that indirect rule was supported by "all competent anthropologists" as the best means for "the control of Natives." Indirect rule has frequently developed into a policy of "selective emphasis" (Keesing and Keesing 1941:81–95) of tribal culture, or "growth from within" (Elwin 1959) which would at least temporarily preserve what is thought to be the best from the traditional culture and promises to combine "the best of both worlds," as in South Africa where:

The aim . . . is to take from the Bantu past what is "good" and, together with what is "good" for the Bantu in European culture, build up a new distinctive culture (Schapera 1934:x).

As Elwin (1959:44) puts it:

We believe that we can bring them the best things of our world without destroying the nobility and the goodness of their's.

In the northeast frontier areas of India this approach has been applied in its most extreme form to purposefully create pleasing, tailor-made cultures. Very careful cultural modification policies were instituted under Elwin's guidance aimed at improving the "quality of human beings," bringing "*more* colour," "*more* beauty," and "a wider view and a purer conception of God and man" (Elwin 1959:136, 215–216). Of course, at the same time these tribal peoples were urged to become loyal Indian citizens and participants in industrial civilization. Where selective emphasis has been applied in other areas, it has been widely criticized as an attempt to keep the natives backward and subservient (Keesing and Keesing 1941:81–95; Mead 1961:369) and thereby facilitate their exploitation. At the present time most "realistic" anthropologists, concerned over possible racism charges, seem much less concerned with preserving and improving elements of tribal cultures, and instead appear to favor letting economic development follow its "natural and inevitable" course from integration to eventual full assimilation, because this is thought to be truly in the best interests of tribal peoples. The only difficulty with such a view is that it disregards the rights of the peoples really concerned to make the basic decisions.

Throughout the integration process "free choice" is generally called for. We are told for example that "choices must lie with the indigenous people themselves" and:

. . . it is the responsibility of the governing people, through schools and other means, to make available to the native an adequate understanding of non-native systems of life so that these can be ranged alongside his own in order that his choices may be made. (Keesing and Keesing 1941:84, citing the "pragmatic" view of a 1935 international seminar on education in colonial dependencies.)

Even the 1968 IUAES Resolution on Forced Acculturation calls for "just and scientifically enlightened programs of acculturation which allow the peoples concerned a free and informed basis for choice" (Sturtevant 1967:160). We are not told what to do in cases involving small, truly isolated tribal societies, such as those in Amazonia which are attempting to avoid contact with civilization and where the degree of contact necessary to provide them "a free and informed basis for choice" would unavoidably overwhelm them. In practice, of course, it becomes clear that there is really only one choice presently allowed to tribal people. Bulmer (1971:18), for example, warns against doing anything that would prevent New Guinea tribal peoples from "exercising to the greatest extent possible their free choice in joining the modern world," and Métraux (1953) tells us that the members of any culture have the right to reject it outright "if they think fit." Tribal peoples are only given freedom to choose "progress":

For practical purposes, societies have little choice but to come to terms with development: they simply are not free to reject it outright (Goulet 1971:93).

I take it for granted that in a complex society and a complex world it is utopian and unrealistic to assume that people can live without intervention (Foster 1969:174–175).

Like a clever advertising agency for industrial civilization, much of applied anthropology has been devoted to supporting cultural modification policies with the techniques necessary to make sure that tribal peoples make the only correct choice. Change agents are advised to destroy self-esteem and create dissatisfactions among people so that they will come to desire change (Goodenough 1963:219) which of course "must be accepted voluntarily" (Arensberg and Niehoff 1964:3). This scientific "get the natives to do it to themselves" approach was anticipated by earlier colonial authorities:

By teaching and education you may subtly incline the natives to give up their ancient traditions without their feeling that they have done so under pressure (Maunier 1949:506).

Anthropologists apparently continue to assume that those in other cultures realize their "obsolescence" and "inferiority" and eagerly desire progress toward the "better life" as defined by industrial civilization. Anthropologists seem unable to recognize the ethnocentrism and hypocrisy of the "choice" argument that permits only one choice. It is forgotten that peoples who have already chosen their major cultural patterns, and who have spent generations tailoring them to local conditions, may not even wish to consider adopting another life-style.

THE CULTURAL AUTONOMY ALTERNATIVE

While discussing a specific ethnocide problem in Amazonia I (Bodley 1972) recently called for government support of tribal efforts to retain a traditional life-style. It was proposed that development programs and other outside intrusion into traditional areas be halted, and that official recognition be given to tribal rights to land and continued cultural autonomy. This radical proposal, which could be called the *cultural-autonomy* alternative, might perhaps be extended to specific ethnocide problems in many parts of the world. The cultural-autonomy solution would specifically recognize a tribal culture's right to remain permanently outside of any state political structure and to reject further "development" along the lines that would otherwise be forced upon it by outside powers. Three specific points are involved:

(1)   the recognition and support, by national governments and international organizations, of tribal rights to traditional land, cultural autonomy, and full local sovereignty;

(2)   the responsibility for initiating outside contacts must rest with the tribal people themselves: outside influences may not have free access to tribal areas;

(3)   industrial states must not compete with tribal societies for their resources.

In actual application this proposal will undoubtedly involve many serious difficulties which cannot be discussed in detail here, but will need to be treated individually with reference to specific cases. However, broad outlines for its operation can be suggested. Cultural autonomy would perhaps best be implemented through the United Nations, which would be authorized to designate Tribal Autonomous Regions to be permanently withdrawn from the sovereignty of the nations which now happen to claim control over them. Border defense would be handled by international peacekeeping forces and health assistance could be supplied to tribal peoples requesting it by the World Health Organization. While many criticisms will be raised against a cultural-autonomy approach, it seems to offer the only clear alternative to ethnocide and if put into effect would permit many tribal peoples to carry on their traditional life-styles.

The cultural-autonomy alternative has been consistently misunderstood and rejected by anthropologists who have obscured it under the misleading category of "isolation policies" where it could be ridiculed with false emotional arguments about "human zoos" and "living museums." As a so-called human-zoo policy, cultural autonomy has been criticized as "sheer cruelty" (Williams-Hunt 1952:79) because it would "deny them the chance to progress"; and has been labeled "inhuman and inefficient" and "morally wrong" because it would perpetuate famine, disease, and ignorance (Goulet 1971:208, 249); and a "retrograde step" that would stifle "the right of people to mould their lives according to their light" (Ghurye 1963:193, 172–173). It has also been called simply "impossible" (Elwin 1959:59) and those who would propose it are accused of not believing the tribals capable of "advance" or wishing to keep them in their place, or else their sanity is questioned and they are accused of other inhuman motives:

No reasonable person could suppose that it would be possible to turn vast areas of the world into preserves for the protection of native cultures (Métraux 1953: 883–884).

No sane, humane and well-informed scientist or scholar could possibly argue that in the interests of the ethnological or cultural record any part of New Guinea should be preserved as a cultural museum or human zoo . . . (Bulmer 1971:18).

In the first place it must be emphasized that cultural autonomy would permit tribal peoples to choose the degree of isolation they wished to maintain; it would not lock them in cages. It could hardly be considered a human-zoo approach unless people were deliberately confined against their will for display and scientific observation. Such criticisms might be expected from those who have difficulty viewing different cultures as something other than objects for study and who are too ethnocentric to recognize that other peoples might actually wish to maintain their own life-styles.

Some will feel that the principle of cultural autonomy may have merit, but that it is too late to apply "because of potent changes in native life and desires" (Keesing and Keesing 1941:81–82). This argument about the supposed futility of attempting to "turn back the hands of the clock" (Smith 1934) has been used for years, even when there were still very large populations of essentially "untouched" tribal peoples. In 1956 Barnett (1956:62) stated that anthropologists "appreciate the futility of advocating a restoration of an extinct way of life." That may be, but the critical question is: at what point are changes caused by outside intrusion irreversible? It must not be forgotten that there are numerous examples of people "reverting" to traditional patterns even after major changes have occurred. This was the case, for example, in many areas of the Pacific when people were forced to rely on their subsistence economies during the economic depression of the thirties (Thompson 1940:92); in the Philippines when political upheaval left tribal peoples on their own (Keesing and Keesing 1934:74); in the Peruvian Amazon when in 1742 the Campa revolted after intensive Franciscan domination and were left to enjoy more than a hundred years of full autonomy (Bodley 1970:3–7); or in the recent case of Canadian Cree "returning to nature" (*Akwesasne Notes* 1972). Judging from these and other similar cases, it might be well to let tribal peoples decide for themselves when their way of life is "extinct."

Those who recognize the validity of a cultural-autonomy approach, but who argue that it would be impossible or impractical to carry out, may be reminded that it has already been applied in a de facto fashion in several parts of the world in recent times. Any areas that have effectively remained outside of government control either because they were too remote or because they contained no valuable resources are, de facto, Tribal Autonomous Regions. Cultural autonomy has also at least temporarily been official policy in some areas, as for example the "inner line policy" of the British in the northeast frontier areas of India (Elwin

1961:43–44); the "uncontrolled areas" policy in Australian New Guinea (Reed 1943:168–169); and the 1822 Native Code of Czarist Russia, which provided a category for Siberian tribal peoples "not completely dependent on the government" (Levin and Potapov 1964:804). When autonomy has been official policy, it has only existed for a limited time and for the convenience of the state. These examples demonstrate, however, that tribal autonomy is neither impossible nor impractical when it is thought desirable.

Another line of argument which has been raised against the cultural-autonomy approach would deny the uniqueness of tribal peoples. According to this view, tribal peoples are no different from any other citizens and should deserve no special treatment. This may be expressed as: "None of the present day needs of Aboriginals are exceptionally 'special'" (Barnes 1968:46), or as in the following reference to a small group of hunter-gatherers in Borneo:

However, at no time have the most "primitive" Punan nomads been treated as a special class of person. They are just inland citizens, with allowances made for the facts of remoteness (Harrison 1967:345).

This kind of argument is a complete denial of the true uniqueness of tribal peoples, and of their right to be different. Some will no doubt argue further that a major weakness of the cultural-autonomy policy is that tribes have never existed in isolated pristine purity. Ghurye (1963:169) takes this view and others agree. Kunstadter (1967:42) argues that the traditional model of tribal society which emphasized uniqueness, isolation, stability, and homogeneity "is no longer acceptable." He feels that minorities are not defined by cultural differences, but rather by *"the patterns of relationship with dominant majorities."* This position sounds very much like the old French colonial method of abolishing tribes by denying their existence:

French courts laid down that the tribes were in no sense collective bodies as understood by French law; consequently they possessed no personality; from a legal point of view, they did not exist (Maunier 1949:572).

The important point that must not be forgotten is that tribal societies are composed of *real* people who are pursuing a unique life-style which they have given every indication they wish to continue to pursue. They should have that alternative.

Perhaps the most important reason for a cultural-autonomy approach, however, is not simply that many tribal peoples have shown repeatedly by their actions that that is what they desire; it may well be that real global cultural diversity will be as critical for the long-run survival of mankind as some suggest (Meggers 1971:166; Watt 1972; Dubos 1965; Rappaport 1971). This argument must be taken with special seriousness now that cultures which specifically reject many of the values resulting in our present worldwide environmental problems are themselves to disappear. We should not forget Tax's recent warning:

I am certain that there is something for us . . . industrialists to learn from the values associated with the tribal life and with the determination of these peoples to preserve this way of life at all costs (Tax 1968:345–346).

If industrial civilization cannot exploit tribal cultures without destroying them and degrading their environments, then perhaps it should leave alone those that remain. Anthropologists, at least, might do well to acknowledge their complicity in the destruction of tribal cultures, and to re-examine the question of alternatives. We might remember that even Alan Holmberg came to regret his "adventures in culture change" with the Siriono:

Today I am frequently disturbed by the fact that I had a hand in initiating some of the changes which probably ultimately overwhelmed them and over which neither I nor they had control. Indeed, when I contemplate what I did, I am not infrequently filled with strong feelings of guilt. *Maybe they should have been left as they were* (Holmberg 1954:113, emphasis added).

REFERENCES

Akwesasne Notes
   1972   Back-to-wild movement attracting more native people in Alberta. *Akwesasne Notes* 4(3):36.
ARENSBERG, CONRAD M., ARTHUR H. NIEHOFF
   1964   *Introducing social change: a manual for Americans overseas.* Chicago: Aldine.
AUSTRALIA
   n.d.   *Report for 1967–1968.* Department of Territories, Territory of Papua.
BARNES, JOHN A.
   1968   Australian aboriginals? or aboriginal Australians? *New Guinea* 3(1): 43–47.
BARNETT, HOMER G.
   1956   *Anthropology in administration.* New York: Row, Peterson and Company.
BERNDT, RONALD M.
   1963   "Groups with minimal European associations," in *Australian aboriginal studies.* Edited by Helen Sheils, 385–408. New York: Oxford University Press.
BERREMAN, GERALD D.
   1968   Is anthropology alive? *Current Anthropology* 9:391–396.
BODLEY, JOHN H.
   1970   *Campa socio-economic adaptation.* Ann Arbor: University microfilms.
   1972   *Tribal survival in the Amazon: the Campa case.* International Work Group for Indigenous Affairs. Document 5.

BRITISH PARLIAMENTARY PAPERS
1836 *Report from the select committee on aborigines* (British settlements). Imperial Blue Book, volume eight, p. 538.
BULMER, RALPH
1971 Conserving the culture: an institute of New Guinea studies. *New Guinea* 6(2):17–26.
CUNNISON, IAN
1967 *Nomads and the nineteen-sixties.* Hull: Hull University.
DALTON, GEORGE
1971 *Economic development and social change: the modernization of village communities.* Garden City: Natural History Press.
DISTROFF
1971 The confusion of cultures: if prosperity is the objective then something has to give. *New Guinea* 6(4):39–42.
DUBOS, RENE
1965 *Man adapting.* New Haven: Yale University Press.
ELKIN, A.P.
1946 Conservation of aboriginal peoples whose modes of life are of scientific interest. *Man* 46(81):94–96.
ELWIN, VERRIER
1959 *A philosophy for NEFA* (second edition). Shillong: J.N. Chowdhury.
1961 *Nagaland.* Shillong: P. Dutta.
FOSTER, GEORGE M.
1962 *Traditional cultures, and the impact of technological change.* New York: Harper and Row.
1969 *Applied anthropology.* Boston: Little, Brown.
GHURYE, G.A.
1963 *The scheduled tribes* (third edition). Bombay: G.R. Bhatkal.
GJESSING, GUTORM
1968 The social responsibility of the social scientist. *Current Anthropology* 9(5):397–402.
GOODENOUGH, WARD H.
1963 *Cooperation in change.* New York: John Wiley and Sons.
GOULET, DENIS
1971 *The cruel choice: a new concept in the theory of development.* New York: Atheneum.
HARRISON, TOM
1967 "Tribes, minorities, and the central government in Sarawak," in *Southeast Asian tribes, minorities, and nations.* Edited by Peter Kunstadter, 317–352. Princeton: Princeton University Press.
HOERNLE, R.R. ALFRED
1934 "Race-mixture and native policy in South Africa," in *Western civilization and the natives of South Africa.* Edited by I. Schapera, 263–281. London: George Routledge and Sons.
HOLMBERG, ALAN
1954 "Adventures in culture change," in *Method and perspective in anthropology.* Edited by R.F. Spencer, 103–113. Minneapolis: University of Minnesota Press.
HUFF, LEE W.
1967 "The Thai mobile development unit program," in *Southeast Asian tribes, minorities, and nations.* Edited by Peter Kunstadter, 425–486. Princeton: Princeton University Press.

KAPLAN, DAVID
1960   "The law of cultural dominance," in *Evolution and culture*. Edited by Marshall E. Sahlins and Elman R. Service, 69–92. Ann Arbor: University of Michigan Press.

KEESING, FELIX M., MARIE KEESING
1934   *Taming Philippine headhunters: a study of government and of cultural change in northern Luzon*. London: George Allen and Unwin.
1941   *The South Seas in the modern world*. Institute of Pacific Relations International Research Series. New York: John Day.

KROEBER, A.L.
1948   *Anthropology*. New York: Harcourt, Brace and World.

KUNSTADTER, PETER
1967   *Southeast Asian tribes, minorities, and nations*. Princeton: Princeton University Press.

LEVIN, M.G., L.P. POTAPOV
1964   *The peoples of Siberia*. Chicago: University of Chicago Press.

LÉVI-STRAUSS, CLAUDE
1966   Anthropology: its achievements and future. *Current Anthropology* 7:124–127.

LINDLEY, M.F.
1926   *The acquisition and government of backward territory in international law*. London: Longmans, Green and Company.

MALINOWSKY, BRONISLAW
1929   Practical anthropology. *Africa* 2(1):22–38.

MANNDORFF, HANS
1967   "The hill tribe program of the Public Welfare Department, Ministry of Interior, Thailand: research and socio-economic development," in *Southeast Asian tribes, minorities, and nations*. Edited by Peter Kunstadter, 525–552. Princeton: Princeton University Press.

MAUNIER, RENE
1949   *The sociology of colonies*, volume two. London: Routledge and Kegan Paul.

MEAD, MARGARET
1961   *New lives for old*. New York: New American Library.

MEGGERS, BETTY J.
1971   *Amazonia: man and culture in a counterfeit paradise*. Chicago: Aldine.

MERIVALE, HERMAN
1861   *Lectures on colonization and colonies*. London: Green, Longman and Roberts.

MÉTRAUX, ALFRED
1953   "Applied anthropology in government: United Nations," in *Anthropology today*. Edited by Alfred Kroeber, 880–894. Chicago: University of Chicago Press.

MURDOCK, GEORGE P.
1965   *Culture and society*. Pittsburgh: University of Pittsburgh Press.

NASH, MANNING
1966   *Primitive and peasant economic systems*. San Francisco: Chandler.

PITT-RIVERS, GEORGE H.
1927   *The clash of culture and the contact of races*. London: George Routledge.

RAPPAPORT, ROY A.
1971   The flow of energy in an agricultural society. *Scientific American* 224(3):117–132.

REDFIELD, ROBERT
1953   *The primitive world and its transformations.* Ithaca: Cornell University Press.
1962   *A village that chose progress.* Chicago: University of Chicago Press.

REDFIELD, ROBERT, RALPH LINTON, M.H. HERSKOVITS
1936   Memorandum on the study of acculturation. *American Anthropologist* 38:149–152.

REED, STEPHEN W.
1943   *The making of modern New Guinea.* Philadelphia: The American Philosophical Society.

RIBEIRO, DARCY
1967   "Indigenous cultures and languages in Brazil," in *Indians of Brazil in the twentieth century.* Edited by Janice H. Hopper, 77–165. ICR Studies 2. Washington, D.C.: Institute for Cross-Cultural Research.
1970   Précis of *The civilization process. Current Anthropology* 11(4–5): 419–421.

SCHAPERA, I.
1934   *Western civilization and the natives of South Africa.* London: George Routledge and Sons.

SMITH, EDWIN W.
1934   Anthropology and the practical man. *Journal of the Royal Anthropological Institute* 64:xxxiv–xxxvi.

STEWARD, JULIAN
1967   *Contemporary change in traditional societies.* Urbana: University of Illinois Press.

STURTEVANT, WILLIAM C.
1967   Urgent anthropology: Smithsonian-Wenner-Gren conference. *Current Anthropology* 8(4):355–361.

TAX, SOL
1968   "Discussion," in *Man the hunter.* Edited by Richard B. Lee and Irven De Vore, 345–346. Chicago: Aldine.

THOMPSON, L.
1940   *Fijian frontier.* New York: Institute of Pacific Relations.

WARD, BARBARA, J.D. RUNNALS, LENORE D'ANJOU, *editors*
1971   *The widening gap: development in the 1970's.* New York: Columbia University Press.

WATT, KENNETH E.F.
1972   Man's efficient rush toward deadly dullness. *Natural History* 81(2): 74–82.

WHITE, LYNN
1966   "The historical roots of our ecological crisis." Paper presented at the 133rd meeting of the American Association for the Advancement of Science.

WILLIAMS-HUNT, P.D.R.
1952   *An introduction to the Malayan aborigines.* Kuala Lumpur: Government Press.

SECTION THREE

The Multinational Corporation and Social Change

The Social Responsibility of Anthropological Science in the Context of Contemporary Brazil

SHELTON H. DAVIS

> SUPYSAÚA is an expression in nheêngatú (Tupi) that means "the truth, only the truth."
>
> FUNDAÇÃO NACIONAL DO INDIO OF BRAZIL (1970)

Over the past fifteen years, a number of reports have documented the tragic, but systematic, extermination of Indian peoples and tribes in Brazil (Fuerst 1972). The first major analysis of the failures of Brazilian Indian policy, in spite of its internationally recognized humane objectives, was a 1957 article by Darcy Ribeiro. Ten years later, a government investigation accused more than one hundred agents in the charge of the Indian Protection Service (SPI) of committing scores of crimes against Indian peoples and their property. "It is not only through the embezzlement of funds," the head of this commission wrote in 1967, "but by the admission of sexual perversions, murders, and all other crimes listed in the penal code against Indians and their property, that one can see that the Indian Protection Service was for years a den of corruption and indiscriminate killings" (Brazilian Ministery of the Interior 1968). In an article dated 1969 and appropriately titled "Genocide," a British journalist recorded the bloody details of ethnic murder and annihilation along the Brazilian frontier (Lewis 1969).

Beginning in 1968, a new government agency was created, the Fundação Nacional do Indio (FUNAI), supposedly to right the wrongs of the past and explicitly to "integrate" Brazilian Indians into national development and growth. Mission after mission was invited to Brazil to observe this new direction in national Indian policy — in 1970, the International Red Cross (Fuerst 1971), in 1971, the Primitive People's Fund/Survival International (Hanbury-Tenison 1971), and in the summer of 1973, a four-member team from the Aborigines Protection

Society of London (Brooks 1973b). Each of these commissions exonerated the Brazilian government from international charges of "genocide" while documenting a continuing pattern of native disease, dislocation, and decimation. Land robbery, highway invasions, development projects, forced removals, and medical neglect, these commissions noted, were generating the same effects as government policy in the past. Most recently, Edwin Brooks has analyzed the effects of Brazilian Indian policy and practice in a first-hand report titled "The twilight of Brazilian tribes" (Brooks 1973a). Using newspaper reports, I have provided similar documentation in an article titled "Custer is alive and he lives in Brazil" (Davis 1973).

From these reports, and drawing upon historical knowledge of other indigenous areas of the Americas, such as the nineteenth-century western frontier in the United States, three predictions seem reasonable concerning the fates of Indian peoples in Brazil. First, in the next decade we shall hear more reports of the rapid population decline and extinction of Indian tribes. This is particularly true in the far northwestern Amazon region, now being invaded by the uppermost perimeter of the Trans-Amazonic Highway and inhabited by an estimated 30,000 Indian people comprising over 100 tribes. Second, a large number of other tribes, possibly numbering 50,000 people, will be "integrated" into Brazilian rural society, but as wretched, poverty-stricken, and destitute populations in an expanding and wealth-producing frontier. And third, those remaining tribes, in spite of government policies of assimilation or acculturation, will cling tenaciously to their ethnic identities, while accommodating to the highly intrusive and exploitative national society in their midst. Many tribes, in other words, will become extinct, but Indian peoples will not vanish from the face of Brazil. Again, all of these statements appear reasonable given the historical experience of Indian peoples faced by similar colonial conditions in other parts of the Americas.

The question I would like to pose here, though is this: What is the social responsibility of anthropologists in the light of these destructive forces now encompassing the interior of Brazil? Cynically, one might argue that as anthropologists we have no responsibility except to get on with the everyday work of ethnological science, to study these native peoples as objects before they vanish, like some nonrecurring astronomical phenomenon, from the purview of other and more technologically powerful human societies such as our own. As the argument goes, the aboriginal world is a world on the wane, and the responsibility of ethnologists is to record the cultures of that world before they vanish out of view. The point, in other words, is to place nasty ethical considerations to one side and proceed with the work of science for science's (or Western society's) sake.

Recently Professor Joseph G. Jorgensen has provided convincing logical argument against the case, on the grounds of science, for avoiding the ethical responsibilities of anthropological research (Jorgensen 1971). For Brazil, the issue was highlighted to me in a conversation with a Brazilian anthropologist who had spent many years among a Gê-speaking tribe. "First," my friend claimed, "the missionaries went to this tribe and robbed these people of their religious beliefs. Then the government came and took away their independence. Then the land grabbers came and robbed their lands. Now, I come, and rob their minds." To forsake the ethical responsibilities of our research, I would argue, is to join in the same expropriative process in which our society encounters other peoples and cultures of the world, to bastardize the premises on which any human science must be based, and to collaborate, in the name of anthropological science, in the imperial process itself. Hence, the questions for us cannot remain on the philosophic level of whether or not we have a responsibility to the peoples whom we study. To the contrary, our decisions, I would argue, are essentially political and pragmatic ones. Namely, what are we to do?

In the brief paragraphs that follow I shall argue that the basic responsibility of anthropologists who possess knowledge of the situation of Indian peoples in Brazil is, to use the Tupi phrase, to speak and write "the truth, only the truth." This may sound simple and trite, but it appears that what is needed at present is to document just what is happening to Indian peoples in Brazil, to counter the fallacious claims of governments and other agencies, and to raise to public and international attention the real conditions of native people in Brazil and other parts of the world. What I am claiming, in other words, is that anthropologists begin to document the social realities of the peoples they study rather than continue to see their work as a contribution to a supposed science which more often than not obscures the existential conditions of the subjects of anthropological research. In the case of contemporary Brazil, where to speak or write the truth about social reality may mean censorship, exile, imprisonment, or torture, this is a dangerous task. Hence, those of us outside of Brazil must accept, both individually and collectively, certain added responsibilities, which at present cannot without serious repercussions be assumed by our anthropological colleagues in Brazil. Specifically, I would like to note only four of many areas which demand the strong, committed, and partisan voice of anthropologists at the present moment in time.

First, anthropologists who have done or are doing ethnographic fieldwork in Brazil must provide complete and exact accounts of present tribal territories, land and property systems, and social and economic patterns of environmental adaptation. Although a vast literature exists on the Indian tribes of Brazil (see Baldus 1968), it is surprising how little information has been collected and is available on aboriginal systems of territory, property, and land tenure. Unfortunately for the peoples involved, we know more about the important but impenetrable exotica of native myth, ritual, and symbolism than we do about the hard facts of native material and ecological existence. The domain of ecology has been left to other scientists working in such places as the Amazon region (see Meggers 1971: preface), and we find ourselves in a situation of ignorance similar to that described by an eminent lawyer of federal Indian law preoccupied with the aboriginal property rights of North American tribes. This lawyer claimed:

The extent of our ignorance of the basic facts of Indian land tenure is amazing. One might read in an hour all that anthropologists have had to say on the subject. Administrators and research workers alike have usually dismissed the subject with the observation that private property in land did not exist. This is a misleading half-truth. . . . Unless this lack of knowledge can be remedied, the drive towards imposition of white concepts of private property, in the form of the allotment system, is likely to be resumed (Cohen 1960:218–219).

Knowledge of the exact territorial limits of these tribes could serve as crucial information in legal briefs, either national or international, in support of the aboriginal property rights of Brazilian tribes. Although recognized by both national (article 198 of the Brazilian Constitution) and international law (the Geneva Accords of June 1957, ratified by President Castelo Branco in December 1965), it is a known fact that those few landed areas now being reserved for Indians severely underestimate or absolutely do not coincide with aboriginal territorial boundaries. Further, in a number of cases, such as that of the Xavante, lands reserved for Indians are in conflict with titles later granted to Brazilian ranchers (Bishop of São Felix 1971).

Edwin Brooks, for example, notes the following concerning land reserved for the Yanomami Indians along the Venezuelan border in northern Brazil:

It is most disappointing to find that the Yanomami Reserve proposed by the government contains, at a generous estimate, no more than 300 of the 4000–5000 members of the tribe living in this frontier region of Brazil. . . . The boundaries of the reserve perversely exclude every single village as identified by FUNAI itself. Far from safe-guarding the Yanomami — who are after all one of the largest tribes of unacculturated Indians anywhere in South America — such a reserve would endanger them, and there is an overwhelming case for extending its limits substantially, and indeed for having a joint policy with Venezuela for protecting these remarkable border people (Brooks 1973a:310).

Ethnographic data is critically needed on the exact territorial limits, needs, and rights of peoples such as the Yanomami. This data must be used, in the first instance, to convince the Brazilian government to legally demarcate and protect Indian lands according to its own national law; or in the last instance, to hold that government accountable in the international arena of law, criticism, and debate.

Second, anthropologists must mount an aggressive campaign against all attempts to forcibly remove or relocate Indian peoples from their aboriginal territories and lands. The forced removal and settlement of native populations is a tested repressive technique of colonial governments which dates from the Spanish *reducciones* of the sixteenth century and Andrew Jackson's Indian policies of the early nineteenth-century United States. Evidence exists that a similar policy is being followed in contemporary Brazil (Davis 1973; Brooks 1973b). Tribes such as the Nhambiquara in Mato Grosso and the Txucarramae in the Xingu National Park have been forcibly removed by the invasions of state-financed and -constructed highways, leading to rapid disease and near extermination. In turn, the directives of FUNAI are such that Indian peoples are coerced to relocate so as not to serve as so-called obstacles in the way of national expansion and growth (Novitski 1971).

Particularly important in this regard is the new Brazilian Indian Statute, in formulation since 1969 but first publicly announced by the President of Brazil in October 1970 (see *America Indigena* 1971: 451–465). Among other things, article 35 of the new statute empowers the President of Brazil with the right to physically relocate Indian groups under five conditions: (1) in order to terminate a fight between Indian tribes; (2) in order to combat the eruption of serious epidemics which could result in the extermination of the tribe; (3) in order to combat any evil which might jeopardize the integrity of an Indian or the tribe; (4) in order to alleviate any impositions to national security; and (5) in order to promote regional development having in view the higher national interests. It is a known fact that intertribal fighting, serious epidemics, and threats to cultural integrity are more often than not the results rather than the causes of relocation of Indian groups in Brazil. Hence, forced relocation serves as a tool to maintain national security and promote regional development, rather than a positive protection of constitutionally recognized Indian rights. The audacity of the Brazilian government to suggest otherwise, in presenting this document to the Brazilian Congress and the Inter-American Indian Institute, is an affront to the judgment of any rational human being, and a threat to the survival of Indian peoples in Brazil.

To date, the statute has received severe criticism, especially from dissident Indian agents and the National Council of Brazilian Bishops, and at this writing it has not yet been passed into law (*Jornal do Brasil* 1972). Should it be, however, in its present wording it would provide a legislative mandate for the systematic and state-directed extermination of the remaining Indian tribes of Brazil. Anthropologists cannot stand by silently and let this statute pass into law.

Third, anthropologists must begin to publicly document the role of powerful economic interests, often international or multinational in scope, that are directly implied in the malicious and unlawful expropriation of Indian lands. This information-gathering and advocacy function must be particularly assumed by anthropologists in metropolitan centers, such as the United States, where large international mining, timber, and agribusinesses are seeking the wealth-generating resources of the Amazon region (Miliman 1973). A perusal of journals in the business schools of universities where most North American, European, or Japanese anthropologists work would indicate the parasitic role which these corporations have assumed in Brazil (e.g., see Thayer 1972a). Documentation, for example, exists on the presence of Swift, Armour, and King Ranch on the lands of the Tembe-Urubu Indians (*Editora Abril* 1971:187), of United States Steel Corporation in the territory of the Xikrin Indians (Thayer 1972b), of several tin-extraction companies, such as W.R. Grace and Royal Dutch Shell-Billiton, on Indian territories in Rondonia (Visão 1972:94–100), and of a number of international aerial photograhic, engineering, and heavy-equipment outfits contracted for the building of the Trans-Amazonic Highway (*Business Week* 1972:34).

Over the past few years, every legislative and administrative technique has been used by the military government of Brazil to give these corporations free and open access to the resources of the Amazon (see *Business Latin America* 1972:385–388). More often than not, such legislation has jeopardized the property rights of Indian peoples, and been followed by angry, but immediately repressed, denunciations of state participation in the "denationalization" of the Brazilian territory. Further, in the case of corporations based in the United States but with thinly disguised subsidiaries in Brazil, these powerful economic institutions have purposely evaded our own anti-trust and environmental protection laws. The public documentation of the scope of these environmentally wasteful and humanly destructive, profit-seeking corporations, I would argue, lies with socially responsible scholars in the countries from where they come.

Fourth, and as our most immediate task, anthropologists must begin to counter scientifically the various disguised ideologies of forced acculturation and assimilation, euphemistically called "programs of national integration," which legitimize state Indian policy in Brazil and other countries of the Americas (see, e.g., Congreso Indigenista Interamericano 1972). It is one of the paradoxes of the history of our discipline that our own unvalidated theories are being used to rationalize state Indian policy and practice leading to the most physically destructive and culturally negating effects. If one reads the history of anthropology it becomes clear that at present various so-called scientific theories of acculturation are being used as a defense for government programs of directed cultural change. These programs, I would argue, are moral rather than scientific in nature, and not strikingly different, except for their language, than the evangelical projects of the past. In spite of their possible well-meaning intentions, they implicitly assume the universal validity of our own way of life and values, and coerce Indian peoples, in the name of "national integration," into a status of colonial wardship and dependency (see Barbados Symposium 1971:6,7). Further, in most concrete cases, such as that in the Amazon region of Brazil, "national integration" is merely a spurious humanistic cover for the robbery of Indian territories and land.

The issues here, it appears to me, are neither ones of romantically supporting the physical and cultural integrity of Indian tribes for purposes of anthropological study, nor espousing a system of ethnic apartheid for Brazil that goes counter to its self-proclaimed position of "racial democracy." Nor in critically challenging the integrationist directives of state Indian policy am I suggesting that the majority of Brazilian people do not have a right to economic prosperity, progress, and growth. These, I would argue, are in large measure philosophic questions which tend to obscure rather than clarify the issues of Indian policy in Brazil. The critique of integrationist ideology arises from nothing less than a knowledge of the nature of historical facts, and an analysis of contemporary political and economic realities in Brazil (see Davis 1971).

As far back as 1957, Darcy Ribeiro provided impressive statistical evidence to show that the political and economic integration of formerly isolated Indian tribes into Brazilian national society was merely a whimsical characterization of the historic process whereby these tribes were becoming physically and culturally extinct. Between 1900 and 1957, some tribes which only maintained intermittent contact with Brazilian society were able to weather this historic process, but a high proportion of other tribes (between 40 and 70 percent) in permanent or total contact encountered rapid disease and extermination. The Kaingang of São Paulo, for example, were reduced from 1,200 to 87 persons, the Xokleng of Santa Catarina from 800 to 189 persons, the Umotina of Mato Grosso from 1,000 to 200 people, and nearly one half of Brazil's contacted tribes passed out of existence. National integration, a concrete political and economic experience for these tribes, meant a series of constant conflicts with the agents of civilization, including the Indian Protection Service itself, and produced an astounding rate of demographic decline due to epidemics, starvation, slavery, murder, and the like.

The so-called integrated tribes in Ribeiro's sample had become a "reserve labor force" in an underdeveloping rural economy. Ribeiro wrote:

Of all the survivors, these *integrated tribes* were enduring the most precarious conditions of life in the greatest dependency and misery. Between these contemporary Indians and their isolated ancestors — in some cases members of the preceding generation — there was an enormous gap. . . . These tribes had run the gamut of acculturation. But some imponderable obstacle blocked their assimilation; there was a final step that they were unable to take.

As an "unwanted minority, restricted to segments of the lands they formerly held or cast out of territory rightfully theirs," these remnants of aboriginal tribes became ethnic enclaves, forced to adapt to parasitic and exploitative regional economies in a struggle in order to physically survive.

Professor Paulo Nogueira Neto, a well-known zoologist at the University of São Paulo, summed up the uses which are made of this integrationist ideology in the following terms:

It is astonishing what is being claimed in the so-called "defense of acculturation" of the Indians. No one is obliged to know history, but a person who occupies an important public charge within indigenous affairs must know the historical antecedents of the problem. It is sad to see the number of untruths that are proclaimed in defense of the policy of immediate contact with the Indians. It is a mistake that has simply been repeating itself for more than 100 years (*O Globo* 1971).

An agent of FUNAI with years of experience among both isolated and contacted tribes analyzed the situation in an interview in somewhat different, but nevertheless revealing, terms (*Editoria Abril* 1971):

Q.   Does the government have conditions to resolve the Indian problem in the Amazon principally now, when it is planning the occupation of the region?
A.   If the government does not have conditions to resolve the social problem of our large urban centers how is it going to resolve the problem of the Indian in the forest?
Q.   In front of this problem, what will the government do?
A.   It will attempt to reconcile its policy of expansion and development with the integration of the Indian. That is the Indian will be forced to rapidly integrate or face eventual extermination.
Q.   But won't such rapid integration place the Indian as a marginal to white society?
A.   My son, 90% of the Brazilian population is marginalized from progress and society. Take a trip here in Porto Velho and observe the state of the population. The Indian will not obtain a better place than the majority of Brazilians.

In a situation where the Brazilian government provides Indian peoples with a choice between extermination or rural poverty and destitution, anthropologists, I believe, have a special responsibility to support other alternatives and challenge present policies of rapid national integration. These alternatives are contained in the ways of life and structures of Indian societies themselves, and reflected in the precarious existence of the Xingu Indian Park. An anomaly in present-day Brazil and throughout the Americas, the founders of the Xingu Park, Orlando and Claudio

Villas Boas, base their work on the living authenticity of Indian societies, and have consistently struggled for these societies' rights to sovereignty, territory, and existence. Believing that modern medicine and legal protection are perhaps all that our society has to offer these people, they have created an alternative to contemporary Indian policy in Brazil. At a time when the Xingu Park has been invaded by highways and criticized by government spokesmen as a "false experience prejudicing the integration of Indians and the security and development of the country," the support of the Villas Boas brothers in their work is a responsibility which falls upon us all (see Hanbury-Tenison 1971:9, 10 and 30).

CONCLUSION

Let me conclude by merely restating a point made earlier in this essay. As anthropologists, I believe our primary contribution to the rights of indigenous peoples lies in independently and publicly documenting the social realities that these peoples face. Given the nature of political repression in contemporary Brazil, this documentation function is a vital task. Political secrecy and repression have become institutionalized aspects of both the Brazilian government and my own, and we can do no less, as scientists and citizens, than make known what our governments would wish left free from public scrutiny, action, and debate.

REFERENCES

AMERICA INDIGENA
   1971   Estatuto del indio de Brazil. 31:451–465.
BALDUS, HERBERT
   1968   Bibliografia critica da ethnologia brasileira. *Volkerkundliche Abhandlungen.* Hannover.
BARBADOS SYMPOSIUM
   1971   *Declaration of Barbados.* Copenhagen: International Work Group for Indigenous Affairs.
BISHOP OF SÃO FELIX
   1971   *Latifundismo e marginalização social na Amazonia.* Mato Grosso, n.p.
BRAZILIAN MINISTERY OF THE INTERIOR
   1968   *Diario oficial da republica.* Section 1:8046 and foreword. September 10.
BROOKS, EDWIN
   1973a The twilight of Brazilian tribes. *The Geographical Magazine.*
   1973b Prospects of integration for the Indians of Brazil. *Patterns of Prejudice.*
Business Latin America
   1972   "Profitability in Brazil looms high as companies continue to cash in on boom." *Business Latin America.* December 7.
Business Week
   1972   "Cats slice out a highway in the jungle." *Business Week.* January 8.

COHEN, FELIX S.
1960   "Anthropology and the problems of Indian administration," in *The legal conscience: essays of Felix Cohen.* Edited by L.K. Cohen, 213–220. New Haven: Yale University Press.
CONGRESO INDIGENISTA INTERAMERICANO
1972   Declaración de Brasilia. *America Indigena* 32:225–258.
DAVIS, SHELTON H.
1971   "Primitive" peoples and "civilized" ideologies in Brazil. Unpublished manuscript.
1973   Custer is alive and he lives in Brazil. *The Indian Historian* Spring.
Editora Abril
1971   Amazonia. *Realidade.* Rio de Janeiro.
FUERST, RENE
1971   *Provisional report on the present situation of the Indians of the Brazilian Amazon region.* Geneva: Amazind.
1972   *Bibliography of the indigenous problem and policy of the Brazilian Amazon region (1957–1972).* Geneva: Amazind.
FUNDAÇÃO NACIONAL DO INDIO
1970   *Supysaúa, o indio brasileiro.* Rio de Janeiro: Editora Vecchi.
HANBURY-TENISON, ROBIN
1971   *Report of a visit to the Indians of Brazil.* London: Primitive Peoples Fund/Survival International.
JORGENSEN, JOSEPH G.
1971   On ethics and anthropology. *Current Anthropology* 12:321–334.
Jornal do Brasil
1972   "Estatuto indigena gera discordância." *Jornal do Brasil.* July 25.
LEWIS, NORMAN
1969   Genocide, from fire and sword to arsenic and bullets — civilization has sent six million Indians to extinction. London: *The Sunday Times.* February 23.
MEGGERS, BETTY J.
1971   *Amazonia, man and culture in a counterfeit paradise.* Chicago: Aldine.
MILIMAN, MARSHA
1973   "Brazil: let them eat minerals," in *Brazil: Development for whom?* Berkeley: North American Congress on Latin America.
NOVITSKI, JOSEPH
1971   "Brazil is seen moving toward forced relocation of tribes." *The New York Times.* July 14.
O Globo
1971   "Naturalista preve fim do indio com a estrada." *O Globo.* March 17.
RIBEIRO, DARCY
1957   Culturas e linguas indigenas do Brasil. *Educaçãe e Ciencias Socials* 2:4–102.
THAYER, YVONNE
1972a The Amazon catches up with the 20th century. *Brazilian Business* 52:8–15.
1972b The Carajas iron ore project — a boost to Amazon development. *Brazilian Business* 53:13–14.
VISÃO
1972   Rondonia, capital do estanho. *Quem e Quem na Economia Brasileira.* 41:94–100.

New Strategies for Multinational Enterprise in the Third World: Deltec in Brazil and Argentina

DELTEC RESEARCH PROJECT

Deltec[1] is primarily a merchant banking and brokerage firm, but in addition to its financial and capital market operations it has extensive real estate holdings in Brazil and elsewhere in South America and an international distribution and marketing system for processed foods (especially meat). The latter is directed toward the European and North American markets but draws its supplies from Latin America, Eastern Europe, Australia, and New Zealand. The bulk of Deltec's financial and capital brokerage business is done in Latin America, but it is currently expanding into Southeast Asia.

No paper of the present size and scope could adequately describe, let alone analyze, all of Deltec's holdings and activities and their effects upon the societies in which Deltec operates. Such an attempt is, in any case, unnecessary to gain an understanding of Deltec's basic strategy and tactics. These may be inferred from a close examination of Deltec's operations in Brazil and Argentina, the countries where Deltec began and where it developed the strategy it has applied in its activities in other

The members of the Deltec Research Project include Ahamed Idris-Soven, Anne Lonigro, Colleen Reeks, Terence Turner, and others who must remain anonymous. They wish to express their thanks and acknowledge their debt to the North American Congress on Latin America for its generous and invaluable help in giving them access to its files on Deltec and the meat industry; to the Amalgamated Meat Cutters and Butcher Workmen of North America for the cooperation and advice given us by its research staff; and to Peter Aaby of the University of Copenhagen and International Work Group on Indigenous Affairs (IWGIA) for many helpful comments on the draft.

[1] Deltec has numerous subsidiaries in various countries, only some of which bear its name. All of the subsidiaries are owned and controlled by Deltec Panamerica, S.A., a holding company with headquarters in Nassau, Bahamas. All references to Deltec by name in this paper may be taken as referring in a specific sense to Deltec Panamerica, S.A., as the controlling and policy-making center of the Deltec organization as a whole, unless otherwise indicated. The description of Deltec refers to the period up to 1975 when this study was written. Facts have not been updated since then.

parts of the world. This paper, accordingly, focuses on Deltec's operations in these two countries.

DELTEC IN BRAZIL: THE UNIQUE INTEREST OF DELTEC AS A CASE STUDY IN MULTINATIONAL ECONOMIC PENETRATION

Deltec's Basic Strategy: Double Envelopment of Third World Economies through Domination of Capital Markets and International Distribution of Manufactured Export Goods

Although it is listed by *Fortune* as one of the 200 largest corporations in the world, Deltec is far from the largest or most powerful corporation operating in Latin America, let alone in the Third World as a whole. It is nonetheless one of the most interesting as a case study of some of the more sophisticated forms taken by the economic penetration and domination of the Third World by North American and international capital.

Deltec began as the vision of Clarence Dauphinot, a U.S. citizen who started his business career as a bond salesman for Kidder-Peabody in Brazil during World War II. Dauphinot was impressed by the prospects of Latin America in general and Brazil in particular for rapid economic development after the war. Dauphinot's vision of capitalist development in Brazil, Argentina, and the other larger Latin American nations was, however, considerably more sophisticated than that of many of his contemporaries in the North American business community, with their relatively traditional notions of extraction and export.

Dauphinot's basic idea, which has remained the basis of Deltec's strategy to the present day, was that the economies of the Latin American nations would never develop into full-fledged capitalist systems until they developed capital markets of their own. Only this would permit the growing middle classes of those countries to invest in the development of their own national economies. The originality of Dauphinot's vision was in seeing a unique opportunity for the foreign capitalist in the promotion of modern capitalist economies in Latin America. Dauphinot's approach diverged significantly from the traditional forms of overt domination by foreign capital of agricultural, manufacturing, extractive, and capital marketing activities in those countries.

At the time Dauphinot began his career, no Latin American country, with the partial exception of Argentina, possessed the legal, institutional, and financial structure necessary for an internal capital market of its own. Dauphinot saw an opportunity for himself, with his experience and connections in the bond-selling and brokerage business, in helping to bring about the necessary internal structural and financial developments for the emergence of capital markets in the later South American countries while simultaneously acting as middleman between the nascent capital markets of countries like Brazil and Argentina and investors from the capital-exporting nations of North America and Europe. Dauphinot's plan, in short, was to combine the roles of domestic and international investment banker and broker while acting as a catalyst for the development of internal capital markets in the larger Latin countries.

Immediately after the war, Dauphinot persuaded his bosses at Kidder-Peabody to back him for six months while he got himself set up as a broker and financial operator in Brazil. Things did not go quite according to schedule: it took two and a half years to get the necessary license to engage in financial and brokerage operations. Dauphinot, however, stuck it out, selling frying pans and Old Crow whiskey in the meantime. He finally hit pay dirt in 1947, when, with his newly acquired license, he managed the sale of a stock issue for the Brazilian Light and Traction Company. "Light," as it is known in Brazil, is a subsidiary of BRASCAN, a Canadian-owned firm with extensive holdings in Brazil. Dauphinot's fortunes have been closely linked with BRASCAN ever since.

Dauphinot's conception of his combined role as capital broker and investment banker must now be more fully explained, for it set the pattern of Deltec's subsequent financial operations in Brazil and elsewhere. His first task was to persuade national governments and firms, or foreign-owned firms operating in the countries in question, to "go public" and allow him to manage the sale of their paper (short-term loan notes, equity stocks, or bonds). He would then sell the paper, either to buyers within the country or to foreign investors (either on the U.S. and European exchanges or directly to banks and other private sources of investment capital). In the same way, he could arrange loans for national enterprises with a potential for expansion from either domestic or foreign sources or have Deltec itself make the loan out of its own capital. In some cases he could combine the two operations, making a loan to a firm for which he would also manage a sale of commercial paper. In others he might simply buy the firm outright, recapitalize and reorganize it, and sell it, if possible, to local corporations or investors to whom he could lend the necessary money. As lender, as underwriter, or as both at the same time, Deltec would be in a position to demand administrative control, or at least certain policy commitments consistent with its larger plans, from the native firms, without buying them outright or taking on the "high profile" roles of owner of national enterprises, extractor of national resources, or employer of local labor.

Such was the original vision upon which Deltec was built. Established in 1949, the first twenty years of its corporate life were spent almost exclusively in capital market brokerage, underwriting, and investment banking operations. These activities are still Deltec's biggest sources of income. Its major business continues to be done in government bonds or the short-term commercial paper of Latin American firms, which it sells at a markup on the European and U.S. capital markets.

It was a short step from such tactics to a second major strategy that has played an increasingly prominent role in Deltec's operations over the past decade (a third of its corporate existence). Deltec has consistently been aware of the political dangers of outright ownership or effective minority control of basic resources and extractive or manufacturing operations in the increasingly nationalist climate of Latin American societies. It has occasionally acquired outright ownership or a controlling interest in major productive enterprises, but such instances are the exception and have almost invariably been temporary, with relatively rapid divestiture and resale envisioned at the time of purchase. If Deltec buys a company (e.g., flour mills in Brazil or meat-packing plants in Argentina), it is usually only for the purpose of capitalizing and perhaps technologically renovating it to the point at which it can be resold to local capitalists at a profit, if possible lending them the money for the sale and thus retaining a line on the company as a secured creditor. Deltec may also be interested in setting up an international distributive network for the product of the firm, developing markets and a product mix for the industry in question. By retaining a creditor's lien on the business, and/or by managing the domestic and foreign sale of the firm's equity stock, loan certificates, or other types of commercial paper, Deltec can reasonably hope to keep the enterprise dependent enough to ensure that it remains a supplier of manufactured products for its export and overseas distributional system. If Deltec is not interested in exporting or marketing the firm's product, it may simply allow the enterprise to flounder under its new management. The latter, lacking Deltec's resources of capital and managerial talent, may not be able to maintain the company at the peak of productive performance, and hence of value, to which it was built up for purposes of resale by Deltec. Deltec, as creditor, may then be able to regain control of the company and repeat the process with yet another native buyer.

An instance of this process of "gold-plating" (i.e., increasing the value of a firm by relatively superficial or temporary infusions of capital, management, technology, manipulation of inventories, etc., for purposes of resale, followed by repossession of a firm from the new management upon bankruptcy), is provided by the Dominium scandal related below. In the alternative type of case in which Deltec attempts to retain a manufacturing firm that it has sold to new management as a supplier for its international export and distributional system, it is able to skim off the lion's share of the profits at both ends of the productive process (financing the sale and raising capital for the firm on the one hand, and marketing its product on the other).

From this point of view, Deltec's policy of developing an export capacity for capital-intensive manufactured goods in the larger Latin American countries comes into somewhat sharper focus. As Dauphinot and other top Deltec spokesmen have repeatedly stressed, to develop into viable capitalist economies, countries like Brazil and Argentina, while necessarily remaining for some time primarily importers of capital, must begin to export capital-intensive manufactured goods as quickly and in as large quantities as possible. True to its policy that what is good for the capitalist development of the Latin American countries is also good for Deltec, Deltec has moved shrewdly to dominate the largest and most practicable mode of export available to these countries at their current stage of development: the export of processed food products.

The trade in processed food products offers perhaps the most promising opportunities for exploitation from the standpoint of this strategy for several reasons: (1) the rapid growth in world demand for food; (2) the prominence of agricultural commodities in almost all Third World economies; (3) the recent technological revolution in methods of processing and preserving food, which makes practicable the processing of many types of food, such as meat, at the source of supply, rather than at the point of final distribution and consumption; (4) the greater suitability of processed food products for international trade and distribution, down to the wholesale and retail levels, than raw commodities like grain or fresh meat; (5) the correspondingly greater dependence of such processed food products on sophisticated distributive and marketing systems; and (6) the ability of a financially oriented and sophisticated management, such as Deltec, to take advantage of the high volume of the food trade.

The trade in processed food products, then, seemed historically ripe for the advent of Deltec and its particular version of "partnership in development." Over the past seven years, Deltec has pushed the development of sales networks for food products in Europe, North America, Latin America, and Africa; has vigorously developed a diversified network of suppliers of products for its distributive network; and has developed whole product lines for particular markets, which it has then persuaded its suppliers to manufacture.

The latter aspect of its operation has in fact taken on the form of a full-fledged technical assistance program, which Deltec markets as a service to prospective suppliers. The description of this service in Deltec's 1972 annual report is as follows:

Deltec is in a uniquely advantageous position to offer a combination package of technical, commercial and financial services to the food industry, particularly in developing nations seeking export earnings. . . . This capability has evoked considerable interest . . . and could well become an important factor in the further development of our food distribution business. Deltec can make available a broad range of technical expertise in the organization of efficient food production facilities; can provide know-how in processing and packaging techniques and in the development of a product mix geared to the requirements of specific markets; can finance the purchase or construction of the facilities, the procurement and installation of necessary equipment and other costs of establishing an operation; can offer a repayment program in the form of cash or finished product at the election of the client and, in either case, can utilize its international facilities for marketing the product in the areas of major consumption (Deltec 1972:19).

The profits in the export trade in simple manufactured goods such as processed foods (e.g., precooked, canned, or frozen beef or instant coffee, the products upon which Deltec has concentrated) go overwhelmingly to the middleman. Best of all, just as financial capital and brokerage activities make difficult targets for nationalization or even political opposition within a country, so an international distributive network remains effectively outside the control of any national government and is thus nationalization-proof.

Deltec's strategy has thus come to be based, in its current, mature phase, on the principle that the combination of roles of exporter and capital broker-financier most effectively minimizes the danger of nationalist or leftist interference and expropriation, while maximizing Deltec's opportunities for control of and profit in both the national economy and international trade. In operational terms this strategy can be described as an orchestration of middleman roles: as middleman between the governments and firms of capital-importing nations and investors from the capital-exporting nations; as middleman between nationally or foreign-owned enterprises operating within Third World nations and national bourgeoisies with capital to invest; and as middleman between Third World manufacturing enterprise and the market of the capital-exporting nations for certain types of capital goods. It is this system of middleman roles, and its relative immunity from effective control by the nations in which it operates, that Deltec spokesmen call their "low-profile" policy.

There is another aspect of this low-profile policy that deserves emphasis. Deltec has consistently placed great emphasis on the recruitment of nationals from the countries in which it operates for top managerial posts. Over and beyond this it has set up close working partnerships with prominent national figures and financial institutions. Deltec's top management is about one-third North American, one-third European, and one-third Latin American, which Dauphinot claims corresponds to the proportions of Deltec capital owned by these three regional blocs.

To help assure its supply of native managerial personnel, Deltec has instituted a training program for Latin American executives at its headquarters in Nassau. Some comments made by Dauphinot about this program in a newspaper interview are interesting for the light they throw on Deltec's general policy and approach:

There is no question that if someone from, say, Colombia, comes up to Nassau when he is about 25 years old and has the capacity to learn and sticks it out for two or three years . . . when he returns to his country, you can bet that he is going to be a far better and more dependable citizen than he ever was before. . . . I suppose it takes a certain type of person to make this kind of investment in time and effort and then return home. He must be a dedicated person — a sort of business missionary. Don't laugh; they exist; we have had them . . . (*Peruvian Times* 1969).

Deltec's interlocking system of financial, capital marketing, and international distributive operations is a far cry from the simple extractive or vertically integrated capital-exporting activities that have been the major forms of dominance by North American and European capital over the Latin American economies. Far more than such familiar types of multinational enterprise, Deltec has built its business strategy upon a sophisticated and farsighted analysis of the internal structural requirements for the capitalist development of the national economies of the Latin American countries considered in global, systematic terms. The concentration on export and international distribution as a technique for outflanking nationalist expropriation, and the combination of this with financial and capital marketing techniques for controlling domestic extractive and manufacturing enterprise within Third World countries in place of outright ownership, which are the hallmarks of Deltec's strategy, exemplify a pattern being followed, to a greater or lesser degree, by an increasing proportion of transnational capitalist operations in the Third World.[2] We have attempted to outline the main elements of these strategies in the preceding pages. In what follows, we shall examine the application of these general principles to concrete cases in Brazil and Argentina.

Investment Banking and Real Estate Operations in Brazil

INVESTMENT BANKING. Deltec has undeniably had a major impact upon the development of the Brazilian capital market since World War II and has played a significant role as an investment banker. It has, in short, largely fulfilled its basic strategy as described in the preceding section. The effects of its success have been, on the one hand, to catalyze the development of Brazilian capitalism and to involve a greater percentage of the Brazilian middle and upper classes in investments in productive

---

[2] See, for example, Stephen W. Langdon, "Export oriented industrialization through the multinational corporation: evidence from Kenya," in this volume.

enterprise within the country. On the other hand, they have tended to maximize Deltec's ability to manipulate both domestic and foreign investment capital, to gain control over national firms by serving as the middleman between them and the financial and capital markets, and to skim off the lion's share of the profits at the other end by serving again as the middleman in the international distribution and marketing of their products.

A brief history of Deltec's career in capital brokerage and investment banking in Brazil will illustrate the nature and scale of its operations in these fields. Deltec, as has been pointed out, originated in Brazil and still does more of its business there, especially in the banking, brokerage, and real estate fields, than in any other country.

For some time after its first big break in 1947 (managing the sale of stock for Brazilian Light and Traction referred to above), Deltec did virtually all of its business in Brazil selling commercial and government bonds and short-term, low-risk loan notes, mostly to U.S. and European customers. Goulart's succession to the presidency of Brazil in 1961 led to a temporary suspension of these operations and, incidentally, the removal of Deltec's headquarters from Brazil to Nassau (where, because of Nassau's merits as a tax haven, it has remained ever since). After Goulart's overthrow in 1964 Deltec resumed its Brazilian operations. It expanded rapidly, prospering under the hothouse conditions for both domestic and foreign investment provided by the development-oriented military regime.

In 1967, Deltec joined with its old client, BRASCAN, and the Rockefeller investment bank IBEC (International Basic Economy) as well as a number of other foreign and domestic banks[3] to form the Banco de Investimento do Brasil, S.A. (BIB). BIB swiftly became the largest private noncommercial banking and financial institution in Latin America. It has played a major role in the development of the Brazilian money and capital markets. A significant proportion of BIB's activities were carried on through its three prosperous mutual funds: Fundo Cresinco (the largest mutual fund in South America), BIB-Cresinco (Brazil's largest tax-incentive fund), and Condominio Deltec (the mutual fund with the highest rate of return in Brazil).

The opportunity for forming this bank came with Resolution 18 passed by the Brazilian government in 1966, which allowed the establishment of private investment/development banks. BIB and a half-dozen other major investment/development banks were set up at this time. Resolution 18 made possible the formation of centralized coalitions or groups of smaller investment banks/financial corporations in order to

---

[3]   These included Credit Suisse, Kommerzbank A.G., and Deutsche Bank A.G. of Germany, União de Bancos Brasileiros, the Antunes Group, Rafinaria União, and 5,000 public shareholders. Each of the three primary shareholders controlled 20 percent of the equity.

strengthen control of Brazil's finance/capital market by the National Monetary Council, which is composed of big bankers, mostly from São Paulo.

BIB resulted from the complementary interests of Nelson Rockefeller's Brazilian Bank IBEC, which sought management capable of more dynamic capital manipulation and growth, and Dauphinot's need for a large capital base to manage. Under these circumstances Nelson Rockefeller permitted the formation of a coalition with Deltec.

Moreira Salles's group provided the crucial Brazilian banking connections and the legally necessary Brazilian majority partner (60 percent of equity). Moreira Salles sought to break Deltec's managerial control of BIB, probably because he was discontented with the passive role he was forced to play in BIB. There was an intense struggle, ended with a public announcement by Salles that BIB was merging with BRADESCO, to be represented by Salles.[4] Deltec then left BIB. Losing Salles was a setback for Deltec, which desperately needed a Brazilian partner for its investment banking operations. Therefore, shortly after its exit from BIB in 1972, Deltec joined Gaston Vidigal's Banco FINASA in São Paulo. Vidigal was an old partner of Dauphinot in Deltec who had split with him and Deltec in 1960 over financial policy — Vidigal had opposed Dauphinot's decision to deemphasize short-term Brazilian currency transactions and concentrate on long-term dollar-loan business. There may also have been sharp differences in business style between the relatively fastidious Vidigal, who for almost fifteen years has been a powerful member of Brazil's National Monetary Council, and the relatively piratical Deltec. The remarriage of Deltec and FINASA lasted only one year — they broke up (again) in 1973.

The complex relations of Deltec with Brazilian banks provide a good example of both the close interdependence and the tensions between multinational corporations (MNC's) and national capital. National finance capital needs the capital resources and international and national market connections (e.g., in the latter case, with other MNC's operating within the country), and, to varying degrees, the managerial skills of the MNC. At the same time it resists (again, to varying degrees) the loss of independence that a close relationship with an MNC typically brings. The MNC, on the other hand, needs the connection with the national institution for legal and political legitimacy, for protection against national regulatory agencies, and for access to local networks and markets. Moreover, the MNC typically fears to commit itself to partnership with a powerful national institution that it cannot control and thus attempts with varying success and to varying degrees to assert control over it. The result

---

[4] This merger never came off, with the result that after Deltec's departure (provoked by the announcement of the impending merger) Moreira Salles was left in sole control of the flourishing BIB.

is a typical conflict in which each partner attempts to use the other while blocking the other's efforts to assert its control (on the MNC's side) or independence (on the national firm's side). The unequal conflict usually results in the domination of the national firm by the MNC, but Moreira Salles's triumph in wresting control of BIB from Deltec shows that in special cases the MNC may find itself used and (at the point where it is no longer needed) rejected by the national firm.

Besides its own mutual funds and its underwriting of the financing of other companies, Deltec makes extensive loans from its own funds. These are of two types, each identified by the number of the Brazilian law regulating it. Law 63 loans comprise those made directly to banks, which then lend the money out in small lots to local customers. Law 4131 loans (by far the more common type) are those made directly to state or national government agencies or to undercapitalized businesses. In the case of Law 4131 loans to private businesses, if Deltec has only arranged the loan of funds from another source it simply takes a percentage commission off the top. If it has made the loan out of its own funds it insists on effective administrative control of the business for the duration of the loan.

Deltec has been known to combine its financial and capital-brokerage roles in relation to the same corporation — in other words, to lend money to the same firm for which it helps to float an issue of commercial paper. In either or both roles Deltec is in a position to affect or control the policies and operations of the firm, while the firm remains under its original ownership. One of the ways Deltec has used the leverage from its financial and brokerage activities has been to line up native suppliers for its international distributional and marketing operations in the processed-food business. Before taking a closer look at Deltec's operations in this field, however, its Brazilian real estate operations deserve some examination.

REAL ESTATE. The center of Deltec's real estate operations in Brazil is the city of São Paulo, one of the fastest-growing cities in the world. São Paulo's population is expected to be increased by a fantastic 500,000 immigrants per year during the 1970's. There is thus a very favorable demographic basis for real estate development in the city.

Deltec's major coup in the real estate field was to acquire control of the Companhia City do Desenvolvimento, a previously British-owned São Paulo firm that had pioneered in building the "garden suburbs" that are now the choicest dwelling areas in the city. Deltec bought a controlling interest in the company (now the fourth largest real estate company in Brazil) in 1957. Though Companhia City, Deltec gained ownership of the choice Anastacio tract, 1,500 acres of prime land in the north-western part of São Paulo and the last undeveloped tract of anywhere near that size in the whole urban area. It also acquired choice commercial and industrial tracts in the down-town area and land outside São Paulo for a satellite city of 5,000 housing units. All of these holdings are currently being developed, either through the construction of dwellings and office buildings or the preparation of industrial sites.

Another venture elsewhere in São Paulo state is Deltec's project in Piracicaba, the major sugar-processing center of Brazil, which is currently undergoing rapid expansion. Deltec now owns 15 percent of the total urban area (about 600 acres) and is constructing a residential, industrial, and commercial complex there. This development, too, is coordinated through Companhia City.

It is typical of Deltec that it has not only used Companhia City as an instrument for conventional developments of the types mentioned above but has also renovated and strengthened its management and added a new line of design, planning, sales, financial, and other real estate services that has become a major business in itself. Deltec contracts these services to third parties in other parts of Brazil and draws upon them itself for its operations elsewhere in São Paulo state and other areas.

As Dauphinot pointed out in a recent interview, "the building industry is, in fact, the most important activity in the nation."

> The interest, encouragement and support of the Brazilian government in developing its housing needs have opened to private industry and investor business opportunities in building and property development that are unparalleled elsewhere in the world today (*American Banker* 1973).

The Brazilian government has, in fact, established generous credit facilities for middle-income housing through its National Housing Bank. Once again, Deltec has managed to cash in on a top priority aspect of the national development effort, in a sector where it can deploy its financial assets and capabilities to great advantage.

It might appear that Deltec's heavy investment in real estate in Brazil and in some other parts of South America[5] constitutes a major exception to its grand strategy, as outlined above, of not sinking capital into fixed assets that might become the objects of nationalist agitation and expropriation. Deltec may indeed have passed some uneasy moments during the Goulart regime, under which large foreign land holdings in Brazil came under much scrutiny and criticism. The exception, however, is more apparent than real. At most, Deltec's real estate operations represent only a somewhat longer-term commitment of capital to fixed assets than in, say, some of its ventures into the temporary ownership of food-

---

[5] Deltec is also engaged in constructing a huge commercial building in downtown Caracas and has developed a large resort, Treasure Cay, in the Bahamas.

processing facilities of various kinds to be discussed in the following sections. The object of its real estate developments, both in private housing and commercial and industrial properties, is sale to Brazilian clients and eventual total divestiture of any particular block of land. Above all, urban real estate development and construction, unlike extractive or manufacturing industry or agricultural production, does not involve the extraction or diminution of national resources and does not involve Deltec directly in the employment of large forces of local workers. Construction can be carried out through Brazilian contractors, who can be left to handle their labor problems in their own way and to absorb whatever pressures unions or governments are capable of mounting on the workers' behalf. Urban real estate, therefore, can be considered a commodity consistent with Deltec's low-profile strategy.

Deltec's experience in real estate has been highly successful (which is doubtless why it is currently expanding its holdings and activities in this sector). By contrast, its major ventures into industrial production, which have been concentrated in processed foods (specifically, instant coffee, flour, cookies, and precooked and frozen beef), have been checkered with economic and political disasters of large proportions. Let us turn, then, to a review of Deltec's adventures in the processed-food business.

DELTEC IN THE FOOD BUSINESS

The Dominium Scandal: Deltec's First Foray into the Processed Food Business in Brazil

Deltec's ventures into the production and marketing of processed food-stuffs represent its second most important activity after its operations in finance and capital marketing. As such, the manufacture and distribution of processed foods provide the major instances of Deltec's application of its general strategy to the development and exploitation of a concrete sector of economic activity. A careful examination of Deltec's activities in this field provides an object lesson in some of the major manipulative and exploitative techniques now being developed by MNC's for dealing with the increasing economic nationalism of Third World countries.

Deltec's first major move into the food business was a financial success, a textbook example of some of the pragmatic implications of its grand strategy of "missionary capitalism." It was also, however, the biggest business scandal Brazil had experienced in three decades.

It all began in 1966 when Deltec paid $2.3 million for a British-owned complex of five flour mills, a textile mill, and a cookie factory called Moinho Inglés from S.G. Warburg, the British investment banking firm (itself an important Deltec shareholder). Deltec's purpose was to resell the mills to Brazilian owners, meanwhile developing financial liaisons with the buyers and distributive facilities for the products (of which it would retain ownership). Within a few months Deltec had sold off four blocks of Moinho Inglés holdings and facilities for a total of $3.6 million, while retaining control of the principal facility, a big flour mill in São Paulo, the Aymoré S. A. cookie factory, and certain other holdings with a total valuation of $3.3 million. Deltec thus had, in a few months, realized a profit of 200 percent on its initial investment, both directly in the form of sales prices and implicitly in the form of the assessed value of its remaining holdings. These facts by themselves caused considerable indignation on the London Stock Exchange and among British investors, who (understandably) felt they had been left holding the bag for Deltec (*London Sunday Times* 1968).

Deltec next (in July 1967) succeeded in unloading the São Paulo flour mill (Moinho Inglés, the namesake of the original combine) to the Brazilian Mineral and Metallurgical Company, a company in which Deltec held a dominant interest.[6] The property was then immediately resold to a group of private Brazilian buyers consisting of the Paula Ribeiro brothers and their cousin, Eduardo Guinle. A brief exposition of the background and purpose of their purchase of Moinho Inglés will be necessary in order to make the spectacular results of the sale comprehensible.

The Paula Ribeiro brothers were the directors of Dominium, the first coffee firm in Brazil to manufacture and export instant coffee, and at the time (July 1967) still by far the largest of the three Brazilian companies licensed to do so. Founded in 1965, Dominium by 1967 was exporting $18 million worth of instant coffee a year, accounting for 60 percent of all Brazilian exports of instant coffee. All of this went to the United States, where it accounted for 12 percent of total U.S. consumption of instant coffee. The profits were immense, and both Guinle and the Paula Ribeiros, particularly the former, attracted attention even in Rio de Janeiro for their spectacular standard of living. Guinle's high living apparently led to a feeling on the part of the Paula Ribeiros that he was not pulling his proper weight in the company. This led to a dispute that exploded into a ferocious rivalry in which both Guinle and the Paula Ribeiros attempted to buy up a majority of the company stock to force each other out of control of the business. Exorbitant prices were paid for the stock by both sides. This put a serious strain upon Dominium's resources. The firm had originally been capitalized at only $9 million and

---

[6]   According to its own 1967 annual report, Deltec headed the syndicate that purchased this company on the London Stock Exchange from Warburg. The purpose of the purchase was stated to be the same as that of Moinho Inglés: that of "transferring it under Brazilian laws and expanding its operations."

Dominium's success in the U.S. market had become in itself a source of demand for increasing capitalization.

The Paula Ribeiros bet upon an ingenious strategy for simultaneously forcing out Guinle and recapitalizing Dominium. This strategy was based upon the acquisition of Moinho Inglés. If the plan had worked, the brothers would have been able to have their cake and eat it too; i.e., to gain definitive control of Dominium, force out Guinle, and at the same time float a large stock issue aimed at recapitalizing Dominium at $35 million in 1967. A stock issue of $20 million was floated, aimed at small investors to minimize the potential threat to the brothers' control. This stock issue was sold through Dominium's subsidiary *ad valorem*, which in turn employed another stock-distributing company CBI (Companhia Brasileiro de Investimentos) to handle the sale to the public. The establishment of this indirect relationship between Dominium and the company actually responsible for selling its stock was, as we shall see, an integral part of the Paula Ribeiros' plan. A further relevant detail: the Paula Ribeiros were also directors and majority stockholders of CBI.

To make the Dominium shares attractive to buyers and thus guarantee a quick sale, they were offered on terms unprecedented in Brazilian financial history. To begin with, they were offered as loan certificates with a guaranteed fixed interest rate of 3 percent per month (36 percent per year, well above the inflation rate of 24.5 percent). In addition, they were stamped redeemable at par upon presentation at any CBI office, thus defining them as direct obligations of CBI and removing them altogether from the category of risk capital. The latter represented a flagrant violation of accepted Brazilian financial practice, but strangely the Central Bank of Brazil, the national regulatory agency, failed to take notice.

It seems clear in retrospect that the Paula Ribeiros were hoping, through these extraordinary measures, to use CBI's capital as a foundation for guaranteeing a rapid sale of shares to small investors (through the free redemption-at-par provision), for the brief time necessary to generate enough capital for them to acquire control of a dominant block of the shares themselves and thereby zap Guinle. Having done this they would be in a position to suspend the fixed interest and open redemption provisions and thus return to normal operation with themselves more firmly than ever in control of a recapitalized Dominium. This scheme presupposed a continued level of successful export performance by Dominium and its product until the required maneuvers could be completed, to make possible continuing interest payments or annual interest or dividends when the shares would later be converted into orthodox form. This presupposition, however, seemed reasonable in the light of Dominium's record to date.

In July 1967, the brothers put the next step of their plan into operation. They purchased Moinho Inglés from the Brazilian Mineral and Metallurgical Company, for $2.6 million. The purchase was in their own names, with money borrowed for the purpose from Deltec, the loan guaranteed by Dominium on the basis of the new stock issue and the guarantee signed by themselves as directors of Dominium (!) The latter step, although unusual to say the least by ordinary business standards, was apparently not specifically excluded by Dominium's bylaws. As security for its loan, Deltec retained a mortgage on Moinho Inglés.

Directly following their purchase of Moinho Inglés, in August 1967, the Paula Ribeiros called a Dominium stockholders' meeting. "Called" is perhaps not the appropriate term: the legally required announcements of the meeting were placed on the back pages of a few little-read journals, so that the public at large was in effect not informed. The brothers then proposed to the packed stockholders' meeting that Dominium acquire Moinho Inglés for the price of $9 million (3.5 times the price they had just paid for it). The purchase would take the form of new Moinho Inglés shares issued to Dominium to be paid for with Dominium shares issued directly to the Paula Ribeiros as owners of Moinho Inglés. The proposal was approved by the stacked meeting. The Paula Ribeiros thus acquired 45 percent of Dominium's new stock issue, guaranteeing their own control of Dominium and incidentally making themselves $9 million richer, while not directly laying out one cruzeiro of their own money. The $2.6-million loan from Deltec was, to be sure, issued to them, but, if worse came to worse it was secured by a mortgage on Moinho Inglés, which was now no longer the property of the Paula Ribeiros but of Dominium, the guarantor of the loan. As directors of Dominium, furthermore, the Paula Ribeiros were in a good position to see that Dominium would not press them overly hard for payment against its guarantee should they default upon their payments to Deltec.

Not content with their coup in the Moinho Inglés affair, the Paula Ribeiros repeated the maneuver a little later with a real estate property that they bought for $300,000 but resold to Dominium for $3 million, ten times its original price. At about this time it was publicly announced that Eduardo Guinle had resigned the directorship and left Dominium.

Within a month after these bold if unsavory tactics had ensured their control of Dominium, the Paula Ribeiros, as directors of Dominium, suspended without notice both the fixed monthly interest and the free redemption features of all Dominium shares. The Central Bank, called upon from many quarters to take some action or at least official notice, blandly insisted that the move was outside its proper authority and continued to take no action.

A cloud considerably larger than a man's hand had meanwhile appeared to cast a shadow over Dominium's prospects. The Brazilian government changed its policy of financing the export of coffee, leading to a serious shortage of foreign exchange on the part of the exporters. In addition, perhaps responding to pressure from U.S. interests but also presumably in order to divert a larger share of national instant coffee production into the domestic market and thus cut down on imports, the Brazilian government imposed an export duty on instant coffee. This hurt Dominium's competitive position in the U.S. market, which had been based upon the principle of higher-quality-for-the-same-price. With its capital base overextended by its recent stock issue, and depleted by the machinations of its own directors, Dominium's reserves proved inadequate to the strain imposed upon them by the resulting squeeze. On May 6, 1968, Dominium shut down its operations, laid off its 1,000 workers, declared bankruptcy, and asked for receivership. This move left 25 banks, 15 finance companies, and 45,000 private investors caught with a total of $12 million owed to them. It also left Moinho Inglés with no money to buy grain to mill, so that it too was forced to shut down, throwing an additional 1,000 workers out of work.

The shock to the Brazilian domestic financial and political system was intense: the scandal was called the largest in the past twenty-five to thirty years. The president of the nation ordered a full investigation to determine "the civil and criminal responsibilities of those involved." The eventual result of this investigation was that Moinho Inglés was declared a national patrimony, that is, a firm so vital to the national interest that the government should step in to get it going again in spite of its bankruptcy.

Moinho Inglés, meanwhile, had reverted to the ownership of Deltec, which held the mortgage on it as security for its loan to the Paula Ribeiro brothers. Deltec had already received 21 percent of the price in payments; now, as a secured creditor, it regained total control of the property, with the Brazilian government assuming the responsibility for getting it back into production after Dominium's collapse.

Deltec thus emerged from the Dominium disaster with its fortunes considerably enhanced. This fact was not lost upon Brazilian observers, who tended to charge Deltec with complicity in, if not with plotting, the entire affair. One point that was raised against Deltec concerned the extent of its knowledge of the Paula Ribeiro brothers' plans for Moinho Inglés at the time it sold the mill to them. Deltec disclaimed any prior knowledge of the amount at which the Paula Ribeiros planned to capitalize Moinho Inglés for its merger with Dominium. But if Deltec had had no inkling that such a deal was in the works, why had it gone to such elaborate lengths to avoid the appearance of a direct sale of Moinho Inglés to the Paula Ribeiros (a sale for which it was itself providing the financing)? Why, in other words, did Deltec sell Moinho Inglés to Brazilian Mineral and Metallurgy, a company under its control, only to have the latter immediately resell to the Paula Ribeiros? The elaborate process of sale and resale seemed to some to suggest that Deltec, knowing at least the gist of the Paula Ribeiros' plans, had sought to avoid the appearance of direct dealings with the latter, at least on the sales end of the operation.

The strongest public grounds for suspicion of a conspiracy between Deltec and the Paula Ribeiros was the incontrovertible fact of Deltec's strong prior connection with Dominium itself. Deltec had acquired a 49 percent ownership in Dominium International Incorporated of New York, the exclusive distributor of all Dominium instant coffee imported into the United States. Deltec, with its substantial banking and credit facilities, had been financing Dominium International's imports from its parent company as well as related transactions and operations such as the carrying of instant coffee stocks.

Dominium International, while under Deltec's control, had been charged with certain illegal ploys typical of the distributive phase of the operations of MNC's. One of these was the building up of credit balances vis-à-vis its Brazilian parent company by charging it 5 percent sales commission against the less-than-1-percent rate prevailing in the coffee trade. Deltec officials in São Paulo claimed that the 5 percent commission included interest on opening letters of credit, freight, and other expenses. In fact, the arrangement had all the earmarks of the common ploy of MNC's whereby profits are transferred out of the country in which the productive operation is located to the distributive subsidiary abroad, thus avoiding taxation in the country of production.

Dominium International had also been accused of practicing the so-called Portuguese Exchange, an illegal though widespread device whereby the foreign distributive subsidiary remits to its Brazilian company less than the $.87 per pound f.o.b. Santos minimum export price set by the Brazilian coffee institute whenever the New York price is lower. The Brazilian company then makes up the difference with dollars purchased on the black market in Brazil. This device, like the high commissions cited above, has the effect of maximizing the interest of the foreign distributor at the expense of the national productive and exporting operation, in this case Dominium-Brazil. It is a pattern that has marked other Deltec operations in South America, as we shall presently see.

From a different quarter, it should be noted that several Deltec officials were intimately acquainted with Guinle and the Paula Ribeiros and knew the details of their feud. The Deltec leadership must thus have been aware of the Paula Ribeiros' motives for the acquisition of Moinho Inglés and their need for secrecy to conceal their plan from Guinle until it was too late for him to stop them.[7]

---

[7]   Personal communication from an ex-employee of Deltec who had a position of authority in Deltec's Brazilian operation during the preliminary stages of the Dominium maneuver. The identity of our Deltec informant is withheld at his request.

Deltec, having acquired financial control over Dominium's export and distribution operation, must have seen an opportunity to use the Guinle–Paula Ribeiros dispute, and specifically the Moinho Inglés deal, to bring the present company also under its control. The terms upon which the Paula Ribeiros were able to carry out their scheme were Deltec's terms. Deltec financed the plan and retained the favored position of secured creditor with its mortgage on Moinho Inglés. Deltec, in other words, promoted the Paula Ribeiros' plot to gain total control of Dominium in order to gain control of the Paula Ribeiros, and through them of Dominium. The Brazilian government stepped in and took control of Dominium as *patrimonia nacional* to forestall this possibility. It was only this action that frustrated Deltec's plan. The government's investigation stopped short of (publicly) involving Deltec. The circumstantial evidence, however, reinforced by the account of a former Deltec employee, strongly indicates that Deltec's "low-profile" partnership with Dominium was in fact part of a plan to seize control of the corporation by covert manipulations that would result in damage to the national economy of Brazil.

The Dominium case was in this respect quickly overshadowed by Deltec's performance in Argentina, which made the Dominium scandal seem like a mere warm-up.

Deltec in Argentina: the Case of Swift de la Plata

Coordination of covert financial manipulation, illicit foreign profit transfers, and tacit blackmailing of national regulatory agencies and governments through threatening local enterprises important to national employment and foreign trade, characterized Deltec's strategy in the Dominium scandal. This strategy reappeared on a far grander scale in Deltec's attempted coup in the affair of Compañia Swift de la Plata in Argentina in 1970–1971. Largely as the result of a courageous judge and the leftward and nationalist trend of Argentine politics in those years, however, the result was the opposite of the Brazilian experience: a stunning setback for Deltec.

Deltec's ventures into manufactured grain and coffee products in Brazil in the late 1960's were only in the nature of exploratory raids into the manufactured-food-products market. In 1969 Deltec made its major move — the acquisition of International Packers Limited (IPL), the combined overseas operation of the U.S. Swift and Armour meat-packing corporations.[8] Deltec saw IPL (then the world's largest processor and marketer of beef and other meat products) as its entrée into the

[8]   The price paid by Deltec was $20 million: IPL had a book value of $100 million (*New York Times* 1971c; see also *New York Times* (1968) and *Wall Street Journal* (1968).

international manufactured food market (*Peruvian Times* 1969a). IPL had large holdings in Brazil but even larger ones in Argentina: Compañia Swift de la Plata (its major Argentine operation) employed 18,000 workers and had an output of $120 million, or 30 percent of Argentine meat exports (which taken together comprise 26 percent of Argentina's total exports) (*New York Times* 1971c). Swift was thus Argentina's largest single private employer and by itself accounted for one-twelfth of the nation's total export earnings.

IPL was an ungainly giant, with a large amount of capital sunk into fixed production facilities and wages and dependent for its slender profit margins (or, often, losses) on fluctuations in supply and international exchange rates. At the time Deltec acquired IPL (November-December 1969) it had been losing money for six straight months, according to Deltec's own account, in spite of relatively low cattle prices (0.69 Argentine pesos per kilo) (Deltec International Ltd:1971a:1).[9] Its purchase by Deltec therefore caused some surprise in financial quarters. Those who raised their eyebrows, however, failed to grasp the nature of Deltec's plans for IPL.

As a *New York Times* correspondent filing from Buenos Aires put it,

Deltec, according to its officials interviewed here, had a dream. It would acquire Argentina's largest meat packing and exporting concern, Swift de la Plata, which had fallen upon hard times. Using their financial expertise gained elsewhere in Latin America, Deltec planned to install a new management, rehabilitate the company and sell it to local investors (*New York Times* 1971c).

Deltec's "dream" was based on several shrewd calculations. The meat-packing industry in the United States had just undergone a major revolution. Once a volume-oriented business with operations focused on the distribution of a basic commodity to retailers, who did the most expensive work of butchering and preparing cuts for sale, it had become a profit-oriented industry focusing upon performing all operations from slaughtering to butchering and packaging cuts for sale at the source of supply. This allowed growers to market branded (manufactured) products rather than merely a basic commodity (i.e., raw material). The key to this change was the development of new freezing and shipping techniques, notably Iowa Beef's Cryovac Process.

IPL had just adopted this and other technological innovations of the U.S. meat packing industry. Deltec could hope to be the midwife of a similar production revolution, financing it from its considerable financial resources while setting up an international distributive apparatus to accommodate the new form of branded-manufactured, precut, and frozen

[9] *Compañia Swift de la Plata: Summary History* is the official Deltec account of the Swift de la Plata case.

(or frozen precooked) meat products. With the meat business put on a steadier, more consistently profitable basis, the high-volume cash flow could be used by a clever financial combine a lot more profitably than by a commodity-oriented packing and shipping management. Finally, selling out the business, once reestablished on the new, technologically transformed and profit-oriented lines, to local management would avoid the danger of nationalization threatening foreign-owned production operations while providing a handsome profit that could be used to fortify the relatively nationalization-proof (and more profitable) international distribution network.

One of Deltec's first major changes in the company was to replace its top management (U.S. and British) with Argentines. Enrique Holmberg, an Argentine, was made president: Deltec has pointed to this move as an instance of its efforts to "Argentinize" Swift de la Plata (Deltec International Ltd. 1971a:7), but it should be noted that Holmberg was already a Deltec man, and president of Deltec's Argentine financial arm (Argentaria S.A. de Finanzas).[10] True to Deltec policy, Holmberg's first assignment was to assemble a group of Argentine investors to whom Deltec could sell the company. These efforts failed, partly because, Deltec claims, "potential investors were never able to ascertain that, upon their purchase of control, Swift de la Plata would be treated as an 'Argentine company' for all purposes [of governmental credit assistance, subsidies, etc.]" (Deltec International Ltd. 1971a:2). Since Deltec would have financed a considerable part of the purchase, retained control of the foreign distribution of the product, installed its own executives in positions of managerial control, and identified these same executives as the prime prospective customers to whom it was trying to sell the company (Deltec International Ltd. 1971a:2), the Argentine government may perhaps be forgiven for having its doubts.

Holmberg's second assignment was to increase profits. This he did, by Deltec's own account, with spectacular success. Confronted with a steady rise in cattle prices (they virtually doubled, from 0.69 pesos per kilo in November-December 1969 to 1.30 pesos per kilo in September-October 1970), Holmberg more than doubled production of frozen cooked beef, the most remunerative export product (from 2 million pounds to 4.8 million pounds per month) in his first three months on the job (May-July 1970). Profits in the same period (May-August 1970) shot up to an average of 816,250 pesos per month, while costs were reduced at a rate projected at $12 million per year (Deltec International Ltd. 1971a:2). This reduction in costs was achieved chiefly through massive layoffs of packinghouse workers — the work force was reduced from 18,000 to between 12,000 and 13,000 in one year (*New York Times* 1971c).

---

[10]   Holmberg is also a first cousin of the then president of Argentina, Lanusse.

In late 1970 it appeared that Deltec's "dream" might turn into a nightmare. The immediate cause was an acute shortage of Swift's basic commodity — beef. The unprecedented phenomenon of a beef shortage in Argentina had been brought about by the government's attempts to flood the beef market in the preceding year as a means of keeping domestic prices down. It levied a tax on cattle herds to force ranchers to sell their stock, choosing a time when the cattle-producing regions were being hit by an intense drought. As a result of the military junta's shortsighted anti-inflationary policy, the number of cattle of marketable size was greatly lowered in the following year, building inflationary pressures to a far more intense pitch, and incidentally squeezing the packinghouses engaged in the export trade between rapidly rising domestic beef prices and the relatively fixed foreign market price. Domestic retail prices for beef (a staple of the Argentine worker's diet) also doubled. The government at first sought to deal with the situation by imposing price ceilings in the wholesale cattle markets, but these were ineffective. Suppliers simply held their stocks off the markets altogether. In desperation the government decreed that every other week was to be a "meatless" week for the Argentine consumer, an utterly unprecedented measure in a nation whose depleted cattle herds still outnumbered the human population by two to one (*New York Times* 1971a and 1971b).

As the price of cattle went up, Swift and the other large packing-houses and exporters set up a great outcry about the squeeze in which they were being placed between rising costs and competitive prices in the international market. The political form taken by this outcry was strong pressure for a new devaluation of the peso. This solution would, of course, amount to the assumption by the national government and the economy as a whole of the sacrifice necessary to maintain what the companies considered an adequate profit margin in their international operations.

When cattle prices reached and passed the level of 1.30 pesos per kilo in September 1970 and the government still refused to devalue the peso, Swift and most of the other large export packinghouses suspended operations in an attempt to force the government's hand. The government responded by making credit available through the official banking institutions to companies more than 51 percent Argentine-owned. This prerequisite could not, of course, be met by most of the packinghouses, which are British or North American–owned. Virtually the entire meat-export industry in Argentina then closed down — temporarily — throwing tens of thousands of workers out of work and raising devaluation pressure to fever pitch (*Wall Street Journal* 1973).

The massive unemployment created by Swift's layoffs as part of its efficiency and economy drive of 1970 was doubled by the layoffs following the new shutdown. Although Swift managed to keep between three and four thousand workers busy subcontracting for various domestic suppliers, it threw a further 8,000 workers out of their jobs (*New York Times* 1971a), raising the total number laid off in little more than a year to 14,000. Most of the unemployed were concentrated in and around Rosario, where Swift's largest plants were located. Rosario was transformed into an economic disaster area.

It was in this context, in May 1971, that Stanley M.F. Sylvester, one of the directors of Swift de la Plata, was kidnapped by the Argentine People's Liberation Army. This kidnapping was widely publicized in the United States at the time, but with Sylvester almost exclusively described in his other capacity as honorary British consul in Rosario rather than as a director of Swift and thus in the upper echelons of Deltec's Argentine operations. Yet it was Sylvester's Swift-Deltec role that was primarily behind his kidnapping. The ransom demanded (and agreed to) was from Swift de la Plata itself (it was the first time that a ransom had been demanded directly from a private corporation, rather than from a foreign government, in an Argentine political kidnapping). It consisted of $62,500 worth of food, blankets, and clothing to be purchased by Swift de la Plata and distributed to the unemployed poor of Rosario. Supplementary demands, to which the company also agreed, were that it hire back hundreds of workers who had been laid off, give them back pay, and make a number of health-and-safety and other internal improvements in the plants. This successful action was effective, not only in gaining its immediate goals (the ransom) but in focusing national attention upon the plight of the unemployed cattle workers and the irresponsibility of their chief ex-employer, Swift de la Plata (*Miami Herald* 1971; *New York Times* 1971b).

A number of the other foreign-owned plants settled their liabilities and slowly resumed production. Swift chose a different course of action. With 6,000 workers out of work (12,000 if the earlier layoffs are included) and a major piece of the nation's export earning capacity, it still had strong cards to play. The tactic it decided upon was (1) to claim it was being forced into bankruptcy by the high cattle prices, by the Argentine government's refusal to devalue the peso, as well as by its outstanding debts; (2) that its major creditor (more than $10 million, or one-third of the total debt) was none other than Deltec (that is, various Deltec financial and other subsidiaries in Argentina); and that (3) the government should intervene to permit Swift's continued operation (under its own management) while repaying its debts to both national and international creditors at very favorable terms of time and interest. The terms Deltec actually proposed were that it should repay 10 percent of its debts in the first year, 20 percent in the second, 30 percent in the third, and 40 percent in the fourth, at an annual rate of 12 percent on Argentine peso debts (this was close to the annual rate of inflation at the time) and 3 percent on international debts.

To implement this policy Deltec-Swift applied to the Commercial court in December 1970 for a legal declaration of insolvency (a *"convocatoria"*). This procedure involves (1) an immediate cessation of payment on all non-secured and nonpreferential debts; (2) the continuation of the business under its own management; (3) the appointment by the court of a referee to report on the business and the nature and amount of its assets and liabilities; (4) the proposal by the management of a creditors' agreement for the orderly repayment of the debts; (5) a meeting of creditors to accept or reject the proposal; and finally (6) the approval or disapproval of the agreement by the court. Rejection of such an agreement by the creditors or disapproval by the court automatically results in bankruptcy (Deltec International Ltd. 1971a:2).

It is important to grasp the difference between "convocatoria," the type of arrangement for which Swift applied, and bankruptcy per se. Convocatoria is in the nature of a provisional breathing space during which a company has an opportunity to work out an agreement with its creditors on its own terms and under its own management without going into bankruptcy.

The convocatoria was duly declared by Judge Salvador Maria Lozada, who set the following October (October 4, 1971) as the date of the creditors' meeting.

The main issue upon which the convocatoria and its outcome depended was the status of Swift's (and Deltec's) claim that the $10 million to $14 million worth of credits (mostly for purchases of cattle and seed grain) extended by Deltec's international financial and various Argentine operations to Swift represented "debts" of Swift to Deltec. Deltec, in its official history of the affair, claims that of the $10 million it lent to Swift between March 1969 and December 1970 (i.e., from the time of its acquisition of Swift to the convocatoria) it "never received one centavo of its own money back in either this period or in any previous or subsequent periods" (Deltec International Ltd. 1971a:2).

These claims are debatable on several grounds. The most fundamental of these is that Swift formed a part of Deltec's overall organization, and that transfers of money or credits from others of its subsidiaries to Swift, like transfers of profits from Swift to other Deltec subsidiaries, must therefore be regarded as aspects of an integral operating budget of a single organization, rather than as externally (i.e., legally) enforceable "debts" between two independent organizations. From this point of view, Swift's plea for a convocatoria to pay off its debts to Deltec as well as its other creditors appeared as a maneuver designed primarily to gain official sanction for sending out of the country to its international financial operation money that it had in effect already recouped in the normal course of operations by diverting profits from Swift into its other Argentine financial subsidiaries, and at the same time bilking its other creditors (mostly Argentine firms) by artifically extending the period of repayment, and depressing the rate of interest, on their credits and sales to Swift. Both the period necessary for repayment and the lower interest rates were calculated, of course, in relation to the artifically distended (by one-third) amount of Swift's total debt created by including the Deltec credits within it.

As a second point, on the other hand, if Swift's "debts" to Deltec were not really debts, then could Swift really be considered insolvent? From the critical point of view outlined above, which sees Deltec-Swift's appeal for convocatoria as a tactic to exploit the national economic crisis and its own social and economic importance to Argentina in order to short-change its creditors, "repay" itself twice, and transfer the second repayment out of the country under official auspices, and answer is, clearly, no. Should Deltec persist in refusing to accept this interpretation of Swift's "debts," however, and continue to insist on Swift's insolvency because of its inability to repay the "debts" to Deltec, then a court taking this critical point of view would be left with only one alternative: disallow the convocatoria, declare Swift bankrupt outright, and hold Deltec responsible for all of its debts. The political, social, and economic implications of such a decision can perhaps be imagined in U.S. terms by substituting General Motors in the role of Swift. Such a step was unprecedented in Argentine history and seemed inconceivable in the political climate of Argentina since the fall of Peron.

The point should also be made that Deltec-Swift had made no substantial capital improvements in its meat-processing facilities in Argentina. The Deltec "loans" were used for routine operating expenses like the purchase of cattle and seed, and the payment of wages. Why then were such loans necessary when the company was running at a profit? Because the profits of Swift were being diverted into other Deltec financial subsidiaries in Argentina, chiefly Argentaria S.A.[11]

After the formal beginning of the convocatoria process in December 1970, Swift reopened and slowly resumed operations. By April 1971 production was back to normal and the rate of profit higher than ever, in spite of the fact that cattle prices had risen higher than the levels they had reached at the time Swift and the other internationally owned packing-houses had shut down on the grounds that the high price of cattle had made continued export operations "economically unfeasible" (prices reached 1.50 pesos per kilo in March 1971 and 2.00 pesos per kilo in August). Swift's profits, in fact, were such that in spite of having been virtually shut down for almost six months, it was able to report in its

[11]   Deposition of the Argentine delegate, O. Valdovinos, in International Union of Food and Allied Workers Associations (1971).

statement for the year ending August 31, 1971, the small loss of only 1,170,000 Argentine pesos for the entire period! In the last four months of the same period, furthermore, the firm's assets, in the form of cash inventories and accounts receivable, grew by a total of 17 million pesos (Deltec International Ltd. 1971a:2, 3).

One of the maneuvers through which Swift sought to recoup its high profit rates immediately following the convocatoria is a textbook case of one of the main ploys developed by international enterprises to bilk their national productive operations and avoid the necessity to remit profits to the countries in which they are located. Swift made a deal with a European buying group for 477 tons of meat extract. It had just completed a contract with the same group for meat extract at the rate of between $3.60 and $3.80 per pound, but the price arrived at for the new contract was only $3.30 per pound. Swift explained that it had settled for the low price because, having completed its original contract by June 1971, "it found itself in the unique position of having produced additional quantities while other producers were still delivering against their original contracts" (Deltec International Ltd. 1971a:3). Having "found itself" in this "unique position," and recognizing that "Swift did not have the financial capacity to carry the extra inventory" and thus could not hold out for prices as high as those of its original contract, it had been forced to settle for less. The Argentine National Meat Board (Junta Nacional de Carne) suspected otherwise. It turned down Swift's proposed sale on the grounds that the price was too low. The underlying suspicion was that the low purchase price, which represented no profit or possibly a loss to Swift, had been negotiated by Deltec as the middleman between Swift and the European buyers' group in order to put itself in a position to rake off high profits by reselling to the Europeans at going high prices.

Judge Lozada described this maneuver in a later interview in the journal of the Argentine meat workers' union as the "subfactoring" of sales between subsidiaries of the same multinational firm, noting that the practice was particularly rampant among the foreign-owned meat-packinghouses operating in Argentina. Lozada described the total process in the following words:

Suppose that the [production] cost of a unit good is 50; the packing house sells to an enterprise belonging to the same corporation, located in the Bahamas, Liechtenstein or Switzerland for the price of 40, thus devaluing the cost of the unit by twenty per cent, so that the firm that produces the unit either sustains a loss or at most obtains no profit. In this way the latter escapes paying taxes to our country and, owing to its size and scale of employment (in other words, to the "great social cost" of shutting down some of its plants) it is then able to gain huge credits at very low interest. These, however, it does not apply directly to overcoming the crisis but channels them through some financial institution of the same group.

Afterwards [i.e., after the original sale of the low price of 40 to its foreign subsidiary], the goods are resold to retail firms, also subsidiaries of the same company, for a price of 80 or 90, and these in turn sell to the consumer for a price of 100. It is clear that the only component of the process to make important profits is the intermediary company (i.e., the foreign wholesaler subsidiary), which is located outside the country and which therefore either pays no taxes or, at most, a negligible duty.

Exports of meat from the [foreign-owned] packing companies account for 28.9 per cent of all national exports, amounting to a total of $350,000,000. If we consider that rather more than 10 per cent of this amount is "sub-factored," over $40,000,000, or approximately 40 billion pesos Argentine, is transferred out of the country each year in the form of unremitted profits while paying no taxes (Lozada 1972:14–15).

As the date for the creditors' meeting (October 4) approached, Deltec submitted its repayment plan (including the figures on interest rates and percentage to be repaid per year cited earlier). It was jolted, however, when Judge Lozada refused to allow Swift's claimed debts to Deltec as genuine debts. He flatly rejected a $12 million claim by a Deltec-affiliated banking group and allowed only $1 million of a $3 million claim by the same group. He accepted $20 million in other debts — $7 million from cattle dealers, $7 million from banks, and $6 million from other accounts. The grounds for refusing the Deltec-Swift debt claims were substantially those cited above.

Judge Lozada's decision directly threatened Deltec's ability to secure the necessary 80 percent majority approval for its repayment plan at the coming creditors' meeting. It resorted to attempting to buy the votes of other creditors for its plan but was caught at it and ordered to desist by Judge Lozada. Nevertheless, whether as a result of these efforts or not, Deltec received an 85 percent vote of approval (in both numbers of shares and creditors) for its plan at the meeting — a major victory. Coming on the heels of a rousing vote of confidence from its own employees for continuation of operations under its own management, Deltec-Swift was in a strong position before Judge Lozada (*New York Times* 1971c). As a *Wall Street Journal* columnist noted, since Argentine national and state banks were among those voting in favor of the Deltec-Swift plan, it seemed doubtful that Lozada would reject the plan (it should be recalled that the approval of the agreement between debtor and creditors by the court is the final step of the convocatoria process) (*Wall Street Journal* 1971).

Also weighing heavily in Deltec's favor was the report of the court-appointed referee on the financial and economic situation of Swift. Judge Lozada, in a sudden move less than two weeks before the creditors' meeting, had replaced Swift's Board of Directors with court appointees, directing them to report on the financial viability of Swift to the court. Their report showed that Swift had total assets of $111 million (of which $97 million represented fixed assets) and total indebtedness (including Deltec group claims) of about $35,000,000, thus a "going concern" value to its equity of $86 million (Deltec International Ltd. 1971a:3). The report amounted to a strong brief for the economic viability of Swift and therefore the excellent prospects of success for the repayment plan.

On November 8, Judge Lozada electrified the nation (not to mention the directors of Swift and Deltec) by rejecting the creditors' agreement and declaring Swift bankrupt. Lozada, in his decision, reaffirmed that Swift and Deltec were the same thing. He therefore chastized Deltec's claim that the credits it had extended to its subsidiary, Swift, were "debts" on a par with those owed to independent creditors as an instance of bad faith. He noted that the payment plan proposed by Deltec-Swift including the Deltec debts, which amounted to over one-third of the total, would have meant, in effect, robbing the other creditors of almost half of what was owed them in effective interest (by both lowering the rate of interest and prolonging the terms of payment). Lozada castigated Swift's man-euvers of selling at artifically lowered prices to foreign branches of Deltec as a major factor in its pretended insolvency. He condemned Deltec's attempts to subvert and defraud the creditors' meeting, or *concordato* phase of the convocatoria procedure, by buying the votes of more than ninety of Swift's creditors through promises of preference in the payment of their claims in advance of those of the other creditors (Treviño 1972:181–182).

For these and other reasons, Lozada concluded, the survival of Swift under its own management was not in the interest of the nation as a whole, and the national interest must take precedence over that of the creditors. This decision automatically threw Swift into bankruptcy, and he appointed the national government as liquidator. The government immediately appointed an intervener and directed him to continue the operations of the company. A few days later Lozada followed up his decision by holding Deltec's other subsidiaries in Argentina responsible for all of Swift's legal debts (Treviño 1972:181).

Swift and Deltec appealed the decision, but a court of appeals and finally the Argentine Supreme Court sustained Lozada, on June 6, 1972, and September 5, 1973, respectively. The Supreme Court specifically reaffirmed Lozada's ruling that all Deltec assets in Argentina be available to be liquidated against the debts of Swift. This decision was followed up two days later by court-ordered bankruptcy proceedings against all Deltec affiliates in Argentina. This move was designed to achieve at least temporary state control of these operations. Clarence Dauphinot, Deltec's president, qualified these decisions as "ourtageous, unfair, and, I might add, unprecedented," and predicted darkly that the decision would have "very far-reaching consequences for any international company doing business in Argentina" (*Wall Street Journal* 1973; *New York Times* 1973a, 1973b).

The effect of this series of court decisions has been in effect to nationalize Swift de la Plata. Deltec officials have recognized that it is uncertain when, if ever, Deltec can regain control of Swift.[12] The impact of Lozada's decision, and its subsequent upholding by the higher courts, upon Argentine consciousness and politics was profound. As one Argentine commentator remarked:

> Many have called the Lozada Decision "historic." There can be no doubt that the history of the cattle industry in Argentina will be divided in the future into the periods "before Lozada" and "after Lozada" (Treviño 1972:182, original emphasis).

Deltec and IPL in Brazil

IPL had extensive holdings in Brazil over and beyond its Argentine operations. When Deltec purchased IPL in 1969, it acquired the Swift and Armour operations in Brazil. Taken together, these two made up by far the largest productive force in Brazil's burgeoning meat-export industry. Swift owned three slaughtering and refrigerating plants, a vegetable oil and detergent factory, and several cattle ranches. Armour owned one slaughtering and packing plant, two can factories (to manufacture the cans used in packing the beef), and several ranches. Some notion of the relative importance of these two companies' holdings in the Brazilian meat export industry can be gleaned from the following figures. In 1971 in the state of Rio Grande do Sul, the chief cattle-producing state, the five principal employers were Armour (2,400 workers), Swift (2,100 workers), and the remaining three with 800, 450, and 400, respectively (International Union of Food and Allied Workers' Associations 1971). In 1972 the value of the capital assets of Swift and Armour was more than 150 million cruzeiros combined, or about double that of their nearest competitor (*Jornal do Brasil* 1972; *Brasil Exportacão* 1972:196). In addition to these holdings, Deltec, in partnership with King Ranch of Texas, began to acquire vast tracts of "virgin" territory as potential ranch land in the Northern Brazilian states of Pará and Maranhão (Deltec 1970:18; Deltec 1971b:17).

"Virgin" is in quotes because not all of the land acquired by Deltec was unoccupied or unutilized by human beings. The human beings were, it is true, Indians, which in Deltec's eyes evidently made them something of an exception; an exception, that is, to the category of human beings.

The story is one that can be told hundreds of times over, changing only the names of the particular private company or entrepreneur, Indian bureau, and government minister involved, in the modern history and development of Amazonia. The military government that took over

---

[12]   Private correspondence with members of the Deltec research project.

Brazil in 1964, in its effort to attract capital to Amazonia, set up a tax-rebate scheme whereby any corporation investing more than a certain percentage of its income or assets in the development of the region could qualify for a rebate of 50 percent on its corporate taxes, provided the government's regional developmental authority approved the investment. To secure the requisite approval the National Foundation for Aid to the Indian (FUNAI) must certify that the investment did not involve land inhabited by Indians.

It so happened that one of Deltec's proposed land purchases lay for the most part within the boundaries of the reservation of the Urubu-Kaapor tribe. This reservation, located on the Maranhão–Pará border; had been officially proclaimed more than thirty years ago by the Brazilian government. It was, in fact, one of the very few Indian reserves in Brazil to have been legally established and demarcated in this way. The reservation had been established to protect the Urubu–Kaapor and the scattered remnants of a related tribe, the Tembe, from the encroachments of small ranchers, nut-gatherers, and rubber-gatherers. Small-scale ranchers and itinerant gatherers have little political clout. Deltec is another story. FUNAI was ordered directly by the office of the Minister of the Interior (under whose administrative jurisdiction it lies) to issue the certification that the land was virgin and uninhabited by Indians, in spite of the existence of the government-owned reservation on the land. The lawyer hired by Deltec to represent its interests in this matter was, incidentally, the son of the Minister of the Interior, which may not have been wholly coincidental. To their credit, officials of FUNAI objected strenuously. They were, however, overridden by their own chief, the redoubtable General Bandeira de Melo, who has made a name for himself for protecting Indian interests with all the zeal and scrupulousness with which former U.S. Attorney General John Mitchell prosecuted anti-trust cases against corporations that had contributed heavily to the Nixon election campaigns. Bandeira de Melo approved the minister's plan to transfer the FUNAI post that administered the reservation to the jurisdiction of the state of Maranhão. It is a frequently used ploy to get Indian lands into the hands of state governments, which invariably prove willing to sell them off to private investors. The state of Maranhão duly agreed to the sale, and the Indians were loaded into trucks, taken to the edge of their ex-reservation, and dumped off. The reservation thereby magically reverted to a state of virginity.

The case of Deltec and the Urubu–Kaapor deserves prominence as a textbook example of the ruthless expropriation of the remaining native peoples of Amazonia by capitalist "developers," both domestic and foreign. That this particular instance was planned and carried out by some Deltec "business missionary" presumably made little difference to the Urubu–Kaapor.

In early 1971, at the same time it was ramming through its theft of the Urubu–Kaapor reservation, Deltec was announcing plans to build the world's largest meat-packing and processing plant on Marajó island, at the mouth of the Amazon River. This announcement also coincided with Deltec's call for a pre-bankruptcy proceeding (convocatoria) for its Swift de la Plata meat-packing facilities in Argentina. It is easy to speculate that the two moves may not have been entirely unrelated. The announcement of Deltec's Brazilian plans must have put great pressure on the Argentines, who depend on beef exports for 30 percent of their export earnings and who knew that they were the prime target of Brazil's drive to make itself the number-one meat exporter in South America, to settle favorably on Deltec's terms. It is also conceivable, on the other hand, that Deltec's Argentine maneuvers may have been part of some sort of deal with the Brazilian government to transfer its major meat-processing and export operations from Argentina to Brazil. The simultaneous announcement of its big plans for new facilities in Brazil and its refusal to invest any of the resources it was planning to channel into the Brazilian facilities in its already existing Argentine operations are certainly consistent with such a theory. There is no hard evidence to support either hypothesis, however.

In the following year (1972) Deltec decided to divest itself of IPL and all its holdings in Brazil. This was part of a general decision to get out of direct involvement in the production of processed foods and to concentrate entirely on distribution and marketing in the North American and West European markets. Deltec's holdings in Australia and New Zealand also were affected by this decision, so it is unlikely that it was merely a reaction to South American conditions, such as Deltec's unpleasant experience in Argentina. Deltec's account of the decision in its own annual report, as usual, gives no reason for the move. The decision is, however, in line with general Deltec policy. As we have observed, the big profits in the international processed-food business are garnered by the middleman, that is, the exporter, importer, and distributor, not the producer. Deltec had, during its brief period of ownership of IPL, done much to modernize and improve the management of its facilities, and it had laid the foundations for vastly increased cattle production with its land purchases in the North, in partnership with King Ranch. It was, as a result, in a position to sell these holdings at a profit. Its long-run interest in these operations, however, had all along lain not in their immediate profitability, but in their potential as suppliers for the international distribution system upon which Deltec was concentrating its main attention. This network was already well established by 1972, and this may have been the decisive consideration leading Deltec to decide that the time had come to get out of production.

Deltec managed the divestiture of its IPL holdings in characteristic fashion. Before selling them off to its old cronies in BIB, Antunes and BRASCAN, Deltec merged Armour and Swift in Brazil as Swift/Armour Industria e Commercio, S.A. (February 1972). It floated a public stock issue in the new company through BIB, of which it was still a member (*Jornal do Brasil* 1972; *Wall Street Journal* 1972). Deltec thus profited by the public capitalization of Swift/Armour and by its sale to a Brazilian group (Antunes) and another long-time associate (BRASCAN), with whom it could expect to work smoothly as suppliers for its export and distribution operations. Far from representing a reverse of policy or a failure, therefore, Deltec's exit from direct ownership and involvement with meat-processing facilities represents an excellent example of Deltec's basic strategy.

REFERENCES

American Banker
  1973 November 28.
DELTEC INTERNATIONAL LTD.
  1970 Annual report.
  1971a *Compañia Swift de la Plata: summary history*. December 15.
  1971b Annual report.
  1972 Annual report.
INTERNATIONAL UNION OF FOOD AND ALLIED WORKERS' ASSOCIATIONS
  1971 *Proceedings of the convention*. Mimeographed. Chicago.
Jornal do Brasil
  1972 June 8.
London Sunday Times
  1968 October 27.
MARIA LOZADA, SALVADOR
  1972 Las Empresses sin Patria. *El Trabajador de la Carne*. No. 1 (n.s.)
    October: 14–15.
Miami Herald
  1971 May 31.
New York Times
  1968 June 19.
  1971a March 14.
  1971b May 31.
  1971c October 17.
  1973a September 6.
  1973b September 8.
Peruvian Times
  1969a May 16.
  1969b May 19.
TREVIÑO, PEPE
  1972 *La carne podrida*. Argentina: A. Peña Lillo.

Wall Street Journal
  1968   June 19.
  1971   October 7.
  1972   December 18.
  1973   September 6.

The "Native Reserves" (Bantustans) and the role of the Migrant Labor System in the Political Economy of South Africa

BERNARD MAGUBANE

> The Colored people are generally looked upon by the Whites as an
> inferior race, whose interests ought to be systematically disregarded
> when they come into competition with their own, and should be
> governed mainly with a view to the advantage of the superior race.
> For this advantage two things are considered to be especially neces-
> sary: first that facilities should be afforded to the white colonists for
> obtaining the possession of land theretofore occupied by the Native
> tribes; secondly: that the Kaffir population should be made to furn-
> ish as large and as cheap a supply of labour as possible.
>
> EARL GREY (1880; quoted in Morel 1969:30)

In the study of reserves and migrant labor we have inherited a distorted
understanding of their role in relation to the large capitalist economy.
The reserves, we were told, were merely places in which Africans were to
be protected for their own sake in the era of white conquest, and now the
reserves are being seriously developed for eventual autonomy. Thus the
reserves and the larger society are considered as separate entities, rather
than as two sides of the same coin: development and underdevelopment,
affluence and poverty. In this paper I will illustrate that the reserves are
the method by which capital exploits labor to reap super-profits.

The statement quoted above, made by an agent of British imperialism,
in actual fact sums up the essence of what South Africa calls her "native
policy." If the capitalist mode of production was to appear and develop it
was necessary to do more than deprive the immediate producers of the
means of production and make them "free" paupers; wealth had to be
concentrated in the hands of the conquering settlers. The process of
"imperialization" involved the restructuring of African subsistence society in such a way that peasants in the reserves could never become
economically self-sufficient again. The process that deprived Africans of
their means of subsistence and reduced them to wage labor is not unique.

Marx wrote that one of Wakefield's great merits is connected with his discovery regarding the colonies:

First of all he discovered that in the colonies the ownership of money, the means of subsistence, machinery and other means of production, do not suffice to stamp the owner as a capitalist unless there exist, as a correlative wage workers, other persons who are compelled to sell themselves "voluntarily." He made the discovery that capital is not a thing, but a social relation between persons, and a relation determined by things. Mr. Peel, he says lamentingly, took with him from England to Swan River, Western Australia, means of subsistence and of production to the value of £50,000. He had the foresight to take with him, in addition, 3000 persons, men, women and children, members of the working class. But, on arrival at his destination, Mr. Peel was "left without a servant to make his bed or fetch him water from the river." Poor Mr. Peel, who had provided for everything, except for the export of the English relations of production. He had forgotten to bring these with him to Swan River! (1957:850).

When the English appeared in the Cape Colony in 1906, they brought settlers with capital who were expected to find their workers among the indigenous population. Their problem then was how to avoid the fate of Mr. Peel. Behind the wars of conquest and the "setting" aside of areas for African occupation is a more pervasive and sinister aspect of capitalist society — the need for a class of laborers to be exploited. For British imperialism, Africans were not just going to be conquered and decimated: they were to be relegated to a condition in which they would be dependent in every aspect on their conquerors for their livelihood. The imposition of capitalist productive relations engendered a profound crisis in African societies that were now being confined in the reservations.

One of the great achievements of Marx was to show that the specific exploitative relations of capitalism are recreated in the colonies in a different manner than in the metropolis:

It is otherwise in the colonies. There the capitalist regime encounters on all hands the resistance of producers who own the means of production with which they work, and who can gain wealth for themselves by their own labour instead of working to enrich a capitalist. The contradiction between these diametrically opposed economic systems works itself out in practice as a struggle between the two. When the capitalist is backed up by the power of the mother country, he tries, by forcible means, to clear out of his way the modes of production and appropriation that are based upon the independent labour of the producers. Whereas in the mother country, self-interest constrains the political economist, the sycophant of capital, to declare that the capitalist method of production is theoretically identical with its opposite; in the colonies, self-interest compels him to make a clean breast of it, and to acknowledge frankly that the two methods of production are antagonistic. To this end he shows that the development of the social productivity of labour, cooperation, the division of labour, the large-scale application of machinery, and the like, are impossible without the expropriation of the workers and a suitable transformation of their means of production into capital. In the interest of what is called "national wealth", he casts about for artificial means which will ensure the poverty of the common people. His apologetic armour, therefore, crumbles away bit by bit, like touchwood (1957:848–849).

The last sentence is extremely important. From the very beginning of white-settler colonization, the colonists decided that the African population was suitable for the most brutal, insidious, and cruel spoilations. In the process of harnessing their labor, a policy of conquest was begun that would not destroy the population but that would deprive it of its land and subsistence and thus reduce it, in effect, to a mere instrument in the process of capitalist prosperity. The Africans were subjected to both expropriation and appropriation. That was the secret alike of conquest and of the setting aside of the reservations in which they would find it hard to continue any form of independent subsistence. From their labor the settlers secured the surplus that provided them with the much-needed capital. In his article, Mafeje (1973) describes the objectives of capitalism in the colonies:

In its imperialist form the objective of West European capitalism was *not* transformation of traditional societies, wherever it found them, but rather their incorporation so as to secure markets and supplies of raw materials. . . . It did this by undermining or reconstructing traditional society in such a manner that it could satisfy its needs, without necessarily reproducing itself as a genuine mode of production. The primitive accumulation it engendered via the world market did not lead to a new and expanding *social* division of labour as in Europe. Instead, it contrived to maintain some semblance of traditional society on non-traditional terms. . . .
We, thus, see that in these countries the logic of predatory capitalism has not been a replacement of the old social formations by new ones but rather an establishment of a hybrid social formation (original emphasis).

By analyzing the history and evolution of the so-called native reserves, I hope to demonstrate in this chapter how these hybrid forms are created and maintained.

The great advantage of confining African labor in the reserves is this: there not only are Africans who are to become wage workers reproduced cheaply over and over again, but the reserves are also used as dumping grounds for the human waste that is discarded in the urban and mining industries. As a result a "perfect" number is maintained of the needed African labor in the so-called white areas. The so-called African areas suffer from the indispensable economic and social dependence on the white areas — a dependency that the capitalist sector wants to maintain by all the political means at its disposal and that the social scientist falsely represents as an aspect of a dual society or a plural society.

In a prototypical essay, W.A. Lewis characterized the economic relations of what he calls a dual society as follows:

The fact that the wage level in the capitalist sector depends upon earnings in the subsistence sector is sometimes of immense political importance, since its effect is that capitalists have a direct interest in holding down the productivity of the subsistence workers. Thus, the owners of plantations have no interest in seeing knowledge of new techniques or new seeds conveyed to the peasants, and if they are influential in government, they will not be found using their influence to expand the facilities for agricultural extension. They will not support proposals for land settlement, and are often instead to be found engaged in turning peasants off their lands. (cf. Marx on "Primary Accumulation"). This is one of the worst features of imperialism, for instance. The imperialists invest capital and hire workers; it is to their advantage to keep wages low, and even in those cases where they do not actually go out of their way to impoverish the subsistence economy, they will at least very seldom be found doing anything to make it more productive. In actual fact the record of every imperial power in Africa in modern times is one of impoverishing the subsistence economy, either by taking away the people's land, or by demanding forced labor in the capitalist sector, or by imposing taxes to drive people to work for capitalist employers. Compared with what they have spent on providing facilities for European agriculture or mining, their expenditure on the improvement of African agriculture has been negligible. The failure of imperialism to raise living standards is not wholly to be attributed to self-interest, but there are many places where it can be traced directly to the effects of having imperial capital invested in agriculture or in mining (1954:139).

The dependence of wages in the capitalist sector upon earnings in the subsistence sector is reminiscent of the development of German capitalism in the nineteenth century as described by Engels:

Here we see clearly: that which at an earlier historical stage was the basis of relative well-being for the workers, namely, the combination of agriculture and industry, the ownership of house, garden and field, and security of tenure in the dwelling-place, is becoming today, under the rule of large-scale industry, not only a worse hindrance to the worker, but the greatest misfortune for the whole working class, the basis for an exampled depression of wages below their normal level, and that not only for individual districts and branches of enterprise, but for the whole country. No wonder that the big bourgeoisie and petty bourgeoisie who live and grow rich from these abnormal deductions from wages are enthusiastic over rural industry and the workers owning their own houses, and that they regard the introduction of new domestic industries as the sole remedy for all rural distress (n.d.:15).

The genesis of capitalism in South Africa in some respects was not unique. It had aspects similar to the German variant but sharply differed from it both in the cause of development and ultimate results. The capital that was invested in the development of South Africa's rich mineral resources was mature capital and it depended for its super-profits on the impoverished masses of African workers confined in the reserves. The chief characteristic of the labor from the reserves has been its inability to meet even the minimum African subsistence needs.

The process that transforms, on the one hand, the social means of subsistence and production into capital and, on the other hand, the immediate producers into wage labor, differs under different circumstances. Engels, for instance, points out that:

When in the decline of the Roman Republic, the free Italian peasants were expropriated from their land, they formed a class of "poor whites" similar to that of the Southern Slaves before 1861; and between slaves and poor whites, two classes equally unfit for self-emancipation, the old world went to pieces. *In the middle ages, it was not the expropriation of the people from, but on the contrary, their appropriation to the land which became the source of feudal oppression.* The peasant retained his land, but was attached to it as a serf or villein, and made liable to tribute to the lord in labor and in produce. *It was only at the dawn of modern times, towards the end of the fifteenth century, that the expropriation of the peasantry on a large scale laid the foundation of the modern class of wage-workers who possess nothing but their labor-power and can live only by selling that labor power to others.* But if the expropriation from the land brought this class into existence, it was the development of capitalist production, of modern industry and agriculture on a large scale which perpetrated it, increased it, and shaped it into a distinct class with distinct interests and a distinct historical mission (Marx and Engels 1962:10–11; emphasis added).

The development of capitalism in South Africa shared these general patterns. As long as Africans had free access to (relatively) plentiful land it was difficult for mines and agriculture to satisfy their labor needs. The methods had to be devised to create free-wage labor for diamond and gold mines, and these methods illustrate how basic the land question was.

Marx laid down the axiom of the genesis of capitalist relations of production. That is for capitalist accumulation to work, two different kinds of commodity possessors must come face to face: on the one hand, owners of money, means of production and subsistence, who are eager to increase their capital by buying other people's labor; on the other hand "free" laborers, the sellers of their own labor power, in a double sense (that is, they themselves neither form part and parcel of the means of production, as in the case of slaves and bondsmen, nor own any means of production, as is the case with peasant proprietors; they are, therefore, "free" and unencumbered by any means of production of their own).

In the opening passage of the *Pre-capitalist economic formations*, Marx puts it this way:

One of the prerequisites of wage labor and one of the historic conditions for capital is free labor and the exchange of free labor against money. . . . Another prerequisite is the separation of free labor from the objective conditions of its realization — from the means and material of labor. This means above all that the worker must be separated from the land, which functions as his natural laboratory. This means the dissolution both of free petty landownership and of communal landed property, based on the oriental commune. In both these forms the relationship of the worker to the objective conditions of his labor, is one of ownership: this is the natural unity of labor with its material prerequisites. Hence the worker has an objective existence independent of his labor. The individual is related to himself as a proprietor, as master of the conditions of his reality. The same relation holds between one individual and the rest. . . . (1965:67).

As the South African capitalist economy developed, peasants were progressively pushed to the reserves where they were then recruited to spend a large portion of their time working for wages. The peasants drawn into the capitalist market became willy-nilly imprisoned by their dependency on wages which in turn perpetuated their exploitability.

As the cash nexus was firmly established, migrant labor relations were structured as a permanent way of life for people in the reserve. The circulation of labor between mine-head and the reserves was maintained and reproduced on a continuously expanding scale by various economic and "legal" means to meet mining and other industries' need for cheap labor.

Rosa Luxemburg demonstrated how mature capital, greedy for super-profits, depends in all respects on the exploitation of noncapitalist strata and social organizations existing side by side with, and integrated into, the capitalist structures.

Since the accumulation of capital becomes impossible in all points without non-capitalist surrounding, we cannot gain a true picture of it by assuming the exclusive and absolute domination of the capitalist mode of production. . . . Capital needs the means of production and the labour power of the whole globe for untrammelled accumulation; it cannot manage without the natural resources and the labour power which all territories provide. Seeing that the overwhelming majority of resources and labour power is in fact still in the orbit of pre-capitalist production — this being the historical milieu of accumulation — capital must go all out to obtain ascendancy over these territories and social organizations. And in fact, primitive conditions allow of a greater drive and of far more ruthless measures than could be tolerated under purely capitalist social conditions (1965:395–400).

The exploitation of gold mining accelerated the incursion and penetration of the "native" reserves by labor recruiters who siphoned off the so-called able-bodied males for labor in the mines.

The relations between the capitalist gold-mining sector and the reserves are a classic demonstration of the workings of internal colonialism as well. André Gorz has advanced the important concept that colonialism is not simply the external practice of one country against the interests of another. On the contrary, he maintains, and rightly, that it is from the first an internal practice (Gorz 1971:22–28). That is, the capitalist state invariably internalizes the colonial form of exploitation for certain areas and people.

When diamond- and gold-mining developed between 1864 and 1900, it constituted the first genuine branch of capitalist industry in South Africa. The internal colonialism that is articulated in the reserve system was simultaneously a way of prolonging the life of mining capitalism, and a way of very effectively limiting the development of these areas. Only the manpower of these areas had to be "set free" in order to be enrolled in the active sphere of capitalist production. As Rosa Luxemburg explains:

The emancipation of labour power from primitive social conditions and its absorption by capitalist wage system is one of the indispensable historical bases of capitalism. For the first genuinely capitalist branch of production, the English cotton industry, not only the cotton of the Southern states of the American Union was essential, but also the millions of African Negroes who were shipped to America to provide the labour power of the plantations, and who later, as a free proletariat, were incorporated in the class of wage labourers in a capitalist system. Obtaining the necessary labour power from non-capitalist societies, the so called "labour-problem", is even more important for capital in the colonies. All possible methods of "gentle compulsion" are applied to solving this problem, to transfer labour from former social systems to the command of capital. This endeavor leads to the most peculiar combinations between the modern wage system and primitive authority in the colonial countries (1965:362–363).

Rosa Luxemburg illustrated the last point by quoting Bryce, an English Minister who had visited South Africa and who described a model pattern or a hybrid form of incorporation of the African in the diamond mines.

When Africans were first pressed to labour in the mines as wage earners, they were retained for six or nine months. In the rest of the year they were supposed to take part in their traditional subsistence, based on land. But the major portion of African lands, as we have seen, had been seized in the wars of conquest. The remaining land soon became overworked and "over" populated. Thus with the opening of diamond and gold mining wage labour became a major source of subsistence and urban areas the main areas for earning a livelihood. The most striking sight at Kimberley, and one unique in the world, is furnished by the two so called "compounds" in which the natives who work in the mines are housed and confined. They are huge enclosures, unroofed, but covered with a wire netting to prevent anything from being thrown out over the walls, and with subterranean entrance to the adjoining mine. The mine is worked on the system of three eight-hour shifts, so that the workman is never more than eight hours together underground. Round the interior of the wall are built sheds or huts in which the natives live and sleep when not working (quoted in Luxemburg 1965:363).

To develop the mineral-rich Witwatersrand, the government and the mine owners resorted to political and economic measures unheard of in England: they transported on a temporary basis tens of thousands of peasants who had been forcibly robbed of their land and freedom. The migrant labor system created conditions in which African labor would be reduced to a pure commodity, while maintaining an illusion of respect for traditional authorities. The communal ownership of the land called the reserves is perfectly suited for this illusion. In these areas, the conquerors have maintained, as far as possible, the outward structure and genealogy of traditional African systems of authority, i.e., the kings or chiefs and emasculated traditional institutions. But all these functions are subject to the ultimate authority of the Minister of Bantu Affairs, who can veto what he finds inimical to the interests of the larger capitalist reality for which the reserves were created in the first place. As a result of this and subsequent measures of the colonial state, African exploitation became more intensive.

When pre-capitalist societies are confined and objectified in the way they are in the reserves, they experience regressive decay. Whatever institutional growth they may require either is denied, because it departs from ancient ways, or is distorted to serve the objective aims of the colonizer. The formalized structures of the decaying traditional institutions are maintained as means of social isolation. People of the reserves are sealed off from relationships with people in other communities, in particular, those in urban areas. They are even sealed off from a relation with their physical environment. The reserves meant, among other things, that Africans after being forced off the land that they had traditionally occupied, could not move to areas of economic growth except as temporary migrants. The reserves are an "original" form of creating cheap labor in South Africa.

Even as early as the middle of the nineteenth century, when Africans were being dispossessed of their best lands, one of the main determinants of the extent of land appropriation was the amount of African labor to be made available to the white settlers. This explains the scattered, spotty nature of the reserves today. The policies adopted in different places at different periods with regard to the maintenance, disposition, and size of the reserves were determined by the economies of the regions. When Natal began to develop sugar-cane plantations, allowing for the presence of a sufficient number of Africans in close proximity to potential white exploiters was a basic strategy in carving up the lands of the Zulu people. For instance, in rejecting Sir Harry Smith's policy of segregation, Earl Grey suggested that natural and permanent locations for Africans be established with sufficient intervals between them for the spread of European settlements, in order that "each European emigrant would thus have it in his power to draw supplies of labor from the location in his more immediate proximity" (quoted in Van der Horst 1971:16). Sheila Van der Horst explains that the same policy had been followed earlier in the Eastern Cape:

In embarking upon the policy of introducing European settlers into Victoria East and later into British Kaffaria, the administration was in fact creating what were to become in part pools of labour, even though at the time the predominant motive was to achieve security by breaking up the cohesion of the tribes and introducing European ideas and institutions (1971:17).

What is called *native policy* in South Africa was a strategy with three aims: breaking up the military might of the African kingdoms, laying the foundations of "law and order" required for a maturing of the new "economic" ways of exploitation, and creating conditions that facilitated both the incorporation of Africans as labor power and the creation of class support in the persons of "reformed" traditional rulers entirely dependent on the British.

The consequences of the policy of juxtaposing African reserves and areas settled by whites are described as follows by Van der Horst:

The effects of the intermingling of Europeans and Native settlements and the imposition of European government were many-sided. The mode of living of the natives, who had combined agricultural and pastoral subsistence farming, had to be modified. For one thing, it required more land than was now available. But, in the Cape Colony, the contact with Europeans tended for other reasons also to break their former self-sufficiency. New wants were awakened and new obligations, notably taxation, were imposed. All these developments necessitated change, the abandonment of that condition of self-sufficiency in which each household had produced the greater part of its own requirements (1971:25).

As a result of these internally contradictory developments, changes occurred in the structure of African societies: a large part of the male population was set free to be enrolled as a class of wage earners in mining and other industries. Alienated from subsistence, this class cultivated desires and habits which made it look upon the substitution of its subsistence with consumption of capitalist goods as natural. Once the organization of the capitalist process of production is fully developed, its momentum breaks down all resistance by the precapitalist mode. The basic compulsion of economic needs ushered in the process of "voluntary" subjugation of the peasants to the capitalist milieu. But as Rosa Luxemburg points out:

Direct force, outside economic conditions, is . . . still used, but only exceptionally. In the ordinary run of things, the labourer can be left to the "natural law of production" i.e., to his dependence on capital, a dependence springing from and guaranteed in perpetuity by the conditions of production themselves (1965:364).

The reservations were thus designed to deal with economic as much as with political and strategic consequences of colonial economic integration. However, for reasons ideological or otherwise, there is a general reluctance among bourgeois theorists to analyze the South African reserves as an aspect of capitalist society, and hence there is a refusal to see the poverty of the reserves as having been generated by forces inherent in the characteristic features of the accumulation process of capitalism.

Before they were physically subdued, African traditional societies with plenty of land confronted the requirements of capitalism with difficult problems. The wants of an African living within his subsistence agriculture, cultivating his *mealies* (corn), were confined to a *kaross* (skin cloak) and some pieces of home-made cotton cloth. The prospects of leaving his family to work in a mine, in order to earn wages with which he could buy things he had no use for, did not at once appeal to him. James Bryce observed that:

The white men, anxious to get to work on the goldreefs, are annoyed at what they call stupidity and laziness of the native, and usually clamour for legislation to compel the native to come to work, adding of course that regular labor would be the best thing in the world for natives. Some go as far as to wish to compel them to work at fixed rate of wages, sufficient to leave good profit for the employer (1969:23).

In the struggle between the traditional and capitalist modes, the white-settler government created the laws to make it easy for the capitalist mode to win. The effective reduction of land for African occupation necessarily limited development of the subsistence sector. In the process, earning money became an unavoidable necessity. In the impatience of the employers, the unavoidable cruelties of capitalism revealed themselves in full glare of day in the methods used to recruit labor for the gold mines. By force and coercion Africans were divorced from their former means of subsistence in a most frightful manner. The record, so far as the activities of the Chamber of Mines is concerned, is stained with pages almost as dark as those which disfigure the earlier records of imperialism in India and America. Rosa Luxemburg, quoting Bryce's observations in South Africa, tells us that:

Here we see that the Negroes are compelled to work in the mines and plantations of Kimberley, Witwatersrand, Natal, Matubelaland, by stripping them of all land and cattle, i.e., depriving them of their means of existence, by making them into proletarians and also demoralising them with alcohol. (Later, when they are already within the "enclosure" of capitalism, spirits, to which they have just been accustomed, are strictly prohibited — the object of exploitation must be kept fit for use.) Finally, they are simply pressed into the wage system of capital by force, by imprisonment and flogging (1965:364).

With the discovery of diamonds in 1866 and gold in 1884, the evolution of the "native policy," i.e., the creation of the native reserves, began to take shape. The entire country having been conquered and brought under a unified system of government, an effort was made to avoid competition among the various employers and to streamline the method of distributing African labor among hitherto competing employers. Van der Horst wrote that before 1910:

The mines, and the expanding industries which served them, competed for the factors of production, for land, for capital and for labour. Complaints about the scarcity of labour became widespread, particularly in the coastal colonies where the construction of railways and harbours and the needs of the growing towns competed with the farmers in the market for native labour. In Natal the government renewed the efforts which it had already made to increase the labour supply by limiting the rights of natives to occupy land outside the reserves, by taxation, and by the importation of Indian indentured labourers. In the Cape Colony, which was granted responsible government in 1872, attempts were made to promote the supply of native labour by legislative and other administrative action of one kind or another. The South African Republic tried to meet its own labour needs by intercepting natives who were making their way to work on the diamond-fields (1971:64).

One of the reasons for the creation of the union was the need for a unified native policy to avoid such competition. Only a centralized administration, it was argued, could apportion African labor to satisfy the conflicting claims made upon it. Cecil Rhodes had already amalgamated the rival diamond-mining companies to form the DeBeers monopoly in 1889. After the formation of the Union in 1910, Africans were soon to learn that their new masters had harsher ways of dealing with problems of "laziness" and labor scarcity. The cornerstone of Union native policy was to have total control over African labor and to distribute it in an authoritarian way among the different industries.

Historically, several mechanisms of forced labor have successfully supported primary production like mining and cash-crop farming. The native reserves and migrant labor became but one version of the classic instances for creating a sufficiently large labor force that is not "completely" dependent on wages and for which the employer can deduct the whole surplus value by paying only supplementary wages for what the worker produces in the land. In the reserves it is always easy to impose noneconomic "inducements" and to institutionalize working-class powerlessness. That is the secret of the extraordinary persistence of the reserves.

Though Cecil Rhodes has been called the father of the native reserves and the migrant labor system, English settlers in Natal, faced with the refusal of the Africans to work in the sugar-cane plantations the colonists were establishing and lacking the means to compel the Zulu people to work for them, had forced the British government to import 6,500 indentured Indians between 1860 and 1866. Sir George Grey had seen the results of the use of indentured labor in the cane fields of Mauritius, and when he visited Natal in 1855, he approved the importation of Indian laborers. He reported to the Secretary of State that:

One measure which would greatly tend to promote wealth and security of that Colony [Natal], and render it of value and importance to Great Britain, would be to encourage the introduction of coolie labourers from India (quoted in Van der Horst 1971:61).

This scheme, however, could only be a stopgap measure. In the diamond mines an average of 30,000 Africans were employed annually in the first seven years of production. And the discovery and exploitation of gold only aggravated the shortage. Thus it became increasingly necessary to begin a crash program to manufacture a labor force out of African peasants. In 1876, Mr. M.X. Merriman was under extreme pressure to bring in Chinese coolie labor, and he wrote:

In the Cape the government is called upon to survey mankind from China to Peru in the hope of creating and maintaining a class of cheap labourers who will thankfully accept the position of helots and not be troubled with the inconvenient ambition of bettering this condition (quoted in Van der Horst 1971:118).

Instead of looking to India and China for labor, a commission was appointed in 1893 — the Commission on Labour in the Cape Colony — which made suggestions that every male African should be taxed, with full remission if he could show he had been away from home in employment during the year. So in 1894, as Prime Minister of the Cape Colony, Cecil Rhodes passed the Glen Grey Act. Its objects were (1) to encourage individual land tenure and (2) to establish a simple system of local councils. This became the surest method of accelerating the dissolution of the traditional social structure based on the communal ownership of land. Rhodes wanted to put an end to peasant "laziness." These two provisions (though praised by liberals as progressive) were intended to negate "tribal" communism and to encourage naked self-interest and egotistical calculation based on the cash nexus.

With the creation of local councils, the chiefs became agents of the colonial power. As if this were not enough, the act also imposed a tax of ten shillings on every male African in the reserve who was not employed by a white person or engaged in cultivating an allotment, or who had not worked outside his district during the previous twelve months. Moving the second reading of the bill, Rhodes, speaking as Minister of Native Affairs, explained:

If you are one who really likes the natives you must make them worthy of the country they live in, or else they are certain, by an inexorable law, to lose their country; you will certainly not make them worthy if you allow them to sit in idleness and if you do not train them in the arts of civilization (quoted in Hepple 1968:197).

The agents of British imperialism were past masters in Orwellian talk. The ideology of civilization through work was merely a smoke screen for the most sinister scheme of proletarianization of the African peasants ever developed. What Rhodes was telling the Africans was that the reason for not killing them was to make them work. In time the African would learn the bitter lesson that laboring in the mines at wages that made fortunes for the mining capitalist had become an unavoidable necessity. They would also learn that economic bondage and wage slavery were not spasmodic but permanent features of the new system.

After the Boer War, the mining industry found itself desperately short of laborers. Despite pressure, and mainly because of low wages, Africans were not coming forward in sufficient numbers. In December 1903, a labor commission reported a shortage of 129,000 African laborers in the mines and estimated that by 1908 the shortage would swell to 365,000. The Chamber of Mines, with the support of the press, embarked upon an intensive campaign to win support for the importation of Chinese coolies. The Milner government, which not only saw the gold-mining industry as key to its imperialist ambitions but also believed that the maintenance of British power in South Africa depended on the exploitation of South African gold, agreed to the policy of introducing indentured Chinese labor. As Simons and Simons put it:

> There was no time to spare, in the view of Milner and the owners; they wanted a ready-to-hand proletariat at the lowest possible cost who would restore the mines to full working capacity without delay, satisfy share holders, attract new capital, save Milner's reputation and the Transvaal from bankruptcy. They would not wait for taxation and land seizures to turn African peasants into work seekers (1969:81).

Meanwhile, a commission would look into the best way to structure a political system that would compel the Africans to work whether they liked it or not. The indentured Chinese labor, like the Indian laborers, could not be a permanent substitute for local labor.

Before the Anglo-Boer War, there had been 90,000 Chinese indentured laborers in the mines. During the war they had scattered and only 30,000 remained. After the war, the mines needed some 200,000 laborers at three shillings per day (60 cents), the highest wages the Chamber of Mines was prepared to pay. Quite obviously this demand could not be permanently met by an imported and indentured labor force. Without a scheme to produce abundant, cheap African labor, there could be no extraction of gold on a permanent basis, and therefore no prospect for attracting foreign capital to expand the only industry that could make South Africa a worthwhile part of the British Empire.

The importation of Chinese coolie labor was thus a bad stopgap measure. In fact, the treatment of Chinese laborers had become an important political issue in Britain itself. In the Transvaal, Botha and Smuts, who were elected to the government in 1906, had pledged not only to repeal the Chinese Labour Ordinance but also to admit no more Chinese. The repatriation of those Chinese whose contracts expired began soon thereafter. By 1910 all Chinese had left South Africa except for a handful who evaded the net and became petty traders and shopkeepers (cf. Hepple 1968:201).

Having been deprived of cheap Chinese labor, the Chamber of Mines was forced to turn its eagle eyes on the local resources. In March 1903, the South African Customs conference was convened to discuss the whole question of the shortage of labor in South Africa. Among other things it concluded that the native population of southern Africa south of the Zambezi did not "comprise a sufficient number of adult males capable of work to satisfy the normal requirements of the several colonies, and at the same time furnish an adequate amount of labour for the large industrial mining centers" (Van der Horst 1971:168).

This was a somber conclusion. In July 1903, the Transvaal Labour Commission was appointed. Its terms of reference were "to inquire what amount of labour is necessary for the requirements of the Agricultural, Mining and other Industries of the Transvaal, and to ascertain how far it is possible to obtain an adequate supply of labour to meet such requirements from central and South Africa" (Van der Horst 1971:168). The recommendations of this commission were put into effect three years after the formation of the Union of South Africa, by the passage of the 1913 Land Act. This act became one of the most effective instruments in creating a landless class of Africans who could be easily compelled to take up work with the mines and white settlers who needed their labor.

The immediate object of the act was to abolish the system of "farming-on-the-half" and to eliminate squatter locations. Farming-on-the-half was a system whereby Africans, who owned their own plough and oxen, entered into a partnership with a white landowner and worked the land, sowed their own seed, reaped the crop, and then handed over half of it to the farmer in return for the right to cultivate, graze stock, and live on the land. The abolition of this system uprooted hundreds of Africans from land that had become white-owned farms. These displaced peasants were sent wandering the roads of the country with no place to establish new homes. According to Francis Wilson:

Few laws passed in South Africa can have been felt with such immediate harshness by so large a section of the population. The system of farming-on-the-half which had flourished ever since whites gained control of the interior, was dealt a blow from which it never recovered. The next three decades were to see the almost total elimination of that class of rural Africans who, in the words of Sol Plaatje's policeman, had once been "fairly comfortable, if not rich and [who] enjoyed the possession" of their stock, living in many instances just like Dutchmen (1971:128).

Wilson then deals with long-range effects of the act:

In the longer term, the Act served well to fuse those idealists, who felt that partition alone was a realistic means of protecting Africans from total domination by whites, with those more selfish and more numerous people who wanted economic integration, without the uncomfortable social and political consequences. For the new law set aside sufficient land to tantalize the idealist without providing enough to enable all Africans to make their living there and so to be able to exist without working for the white man on his terms. In later years much political dexterity was displayed in using the reserves to maintain a policy which simultaneously won the support of idealists . . . without alienating the confidence of those voters for whom Africans were primarily units of labour whose presence was essential but only tolerable so long as they ministered to the needs of the white man (1971:131).

The South African version of the enclosure movement was extremely cruel. The expropriation and expulsion of the peasantry from white farms, intermittent but renewed again and again, supplied the mining industry with a mass of proletarians entirely unconnected with the land and unfettered by possession of a house, garden, or field.[1] The thinning out of independent, self-supporting peasants was duplicated in the urban areas in 1923 by the Urban Areas Act and in 1954 by the Western Areas Removal Act, which abolished freehold that Africans had to land in Johannesburg and other areas.

From 1913 on, the Chamber of Mines and the capitalist farmers would have a regular flow of "temporary" labor. Furthermore, economic pressures increased when, in 1922, African taxation was transferred from the provincial administration to the central government under the Native Taxation and Development Act (Number 41 of 1925). In terms of this act, all African males between the ages of eighteen and sixty-five were made to pay a poll tax of £1 per annum. *In addition, a local tax of ten shillings was imposed on every male occupier of a hut in the reserves.* The Native Economic Commission of 1930–1932, surveying the situation after twenty years of active legislation to extract the Africans from their subsistence, commented gleefully:

In the past difficulty was experienced in obtaining a sufficient supply of labour for industries of this country. The native in the tribal Reserves, accustomed to subsistence economy . . . felt no urge to go out to labour. . . . The European Government, wanting labour for their industries, decided to bring pressure to bear on the native to force him to come out to work and did this by imposing taxation (quoted in Hepple 1968:198).

The 1913 Land Act and subsequent acts in that genre proved one thing, if any proof was necessary, namely that "when capital finds itself face to face with relations which stand in the way of its needs for expansion and which would be overcome by economic process only gradually and much too slowly, it appeals to the state power and puts the latter into the service

---

[1] The forcible removal of Africans from one part of South Africa to another that began by the 1913 Land Act is being continued today on an even larger scale. According to a study just published, *Uprooting a nation* by Alan Baldwin, more than 1¾ million Africans have already been uprooted in South Africa and at least another half million stand ready to be moved along. The logic behind the removals is to shift the burden of responsibility to the Bantustans, and because the bulk of industrial growth is based in the white areas, blacks may return to work in a "white area" as migrant labor. "Migratory labor is thus the reverse flow of mass removals: Workers who, with their families, are pushed out of the towns . . . are often allowed to come back to urban areas when work is available, but this time as migrants; they cannot bring their families with them. Thus family life is being deliberately destroyed. . . ." (Baldwin 1974:9).

The twin policies of removal and migrancy are being used as instruments for "transferring onto the newly created Bantustan administrations the problems of unemployment, overcrowding, poverty, and resettlement," the report says (1974:10).

of forcible expropriation which creates the necessary force of wage proletariat. . . ." (quoted in Sweezy 1962:304).

For plantation and mining economies a large supply of cheap labor is a
must. These industries in fact come to set the pattern in the structure of
labor relations, wages, and employment. Cash-crop plantations and
mines are extremely wasteful of manpower and thus always experience a
chronic relative shortage, which impels the government to adopt even
more stringent forced-labor laws. With the ever-increasing importance of
mining in South Africa, it is not surprising that the reserves have been
reduced to an increasing poverty: here the threat of death by starvation
produces more helpless workers for the mines.

The primary responsibility of the mining industry for entrenching the
reserves and migratory labor is not doubted. Hepple writes that:

In view of the considerable use made of migrant labour in the mining industry, its
role in entrenching the system is worthy of examination. From the very beginning
the gold-mining industry clamoured for cheap labour. The Chamber of Mines
urged President Kruger to impose strict control on African labourers. They
complained that because of inadequate pass laws and regulations for the control
of African labour "it is impossible to secure such combination on the part of
employers as would enable native wages to be reduced to a reasonable level." The
cash wage of African miners was at the time about two shillings a day. Kruger
complied with their request and enacted two pass laws (1968:199).

The 1913 Land Act expressed more than anything the extent to which
"King Gold" enjoyed privileges as far as African labor was concerned.
According to Wilson, "At the same time as the land legislation was being
discussed and passed, mine owners were working out, not for the first
time, an agreement whereby the average wage of blacks of any mine
would not exceed a certain maximum, and there is a sense in which the
Land Act was, for farmers, what the maximum-permissible-average
agreement was for the mining magnates" (1971:128).

To sum up, the creation of reserves, where Africans eke out a less than
subsistence existence, became an important factor in South Africa's
gold-labor-market structure. In the reserves, commodity labor power
does not merely exist, it is also *available* in adequate quantities for the
evolving capitalist sector. Starvation is a relentless goad pushing men out
to places where they think they can earn money to support their families.
Internal colonialism is the general result in the integration of non-
capitalist organizations with capitalism. Working in the mines means, to
use Marx's expression, the "martyrdom of the producer." It is inevitably
accompanied by insecure existence for the worker. African existence in
the reserves became vegetative, with no other purpose than to provide
labor for an "exogenous" economy whose products were irrelevant and
unattainable to the African labor force itself.

THE ORIGINS OF THE "NATIVE RESERVES" OR BANTUSTANS[2]

The physical basis of the native reserves is complex: in the era of white-settler colonization, they were initially the areas of the country to which Africans were progressively pushed and confined. According to Van der Horst:

> The "Kaffir Wars" on the eastern frontier during the late eighteenth century and the first half of the nineteenth were essentially a struggle for land; a struggle in which the Bantu were pushed back until it was finally realized that conquest and expulsion proved no ultimate solution, but were the cause of further unrest (1971:13).

Today these areas have been modified by legislation into labor reservoirs and they are the only areas where Africans, whose labor is unwanted in either the urban areas, mining, or farming, are permitted permanent but dubious legal residence.

In 1964, a "new" legal maneuver presented these areas as being prepared for independence. It promised that under certain conditions, they may be allowed to call themselves "independent states." These maneuvers are simply not going to achieve this. The so-called black assemblies are and will remain powerless in matters of substance, since all power still remains in Pretoria. In a resolution 2671 (XXV) adopted on December 8, 1971, the Survival Assembly of the UND condemned the establishment of Bantustans in the so-called reserves as fraudulent, a violation of the principle of self-determination, and prejudicial to the territorial integrity of the state and to the unity of its people.

After each act of conquest, boundaries were fixed by the conqueror, who then occupied some of the best land previously owned by Africans. The changes of the frontiers meant that the amount of land available for African use shrank, while each and every African kingdom and chiefdom was incorporated so that its people could become labor power for the settlers. At no time were the reserves intended to support the population that ostensibly was to live on them, for the allocated land was not only insufficient in extent but also inferior in quality. Moreover, as mere subsistence production was impossible, the creation of surplus with which to pay the white-imposed taxes was wholly out of the question.

From the moment the Africans were pushed into these areas, they became totally and fully integrated into the developing "white" economy. Land scarcity forced them to work in the money economy permanently even though at intermittent intervals. But legislation

---

[2] "Bantustans" is a word coined on the analogy of "Pakistan" to denote the hoped-for "separate" African states within the Republic of South Africa.

decreed the scope, conditions, and specific application of their labor power. The political and social forms of organization that were imposed in the reserves did not grow organically from the indigenous society, nor were European-type institutions grafted onto existing institutions. Whatever institution of rule is used today in the reserves was ruthlessly imposed in the service of the settler economy. In the reserves we can postulate a pure system of subordination achieved after numerous wars. Van der Horst explains:

> Stripped of everything, and weary of war, [Africans] desired nothing better than to repair their fortunes by the labour of their hands, and from the first showed themselves tractable, and even grateful to those who received them; while the latter welcomed with delight skillful shepherds and excellent workmen, who were satisfied with very humble remuneration (1971:15).

The economic integration of the African, far from eliminating traditional dispersion, consolidated it. The British conquerors broke up larger states and created units over whom puppets were installed as rulers. This happened, for instance, in the case of the Zulu Kingdom. Extractive capitalism preferred to adapt the old structures to its needs, and through taxation it facilitated "economic assimilation." The relations between the reserves and white areas symbolized the essence of colonial capitalist relations, that is, relations between the buyer and settler of labor power, the center and metropolis, the colonizers and colonized, the master and servant. Like the relation of capital and labor in capitalist countries, colonial capitalist relations are based on the cash nexus and exploitation. Because they are unequal in structure and reward, they have to be maintained by force.

The constitution of the Union of South Africa, in 1910, was the most striking and specific expression of the fact that Africans were not citizens but a conquered people. Soon after 1910, the acts of parliament would begin to tidy the process of dispossession. In 1903 a government commission (already referred to above) declared (in paragraph 207 of its report) that:

> . . . the time has arrived when the lands dedicated and set apart, as locations, reserves or otherwise, should be defined, delimited, and reserved for Natives by legislative enactment.

Further, it recommended that this should be done "with a view to finality" and thereafter that no more land should be set aside for African occupation. As a slight concession, it suggested that there should not be a prohibition on "deserving and progressive individuals among the Natives requiring land." However, the purchase of land by Africans should be limited in the future to certain areas defined by legislation: tribal, collective, or communal possession should be prohibited.

In 1910, a Parliamentary Select Committee on Native Affairs published a preliminary bill which embodied the conclusions of the commission, specially referring to the abovementioned paragraph 207. Although the bill itself did not become law, the fundamental principle of territorial segregation which it contained became the policy of the government.

The Native Land Act of 1913 was designed as an interim measure to maintain *inter alia* the *status quo* as regards land ownership, until the passing of a comprehensive and final measure: a commission was appointed to recommend the permanent lines of territorial segregation.

The Act stipulated that, without the consent of the Governor General, no African could acquire from a person other than an African (or *vice versa*) any land or interest in any land outside of the scheduled African areas. Nor could any person other than an African acquire any land or interest in any land in a scheduled African area without the approval of the Governor General.

The scheduled African areas consisted of the existing African reserves and locations in the rural areas of the Union, as well as (rural) land privately owned by Africans — a total of 10.7 million *morgen*. Tenure and occupation of the land in the townships was not covered by the Act.

The scheduled areas where Africans would be free to settle amounted to 10.7 million *morgen*, or a mere 7.3 percent of the total land area of the country. A further 5.7 percent of the areas was to constitute "released" areas in which Africans would be freed from the general prohibition on buying land.

White farmers raised an outcry against "released" areas, on the grounds that whites would be prevented from obtaining more farms and that Africans would settle in these areas and cease to provide labor for white farmers.

White politicians began to reassure them that the actual release of the "released" areas would be contingent on the abolition of the voting rights held by Africans in the Cape. But the Act of Union (1910) and the promises not to betray the Africans were still too recent to trample on, and voting rights were not immediately abolished. Neither were the released areas actually released.

As a result, Africans, who were already land-starved, were deprived of the right to freely purchase and acquire land as a prelude to an indefinite promise of land concessions.

The anomaly of the Cape Colony (confirmed by the Act of Union) which gave Africans in the Cape Province the franchise and, thus, a claim to citizenship, was eliminated in 1936 when parliament passed the Hertzog Bills — the Representation of Natives Act and the Native Trust and Land Act. The first act took away the token franchise; in its place the Governor General was made the supreme chief of all Africans, while in parliament Africans were given three white representatives and a representative council to which they could take their grievances. The second act provided machinery for the acquisition and development of the 13 percent of the land intended for the subsistence of Africans when they were not employed in the "white" economy.

The principles laid down in the Native Trust and Land Act went far beyond those of the 1913 Land Act, which forbade the sale or lease of land outside the scheduled areas (that is, reserves) to Africans. The purpose of the 1936 act was essentially political — to establish once and for all that the conquered estate could not be acquired by Africans either through commercial purchase or political means.

The 1936 Native Trust and Land Act also dealt with the important issue of the control and direction of African labor. The Native Service Contract of 1932 was extended from the Transvaal and Natal to the Cape and Orange Free State. According to the Native Service Contract, landowners were obliged to choose between turning their African squatters into labor tenants, subject to the penal sanctions of the master and servant laws, or sending them to a declared native area. If a landowner could not prove that all his labor-tenants had rendered a minimum of 180 days of labor a year, he could be deprived of those considered surplus to his needs. The Native Service Contract complemented the Urban Areas Act of 1923, which declared that all Africans not ministering to the needs of the whites were to depart from urban areas. Thus the Hertzog Bills completed the scenario of conquest.

The struggle for land, which had lasted for three centuries, had now ended. The white settlers had won. Through the 1913 Land Act, the Urban Areas Act of 1923, the Native Service Contract of 1932 and the 1936 acts, the victims of conquest were finally being dispossessed and permanently reduced to "hewers of wood and drawers of water." From now on, they would be available as labor power when it was required by the various sectors of the "white" economy. That, of course, was the original rationale for sparing the lives of Africans — to force them to work for their new masters.

Land alienation transformed once self-supporting peasants into squatters, tenant farmers, or migrant laborers on the ill-gotten settlers' farms or drove them into the mines and cities in search of work. (This section is based on Hepple 1968:Chapter 13, 93–94.) With the passage of the various acts to which we have briefly referred, the Africans, like the Gaels of the eighteenth century, were forbidden to emigrate from the country in order to drive them by force to the mining centers (cf. Marx 1969:23).

In the history of colonization in other parts of the world, the reserves system has been a common device in the control and relocation of native populations by colonial governments. It is a system that is military and political in design but economic in practice. By controlling the movements of indigenous peoples, colonial governments try as far as possible to prevent any kind of political organization among them. At the same time, by leaving so little land available for "native" occupation they force the indigenous peoples to sell their labor, often very cheaply, to build the settler colonial economy which oppresses them further.

The South African Native Reserves (now renamed Bantu Homelands) today are great concentrations of poverty, disease, and ignorance, deliberately enforced in order to create the necessary labor for the "white" economy. They are centers of helplessness, of discouragement of initiative, of forced labor, and of legal repression of all activities or thoughts that the white rulers fear or dislike. The system represents, in a very real sense, the ultimate in deliberate human retardation. The Africans in the reserves are compelled by their physical hunger to do the hardest and the lowest-paying jobs. The political division of the land mass of South Africa into "white" and "Bantu Homeland" exhibits, more than anything else, the structural entrenchment of an inhuman social geography. The Bantu Homelands, in the words of Mbeki, are:

... South Africa's backwaters, primitive rural slums, socially eroded, and underdeveloped, lacking power resources and without cities, no industries and few resources of employment. They are congested and permanently distressed areas where the inhabitants live on a narrow ledge of starvation, where a drought . . . leads inevitably to famine. They are areas drained of their men folk, for their chief export is labour and while the men work on white owned farms, in mines and industry, their women folk and old people pursue a primitive agriculture incapable of providing even subsistence. The "homelands" are mere reserves of labour, with a population not even self-sustaining, supplying no more than a supplement to the low wages paid on the mines and farms (1964:82).

To make this system work, the chain of command extends from the State President and Minister of Native Affairs (now called Minister of Bantu Development) through the district commissioners in the reserve areas to the chiefs. By making the chiefs dependent on the salary paid by the government, the settlers transform them into agents for requisitioning labor. The Bantu Homelands reveal the deliberateness and "incompletion" of the project of settlement! The destruction of traditional means of subsistence in order to ensure a constant supply of labor, the restriction of free land ownership to whites only, and the increasing constraints imposed by the towns on African entry and urban occupation, except as hired servants, all served to render Africans submissive and tractable in the hands of their masters, who then employed them as they wished and at the most minimal wages.

Through this deliberate policy, conquerors cultivated the assumption that Africans would be ancillary to European enterprise and yet would continue to live within the social, economic, and political system of the "traditional" society. This persuasion eventually formed part of the rationale for the lie that says that reservations are no longer reserves, but Bantustans.

Bourgeois social scientists have obfuscated the real meaning of the creation of the reserves in South Africa. The importance of the reserves for the whole development of South Africa lies in their "mutual" integration to the economy of the "white" state. It is a relationship based on a classic division between superiors and subordinates, between those who own capital and means of production and those who own nothing but their labor power. What would it mean to the mining and agricultural industries to be without reserve labor? The black worker confined in the reserves is the cornerstone of the two industries: gold-mining and agriculture. African labor means the difference between profitableness and bankruptcy. From the exploitation of reserve labor comes the surplus value that is converted into capital invested in the urban-based industries.

In the light of the current debate regarding the future of these areas, I cannot overemphasize the fact that these areas, with a few exceptions, are the shrunken remnant of territories once occupied by Africans and are unevenly scattered over South Africa. The "white" state is a continuous land area, containing most of the natural resources, and most of the results of advanced development secured by the labor and skill of black and white workers — the most exploited of whom are, of course, the Africans. The so-called white area includes all large cities, seaports, harbors, airfields, and areas served by key railways, main roads, power lines, and major irrigation schemes. The enormously rich gold, diamond, and coal mines are located there, as are all main industries and seaports, worked by cheap black labor. The white area includes, as well, the best and most fertile lands for agricultural use (Mbeki 1964:82).

This asymmetrical economic geography is explained in official South African propaganda as the accomplishment of white capital, enterprise, and skills in exploiting the mines, agriculture, and industries; yet no mines or industries would ever have existed without the unceasing exploitation of black labor. In bourgeois social sciences the asymmetrical geography is explained as an example of plural or dual society. The far-reaching discriminatory laws and permanent violence that sustain the brutal exploitation of the Africans, making their tenure in any sphere of South African life extremely precarious, are thus observed. In fact, the superfluity of the white area issues out of the hunger of the blacks, its prosperity out of the exploitation, impoverishment, and subjugation of millions of Africans, its exaltation out of debasement. Once the determinant influence of capitalist relations of production on the allocation of land and social resources is recognized, the surface irrationality and the amoral impoverishment of the reserves find their rational explanation.

The Afrikaans expression "too little to live on, too much to die from" is an apt description of the conditions in the reserves, where individuals exist in forced assemblage as groups to which extra-economic coercions and controls can be swiftly applied. The reserves should be conceptualized therefore as dormitories for cheap labor — severe handicaps are imposed on the African people, which depress their earnings, deny them skills, and put a premium on instability. With only a paltry budget and a pseudo-political status, the reserves are rural slums whose rhythm of toil is at the mercy of what happens in the mines and urban areas of what is called "white" South Africa.

In the reserves, we are dealing with regions whose social structures have been influenced a great deal by the demands made on their labor by the mining and cash-crop industries. With this recognized, the real dynamics of capitalist development and the structural imperatives behind the creation of the reserves are opened for analysis; then (and only then) does it become possible to assess the real significance of these areas in a way that does not mistake appearance for reality or mere surface phenomena for structural depths.

With the development of secondary manufacturing, a new demand for African labor was created. The problem of labor in one sector of the economy cannot be separated from its distribution in another. Because secondary industry is in general an urban phenomenon, requiring an infrastructure of services and supplies, urban counterparts to the Bantustans have developed. These are the "locations" or townships which are physically demarcated from the "white" cities whose labor they largely provide and in which all Africans are required to live under stringently restricted conditions. Needless to say, amenities are minimal and slum situations prevail. The structural relationship between the rural Bantustans and the urban locations is crucial here. While the migrants supply labor for the mines, those who are allowed to settle in towns supply labor to the secondary industry which is gaining in importance in the South African economy. The presence of Africans in urban locations demands day-to-day regulation; the pass system, the service contract, and other documents of eligibility demand an enormous police force and such a force is manned at strategic points by poor whites.

MIGRANT LABOR

Now that we have considered the forcible creation of the reserves as pools of labor and places where conquered African societies were confined, let us discuss the methods by which Africans were incorporated into the economy. Export of cheap migrant labor is not a purely South African phenomenon. Such highly developed countries as Germany, France, Belgium, the United States, etc., take thousands of migrant workers from the less-developed countries on their periphery every year. As Castles and Kosack point out:

The employment of immigrant workers in the capitalist process is not a new phenomenon. The Irish played a vital part in British industrialization. Not only did they provide a special form of labour for heavy work of a temporary nature on railways, canals and roads; their competition also forced down wages and conditions for other workers. Engels described Irish immigration as a "cause of abasement to which the English worker is exposed, a cause permanently active in forcing the whole class downwards" (1972:6).

Migrant workers in Europe have long filled the lowest-paid jobs in city services: sweeping streets and mending roads. In the United States, migrant workers are employed to harvest vegetables, fruits, and tobacco in such states as California and Connecticut.

Labor migration in South Africa, although superficially similar to all capitalist societies in search of cheap labor that can be disposed of easily in times of economic crisis, has certain distinctive features of its own. Woddis has described the unique features of South Africa's migrant labor system:

First, it is a migration *almost overwhelmingly of adult males*, single men, or husbands unaccompanied by their wives and children, who have been left behind in the ruined countryside. Secondly, the migrants usually *take up employment for a strictly limited duration* — six months, a year, two years, but seldom longer. Thirdly, *the migration is repeated again and again in the life of the individual peasant-worker*, his career consisting of numerous short terms of employment alternating with periods at home in his village or the Reserve. Fourthly, whether he migrates from the countryside to a town or mining area within the same territory, or whether it is a question of "alien migration" across frontiers, it is *on foot*. Fifthly, it is frequently *connected with various forms of labor recruitment* which sometimes tend to be disguised forms of forced labor. *And sixthly, it is on such a scale and of such a character that it produces a completely disproportioned population both in the towns and in the rural areas, aggravates terribly the already acute agrarian crisis, and leads to a total disharmony of the economy of the African territories most affected by it*. From the standpoint of labor it has three further results; the constant change of personnel in employment which arises from this system *makes difficult the acquisition of labor skill, creates enormous difficulties for trade-union organization, and tends to depress wages* (1960:82; original emphasis).

Never in modern times has a country based its policy of employing more than 70 percent of its labor on such an extensive use of migrant labor as has South Africa. Why? What does it mean? We think of "modernizing societies" as societies in which there is a permanent shift of population from agriculture to industry. What about South Africa? South Africa of course is one country in the world that has a monopoly of gold, a mineral in universal demand, and it is this mineral that most heavily relies on migrant labour.

To begin with, let us view the use of migrant labor in mining in historical perspective as provided by Maurice Dobb. In England, he writes:

When the supply of labour for any new enterprise was insufficiently plentiful, for example in mining, it was not uncommon for the Crown to grant the right of impressment to the entrepreneur or to require that convicts be assigned to the work under penalty of hanging if they were refractory or if they absconded. This was done in the case of South Wales lead mines leased to royal patentees in Stuart times; from which apparently numerous convicts ran away, despite the threatened penalty, declaring that "they had better have been hanged than to be tied to that employment." Throughout this period compulsion of labour stood in the background of the labour market. Tudor legislation provided compulsory work for the unemployed as well as making unemployment an offence punishable with characteristic brutality (Dobb 1963:233).

In this passage Dobb draws attention to two facts — scarcity of labor in mining and the right of impressment granted by the Crown to the entrepreneur. We have already examined the considerable use of migrant labor in the mining industry, and its role in entrenching the system, despite many tongue-in-cheek denials, is crucial. On June 20, 1955, in a paper entitled "Development and progress in Bantu communities," the late Prime Minister, Dr. Verwoerd, stated the reasons for the preference for migrant labor:

The migratory labour system under which the Bantu sell their working power and labour far from their homes, has been in force for generations. *We all know that for mining labour it is the best and presumably only practicable system.* It is my contention that strengthening of this system and its extention to most other fields of labour would benefit the Bantu, because the established business interests in the European towns will never permit the urban locations to grow into fully independent Bantu towns and because such development would, in any case, be contrary to government policy (1968 [1955]; emphasis added).

The hypocritical character of the assertion that migrant labour benefits the African is too obvious. But the statement also touches on the fundamental principles on which the migrant labor system is based: the need of gold mining for cheap labor. Furthermore, there is, on the one hand, the fear of a permanently settled African proletariat in the towns. That is, that migrant labor creates conditions in which the African working class is kept in a state of permanent disorientation, unable to organize and confront white supremacy where it is weakest. Hepple describes the advantages of migrant labor this way:

There is no doubt that the advantages of this kind of labour to employers are considerable. African mine workers are prevented from forming trade unions. Being compounded immigrants, they are insulated from the influences of trade unionism among free workers. Attempts to establish unions are quickly scotched, and the organizers severely dealt with. The exclusion of trade unionism has created the extraordinary situation that the industry is organized only to the extent of its white employees, who comprise a mere ten per cent of the workers employed (1968:204–205).

Other advantages of the migrant labor system are that African labor can be rationed and moved from one employer to another and from one branch of industry to another as required by the developing and expanding economy. In times of work shortages, Africans can be thrown out of work and dispatched to the reserves without causing social tensions. The system of labor bureaus facilitates the mobility of African labor. Describing the system of labor bureaus, the *South African yearbook* stated in its 1956–1957 issue:

The main object of the labour bureaux scheme is to canalize Native labour in accordance with the demand therefor. In order to facilitate matters for both employer and workseeker, each labour bureau is intended to form an avenue of contact between employer and workseeker. For this reason, employers are required to perform all their transactions in connection with the employment of native labour through the medium of the appropriate labour bureau. Such a bureau, being linked with the general network of labour bureaux, not only provides a system of contact between employers and workseekers — the only effective means of communication regarding Native workseekers — but also knows from day to day what the demand for Native labour is in various fields of employment. Hence a workseeker, either in the rural areas, or in an urban centre, is advised of the work available and the conditions of service attached to each category of employment. Once he decides to accept the employment offered to him, he is able to proceed directly to his employer, thus avoiding the frustration previously experienced by workseekers who failed to find employment on their own. Although it cannot be claimed that the labour bureaux provide for all the needs of every employer or satisfy the wishes of every workseeker, it can nevertheless be stated that 'their scope is tremendous. During the period July 1955–June 1956, altogether 1,016,378 Native male workseekers were placed in employment through the labour bureaux (1956–1957: 361).

Here then we have a full picture of how the African population is organized with maximum efficiency and bottled up in labor reservoirs. From the reserves, channels are created leading up to white farms and mines and wherever African labor is needed. As the secondary economy grew and the mining kingdom expanded, an unemployed (that is, "idle") African was an anomaly, a threat, and a menace. He must not be. He must be enrolled in the form of prison labor or free labor; if not, he must be weeded out and sent to the reserves to starve. Again I quote the *Yearbook*, which states:

The large number of unemployed Natives, especially juveniles, found in practically every urban area in the Union, is steadily being diminished through the efforts of both local and district labour bureaux. Large numbers of Native youths previously regarded as unplaceable and labelled as *tsotsis* (gangsters) are now being engaged for work and most employers have intimated that they are satisfied with the services of these juveniles (*South African yearbook* 1956–1957:360).

Since the famous declaration of the Stellard Commission in 1922, the migrant labor system and the rightless status of Africans working in white areas have been secured and entrenched by a complex system of laws and regulations that severely restricts the rights of African workers anywhere. Some of the laws recently passed are the Bantu Laws Amendment Act of 1964 and the Bantu Labour Regulations. A watershed in racial labor policies was passed on April 1, 1968, when the government finally established migrant labor as the only form of employment for Africans in urban areas. According to the terms of these regulations, all blacks entering the white areas to work may do so only on one-year contracts. While they may, and often do, return year after year, they can never qualify for permanent residence under Section 10 of the Urban Areas Act. A government minister declared that through these regulations "we now give judicial recognisance of our expressed policy of building our economy on contract labour" (quoted in *Financial Mail* 1968: 198).

The true intent of the regulations introduced in 1968 was the abolition of Section 10 of the Urban Areas Act, which until then had made it possible for an African born in town or employed continuously by one firm or employer for ten years to qualify for permanent residence in the town. Through the pretext that all Africans are migrant laborers, the government is in fact reducing them to what the late Prime Minister Verwoerd called "interchangeable" units of labor.

Given the political aims of the white state, an African with permanent rights in the city was a contradiction. As a vagabond he could threaten individuals in society; but as an educated property holder, a successful engineer, or a businessman, he undermined and threatened the whole superstructure of settler society. Therefore, patiently and systematically, all the anomalies and loopholes of 1910 are being removed.

The reserves cannot be treated solely as reservoirs for cheap labor. Nor can migrant labor be considered as an economic anomaly. South Africa's capitalism cannot be understood as an "economic" system in the narrow sense, divorced from the total social framework within which it grew and which sustains it. In a settler society likely to be threatened by African revolt, economic calculations mix with political and strategic considerations. The white settlers suffer from what may be called a minority status syndrome. They have always feared that someday they will be overwhelmed by African political power, if the various social and "racial" groups shared South Africa as a unified political state. To cope with this problem the various South African governments followed a strategy of "divide and rule." The various ethnic groups that made up the country were to be isolated from one another for the purpose of control and containment.

Thus the economic, political, and strategic motives are inextricably intertwined in the establishment of Bantustans. The often-quoted Landsdown Commission of 1944 particularly stressed the economic motives, especially the crucial importance of the gold-mining industry:

The goldmining industry of the Witwatersrand has indeed been fortunate in having secured, for its unskilled labour, native peasants who have been prepared to come to the Witwatersrand for periods of labour at comparatively low rates of pay. But for this fortunate circumstance, the industry could never have reached the present stage of development — some mines would never have opened up, many low grade mines would have been unable to work with any prospect of profit; in the case of the richer mines, large bodies of ore, the milling of which has been brought within the limits of payability, could never have been worked, with the result that the lives of the mines would have been considerably reduced.

That the results accruing from this cheap native labour supply have had a profoundly beneficial influence on the general economic development of the Union is a matter that needs no demonstration. Not only has the earth yielded up a great body of wealth which would have remained unexploited, but vast amounts of money have been paid away in wages and put into circulation for the acquiring of equipment and stores necessary for the working of the mines and this, in turn, has had the beneficial effect upon the development of secondary industries (Union Government 1944: parts 70–71).

The significance of the availability of "unlimited" supplies of cheap labor lies in the fact that only one portion of the capital invested in any productive undertaking directly contributes to the production of surplus values, and that is the capital laid out in the purchase of labor. Marx' categories of *constant* capital (i.e., capital invested in machinery, raw materials, and other accessories of labor) and *variable* capital (capital that is not only reproduced but is at the same time the direct source of surplus value) apply with particular cogency to the role played by reserved migrant labor in subsidizing the growth of industry in South Africa. According to Maurice Dobb:

It has always, of course, to be borne in mind that, when they spoke of plenty in connection with supply, both economists and factory-kings had in mind not only quantity but also price; and that they required the supply to be, not merely sufficient to fill a given number of available jobs, but in sufficient superabundance to cause labourers to compete pitilessly against one another for employment so as to restrain the price of this commodity from rising with its increased demand (1963:275).

That is, labor is cheap from the employer's point of view, when he contributes the least possible amount to the subsistence and upkeep of the laborer and when he can use the services of the laborer for the longest possible period, and in excess of the necessary labor time, to earn his upkeep. Slavery provides the most extreme and the most straightforward example of the process of exploitation. Slave labor was undisguised forced labor. Not only the means of production but also the workers were the property of the exploiting class. Everything created by the labor of slaves belonged to the slave owner. He supplied the slaves with the instruments and materials of production, and distributed work and the means of subsistence among them as he wished.

Migrant labor, confined in the reserves, is a variant of forced labor — hence its cheapness. Its resemblance to slavery is obvious at a glance. The fact that African migrant laborers are paid subsistence wages, as distinct from slaves or those working under forced-labor conditions, does not minimize the similarity. African migrant laborers are paid at the minimal subsistence level for single men, even when their families live with them in town. The rationale behind the wage structure is that wages merely supplement African susbsistence farming in the reserve. The Native Recruiting Corporation told the Economic and Wage commission of 1925:

The social and economic position of the Native is such that he is able to satisfy his needs by intermittent periods of service. Generally speaking, the Native postpones going out to work until the last possible moment, and the possession of additional funds merely enables him to remain in idleness a further period. . . . The Corporation is convinced that any increase in the level of Native wages would be followed, to only a small extent, by an increase in the Native standard of living; that the main result would be that the Native would work for a shorter period than at present; and that consequently the Native labour available to industry in the Union would be reduced (Union Government 1944:66).

The close connection between land scarcity and availability of cheap labor was the cornerstone in the creation of reserves and use of migrant labor — hence the restriction on entry and permanent residence of Africans in towns.

By confining Africans to the reserves, where they were free to starve and die, the transition from exploitation of slave labor to that of forced labor was disguised. Under slavery each worker represented a substantial initial investment for the owner/employer; thus it was in the interest of the owner of slaves to provide them with a satisfactory subsistence for themselves and their families in order to maintain their productivity and to assure their reproduction and replacement. This entailed additional investment beyond the purchase price. The reserve and migrant labor system in South Africa freed the employer of any expenses for the upkeep of his laborers. In the migrant laborer he bought only labor power and paid only for the laborer's subsistence, without heed to his family needs or further reproduction of new proletarians.

In general, the capitalist class under any circumstance goes to extremes to prevent the worker from selling his labor power above value. It often reenacts the violence of "primitive accumulation" to swell the ranks of the proletariat and to ensure that there are always more workers than jobs, or what is called the "reserve army of labor." The existence of a mass of dispossessed workers, "free" to work or starve, is a necessary condition of capitalist production and accumulation. Under the political economy of South Africa, this general law is facilitated by the native reserves, legal-political enforcement, and the migrant labor system. The migrant laborer, to paraphrase Marx, stands in absolutely no relation to the objective condition of his labor; it is rather his labor power itself, which is placed in an organic relation to production alongside the other natural implements, e.g., cattle which are regarded as an appendage of the machinery if used as draft animals.

Besides economic benefits, there are psychological reasons why migrant workers are preferred for South Africa's political economy. In order to undercut the migrant laborer's claim to urban residence, he is forever forced to repeat the short history of his origin. Whereas, in the manufacturing sector a class of hereditary proletarians has crystallized out, having made a complete break with the country, in the mining industry the typical laborer is forced to be half-proletarian and half-peasant. A yearly outflow of the labor force from the reserves to the mining industry, depleting these communities of their manpower resources, results in a radical change of traditional attitudes and way of life without at the same time compensating for the distintegration of the old order. Periodically returned to what are called homelands, the migrant, to a greater or lesser degree, acquiesces in his subjugation. According to Harris (1966:98), the sociological and psychological effects of migrant labor are that the peasant, who has been forcibly uprooted from subsistence and made a wage earner, is widely separated in space from his family; but this separation, while lasting for an uninterrupted period, is yet not so long as to break ties binding him to his family and the reserves.

The use of migrant labor shows that the domination of the working masses by capital is never based on violence alone. Capitalist rule is based on a whole range of mechanisms, some objective products of the economic process and others subjective phenomena arising through the manipulation of attitudes. Migrant labor is thus a deliberately contrived system whereby surplus value is extracted from the peasantry without incurring the political and economic consequences of a fully fledged and integrated proletariat.

Thus the employers of migrant labor enjoy many advantages: the initial investment required to obtain slave laborers is eliminated (police costs for maintaining and regulating this labor are high, but they are borne by the state as a whole and therefore do not enter into the profit calculations of individual firms), as is the necessity of maintaining their health and family through further investment. If a migrant laborer becomes unproductive or dies because his wage is not sufficient to meet his subsistence needs, he can be replaced with no additional capital simply by pressuring the government to make the necessary labor available. The cost of labor is thereby reduced to or below the cost of the individual laborer's subsistence. Burnett explains further:

Confined to a "reserve" of one form or another, the peasant is confronted with an insufficiency of land for the profitable pursuit of his traditional methods of shifting cultivation and pasturage, an insufficiency of capital and technical training to turn to a more advantageous form of agriculture or animal husbandry, and a resulting insufficiency of produce to feed his family and exchange for the cash required to pay his taxes and make the necessary purchases of imported goods. It is this condition which necessitates the outward flow of male, and to a lesser extent female, labor from the peasant communities into the European industrial centers. Low wages, short term contracts and other devices calculatedly prevent the vast majority of Africans from taking up permanent residence with their families in their place of employment, forcing them to leave wives and children at home and return to the reserves themselves after relatively short and intermittent periods of wage employment. This has resulted in what Wilson so vividly described as the "hungry, manless areas" of Africa in which peasants buy "clothes with hunger" (1973:22–24).

The "hungry, manless" reserves are in a worse position than ever. In 1939 a government white paper on land policy said of the Reserves that "speaking generally," they were "congested, denuded, overstocked, eroded, and for the most part in a deplorable condition." Another typical and authoritative opinion was expressed in the ninth report of the Social and Economic Planning Council, an official body, which called attention to "the incapacity of the Native Reserves to provide even the minimum subsistence requirements under present conditions" (Davidson 1952: 62). The African in the reserves is thus often pushed to work for menial wages by the real threat of death through starvation. The physical conditions in the reserves force streams of men into a search for casual employment in European domains or an outright exodus to the towns.

There is some similarity between the position of the Africans, as both tenants on the farm and migrant workers in the reserves, and that of former serfs in the agrarian centers of Europe at the beginning of the industrial revolution. Dobb gives two examples from the Russian and Prussian Empires; we quote him to stress the similarity. In the Baltic States, following the emancipation of serfs, the emancipated peasants were precluded from moving away from the locality, in order that they would remain as cheap laborers for the large estates. "In other parts of the Russian Empire after 1861 the institution of the village commune, with its collective obligations for taxes and other obstacles in the way of transfer of holdings of a peasant household — served to retard the flow of labor from the village to the towns [in order to be sent] from regions of surplus labor to the regions of growing demand in mill or mine" (Dobb 1963:275).

The extensiveness of the migratory labor system as used in the gold-mining industry has been described by Houghton as probably the most fantastic labor setup of any industry in the world:

Imagine an industry located in Paris drawing some 340,000 workers from as far afield as England, Scotland, Norway, Poland, Germany, Italy and Spain, and returning them to their homes once every year or eighteen months, and you have a European equivalent (1967:66).

Given this most peculiar situation, social scientists have been primarily interested in asking: what makes Africans travel thousands of miles to the South African gold mines? As with Houghton, they also often make comparison with some situations from the Western experience purely for purposes of dramatization and to denounce the evils of the migrant labor system without affecting the system in the slightest. However, the scope and extent of the migrant labor system in South Africa lead to the posing of far more fruitful questions. For example: What are the structures of command that compel men to leave wives and children and to travel great distances just to work under the most difficult conditions? Why should employers of African labor tolerate such a situation if in fact it has the disadvantages that bourgeois economists say that it has?

In the vast literature on this subject (some of which we have had the occasion to criticize [Magubane and O'Brien 1972:88–103]), the dynamics of the migrant system are often reduced to the motivations of Africans who "shuttle" between areas of work and the reserves because this helps (it is said) to stabilize their families. The causes of migration thus have been described as economic (e.g., the Africans' need for money to pay taxes and *lobola*); or political and social (e.g., the desire to escape from "tribal" obligations or from the dull routine of the "tribe"). Such subjective conceptions of migrant labor became most useful against those who criticized the migrant labor system, and these ideological assertions were repeated so often that they are now accepted as true. They have congealed to become the cruel folklore which must be debunked in order to illuminate the forcible expropriation of the migrants and their oppression.

Thus, for example, when discussing the effect of the reserves and recruiting system on the economic status of the urban African workers, Houghton reaches this comfortable conclusion:

The recruiting system has had important economic and social consequences. It does not create a permanent class of town dwellers, but is in effect the temporary transference of reserve Natives to the industrial centers to work for a period of nine months or more, after which they are returned to their homes in the Native territories. The recruited labourers *are not wholly dependent* upon their possessions in the reserves. They go to the mines to obtain cash to augment their farming income. *They can, therefore, accept wages that are less than sufficient to support a man and his family dependent entirely upon their urban earnings* (1967:36; emphasis added).

And later, he says that in addition to urban and recruited Africans:

There are a large number who, while they have come to town of their own accord, still have economic interests in the reserves and intend to return there eventually. These exert a depressing effect upon urban wages in much the same way as recruited labourers, for like them they are not wholly dependent on their urban earnings (1967:57).

These conclusions do not simply fail to weigh the effects of political manipulation — they never raise any serious questions about methods of compulsion on the determinant structures of the capitalist system. When Marx (1957) said that in the tender annals of bourgeois political economy, the idyllic reigns from time immemorial, he was referring to analyses like the above. We have seen that (in the actual evolution of South Africa's political economy) conquest, enslavement, robbery, and force played a great part in the production of cheap labor. To those facts the political economist applies the method of psychoanalysis to individuals who are victims of the system. The more loudly the facts cry out in the face of his ideology, the more the apologist of the system is forced to produce obfuscating psychological explanations.

Like "skill," the category "migrant labor" in South Africa has rarely been used to describe a real economic fact. As a descriptive term it is used for political and propaganda purposes, to justify low wages and labor regulation. Houghton writes:

Migratory labour cannot suddenly be abolished because the very survival of both black and white depends upon it, but it should be recognised for what it is — an evil canker at the heart of our whole society, wasteful of labour, destructive of ambition, a wrecker of homes and a symptom of our fundamental failure to create a coherent and progressive economic society. . . . This institution is a symptom of a deep underlying weakness in the whole national structure. Perhaps the most insidious effect of the migrant system as a whole is that it perpetuates poverty, and prevents the raising of consumption standards of the mass of our population (1967:95).

Very little reflection is needed to understand that here we face not only a false conclusion, but also a deliberate apology. Any serious study of the migrant labor system must, of necessity, depart from an analysis of the superficial and must analyze migrant labor and "Native" reserves in the context of conquest and the labor requirements of extractive capitalist industries. That is, migrant labor is part and parcel of the political economy of capitalism and is a system devised and fostered by the state as an organ of capital. The decision to work as a migrant is not in the hands

of African workers. Instead, this crucial set of decisions is mainly determined as a by-product of policies over which he had no say. In 1947,
Schapera argued this point for the South African gold mines:

It is clearly to the advantage of the mines that native labourers should be
encouraged to return to their homes after the completion of the ordinary period of
service. The maintenance of the system under which the mines are able to obtain
unskilled labour at a rate less than ordinarily paid in industry depends upon this,
for otherwise the subsidiary means of subsistence would disappear and the
labourer would tend to become a permanent resident upon the Witwatersrand,
with increased requirements. . . (quoted in Wolpe 1972:434).

H.J. and Ray Simons agree with Schapera, but not for apologetic reasons:

The owners [of the mines] contended that the migratory system was "a fundamental factor" in the mining economy and essential to their prosperity. If the
African "has not got the reserve subsistence to go back to" said Gemmil, the
secretary of the Chamber, "we cannot afford a wage to make it possible for him to
live in an urban area" (1969:86).

Gorz has examined the way in which the political and economic advantages of migrant labor work to subsidize capitalist accumulation in geographically selected areas. That is, migrant labor causes an artificial modification of the social and political structure of the indigenous and colonized population. And the migrants, fragmented and exploited, can be
excluded from trade-union action, which means a considerable decrease
in the political and electoral weight of the working class and the
weakening of its ideological force and cohesion. Economically, the
importation of "ready-made" workers amounts to a saving for the "country" for which the migrants work. The country of immigration does not
have to pay for the childhood and adolescence of migrant workers, nor
will it be responsible for supporting its migrant workers in their old age.
The fact that most migrant workers are not accompanied by their families
brings the "country" of immigration an additional and substantial saving
in social capital (housing, schools, hospitals, transport, and other infrastructural facilities).

On these counts alone — not to speak of the under payment of immigrant labor
power, immigrant workers are super-exploited by the capitalist class i.e., they
are a source of additional surplus value (Gorz 1970:70).

The contribution of the migrant laborers to the prosperity of the gold-
mining industry has been decisive. Brought up in the reserves in their
youth and shipped back there in their old age, the urban-based capitalist
industries save a whole range of social costs, and in fact shift the burden
of these costs to the poverty stricken and underdeveloped "reserves." All

that is produced over and above what is required to provide a bare living for migrant workers goes to the mine owners — this constitutes their profit, their "income." The reserves provide the towns their labor power and their men, without themselves having a right to the social benefits that are a spin-off from the capital accumulated through their activity. The reserves are made to fulfill the functions that capitalism prefers not to assume — the functions of social security for the migrant workers.

The development and prosperity of the settler sector depended directly and heavily upon the existence of labor from the reserves. Dr. Margaret Mead points out that:

White employers on the whole are ready to put up with migrant labour provided the supply is constant, for the important reason that migrant labour is likely to be cheaper in the long run than permanent labour. Apart from a rising scale of wages, a permanent labour force would require social amenities, such as housing and recreation, of a more extensive and costly type than the migrant labourer will accept. Even more costly, whether at the employers' or the government's expense, would be the necessary provision for old age and unemployment. The white employers, provided they can get their labour at what they consider to be "reasonable wages", do not, naturally, concern themselves with the problem of whether the African working for them is undermining the economic life of his own village (quoted in Woddis 1960:94).

The studies of migrant labor by liberal sociologists, anthropologists, and economists discuss at length the effects of migration on the family life, the social structure, the economy, and the values of migrants, and they examine its consequences for the attainment or lack of skills among Africans, but they omit important questions regarding the profits that capitalists derive from this labor. At the same time, the conventional approach has tacitly accepted and thus reinforced ideas of the system of labor migration as a necessary evil, for it says that the reserves provide a place where Africans can have land free from fear of expropriation by whites.

By failing to come to grips with the political economy of the system of capitalism, social scientists have missed the underlying logic that has allowed such an obvious evil to continue for such a long time. The labels "homeland" and the "dual" or "plural" society are metaphorical terms for describing concrete policies for robbery and death. In the reserves, the specific meaning of a "dual" society can be observed at close quarters.

Davidson explains why migrant labor has continued:

Earnest commissions of medical men, missionaries, social workers, and officials have debated and debated on the disease, the abandonment of family life, the decay of agriculture, the breakdown of all serious tribal tradition, that are present in central and southern Africa today, and are intimately associated with the provision of cheap labour for the gold fields of the Rand. *The method of this provision — migratory labour — has been several times condemned by official investigations. But the Chamber of Mines has laid great stress on the fact that its policy was to employ cheap native labour; and the Chamber has had its way* (1952:94; emphasis added).

Houghton's description of migrant labor as a necessary evil reveals the dilemma facing bourgeois thought: that it must stop in theory where it must stop in social practice, i.e., it cannot supersede the reality from which its status and livelihood are derived (cf. Korsch 1970:47).

South Africa does not have two economies or two social systems, nor does it have "black" and "white" areas. Economically, socially, and politically the "Bantu homelands" and "white" areas are dovetailed parts of the larger imperial system, and any attempt to obscure this is an exercise in intellectual mystification. It is particularly important to emphasize this in the light of a school of thought that sees South Africa in terms of a "plural or dual society" distinguished by cultural cleavages. The Bantu Homelands and the migrant labor system are as much a problem of political economy as they are a problem of technology, town planning, or a strategic problem to contain revolutionary possibilities.

Marx rightly points out that the bulk of the labor force in capitalist society comprises unskilled workers expending time on routine operations. "Skilled labour counts only as simple labour intensified, or rather, as multiplied simple labour, a given quantity of skilled labour being considered equal to a greater quantity of simple labour. . . . The different proportions in which different sorts of labour are reduced to unskilled labour as their standard are established by a social process that goes on behind the backs of producers, and consequently appears to be fixed by custom" (quoted in Eaton 1963:34).

The Carnegie Commission, appointed to investigate the "poor white" problem in the early 1930's, pointed to the characteristic rigidity and inflexibility of the labor market in the mining industry:

It is . . . quite certain that the task at present performed by Natives could not simply be transferred to White men, even if we were optimistically to assume that White men (under the conditions in the Witwatersrand mines) would achieve in larger output in purely normal labor. In 1930 in all the Transvaal gold mines non-Europeans received in wages over £7,000,000. A doubling — let us say — of these labor costs, the mining industry could not bear. But even twice the average native wage could not support a White family, for the average earnings of the non-Europeans were £33-8s per annum (Carnegie Commission n.d.).

Houghton and Horwitz directed their analysis to symptoms rather than primary structural causes of the migrant labor system. The socioeconomic conditions that prevail in the reserves or Bantu Homelands are conditioned by the need of cheap labor in the so-called white economy to which the reserves are subjected. The need for migrant labor lies deep in the nature of the South African capitalist system. Specifically it lies in the difference the use of migrants makes for the profitableness of the mines.

Through centralized recruitment and wage fixation by the Witwatersrand Native Recruiting Association and the Native Recruiting Corporation, both under the auspices of the Chamber of Mines, mine owners were able to establish a monopolistic position in relation to unskilled African labor. Moreover recruitment was not confined to South African territories alone (as we have seen), which would have limited the available supply and favored the possible bargaining power of the workers, but was extended throughout East and Central Africa, including the Portuguese territories and what were then British protectorates. Thus, by eliminating competition among the mining companies, the government and the Chamber of Mines instituted a method of collective exploitation which is greatly facilitated by the reserves and migrant labor.

Yet, when South Africa's political economy is discussed, the role of the state in providing the political framework for the social relations of collective exploitation obtaining in the mines is usually deemphasized or even omitted. Alternatively, those analyses which recognize government influence almost invariably assume a conflict of interests between economic growth and political legislation. Such perspectives lead to severe limitations on a thorough understanding of apartheid labor policies, for it has been particularly in this significant area of labor recruiting that government labor policies have *not* been in conflict in any major way with those of the employers. Labor legislation is enacted as much in the immediate interest of the capitalist class as in the interest of the white settlers' state in general. Even Houghton recognized that the labor going to the mines was not subject to influx control laws:

Finally, perhaps one of the most powerful forces of all is the fact that legislation restricting the movement of Africans into urban areas does not apply to mine workers. Thus general influx control, by diverting men into mining, who might otherwise have sought employment in some other field, tends to increase the supply of mine workers and thus to depress wages in mining (1967:162).

The gold-mining industry, the original focus and foundation of South African economic development, has waged fierce war against the peasant societies of southern Africa. It has fought to buy African labor as cheaply as it is possible; and it has enjoyed a favored position, always receiving priority in fulfilling its labor requirements. The mining industry will defend its sources of cheap labor with all its might. On a few occasions, when laborers in the mines demanded better conditions, the armed might of the state was used with untold ruthlessness to suppress these workers. Migrant labor and slave wages will be eliminated only when the gold industry belongs to the people, and when the African people assume their rightful place. The impending death of an illusion.

The migrant labor system draws Africans from all over South and Central Africa into the capitalist economy. Thus the migratory labor has created conditions which have spread the effect of capitalist exploitation over a far wider territory than anywhere else in the world. Since 1963, Mozambique (from where more than 100,000 migrant workers are recruited annually) has been in the grips of a successful war of liberation. Recently this movement caused the fall of the Portuguese government. In southern Africa, the revolutionary working class has been spread over every part of the country instead of being confined exclusively to the urban centers. This explains the steady, certain, and irresistible progress of the revolutionary struggles in the late 1950's and early 1960's to the most remote corners of the country. In southern Africa it is perfectly clear that a victorious movement in Mozambique will be felt even more in South Africa. The interests of South Africa in the Portuguese territories of Angola and Mozambique were not only confined to the labor these territories supplied, but the areas also provided a *cordon sanitaire* against the spread of guerrilla struggles to South Africa itself. If FRELIMO can gain control in Mozambique, it will not only stop the flow of labor to South Africa, but it will provide fraternal support to South African insurgents, who will establish bases and lines of infiltration to South Africa. Nusey (1974) writes, "In five swift weeks [the April Coup in Portugal] has stripped away the comforting security of Mozambique and Angola, shaken the delicate coexistence between Black States and White States throughout Southern Africa, drastically bruised the White and boosted the Black morale and thrown the future into doubt."

The success of the guerrilla struggle in Mozambique and Angola, and recently in Zimbabwe, will have a definite impact on the South African labor market. Of the 370,000 Africans who work in the mines, only about 100,000 come from within South Africa, mostly from the Bantustan of the Transkei and Ciskei. The majority of the miners are what South African law classifies as "foreign natives," recruited from Malawi, Mozambique, Lesotho, and Botswana. James Gemmill, general manager of the mine labor organization, expressed the fear of the miners in these words, "If we were thrown on our own devices for labor, we'd be busts" (Gemmill 1973).

When the struggle does get underway the revolutionary struggle of the urban areas will never be in a position to suffer defeats by the reactionary rural areas thanks to the mining industry and the migratory labor system.

In conclusion, the labor used in the gold mines reveals the most carefully planned structures of exploitation. The big mining companies are impersonal, professional corporations. They are rationalized in terms of personnel, production, marketing, advertising, etc. At all times the need to reduce costs gave mining capitalism its drive toward expansion and domination of the whole African labor force in South Africa. In the growth and entrenchment of migrant labor, we see how the super-structure was created by individuals capable of consciously planning the exploitation of resources to eternity, based always on social domination of the Africans.

Finally, in view of the greater expansion of the mining industry due to the external demand for gold, the domestic labor force will be subjected to even greater regulation and exploitation, especially when the guerrilla movement in Mozambique makes it impossible for South African recruiting agencies to get the necessary labor. This will create even more tensions in the domestic labor scene and negate even more the whole bogus idea of Bantustans.

REFERENCES

BALDWIN, ALAN
　　1974　*Uprooting a nation*. African Publications Trust.
BRYCE, JAMES
　　1969　*Impression of South Africa*. New York: New American Library.
BURNETT, DON
　　1973　*Peasant types and revolutionary potential in colonial Africa*. Richmond, B.C., Canada: L.M.S. Press.
CARNEGIE COMMISSION
　　n.d.　*The poor white problem in South Africa*, volume one. Carnegie Commission Report.
CASTLES, STEPHEN, GODULA KOSACK
　　1972　Common Market migrants. *New Left Review* 73:3–22.
DAVIDSON, BASIL
　　1952　*A report on southern Africa*. London: Jonathan Cape.
DOBB, MAURICE
　　1963　*Studies in the development of capitalism*. New York: International Publishers.
EATON, JOHN
　　1963　*Political economy*. New York: International Publishers.
ENGELS, FRIEDRICH
　　n.d.　*The housing question*. New York: International Publishers.
Financial Mail
　　1968　Page 198. *Financial Mail*, July 19.
GEMMILL, JAMES
　　1973　Article in the *New York Times*, October 23.
GORZ, ANDRÉ
　　1970　Immigrant labor. *New Left Review* 61:70.
　　1971　Colonialism at home and abroad. *Liberation* 15(6):22–28.
HARRIS, MARVIN
　　1966　"Labor emigration among the Mozambique Thonga: cultural and political factors," in *Social change: the colonial situation*. Edited by E. Wallenstein. New York: John Wiley and Sons.
HEPPLE, ALEX
　　1968　*South Africa: a political and economic history*. New York: Praeger.

HOUGHTON, D. HORBAT
1967   "Some economic problems of the Bantu in South Africa," in *The political economy of South Africa*. South African Institute of Race Relations, Monograph Series 1.

KORSCH, KARL
1970   *Marxism and philosophy*. New York: Monthly Review Press.

LEWIS, W.A.
1954   Economic development with unlimited supplies of labor. *The Manchester School of Economic and Social Studies* 22(2):139.

LUXEMBURG, ROSA
1965   *The accumulation of capital*. New York: Monthly Review Press.

MAFEJE, ARCHIE
1973   "The fallacy of 'dual economies' revisited: a case for east, central Africa and southern Africa." Unpublished manuscript.

MAGUBANE, B., J. O'BRIEN
1972   Migrant labor in Africa: a critique of conventional wisdom. *Critical Anthropology* 2 (2):88–103.

MARX, KARL
1957   *Capital*, volume one. London: Everyman's Edition.
1965   *Pre-capitalist economic formations*. Translated by Jack Cohen, edited and with an introduction by E.J. Hahsbown. New York: International Publishers.
1969   *Genesis of capital*. Moscow: Progress Publishers.

MARX, KARL, FRIEDRICH ENGELS
1962   *On Britain*. Moscow: Foreign Language Publishing House.

MBEKI, GOVAN
1964   *South Africa: the peasants revolt*. Baltimore: Penguin African Library.

MOREL, E.D.
1969   *The black man's burden*. New York: Monthly Review Press.

NUSEY, WILF
1974   Johannesburg *Star*. June 8.

SCHAPERA, I.
1947   *Migrant labour and tribal life*. London: Oxford University Press.

SIMONS, H.J., RAY SIMONS
1969   *Race and class in South Africa, 1850–1950*. Baltimore: Penguin African Library.

South African yearbook
1956–1975   *The official year book of the Union of South Africa and Basutoland, Bechuana Protectorate and Swaziland* 29. Pretoria.

SWEEZY, PAUL M.
1962   *The theory of capitalist development*. New York: Monthly Review Press.

UNION GOVERNMENT
1944   *Landsdown Commission*. Union Government Report 21.

VAN DER HORST, SHEILA T.
1971   *Native labour in South Africa*. London: Frank Cass.

VERWOERD, H.F.
1968 [1955]   "Development and progress in Bantu communities," quoted in *Daily Dispatch*. April 12, 1968, East London.

WILSON, FRANCIS
1971   "Farming 1870–1966," in *The Oxford history of South Africa*, volume two: *South Africa 1870–1966*. Edited by Monica Wilson and Leonard Thompson. New York: Oxford University Press.

WODDIS, JACK
1960 *Africa: the roots of revolt*. London: Laurence and Wilhart.
WOLPE, HAROLD
1972 Capitalism and cheap labour power in South Africa: from segregation to apartheid. *Economy and Society* 1(4).

Export-Oriented Industrialization Through the Multinational Corporation: Evidence from Kenya

STEVEN W. LANGDON

Multinational corporations (MNC's) are increasingly recognized as important and relatively distinctive factors in the international economy. Because of their size and transnational character they are able to escape many of the conventional constraints imposed on firms by the marketplace and the nation-state (Behrman 1969; Hymer and Rowthorn 1970; Vernon 1971; Paquet 1972). The operations of such firms are therefore clearly relevant to the problems of less-developed countries. Multinationals dominate the international transfer of technology (Cooper 1970); they organize much of international trade within their corporate structure (Helleiner 1972:2); and they often undertake the bulk of manufacturing investment in developing countries, organizing some 60 percent of such investment in Kenya, for instance (ILO 1972:442).

How should this multinational role be analyzed? Until recently MNC operations in the less-developed world have been rather uncritically assessed by economists (Kamarck 1967; Kindleberger 1969; Hirschman 1958), despite some probing questions about foreign resource-extraction firms (Singer 1950) and some attention to the inequality in negotiating ability and power between MNC's and their host governments (Perroux and Demonts 1961; Seers 1963). Recently, however, a more critical perspective has been emerging (Hirschman 1969; Vaitsos 1970; Van Arkadie 1969; Tanzer 1970; Rweyemamu 1971; Streeten 1972; Weeks 1972), emphasizing the ambiguities and distortions implicit in many MNC investments, the considerable costs often associated with such projects (in terms of both surplus loss [see Vaitsos 1970] and the undercutting of local entrepreneurship [Van Arkadie 1969]). My research in

IDR Internal Paper E 74.5 of the Institute for Development Research, Copenhagen, Denmark.

Kenya suggests that this critical perspective provides a more valid starting point for analysis, though perhaps requiring somewhat better definition than it has received.

I start with how the institutional nature of the MNC seems to be emerging. Two points are important. First, centralized, coordinated control is typically exercised by the head office over subsidiaries throughout the MNC (Behrman 1969; Aharoni 1966; Dunning 1971). This puts institutional pressures and constraints on subsidiaries in a less-developed country that differ from the forces shaping behavior of a locally controlled firm. Second, MNC investment transfers a whole package to the less-developed world, not just capital, for instance, as in the days of British railway investment abroad. This package represents a whole way of doing business that has given the MNC the monopoly power elsewhere that underlies its world expansion (see Vaitsos 1970; Hymer and Rowthorn 1970; Galbraith 1969). This provides MNC's with special strength compared to local firms, and it also results in distinct business behaviour — subsidiaries tend to undertake only the exact reproduction locally of particular, trademarked, Western-type products; they actively promote the transfer of tastes for such products; they use managerial/ technical/marketing skills based on experience in advanced economies, etc.

These institutional realities shape the MNC role, and so does the powerful influence in the local political economy that the MNC subsidiary typically carries by virtue of its considerable world resources, bargaining skills, etc. In Kenya, for instance, the MNC sector has clearly entered a "comfortable symbiosis" with the locally dominant political-bureaucratic bourgeoisie (Langdon 1974). As a result the MNC sector obtains important favors in terms of market protection, access to local finance, duty exemptions, etc.; and the local bourgeoisie strengthens its internal dominance via the resources and opportunities its close relationship with the MNC sector provides (through minority shareholding, directorships, special contracts, etc.).

The MNC institutional characteristics, in such a political economy context, generate significant weaknesses in the structure of industrialization. My research illustrates the importance in Kenya of the following problems (see Langdon 1973b): (1) MNC product and taste transfer patterns, combined with head-office pressures, lead to choice of highly capital-intensive techniques in many MNC subsidiaries, with adverse employment consequences; (2) this capital intensity, MNC taste transfer, and head-office emphasis on intrafirm trade all inhibit linkages, especially backward linkages, that could generate considerable economic growth; (3) taste-transfer efforts, and the product differentiation that goes with them, result in wastage of resources on advertising expenditure and changeover costs; (4) these activities can serve to undercut local

industry and/or force it into the same inappropriate sorts of industrialization as the MNC sector (illustrated for Kenya's soap industry in
Langdon 1973a); (5) capital intensity, product/taste transfer, and the
imperatives of communication with the head office, all favor the centralized location of subsidiaries in Nairobi and Mombasa, as one aspect of
the inequality MNC's generate through concentrating their benefits very
narrowly; and finally, (6) the MNC sector's political strength, the favors
that it establishes, and the marketplace advantages of the MNC package
all give subsidiaries marked local monopoly power, which results in
considerable surplus appropriation and repatriation and in turn contributes to Kenyan balance-of-payments difficulties (especially given
head-office export restrictions on many subsidiaries). Such difficulties, it
should be added, may in turn make incoming MNC investment more
essential, thus increasing the bargaining strength of MNC's, thus
encouraging greater favors, thus producing higher surplus drains, and so
on in a vicious circle.

The evidence of such distortions and weaknesses is considerable. But
some economists have responded by suggesting the problem is not the
MNC's institutional nature per se, but the *import substitution strategy*
within which those MNC's operate. Imports, the argument goes, are
inevitably Western-type products, requiring advanced technology to
produce, relying on foreign inputs, and carrying with them market-power
characteristics; so to choose to reproduce imports locally is to choose high
capital intensity, low linkage effects, and balance-of-payments difficulties
regardless of the auspices under which import-substitution is conducted.
Such arguments conclude that export-oriented industrialization, *under
MNC auspices*, will avoid such distortions; such an approach, it is
claimed, uses labor-intensive techniques, relies on local inputs, operates
in decentralized rural areas, holds no monopoly power on a world market, and contributes valuable export earnings to the balance of payments.
So discourage MNC import-substitution but encourage MNC export
processing and production — this is the message of the recent ILO Report
on Kenya (ILO 1972: 178–192); and the Kenyan government's 1973
budget speech suggests the message has been received (Kenya
1973:7–8).

Is this argument justified? The following sections suggest not. They
draw on evidence from Kenya to show that the institutional nature of the
MNC, in the context of Kenya's political economy, builds weaknesses and
costs into both export-oriented and import-substitution industrialization,
under MNC auspices. I examine the behavior of ten MNC subsidiaries
that are active in export-oriented processing and/or production in Kenya.
These firms range from a small fish-freezing plant to a giant agricultural
conglomerate, and include four other agricultural producer/processors,
two mineral extraction/processing firms, one tannery, and one cement-

manufacturing exporter. Managerial control is exercised by British parents in two cases, U.S. parents in two cases, a Swiss parent in one case, a Danish parent in another, and British-Dutch, British-Swiss, Japanese-British, and Belgian-French interests in the others. Altogether the firms permanently employ more than 23,000 workers (more than 5 percent of all Kenya's private-sector employment) and represent capital employed of over K£25 million. The sample includes the largest foreign-controlled firm in Kenya in each of tea production and processing, coffee production, fruit and vegetable canning, passion-fruit processing, horticultural production, mining, tanning, and cement manufacturing. In short, the sample covers most of the country's principal export-oriented MNC's and should therefore provide a comprehensive indication of the performance of export-oriented industrial subsidiaries in Kenya.[1]

AN OVERVIEW

At first glance the sample seems to offer evidence supporting the ILO argument. In terms of capital intensity, for instance, the export-oriented MNC's show up much better as creators of employment than do their import-substituting MNC counterparts. Capital employed per employee averaged K£1,130 for the ten firms in the sample as compared with an average of K£4,060 for the fifteen largest import-substituting subsidiaries from which statistics were obtained in my general survey.[2] The export-oriented firms showed some willingness, too, to develop backward linkages in their operations, especially in the case of enterprises remote from the centers of import supply. One isolated large agricultural processor, for instance, has its own engineering section (employing 350 workers and making truck frames, boxes, buildings, etc., for its operations), its own dam and generating station, its own timber plots for fuel, its own printing facilities, etc. Another agricultural-producing firm has invested in ranching, primarily to provide inputs for its other estates. The cement company, too, has invested in resource-extraction ventures that will supply it with local inputs.

Nor do these firms waste resources in advertising, since most of their production is exported. Changeover costs in promoting product dif-

---

[1]   Note, however, that the sample includes no real examples of export-processing-zone manufacturing, as discussed in Helleiner (1972). No sign of this has appeared in Kenya as yet, although the ILO Report (1972) has recommended its consideration.
[2]   Defining capital employed as fixed assets plus current assets minus current liabilities. The fifteen import-substitution subsidiaries were: BAT Kenya; East African Packaging Industries; Metal Box Kenya; East African Industries; East African Portland Cement; Cadbury-Schweppes Kenya; Coca-Cola Bottling Co. of Nairobi; Brollo Kenya; Leyland-Albion East Africa; Kenya Toray Mills; East African Oxygen; United Textile Industries; Firestone; East African Oil Refineries; and Kisumu Cotton Mills.

ferentiation are rare. The benefits of export-oriented MNC's seem more widely shared, too. None of the sample companies had a significant portion of its productive activity centered in Nairobi (unlike the bulk of import-substituting manufacturing subsidiaries), and only two firms were centered in Mombasa, with the rest providing employment opportunities in poorer areas like southern Machakos, Kericho, the Kerio Valley, Kisii, the Magadi-Kajiado area, and Thika. For most of the firms, the argument that multinationals concentrate benefits among a small "labor aristocracy" (Arrighi 1970) would also be invalid. Basic wages in the agricultural processing firms vary from K.Shs 98/ to 117/ a month, compared with an average of close to K.Shs. 400/ a month in large import-substituting subsidiaries.[3] A large number of people are employed at lower wages, rather than a small number of people at higher wages.

Finally, all the firms, of course, are significant foreign exchange earners through their production and processing for export.

The case may seem unambiguous. However, these favorable effects should be seen as consequences of export-oriented industrialization per se, rather than of the *MNC auspices* under which the growth is taking place (turning around the ILO argument). As the evidence is examined in more detail, some serious costs of relying on those MNC auspices emerge. The following sections distinguish and discuss some of them.

MNC EXPORTING, CAPITAL INTENSITY, AND IMPORT INTENSITY

As among import-substituting subsidiaries, a considerable trend toward higher capital intensity (and reduced employment effects) is evident in most of these export-oriented subsidiaries (particularly in their industrial-processing operations). At the same time considerable import intensity is growing in some enterprises (with inhibitions on backward-linkage effects). These weaknesses seem to be consequences of the MNC institutional structure within which the subsidiaries are operating.

Take, for example, one agricultural-processing enterprise in the sample. Its Kenyan subsidiary was established solely to supply Europe with the MNC's international trademark product. This directly imposed international production techniques on the subsidiary, as the local managing director explained:

We must use the same growing and canning techniques as in our operations in developed countries. In exporting under our brand-name, our product must be

---

[3] The import-substituting subsidiaries covered: BAT Kenya; East African Industries; Cadbury-Schweppes Kenya; Brollo Kenya; Bata East Africa; Firestone; and East African Oil Refineries. The statutory minimum wage, for comparison, was K.Shs. 175/- a month in Nairobi and 70/- a month, for unskilled males, in rural areas (ILO 1972:256–257).

identical. When the can is opened in Europe, the customer must not be able to tell where it comes from — our subsidiary here or our subsidiaries elsewhere (personal communication).

As in many import-substitution subsidiaries, the parent company keeps a close check on quality control to enforce this identity of product and production technique. A plantation system is therefore used, rather than a more labor-intensive peasant production of food. The machinery used in processing, too, is therefore standard, highly mechanized canning equipment and must thus be imported (some of it from associate companies, which in itself provides another pressure toward capital intensity, based on MNC preferences for intrafirm sales).

This pattern places other constraints on the subsidiary, too. Sugar inputs for cans, for instance, must also be identical; this means that the unrefined sugar manufactured in Kenya is unacceptable as an input, and so refined sugar must be imported. The package nature of the production system transferred from abroad means that there are no possibilities for local subcontracting (which could develop local indigenous entrepreneurship [ILO 1972:195]): "Because we are here as an integrated operation," the managing director noted, "there is no gap in our process to be filled." In short this MNC has, on a world basis, developed a differentiated product demand and a system of meeting it. The subsidiary has transferred that particular demand to Kenya and reproduced precisely the system that meets it, thereby establishing developed-country production techniques locally and inhibiting potential linkage to the indigenous economy. This is the exact parallel of taste transfer in the import-substitution MNC sector and has similar consequences.

Cement production offers a somewhat different but related example. Much of the Kenyan subsidiary's exports go to U.S. multinational oil installations in the Persian Gulf (in fact the subsidiary has just taken over the production of a special oil-well cement formerly supplied directly from its parent). Such production must meet rigorous, externally imposed standards, laid down, for instance, by the American Petroleum Institute. This generates considerably increasing capital intensity. Until recently the company used six shaft kilns to turn its basic material mixture into cement clinker; some ten to twelve men were required for each shift to produce 1,100 tons daily. But the firm has now introduced a huge, very expensive rotary kiln, employing only three men per shift to produce 1,000 tons daily. Company officials advanced two main reasons for the change. First, they suggested, the quality from the advanced kiln was superior; they wouldn't be able to meet U.S. cement standards in the Gulf nor to produce the "lucrative" oil-well cement without it. They conceded, however, that the shaft kilns could produce as high a quality cement, if even more labor were used on them. But this possibility fell foul of a second MNC institutional reality: the insistence of one parent company that labor consistently be reduced to a minimum, an attitude based explicitly on European experience. The result of such pressures showed up in a capital-employed-to-labor ratio of K£6,200.

Another agricultural-processing company showed the impact of similar parent-imposed labor-reduction priorities. In this case the company concerned had seen its employment policies in other less-developed countries subjected to strict regulation as local unemployment grew; it had been forced to retain many more workers in those countries than it wished to. The Kenyan subsidiary anticipated similar restrictions in the future, and with the assistance of head-office technical experts it was reducing its labor force to a minimum while it still was free to do so. In one of its processing factories, for instance, where output had increased considerably, the number of production workers had been cut from 100 to 48 over the last five years.

These sorts of pressures may help increase the import-intensity of agribusiness, too, as subsidiaries substitute herbicides and fertilizers for labor. In one large subsidiary, for instance, there has been a drop in labor input from 2.9 to 1.5 workers per hectare between 1958 and 1973, all of it permitted by great escalation in chemical inputs. Production on estates therefore becomes more and more import intensive than the peasant production equivalent.

More direct parent-company decisions may generate heavy import intensity, too. In one recently established project the main foreign shareholders (including a large trading concern) brought in the whole plant, right down to simple tables, from their home country. In such cases parent trade objectives clearly prevent the development of easy and obvious local linkages.

There are, then, costs in the behavior of export-processing subsidiaries. The institutional nature of the MNC places pressures on the subsidiaries for reducing their labor force and relying on imports, particularly when the market they serve has already been defined and differentiated by the operations of their parent organization in the developed economies.

INHIBITIONS ON FORWARD LINKAGES

Since Singer (1950) it has been recognized that foreign-owned extraction and agricultural firms in poorer countries have a tendency to concentrate their further-processing and other forward linkages in the developed countries. The evidence from Kenya suggests that this is still a significant weakness in the behavior of export-oriented subsidiaries, even though a number of companies in my sample now *are* making forward-linkage investments. (Brooke Bond is building an instant tea factory, the cement firm is a shareholder in an asbestos-cement operation, and the tannery has begun to manufacture shoes from its own leather).

Other firms were less energetic. Again, their weaknesses seem implicit in the MNC institutional structure. One agricultural-processing firm, for instance, has started growing cinchona trees (the source of quinine). However, no processing plant for the cinchona bark has been planned for Kenya. When asked why, the subsidiary chairman explained:

... because by the terms of our original agreement, we agreed to supply two firms — one in Germany, one in the UK — and it was part of the agreement to plant in Kenya that they would take the crop and they in fact required that crop to keep their own factories viable. They were looking throughout the world; they needed to insure their future supplies; and we tied in with the pattern (personal communication).

Thus, worldwide MNC perspective has inhibited possible forward linkages, at least up to now. New economic arrangements between East Africa and the European Economic Community (EEC), as well as changing cost considerations, underlie possible changes in MNC world perspectives, though; in this case the European processors have begun to examine the possibility of processing the cinchona bark in Kenya. But the critical fact remains that they will break their restrictive agreement only if it is in their *own external interests*. They might as easily choose not to do so and leave Kenya exporting no more than the basic raw material.[4]

Another interesting case is provided by the fish-freezing plant. Such a facility might have been part of a well-planned effort to develop an indigenous fishing/canning industry in Kenya. Arrangements could have been made to draw on the centuries-old skills of Kenyan coastal fishermen (redirected, perhaps, more toward deep-sea fishing in locally manufactured ships) and to can the fish locally for export. The Japanese companies that initiated the project, however, were primarily concerned with supplementing their existing pattern of fish receiving and freezing facilities throughout the Pacific and with preventing other fishery firms from setting up competitive operations in Mombasa. So the fish-freezing plant has no forward or backward linkage effects at all. No development of local fishing has taken place (the plant depends on foreign trawlers calling at Mombasa), and the construction of a canning factory has little priority. Nor does Kenya even earn significant foreign exchange from the operation — the payments and receipts for all transactions go through Tokyo, with Kenya receiving only a small fee for the freezing services. This is a classic enclave investment — an example of the weaknesses

[4] This case has interesting implications, in that the restrictions could conceivably have been as well applied to locally owned cinchona producers, by the powerful external MNC processors, as to the Kenyan agricultural subsidiary. The world MNC pattern can thus generate weaknesses in less-developed country industrialization through other than direct investment.

generated when a sensible project is shaped in the interests of world-straddling MNC parents rather than in the interests of the indigenous economy.[5]

Perhaps the most prominent example of reluctance to provide for forward linkage in Kenya is represented by ICI and its subsidiary, the Magadi Soda Company. The Kenya government has found the company very uncooperative in developing linkages from its soda-ash production.[6] As Reichhelt notes:

The domestic market for soda ash would be greatly increased if the production of caustic soda on the basis of soda ash would be started in East Africa. Caustic soda (NaOH) is a basic inorganical chemical with a wide application in a large number of industries which are already established in East Africa, like the textile, soap, petroleum and vegetable oil milling industries (1970:138).

A Kenyan government report has concluded that production (for the whole East African market) would be viable. But ICI seems not to accept East Africa as a likely future market, and seems unwilling to produce caustic soda there on a large-scale basis for export. The complex economics of caustic production in part underlie this reluctance;[7] but the fact also is that ICI already makes a great deal of caustic soda for the world market, and a Kenyan subsidiary, using cheap soda-ash inputs, might complicate that market. So parent considerations inhibit potential local linkages. This reality, the evidence suggests, is a continuing weakness in the behavior of export-oriented subsidiaries generally in Kenya.

MARKET ACCESS, POLITICAL POWER, AND MNC SURPLUS REPATRIATION

Even more serious weaknesses are generated by the complex interplay

[5] Among the critics of this truncated project is the international can-making subsidiary in Kenya. It has pushed government to force forward a canning operation, to which it would supply the cans.
[6] Interview with D. Steele, IDS, a former adviser in the Ministry of Commerce and Industry, Kenya.
[7] Two processes exist for producing caustic soda. The first, electrolysis of salt, depends on world detergent production, which generates a demand for chlorine, the main product of electrolysis. The older method, based on soda ash, becomes competitive only when world detergent demand falls reducing related caustic-soda production and raising world prices for it. However, recently a project was seriously considered in which Magadi would supply an Australian factory with soda ash to use for old-style caustic-soda production on a large scale. Surely if such a project was considered viable enough for serious investigation, a similar factory in Kenya, closer to the sources of raw material, could be even more viable. It would seem that other factors are behind ICI's not considering that option, perhaps ICI's reluctance to invest a large sum in a potentially "risky" less-developed country to produce exports it already supplies from elsewhere in the MNC organization.

among three factors: MNC control over the marketing institutions for subsidiary exports, MNC influence in the local political economy, and the set of concessions to subsidiaries that accordingly emerge. This interplay generates considerable surplus appropriation and repatriation, much of it possibly disguised.

What the export-oriented multinational particularly offers, aside from the usual technology, managerial skills, and capital, is well-developed access to advanced-economy markets for processed goods. It provides "expertise in world marketing, advantages of brand names and so forth," says the ILO Kenya Report in recommending export agriprocessing under MNC auspices (1972:186). The source of this strength, however, lies abroad, in the parent organization's marketing system. Multinationals in Kenya have been very careful to keep that source safely abroad. In six firms in my sample *all* export marketing is done by other parent agencies in Europe, Japan, or the United States. Kenyan subsidiary exports are usually "sold" directly to those agencies, which market them in turn as they see fit.[8] In two other subsidiaries the Kenyan firm relies very considerably (though not exclusively) on its associate companies abroad for marketing.

This pattern is one basis for considerable power by the MNC subsidiary in the Kenyan political economy. It means that local benefits of export-oriented industrialization remain dependent on access to MNC-controlled markets. The center of that control is abroad and therefore free from direct sanctions or threats from the Kenyan government (unlike the situation in import-substituting industrialization, where the government's control over market access is *its* critical source of bargaining strength). In export-oriented industrialization, market access provides subsidiaries with local power, a point made explicitly, for instance, by one subsidiary's managing director, when asked his firm's possible reaction to tougher Kenyan regulation of its activities: "We have a strong bargaining position in any fight, because we sit on the marketing system in Europe. So it would be senseless of them to demand and force changes" (personal communication).

To this institutional source of power is added the close informal contacts and influence that subsidiaries can develop with the dominant African political-bureaucratic bourgeoisie in Kenya, an ability based on the size of their operations in Kenya and on the resources and opportunities such large operations can provide this bourgeoisie. Seven firms in my sample reported they had such close, informal contacts and influence — which they use in their dealings with government. Another firm

---

[8] In one case the parent company is sole marketing agent for the subsidiary rather than sole buyer; in the other case, already cited above, the goods being processed are not actually bought or sold in Kenya at all.

frankly illustrated MNC thinking on the issue in discussing its *lack* of such informal links with government:

In what is after all a very parochial environment I feel that this is important. I would say that we haven't cultivated this side enough, and we're taking steps to do so. Informal contacts with people in government are extremely important — far more important than we realize. Because when you do run into trouble as we have over [certain expatriate staffing] points [recently], you feel that you want friends in court. And I think again we've neglected the cultivation of the right contacts — that's not to say we don't have a number of friends. But on the whole, it's my feeling it's better to be well known and have influence with people at Permanent Secretary level — the real people behind the scenes that do the work. . . . I feel just going door-to-door to Ministers is not the right way; it's better to make yourself felt and known in a more subtle manner (personal communication).

These sources of MNC political power — Kenya's dependence on MNC overseas marketing networks, the strategy of informal influence, and the resulting comfortable symbiosis between MNC's and the dominant local bourgeoisie — all combine to generate large concessions for subsidiaries entering Kenya and ongoing favors for subsidiaries already in the country. This may be measured by the government's having provided finance (either equity or loan) to seven of the firms in my sample; permitted generous exemptions from Kenya's restrictions on local borrowing rights for foreign companies for many of them; provided other exemptions from import restrictions or levies on inputs or equipment; given land on long, generous leases; and exempted some firms from any future legislation that might otherwise affect them.

Some particular cases from the survey graphically illustrate this point. One firm has a ninety-nine year lease, given in colonial days, to land on which valuable resources exist. Sections of the government have been pushing the firm, so far unsuccessfully, to develop forward linkages; other government spokesmen have called, also unsuccessfully, for a significant expansion of the company's extractive capacity and output (*East African Standard* 1973). But the government as a whole has not been prepared to move effectively against the firm by forcing renegotiation of its lease. One reason: the subsidiary's parent controls much of the world market for present production and for related potential linkages, and Kenya feels an attack on the lease would therefore seriously hurt its access to that market.[9] Another reason: the subsidiary has considerable informal influence with key political-bureaucratic figures. At one stage, for instance, an expatriate adviser in the Ministry of Commerce and Industry began investigating the subsidiary's reliance on parent overseas agents for

---

[9] Interview with D. Steele, IDS, former adviser, Ministry of Commerce and Industry, Kenya.

marketing, but the company's manager simply approached one of his informal contacts — the Permanent Secretary in that Ministry. As the subsidiary manager explained: "This straightened out the problem because he kept the man in check." So the subsidiary maintains its privileges unmolested.

Another case involves a firm that planned new export facilities in Mombasa. These required a K£1.5 million expenditure by the East African community on related dock installations; but Tanzania objected strongly, and the project seemed to have been rejected. The subsidiary, however, was able to use its informal political contacts, and emphasizing its foreign-exchange earnings thereby persuaded President Kenyatta to intervene personally and push the expenditure through.

Then there is the case of the Fluorspar Company of Kenya, Ltd. Because of its world expertise in producing and selling fluorspar and its close relations with the quasi-public Industrial and Commercial Development Corporation (majority shareholder in the Fluorspar Company of Kenya), the U.S.-owned Continental Ore Company has been able to shape an extremely favorable role for itself in this new enterprise. As the fluorspar project was first financed, Continental Ore was *guaranteed* a yearly return, via management fees alone, of K£20,000 on a total investment of less than K£80,000 (the gearing ratio for the project was very high, with Continental Ore providing none of the loan capital). On top of this, Continental Ore in New York was to be the exclusive marketing agent of the K£4 million of fluorspar exported each year, at a fee of 5 percent of the selling price (though some of the financing of the exports must be done with that fee).[10] This agreement was questioned by Kenyan Treasury representatives in the government's New Projects Committee when it was submitted for approval; but the objections were overridden by the politically powerful allies of Continental Ore in the ICDC.[11] Some refinancing of the project has since been necessary (because local banks considered the gearing ratio too high); and this will mean that Continental Ore's equity participation, at 24½ percent, will ultimately rise to K£200,000. But with a K£350,000 profit expected the first full year of integrated operation (1975–76), *plus* the management fees (the K£20,000 or 2½ percent of pre-tax profits, whichever is higher), *plus* the sales contract, Continental Ore has clearly won itself a very favorable position in Kenya.

Finally one might note the wide concession won by another firm in my sample, DCK, as described by Carlsen (1973:35, 44, 53): a twenty-five year agreement by which the company is exempted from future tax, tariff, or financial-incentive changes; has work-permit guarantees for at least

---

[10]   Interview with J. Lang, Managing Director, Continental Ore Kenya Ltd., Nairobi, July 26, 1973.
[11]   Interview with U.S. Embassy officials, Nairobi.

ten expatriates, or 2 percent of the total labor force; and enjoys a ban on any competition (local or foreign) in Kenya for eight years.

This multinational bargaining power and these concessions result in considerable surplus appropriation and repatriation by export-oriented subsidiaries in Kenya. This is evident from their financial accounts. Comparison is possible for seven subsidiaries and their parents in similar financial years (see Table 1).[12] Table 1 shows clearly that Kenyan subsidiaries appropriate much higher profits than their parent organizations

Table 1. Profits and dividends, 1971/72

(a) Category	(b) Capital employed (K£000)	(c) After-tax profit	(d) (c) as percent of (b)	(e) Available dividends	(f) Dividends (K£000)	(g) (f) as percent of (c)
Seven parent firms	2,168,473	128,109	5.9	112,054	73,238	65.3
Seven sub-sidiaries in Kenya	20,249	2,314	11.1	2,314	1,817	78.5

as a whole, and that they retain a smaller portion of those profits for reinvestment than is the norm for their parent organizations. Nor are declared profits, in the case of export-oriented multinationals, likely to be a full measure of surplus appropriation. Extra external payments, in the form of technical, management, and service fees, exist in seven of the firms in the sample; taken together in the last comparative financial year, they accounted for a figure of some K£240,000, or more than 13 percent of subsidiary dividend payments. This figure ignores marketing commissions paid to associate companies abroad.[13]

[12] Statistics on subsidiary operations are from interviews in Kenya and from the files of the Companies Registry in Nairobi; on parent firms, from annual reports and other information in the Corporate Library of the London Graduate School of Business, and in the IDS Library, Sussex, both in the United Kingdom. In the table, capital employed comprises fixed assets plus current assets less current liabilities (except in the case of two Japanese parent firms — of one subsidiary — where the only available figure was "net worth"; as this excludes long-term loans to the parent, my analysis may slightly overstate the profitability of parent firms as compared with their subsidiaries). The column "Available for Dividends" excludes minority interests in parent-company profits. The figure for dividends ignores the $12\frac{1}{2}$ percent withholding tax introduced by Kenya in 1971.
[13] Another complication in measuring comparative rates of profit arises from revaluation of fixed assets. For instance, Brooke Bond Liebig Kenya added K£4,166,000 to its group fixed assets by this means between July 1, 1969, and June 30, 1971. Its capital employed on June 30, 1971, was therefore K£8,217,076, of which group after-tax profits of K£1,102,527 represented some 13.5 percent, substantially but perhaps not excessively higher than parent profits of 6.1 percent of capital employed. Using the former valuation, however, the subsidiary profits would have represented 27.2 percent of capital employed, a much more

A more serious complication for analysis, however, is the unique possibility for transfer accounting in export-oriented subsidiaries. By underpricing exports to its parent, a subsidiary may appropriate and repatriate surplus by other than dividends or fees (see Lall 1973). The critical importance of parent control of the world marketing network emerges here again — especially in those four firms in my sample in which the subsidiary "sells" *all* its exports to the parent company — and also in companies that sell a significant proportion of exports to or through foreign associates. Inevitably price setting is arbitrary in such a relationship, and the prices established will reflect parent views of where it prefers to declare profits rather than imposed market conditions. The managing director of one agriprocessing subsidiary, for instance, described price-setting in his case as follows:

> The organization usually prepares a budget, sees what our costs are, then prepares a price to see we'll make some money out of it here. [The managers of the parent company] do say what is going to be the price, and in fact the local directors accept it, as being reasonable (personal communication).

Such arbitrary decisions shape the behavior of other firms, too.

Even where ruling commodity prices exist on a world-market basis, ambiguities endure. There may be, for example, a going rate for canned pineapple per se in the international marketplace. But who can say what the price should be for such cans under a special, differentiated trademark? That trademark, after all, is considered a premium point, one of the advantages of projects under MNC auspices, something that increases a less-developed country's access to advanced-economy markets (ILO 1972). But if a Kenyan subsidiary sells such brand goods to its parent at the ordinary nondifferentiated commodity price, then all of the "premium" profit is being taken abroad rather than shared with Kenya. One also has to take account of discounts offered for bulk purchases, perhaps premiums paid for long-term agreements, etc. Other companies may claim to be following a long-range strategy in their pricing, aiming, for instance, to keep their materials priced low enough to discourage customers from switching to synthetic substitutes; they may justify paying below-market prices to their Kenyan subsidiaries in terms of that strategy. So it becomes very difficult to determine what ruling prices *should* be for any given Kenyan export-processing subsidiary.

One consequence of this situation deserves special emphasis. Regardless of whether Kenyan exporting subsidiaries are *now* using transfer pricing to repatriate profits, it is clear they *could* use the technique

---

dramatic rate of return, especially since virtually all the profits were repatriated as dividends. See Brooke Bond Liebig Kenya Ltd. (1972a, 1972b) and Brooke Bond Liebig Co., Ltd. (1972).

anytime in the future. This is yet another factor in the bargaining strength multinational export processors carry into the local political economy; it gives them yet another escape route should the authorities attempt to regulate them more effectively.

There is some evidence suggesting that such transfer pricing is already taking place in Kenya. One firm in the sample conceded that it sometimes slightly underinvoices its exports to associate firms in Europe. Carlsen's information (1973:53) on DCK also shows substantial underpricing of subsidiary exports from Kenya. Two other firms in the sample have been seriously investigated by the Kenyan government for possible under-pricing. And questions have also been asked (by another government official interviewed) about the low prices at which a further company in the sample has exported its production. A more substantive indication of underpricing, perhaps, is the fact that all three of those agricultural export subsidiaries that supply only their parent marketing systems have been operating consistently at a loss since they began production. What is probably happening is that the parent firms are content to absorb small losses or make minimal profits on their Kenyan subsidiary operations because the low-cost secure inputs these operations provide can be sold in Europe at a handsome profit to the MNC marketing subsidiaries there. This amounts to the same thing as transfer-pricing, and it means that loss of significant potential surplus to the Kenyan economy.

One question occurs, however. Why should parent firms effectively take their profits in Europe (or North America) rather than in Kenya, given Kenya's relatively low corporation and withholding taxes (40 per-cent and 12½ percent respectively) and its freedom of remission for dividends? A number of reasons are suggested by this study. First, there are occasions when Kenyan exchange control may block payment of subsidiary dividends, as when, for instance, a subsidiary has been given special rights to borrow locally beyond the 20 percent of parent invest-ment to which it is entitled by Exchange Control Notice No. 19 (Kenya 1971). This is the case for the one sample firm that conceded it sometimes slightly underprices its intrafirm exports. Second, assuming that sub-sidiary fee payments actually make a contribution to parent overheads, the Kenyan tax system (with its 20 percent tax on fees) makes it pre-ferable for companies to abolish those fees and cover overhead costs by underpricing exports. Third, these subsidiaries in Kenya typically involve minority (often government) shareholders. Transfer pricing permits par-ents to accumulate most of the profits from a venture themselves rather than having to share these with their minority partners. Fourth, there is a risk factor that parent companies perceive. They probably feel much more certain of getting their dividends from profits that are being "made" in the advanced capitalist world. A "Uganda" could always occur in Kenya, they fear, and their subsidiary assets be frozen; or short-term foreign-exchange shortages could, as in Tanzania, suddenly restrict possible dividend repatriation. These uncertainties are avoided if profits are accumulated outside Kenya. Fifth, there are tax havens around the world, and it is easy enough for an MNC to use transfer pricing across the corporation to concentrate its profits in such havens, even if the Kenyan subsidiary, for instance, is not selling directly to an associate in such a haven. A final point should be made. Overpricing of intrafirm inputs by import-substituting subsidiaries may also camouflage surplus repatriation from Kenya. But as a rule such overpricing at least results in higher tariff receipts in East Africa. No such constraint operates on subsidiaries' underpricing of exports. Indeed, such under-invoicing may even reduce parent duty liabilities on entry to developed-economy markets.

Overall, then, it is clear that export-oriented industrialization under MNC auspices can be costly to an underdeveloped country. The MNC's institutional structure gives it international market-access power. That externally based strength, plus careful political tactics, give many subsidiaries great bargaining power in the Kenyan political economy. That, in turn, generates considerable concessions. And these concessions result in marked surplus appropriation and repatriation by export-oriented subsidiaries. The MNC institutional structure gives these subsidiaries both the means and the motivation to undertake that repatriation surreptitiously, via transfer pricing, and thus reduce Kenyan tax revenue and foreign-exchange earnings.

THE MNC vs. LOCAL ENTREPRENEURS

The costs of MNC reliance must be measured in more than the drain of potential surplus from Kenya. The MNC's bargaining strength and political power can also have a severely negative impact on the development of indigenous entrepreneurship in the country. This is particularly the case, it seems, where MNC and local entrepreneurs compete over potentially very important economic opportunities; i.e., such competition can arise especially in the context of large-scale export-oriented projects.

Carlsen's analysis (1973:44) of DCK shows how the concessions that firm won from government have blocked local entrepreneurs from following up important opportunities. There are other firms in my sample that have had the same negative impact on indigenously based development.[14] But this section will concentrate on a single recent case of MNC-local competition in Kenya. The case illustrates the determination of

[14] Historically, for instance, foreign-owned estates blocked African rights to cultivate coffee until the 1950's (Rosberg and Nottingham 1966:84, 159, 207). In the present, too, MNC agricultural subsidiaries often see smallholder expansion as a threat to world market prices, and may therefore discourage it. The capital-intensive, plantation approach to other

MNC's when faced with large-scale resource opportunities, the political strength they seem able to mount in seeking their objectives, the importance and intimacy of the MNC symbiosis with Kenya's political-bureaucratic bourgeoisie, and the blow this pattern can strike at indigenous entrepreneurs.

The case concerns the large deposits of fluorspar now being exploited in the Kerio Valley by the Fluorspar Company of Kenya, Ltd.[15] These deposits were first found in the late sixties by an indigenous Swahili entrepreneur, M.M. El-Amin. He took ore samples to the government Department of Mines and Geology in the Ministry of Natural Resources in Nairobi; but they told him he was wasting his time, that the ore was not fluorspar, as he had claimed. El-Amin, however, persisted, sending the material off to analysts in Europe, who proved that very rich deposits were involved. (It is now estimated that eight to ten million tons of fluorspar exist in the deposit, at an average export value of some £20 per ton.)

It is common for small-scale prospectors to sell such claims once they are proved. But El-Amin was an entrepreneur as well as a prospector, and his purpose was to help the resource. One senior Mines and Geology official later said, that "El-Amin did more for mining as a small man than anyone has ever done here — because he pushed so hard." El-Amin hired his own graduate Kenyan geologists and mining engineer, invested in trucks and road building to get the ore out sixty torturous miles, and began to regularly supply the fluorspar needs of the cement manufacturer in Mombasa. By July 1970, El-Amin's project was producing 470 tons of fluorspar a month, using very labor-intensive hand-picking and hand-crushing mining methods only. The man was also actively investigating ways of developing the deposit on a larger scale for export, even negotiating with a Hungarian state corporation over the equipment and expertise he might need.

This evidence suggests that El-Amin was trying to develop the resource as quickly and fully as possible. He clearly recognized the need for some foreign technology and technical assistance, but at the same time he wanted the development to remain under indigenous Kenyan control. (By late in 1970 he had accordingly placed orders for K£150,000 worth of drills, compressors, and other mining equipment with Holman Bros. (EA), Ltd., who had accepted a K£100,000 debenture from El-Amin's company in part payment.)

---

crop production, too, may block off the option of indigenously organized smallholder production, especially since government resources and attention are consequently directed toward the former rather than the latter.
[15] This analysis is based on interviews with my sample of export-oriented multinational subsidiaries, with officials in the Kenyan Department of Mines and Geology, with officials in the U.S. Embassy, and with certain local entrepreneurs.

Cooperation with a multinational firm was another possibility El-Amin had investigated from the beginning, on the advice of Mines and Geology officials. He wrote, for instance, to the German firm of Fried Krupp; but they insisted on control in a joint venture before they would proceed. El-Amin refused, emphasizing his commitment to Kenyan entrepreneurial control of the project — and its benefits.

As news spread of the large fluorspar deposit, however, the concerted attention of a considerable number of resource-oriented multinationals began to converge on Kenya, showing the determination with which international capital can respond when important resources become available in a less-developed country. El-Amin was approached by, among others: Falconbridge of Canada, who controlled the Kilembe mines in Uganda; Lonrho, of the United Kingdom; the Continental Ore Co. of the United States; Associated Portland Cement Manufacturers (APCM) of the United Kingdom, through their Kenyan subsidiary; and the American Steel Corp. The strategy of each MNC was to win majority control of the project, but El-Amin continued to refuse this as undesirable for Kenya. Continental Ore, for instance, offered El-Amin a 50/50 partnership, which he accepted, but only if he retained managerial authority. Continental Ore refused to accept this.

El-Amin also had other options. Various multinational commercial companies were interested in purchasing the ore for export, perhaps also supplying technical personnel and machinery for production but leaving actual management and equity control with El-Amin. In a series of complicated negotiations El-Amin explored this option with Ataka & Co., the large Osaka trading firm, throughout 1970. Chori Co., Ltd., another large Osaka commercial company, also approached Amin, as did Iwatani & Co., Ltd., yet another sizable Osaka-based firm.

This commercial option would also have involved some dependence on international firms, who were prepared to use their bargaining power to force El-Amin into concessions. Ataka & Co., for instance, in preliminary negotiations insisted on exclusive rights to export and sell the fluorspar produced and on El-Amin's covering all costs of the Japanese company's project investigation, in return for Ataka arranging to supply all necessary equipment for the enterprise. El-Amin felt that even such concessions would leave him more benefits and safeguards than would minority participation in an MNC-controlled joint venture.

The pressure of the big multinational grew as it became apparent that El-Amin might be able to arrange an alternate option for development. This pressure, however, was increasingly directed through the Kenyan government. The APCM subsidiary had a close, informal relationship with the government. Lonrho, too, had influential channels to senior government personnel, and Continental Ore's Kenyan subsidiary had already developed friendly, informal relations with the influential directors of the ICDC. These multinationals, too, could stress their market access — and their experience and expertise. They argued that they would be able to develop the fluorspar for export much faster than El-Amin could. There were, moreover, reasons for the dominant political-bureaucratic bourgeoisie to favor reliance on the multinationals; that bourgeoisie might obtain benefits through new arrangements for exploiting the resource, benefits it was unlikely to obtain while the project was directed by El-Amin, a relative outsider, an independent entrepreneur, and a Swahili (whose allies were out of favor with the country's dominant Kikuyu, coastal politicians and businessmen).[16]

By the middle of 1970 this pressure was having an effect. In June, for instance, the Commissioner of Mines wrote officially to one of the resource-oriented multinationals (with copies to other Ministries and to El-Amin) describing El-Amin's negotiations with Ataka, saying these didn't have his approval, and endorsing the idea of that multinational and El-Amin jointly developing the project. But still El-Amin resisted.

Finally, the government moved decisively. Without even consulting most of the senior officials in the Department of Mines and Geology to get their assessment of El-Amin's development activity, the government stripped him of his claim and established the new Fluorspar Company of Kenya, 51 percent ICDC-owned, with a 24½ percent share for the APCM subsidiary, and a similar share, plus management and marketing contracts, for Continental Ore. (Lonrho found itself out-maneuvered in the end, as Continental Ore was prepared to see an ICDC majority share in equity and had skillfully brought the APCM subsidiary into an alliance with it.) The justification for the takeover, according to the Minister of Natural Resources, rested on the fact that El-Amin's company was not in a healthy state and "the fact that efficiency is now necessary in the further development of the fluorine deposit."[17]

The implication is that El-Amin could not have organized full extraction and export of the mineral, while the MNC-run venture could. Was the stated government view justified? Almost certainly not. A senior expatriate official in the Department of Mines and Geology, who was a close spectator of the whole affair, probably provides the most disinterested judgment: "It was coming to a point where we had to push

[16] One rather obvious example of the benefits the new African political-bureaucratic bourgeoisie could receive: under a new arrangement ICDC could have a large shareholding in the resource development and receive generous dividends, thanks to the managerial/marketing expertise of its MNC partner(s). Such dividends could finance ICDC loans, many of which go to prominent members of the political-bureaucratic bourgeoisie (as is evident from my research in the Companies Registry, Nairobi). The dividends could also be shared with the ICDC Investment Company, an ICDC-associated company through which prominent private African shareholders have shares in the operations of many nonpublic MNC subsidiaries.

[17] One M.P. claimed that the Minister "had been instructed by some people at the top in this country . . ." (Republic of Kenya, n.d.)

El-Amin somewhat. But there were not grounds for slinging him out."
El-Amin still had commercial company options to explore (though Ataka
had withdrawn at this stage); he had arranged the debenture with Holman's; and, perhaps most significant, he was in contact with a large MNC
consortium that was prepared to work with him without insisting on
managerial control.

By mid-October, AKZO, the large Dutch chemical firm, had told
El-Amin that an MNC group was prepared to give him financial and
technical help to build a large-scale mine, a 100,000-ton flotation processing plant on the site, and, as a forward linkage at a later stage, a
chemical-manufacturing plant to make kryolith, or aluminum fluoride,
from the fluorspar. The financing would be by loan, or an advance on
production, and/or by equity participation, whichever El-Amin preferred. The consortium would guarantee to sell the total production in
Europe (or elsewhere if Amin wished), to provide all necessary expatriates, and to train Kenyans to replace them. Besides AKZO, the companies involved included a subsidiary of Alcan (which is the only significant fluorspar producer in Canada), and the German state-owned
Vereinigte Aluminium Werke (which operates fluorspar flotation mills in
Germany) (Hodge 1973). So there is no doubt the consortium could have
provided the technical skills and experience needed. Significantly, El-
Amin's tough bargaining position in his negotiations for foreign technology and market access had resulted in a proposal that would have left
managerial authority (and more benefits) with Kenyans and was planned
in terms of extensive forward linkages.

The project was not to be pursued, however. El-Amin's company
pleaded with the government to participate with it in such an alternate
venture, but to no avail.

A dismal denouement; El-Amin's compensation was determined by
arbitrary action, without any visit to the site of his undertaking, without
any reference to most of the chief officials in the Mines and Geology
Department. One of those officials (the disinterested expatriate noted
above) estimates the value of El-Amin's investment at some K£250,000;
but he was given only K£50,000, out of which his firm's current liabilities
had to be settled. El-Amin's effective compensation, for finding and
developing, in the face of government discouragement, a mineral deposit
valued at some K£200 million, was about K£30,000.

And a dismal footnote: the Commissioner of Mines who first told
El-Amin his ore was worthless, who tried to pressure him into a joint
venture later, and who arbitrarily calculated the compensation El-Amin
received, is now an official on the staff of the Continental Ore Co. of
Kenya, Ltd.

What are the consequences of such patterns of MNC pressure and
political economic symbiosis? I have already noted the very favorable

concessions Continental Ore got for itself in the new firm. The APCM subsidiary, as another shareholder, also won special benefits, in the form of a percentage fee on all fluorspar exports, since its Mombasa port installations are used for such shipments. Overseas marketing rests with Continental Ore, which has considerable control over export prices. So all the ingredients are present of the market control/dependence/surplus loss bundle. Kenya may export more fluorspar now than it might have with El-Amin in charge; but it is unlikely to receive as great a proportion of the financial return from those exports.

Even more obvious is the heavy negative impact on local entrepreneurship. Independent risk-taking innovation has been shown not to pay, even when the *business* risks work out. El-Amin will certainly initiate no more mining enterprises. And there is evidence of other local entrepreneurs drawing the same lesson from El-Amin's case.

MNC EXPORT-PROCESSING AND KENYAN UNDERDEVELOPMENT

The evidence from firms in my sample clearly suggests that the performance of export-oriented multinationals can further Kenyan underdevelopment, just as MNC import substitution does. The institutional nature of the MNC can impose increasing capital- and import-intensity in Kenyan subsidiaries, restrict forward-linkage effects, deepen Kenyan dependence, and thereby generate considerable (though potentially disguised) surplus repatriation from the country. Further, the strength the MNC's position gives it within the local political economy can block the development of independent indigenous entrepreneurs in Kenya.

This evidence raises an interesting issue. I have suggested earlier that export-oriented industrialization per se offers many benefits to Kenya, in terms of the growth of more labor-intensive, decentralized production, with clear potential linkages and marked foreign-exchange earnings. But reliance on MNC firms can distort and seriously misshape this impact. Such reliance, however, in the present international economy, often seems a *condition* of market access. So in that sense the MNC-imposed distortions may be more implicit in the *strategy* itself than is the case in any import-substituting strategy of industrial growth. That may be a reason for less-developed countries questioning the current conventional wisdom that favors an export-oriented strategy, at least where that strategy is oriented toward advanced-economy markets.[18] The firms

[18]   And given that MNC's dominate import-substitution in many less-developed-country markets, and that they emphasize the transfer of advanced-country tastes to those markets (Langdon 1973b), even many less-developed-country markets are effectively "advanced economy markets," so far as exporting to them is concerned.

whose auspices must be used to gain market access, the products those firms produce, the means by which they produce them, their preferences about where to take profits, their competition with local entrepreneurs — all these factors carry the ingredients of restricted, inhibited, weak, and underdeveloped industrialization into Kenya's economy.

An ultimate answer may be an internally oriented industrialization on an integrated continental African (or Afro-Asian) basis. But here another difficulty with MNC reliance emerges. MNC export processing is typically advanced-economy oriented, and it locks its host country into that orientation because of the sizable costs of transition involved in any change. So MNC reliance inhibits movement to that wider strategy.

An even more important block to any such reordering of priorities and plans is evident in terms of our political-economy approach. The comfortable MNC symbiosis with the dominant local political-bureaucratic bourgeoisie gives the latter a noticeable stake in MNC operations, and insofar as transition would threaten the MNC, it would threaten the bourgeoisie's position too. That's an inhibition to change. Moreover, the resources the MNC's provide that bourgeoisie give it more power within the political economy, and make its resistance to change more potent. So the basis of present underdevelopment and dependence is perpetuated. Kenya remains tied to its satellite-metropolis relationship with the advanced capitalist economies. And the mass poverty associated with that orientation endures (Langdon 1974).

SOME INTERIM CONCLUSIONS

This paper has stressed the costs of export-oriented industrialization through MNC's. What tentative conclusions might be drawn from the analysis?

First, a less-developed country seems likely to maximize its chances of *dynamic* industrialization (i.e., growth with wide distribution and linkage effects, maximum surplus retention, and optimal impetus for local entrepreneurship) by minimizing its reliance on MNC's, in export-oriented as in import-substitution projects. Second, insofar as participation of multinationals is necessary in particular export projects, a first priority of less-developed-country strategy must be to develop indigenous control of the marketing system used by the project throughout the world. That marketing structure is usually the critical source of MNC bargaining strength, and so long as the MNC has exclusive information and expertise on its workings, the less-developed country is vulnerable and dependent — as the concessions in Kenya show. Such indigenous participation in world marketing is also essential to prevent intrafirm transfer pricing. Third, there clearly are weaknesses in the export-oriented strategy of industrialization because of the dominance of MNC's in world trade. This suggests that African countries should avoid shaping their economies around such a strategy, especially as that strategy helps preclude the more positive option of internally oriented, continental industrialization.

This doesn't mean that *no* export-oriented industrialization should be done, nor that rigid exclusion of multinationals should become the norm. But it does mean less-developed countries should not *rely* on either the MNC sector generally or MNC export-processing particularly as a central element in industrialization and development strategy. Much more selectivity of projects should be practiced in the context of much firmer regulation of and bargaining with multinationals. The basis of selectivity should include a wide analysis of alternate uses of the land, labor, and capital resources to be involved in any export project; and it should recognize the differing ways in which possible relations with MNC's on the world market may be organized, through equity participation, management contracts, or long-term sales contracts, among others.

A fourth conclusion is relevant for aid agencies in more-developed countries: a priority for assistance to the poorer nations would seem to be market access (perhaps state trading corporations) that would reduce the less-developed countries' need to rely on the MNC to sell their exports.

Finally, this whole issue demands much more research. We need more systematic investigation of the relationship of small-scale entrepreneurs to multinational export-processing; e.g., how have small-scale tanneries been affected by the large subsidiary in my sample? How have small-scale tea operations been influenced by Brooke Bond? We also need careful investigation of transfer-pricing in export processing firms; this will require detailed research at the European end of MNC operations as well as in Kenya. And we need considerable information on relative strengths and weaknesses of alternatives to MNC reliance in this area. This paper has aimed at giving impetus to such detailed work through evidence that questions the advantages of export-oriented industrialization through the MNC.

REFERENCES

AHARONI, Y.
  1966   *The foreign investment decision process*. Boston.
ARRIGHI, G.
  1970   "International corporations, labour aristocracies and economic development in tropical Africa," in *Imperialism and underdevelopment*. Edited by R.I. Rhodes. New York.
BEHRMAN, J.N.
  1969   *Some patterns in the rise of multinational enterprise*. Chapel Hill, N.C.: University of North Carolina Press.

BROOKE BOND LIEBIG, LTD.
1972   *Annual report for year ending June 30, 1972*. London.

BROOKE BOND LIEBIG KENYA, LTD.
1972a *Prospectus for public share issue* March 22. Nairobi.
1972b *Annual report for year ending June 30, 1972*. Nairobi.

CARLSEN, J.
1973   *Danish private investment in Kenya*. Institute for Development
         Research. Paper D 73.1. Copenhagen.

COOPER, C.
1970   *The transfer of industrial technology to the underdeveloped countries*.
         Bulletin 3:1. Institute of Development Studies.

DUNNING, J., editor
1971   *The multinational enterprise*. London.

GALBRAITH, J.K.
1969   *The new industrial state*. London: Hamish Hamilton.

East African Standard
1973   "Company urged to raise production." *East African Standard*. Feb-
         ruary 23.

HELLEINER, G.K.
1972   "Manufactured exports from less developed countries and multi-
         national firms." Mimeographed.

HIRSCHMAN, A.O.
1958   *The strategy of economic development*. New Haven. Yale University
         Press.
1969   How to divest in Latin America, and why. *Essays on international*
         finance 76. Princeton University.

HODGES, B.L.
1973   World fluorspar developments. *Industrial Minerals*. May and June.

HYMER, S.H., R. ROWTHORN
1970   "Multinational corporations and international oligopoly: the non-
         American challenge," in *The international corporation*. Edited by C.P.
         Kindleberger. Massachusetts Institute of Technology.

INTERNATIONAL LABOR OFFICE
1972   *Employment, incomes and equality: a strategy for increasing productive*
         employment in Kenya. Geneva.

KAMARCK, A.M.
1967   *The economies of African development*. London.

KENYA, REPUBLIC OF
1971   *Exchange control administrative notices and instructions*. Nairobi.
1973   *Budget speech for the fiscal year 1973/74*. Nairobi.
n.d.   *The National Assembly: official report*. Volume twenty-one, part two.

KINDLEBERGER, C.P.
1969   *American business abroad*. New Haven: Yale University Press.

LALL, S.
1973   Transfer-pricing by multinational manufacturing firms. *Oxford Bulletin*
         of Economics and Statistics 35(3):173–195.

LANGDON, S.W.
1973a *Multinational corporations and "appropriate technology": a case study*
         from Kenya. Appropriate Technology Conference. Paper PE/S 12.
         Edinburgh University.
1973b "Multinational corporations and 'taste transfer' to Kenya." Mimeo-
         graphed.

1974   The political economy of dependence: notes toward an analysis of multinational corporations in Kenya. *Journal of East African Research and Development*.

PAQUET, G.
1972   *The multinational firm and the nation state*. Don Mills, Ont., Canada.

PERROUX, F., R. DEMONT
1961   Large firm — small nation. *Présence Africaine* 10(38).

REICHHELT, H.
1970   "The chemical and allied industries in Kenya," in *Studies in production and trade in East Africa*. Edited by P. Zajadasz. Munich.

ROSBERG, C.G., JR., J. NOTTINGHAM
1966   *The myth of "Mau Mau"*. Nairobi.

RWEYEMAMU, J.F.
1971   The political economy of foreign private investment in the underdeveloped countries. *The African Review* 1:1.

SEERS, D.
1963   Big companies and small countries: a practical proposal. *Kyklos*. 16(4).

SINGER, H.
1950   The distribution of gains between investing and borrowing countries. *American Economic Review*, 2(2).

STREETEN, P.
1972   "New approaches to private investment in less developed countries", in *International investment*. Edited by J. Dunning. Harmondsworth.

TANZER, M.
1970   *The political economy of international oil and the underdeveloped countries*. Boston: Beacon Press.

VAITSOS, C.V.
1970   *Transfer of resources and preservation of monopoly rents*. Development Advisory Service. Paper 168. Cambridge, Mass.: Harvard University.

VAN ARKADIE, B.
1969   "Private foreign investment: some limitations," in *Private enterprise and the East African Company*. Edited by P.A. Thomas. Dar es Salaam.

VERNON, R.
1971   *Sovereignty at bay*. New York and London.

WEEKS, J.
1972   Employment, growth and foreign domination in underdeveloped countries. *The Review of Radical Political Economies*. 4(1).

Plantations, Peasants, and Proletariat in the West Indies: An Essay on Agrarian Capitalism and Alienation

GEORGE L. BECKFORD

The economic plight of the majority in the West Indies is a direct result of the dominance of agrarian capitalism, in the form of the modern plantation.[1] Persistent material poverty is obvious among the rural proletariat and the peasantry. Malnutrition, poor housing, illiteracy, and disease are in evidence everywhere.

The thesis of this paper is that the chief cause of poverty in the West Indies is the monopoly of land and capital by plantations. This monopoly has intensified over time, thereby leaving rural population groups with increasingly fewer resources with which to secure their own economic and social advancement. The effects of this process of alienation have been most severe in those island economies where land is in short supply. Where fertile, arable land is in abundance, the effects are less stark; but they are evident nonetheless.

The analysis in support of the theses outlined is sequenced as follows: the genesis of agrarian capitalism is briefly described in the first section; the second section analyzes the ascendancy of monopoly capital during the twentieth century. Subsequently, patterns of alienation and of resistance are considered in the third and fourth sections. And finally, the fifth section describes the situation at present and speculates, briefly, on the possibilities for change.

---

[1] The term "West Indies" is used here to denote the English-speaking territories of the Caribbean, South America, and Central America. Sugar is the major plantation crop in Guyana, Trinidad-Tobago, Barbados, St. Kitts, Antigua, Jamaica, and Belize. Banana is the main crop in the Windward Islands where both plantations and peasants engage in its production. Emphasis will be placed on the sugar plantation in the present exercise, because the banana industry is of recent vintage — having replaced sugar in the Windward Islands during the last two decades.

THE GENESIS OF AGRARIAN CAPITALISM

Contemporary West Indian economy and society are a legacy of the slave plantation system which was introduced by European colonizers in the sixteenth century and which lasted until the mid-nineteenth century. That system of agricultural organizations was based on the production of staple commodities (chiefly sugar) for export to Europe. European colonizers captured the land from the indigenous Indian peoples, and they then established a system of large-scale agriculture utilizing the slave labor of African peoples secured from the Atlantic slave trade.

In that system of production, the European capitalists owned the slaves (the labor power), the land, and the capital stock built by the slaves. The surplus realized from that production accrued entirely to the European owners of the means of production. The slaves received only what was required for subsistence. Alienation and mass poverty was at its extreme during that period of history.[2]

Caribbean economy during the era of the slave plantation was simply an overseas branch of European economy. The Caribbean was a locus of production of agricultural staples for transshipment to Europe. The Caribbean was in reality part of the agricultural sector of European economy. Production carried on in the region did *not* generate any income for its inhabitants. The slaves were essentially part of the capital stock, maintained by subsistence levels of consumption, depleted by runaways (the Maroons), and increased by new purchases and natural increase. The owners of the means of production were, for the most part, non-resident: and managerial staff were temporary residents.

In the circumstances the economy generated no *national* income from slave plantation production.[3] Only the marginal subsistence activity of the Maroons and of free yeoman farmers provided any real income. Dependent underdevelopment was at its zenith during that period of Caribbean history.

Emancipation came in 1838 and changed things a bit — but only a bit. After that date, black people were legally free; in a sense, free to starve, as no resources were provided for their independent survival. As the plantations had engrossed all the arable land in some places (notably the Leeward Islands), black people were forced to continue working on the plantation for subsistence wages. As the planters had monopsony power in the labor market, there was no need for them to pay wages higher than

---

[2]   For an excellent analysis of the slave plantation case, see Williams (1964). New World slavery is the earliest form of capitalism and it is the pillar on which European and American capitalism was built.

[3]   For a formal exposition of the structure and functioning of slave plantation economy, see Best (1968).

subsistence. The only alternative open to black people in those circumstances was emigration.

Elsewhere in the Caribbean where some land was available, the economic position of black people was slightly better. In places like Jamaica, the Windwards, Trinidad and Guyana, they were able to find some, though not the best, land on which to settle independent of the plantations. Through individual and cooperative effort, black people bought or captured what marginal lands they could find. And eventually a peasantry emerged. But because of numerous legislative obstacles introduced by the planter-controlled governments, land was hard to secure. So continued dependence on plantation wage work was the lot of most black people.[4]

Wherever land was still available after Emancipation, the plantations had great difficulty in securing the labor services of the ex-slaves. Poll taxes were introduced to induce people to work for wages; land alienation by ex-slaves was prohibited in some places; legal sanctions against squatting were rigidly enforced; and sharecropping was introduced in some places. In spite of these measures, the planters still experienced labor shortages in the larger territories. Consequently, indentured East Indian laborers were brought in to work on the plantations — particularly in the newer plantation colonies of Trinidad and Guyana; but also, to a lesser extent, Jamaica and the Windward Islands.

The peasantry that emerged under the circumstances is a product of, and is dependent (to a certain degree) on, the plantation system of capitalist organization. And, by and large, the fortunes of the peasantry have been linked with booms and depressions in the plantation sector. So too has been the lot of the rural proletariat — those who, by force of circumstance, continue to work on the plantations for wages.

Booms in the sugar industry resulted in large profits for the plantations. Wage workers receive bonus payments under these circumstances. But peasants suffer as the plantations engross more land for sugar production. Depressions in the sugar industry produced opposite effects: wage workers suffered from unemployment and lower wages for those still employed; while peasants benefited, as more land became available to them when some plantations were forced out of business. This general pattern has persisted right up to the present time.

Rural society in the West Indies today consists of two major social groups: the peasants (small farmers) and the rural proletariat (wage workers). The peasantry may be subdivided into "big," "middle," and "small." In such a breakdown we would find that the "small" peasant

---

[4] Peasant farmers in the West Indies to this very day still rely on plantation wage work to supplement the meager incomes generated from production on their small infertile holdings.

comprises the bulk of the peasantry (see Table 2 under "Patterns of alienation"). The historical pattern of alienation of these groups persists to the present time. The pattern has been accentuated by the ascendancy of monopoly capital since World War I.

THE ASCENDANCY OF MONOPOLY CAPITAL

During the slave plantation era and up to the first decade of the twentieth century, the dominant ownership pattern of West Indian plantations was individual (or family) proprietorship. Today, corporations dominate the picture. And among these, the multinational corporation (MNC) reigns supreme.[5] This transition is of profound significance in understanding the deepening process of alienation which has pushed the majority of West Indian peoples further onto the margins of existence, indeed of survival.[6]

Two distinct trends are associated with the transition noted above. One is internal, the other external. The distinction is really heuristic, as there are obvious interrelationships between internal and external factors, more so in economies which are, in essence, extensions of metropolitan (i.e., British) economy.[7]

Internally, the emancipation of slaves served to push up costs of production, as labor then became relatively scarce. That was one signal for the rationalization of production to keep costs down. The situation created by Emancipation was aggravated by three subsequent external events. First, the British equalization of tariffs in the 1840's exposed West Indian sugar planters to competition from non-British sources of sugar. The slave sugar economies of Brazil and Cuba thus had equal access to the British Market.[8] Second, the opening of the Suez Canal in 1869 improved the competitive position of tropical Asia as a source of sugar. Third, beet-sugar production in Europe was on the ascendancy. And this further expanded the world supply of sugar. Consequently, the pressure was intensified for rationalization to keep down production costs in the West Indies.

Other external events helped to provide an answer. The introduction of

[5]   Some writers prefer the term "transnational corporation." Both terms refer to the same thing — a corporate enterprise with subsidiaries in many countries (nations), usually with the parent company registered in some metropolitan country (nation). The operations of these enterprises call into question the relevance of the nation-state as a useful analytical construct for economic analyses in the contemporary world economic order.
[6]   The distinction between "existence" and "survival" is critical to our analysis. It is being suggested that, whereas the existence margin is "tolerable," the survival margin is not. And it is on the latter margin that social breakdown is inevitable. (See the sections that follow.)
[7]   Nineteenth-century British economist J.S. Mill correctly described the West Indies as a place "where England finds it convenient to carry on the production of sugar, coffee, and a few other tropical commodities."
[8]   Slavery was not abolished in Brazil and Cuba until the 1880's.

steam as a source of power transformed the technology of processing sugar and of transporting sugar cane to the factories. And the invention of the centrifuge and the vacuum pan elsewhere showed the way for modernizing processing, in a way that would produce higher yields of sugar from the cane and thereby reduce processing costs. But these new technological developments involved finance capital of a kind that could hardly be mobilized by plantation proprietors operating on the margin.

To make matters worse, the international sugar market in the latter half of the nineteenth century was characterized by falling prices (as a result of developments, noted earlier, which contributed to supply outpacing the growth of demand). With falling prices, rising costs of production arising from labor shortages, and large-scale capitalization as the only solution, many individual (and family) proprietors were unable to remain in business. Their estates went into receivership to creditors in Britain. And these estates were either sold in the West Indies — intact to other estates or subdivided for sale to the peasantry (ex-slaves).

Other external currents explain the ascendancy of monopoly capital. The efficacy of the joint-stock company (corporate enterprise) had become established in metropolitan capitalist centers by the turn of the century. Additionally, capitalism in Europe had reached a mature stage; and overseas investment opportunities were being sought. This situation was aggravated by World War I and events leading up to it. Shortages of tropical raw materials, and the associated competition among metropolitan firms engaged in the elaboration of these products, led to a drive by these firms to secure their own sources of raw materials. All these occurrences laid the foundation for the emergence of the MNC and the associated ascendancy of monopoly capital.[9]

Trends in the ever-increasing concentration of capital in the West Indian sugar industry can be discerned from the dramatic decline in the number of estates (and factories). Table 1 provides some evidence for

Table 1. Sugar estates (factories) in Jamaica, 1836–1970 (data to 1930 are from Eisner [1961] and data for 1970 are from 1967 from the Mordecai Sugar Commission Report [1967:87])

	Number	Average size (acres)	Total acreage
1836	670	—[a]	—[a]
1865	300	—[a]	—[a]
1900	111	196	21,756
1930	39	661	25,779
1970	18	11,112	200,000

[a] Data not available

[9] For a more detailed discussion in relation to international agrarian capitalism, see Beckford (1972:chapters 4 and 5).

Jamaica. The process of amalgamation (through the merger of adjacent estates) began right after Emancipation, accelerated toward the end of the nineteenth century, and continued at least until the 1930's. Since then, the industry has expanded the acreage that it controlled almost eightfold, with an attrition rate of roughly half for the number of factories.[10] This was a result of the incursion of international monopoly capital.

The MNC reared its ugly head during the 1930's. Tate and Lyle, the giant British sugar refining enterprise, bought out large areas of land in Jamaica and Trinidad and established subsidiary companies for the production of sugar cane and raw sugar. Today, that particular corporation produces 100 percent of sugar output in Belize, 92 percent of output in Trinidad, and 60 percent of output in Jamaica. And in Guyana, another British corporation — Booker McConnell Limited — produces 98 percent of that country's sugar output. Together these two enterprises account for over 90 percent of West Indian sugar production.

As international monopoly capital engrossed more and more of the farmlands throughout the West Indies, less and less land was left for the peasants. Meanwhile peasant population expanded rapidly, so increasingly small acreages had to sustain each peasant family, and in the absence of dramatic improvements in small-farm productivity, independent peasant economic existence became increasingly precarious. As a result, many peasants are forced to supplement their incomes with wage work on plantations or elsewhere.

The plantation incursions on the land have been buttressed, more recently, by other nonagrarian invasions of monopoly capital. Mining (bauxite and petroleum) and tourism now occupy large areas of land in many of the islands. Consequently, the peasants are forced further onto the margins of these societies. The position of the rural proletariat is even worse that that of the peasantry.

PATTERNS OF ALIENATION

The plantation system alienates West Indian peoples from their resources. The two groups most directly affected are the peasants and the rural proletariat. In general, they exist on the margins of society. For purposes of our analysis, it is useful to make a distinction between "the margin of subsistence" and "the margin of survival." The margin of subsistence represents levels of living (consumption) which are barely tolerable by civilized human standards. The margin of survival represents

[10]   The eighteen sugar estates occupy about 12 percent of *all* farmland in Jamaica (1.7 million acres). The cultivated area of these estates is about 20 percent of total cultivated area in the country as a whole.

levels which are intolerable. The individual on the margin of survival scrapes to achieve a level of consumption which is just enough to survive.

For the West Indies as a whole, the "small" peasant is on the margin of subsistence. (Middle and big peasants who have sufficient land resources to be able to hire wage labor and/or to secure machine capital generally achieve decent levels of living. But these are a minority of the peasantry.) The rural proletariat are, for the most part, on the margin of survival. Over time, the position of the peasantry shifts with changes in the fortunes of the plantation sector. During periods of plantation expansion the peasantry is forced back closer to the margin of survival. The opposite shift takes place during periods of plantation contraction. The position of the rural proletariat remains static over time — on or about the margin of survival.

Tables 2 and 3 provide a summary of census and survey data showing the position of the peasantry in relation to land, and relative to plantations. The small peasant is assumed to correspond to the size group less than five acres; the plantation falls in the size group over 500 acres. (Exceptions to this general rule of thumb should be made for places like Barbados where a farm over 100 acres is a plantation. But no effort is being made for that kind of refinement in the present exercise.) Table 2 shows the size group distribution of all farms, by territory. And Table 3 shows a similar distribution of the area in farms, again by territory.

Table 2. Proportion of total number of farms by size group and territory

Year	Territory	Size group (acres)					Total (per-cent)
		<5	5–<25	25–<100	100–<500	>500	
—	Belize[a]	—	—	—	—	—	—
1961	Barbados	98.3	0.8	0.2	0.5	0.2	100
1961	British Virgin Islands	36.6	52.7	9.5	1.3	0.0	100
—	Guyana[a]	—	—	—	—	—	—
1968	Jamaica	78.6	19.4	1.6	0.4	0.2	100
	Leeward Islands						
1961	Antigua/Barbuda	91.1	7.7	0.59	0.4	0.26	100
1961	Montserrat	92.7		6.5		0.7	100
1961	St. Kitts/Nevis/Anguilla	94.5	3.9	0.7	0.5	0.45	100
1963	Trinidad and Tobago[b]	46.5	46.8	5.3	1.1	0.3	100
	Windward Islands						
1961	Grenada	89.7	8.8	0.9	0.5	0.1	100
1961	Dominica	75.2	21.5	2.3	0.8	0.3	100
1961	St. Lucia	82.5	14.9	1.9	0.6	0.2	100
1961	St. Vincent	89.0	10.1	0.6	0.2	0.1	100

[a] Data not available
[b] Provisional estimates for holdings of one acre and over (excluding land owned by government)

Table 3.   Proportion of total area in farms by size group and territory

Year	Territory	Size group (acres)					Total (per-cent)
		<5	5–<25	25–<100	100–<500	>500	
—	Belize[a]	—	—	—	—	—	—
1961	Barbados	13.4	2.4	2.5	50.4	31.3	100
1961	British Virgin Islands	5.7	43.7	34.2	16.4	—	100
—	Guyana[a]	—	—	—	—	—	—
1968	Jamaica	14.9	22.1	8.3	9.9	44.9	100
	Leeward Islands						
1961	Antigua/Barbuda	26.7	9.7	4.4	17.1	42.2	100
—	Montserrat[a]	—	—	—	—	—	—
1961	St. Kitts/Nevis/Anguilla	15.0	5.2	4.3	18.9	56.6	100
1963	Trinidad and Tobago[b]	6.9	30.7	15.1	16.2	31.1	100
	Windward Islands						
1961	Grenada	23.9	19.7	10.3	31.1	15.0	100
1961	Dominica	13.2	21.0	12.2	21.3	32.2	100
1961	St. Lucia	18.0	19.6	0.2	17.9	33.8	100
1961	St. Vincent	27.0	24.5	7.69	16.0	24.2	100

[a] Data not available
[b] Provisional estimates for holdings of one acre and over (excluding land owned by government)

Comparing the data in these two tables reveals the dismal position of the peasantry. Everywhere the small peasants (less than five acres) dominate in numbers but they have only a small proportion of the farmland. On the other hand, plantations (over 500 acres) are few in number but they have a large proportion of farmland. Barbados is perhaps the extreme case. There, small peasants are 98 percent of all farmers and they exist on 13 percent of all farmland; while the plantations (over one hundred acres) are less than 1 percent of all farmers with 82 percent of all farmland. These tables clearly reveal the existing alienation of the peasantry throughout the region.

It was suggested earlier that alienation of the peasantry has been increasing as a result of the incursions of monopoly capital. Table 4 provides some evidence of this for Jamaica. There we see that the number of small peasants and the acreage farmed by them increased between 1943 and 1961; but average farm size remained virtually unchanged. Over the same period, the number of plantations declined drastically; acreage farmed also declined, but not to the same degree; so that average farm size increased appreciably. It is important to note that the total area in farms declined, at about one-half the rate of decline in plantation land.

Now these trends tell a story. Nonagrarian capitalism (mining and tourism) came on the scene in Jamaica during the period covered by the data. Also, the revolt of 1938 (to be discussed later) resulted in intensified government policy to provide land for the peasantry — through

Table 4. Peasant and plantation land and labor, Jamaica, 1943–1968[a]

	1943			1961			1968		
	Small peasants	Plantations	Total	Small peasants	Plantations	Total	Small peasants	Plantations	Total
Number of farms	116,200	532	149,142	113,239	350	158,938	149,703	295	190,582
Area (acreage)	157,363	1,068,000	1,836,668	201,093	774,000	1,706,561	223,818	676,426	1,508,000
Average size	1.4	2,000	—	1.8	2,210	—	1.5	2,340	—
Employment (number per 100 acres cultivated land)	69	17	44	84	17	42			

[a] Census survey data. "Small peasants" refer to farm size group of less than 5 acres. "Plantations" refer to farm size group of more than 500 acres. The "total" colums refer to all farms; it thus includes size groups not shown in Table (i.e., farms of 5–500 acres).

"land settlement" schemes. Additionally, the population of Jamaica increased from 1.3 million in 1943 to the present two million.

The decline in total farmland shown in Table 4 is chiefly a result of mining developments. Metropolitan (United States and Canada) bauxite companies purchased considerable areas of land. And a good share of this was former plantation land — particularly in St. Ann, traditionally a plantation ("pen-keeper" — i.e., livestock ranch) parish. Nevertheless, the average size of plantations increased as the remaining plantation land became more concentrated among fewer plantations. The marked increase in small-peasant acreage between 1943 and 1968 is directly attributable to the government land-settlement scheme. The government purchased several derelict plantations and subdivided them for sale to peasants. The decline in plantation acreage, then, is partly a result of the invasion of nonagrarian capitalism and partly a result of peasant substitution.

Although peasant acreage increased, the average size of peasant holdings remained static. In short, the rate of growth of peasant farmers kept pace with the rate of growth of land operated by them. This is a *crude* indication that the economic position of the peasantry has remained virtually unchanged since 1943.[11] If we assume that the average household size of small peasants is five, then in 1968 the 150,000 small farms provided subsistence for 750,000 people on 15 percent of Jamaica's farmland. At the same time, 350 plantation owners luxuriated on 45 percent of all farmland.

Back in 1943, 530 plantation owners earned profits from 60 percent of all farmland. Also, they benefited from capital gains on land values since that time. Census data reveal that productivity of plantation farmland tripled between 1943 and 1961. It is clear, then, that the economic position of plantation owners has improved appreciably, in both absolute and relative terms.

To return to the general West Indian situation, and the special case of the sugar plantation, we find an interesting interplay between plantations and some of the peasantry — i.e., those engaged in cane farming. In that game, plantations win again; and peasants lose. During the plantation labor crisis following Emancipation, and after numerous efforts to solve that crisis, plantation owners finally resolved to encourage peasant production of cane to provide the necessary throughput for their factories. This is the genesis of peasant cane farming in the West Indies. It began toward the end of the nineteenth century and today cane farmers (many of whom are peasants) produce one-half of sugar cane output in Jamaica

[11] This inference is reasonable unless it can be demonstrated that land productivity on small farms improved substantially *and* that the terms of trade have shifted in favor of the peasant. Census data indicate a decline in land productivity. In any case it is clear that the position of the peasantry relative to the plantation has deteriorated over the period.

and significant shares of output in Trinidad and Belize. (Ironically, the Guyana government is now encouraging peasant cane farming, which never existed there before.)

Johnson has analyzed the origins of cane farming in Trinidad. He demonstrates the importance of the planter class to its development. Planters around the turn of the twentieth century

often provided land, as well as advancing capital, and sometimes even supplied labor to the cane farmers. Their encouragement of cane farming is explained by the fact that they anticipated certain benefits from its establishment. . . . Low prices emphasized the need for more economical sugar production. However, the savings effected were mainly in the manufacturing process (Johnson 1972:59).

Cane farming involves more risk than processing. Furthermore, since factory owners are in a monopsonistic position they can determine the price paid to farmers growing cane. From the beginning, until now, the price was set at a disadvantage to cane farmers. Johnson concludes that "the cane farmer was plagued with three major problems — lack of capital, inadequate transport facilities and an unsatisfactory cane-price formula. These difficulties have persisted up to the present" (1972:73). The cane farmer is, in essence a plantation worker who works for the plantation on his own land. His fortunes are bound up directly with those of the plantation.

The rural proletariat suffers a greater degree of alienation than the peasantry. Plantation strategy since Emancipation is to create a labor surplus in each economy. This was engineered by importing labor (under indenture) and by land monopoly. A more recent strategy is mechanization — the substitution of capital for labor, as the labor force became unionized after the revolts of the 1930's. According to Table 4, plantations in Jamaica maintained the same rate of employment per 100 acres of cultivated land in 1961 as in 1943. With the increase in cultivated acreage, the number of workers employed increased from about 27,000 in 1943 to about 32,000 in 1961 — nearly 20 percent. Meanwhile output per man working on plantations rose about 64 percent over the same period. The *real* wage of plantation workers has remained virtually static.

In Jamaica, cultivated acreage on plantations actually increased during this period (from 160,000 acres to 191,000 acres). It will be recalled that total plantation farmland decreased. Improvements in technology, both mechanical (labor-saving) and biological-chemical (land-saving), explain the sharp rise in productivity, per man and per acre. But the plantation worker has gained nothing from these improvements.

It is important to note that most of these improvements resulted from public-sector investments, and that the industry is subsidized by governments throughout the region. The technological improvements have served to aggravate the unemployment situation. Machine capital displaces labor directly. So too does chemical technology which replaces workers with weed killers.

West Indian economies are all labor-surplus economies. McFarlane (1970) provides the following estimates for 1960 of open "long term unemployment":

	Percent of labor force		Percent of labor force
Jamaica	23.4	Grenada	22.3
Trinidad-Tobago	15.6	St. Vincent	22.8
Barbados	19.5	Dominica	16.1
St. Lucia	17.5	Others	not available

In such situations monopsonistic buyers of labor services, as plantations are in specific localities, do not need to pay wages higher than survival levels, the more so where plantations and other capitalists monopolize land (thus restricting labor from own-account production) and where there are limited job opportunities available elsewhere.[12]

The rural proletariat earns income working on the plantation, on the wharves shipping plantation products, and in other plantation-related activities; they work as well with middle and big peasants, with other small capitalists, and with government and the petty bourgeoisie (service activity). The plantation worker suffers the most. Income is seasonal and out-of-crop; the worker lives off credit in order to survive. Crop-time work pays back this credit in good years; and it may not during bad years. The margin of survival is most pronounced among this category of workers. But all rural workers are pushed onto the margin of survival when there is depression in the plantation sector. For it is in that sector that economic action begins to multiply and to decelerate. Many small peasants are wage workers on plantations. They suffer as both peasant and proletariat.

PATTERNS OF RESISTANCE

Alienation induces resistance on the part of those who are pushed onto the margins of society. Resistance takes different forms — trade-union

---

[12]   Government public works programs are the only real alternative in rural areas. Otherwise the suffering plantation worker must learn some artisan trade. But even when that skill is acquired, the market for the skill is largely determined by the economic achievement of peasants and the rural proletariat. They depend on the artisan for house construction, tailoring, dressmaking, shoemaking, furniture, and so on.

organization, political mobilization, formation of peasant associations, and at the extreme, social revolt or revolution.

At one time or another in the West Indies, peasants and proletariat have engaged in all these different patterns of resistance. As indicated earlier, the West Indian peasantry normally exists on the margin of subsistence while the rural proletariat stands on the margin of survival. Whenever the economic situation has forced the peasantry down to the margin of survival, widespread social unrest has been the result. The confluence of degrees of hardship suffered jointly by peasants and proletariat creates a powerful force for social change to alleviate mass suffering. Revolts and rebellions in West Indian history occurred within that context.

The 1865 rebellion in Jamaica is one case. Declining estate wages resulted from falling sugar prices and placed the rural proletariat in a precarious economic position. Meanwhile drastic measures were introduced to curtail peasant squatting on estate land. Low prices, low wages, increased taxation, and insecure land tenure for the peasantry created an economic crisis for peasants and rural proletariat alike, and a violent rebellion was the natural outcome.

Again, economic crisis during the 1930's heightened the alienation of peasants and rural proletariat to a degree that social upheaval occurred throughout the region, beginning with St. Kitts in 1935 and ending with Jamaica in 1938. Post (1969) has analyzed the 1938 rebellion in Jamaica. He identifies six groups of "demonstrators" involved in the protest:

(1) workers at the new Tate and Lyle sugar estates;
(2) dockers at the city port;
(3) public-works laborers;
(4) ex-servicemen settled on government land grants;
(5) sugar cane workers;
(6) banana workers.

The most militant of these groups were the banana workers who were, for the most part, peasant farmers as well.

According to Post:

... It is not primarily as wage workers that the banana plantation workers must be seen, but as peasant farmers. . . . I would argue that it was this hunger of land — either to add to an existing plot or to turn a landless labourer into a proprietor — which was the main force of the strikers in the banana areas (1969:379).

Both peasants and proletariat were involved in the 1938 rebellion. Economic crisis in the plantation sector resulted in equal hardship for both groups. And their joint resistance created the social crisis.

It is instructive to consider, briefly, the economic background to the

West Indian revolts of the 1930's. Indentured East Indian labor had provided a prop to the sugar industry after Emancipation. But the Indian government terminated the scheme in 1917. Sugar prices rose sharply during the 1920's, but they fell drastically with the depression of the 1930's. It was during that decade that the MNC came on the scene and plantation land monopoly intensified. Peasant access to land was thereby further restricted and low sugar prices meant low wages (and unemployment) for plantation workers. Thus economic crisis reached a peak throughout the rural sector.

The revolts of the 1930's subsequently led to less-violent patterns of resistance: trade-union mobilization of the rural proletariat, political (constitutional) change, and the ascendancy of peasant organizations. Trade unions sprang up everywhere out of the ashes of the revolts, and these have developed into powerful bargaining agents on behalf of the rural proletariat. Also, the trade-union movement throughout the West Indies has been instrumental in promoting constitutional change. In most places, trade unions are associated directly with political parties which spearheaded the movement from crown-colony status to constitutional independence, under universal adult suffrage. Today most heads of governments throughout the West Indies are (or were) trade-union leaders — most of whom were associated with the revolts of the 1930's and the subsequent growth of the trade-union movement.

Peasant associations also mushroomed after the disturbances. Agricultural societies, cane farmers' associations, banana growers' associations, citrus growers' associations, and farmers' unions flourish today in most places, and these operate as powerful political lobbies, in addition to providing economic assistance and bargaining strength for member farmers. Small peasants are the majority of members in these organizations although leadership is usually concentrated among middle and big peasants.

As mentioned earlier, monopoly capital has increased its stranglehold over rural resources in the West Indies over the last three decades or so. The resulting alienation of peasants and proletariat has induced different forms of resistance. Trade-union organization is perhaps the most important of these. Throughout the region, unions have managed to secure periodic wage increases for workers, at least to keep money wages in step with the rising cost of living. Unions have managed as well to prevent large-scale substitution of machine capital for labor, thereby preventing a greater increase in the rate of unemployment. But the efforts of trade unions have failed to eliminate widespread unemployment as the growth of population (and labor force) outpaced the growth of new employment opportunities. Consequently, the rural proletariat continues to exist on or about the margin of survival.

SITUATION AND CHANGE

In spite of organized resistance, the peasantry also remains in a precarious position throughout the West Indies. New incursions of monopoly capital in rural areas (for mining and tourism) have reduced the land area available to peasants. At the same time, peasant population expanded rapidly. The resultant decline in resources per peasant household intensifies rural poverty. However, this situation has been tempered by large-scale emigration from rural areas.

Throughout the present century, emigration has been one of the main avenues through which the rural population of the West Indies managed to escape alienation by agrarian capitalism. Large numbers migrated to Central America to provide labor for the establishment of banana plantations and for building the Panama Canal. Many went to Cuba to work on the sugar plantations in the early decades of the twentieth century. Movements from smaller islands to larger ones were always significant. And during the past few decades, migration to advanced industrial countries and from rural to urban areas within individual West Indian countries has been very substantial.

The economic situation of peasants and rural proletariat in the West Indies would have been far worse today were it not for the persistent migration from rural areas. Without migration, resource pressure would have been far more intense and rural poverty more pronounced. In this connection, it is important to note that migrants provide substantial income flows for those remaining on the land. Remittances from migrants abroad to relatives at home exceed inflows of foreign capital in most territories; and in some smaller ones, remittances may be greater than total income generated in production.

In spite of resistance and migration, the economic position of peasants and proletariat remains precarious throughout the region. The unequal pattern of land distribution everywhere results in poor distribution of wealth and income, with proletariat and peasants at the bottom of the economic (and social) ladder. The solution to this problem will come through either reform or revolution.

The Cuban revolution served to eradicate extremes of mass rural poverty. Unless West Indian governments implement major programs of agrarian reform, it seems certain that increasing alienation of peasants and proletariat will eventually result in revolution. If history is any guide, that will occur whenever the peasantry is forced back from the margin of subsistence to the margin of survival.

REFERENCES

BECKFORD, GEORGE L.
1972 *Persistent poverty*. New York: Oxford University Press.
BEST, LLOYD
1968 Outlines of a model of pure plantation economy. *Social and Economic Studies* 17.
EISNER, G.
1961 *Jamaica 1830–1930*. Manchester: Manchester University Press.
JOHNSON, HOWARD
1972 The origins and early development of cane farming in Trinidad 1882–1906. *The Journal of Caribbean History* 5.
MCFARLANE, CARMEN
1970 "The employment situation in overpopulated territories in the Commonwealth Caribbean," in *Human resources in the Commonwealth Caribbean*. Edited by Jack Harewood. St. Augustine, Trinidad.
POST, K.W.J.
1969 The politics of protest in Jamaica, 1938. *Social and Economic Studies* 18.
MORDECAI SUGAR COMMISSION
1967 *Report*.
WILLIAMS, ERIC E.
1964 *Capitalism and slavery*. London: Deutsch.

The Role of Peasant Organizations in the Struggle Against Multinational Corporations: The Cuban Case

GERRIT HUIZER

In some of the so-called underdeveloped countries, the struggle against multinational or transnational corporations has gradually evolved from relatively weak efforts to gain concrete benefits to outright revolutionary action. This kind of evolution was not the result of a clear theoretical consciousness of peasants and workers of the role of such corporations, but was a reaction to the rigid and crude forms of exploitation and domination maintained by these corporations at all costs. Examples are the struggle of the peasant workers in the Laguna area in Mexico in 1936 against the Anderson Clayton and other cotton producing and trading companies, leading to the almost complete expulsion of these companies from the region; the land invasions organized by the Union General de Obreros y Campesinos de Mexico (UGOCM) in 1958 against the Cananea cattle company in Sonora; and the actions of the *comunidades* of Pasco and Junin, Peru, against the Cerro de Pasco Corporation (Huizer 1972b). A particularly clear example is the gradually escalating struggle of the Cuban peasants against national and foreign landowners and plantation companies.

In the developing countries, the ill effects of transnational corporations have often been felt more strongly in agriculture than in other fields of the economy. In the mining, and particularly in the manufacturing and oil industries, the transnational corporations can claim that certain and even considerable benefits accrue to the countries where they operate, in spite of the huge profits made by these corporations. In agriculture, however, the exploitation of the host country and its population is more clear-cut and brutal. Protest against inhuman working conditions in the mining,

The author is heavily indebted to the Asociación Nacional de Agricultores Pequeños Havana, which supplied him with data on the Cuban peasant struggle through interviews and training material (e.g., Regalado 1973).

manufacturing, or oil industries, can often be neutralized by giving in to certain material demands, such as wage increases or higher taxes or royalties. This is more difficult in the plantation economy. Although simple wage demands can be met, the demand for land by peasants whose forefathers or who themselves have been evicted by the plantations when these were introduced cannot be fulfilled unless the agrarian structure as such is radically changed. There are numerous cases where the demand for land has aroused the population of developing countries to strong resistance movements against the transnational corporations. A main reason for this fact is that in the past or even recently the transnational corporations have displaced or evicted the indigenous peasant population in order to get good lands to create the plantation system. The initiation of the plantation economy has often been felt as an intrusion and, in fact, often consisted of simple usurpation of lands originally belonging to local peasants or communities.

Thus from the start many plantation corporations have been a source of frustration for the local population, and on the whole they have done very little to compensate for this. On the contrary, they have often aggressively continued the trend set at their initiation. Formerly independent peasants who were forced to work on the plantations were badly paid and housed. If more lands were needed, because of the profitability of the plantation agriculture, the same rude means of usurpation or similar doubtful approaches were used to get these lands from neighboring peasant communities. Whenever movements to correct these practices were initiated by the victims or those who were interested in helping them, the counterreaction of the corporations was out of proportion. Thus the moderate efforts of the Guatemalan government in 1953 to expropriate some of the unused lands of the United Fruit Company (UFC) for distribution among landless peasants led to international action to defend the UFC's interests, going as far as overthrowing the Guatemalan government and installing a military dictatorship which has caused the deaths of numerous peasant and labor leaders until today. In several developing countries the plantations are a strongly dominating force, virtually unchallenged.

The influence of transnational agricultural corporations in some of the smaller developing countries comes out clearly in Table 1 from Beckford (1970:448).

In some cases resistance to change by the corporations and their increasingly violent reaction against legitimate demands has led to an escalation of the peasant and worker resistance against them. The resistance of the peasants organized by Viet Minh against Michelin and other foreign powers is probably the most notorious, but also certain peasant movements, e.g., in the Philippines and Cuba, which later became more or less violent revolutionary movements, should be mentioned. The process by which moderate, legalistic peasant interest groups, in their

Table 1.   Big companies and small countries: a comparison of company activity data and national aggregates for selected plantation economies 1967–1968 (million dollars U.S.)

	Company		Country		
	Annual sales	Net income	National income	Exports	
				Total	Plantations[a]
Booker	198.6	11.5			
Guyana			162.5	108.2	31.8
Tate and Lyle	549.2	27.1			
Jamaica			787.2	219.5	44.9
Trinidad			569.0	466.2	24.2
United Fruit	488.9	53.1			
Panama			634.0	95.2	55.6
Honduras			649.0	181.4	85.4

Source: All country data from International Monetary Fund, International Financial Statistics, January 1970. Company data are from respective company annual reports.
[a] Plantation exports refer to exports of the commodity produced in the particular country by the relevant metropolitan enterprise.

demand for justice and recognition of rights, became an outright revolutionary movement as a reaction to the intransigence of the established elite and the corporations is well illustrated with the case of Cuba.

As in several other Latin American countries, in Cuba the struggle of peasants against large estates and corporations has a tradition which goes back to the colonial period. In Cuba it started particularly after the introduction of railways around 1830 made the cultivation of sugar cane profitable. The owners of sugar estates then started to extend their lands aggressively at the cost of the small tobacco-producing farmers, through eviction and usurpation.

Peasant resistance was initially sporadic and isolated. When, however, the armed struggle for independence started in 1868, the peasants joined this movement. Although this struggle was repressed, many peasants participated again in the Mambi army, in the revolution of 1895 against the Spanish regime. As a counteraction the peasants were "concentrated" by the colonial regime in villages; because they lost even more lands through this form of eviction, they joined more massively the liberation struggle until it ended because of the American intervention. The Americans took more and more power in Cuba, replacing the colonial forces. Instead of institutionalizing the armed forces of the liberation as a national army, as was proposed by the Cubans, they created the Guardia Rural (Rural guards) with elements which were not identified with the peasantry. Supported by this Guardia Rural, the process of eviction of peasants from communal lands and small private plots went on, creating more and more plantations in the hands of American companies or individuals. By 1905 there were 13,000 American properties in

Cuba, covering almost 10 percent of the total surface of the country. The estates were dedicated to sugar cultivation or cattle. Moreover, the promises made to those who struggled in the liberation war to get uncultivated land were not kept. Many of the veterans went to the Oriente province and took idle lands. Officially this was made possible by a law in 1904, but, in fact, large landowners took away those lands from the peasant occupants. Protest against these activities was initially sporadic.

Between 1910 and 1920 the peasant struggle in Cuba became somewhat influenced by the growing urban labor movement and by socialist and communist ideas. A greater effectiveness and increasing radicalization of the peasant struggle was, however, particularly a reaction to the rapid expansion of large estates which took place between 1915 and 1925, mainly in Oriente province and Camagüey. Thousands of peasants were evicted and pushed into the mountains or forced to work as laborers on the estates or in the large sugar factories, often owned by foreign companies. There was a close collaboration between the companies and the Cuban government. President Garcia Menocal, for example, was linked to the Cuban American Sugar Company, the second largest American sugar enterprise in the country. In 1923 there was a massive mobilization of peasants against the usurpation manipulations of an American company in Caujeri, Oriente province. Peasants were willing to defend their lands by armed force. The same happened in Sagua de Tánamo.

Although peasants often had started to defend their rights through legal action in the courts, they were able to use more radical means since many of them were veterans of the Independence struggle. Unrest went on for years in one or another part of the country. In 1928 the peasants mobilized to get back lands or prevent usurpation by the United Fruit Company, which received help from the Guardia Rural, in several places at the north coast of Oriente province. By 1933–1934, however, the peasants had become more formally organized and were able to struggle more effectively in a coordinated way. One outstanding leader, a veteran of the 1895 revolution, was Lino Alvarez. His strategy, particularly at the beginning, was to try all the possible legal means to defend the peasants' lands. More radical leaders denounced his "excessive legalism," but it gave time to organize the peasants effectively and mobilize them into big demonstrations when it became clear that the legalistic approach dismally failed. The peasants then felt better prepared to initiate more radical and extralegal actions such as invasions of land.

During the twenties and thirties the sugar workers also had been organized through the Confederación Nacional Obrera de Cuba (National Workers' Confederation of Cuba) connected with the Communist party which had been created in 1925. Sugar workers and cane-cultivating peasants worked together in the struggle against the owners of plantations and sugar mills, such as the United Fruit Company. This struggle became particularly acute when the repressive Machado regime was overthrown through a general strike in 1933. The peasants had their own demands, increasingly radical, such as "land to the tillers," and "school for the children." At the Second Congress of the Communist Party of Cuba in April 1934 the slogan "Agrarian and anti-imperialist revolution" was launched, and mass meetings of peasants, at times supported by rallies or movements in the towns, were organized around this slogan. Trade-union leaders and Communist party cadres who went out into the rural areas were surprised by the force of such peasant movements as those in the mountainous areas of Oriente province.

In some areas, such as Camagüey, the peasant struggle initially took the form of the creation of pro-school committees. The joint efforts as such and the difficulties encountered had a solidifying and radicalizing effect on these groups. These committees from Camagüey, supported by the Communist youth organization, initiated a First National Peasant Congress in 1937, to coordinate peasant activities all over the country. After this congress in Havana many peasant committees and associations were created in different provinces, where they did not yet exist.

Elsewhere they were brought together regionally. Thus, in 1939, the Peasant Federation of Oriente was created at a peasant congress there. The struggle everywhere for concrete and moderate demands encountered such a rigidly negative reaction from the landowners and companies that the peasants realized that these were their class enemies. As a result of this awareness, the small local groupings saw the need to become more strongly and rationally organized and to give a more radical content to their demands. Thus, a more or less organized struggle emerged gradually. At the Second National Peasant Congress in Havana in 1941, in which over 800 peasant delegates participated, the Asociación Nacional Campesina (National Peasant Association) was created. The main struggle of the Association and its affiliates all over the country was against the numerous evictions of peasants by the large owners or companies. In the following years the efforts of the estate owners or companies to evict peasants and usurp their lands became increasingly violent. Many peasant houses were destroyed, several peasant leaders who led the resistance against such activities were assassinated, such as Niceto Pérez García in 1946 and Sabino Pupo Pillán (leader of the struggle against eviction by the Manati Sugar Company) in 1948. By 1944 the Asociación Nacional Campesina denounced the fact that altogether about 40,000 families were threatened with eviction. Mass meetings and demonstrations were organized in several parts of the country against the eviction threat.

The need to demand such fundamental changes in the rural social structure as agrarian reform rather than small gains was felt increasingly by the peasant associations. Under the governments of Grau San Martin and Prio Socarrás, promises about land reform were made and some action, though weak, was taken in that direction. Efforts to neutralize the radicalization of the peasant movement and the increasing demands for structural change were also made through the creation of an alternative organization, the Confederación Campesina de Cuba (Peasant Confederation of Cuba), led by persons related to the government. Also, the Banco de Fomento Agrícola e Industrial de Cuba (BANFAIC, Agricultural and Industrial Development Bank of Cuba), created in 1950, tried, with some success, to give the impression that a new reform-oriented policy had been initiated. Another institution created with that purpose was the obligatory membership of producers of certain products, such as tobacco, in a corresponding national organization, such as the tobacco growers. Although at the village level these organizations were sometimes led by small farmers, nationally they were dominated by the large producers. Members of the radical Asociación Nacional Campesina tried to take over more and more leadership in these organizations, rather than struggling against them.

After the coup d'etat which brought Batista to power as president in 1952, the struggle of the peasants again became more outspoken because large landowners and companies started to increase their demands. The Asociación Nacional Campesina organized many meetings, and pro-land-reform committees were created in many sugar areas. The attack on Moncada barracks by young revolutionaries headed by Fidel Castro on July 26, 1953, had a considerable impact on the militancy of the peasants and workers. The sugar strike of 1955, which paralyzed over a hundred sugar mills, was an expression of the radicalization trend. So was the confrontation of the peasant associations with the King Ranch (from Texas) when it tried to usurp lands in Adelaide, Camagüey province, in 1954, and against the Francisco Sugar Company which tried the same in 1958. After the men were imprisoned when they tried to prevent these companies from taking their lands, women took over and tried to halt the bulldozers that came to destroy their houses and crops. Similar activities were continuously taking place in Oriente province. When the small group of revolutionaries headed by Fidel Castro started a guerrilla struggle in Oriente province after their landing with the Gramma in December 1956, they found the peasantry ready for insurrectionary action. The tradition of resistance against the violence of the large landowners and companies had radicalized the peasants to such an extent that they were prepared to support or even to join the guerrilla forces.

The repressive action of the Batista regime, trying to concentrate the rebellious peasants in areas where they could give no support to the guerrillas, only radicalized their resistance. The careful way in which the guerrilla forces approached the peasants in the areas they dominated, and the reform measures they encouraged, found immediate support from the local peasant associations. In particular, Law No. 3 of the Rebel Forces, promulgated October 10, 1958, giving the land to its cultivators free of charge (up to twenty-six hectares) helped to mobilize the peasantry behind the revolutionary forces, which gained a victory on January 1, 1959.

Soon after the revolutionary regime came to power, a land-reform law was promulgated (May 17, 1959) which prohibited the possession of land beyond the size of thirty *caballerías* (about 390 hectares). More than 100,000 tenants, sharecroppers, and other precarious cultivators became proprietors of their plots.

The large company-owned estates were expropriated and transformed into cooperative or state farms. Efforts to turn the clock back, by overthrowing the government, as was done in Guatemala in 1954, were undertaken in 1961, through the invasion of Playa Girón. This effort failed and Cuba became the first Latin American country to eliminate drastically the influence of multinational corporations (MNC's).

The next country to take serious steps in this field was Peru. The 1969 land reform, introduced by a "revolutionary military government," dealt in the first place with the huge sugar estates of such MNC's as W.R. Grace, Gildemeister, and others in the northern coastal regions. It should be noted that the military forces, which made up the Peruvian government from 1968 onward, in earlier years had been made aware of the serious problems created by the large estate system, when they had to confront massive peasant movements and land invasions involving over 300,000 peasants (including the occupation of the estate of the Cerro de Pasco Corporation).

In the struggle against the increasing influence of MNC's, peasant resistance movements have played a crucial role and will probably continue to do so in the future. As clearly demonstrated by the Cuban case, the intransigent reaction of the companies and large estate owners to the reasonable and legitimate demands of the peasants and workers led to a radicalization of the peasantry in demands as well as means of struggle. This process of escalation introduced by the established powerholders eventually led to their own destruction.

REFERENCES

BECKFORD, GEORGE
    1970   The dynamics of growth and the nature of metropolitan plantation enterprise. *Social and Economic Studies* 19:4. University of West Indies, Jamaica.

HUIZER, GERRIT
1972a Land invasions as a non-violent strategy of peasant rebellion. *Journal of Peace Research* 3.
1972b *The revolutionary potential of peasants in Latin America*. Lexington, Massachusetts: Heath Lexington.
REGALADO, ANTERO
1973 *Las luchas campesinas en Cuba*. Havana.

Taxes, Tourists and Turtlemen: Island Dependency and the Tax-Haven Business

MINA DAVIS CAULFIELD

Grand Cayman, a small island in the western Caribbean, just twenty-two miles long and eight miles wide, is currently a hot spot on the international tax-evasion scheme. Together with two smaller islands, Little Cayman and Cayman Brac, it is a British Crown Colony, having opted as recently as 1962 to become a colony on its own rather than continue as a dependency of Jamaica when that country became independent. Isolated from and ignored by the outside world for centuries, Caymanians are now undergoing a rediscovery of their homeland; a number of previously unnoticed resources are now being exploited in what appears to be a carefully thought-out pattern. One resource is the colony's total absence of taxation; another is the historical absence of the typical West Indian plantation society, which means a relative lack of class and racial antagonism. A third resource is the land itself, relatively infertile, which the islanders have traditionally considered as worth little, since they have always been seafarers, specializing until recently in hunting the giant green turtle. This combination of resources has proved extremely attractive to the rapidly expanding international tax-haven business, and drastic changes have occurred in island life as a result. A new kind of dependency has been fostered in this miniature society of only 10,000 people, a dependency that is incredibly profitable to some of the world's wealthiest corporations and individuals. I will try to outline here some of the main features of this development.

Four hundred and fifty years after Columbus sighted the Caymans in 1503, Grand Cayman suffered its second "discovery." In 1953, after several years of irregular communication by light seaplane between Georgetown (the capital) and Jamaica, work was finished on an airstrip. Development of the tourist industry, virtually nonexistent before this, was clearly one motive in building the airstrip, but it is also clear that at least an equal motivation was the desire to expedite the transport of Caymanian seamen to Panama, New York, Miami, and the Gulf ports of the United States. The Colonial Office Report for 1953–54 puts it succinctly:

The business of the Dependency [Cayman was at this time a dependency of Jamaica, which was itself a British colony] is no longer turtle fishing, or rope making, or shipbuilding, though these still make an important contribution towards income. The business of the Dependency is nowadays the export of seamen. With the new accessibility of the Dependency and with the co-operation of one of the leading American tanker companies, some hundreds of additional seamen have been enabled to obtain remunerative overseas employment. . . . At the end of 1954 one Company alone employed over 600 Caymanians (H.M.S.O. 1956:4).

The "cooperation" supplied by the American tanker company is not specified. But in view of the intense interest shown in Cayman as a supplier of cut-rate labor by the National Bulk Carriers Co., it is likely that the construction of Cayman's airport was undertaken with the urging, or even the financial backing, of D.K. Ludwig, one of the world's richest men, of whom we will hear more later.

The year the airport was completed also marked another prophetic first in the islands — the first bank, a branch of Barclay's, D.C.O., in Georgetown. Three years later, the first large hotel opened on the Seven-mile Beach, a part of the coast that had always been all but deserted, since virtually nothing will grow there and the white sand is unsuitable for the ingenious davits rigged for the landing of small boats. What the Caymanians saw as barren land, foreign capital moved to exploit, and the discovery of Grand Cayman as "the island that time forgot," "the last of the unspoiled Caribbean paradises," led to rapid resolution of some long-standing "licensing and other difficulties" that had existed with regard to air travel with the United States. By 1965 there were six hotels on Seven-mile Beach, the total number of beds available to tourists in hotels, cottages, and clubs on all three islands was 532 — not a great number, but growing every year.

It is not clear exactly when the most significant discovery about the Cayman Islands was made: that it was an ideal tax haven. By 1966 it was being widely advertised in business journals, and in 1970 it was already reported to be taking over the major part of the tax-haven business from the troubled Bahamas. It is the story of this strange "business" that I will now review; first, as it has affected the people of the islands, and second, as it operates for the benefit of international corporate capital. To the cosmopolitan seekers of tax loopholes and means to ease the flow of capital into investment centers around the world, Grand Cayman exists largely on paper: it is not a center for commercial or industrial investment in itself. But thousands of companies, trusts, and corporations name it as their base. To the inhabitants of the islands, on the other hand, the fact that these companies are based in their islands is very little known and scarcely regarded as important by anyone beyond the few Caymanians employed in the banks and office buildings, and the tiny native elite, including a few new political leaders. The fact that their lives have been altered by this last "discovery" of their home is hardly perceived by most islanders, who attribute the changes to "progress," "modernization," and the ubiquitous "visitors."

Tourism had already begun to cause major changes in the lives of the inhabitants before the tax-haven business got into full swing. It would be difficult to separate out the effects of the two sources of intrusion. There can be little doubt that the growth of tax-related activity has been the occasion for a very considerable immigration of tax lawyers, accountants, and clerical staff, and more significantly, a huge number of short-term visitors who combine business with pleasure, living in the luxury hotels while they set up their trusts, often adding a little real estate speculation on the side. It is certainly true that the invasion of outsiders took a drastic upswing in the late sixties and early seventies, coinciding exactly with the tax-haven boom. In 1970 it was estimated that 20,000 visitors came and went from the islands — double the number of permanent inhabitants. In assessing the impact on the lives of Caymanians, I will consider tourism and the tax-haven business as a single phenomenon, as they are experienced by the people.

THE BAHAMAS AND THE CAYMANS: "MISTAKES" CORRECTED

Caymanians are fond of comparing their islands to the Bahamas, pointing out, in most cases, how the permissive attitude to gambling in the Bahamas has led to their "downfall." The boom-and-bust cycle of Nassau, however, is more complex. A variety of "mistakes" made in managing the tax-haven business in the Bahamas are frequently cited in the business journals, but casino gambling is not one of them. The most glaring factor, in the eyes of the international money market, is the Bahamian independence and Black Power movement, which had the "disastrous" consequence of limiting the "freedom" of foreigners to conduct their business as they see fit. Not only has there been talk of nationalizing the lucrative tourist industry, but some extremists have even suggested that the poverty-stricken islanders should have a share in the profits of the tax-haven business, at least to the extent of getting jobs in the offices and banks. The problem of unemployment, which has been endemic to the Bahamas since wage labor was introduced there, has become rather suddenly a major concern of the foreigners, who find that when a powerful political movement undertakes to tackle the question things can indeed become sticky. The work-permit restrictions imposed by the Bahamian government reached a point in 1971 where it was announced that no expatriate could expect to remain more than five years. The antiforeign sentiment of the people has become so extreme as to penetrate even the barbed-wire fences that enclose most tourist beaches. The response has been not to rectify the situation in the Bahamas, but to move on to a fresh field.

The Caymans certainly lacked the sparkle and glamor of the Bahamas, having been for 150 years virtually isolated from regular contact with the outside world. Since Cayman had never been a plantation colony, Caymanians have never experienced the British, or any foreigners, as exploiters until the recent period. Furthermore, their traditional mode of economy, based on independent fishing enterprise in home-built sailing vessels, supplemented on occasion by smuggling, wrecking, and piracy, never lent itself to the development of a well-defined class structure. Any man could be lucky or skilful in his struggles with the sea, and besides there were no large fortunes to be made, once the true buccaneering age was past, with which to capitalize a modern profit-making enterprise. Caymanians, in short, were virtually uncolonized colonials, with little or no experience in politics beyond the town-meeting variety and no tradition of class or imperial oppression to compare with the typical West Indian society.

When Cayman became a Crown Colony, it had a modern airport, the modest beginnings of a tourist trade, and a population just starting to taste the temptations of modern commodities. The shift from island-based fishing to wage labor on U.S. cargo ships has increased in momentum. The coming of air transport, with fares paid by the shipping agents who employed the seamen, accelerated the pace. By the mid-sixties the turtle- and shark-fishing fleets were beginning to falter. Local agriculture, never a major preoccupation for Caymanians, was declining. The process of proletarianization, especially among seamen and almost exclusively with one shipping firm (National Bulk Carriers), was well on its way. By the end of the decade it was virtually complete: in 1971 I saw the last island-built schooner depart on its last turtling voyage; all the other seamen worked for wages (turtlers worked on shares, as their buccaneering forefathers did).

This pattern of employment, which made the population dependent on foreign companies, also made the control of problems of large-scale unemployment relatively simple. Unlike colonized peasant populations, caught in the squeeze between alienation of their land and capital-intensive industries that do not provide enough jobs, the relatively small population of the Caymans has been readily absorbed — so far — by the "runaway shops" of the shipping industry, the U.S.-owned lines flying Liberian and Panamanian flags of convenience.

With the discovery of Cayman's tax-haven potential came an almost immediate boom in construction. Land prices rose phenomenally in the mid-sixties; hotels and cottages for tourists, new banks and office buildings, supermarkets and night clubs all went up at once, creating a huge demand for construction workers. Cayman became another kind of anomaly in the Caribbean: a colony of *over*-employment. Overemployment, which forces wages up, is of course bad for business — but only for those businesses that make profits by extracting surplus value from the workers. If major profits are made in other ways, as in the case of the tourist and tax-haven industries, underemployment can be a much worse problem, as the experience in the Bahamas had amply demonstrated. In a situation where it is essential to import a fairly large number of skilled office and professional staff, the existence of an army of indigenous unemployed can make for "social unrest," which tax-haven experts have come to regard as the one most dangerous condition in the havens of their choice. Furthermore, a working population in which a large proportion of the men are always away at sea, working at what is in relation to their previous incomes a very good wage (though it is only about one-third of the wage commanded by U.S. seamen), is far less likely to stir up trouble at home.

Caymanian legislation, geared since the early sixties toward accommodating the tax-haven business, has carefully excluded the possibility of changing this overemployment pattern. Although Jamaicans, suffering from the long-standing crushing underemployment generated by the plantation economy, are always anxious to emigrate to any spot where jobs are available, Cayman has strictly enforced its work-permit regulations *as they apply to other West Indians.* Any Jamaicans caught looking for jobs in Cayman — though there are many jobs open — are jailed and deported, even if they have entered the island legally.[1] Workers in the tax-haven business suffer no such restrictions; on the contrary, they have come to constitute a significant proportion (more than one-tenth) of the total permanent population. One such immigrant banker, writing in a business journal of the advantages Caymanian banks enjoy over those in "other territories," exults:

The population is small and a good proportion of its growth is attributable to the influx of expatriates skilled in banking, insurance, mutual funds, government and communications (over 1,000 during the last five years). With a small population, the social problems are greatly diminished and when existent are easily solved (Doucet 1971:513).

[1] A Jamaican friend of mine, who was living with us on our boat at anchor off Grand Cayman, was seen talking to a construction worker ashore; within hours, he was picked up

THE VIEW FROM BELOW: DEVELOPMENT OF A "SERVICE CULTURE"

Proletarianization: Women and Men

The trend toward proletarianization of the Caymanian work force has already been discussed as it applies to the takeover of seagoing workmen by large shipping corporations. The other half (actually more than half) of the work force, the Caymanian women, has undergone a corresponding transformation in occupation. In the traditional fishing economy of the islands, women played an essential role, almost completely separate from the activities of the men but in no sense secondary or supplementary. Despite the unproductive land, cultivable only in small "pockets" widely separated by rock and swamp, subsistence farming until recently was the source of most of the daily food intake, excluding protein, of the majority of the population. Since women traditionally have no truck with boats, all the fishing, including small-boat fishing just off shore, has always been done by men; but aside from clearing brush and breaking ground men have not taken part in agriculture except when, for one reason or another, they have been unable to go to sea.

In addition to the crucial role they played in food production, women have specialized in the crafts associated with boats and fishing: home manufacture of nets, baskets, and especially the strong, rot-resistant thatch rope used almost exclusively for rigging until recent years. As early as the turn of the century, thatch rope produced by Caymanian women was exported to Jamaica, bringing in £586 as early as 1905 (Williams 1970:66). By mid-century it was actually a major item of exchange, usually by barter rather than cash, with the outside world. In 1964, as the islands moved into the tax-haven period, thatch-rope exports almost exactly equaled the export value of all turtle and shark products; the women produced and sold (in addition to what was used in Cayman) 1,302,750 fathoms of rope for a cash value of £15,740 — earning an estimated 3½ to 4 pence *per day* (H.M.S.O. 1967:16).

The following year both fishing and thatch rope exports dropped drastically, although the demand was reportedly increasing for all of them. Turtle and shark exports declined in one year from a value of £15,830 to £12,256, while thatch-rope products dropped from £15,740 to £8,865 (H.M.S.O. 1967:16). Meanwhile, the value of imports into the islands was rising steadily, reaching more than £1,000,000 in 1965. Although a significant portion of the imported goods were consumed by the tourists and expatriates on the islands, this large discrepancy also

---

by the police, and only released in our custody on condition that we guarantee he would never go ashore!

reflects the important shifts in occupational patterns taking place among Caymanians. On the one hand, more and more men were working for wages on foreign-owned ships and in construction; on the other, more and more women were taking employment as domestics, retail clerks, and waitresses in the tourist industry. When I visited the island just five years later I was able to locate only one woman who still made thatch rope, and she produced only short lengths for sale to tourists as souvenirs. "You can put it on bar stools," she said. "Looks pretty." Every woman I spoke to over the age of thirty had made rope in the past and spoke with mingled distaste and nostalgia about the work. The rewards were pitifully small, the work of cutting, splitting, drying, and twisting was backbreaking; but the pride in skilled workmanship and the pleasure of the group process (usually done in cooperative holiday style similar to "morning sport" work gangs in Jamaica) were considerable. Many women still make baskets for a variety of uses: fish baskets, sand baskets, lunch baskets, book baskets, etc., and of course baskets for the tourists. Government "development experts" brought in a Trinidadian crafts expert a few years ago to teach Caymanian women how to make the kind of baskets tourists want: lots of colored raffia decoration, simple quick plaits of inferior thatch. The classes were not a success, and all the colorful baskets I saw for sale in tourist shops had been made in Jamaica. Caymanian women make superb, closely plaited baskets that are designed to carry heavy loads and not wear out.[2]

The decline of female crafts has not meant, of course, that Caymanian women no longer contribute importantly to household income. The extreme exploitation of their skilled labor in the thatch-rope trade made their earnings, in cash or barter, meager indeed; they were quick to shift to wage work at £15 per month when it became available. This is still less than half of what unskilled male labor commands in the islands, and of course it is full-time work in most cases. The decline in local agriculture, which makes ever-increasing prices of basic foodstuffs a daily problem for households, is clearly related to this occupational shift among women, who no longer have time for either craft production or subsistence agriculture.

Food: Dependency and Inflation

Today Grand Cayman imports almost all its food, and canned or frozen U.S. products have become the prestige eatables. Caymanians have always eaten some imported food, primarily rice, beans, and sugar; now

---

[2]   A common use in the old days was to carry 50-lb. loads of sand from the beach to smooth out in one's front yard, analogous to the lawn grass that won't grow without water. Today most women use plastic buckets to carry their sand.

they buy even plantains, chochos, and pawpaws imported from Costa Rica, and their eggs, milk, and meat are flown in from Florida. Prices, predictably, are very high indeed, an estimated 10–20 percent higher than the same items in the United States.

An important element in this high cost of living is the import duty. Since there are no taxes on Cayman, the government expenses are paid almost exclusively from import duties; when almost everything is imported, this has the same effect as a sales tax, the most repressive form of taxation for the low-income consumer. And naturally, the costs of running the government have risen in direct proportion to the "economic development" of the territory. Airport, paved roads, mosquito control, schools, vastly increased police "protection," improved harbor facilities, a government hospital, a new mansion for the administrator — the list is long, but the islands were, after all, very "backward" prior to the 1960's, and the demands of the visitors are commensurate with *their* accustomed standard of living.

The occupational shift to wage labor has also affected the availability of low-cost protein in the diets of Caymanians. Fish has traditionally pro-vided an ample supply of protein, but fish are no longer so easy to come by. Every family either owns or has access to a dugout, catboat, or small outboard skiff, and fishing from these craft is a favorite off-hours occu-pation for almost all men. In "days gone by," as the islanders say, the turtling schooners would bring home not only enormous catches of the giant green turtle, the favorite food of most Caymanians; each man would bring back a large supply of salt fish caught with hook and line during lulls in the turtling. The locally caught fresh fish were never more than an occasional supplement to these staple supplies of preserved fish. Today, not only are the turtles and salt fish gone, but also the tourist hotels are paying good stiff prices for the fresh fish caught in small boats; the local waters are already nearly fished out.

In addition, the visitors have introduced a great new sport to the islands: skin diving and spear-fishing. The shallow-water Langouste, or "lobster," always an easily caught addition to any Caymanian dinner, has all but disappeared under the onslaught of this diversion. Similarly, the large conches, edible shellfish which were so plentiful in former days that every front yard was decorated with rows of the colorful remains of past meals, have been snatched up by eager tourists, who disdain to eat the meat but carry the shells home with them. Party boats for sportfishers have reduced the supply of wahoo, or "queen fish," as well as the barracuda. In short, virtually all the cost-free protein that Caymanians still regard as a natural part of their diet has disappeared, in the space of just ten years. A can of Franco-American spaghetti or a tiny jar of cocktail sausages frequently replaces the turtle steak or lobster on the typical island dinner table.

Tourist-board and tax-haven enthusiasts are fond of quoting figures showing that the Cayman Islands have the highest standard of living in the Caribbean, and indeed Caymanians themselves are still somewhat dazzled by the unheard-of amounts of cash they can bring home, but it never seems to go as far as it should, and in terms of the typical diet of most households they have suffered a great loss.

The Homeland: Sea

Fished-out waters can recover, in time, if the underlying food chain is not disrupted, but Grand Cayman's magnificent coral reef is dying. Pollution from the increasing number of cargo vessels and cruise ships is mostly confined to the west side of the island, where only the white sand beaches are affected; but other kinds of pollution are literally muddying the waters of the great North Sound and spilling out into the long reef running along the north coast. Several land developers have bought up cheap swamp land in the interior, along the shores of the Sound, and are busily dredging the swamps to produce dry land (albeit still mosquito-infested) for U.S.-style tract homes. The immense quantities of suspended silt that this activity produces wash in and out of the Sound with every tide, directly over the living coral, and the results are disastrous. To make matters worse, an "ecologically minded" U.S. firm has undertaken to save the threatened green turtle by establishing an extensive turtle farm on the Sound.[3] Daily pumping of the huge tanks has so fouled the waters surrounding the farm that turtle grass is dying off and the farm must buy Purina Rabbit Chow to feed the turtles. The effects on the coral are similar to those produced by the dredging.

The East End reef appears, so far, to be safe, and East Enders, generally regarded as the "backward" part of the population, still bring in good catches of lobster, snapper, and jack, blowing a conch shell horn to announce to their neighbors that fresh fish is available. But these days a tourist is likely to beat them to it, and the lobster will most likely be sold for a beach cookout rather than given (with reciprocity assumed) to an island dinner table.

The Homeland: Shore

Caymanians are rather suddenly losing their beloved home waters, having already lost their former turtling haunts among the banks and cays of

---

[3]   The turtle meat thus produced has proved to be so expensive that it is sold exclusively to posh restaurants.

the Honduran and Nicaraguan coasts; they are also losing their very islands. Starting in the mid-sixties there has been a tremendous real estate boom on the islands, particularly Grand Cayman. Caymanians had never considered their land to be particularly valuable; island custom decreed that if any family member needed a place to live or a lot to build on he or she could simply apply to the nearest relative. There was no immediate concern about selling off plots of land, or even houses, to the eager buyers so "free" with their money. Not surprisingly, many property owners were unconscionably fleeced, especially those with supposedly worthless beach land. As more and more land went into the hands of developers and speculators and the prices offered began to rise, families experienced two kinds of trouble. In the first place, they began for the first time to be crowded. If a man, for instance, decided to sell his house and lot to a developer for an amount of money he had never in his life contemplated before, he would quite naturally tell his sister, or mother, or uncle that he and his family would be living with them until he built a new house with a part of the money. House building goes on regularly in the islands and normally is a project of several years' duration, involving family labor sandwiched between other occupations. Wage labor is not so flexible in regard to time off as locally based enterprise, however, and also building materials were suddenly in very short supply, with first choice going to the big hotels and office buildings. Furthermore, finding a lot to build on once he had sold his own turned out to be more expensive than he had thought, since others were cashing in on the same kind of deal. Renting a house was out of the question, considering the prices U.S. visitors were willing to pay. The welcomes afforded to visiting relatives began to wear out.

In addition, the sister, or mother, or uncle so solicited for a temporary lodging might well feel that the man who sold his land to outsiders was acting unfairly to begin with. Family land, by tradition, belongs in Cayman to "all the children," rarely if ever to one person alone, man or woman. If you build a house on family land, the house belongs to the builder and his or her children, but it is still family land, and a sale is, or should be, a matter for general family agreement. Deeds, titles, and surveys play no part in this system of land tenure; everyone in the community knows the boundary markers ("the north end of the rock face to the middle of the swamp"), and in fact the genealogy of every quarter-acre ("This little piece belongs to me and my cousin who lives in Brooklyn now because my mother and her mother were the only children of old John Bush. Her daughter and grandchildren might be coming back here one day; we'd put up a pretty little house right on this spot . . ."). Individual private property in land, and especially the idea of land as a profit-making asset, had died out of this culture even before the end of slavery; there were enough provision grounds for anyone who wanted to grow a few yams and plantains; everyone, after all, had multiple claims to family land.

Until the land boom in the sixties, the fact that the British and Americans had different ideas about land was of no practical interest to anyone. It is easy to understand how the increasing sale value of land of all sorts could lead to disputes, the basic point of which was the difference between the legal (British) system and the actual (customary) system. The new law passed in 1960 calling for registration of land transactions acted to legitimize a large number of transactions in which land of questionable "ownership" passed into the hands of speculators, mainly foreigners but also some Caymanians. Intrafamily disputes over land became widespread and bitter and continued throughout the decade to create major rifts in families, both extended and nuclear. Speculators resold land at profits of as much as 500 or 600 percent.[4] In the process, of course, more and more land passed out of even potential agricultural use.

Toward the end of the decade the furious pace of speculation had calmed somewhat, and Government, in the person of the British Administrator, moved to set up machinery for regulating actual development, accomplishing the accurate surveying and registration of titles, and ensuring "that the Crown's rights in land are not ignored or abused" ("Speech from the Throne" of Administrator A.C.E. Long, February 1969). By this time, however, there had developed a new phenomenon in the islands: a political faction, openly and indignantly opposed to any move by the Crown to limit the freedom of real estate operators in their often underhanded methods of acquiring some kind of title to land. This same faction had been outspoken against the Statistics Law, arguing that the interests of tax-haven users were threatened by any investigation of economic matters in the territory. On both issues these men and women represented themselves publicly as standing up for the rights of the "little man" as against the increasing encroachments of an oppressive government run by the hated "limeys." Crown land was a sensitive issue, since according to the interpretation of the British all "unclaimed" land reverted to the Crown, and there is more than a little evidence to indicate that the government had in mind precisely the takeover of a huge amount of interior swamp land for which no registered title existed, but which had always "belonged" to a large number of Caymanians who lived on the shore but farmed in the interior.[5]

A public demonstration by these protesters was eventually organized

---

[4]   In 1970 beach frontage in West Bay, Grand Cayman, was reportedly selling for $1,000 per *foot*.

[5]   When I visited the Regional Planning Officer in his office in 1971, I commented on a large map of the island that had recently been removed from the wall. The whole interior portion of the island was colored a lovely green and labeled "CROWN PARK LAND." The Planning Officer refused to answer any questions about it, saying simply that he was not using that "projection" any longer.

against the government's new set of "Development Planning" regulations; for the first time the much-touted "political stability" of the islands seemed to be a trifle threatened. The Crown reacted promptly: within a few days a naval warship was lying at anchor off Georgetown — perhaps a rather extreme response to an orderly march of at most 500 people to the government offices. The issues and events surrounding this dispute are too complex for any complete analysis here; the main point is that feelings on the subject of land were more volatile than on any subject in the island's history. Anti-British and anti-foreign sentiment was extreme, although confused because in the end the basic problem remained: land was steadily and inexorably passing into the hands of foreigners, often using Caymanian agents. The Crown, however, suffered a major defeat in its attempts to take over a large bloc of land. Perhaps the most influential leader to emerge from this, as well as from a similar protest a year later, was a Caymanian real estate operator with U.S. citizenship, who argued forcefully in public meetings that no regulations should be passed that would make foreign investors stay away.

The Homeland: Fresh Water

Not only are Caymanians fast losing their sea resources and their land, but they are in grave danger of losing their fresh water as well. Grand Cayman is a flat, low-lying island with no streams or rivers and relatively sparse rainfall. Traditionally, fresh water for human and animal consumption has been secured by householders from roof catchments that retain water during the rainy season. Each house has its cistern dug into the ground where the accumulated rainwater is stored, and even in the driest of dry seasons there was never, until recently, any problem. In addition, many households dug wells to tap the ground water, mostly for purposes of watering cattle, or in some cases to supplement the catchments. Water requirements were not great for the majority of the islanders; there were no flush toilets, showers, or washing machines except in the homes of the few more affluent merchants.

The decade of the sixties saw a major change in this situation. Hotels, condominia, and vacation homes all used immense quantities of fresh water, which they took from wells, scorning the "primitive" arrangement that appeared highly unsanitary: who wants to drink water collected from the roof? Furthermore, a large number of Caymanians, suddenly in possession of unexpected cash incomes, quickly installed flush toilets and showers themselves, and correspondingly dug new wells.

Many of these new conveniences now stand unused and unusable. In many areas of the island the water table has been reduced to levels that allow the inflow of swamp water and sea water, so that the newly dug wells produce an outflow that looks and smells like sewage. Rainfall hasn't been as heavy in recent years either, and some Caymanians attribute the passing-by of the annual squalls to the felling of so many large trees on the island. Whether this bit of folk wisdom has any truth or not (and it seems not entirely impossible), the cisterns have been running dry long before the end of the dry season, and householders must "borrow" water from those who still have it, or as a last resort buy it, as the Americans do. Pasturage for the cows has withered in the drought, and their owners sometimes "accidentally" leave gates open so the animals can look for water and forage along the roads, with the result that half-crazed cows have become a hazard to pedestrians in the dry season.

This section was intended to present an overview of the ecologic, economic, social, and cultural changes that have taken place in the Caymans in the few short years since their discovery as a base for the international tax-haven business. The shift in occupational patterns for men has occurred over a longer period than this and represents the long-delayed demise of a way of life organized around the values and economic relations of the buccaneers of the New World. The acceleration of the process under the aegis of U.S. shipping interests, however, has been very recent. The culminating force that made firm the wage-labor pattern was the construction boom with its exhilarating, albeit necessarily temporary, overemployment.

A kind of dependency has been fostered on these tiny islands that is different in kind from other situations of neocolonialism today. Caymanians now find themselves transformed into a service community: part working-class residential community — almost a company town considering the control that a single shipping company wields over the employment chances of the men; part luxury accommodations for the patrons and high-salaried employees of one of the world's strangest "industries"; and part extension of the far-flung North American "vacation home" complex, complete with tract houses that look for all the world like an arm of Miami's urban sprawl. A tropical paradise indeed.

THE VIEW FROM ABOVE: TAX HAVENS AND THE MODERN CAPITALIST STATE

We have seen some of the "benefits" Caymanians experience in their entrance into the modern world. The benefits on the other side of the ledger are less clear, for the identities and modes of operation of tax-haven users are by their nature shrouded in secrecy. What, in fact, is a tax haven? The simplest answer is that it is any principality offering a better tax "deal" than one's own country. In Grand Cayman, for example, there are just *no* taxes — no property tax, no income tax, no estate tax, no capital gains or business tax, no sales tax, no death duties, and no inheritance or gift taxes. There is a nominal head tax, £1 per year, for all Caymanian males (not visitors) between ages eighteen and sixty.

The use of tax havens by commercial companies dates back a long time. Switzerland is perhaps the most well-known example, although it has existed primarily as a haven for capital rather for taxes in the usual sense. Going back to the Middle Ages we find that the Hanseatic traders frequently were accorded favorable tax treatment in various places, presumably to encourage their business. The City of London, for example, exempted members of the Hanseatic League resident in London from all taxes. Until recently the Vatican operated as a classic tax haven (Doggart and Voûte 1971:1). The big boom in the use of tax havens, however, has come in the period following World War II, when Switzerland, the classic depository for secret accounts, was eclipsed by a host of newcomers, from the Bahamas to the New Hebrides. The latest addition, Minerva, the world's first underwater tax haven, is a submerged coral reef between Tonga and Fiji, which an American syndicate calling itself the Ocean Life Research Foundation has undertaken to dredge, creating a new island of 400 acres and no taxes (Doggart 1972:539).

The rapid growth of interest and activity around tax havens corresponds to a growth of taxation in the major capitalist countries of the world. Business spokesmen explain the phenomenon in terms of the normal self-protection of private enterprise. As one commentator said:

Tax havens meet a basic need. They exist to enable individuals to increase or dispose of wealth they have won as they see fit and not at the whim of their rulers. Thus, tax havens exist not only as a result of world-wide increases in taxation; they are also refuges from political intervention with private property. . . . Statistics prove that excessive taxes are hampering capital growth. . . . It is not surprising that many law-abiding citizens have begun to think of tax avoidance as less than sinful (Doggart and Voûte 1971:1–3).

If we were to accept this type of analysis, we would say that tax havens have become so phenomenally popular because of the unreasonable demands of state spending on private capital; that the only way to avoid a disastrous recession (the "inevitable" outcome of "hampered capital growth") is for private business to systematically avoid paying the taxes that the state demands. This line of reasoning is implicit in the large literature on tax havens in the business journals.

However, the evidence, at least in the case of the United States, seems to indicate another explanation for the rise of tax-haven activity.[6] In this

---

[6]   This discussion will be limited to the United States, not only because this is the most developed capitalist country in the world but also because the use of tax havens in general and Grand Cayman in particular is largely, if not predominantly, by U.S. companies and individuals.

country, government spending has certainly tended to rise dramatically as a proportion of total spending in the whole period since the Great Depression. Far from constituting a threat to the system, however, such increased spending can be seen to be integrally related to the process of consolidation and growth of the giant corporations. As James O'Connor outlines in his *The fiscal crisis of the state* (1973), the growing interdependency of capitalist production processes has made the growth of state spending an economical, even a necessary, form of providing the social capital needed for continuing expansion in the monopoly sector. Infrastructural needs for this increasingly interdependent production — transportation, communication, research and development, education, etc. — as well as social consumption needs — insurance for workers against sickness, old age, and economic insecurity, public housing, recreational facilities, etc. — are indirect costs of production in modern capitalism, and they are not paid for by private capital but are socialized, or paid for by the state. As O'Connor says:

Unquestionably, monopoly sector growth depends on the continuous expansion of social investment and social consumption projects that in part or in whole indirectly increase productivity from the standpoint of monopoly capital. In short, monopoly capital socializes more and more costs of production (1973:24).

Investment by the state in various forms of social capital has the clear advantage, from the point of view of capital, of providing essential goods and services on a permanent basis at a stable, minimal cost. Further, the projects are usually far too costly on a short-run basis for an individual company to finance. Finally, they need not meet the test of the market: they may be, and often are, wasteful and inefficient. A 1967 study by the Congressional Subcommittee on Economic Progress estimated that the U.S. economy would require an annual investment of $50 billion in physical social capital between 1966 and 1975 (U.S. Congress 1968). As O'Connor notes (1973:37), "If investment in 'human capital' was added to investment in physical capital, and if the volume of social capital in relation to total capital were calculated, social investment no doubt would prove to be considerably greater than private investment."

If, as O'Connor argues, capital investment for the growth of monopoly production is coming to be largely provided by the fiscal resources of the government, who foots the bill? What is the structure of the tax base that provides the revenue for this enormous and expanding outlay? Several recent studies (Eisenstein 1961; Gurley 1967; Hellerstein 1963; Lundberg 1968; O'Connor 1973; Paul 1954; Pechman and Okner 1972; Stern 1964) have shown the multitude of ways in which the higher-income members of society avoid paying anything approaching their share of the tax dollar, and how the ideology of "ability to pay" as the basis of tax legislation is no more than a pious phrase in the mouths of politicians. Far from acting as a "redistributive system," as one economist has claimed (Buchanan 1960:18–19), these studies show that tax policies and government spending patterns act, in the aggregate, to take from the poor and middle-income population and give to the rich. Lundberg estimates that $27.1 billion per year in scheduled taxes are evaded by the wealthy by means of depletion and depreciation allowances, expense-account deductions, capital-gains deductions, estate-tax evasions, tax-free bonds, undistributed corporate profit, etc. — all perfectly legal according to existing tax law (1968:459–461).

O'Connor shows that the individual income tax, widely believed to represent a "progressive" tax form, i.e., one that is based on the "ability to pay" and whose scheduled rates clearly indicate a much higher percentage taken from wealthier individuals, actually has "encroached more and more on wage income since it was first introduced." According to O'Connor:

The national state systematically reduced personal exemptions and credits for dependents from $4000 (for a family of four) in 1913–16 to $2400 in 1970. In 1913–16, a single person was granted an exemption of $3000; in 1970, only $600. And, until 1943, labor income was taxed at a rate 10 percent lower than profit income because of the absence of comparable treatment of personal expenditures for "business purposes" such as personal depreciation allowances, education expenditures, and so forth. Further, in terms of actual purchasing power, real exemptions have fallen by even greater amounts. Finally, popular consciousness of the tax burden has been reduced by tax withholding — the most subtle form of tax exploitation (1973:210).

O'Connor estimates that the average effective rate of taxation on the highest incomes is no more than 25 percent, despite the much higher schedules already noted. In regard to estate taxes, which show scheduled taxes as high as 77 percent on estates of $10 million or more, the actual average rate is little more than 10 percent (1973:207).

Summing up, O'Connor states:

The tax system performs two major functions. First, it permits monopoly capital to expand its income and wealth, and thus plays an important role in reinforcing it as the dominant class. Even when these outlays nominally are covered by taxes on profits, increased state outlays increase profits and fall on the real wages because corporate taxes are shifted to consumers in the form of higher prices. Second, to meet the costs of social capital and social expenses, the system appropriates capital from small business and the working class. Thus by limiting their ability to accumulate liquid savings, the tax system forces workers to remain workers — and in the long run it compels the working class to be more and more dependent on capital and ultimately on the state (1973:210–211).

Tax havens, then, can be seen, indeed, to "meet a basic need." As monopoly capital tightens its hold on the fiscal policies of the state, more of the social costs of production are met through direct and indirect assessment of the assets of small business and workers. However, in order to prevent a tax "revolt" by these groups, the system is bolstered by the ideology and the appearance of a progressive policy based on ability to pay, which would in theory act as a redistributive mechanism in sharing the wealth. Thus the graduated income tax, hailed as a progressive reform, has from the beginning been systematically evaded by the wealthiest individuals, while capital gains, estate, and profits taxes are either passed on to consumers as price increases or evaded, usually both. Tax evasion is a "basic need" for capital in this sense: consolidation and perpetuation of large accumulations of capital are essential to the continued trend toward monopoly control of the economy, as well as for the individual success of large businesses and business people.

As public financing of capital investment grows, so also does the ingenuity of the wealthy (who of course command the services of the best lawyers, accountants, etc., not to mention the government executives and legislators themselves) in devising means to avoid paying their share of the bill. The political necessity for a publicly proclaimed "progressive" tax structure makes this an increasingly complex task. Furthermore, as the involvement of U.S.-based multinational corporations (MNC's) in the Third World increases, new means have been sought to facilitate the flow of capital that accumulates at fantastic rates of profit in neocolonial countries back into more and more foreign investments, without its becoming subject to taxation at home. From time to time we hear political figures announcing their intentions to close the "loopholes" in the tax system (implying that the system itself is sound, with minor flaws), but somehow the truly enormous swindles like the oil-depletion allowance and other forms of depreciation never do get corrected. The growth of tax-haven activity in the sixties and the seventies is part of the trend, not toward closing the loopholes but toward making the operations of the large corporations virtually invisible.

SECRECY: THE FIRST COMMANDMENT

Any attempt to determine the actual users of tax havens runs immediately up against rule number one: the prime requisite for a reliable tax haven is the guarantee of total secrecy as to the identities of the real (as opposed to the local, token) directors, investors, and trustors. This principle was tested in 1967 when a Congressional committee investigating the affairs of the late Rep. Adam Clayton Powell (D.-N.Y.) ordered the New York branch of Barclay's Bank to produce Powell's Bahamian records. When Barclay's, true to tax-haven principles, refused, an official of the bank reported that "there was a rush of deposits to our New York office for transfer to the Bahamas" (Ferris 1968:103).

Secrecy, of course, is one traditional feature of tax havens; Switzerland has laws dating back to the Nazi era that protect users of its numbered-account system from investigation by the home governments of depositors. However, the Swiss system has serious drawbacks for modern tax evaders, which account for the relative popularity of the Bahamas and other newcomers. Swiss bank secrecy does not apply if the depositor is being investigated for tax fraud. In December 1970, the Swiss Confederation Supreme Court made a significant decision holding that under the provisions of the U.S.-Swiss tax treaty, secrecy would not be honored in tax-fraud cases; these same provisions are present in the treaties between Switzerland and other countries. Although the decision clearly differentiates between "simple" tax evasion and "aggravated tax fraud," the advantages of using a haven with no tax treaties of any sort are significant enough to make them attractive to a growing number of users. Charles Adams of the Euro-Dutch Trust Company in Grand Cayman, writing in the journal *The. Banker*, defends the use of tax havens as "ethical," saying:

It is a well-recognized principle of tax ethics and law that every citizen has a right to rearrange his affairs so as to pay the lowest tax, because taxes are forced exactions by the police power and are not voluntary contributions based upon equity and fair play (1972:533).

Adams evidently includes tax fraud among the recognized rights of every citizen, since he also advises his readers to move their banking activities from Swiss accounts, where tax-fraud investigations could pierce bank secrecy, to "tax havens where there are no tax treaties providing for exchange of information and assistance," such as Grand Cayman (1972:531).

The Cayman Islands have not only no taxes but no tax treaties. The secrecy guaranteed by this situation is further bolstered by extreme precautions that make the line between "simple" tax evasion and aggravated tax fraud a matter of no consequence whatever. The Cayman Islands Banks and Trust Companies Regulation Law (1966) S. 10 states that "no person shall disclose any information relating to the affairs of a licensee or any customer of a licensee,"[7] under penalty of fines and imprisonment. That this law is taken very seriously in Cayman is made evident by an interesting series of events surrounding the taking of the 1970 census in the islands. When the census was taken, the British Administrator pushed through a "Statistics Law" that specified what items of economic data could and could not be gathered; as he pointed out, the wording of the secrecy law was so vague and all-inclusive as to make a census almost impossible. After a protracted struggle, and after

---

[7]   A licensee is any person holding a license to do business.

the census had actually been taken, the Statistics Law was withdrawn at the insistence of the same faction of legislators who later protested the land regulations. These men and women spoke vociferously about the damage the Statistics Law could do to the anonymity and privacy of the offshore companies, at the same time playing on the fact that the Caymanian people are extremely suspicious of the British and fearful that the Crown plans to impose some form of taxation on *them*. When I was doing research in the islands in 1970–1971, I was uniformly told that no information could legally be given out or collected by anyone (including myself) as to the earnings, occupations, or general economic position of any individual or group or the island as a whole. The parts of the census return dealing with these matters are confidential information, and the entire Cost of Living Survey conducted prior to the withdrawal of the law is not to be published or even examined by anyone in or out of the islands. In addition, no breakdown of the census, aside from the male-female and "racial" category data has been released. The Government economic adviser was of the opinion there would be an "indefinite delay" in releasing them.

In view of the overall role of the Crown's Administrator in defending the rights of tax-haven users, it is ironic that his carefully worded "Statistics Law" should have been attacked on these grounds, and by "representatives" of the Caymanian people. We have already reviewed the role of this group of anti-British politicians in the land disputes; here we find them *extending* the principle of secrecy of information to cover all aspects of economic life, including land speculation and price inflation.

THE EMIGRANTS

One group of tax-haven users are the relatively small-time private individuals who, in the interests of protecting their amassed wealth, actually emigrate to the haven of their choice, usually upon retirement, to enjoy the benefits and pass on the inheritance without interference from the tax collector. For these people, the havens of the Caymanian variety are *not* the best deal, although many Americans who have taken Caymanian citizenship were most likely motivated by some such consideration. The primary drawback for the emigrant from the United States is the requirement that to legally avoid taxes he or she must not only change residence but renounce citizenship and then wait ten years. In practice, of course, most emigrants don't do this; they simply ignore the IRS once they have removed their assets. However, this step requires that they effectively cut off business ties, and for the more affluent retirees this is clearly not advisable.

Furthermore, renouncing citizenship and taking up permanent residence in Cayman or other tax havens of the "tropical paradise" variety has proved to be a mixed blessing for many. The simple life in Cayman, especially for expatriates who want a few amenities like hot running water, U.S. foods, and an active nightlife, has the disadvantage of a high and rapidly rising cost of living, a structural feature of a country that has tourism and tax-haven business as its principal industries, as we have seen.

Furthermore, as Doggart and Voûte point out, non-tax havens *with* tax treaties (Mexico, for example) work better for the emigrant:

Apart from the U.S. and U.K. there are few countries which effectively tax the external investment income of a resident of foreign origin. In addition, most non-tax havens will have a network of tax treaties which allow pensions, annuities and dividends to be received gross or subject to a reduced rate of withholding tax, whereas in a typical tax haven such income from abroad will have suffered the full rate of withholding or income tax in the source country (1971:9).

For the retiree living on annuities and dividends, then, the absence of tax treaties is a disadvantage, in contrast to the tax evader who is actively engaged in making his money grow. As one commentator remarks of the tax-haven business generally: "It's a market for the rich, run by banks, trading in large quantities on behalf of clients who, whatever they are, aren't small men" (Ferris 1968:101).

PROTECTING ACCUMULATED CAPITAL: THE FOREIGN TRUST

As outlined above, one of the "basic needs" of the monopoly sector is to negate the apparent intent of estate, gift, and death duties in order to retain intact large accumulations of capital in the control of the 1 percent of the U.S. population that owns more than 70 percent of the nation's productive property. Clearly, were the high estate taxes on the books really collected, large family fortunes would not remain intact over the generations, but there are a variety of means by which these taxes can be avoided. The money can be left to a foundation, as was done with the Ford fortune, then invested by the foundation back into the company, when then continues to be controlled by the family; it may be given in several installments to family members prior to the death of the donor, in which case the much lower gift tax applies; or it may be given in trust to family members, the terms so arranged that the principal remains intact and working for the company for up to one hundred years. Over-depreciated or underassessed real estate or mineral rights make good gifts, since the owner alone knows the true value.

Family trusts are one of the specialties of tax havens, and their uses are by no means limited to the avoidance of estate taxes. The principle behind foreign trusts is simple: the trustors legally divest themselves of their assets and put them, on paper, in the hands of a trustee who is a non-resident alien in every jurisdiction except that of the tax haven, where there are no taxes. The trustees, normally banks, "own" the assets absolutely, and have full discretion to manage, invest, and distribute assets, but such distribution is of course in practice limited to the beneficiaries of the trust, usually family members of the trustor. The total lack of legal rights to trust assets or any profits accruing from their investment makes the trustor and the beneficiaries nonliable for any tax until and unless the trustee decides to distribute them. This is an important point, for some countries tax trust assets that are accessible to owners whether or not they make use of them; modern tax-haven laws such as those of the Caymans make such taxation impossible.

The advantages of such trusts, which after all only protect one's assets until they are distributed, may not be immediately apparent to those of us who perforce pay our taxes as we go. If you can't *have* your money without paying tax, what's the point? But to have the full benefit of one's capital invested wherever in the world one wishes, with no taxes taken out at any time, is an enormous gain when one is dealing in hundreds of thousands of dollars. This is called "tax deferral," and as one expert notes, "as a rule of thumb, practitioners consider that if a tax is deferred for ten years, it is saved" (Adams 1972:531); the use of the capital tax-free for this period makes up for the tax that eventually comes due. However, there is more to it than that. If one is using a tax-haven trust there is no way the revenue collectors can determine how much profit is made, since at the situs of enterprise only the trustee's name appears, and at the tax-haven end strict secrecy is kept. There is thus no way of knowing how much income is totally concealed and never taxed at all, even at the time of distribution.

Cayman Islands Trust Law No. 6 (1967) is cited by experts as "a truly modern law of trusts which is most appropriate for the purpose of an international set-up," combining these crucial features: (1) "speed, ease and flexibility of creating, running and terminating": i.e., the rules are lax in regard to directors, meetings, accounting, and minimum assets from beginning to end; (2) "restrictions on perpetuity periods": i.e., trusts can be exempted from the English common law limitation of the duration of trusts to the lives of certain identifiable persons; and (3) "the possibility of divesting beneficiaries of any legal rights to the capital or income of the trust without in any way endangering their interests" (Spitz 1972:95–98). Furthermore, the Cayman Islands Tax Concession Laws Nos. 20 and 21 (1962) specify that "the Administrator in Council may give an undertaking to any 'exempted' company or trust that no law which is subsequently enacted in the Islands imposing any tax or duty to be levied on profits or income on capital assets, gains or appreciations, shall apply" for periods ranging from fifteen to fifty years in the future. Interestingly, this last provision specifically does *not* apply to any person resident in the Islands.

FOREIGN INVESTMENT: THE OFFSHORE COMPANY

Tax-haven trusts, then, act to insure that large holdings of capital will remain in the hands of a select few, and especially that they will continue to be available for easy flow into investment opportunities anywhere in the world, without possibility of regulation or taxation. Since World War II, U.S. capital has been moving with accelerated pace into Latin America, Southeast Asia, and other areas of the Third World in a variety of foreign investment schemes that have the net effect of increasing the dependency of these economies on the giant transnational corporations. In this period the advantages of tax havens have become more and more important to the process.

Another mechanism useful in the process is the offshore company. An offshore company is, simply, a paper company, or holding company, which is licensed to operate using a tax haven as its home office, but is restricted to operating its actual business outside the territory, or "offshore." These companies are in many ways similar to the foreign trusts: investors are protected with strict anonymity; their profits are held, tax-free, in the company for reinvestment quickly and easily; modern professional services of lawyers, accountants, and investment brokers are readily available; and of course the regulations governing such matters as listing of assets, accounting for sources of money, meetings of directors, etc., are permissive in the extreme. Relatively small investors, without the huge assets which make the establishment of separate trusts advantageous, can place their money with a holding company, which will manage their foreign portfolios, receive the income tax-free, and reinvest without the tax agencies of the home country being any the wiser. Paul Ferris, describing the operations of holding companies out of Luxembourg (a European tax haven), sums up the operations nicely:

The crux of the matter is that when a company is established in Luxembourg for the purpose of receiving income, it can take in the money from abroad, and pay it out again to whoever it likes, without seeing it shrunk by tax. The holding company may retain some of the money, but if it does, and eventually dissolves itself, it can walk off with the money, tax-free as far as Luxembourg is concerned. The income may have been taxed already in the country where it originated; and when it has passed through Luxembourg and is paid over to a citizen of any country, he should pay tax on it in the normal way. But in practice it can be highly advantageous to use a Luxembourg company to collect and distribute money. . . . Even if he must later pay tax, he will think it better to receive the full amount to begin with; and *if his conscience and the tax inspectors don't intervene, he may well be able to conceal the income, and so never pay tax at all* (Ferris 1968:96–97; emphasis added).

The big boom in offshore investment came in the second half of the sixties, with the development of the Eurodollar market providing an added stimulus. Predictably, in such a wide-open field, with secrecy and laxity of regulations built in, an unknown number of "sharp" operators tried their luck, promoting their funds with a "novelty and flamboyance" that shocked the more-established denizens of the financial world (Miller 1971:501–502). Profits were such that new companies proliferated overnight; Cayman became the locale for a large number. By 1971 more than 2,500 companies and 600 trusts had been formed in Cayman; the Bahamas had 12,000; Bermuda, long known for catering only to established banks and reputable dealers, had only 1,700.

Toward the end of 1970 the offshore-fund business suffered a severe scare: a number of large funds collapsed with spectacular losses to investors, and some commentators were of the opinion that the industry was dead. Others, however, see the bust as a positive step toward consolidation in the hands of established, responsible financial groups of a business not only highly lucrative but also crucial to the international development of big capital. Norman Miller, a high-level financial executive, had this to say just following the big collapse:

It would be wrong to suppose that the events of the last year in any way herald the demise of off-shore funds. What has happened has merely strengthened the hand of those established groups who have always kept to the legitimate stage, whose management has been proven, where investment management commands respect and who can be expected to conduct the international side of their business according to the same standards they follow on the domestic side which, by far, is their primary interest. . . . Off-shore funds meet a basic need. It would, therefore, be a pity if the abuses and folly perpetuated by some sharp operators during recent years should call the concept . . . so completely into disrepute that other promoters despaired of every running them with success and eventual profit. Fortunately, this is not the case so far . . . (1971:502).

In Western Europe, notably West Germany, where the "undesirable salesmanship" evidently was allowed much more freedom than in the United States and the United Kingdom, reaction to the bust has resulted in strict new rules. According to some observers,

Certain vested interests in the countries concerned have used the failure last year of some badly managed international funds to regain, through legislation which bears onerously on the foreigner, their former control of the savings and investment business (Miller 1971:505).

This mini-crash has apparently served, like certain other crises in capitalist economies, to strengthen the control over this aspect of international business by the most powerful agents of the large corporations. A certain amount of activity in tax havens by out-and-out con men is perforce tolerated, since real regulation would obviate the crucial functions that tax havens perform; too much of such activity, however, is seen as a threat. This is no small-time industry to be left open to the depredations of fly-by-night operators; estimated assets in the offshore business are projected to reach $20 billion by the end of the seventies (Doucet 1971:515).

BANKING: NATIONALISM AND OFFSHORE BANKS

Banks, too, can operate as offshore entities. The most recent trend in international banking in the Caribbean is a phenomenal growth in such enterprises in the Bahamas and Caymans, paralleling another shift in the non–tax havens of the area. Although the connection between these two modes of growth in banking is not explicitly stated, the fact that they have gone along side by side appears significant. In the non–tax haven areas of the "eighty continent," as international development experts sometimes refer to the Caribbean, the independence and Black Power movements, successful to the extent of achieving nominal independence, have somewhat altered the planning of international bankers. As described by Jean Doucet, chairman of the International Bank, the first offshore private bank to establish itself in the Cayman Islands, local branches of the big Commonwealth banks (Barclay's, Royal Bank of Canada, Bank of Nova Scotia, Bank of London and Montreal) have instituted a "dramatic change in foreign banking approach: a move from ownership to partnership."

While this policy is now promoted by governments of the larger countries such as Jamaica, Trinidad and Guyana, it was started by the banks themselves realizing that it was necessary and advantageous to move with, rather than against, the tide of nationalism and that the alternative to partnership was eventual withdrawal or nationalization (Doucet 1971:508).

The names of the branches are altered slightly (e.g., the Jamaican branch of Barclay's Bank, D.C.O., has become Barclay's Bank (Jamaica), Ltd.; or in the case of a U.S. bank, the Jamaican branch of Citizens & Southern Bank of Atlanta became Jamaica Citizens Bank), and 51 percent of the shares are "made available" to Jamaican nationals. Trinidad and Guyana, whose present governments were elected on specific platforms of nationalization of foreign interests, have themselves gone into the banking business. Here also the Commonwealth banks, which have "gone public" or "sold out to the Government," have simply converted their branches to a "partnership" with nationals in nominal control (Doucet 1971:509).

U.S. banks, now entering the Caribbean field in force, take a similar approach, establishing "correspondent" (as distinguished from "branch") banks throughout the area, in which they "share ownership and management with Caribbean nationals" in the interests of "efficiency and local stability" (Doucet 1971:511). Recruitment programs and management-training programs are instituted to complete the facade, and Doucet reports:

Investment participation and correspondent relationships are . . . growing in popularity and the latter is behind the decision of a number of U.S. banks such as Citizens & Southern Bank of Atlanta and First National City Bank of New York to establish an international division in Miami, the gateway to the Caribbean, to service their correspondent banks in the Caribbean (1971:511).

This "partnership" approach to banking is the same strategy adopted by many MNC's in the region, which counter nationalist demands for an end to foreign domination by appointing local nationals to boards of directors. This strategy has been exposed in the penetrating analysis of Jamaican economist George L. Beckford. Beckford points out that the vertical integration of the MNC guarantees that "the board of directors of the parent company makes all important decisions relating to each subsidiary company and the group of companies as a whole. The day-to-day running of each subsidiary is left to its own board of directors . . ." (Beckford 1972:139–140).

At the same time, multinational banks expand their Caribbean activities by moving into the tax havens as offshore banks. It is apparent that not only tax avoidance is at issue in this move, but again the "danger of political confiscation," or nationalization. As multinationals move into the tax-haven scene (Ferris 1968:101; Doucet 1971:515; Doggart and Voûte 1971:3), the very large pool of assets held and managed from these centers will grow.[8] Rapid transfer of assets into and out of Third World countries to take maximum advantage of changing political climates and to facilitate regional dispersal of manufacturing and resource exploitation is clearly a prime consideration.[9] As Doucet says:

As long as there are taxes and dangers of political confiscation of private properties, tax havens will continue to develop and the pool of money held outside the jurisdiction of high tax countries will continue to grow. Although no precise estimate of the size of the pool is available, some claim that it could amount to as much as 50 billion dollars (1971:515).

[8]   One French economist, noting that the principal tax havens are for the most part under the British flag or under powerful U.S. influence, is of the opinion that they are part of the mechanism whereby "*la Wall Street*" and "*la City*" are imposing on the world "*la hégémonie anglo-saxonne*" (Vernay 1968); a theory which, whatever its merits, fits in with the general tendency toward increasing tax-haven involvement of the multinationals.

[9]   See Mary K. Vaughan (this volume) for an excellent analysis of these developments in multinational planning.

CAPTIVE COMPANIES: INSURANCE AND PENSION FUNDS

Very large corporations can also use tax havens to set up their own "captive" companies for the purpose of selling themselves their own insurance, a fairly widespread practice that saves millions of dollars annually (Doggart 1972:543–544). In the same way they can set up their own companies to collect payments for pension funds for their employees, thus pocketing the profits without tax loss on the assets held. In addition to the tax benefits, such schemes can be initiated in tax havens without undue concern about the amount of assets held to cover claims, since the rules are extremely lax and impossible to enforce.

These same lax rules, of course, make possible a number of fraudulent insurance companies, set up virtually without assets, which then simply fold if claims wipe them out. Insurance regulators in the United States are helpless to stop such practices because of the secrecy laws and essentially are limited to answer inquiries about known professional con men.[10]

LAUNDERING MONEY

One last group of tax-haven users must be mentioned, a group that in the last two years, since the Bahamas tightened up regulations on moving U.S. dollars in and out, has switched allegiances to Grand Cayman. These are the money-launderers, who use the facilities of tax-havens to legitimize incomes that are acquired by wholly illegal means. These people are engaged in gambling, narcotics, and various kinds of organized crime and have need of a cover to explain where the money came from. Offshore companies are ideally constituted for this purpose; there is no way to detect the difference between the "legitimate" investor and the criminal, and the money paid out in "dividends" comes through the process clean — or at least as clean as any tax-haven money can be said to be.

The Bahamas have been for many years the principal locale for money-launderers, a natural outgrowth of the combined tax-haven and gambling specialties of the territory; the shift to the Caymans seems to be going ahead without a hitch, despite the strict rules forbidding gambling in the colony. The firm moralism of Caymanian legislators in uprightly refusing to allow any discussion on changing the anti-gambling laws appears rather pathetic in view of the multibillion dollar "industry" quietly, indeed almost invisibly, racking up the profits in ways that make simple gambling seem almost virtuous.

---

[10] Information provided by an official of the National Association of Insurance Commissioners who prefers to remain anonymous.

CONCLUSION

What lies ahead for the Cayman Islands? This is a question many Caymanians were asking when I visited in 1970–1971. The drastic changes in their way of life are viewed with mixed feelings by some of the older inhabitants, who speak nostalgically of "days gone by" when money was only rarely used by most families, when times were "hard" but food was plentiful, and both the sea and the land were their own territories. They like their high wages, and the commodities that are suddenly accessible, the new schools (overcrowded and inadequate though they still are), the paved roads, the electricity. They even like the visitors — the U.S. ones, if not the British — who are fulsome in their praises of the island's charm and also free with their money. But can it last? Caymanians don't know, and they are becoming aware that they have little if any control over what will happen to their land, their jobs, their entire way of life. The flurries of political activity around the land regulations ended inconclusively. Most Caymanians are confused as to the real issues involved, although they did gain a sense of their potential power when they acted together.

In fact, the dependency of the islands' economy on foreign industry is almost complete. The overemployment due to the construction boom is finite; even if Cayman continues to be the favored tax haven in the Caribbean there is a limit to the number of banks, office buildings, and hotels the islands can house. When the jobs in construction run out, many more men will be looking for their old seafaring jobs once more, and they'll no longer simply be able to invest some of their cash savings in building their own boats and set off for the fishing banks in search of shark and turtle.

Only a few older men still have the skills to build large boats, and in any case the island supply of hardwood, once a major resource, is substantially exhausted; imported lumber is inferior and expensive. Furthermore, turtling on the Honduran and Nicaraguan banks is no longer feasible, since these countries have taken to patrolling their announced 200-mile limit with armed aircraft and gunboats, impounding vessels that violate their waters. Moreover, the waters of the Western Caribbean outside these banks have been effectively preempted by a group of shrimp fishers out of the United States. Having fished out the shrimp in the Gulf of Mexico, these highly capitalized fishermen with their $500,000 boats have been demolishing the supply of langouste on all the outlying banks for the last several years, ironically using the harbor at Grand Cayman as their base of operations. Although these boats occasionally take on Caymanian seamen as deck hands, the whole operation is also finite; already in 1971 they were complaining that the banks seemed about depleted and they were forced to take undersized lobsters and females with roe in order to make ends meet. Caymanian fishermen, with their tradition of fishing in wooden-hulled schooners, can hardly hope to compete with the sophisticated equipment of these big operators. So they will apply to the National Bulk agent in Georgetown, offer him the usual "gifts," and hope.

The job market in the shipping industry is no less subject to foreign control, however, and the factors that will make it more or less secure are outside their realm of knowledge, let alone influence. Bulk shipping (mostly oil) has made fabulous fortunes for a few men — Niarchos, Onassis, and Ludwig are the top three — but the market is a volatile one (Whealdon 1970:47). The flag-of-convenience tactic — another form of tax-haven, incidentally — which enables Mr. Ludwig to ignore environmental, safety, and union regulations on his ships as well as evade taxes, has been under attack in this country from shipbuilders, maritime unions, and others. Should current legislative attempts to limit the practice succeed, much of the cut-rate labor he has been hiring in Cayman might have to be replaced by union labor from the United States. Thus, even the position of Cayman as a company town for National Bulk Carriers is in question.

Dependence on tourism as a basis for the island economy is not only inadequate, even at today's phenomenal rate of expansion; it is also problematic. By its nature, the tourist industry is self-defeating, for as soon as Cayman becomes highly developed it loses a large part of its charm for the seeker after "unspoiled" playgrounds. More importantly, the growth of tourism in this swampy, mosquito-infested piece of real estate is clearly dependent on the boom in the tax-haven business; if that goes, a large proportion of the visitors will go with it.

The tax-haven business itself is of course totally outside the power of the islanders to control. Forces in the international financial world dictate the rise and fall of tax havens, and no amount of effort on the part of the inhabitants can change that. They could drive the business away should they become infected with the "social unrest" characteristic of the rest of the Caribbean, but they can hardly force it to stay if tax laws in a variety of different metropolises should change or if the tax strategies of the multinationals should take a new twist.

Finally, the older pattern of subsistence agriculture combined with local fishing, even were it adequate to support the population without the turtling or wage-labor seafaring, may well be unavailable as a last resort for the population. The ecological changes in the sea and ground water may have gone so far as to be irreversible; in addition, the social and cultural patterns that are an integral part of these occupational specialties have been altered so totally that it is doubtful whether further changes could make them operable again. The younger generation on Cayman not only has no interest in farming, it has no skills for this occupation, and "modern" farming techniques are completely inapplicable to the broken terrain and the scanty rainfall of the territory.

What lies ahead for the Caymanians? Continued dependency, certainly, for a time at least. In the long run it seems that any hope for an end to this dependency must rest with the ability of Caymanians to join forces with other Caribbean nations in breaking the yoke of neocolonialism — in all its variations — which is keeping the whole region firmly in the "underdeveloped" category.

REFERENCES

ADAMS, CHARLES
   1972   Secret account or foreign trust? *The Banker* 122:529–533.
BECKFORD, GEORGE L.
   1972   *Persistent poverty: underdevelopment in plantation economies of the third world.* New York: Oxford University Press.
BUCHANAN, JAMES
   1960   *Fiscal theory and political economy.* Chapel Hill: University of North Carolina Press.
DOGGART, TONY
   1972   *Tax havens — the landscape changes. The Banker* 122:537–545.
DOGGART, TONY, CAROLINE VOÛTE
   1971   *Tax havens and offshore funds.* Revised edition. London: Economic Intelligence Unit, Ltd.
DOUCET, JEAN
   1971   The growth and challenge of Caribbean off-shore banking. *The Banker* 121:507–515.
EISENSTEIN, LOUIS
   1961   *The ideology of taxation.* New York: Ronald Press.
FERRIS, PAUL
   1968   *Men and money: financial Europe today.* London: Hutchinson.
GRUNDY, MILTON
   1972   *Grundy's tax havens.* London: Sweet & Maxwell.
GURLEY, JOHN G.
   1967   Federal tax policy. *National Tax Journal* 20(3).
HELLERSTEIN, JEROME R.
   1963   *Taxes, loopholes and morals.* New York: McGraw-Hill.
HER MAJESTY'S STATIONERY OFFICE
   1956   *Cayman Islands: report for the years 1953–1954.* London: Her Majesty's Stationery Office.
   1967   *Cayman Islands: report for the years 1961 to 1965.* London: Her Majesty's Stationery Office.
LUNDBERG, FERDINAND
   1968   *The rich and the super-rich.* New York: Bantam.
MILLER, NORMAN
   1971   Off-shore investment centres. *The Banker* 121:501–505.
O'CONNOR, JAMES
   1973   *The fiscal crisis of the state.* New York: St. Martin's Press.
PAUL, RANDOLPH E.
   1954   *Taxation in the United States.* Boston: Little, Brown.

PECHMAN, JOSEPH, BENJAMIN OKNER
 1972   *Individual income tax erosion by income classes.* Washington: Brookings Institute.
SPITZ, BARRY
 1972   *International tax planning.* London: Butterworth's.
STERN, PHILIP M.
 1964   *The great treasury raid.* New York: Random House.
U.S. CONGRESS
 1968   *Financing municipal facilities.* Washington: U.S. Government Printing Office.
VERNAY, G.
 1968   *Les paradis fiscaux.* Paris: Editions du Seuil.
WHEALDON, JOSEPH A.
 1970   *Bulk, oil and ore shipping: present and future developments in world markets.* Unpublished M.A. thesis, School of Business Administration, University of California, Berkeley.
WILLIAMS, NEVILLE
 1970   *A history of the Cayman Islands.* Portsmouth, England: Eyre & Spottiswoode.

Notes on a Corporate "Potlatch": The Lumber Industry in Samoa

PAUL SHANKMAN

In anthropological parlance, the potlatch is usually identified with an aboriginal form of feasting and conspicuous giving found among Indian groups of the American Northwest. But during the 1950's and 1960's — the era of "development" — the term *potlatch* took on a somewhat different meaning. Through massive aid and technical assistance programs, underdeveloped countries were to partake in a "global potlatch" that would see them "take off" as a result of the generosity of developed countries. Of course, this use of the term *potlatch* was sheer hyperbole since the global potlatch involved a system of international trade that bore little resemblance to aboriginal forms of exchange and redistribution. For the underdeveloped countries, the global potlatch seemed a program more relevant to the political and economic concerns of Western nations than an altruistic plan suited to the needs of underdeveloped areas. This was especially the case with Western encouragement of private foreign investment in underdeveloped areas, sometimes making it difficult to discern the difference between developmental "take-off" and capitalist "rip-off." And, in spite of the promises of abundance and development implicit in the global potlatch, the rich nations grew richer in both relative and absolute terms.[1]

Research for this paper was made possibly by an NIMH Fellowship and Field Training Grant. My thanks to the several individuals who read earlier versions of the manuscript and rightly disavowed responsibility for it. The paper was originally written in 1971 with revisions in 1973 and 1975. Apologies are extended to readers who may find some of the information a bit dated; multinationals are changing rapidly and this kind of information lag is inevitable.

[1] The term *global potlatch* is borrowed from Manners' early paper (1956) on underdevelopment. The theory of economic "take-off" associated with Rostow (1960) has been the subject of a variety of critiques (Higgins 1968:174–187), Baran and Hobsbawn (1961:232–242), Frank (1969:39–47). For other critiques of development theory, see

One of the major institutions that enabled the rich to grow richer was, and continues to be, the multinational corporation (MNC). This paper is about multinationals and their effects on underdeveloped areas. In it I shall attempt to show how the corporate mode of operation tends to perpetuate underdevelopment, despite public rhetoric to the contrary. We shall also review the case of one multinational's interests in the tiny country of Western Samoa. This corporation is one of the larger wood and wood-products firms in the United States. Ironically, the corporation is based in the American northwest and is named Potlatch — Potlatch Forests, Inc.

Before describing Potlatch's Samoan interlude, some general background may be helpful. The paper is therefore divided into three parts: (1) a discussion of MNC's, their mode of operation, and their relationship to underdevelopment; (2) a sketch of the Western Samoan economy; and (3) the terms of the Potlatch contract with an estimate of the corporation's impact on Samoan society. This paper does not represent a comprehensive review of multinationals or an exhaustive study of Potlatch Forests, Inc., in Western Samoa, but it can be viewed as rudimentary notes on a type of economic organization endowed with powers of an extraordinary kind.

CORPORATIONS AND UNDERDEVELOPMENT[2]

The president of BankAmerica Corporation has said:

The opportunities that international business exploited in the last decade will seem pedestrian when compared with the opportunities that will open up in the next few decades (Clausen 1972:20).

True, and yet how many of us fully understand the implications of this statement? During the last two decades, MNC's have become a dominant feature of the world economy with multinational subsidiaries growing from 1,000 in 1930 to 8,000 in 1970. Some authorities, both conservative and radical, feel that they will become *the* dominant feature sometime between 1985 and 2000 (see for example Brown [1971], Magdoff and Sweezy [1971:106] and Sunkel [1972:523]). Whatever the case, the size

---

Frank (1969), Bodenheimer (1970, 1971–72). Myint (1969), Baran (1957), Batalla (1966), and Griffin (1969:20–50). On the failure of current development policy, see Robert McNamara's address (1972) to the United Nations Conference on Trade and Development held in Santiago, Chile; also Hayter (1971) and the Nultys' (1969) case study of Pakistan.

[2]   This section represents a very brief introduction to MNC's and their relationship to underdeveloped economies. No attempt is made here to cover the field or the literature, each of which would require volumes. Barnet and Miller's *Global reach* (1974) is the best general introduction to multinationals.

of the multinationals and their already existing control of production and markets cannot be underestimated. Of the fifty largest economic entities in the world, forty-two are countries and eight are multinationals; of the top one-hundred, forty-four are multinationals (Brown 1971:178–179). The growth rate of the top multinationals is twice that of the developed nation-states and these giant corporations now account for one-quarter of all production on the world market (Polk in Magdoff and Sweezy 1971:106).

The MNC is not really "multinational" in the sense of ownership or control; it usually represents a nationally based corporation with foreign subsidiaries.[3] Corporations based in the United States comprise a majority of the multinationals with over 3,500 U.S. corporations having at least one overseas subsidiary. Of the world's forty-four largest multinationals, thirty-four are U.S. based (Brown 1971:178–179). Their names are familiar: General Motors, Standard Oil, Ford, General Electric, Chrysler, IBM, Mobil, U.S. Steel, ITT, DuPont, Westinghouse, Boeing, RCA, etc.[4] The exploits of some of these companies are also familiar. One need only consider the incredible power these corporations wield *within* the United States in order to appreciate their influence abroad.[5] Although the total overseas investment by U.S.-based multinationals is relatively small compared to overall investment, it has grown from $7.2 billion in 1946 to over $85 billion by 1970.[6] Each year several billion dollars in investment capital are migrating abroad with income to the multinationals from such investments growing at a rate of $9 billion annually.[7]

The present expansion of U.S. business overseas is not a new phenomenon; its historical roots date back to the nineteenth century (see for example Healy 1970, Julien 1971, or Williams 1971). Nor is it a purely business phenomenon. Throughout the twentieth century, business expansion has been supported and subsidized by the federal government. According to former President Richard Nixon:

As we look to the future, we must seek a continued expansion of world trade, even as we also seek the dismantling of the barriers — political, social and ideological — that have stood in the way of freer exchange of people and ideas, as well as goods and technology.[8]

---

[3] Two notable exceptions are Unilever and Royal Dutch/Shell.
[4] In order of size. Other corporations, such as United Fruit and Firestone, are more notorious (see *Newsweek* 1972a).
[5] See any of the Nader group reports or popular treatment of corporate power like Mintz and Cohen's *America, Inc.* (1971).
[6] The 1946 figure is from Horowitz (1969:17); the 1970 figure is from Fusfeld (1972:6) and represents the book value of direct U.S. investment abroad. Exact figures for this period (1946–1970) vary by a few billion dollars depending on the source.
[7] For exact figures see *Wall Street Journal* (1972:3).
[8] From his speech "The Trade Act of 1969" (U.S. Department of State 1971:468). In this speech, the strategy for supporting U.S. private investment overseas was, in part, laid out.

What is unique about the present and future outlook of American business abroad is not expansion itself, but rather the sheer magnitude of expansion and the increasing reliance of the U.S. economy on multinational investment. As former Secretary of State William Rogers noted:

With . . . half the world's long-term foreign investment and nearly half the developed world's foreign assistance, our economy is inextricably linked with — and in many ways dependent on — that of the world as whole (U.S. Department of State 1971:xv).

If the present policy of replacing foreign aid with private investment continues, the multinationals will play an even more important role in the future.

Although most multinational investment remains in the developed nations, increasing amounts are going to underdeveloped areas. Of course, the primary reason for multinational expansion in underdeveloped areas is the search for corporate profits. Referring to multinationals, former President Nixon remarked, "Venture capital seeks profit, not adventure,"[9] and most businessmen would agree. What is more, the multinationals are quite successful in their search for profits; each U.S. dollar invested in Latin America between 1946 and 1967, for example, returned $2.73 (Dos Santos 1971:232). Annual rates of return on foreign investment often run over 30 percent in underdeveloped countries — rates generally unheard of within the United States. Some countries, such as Nigeria, openly advertise these rates. Nevertheless, there are some observers who contend that the expansion of multinationals is related not so much to the search for profits as to the need for "development" and to "forces inherent in modernization."[10] Accompanying this view is a conception of the MNC as a dynamic "agent of development" (Johnson 1970), exporting American capital, technology, and know-how for the "provision of abundance" (Hobbing 1971:51). Out of the need for development comes a new corporate role based on the alleged global desire for private capital, a desire that American business seems eager to satisfy. As one zealous representative of the U.S. Chamber of Commerce put it:

. . . the thing that has made America great is private enterprise. I think we have something to "sell." I think private enterprise in developing countries is the key to recovery, economic development, and economic growth. That makes missionaries, in a sense, of the business people and the Government people who go to other countries (U.S. House of Representatives 1968:195).

[9] From the proposal to establish the Overseas Private Investment Corporation (U.S. Department of State 1971:460).
[10] The phrase "forces inherent in modernization" is taken from developmentalist Lester Brown (1971).

But private enterprise is not the only key to development. There are other *kinds* of development that place little reliance on private capital (Gurley 1969). The existence of alternative development strategies reminds us that the word "development" is meaningless unless it is related to a particular economic and political context. Without such contextualization, this word has as little substance as its precursors, "civilization" and "progress." In the context of U.S. policy during the 1950's and 1960's, development was used as a gloss for peaceful, gradual, capitalistic change as opposed to violent communist revolution.[11] The current enlistment of private foreign enterprise under the banner of development now helps legitimize a changing policy in the 1970's, but apart from its symbolic value, the business community has shown relatively little concern for any abstract ideal of development. The term was certainly not necessary to rationalize expansion in the past, and if current conditions favor its usage, there is still the question of what "development" means in relation to actual investment policy.

One person who has given some thought to this question is economist Harry G. Johnson, a multinational proponent. According to Johnson, even if private capital, technology, and know-how are the keys to development, it does not follow that multinational investment will bring widespread economic transformations to underdeveloped countries because *the very pattern of multinational operation limits the diffusion and the spread of development.*

The corporation's concern is establishing branch operations in a particular developing economy is not to promote development according to any political conception of what development is, but to make satisfactory profits for its management and stockholders. . . . It has no commercial interest in diffusing its knowledge to potential local competitors, nor has it any interest in investing more than it has to in acquiring knowledge of local conditions and investigating ways of adapting its own productive knowledge to local factor-price ratios and market conditions. Its purpose is not to transform the economy by exploiting its poten-

[11] This has been the essence of Cold War ideology as explicitly stated by each of the post–World War II Presidents. It is also stated in the Program Guidance Manual of the U.S. Agency for International Development, i.e., "Development is not an end in itself, but is a critical element in U.S. policy, for in most countries some progress in economic welfare is essential to the maintenance of free, non-communist societies" (quoted in Hayter 1971:16). The idea of development as an anti-communist, counter-revolutionary strategy was perhaps best articulated in Rostow's *The stages of economic growth: a non-communist manifesto*, although the same theme runs throughout much of the development literature. Adelman and Morris, for example, in their statistical study find a long-term relationship between development and democracy; they conclude that "aid can lead to significant rewards for the Western donor nation in the sense that, *ceteris paribus*, a larger proportion of the world's population will eventually be governed in accordance with participant democratic ideals" (1967:276). Of course, this statistical trend will be of little consolation to people in South Korea, the Philippines, Brazil, and other countries where Western development has been accompanied by authoritarian regimes. And then there are those countries where aid and multinational investment has been unable to produce either development or democracy (see Barnet 1968, 1971).

tialities — especially its human potentialities — for development, but to exploit the existing situation for its own profit . . . (Johnson 1970:26).[12]

Although Johnson admits that this can hardly be called development in the usual sense of the term, he labels the process of multinational investment "profit-motivated development." The direct and visible impact of this process is the creation of a small number of jobs, both skilled and unskilled, in a general environment of low income and heavy unemployment. Any broader effects of "profit-motivated development" will depend on the "exemplary value" of the multinationals for local enterprises and the use of taxes for education and other development expenditures. Johnson warns against incorporating "social justice" into the development process, dismissing economic transformations involving more equitable income distribution, adequate wages, and unionization as being "naive" and grounded on "economically debatable assumptions." The net effect of such "well-intentioned" measures would be to hinder "profit-motivated development," i.e., multinational investment.

Given the exploitative mode of corporate operation, conceded by proponents and critics alike, one may ask whether "profit-motivated development" is not merely a euphemism for capitalist neocolonialism. The answer will depend largely on political tastes, but it should not obscure the fact that the content and consequences of this kind of development are subordinated to corporate interests and favor the perpetuation of underdevelopment.

Realistically, it is unnecessary to speak of development as a goal of multinational investment. The expansion of multinationals is governed by clear-cut economic considerations rather than by whimsical "forces inherent in modernization." This is why multinationals invest in those sectors of under-developed economies that are the most profitable rather than those most in need of modernization or development. The economic considerations involved in overseas manufacturing investment are summarized in a report from *Fortune*:

Typically, U.S. companies first develop a product, produce it in the U.S., and then export it. As the product ages, and the technology becomes more widely available, foreign competitors jump into the business. U.S. companies then find that they can't hold onto their markets if they must continue to face tariff barriers and pay high transportation and labor costs. So they invest abroad (*Fortune* 1972:62–63).[13]

[12]   The idea that corporations should make a profit has fallen into disrepute in some circles, but most stockholder publications assure their constituencies that they are interested in profits. Potlatch's new president, R.B. Madden, says, . . ."I'm not at all ashamed to say that I believe the purpose for any business is to earn a growing profit and a reasonable rate of return on the shareholders' investment in the business" (Potlatch Forests, Inc. 1971:6).
[13]   This report, carried out by Harvard Business School's R.B. Stobaugh, covered nine major industries accounting for 90 percent of all U.S. foreign investment. It attempts to

There is no mention of development here. Technology and know-how are exported to control markets and to lower production costs. The same is true for overseas investment in raw materials, where most multinational investment remains. It is hardly surprising that when former Secretary of the Treasury John Connally spoke of the need for U.S. multinationals and the U.S. government to join forces in securing raw materials, he did so without reference to development (Critchfield 1972:621). With or without the goal of development, multinational investment does have several very specific effects on the economies of underdeveloped host countries involving the structure and direction of the host economy, income and consumption patterns, and more generally, the perpetuation of under-development. Let us examine each of these.

Multinationals alter the structure and direction of the host economy through the sheer size and type of investment they make. Large foreign-owned subsidiaries, whether concerned with raw materials or manu-facturing, are usually export-oriented, with the terms of operation being dictated largely by the corporations. In accommodating the export en-clave, the host economy adapts both internally and externally to a highly specialized export market, thereby becoming less able to diversify and less able to compete with multinational subsidiaries in the same field. When local enterprises do become competitive, they are often bought out or "competed" out (Sunkel 1972:525). By depressing local competition in the most remunerative sectors of the host economy, the multinationals tend to depress the economy as a whole. Over the long term, under-developed areas that have relied heavily on foreign investment to pro-mote a few specialized exports have generally seen underdevelopment exacerbated (Levin 1967, Frank 1969, Resnick 1970). At the same time, the greater the foreign investment, the less likely that country will be to chart an independent economic course. As former Undersecretary of State George Ball inquired:

How can a national government make an economic plan with any confidence if a board of directors meeting 5000 miles away can, by altering its pattern of purchasing and production, affect in a major way the country's economic life? (quoted in Heilbroner 1972:623).

Planning and investment by the host economy are subordinated to multinational objectives in other ways. Infrastructure (power facilities,

---

show, at a time when U.S. multinationals are under fire for exporting capital and jobs, that multinational investment actually helps the U.S. balance of payments and creates jobs in the U.S. Individual corporations, like Union Carbide, are also putting out reports on the importance of overseas investment, including investment in underdeveloped areas, for the viability of the *American* economy. According to an editorial in the *Wall Street Journal* (October 18, 1972), multinationals are "the best thing that every happened to the U.S. balance of payments."

transportation, etc.), for example, can be a costly but necessary part of initial investment by multinationals. However, underdeveloped countries are frequently encouraged to invest in infrastructure as an "incentive" to attract otherwise reluctant multinationals. The burden of expenditure can then be transferred to the host economy through tied loans from various development agencies and developed governments (Hayter 1971). The lending agency or government will extend the loan on the conditions that it is used for specific purposes and that it is repaid in a certain manner. The result is a reduction of corporate costs while increasing the long term balance-of-payments problems for the host country. In underdeveloped areas, debt payments on such loans are increasing at *twice* the rate of export earnings (Critchfield 1972:623), and much current development-loan money is being used to pay off the *interest* on previous loans (World Bank 1971:68).[14]

Income distribution patterns are also affected by multinational presence. It has been assumed that because multinational investment can lead to per capita increases in income (a popular measure of development), multinationals will promote development in underdeveloped countries.[15] As we have seen, though, development is not necessary in order for multinationals to extract large profits. In this case, increases in per capita income may indicate only that the corporations and local elite are growing wealthy more rapidly. *Regardless* of growth rate, the common pattern of income distribution in underdeveloped countries under multinational control is one of little change for the masses and often further destitution and displacement. This pattern is sometimes attributed to "the early stages of industrialization" with the expectation that structural economic differences will gradually be lessened.[16] Yet what seems to be happening is an intensification of income differentials both within and between countries. The conventional examples of intensification within underdeveloped countries come from the oil fiefdoms, agricultural republics, and mining states of Latin America, Africa, and the Middle East, but this pattern is also found in countries that are (or were) considered "development miracles." In Brazil, for example, where development is used as a rationale for repression, there has been a spectacular overall growth rate over the last decade.[17] However, in terms of distribution, World Bank President Robert McNamara noted that:

The share of the national income received by the poorest 40% of the population declined from 10% in 1960 to 8% in 1970, while the share of the richest 5% grew from 29% to 38% (1972:483).

14   Calculations at current levels of aid suggest that by 1977, poor nations everywhere will be paying out more in debt service than they are receiving in aid (Steel 1970:258).
15   On this fallacy see Nulty and Nulty (1969).
16   See Moore (1963:chapter 5) for this type of thinking.
17   The recent growth rate has been about 9 to 10 percent a year (Burns 1972:18).

Even Brazil's president conceded, "The economy is doing well, the people not so well" (Burns 1972:18). The same type of concentration and displacement has also occurred in other "rapidly growing" countries like Mexico, Taiwan, Nigeria, and (formerly) Pakistan. The explosive social and political repercussions of inequitable income distribution require no comment here.

Consumption patterns in the host country are also influenced by multinationals since the corporations have a strong voice in where goods come from as well as where they go. Multinationals prefer to deal with their own branches and affiliates, thereby limiting transactions with the host economy. It has been estimated that one-quarter of all U.S. manufacturing exports are multinational intrafirm transfers, meaning that the corporations are doing business within themselves (*Newsweek* 1972b). Since the corporations set the prices of intrafirm transfers, public and private consumers in the host economy often find themselves paying inflated prices. This inflationary squeeze is not unrelated to the steadily declining terms of trade for underdeveloped countries over the last two decades.

The reader may well ask: if the consequences of multinational investment are so deleterious for host countries, why do they allow multinational investment at all? There are a variety of reasons: prior commitments; already existing dependency and foreign control; the advice of development agencies; the benefits for those closest to the multinationals; the promise of "growth"; and a future with very little hope. Robert Heilbroner believes that the real danger lies in MNC's *not* investing in underdeveloped countries (1972:694). And in fact, there are some benefits to the host country. But these benefits diminish as the multinational subsidiary follows its life cycle. United Nations economist Osvaldo Sunkel found that:

At the beginning the foreign firm may make a substantial contribution in capital, skilled personnel, technology, management, etc. But over time the cash outflow becomes larger than the inflow. Moreover, among the various alternative ways of obtaining external cooperation, direct foreign investment in the form of wholly owned subsidiaries is the one with the smallest educational effect because of its policy of retaining its monopoly on skills and technology. It is only as a consequence of the process of a country's development that local personnel learn modern management and technological skills. Eventually the corporation's net contribution to the development capabilities of the country become negligible or even negative. When the technology of the activities in which the firm operates becomes standardized and well known, the subsidiary becomes an "obsolete" form of foreign ownership . . . (Sunkel 1972:526–527).

Obsolete or not, the corporation is usually unwilling to divest itself of control and the greatest single fear of multinationals is that of local actions which threaten corporate activities.

Economic nationalism is the term applied to various local efforts to curb the power and profits of multinationals. This kind of economic nationalism is not to be confused with so-called nationalistic economic policies that *favor* multinational investment, as in Indonesia and Brazil. The difference between the two is most quickly recognized by corporate spokesmen who dub potentially restrictive efforts as "irrational," "xenophobic," "blind," "authoritarian," "radical," and "against the best interests" of the host country.[18] For those versed in development theory, this invective must seem odd since "self-sufficiency" is supposedly one of the fundamental goals of economic development. Yet when under-developed host countries make autonomous decisions about their economic features, they soon find their corporate "partners in development" wanting an unequal voice in preserving present arrangements (Girvan 1971).

Economic nationalism immediately raises the specter of expropriation and MNC's have used the "risk" of expropriation to rationalize their high profits. A professor of international finance at Columbia explains:

The longer a company is in a nation, the better its chances for expropriation. There has been much more time for the local people to learn how to operate the company. It is therefore in the interest of the American company to maximize profits in the short run, which is just what the foreign governments complain about (*Newsweek* 1972a; Barovick 1970:6).

The idea that high risk requires high profits seems logical enough until one looks at actual cases of expropriation, which are quite rare.[19] Even then, expropriated properties can be covered by the Overseas Private Investment Corporation, which readily insures American companies against losses due to political instability, riots, and revolution, as well as expropriation. There is also the question of why, if the risk of expropriation is so high, the U.S. government offers such a variety of incentives for overseas investment including survey subsidies, direct tax write-offs, and tax deferrals on profits.[20] It seems that the high profits obtained abroad have little to do with "risk" although they may be justified in these terms. What corporations are actually worried about is "creeping expropriation," a quaint phrase used to cover almost any infringements that multinationals deem unfair, but which are the prerogative of national governments. Thus the real question is more one of *sovereignty and*

---

[18]   These adjectives can be found in Johnson (1970) and Boddweyn and Cracco (1972).
[19]   Testimony in House Subcommittee Hearings (U.S. House of Representatives 1968:38): "Now, actually, the number of outright expropriations, where the Government takes a drastic act and really does it, are quite few. You can name almost in 15 or 20 (sic) all of those that have taken place since World War II in the whole world. There aren't very many."
[20]   For example, one such incentive allows corporations to subtract from their tax bills taxes paid to foreign governments instead of deducting them from income as they do with tax payments to states in the U.S.

control than of risk. Virtually all multinational observers wonder who will regulate the corporations as differences between national and corporate interests become increasingly apparent. According to some, the multinationals will have to relinquish some of the *de facto* power they have acquired in expanding (Gabriel 1972a, 1972b). According to others, like Harry G. Johnson, "there will have to be one world, politically as well as economically" (1970:30).[21] Indeed, Ford has already spoken of how its overseas operations promote "peace and unity."[22] And BankAmerica President Clausen feels that:

... the idea that this kind of business enterprise can be a strong force toward world peace is not so farfetched. Beyond the human values involved, the multinational firm has a direct, measurable, and potent interest in helping prevent wars and other serious upheavals that cut off its resources, interrupt its communications, and kill its employees and customers (1972:21).

This brief summary of the corporate mode of operation has dealt mainly with its economic aspects rather than with its social and political aspects. For our purposes it is sufficient to note that the content and consequences of multinational investment are dictated largely by the corporations and that, in spite of rhetoric about development, the structural economic changes initiated by corporations tend to perpetuate underdevelopment and dependency. So far, this argument has been presented in terms of general trends. Let us now turn to Western Samoa and Potlatch Forests, Inc., to see why, in a specific instance, corporate interests and development priorities do not always mesh.

UNDERDEVELOPMENT IN WESTERN SAMOA

The impact of any multinational is dependent not only on the corporate *modus operandi*, but also on the state of the host economy. To many people, the mention of Samoa still conjured up romantic visions of a tropical paradise supporting a primitive economy, but this imagery will not aid in understanding the economic circumstances into which Potlatch ventured. In fact, Western Samoa is an underdeveloped country that falls very much within the orbit of other former colonies. Potlatch is not the first large foreign corporation to enter Western Samoa; this tiny group of islands, with a population of only 155,000, has had over a century of experience with large foreign concerns.[23] Underdevelopment, then, is not

[21] Sherrill (1973) provides a good summary of the corporate position.
[22] This was with special reference to Ford's new investments in Southeast Asia.
[23] On the history of underdevelopment in Western Samoa, see Gilson (1970), Davidson (1967), and Lewthwaite (1962). On the agricultural economy of the islands, see Fox and Cumberland (1962), Lockwood (1971), and Pirie and Barrett (1962).

a pristine state of Samoan society, but rather the result of specific historical processes.

Although it may be difficult to conceive of South Sea islanders undergoing the same historical transformations as people in Asia, Africa, and Latin America, the Samoan economy did pass from a stage of *un*development in which local factors of population, redistribution, and exchange were dominant, to a stage of *under*development relative to the wider political economy into which it was incorporated, and in which foreign factors were dominant.[24] The establishment of a European export enclave in Western Samoa in the mid-nineteenth century, with new land and labor requirements, brought numerous changes to the islands' economy, but the consequences of British, American, German, and finally New Zealand colonial influence were nowhere as damaging as in other parts of the world, including other islands in the Pacific (see Valentine 1970). The Samoans were never defeated in battle and, due largely to the existence of an indigenous hierarchical structure and the exigencies of colonial rule, an early if troubled accommodation was worked out.

Under what might be considered a paradigm of "benevolent" paternalism, the Samoans were incorporated into a European state-level polity and an international agricultural export economy. The stability of the initial Samoan adaptation to the wider world has given this relatively recent social situation an aura of "tradition." Yet what is referred to today as "the Samoan way" or *fa'asamoa* probably had its roots in the "Samoan-mission-trader" equilibrium that developed between 1830 and 1870 (see Stanner 1953:305–323). The persistence of Samoan tradition can be traced to an absence of development beginning in the nineteenth century, with what little development that has occurred being concentrated in the hands of Europeans, who constitute less than 1 percent of the population and, to a lesser extent, the part-Europeans or "halfcastes," who constitute about 10 percent of the population.

For the past fifty years, the agricultural export economy has been dominated by a few large foreign companies, such as Burns Philp and Morris Hedstrom, which have widespread operations in other islands, and by local European firms. These firms market copra and cocoa and supply imports; the government markets bananas. These three cash crops — copra, cocoa, and bananas — have been the primary agricultural exports with the Samoans (about 75 percent of whom are engaged in village agriculture) producing about 75 percent of the total agricultural exports (Fairbairn 1970a) and receiving 50 percent or less of their actual value. Recently tourism and remittances from migrants overseas have changed the national income picture somewhat, but the overall state of

---

[24] This conception of underdevelopment is borrowed from Frank (1969).

the economy is rather grim. Per capita income is below $100. Moreover, the general trends in the economy present a dismal record in historical perspective. Time-series data from 1956 back to 1900 show that levels of production have increased "merely enough to restore production standards obtaining fifty years ago, and not enough, by some 18 percent, to reach the position ruling in the nineteen-twenties" (Stace 1956:71). Between 1956 and 1970, production of agricultural exports declined to levels below those at the turn of the century. While the basis of agricultural-export production had shifted away from the large plantations to the general Samoan population, productivity itself declined.

Incomes for the population as a whole did increase sharply following World War II, but in the last decade they have fallen steadily. Consumption, however, has continued to increase even as agricultural production and income decreased. For the economy this has meant trade and payments deficits. Such production income, and consumption trends indicate that Western Samoa's economy was deteriorating — underdeveloping, if you will — in terms of itself. Comparatively, the islands' position was equally discouraging. Of the seventeen countries participating in the Asian Development Bank's (ADB) regional seminar on agriculture in 1969, Western Samoa shared, with only South Vietnam and Indonesia, the unfortunate honor of having a *negative* compound growth rate per year (1957/59–1964/66) in total exports and agricultural exports (Ojala 1969:59, 62).[25] It had the highest percentage of agricultural imports of any of the ADB member nations and its population growth rate continues to be one of the highest in the world. In 1971 the United Nations identified Western Samoa as one of the sixteen poorest countries in the world.

During the late 1950's and early 1960's, the seriousness of the economic situation was still a matter of debate. As New Zealand's colonial ward until 1962, Western Samoa did not have to face the problem of underdevelopment directly and there were those who felt that better times lay ahead. The situation did not seem acute, as it rarely does in countries living under conditions of "primitive affluence" (Fisk 1962). In such countries, underdevelopment does not entail the kind of poverty that is found in areas with acute land shortages, chronic food shortages, high infant-mortality rates, and short life spans. In each of these respects Western Samoa was relatively well off. The slow economic decline that had occurred over the last half century was not regarded with alarm because its effects were not catastrophic. Hope was not abandoned since quick reversals are possible in such economies, and since there was agricultural growth in the 1950's, continuing growth was expectable.

[25] Ojala (1969:59, 62). This comparison is no doubt highly misleading, but the figures themselves are rather startling.

On the other hand, there were the pessimists — those experts, both Samoan and foreign, who expected a change for the worse. They predicted that the conditions that had led to the long-term decline were likely to continue and that the expansion of the 1950's would be offset by increasing costs. One prophetic analysis warned:

... a combination of unfortunate circumstances in weather, plant diseases, pests, and poor world market prices for two or even three of the major crops would result in a financial crisis for the Western Samoan nation (Gerakas 1964:32).

But the optimists were not deterred, especially the popular press. In 1964, "BOOM IS ON THE WAY" headlined an article in the *Pacific Islands Monthly*. The same caption appeared in an editorial in *Samoana*, a Samoan newspaper, on January 26, 1966. An opinion was offered that things were not as bad as they seemed:

In fact, indications are that this country is on the verge of a boom that in five or six years could transform its economy from that of subsistence to one of the most flourishing in the South Pacific.

The following week Western Samoa was devastated by the worst hurricane in the South Pacific in seventy-five years.

The hurricane underscored the vulnerability of the economy in a manner that left few illusions. The experts had been correct and in the next five years (1966–1971), Western Samoa was to be visited by all the woes prophesized. Hurricanes struck in 1966 and again in 1968. The important banana industry, already decimated by bunchy-top virus disease, was virtually eliminated. The hurricanes curtailed production of the other two major export crops, copra and cocoa. When copra exports made a dramatic rebound in 1971, slumping world market prices reduced the value per ton to less than two-thirds of what it had been the previous year. Trade deficits persisted over the five-year period and payment problems were common.[26]

THE ENTRY OF POTLATCH AND ITS IMPACT

While events were obviating the debate over the seriousness of the situation, plans were being laid to develop the economy. In 1961, just prior to Western Samoa's political independence, a Committee on Economic Development was formed and in 1964 a Development Secretariat superseded the Committee. Much of the support for the Secretariat (known since 1965 as the Department of Economic Develop-

---

[26]   A more optimistic interpretation can be found in Fairbairn (1970b).

ment) came from the United Nations Development Program, which had its regional headquarters for the South Pacific in Western Samoa. With the U.N. staffing the highest positions in the Secretariat, this advisory group set about surveying the islands' resources, determining planning priorities, producing a five-year development program, and selling development to the Samoans.

Following the completion of their surveys, the development group decided that stress had to be placed on improving conditions in the deteriorating village agricultural sector. A lesser emphasis was given to fisheries, tourism, and forestry. One of the reasons that forestry was given secondary attention can be found in a non–U.N. study which reported that local demand alone would put severe pressure on the rapidly diminishing lumber supply:

Western Samoa today possesses inherently poor forest resources which, unless rapid and coordinated preventive and remedial measures are taken, could disappear within two generations because of the ever-increasing demand for timber and cropland (Cameron 1962:77).

This study concluded that large-scale milling and logging operations would not be feasible. Another study carried out under United Nations auspices in 1963 came to the same general conclusions about planning priorities as earlier studies, *except* that large-scale sustained-yield tree farming was viewed as a feasible, though secondary, development possibility.[27] Potlatch cites this study as the beginning of its efforts to help Western Samoa "launch itself into the mainstream of economic development" (Potlatch Forests, Inc. 1971:3).[28]

The exact details of how Potlatch learned of this study and subsequently became interested in the islands are not fully known. In its stockholder publication, *The Potlatch story*, the corporation implies that it was "selected by the Western Samoans" (Potlatch Forests, Inc. 1971:15), but this seems unlikely since the Samoans had no idea of what was being planned on their behalf. More realistically, the connections seem to have been made by Harry Spence, Jr. As head of U.N. regional

[27] This is the Stace and Lauterbach study (1963). Samoan expert J.W. Davidson gave the following assessment of this study: ". . . despite Stace's intimate knowledge of Samoa (and of the Pacific Islands, generally), the report that he and his colleague produced early in 1963 was a disappointing one. Though it was issued in both their names, it consisted of two parts which they had clearly drafted separately. These overlapped and were, to some extent, inconsistent. Much of the analysis was trite or woolly. Many of the recommendations seemed to reflect little more than a simple acceptance of ideas that were already in circulation. The work of the economists was later supplemented by more specialized studies by other United Nations experts; but these, too, failed to relate fact and theory rigorously enough to provide a firm basis for a development plan" (1967:419–420).
[28] The whole issue is devoted to Western Samoa. In 1973, Potlatch Forests, Inc., became the Potlatch Corporation.

headquarters, Spence had a good deal of influence on Western Samoa's development planning, drawing up development guidelines and commissioning the 1963 U.N. study. It seems that Spence mentioned Western Samoa's timber prospects to a friend, who happened to be a Potlatch stockholder.[29] Shortly thereafter, in 1965, and without directly involving the Samoans, Potlatch visited the timber-rich island of Savaii and conducted preliminary tests on twenty-six varies of Samoan hardwoods. In that same year, Prime Minister Fiame Mata'afa Mulinu'u II visited Potlatch operations in the United States and returned home with a glowing endorsement of Potlatch. Mata'afa was to become the most important public advocate of the Potlatch proposal and, soon after his return, a general announcement was made welcoming private foreign investment to the islands.

The welcoming of private foreign capital had been in the wind well before Potlatch. The 1963 U.N. study had recommended that Western Samoa take steps to secure outside capital, but this new policy stood in marked contrast to past policy and the wishes of many Samoans. For some time the islanders have been especially wary of foreign capital and foreign control, a fact sometimes attributed to Samoan "conservatism" or "traditionalism," although experience under colonial rule is probably the more immediate cause. The islanders have seen that they are the last to benefit from such arrangements and have consequently voiced their apprehension about each new attempt to exploit them. In 1947, for example, when Western Samoa was still under New Zealand mandate, a Dominion furniture company was given permission to utilize Samoan timber resources. However, fearing that this would set a precedent for further outside investment, Samoan opposition became so intense that the firm withdrew. The same cautious approach continued through the 1950's and 1960's and, in 1966, was extended to the negotiation of the Potlatch contract.

The delicate and complex business of negotiating the contract began with informal discussions with the members of Parliament by Potlatch's general manager, who received support from Prime Minister Mata'afa and advice from Harry Spence, Jr., now a Potlatch consultant following his retirement from the U.N. several months earlier. It was Spence, in fact, who presented the Potlatch proposal to Parliament, citing as support the very study he had commissioned three years earlier.

Basically, Potlatch wanted to invest in milling operations that would produce fifteen million board feet of lumber per year when at full capacity, with possibilities for further expansion. The operations would be built on the large but sparsely populated island of Savaii at a cost to Potlatch of

---

[29]   This story was told to me by a Potlatch official. Spence's influence is summarized in a brief article in *Pacific Islands Monthly* (October 1965).

$10 million, a figure considerably larger than the value of export production in the islands for any recent year. This enormous investment, later reduced to $6 million (personal communication), would not only create an overseas plant for Potlatch but held the promise of providing jobs for Samoans, supplying revenues for government and villagers, substituting domestic lumber production for lumber imports (which comprised about 9 percent of the islands' total imports in 1970), and promoting development in an undeveloped part of Western Samoa. Potlatch would provide the capital, prepare a plan for forest use, establish logging facilities, and develop roads and power. In order to commence this undertaking, Potlatch requested the following incentives from the government (*Pacific Islands Monthly* September 1966:139):

(1) the establishment of a Forest Service and Land Use Board so Potlatch could lease directly from the government rather than from communal landholders;

(2) renewable leases of twenty years on land in Savaii;

(3) property leases for Potlatch around Asau harbor and the harbor concession to Potlatch;

(4) a tax moratorium, customs exemptions, repatriation of capital, foreign exchange privileges, and personnel privileges;

(5) implementation of reforestation in the areas milled by Potlatch.

These incentives merit a closer look, for the scope of the Potlatch proposal would have broad implications for Samoan land policy, the ecology of the rain forests of Savaii, and the Western Samoan government's future commitment to Potlatch and other multinational investors.

The major difficulty in the Potlatch proposal was leasing land from Samoans. In the past, Samoan customary law prohibited the lease or sale of land to anyone, foreign or Samoan. Of course, without the ability to lease necessary land, foreign investment could not be secure and so, well before Potlatch, the Samoan government modified the law to allow limited leasing for commercial, industrial, and tourist purposes. While this modification did encourage some foreign investors, it was insufficient for the large-scale Potlatch leasing arrangement. By early estimates, Potlatch wished to lease between 100,000 and 160,000 acres of land on the island of Savaii or *between 14 percent and 23 percent of Western Samoa's entire land area* (*Pacific Islands Monthly* December 1968).[30] For a transaction of this magnitude, it was necessary for the corporation to request special leasing provisions that would circumvent restrictions remaining in the Samoan land-tenure system.

The roots of this unusual system lie in the colonial past. Ever since large parcels of land were alienated to European plantation owners in the mid-nineteenth century, Samoans have been acutely aware of the need to

---

[30] By 1973 Potlatch had leased 80,000 acres.

control their land. In 1921, while still under New Zealand mandate, Western Samoa's quasi-traditional system of land tenure was codified into law and now applies to 80 percent of the islands' land. Under this system, extended family units in each village hold title over various plots of land that are owned through use. When not in active use or fallow, the land may revert to the village as a whole or to other families who will use it. To complicate matters, land is jointly owned by the whole extended family, including kin in other villages who have a potential voice in land use even though they do not reside on it. Actual decisions about use lie with an elected family head, or titleholder, who, in consultation with his own family and with other titleholders in the village council, manage land-use policy.[31] If conflicts within families, between families, or between villages cannot be resolved, they are referred to the national Land and Titles Court, an institution set up to handle just such litigation.

As long as land was abundant and was not a commodity, this system of communal land tenure was viable, and conflicts could be kept at a minimum. Although relatively inefficient in strict economic terms, the system supported the Samoans quite adequately, and in the process, the mastery of its labyrinthian complexities helped Samoans to become astute politicians. As land became scarce, however, and as more profitable land-use alternatives were foreseen, the traditional system came to be regarded as a barrier to economic development.

Although limited leasing had been approved in 1962, massive leasing by Potlatch would be a formidable task given the normal conditions under which leasing would take place. If Potlatch wished to lease the land, it would have to negotiate hundreds of leases on a family-by-family and village-by-village basis. Arrangements would have to be made in a foreign language, and contracts would have to be designed to cope with a system in which management and ownership functions were separate. For the foreign investor the system was chaos. To make matters worse, since much of the land was unsurveyed, conflicts over ownership could involve litigation that would prevent the Potlatch project from ever getting off the ground. The 1966–1970 *Development program* reported that:

If a number of such disputes are brought before the court, which must be resolved before Potlatch obtains enough land for its operations, there could be a seemingly interminable delay in getting this operation started (Economic Development Board 1966:33).

To prevent such a delay and to bypass other difficulties, Potlatch asked

---

[31]   The Samoan system of land tenure and social organization is considerably more complex than presented in this article. Such terms as "communal" land tenure and "extended family" are glosses for subjects that deserve much fuller exposition. Among the more detailed accounts are Davidson (1967), Gilson (1970), Nayacakalou (1960), and Farrell and Ward (1962).

that the Western Samoan government set up an agency to act as a land broker on the corporation's behalf.

The issue of leasing was debated at the national level by members of the Samoan Parliament through 1966 and 1967. The Prime Minister assured members of Parliament that leasing would bring economic prosperity to poor Samoans. Noting that there were two economic classes in the islands — the rich but landless Europeans and the poor but landed Samoans — Prime Minister Mata'afa maintained that the Samoans could help themselves by leasing the land on which the valuable hardwoods stood. While the Prime Minister's analysis of economic stratification in the islands was fairly accurate, members of Parliament did not automatically accept his advice and he was even accused of helping himself to Potlatch stock, a charge that was never confirmed.

At the village level, the advantages and drawbacks of leasing were also debated. In the small villages of western Savaii, the island on which Potlatch would set up its operations, the obvious monetary advantages seemed attractive. This area, with about 14 percent of Western Samoa's population, is one of low agricultural potential and low income, so the interest in leasing was understandable. Nevertheless, the villagers considered the possibility that the twenty-year renewable leases would put pressure on remaining agricultural land that could be brought into subsistence or cash-crop production. Although most of the land leased by Potlatch is not suitable for agriculture, villagers feared that in areas where there was potential for both forestry and agriculture, leasing would mean relinquishing their rights to farm the land. In one instance, Potlatch uprooted coconut trees on leased land to make way for a road. The villagers asked to be compensated for their loss at $42 a tree; they received only $7 a tree.

Once the Samoan Parliament approved the Potlatch proposal in 1967, the possibility of leasing sparked a new interest over the use, ownership, and boundaries of land in the villages of western Savaii. Disputes arose as land between villages suddenly became a commodity. Anthropologist Sharon Tiffany describes one case in which two villages claimed title to land long ignored by both. The dispute could not be resolved locally and the national Land and Titles Court finally ruled that neither village owned it (Sharon Tiffany, personal communication). Other means of obtaining land were employed during a minor wave of land speculation; for example, one wealthy titleholder tried to extend his holdings by clearing additional land so that he would have more acreage to lease to Potlatch for tree farming.

The monetary rewards which the Samoans anticipated from leasing did not prove as great as expected. The first property to go was the 181-acre sawmill site owned by the government and leased at a fixed rate of $1,500 a year for a twenty-year period (about $8 per acre), a low sum considering the increasing value of the land over that period of time. The first leases from Samoan peasants were substantially lower: $1.40 an acre. In 1969, Potlatch leased 28,000 acres from a group of seven villages with a total population of about 2,600 people, bringing the average yearly per capita income from leasing to a little under $11. Villages receiving leasing advances in a lump sum can receive much higher amounts. One small village received almost $20,000 in a single payment. But this kind of arrangement masks the annual amounts to be made from leasing, which are not very large even in terms of the low overall income of the peasants. Royalties paid on cut timber may help, but they are also low — about four cents per cubic foot, part of which reverts to the government for reforestation.

The economic effects of the Potlatch operation extend well beyond leasing and royalty fees to villagers; revenues to the government and jobs for Samoans are supposed to help balance the development ledger. Early studies suggested that a nominal investment of $260,000 by the government of Western Samoa in industrial infrastructure, especially the Asau wharf and harbor facilities, would yield about $13 million in revenues from Potlatch over a twenty-year period. Unfortunately, the government's infrastructural estimate turned out to be too low. Building the Asau harbor and wharf facilities for Potlatch's use ended up costing the government almost five times the projected initial figure. By "some incredible engineering miscalculation" (as one reporter put it), foreign engineers failed to carefully examine the harbor bottom that was to be dredged for a shipping channel: it turned out to be solid coral. Instead of the simple dredging that had been scheduled, a lengthy blasting and dredging job was necessary. In 1972, dredging was still under way, even though the wharf had been completed in 1968, and the delays caused friction between Potlatch and the Samoan government. From an economic perspective, the repayment of principal and interest on the loans used to cover these infrastructural developments will cut deeply into the revenues anticipated from Potlatch. By 1970, the government had already concluded that Potlatch's contribution to the country's balance-of-payment problems would be small.

Although direct revenues to the government and help with the balance-of-payments problem did not meet original expectations, by 1975 Potlatch was providing employment for 300 people, making the corporation one of the islands' major employers. Yet, in the context of an underdeveloped economy like Western Samoa's, it is important to understand that these new Potlatch employees were not necessarily unemployed when they were hired by the corporation. What Potlatch did was shift employment opportunities, through training programs, from agriculture, civil service, and light industry to forestry; this can be viewed as an upgrading of the labor force. At the same time though, by leasing enormous tracts of land, Potlatch will, at a certain point, create a situation in which Samoan peasants may not have sufficient land on which to carry out peasant agriculture. Samoans will then begin to lose employment in peasant agriculture, and given the scarcity of land, coupled with population growth, Potlatch may be contributing to unemployment in peasant agriculture while creating employment in forestry.

An additional problem has to do with the rising cost of living as people move from a subsistence-oriented peasant economy to a consumer-oriented wage labor economy. While Potlatch creates much higher incomes than peasant agriculture, Potlatch employees may no longer have the time or the land to cultivate subsistence crops; they must therefore import food and other necessities, paying for them with cash. On a long-term basis this means that the real cost of living is likely to rise and that high wages by Samoan standards may not be able to offset these rising costs. In already commercialized areas of Western Samoa, this trend — rising incomes, coupled with even more rapidly rising costs — has led people to migrate overseas in order to improve their unstable position in a consumer economy.

Apart from its social and economic effects, the Potlatch proposal may have considerable effects on the ecology of the tropical rain forests in Western Samoa. Although at one time rain forests were thought to be an inexhaustible resource, this is no longer the case. Throughout the world, primary tropical rain forests are threatened by human use to such an extent that they are in danger of vanishing by the end of this century (Gómez-Pompa *et al.* 1972). Well before Potlatch arrived, the rain forests of Western Samoa were threatened by such normal processes as population growth, agricultural expansion, and the domestic use of timber. As mentioned earlier, a study conducted almost two decades ago warned that unless rapid and coordinated remedial measures were taken, the forests, which seemed so abundant, could disappear within two generations (Cameron 1962:77). The presence of a large-scale commercial milling operation can only hasten this trend, irreversibly damaging the primary rain forest composition and erosion patterns. Geographer Peter Pirie of the University of Hawaii has observed that the area leased by Potlatch contains the only remaining stand of large tropical hardwoods in the country and that it could be quickly exhausted (Pirie 1970:503).

Potlatch has maintained that its strategy of continuous-resource tree-farming would replace the primary rain forest with rapid-growing timber varieties that would not only regenerate the forests but also be financially remunerative. The reforestation program, however, is not Potlatch's responsibility; as part of the Potlatch contract, the government of Western Samoa has agreed to replant as Potlatch cuts. But in 1973, as Potlatch was getting into its harvesting program, much of the basic research on replanting had not yet been carried out. Some government officials were concerned that further delays could lead to erosion problems and also create undesirable types of secondary growth.

Despite delays, and despite some mutual dissatisfaction of both the Western Samoan government and Potlatch, the Potlatch subsidiary is now operating and should be a financial success. Some idea of the subsidiary's profitability can be gauged from a smaller joint Japanese-Samoan timber venture that made 20 percent profit in each of its first two years and is expecting higher returns in the future (Fairbairn 1971:114). Such rates of profit are not unusual in overseas timber operations; companies in the Amazon can make over 55 percent a year (Anderson 1972:64). If Potlatch should enjoy only a 20 percent rate of profit, it could recoup its initial investment rather quickly, and if proper reforestation is carried out, the company could remain in Western Samoa indefinitely. Yet there is the possibility, acknowledged by Potlatch, that the subsidiary could fail.

There is no guarantee that Potlatch's Samoan subsidiary will be a success. Multinational ventures do not always yield expected profits, and, when a Potlatch subsidiary in Colombia faltered, it was sold by the corporation to cut losses. Although peasant and Indian unions and cooperatives had protested Potlatch's presence, the decision to sell was made on a purely economic basis. This should remind us that behind the promise of abundance there is a calculus of stockholder and management returns, a calculus that becomes most apparent when the corporation is in financial difficulty. Then the same company officials who had publicly embraced the goal of development before signing the contract can be found invoking the inevitability of the balance sheet after commencing operations. Whether Potlatch will alter its commitment remains to be seen, but regardless of Potlatch's success or failure, the corporation has stimulated Western Samoa into opening its door to private capital. Consideration is being given to further timber exploitation and the establishment of a pulp and paper products plant, while tourist investment is booming.

The newly arrived foreign investors present a problem for the Western Samoan government as well as a hope, for the government is aware that these corporations are interested in those sectors of the economy that are the most profitable rather than those most in need of development. While investment in forestry and tourism has been high, the peasant agricultural sector continues to deteriorate. In this respect, the precedent set by Potlatch may not be the one that the government wants others to follow; for while the praise for Potlatch has been high, it is of little consolation to the Samoan peasant. Although Potlatch can hardly be expected to invest in agriculture, its timber-harvesting program has diverted both government attention and funds from the basic problem of agricultural development. Furthermore, to have any effect on the majority of

Samoans, the limited revenues from Potlatch will have to be reinvested in peasant agriculture.

For the Samoans within the Potlatch orbit, there is little concern about the abstract goal of economic development. Their feelings revolve around concrete problems — and these feelings are mixed. There is a general acceptance of Potlatch, especially by the small group that is doing well because of the corporation's presence. But other Samoans have questions concerning the amount of land leased and the prices that Potlatch has paid for both land and timber. Samoans wonder about the pollution at the mill site; there is also some resentment against Samoans from other parts of Western Samoa who are now employed by Potlatch in western Savaii. Generally, Samoans suspect that Potlatch is taking advantage of them as other Europeans have in the past. The depth of these feelings is rarely understood or appreciated by most Europeans.

When all of the economic, social, and ecological costs that could effect the people of Western Samoa due to Potlatch's presence are considered, it is apparent that the Samoans are taking a larger gamble than the corporation. Potlatch can measure the outcome by calculating the financial return on its investment, but no such clear-cut standard can be used by the government or by the people. The question of adequate compensation is a difficult one to answer, especially because there has been no public estimate of the worth of the islands' forests. For most Samoans, Potlatch's promise to help Western Samoa "launch itself into the mainstream of economic development" has brought consequences that were both unanticipated and undesirable.

It would be encouraging to believe that the future will bring more beneficial consequences, but there are no assurances that corporations, even under the best of circumstances, can promote economic development of the type needed in Western Samoa. One need only look at what has happened to the U.S. Trust Territory of American Samoa, seventy miles away. In about the same condition as Western Samoa two decades ago, American Samoa was the beneficiary of two American companies, Star Kist and VanCamp, which set up tuna canneries near Pago Pago. The canneries took advantage of territorial tax status, cheap Taiwanese, Japanese, and Korean tuna catches, and cheap Samoan labor. Several hundred jobs were created by the canneries and the United States committed huge sums of money for welfare measures. Incomes soared to the highest levels in that part of the Pacific, at least fifteen times those in Western Samoa. But this kind of development did not bring financial stability to American Samoa. The *real* cost of living shot up dramatically as American Samoa began importing former subsistence staples, like taro, at exorbitant prices. And Samoan aspirations for motorcycles, televisions, and cars could not be satisfied by even large increases in income.

American Samoans became aware of even better opportunities in Hawaii and the American mainland where they have migrated by the thousands; more than half of the American Samoan population now resides abroad. The economic problems leading to this massive exodus underscore the fact that development has left American Samoans even more dependent on forces over which they have little or no control. With this example in mind, Western Samoans are sometimes perplexed by statements about how Potlatch "will contribute to their economic independence" (Potlatch Forests, Inc. 1971:15).[32]

POSTSCRIPT

The skepticism expressed in this paper may seem unwarranted. Indeed, on the basis of early fieldwork alone, I would be inclined to be more optimistic. I was particularly impressed by one American forestry expert who had reviewed the Potlatch plan and was convinced that it was ecologically and economically sound. He informed me that only selective cutting would take place with smaller trees preserved and watersheds carefully protected. The reforestation program would actually improve the hardwoods of the area as well as helping the timber industry. And I was told that Potlatch would not "make a killing" off the operation given its commitment to sound ecological management. Since I knew virtually nothing about tropical forestry or Potlatch at the time, my optimism was understandable. It was also short-lived.

On returning from the field in 1970, I was surprised to find a full-page Potlatch advertisement in a number of popular national magazines. The ad proclaimed: "IT COST US A BUNDLE BUT THE CLEARWATER RIVER STILL RUNS CLEAR" and was accompanied by a photograph of one of those great out-of-door scenes with beautiful blue rushing waters surrounded by tall, stately evergreens. The ad referred to Potlatch's environmental efforts at its Lewiston, Idaho, plant, which is located near the Clearwater. The pure waters flowing in the ad supposedly demonstrated Potlatch's "total commitment to pollution control" that goes into "all our operations." What Potlatch failed to mention was that the photograph was taken many miles *upstream* from the Lewiston plant and that when the Clearwater did run clear, it had virtually nothing to do with Potlatch's efforts. At the plant itself, Potlatch takes in fresh water and dumps back up to 230 tons of suspended organic wastes daily into the Snake River through a pipe which diverts effluent from the Clearwater (Council on Economic Priorities 1971a:Q-2–Q-6); this section of the Snake is deep brown, turbid, and

---

[32]   In the Caribbean, the process occurring in American Samoa is further along. See, for example, O'Neill's study of the Virgin Islands (1972).

odorous. However, not even the pipe can keep the Clearwater clear, for about once a year it ruptures, gushing the foul wastes into the Clearwater. *Newsweek* described the situation forther:

Aside from the filth that spews into the river, Potlatch concedes, some 2.5 million tons of sulphur gases and 1.8 million pounds of particulates billowed from the plant stacks last year [1969]; in fact, the Lewiston plant enjoys the dubious distinction of being the only industrial mill in the U.S. to have been the subject of separate air- and water-pollution-abatement hearings before Federal authorities. Each day, on leaving the plant's parking lot, employees sluice down their autos with a company-installed car wash to protect the car's paint from the corrosive sodium sulphate that sifts from the air. When an enterprising local college-newspaper editor point out the discrepancy between ad copy and reality, the company responded by cancelling all corporate advertising. As Potlatch president Benton R. Cancell explained it: "We tried our best. You just can't say anything right any more — so to hell with it" (*Newsweek* 1970).

Under federal pressure Potlatch announced plans to spend $9.6 million dollars for pollution-abatement equipment at the Lewiston plant and, recently, there has been improvement. But in January 1972, Potlatch's new president admitted, "Still the wind blows odor from the mill, and the Clearwater ran coffee brown last month" (Council on Economic Priorities 1972:35–36).

During the latter half of the 1960's, when Potlatch was in clear violation of state and national regulations, the corporation used a number of strategies to conceal what was going on. Public relations, as well as political pressure and noncooperation with governmental agencies,[33] was an important tool in molding opinion while at the same time corporate spokesmen were denying, manipulating, and mystifying the facts. Similar strategies were being employed with regard to Western Samoa and again public relations was an important tool. In another advertisement, Potlatch declared that from San Francisco to Samoa, the corporation's products would "help make a better life possible for everyone everywhere." Such extraordinary claims may amuse anthropologists with their obvious parallels to the boasting and conspicuous giving of the aboriginal potlatch. Some Samoans, however, are not amused by parallels with the aboriginal potlatch or, for that matter, with the promises of corporate executives. They remember another day, when natives peoples were alleged to "serve the devil," thereby justifying colonial regimes. Today, they are less likely to believe those who tell them that, because they lack capital, corporate financing is necessary for economic development to "serve the people."

[33] On Potlatch's tactics, see Zwick and Benstock (1971:168–172) and Council on Economic Priorities (1971a:Q-2–Q-6; 1971b:29).

REFERENCES

ADELMAN, I., C.T. MORRIS
1967　*Society, politics, and economic development: a quantitative approach.*
Baltimore: Johns Hopkins Press.

ANDERSON, A.
1972　Farming the Amazon: the devastation technique. *Saturday Review*
55(40):61–64.

BARAN, P.A.
1957　*The political economy of growth.* New York: Monthly Review
Press.

BARAN, P., E.J. HOBSBAWN
1961　The stages of economic growth. *Kyklos* 14:234–242.

BARNET, R.J.
1968　*Intervention and revolution: the United States in the Third World.* New
York: World Publishing Co.
1971　*Can the United States promote foreign development?* Overseas Development Council Development Paper 6.

BARNET, R.J., R. MILLER
1974　*Global reach: the power of multinational corporations.* New York:
Simon & Schuster.

BAROVICK, R.L.
1970　Congress looks at the multinational corporation. *Columbia Journal of
World Business* 5(6):75–79.

BATALLA, G.
1966　Conservative thought in applied anthropology. *Human Organization*
25:89–92.

BODENHEIMER, S.J.
1970　The ideology of developmentalism: American political science's
paradigm-surrogate for Latin American studies. *Berkeley Journal of
Sociology* 14:95–137.
1971–1972　Crucifixion by Adams. *Berkeley Journal of Sociology* 16:60–
74.

BODDWEYN, J., E.F. CRACCO
1972　The political game in world business. *Columbia Journal of World Business* 7(1):45–56.

BROWN, L.R.
1971　"The nation-state, the multinational corporation, and the changing
world order," in *The future of U.S. government: toward the year 2000.*
Edited by H. Perloff. New York: George Braziller.

BURNS, E.B.
1972　Brazil: the imitative society. *The Nation* 215(1):17–20.

CAMERON, S.S.
1962　"Vegetation and forest resources," in *Western Samoa: land, life, and
agriculture in tropical Polynesia.* Edited by J.W. Fox and K.B. Cumberland. Christchurch: Whitcombe & Tombs Ltd.

CLAUSEN, A.W.
1972　The internationalized corporation: an executive's view. *The Annals*
403:12–30.

COUNCIL ON ECONOMIC PRIORITIES
1971a　*Paper profits: pollution in the pulp and paper industry.* New York:
Council on Economic Priorities.

1971b *Corporate advertising and the environment.* Economic Priorities Report 2(3).

1972 *Paper profits: pollution audit 1972.* Economic Priorities Report 3(3).

CRITCHFIELD, R.

1972 The new environment of foreign aid. *The Nation* 214(20):621–623.

CUMBERLAND, K.B.

1962 "Conclusion: the problem reviewed and restated," in *Western Samoa: land, life, and agriculture in tropical Polynesia.* Edited by J.W. Fox and K.B. Cumberland. Christchurch: Whitcombe & Tombs Ltd.

DAVIDSON, J.W.

1967 *Samoa mo Samoa.* London: Oxford.

DOS SANTOS, T.

1971 "The structure of dependence," in *Readings in U.S. imperialism.* Edited by K.T. Fann and D.C. Hodges. Boston: Porter Sargent.

ECONOMIC DEVELOPMENT BOARD

1966 *Western Samoa's economic development programme 1966–70.* Western Samoa: Economic Development Board.

FAIRBAIRN, I.J.

1970a Village economics in Western Samoa. *Journal of the Polynesian Society* 79:54–70.

1970b The Samoan economy: some recent developments. *Journal of Pacific History* 5:135–139.

1971 A survey of local industries in Western Samoa. *Pacific Viewpoint* 12:103–122.

FARRELL, B.H., R.G. WARD

1962 "The village and its agriculture," in *Western Samoa: land, life, and agriculture in tropical Polynesia.* Edited by J.W. Fox and K.B. Cumberland. Christchurch: Whitcombe & Tombs Ltd.

FISK, E.K.

1962 Planning in a primitive economy: special problems of Papua and New Guinea. *Economic Record* 38:462–478.

FRANK, A.G.

1969 *Latin America: underdevelopment or revolution.* Monthly Review Press.

FUSFELD, D.R.

1972 The rise of the corporate state in America. *Journal of Economic Issues* 6:1–27.

GABRIEL, P.B.

1972a The multinational corporation on the defensive (if not at bay) with a reply by Raymond Vernon. *Fortune* 85(1):119–120, 124.

1972b Multinational companies. *Fortune* 85(2):68.

GERAKAS, A.

1964 *Information on economy of Western Samoa.* Development Secretariat Public Bulletin 1.

GILSON, R.P.

1970 *Samoa 1830 to 1900: the politics of a multi-cultural community.* London: Oxford.

GIRVAN, N.

1971 Making the rules of the game: company-country agreements in the bauxite industry. *Social and Economic Studies* 20:378–419.

GÓMEZ-POMPA, A., C. VAZQUEZ-YANES, S. GUEVARA

1972 The tropical rain forest: a nonrenewable resource. *Science* 177: 762–765.

GRIFFIN, K.
   1969   *Underdevelopment in Latin America.* London: George Allen and Unwin.
GURLEY, J.G.
   1969   "Capitalist and Maoist economic development," in *America's Asia.* Edited by E. Friedman and M. Selden. New York: Pantheon.
HAYTER, T.
   1971   *Aid as imperialism.* Middlesex: Penguin.
HEALY, DAVID
   1970   *U.S. expansionism: the imperialist urge in the 1890s.* Madison: University of Wisconsin Press.
HEILBRONER, R.
   1972   *The economic problem.* Englewood Cliffs: Prentice-Hall.
HIGGINS, B.
   1968   *Economic development: problems, principles, and policies.* Revised edition. New York: W.W. Norton.
HOBBING, E.
   1971   The world corporation: a catalytic agent? *Columbia Journal of World Business* 6(4):45–52.
HOROWITZ, D. *editor*
   1969   *Corporations and the Cold War.* New York: Monthly Review Press.
JOHNSON, H.G.
   1970   The multinational corporation as a development agent. *Columbia Journal of World Business* 5(3):25–30.
JULIEN, C.
   1971   *America's empire.* New York: Pantheon.
LEVIN, V.
   1968   "The export economies," in *Economics of trade and development.* Edited by J.D. Theberge. New York: John Wiley & Sons.
LEWTHWAITE, G.R.
   1962   "Land, life and agriculture to mid-century," in *Western Samoa: land, life and agriculture in tropical Polynesia.* Edited by J.W. Fox and K.B. Cumberland. Christchurch: Whitcombe & Tombs, Ltd.
LOCKWOOD, B.
   1971   *Samoan village economy.* Melbourne: Oxford.
MAGDOFF, H.
   1969   *The age of imperialism: the economics of U.S. foreign policy.* New York: Monthly Review Press.
MAGDOFF, H., P.M. SWEEZY
   1971   "Notes on the multinational corporation," in *Readings in U.S. imperialism.* Edited by K.T. Fann and D.C. Hodges. Boston: Porter Sargent.
MANNERS, R.A.
   1956   Functionalism, realpolitik and anthropology in underdeveloped areas. *America Indigena* 16:7–33.
MCNAMARA, R.S.
   1972   Development in the developing world: the maldistribution of income. *Vital Speeches of the Day* 38(16):482–487.
MINTZ, M., J. COHEN
   1971   *America, inc.,* Dell.
MOORE, W.
   1963   *Social change.* Englewood Cliffs N.J.: Prentice-Hall.

MYINT, H.
1969 "The peasant economies of today's underdeveloped areas," in *Subsistence agriculture and economic development.* Edited by C. Wharton, Jr. Chicago: Aldine.

NAYACAKALOU, R.R.
1960 Land tenure and social organisation in Western Samoa. *Journal of the Polynesia Society* 69:104–122.

Newsweek
1970 Page 49. *Newsweek.* December 28.
1972a Pages 80–82. *Newsweek.* April 10.
1972b Pages 66, 69. *Newsweek.* April 24.

NORTH AMERICAN CONGRESS ON LATIN AMERICA
1971 *Yanqui dollar: the contribution of U.S. private investment to underdevelopment in Latin America.* New York: North American Congress on Latin America.

NULTY, J., L. NULTY
1971 Pakistan: the busy bee route to development. *Trans-Action* February:18–26.

OJALA, E.M.
1969 "The pattern and potential of Asian agricultural trade," in *Regional seminar on agriculture.* Philippines: Asian Development Bank.

O'NEILL, E.
1972 *The rape of the American virgins.* New York: Praeger.

POTLATCH FORESTS, INC.
1971 *The Potlatch story.* Potlatch Forests, Inc. October.

PIRIE, P.
1970 "Samoa: two approaches to population and resource problems," in *Geography and a crowding world.* Edited by W. Zelinsky, L. Kosinski, and R. Prothero. New York: Oxford University Press.

PIRIE, P., W. BARRETT
1962 Western Samoa: population, production, and wealth. *Pacific Viewpoint* 3:63–96.

RESNICK, S.A.
1970 The decline of rural industry under export expansion: a comparison among Burma, Philippines, and Thailand, 1870–1938. *Journal of Economic History* 30:51–73.

ROSTOW, W.W.
1960 *The stages of economic growth: a non-communist manifesto.* New York: Cambridge University Press.

SHERRILL, R.
1973 Invisible empires; the multinationals deploy to rule. *The Nation* 216(16):488–495.

STACE, V.D.
1956 *Western Samoa — an economic survey.* South Pacific Commission Technical Paper 91.

STACE, V.D., A. LAUTERBACH
1963 *Economic survey and proposed development measures for Western Samoa.* Legislative Assembly of Western Samoa, Sessional Paper 24.

STANNER, W.E.H.
1953 *The south seas in transition.* Sydney: Australasian.

STEEL, R.
1970 *Pax Americana.* New York: Viking.

STOBAUGH, R.B.
1972   *Fortune* 85(2).

SUNKEL, O.
1972   Big business and "dependencia": a Latin American view. *Foreign Affairs* 50:517–531.

U.S. HOUSE OF REPRESENTATIVES
1968   *The involvement of U.S. private enterprise in developing countries.* Subcommittee on Foreign Economic Policy of the Committee on Foreign Affairs, U.S. House of Representatives. Washington: U.S. Government Printing Office.

U.S. DEPARTMENT OF STATE
1971   *United States foreign policy 1969–1970. A report of the Secretary of State.* Publication 8575, General Foreign Policy Series. 254. Washington, D.C.: U.S. Government Printing Office.

VALENTINE, C.
1970   "Social status, political power, and native responses to European influence in Oceania," in *Cultures of the Pacific.* Edited by T.G. Harding and B.J. Wallace. New York: The Free Press.

VERNON, R.
1969   The role of U.S. enterprise abroad. *Daedalus* 98(1):113–133.

Wall Street Journal
1972   Page 3. *Wall Street Journal.* November 3.

WILLIAMS, W.A.
1971   "The vicious circle of American imperialism," in *Readings in U.S. imperialism.* Edited by K.T. Fann and Donald C. Hodges. Boston: Porter Sargent.

WORLD BANK
1971   *World Bank — International Development Association annual report.* New York World Bank.

ZWICK, D., M. BENSTOCK
1971   *Water wasteland: Ralph Nader's study group report on water pollution.* New York: Bantam Books.

The Nationalization of Copper in Chile: Antecedents and Consequences

AL GEDICKS

On July 11, 1971, the Chilean Congress voted *unanimously* for the amendment to the Chilean constitution that authorized the government to nationalize the holdings of the three largest copper companies in Chile — Anaconda, Kennecott, and Cerro — all U.S.-owned companies. The day this amendment was passed is celebrated in Chile as a "Day of National Dignity." President Salvador Allende declared the event Chile's "second independence," referring to the achievement of economic independence that had been denied Chile since its political break from Spain in 1818. In light of the unanimity of political support for the nationalization of the U.S.-owned copper companies it is very unlikely that the subsequent violent overthrow of Salvador Allende's Marxist government will result in a reversal of that decision. Admiral Ismael Huerta, the junta's foreign minister, said the new regime "never contemplated" returning the copper mines to their original owners although the junta has promised to begin talks with Anaconda and Kennecott about compensation.

The nationalization of copper in Chile has a specific importance in terms of Chile's own historical development as well as a more global importance in terms of the conflict between the natural-resource multinational corporations (MNC's) and the forces of economic nationalism in many Third World countries. Chile's decision to nationalize the copper industry was the culmination of a long history of conflict between the U.S.-owned copper companies of Anaconda and Kennecott and the Chilean government, which started with the *denationalization* of the

This article is reprinted from the Fall 1973 issue of the *Review of Radical Political Economics*. In addition to the *RRPE* editorial board I would like to thank Carolyn Baylies, Bob Griss, Nora Hamilton, Eugene Havens, Ann Seidman, and Maurice Zeitlin for their comments on earlier drafts of this article.

Chilean copper industry in the early years of this century. The conflict between Chile and the copper companies resulted from the organization of copper production whereby the basic decisions affecting Chilean national development were made by foreign corporate officials according to the needs of the vertically integrated copper companies and not according to the needs of the Chilean economy.[1]

At each stage in the development of the conflict between Chile and the copper companies there was an interaction between Chile's knowledge of the technical and managerial functions of the U.S. copper companies and the nature of Chile's bargaining stance toward them. When Chile's knowledge of the industry was very primitive the Chilean government was content to bargain for a higher percentage of the profits. As Chile's knowledge of the industry became more sophisticated Chile's bargaining demands changed from those that called for greater Chilean benefits from the industry to that of demanding total Chilean ownership and control.

In the context of the present U.S.-Latin American relations, the U.S. government and the MNC's are gravely concerned about any precedents that the Chilean nationalization may provide for other Third World countries seeking control over their natural resources.[2] The attractiveness of the Chilean nationalization lies in its orderly, legal character. The possibility that the Chilean nationalization may be used as a model for other Third World countries that are dependent upon a large export-oriented natural-resource industry dominated by foreign companies makes it important to examine the factors that led up to the nationalization of copper and the extent to which the nationalization can be expected to function as a source of internally generated wealth at the service of economic development in Chile.

EARLY HISTORY OF THE CHILEAN COPPER INDUSTRY

Copper has played an important role in the Chilean economy ever since Chile first exported bars to the Viceroyalty of Peru for processing into cannon in 1749. By 1820 Chile's production of copper had increased to 9 percent of the world total. Copper was first shipped as concentrates, but after the 1830's a substantial part was smelted in Chile. Chile's share of world production increased rapidly in the next several decades to a peak

---

[1] The theoretical elaboration of the idea of the corporate economy and the national economy used in this analysis is contained in Girvan (1970).

[2] A perspective on the Chilean nationalization as part of a regional pattern throughout Latin America can be found in Petras (1972). The concern of the U.S. government with recent nationalizations in the Third World can be seen in a recent study by the U.S. Department of State (1972).

of 44 percent in the 1860's (Grunwald and Musgrove 1970:167). In spite of the great distance to the European market Chile's Tamaya mine had the reputation as the world's foremost producer of copper, and the crude "Chile bars" that were produced from Welsh-type reverberatory furnaces in Chile became the standard grade on the London Metal Exchange. Chilean copper provided approximately 65 percent of the needs of British industry and consumption (Pinto 1962:15). A few foreign companies were active in Chile during this later period but 90 percent or more of production was controlled by Chileans. Table 1 summarizes the steady growth of world copper production and the rise and fall of Chile within that international industry.

Table 1. Copper production

Decade	Average annual production	Percent increase	First producer		Second producer		Third producer		Fourth producer	
1801–1810	18,200	—	England	40%	Russia	18%	Japan	17%	Chile	9%
1811–1820	18,850	3.6%	England	44%	Russia	18%	Japan	17%	Chile	9%
1821–1830	27,350	45.1%	England	45%	Japan	16%	Russia	16%	Chile	11%
1831–1840	36,450	33.3%	England	44%	Russia	14%	Chile	14%	Japan	12%
1841–1850	49,381	35.5%	England	31%	Chile	20%	Cuba	13%	Russia	11%
1851–1860	75,908	53.7%	Chile	32%	England	21%	Russia	8%	Cuba	7%
1861–1870	114,934	51.4%	Chile	44%	England	11%	U.S.A.	9%	Spain	8%
1871–1880	142,374	23.9%	Chile	36%	Spain	15%	U.S.A.	15%	Australia	9%
1881–1890	248,859	74.8%	U.S.A.	32%	Spain	22%	Chile	16%	Germany	7%
1891–1900	414,935	66.7%	U.S.A.	52%	Spain	15%	Chile	6%	Japan	6%

Source: Compiled from U.S. Department of Commerce: Department of Mines, *Eco. paper no. 1: summarized data of copper production, 1928*

There have been a number of explanations advanced to explain the collapse of the Chilean export sector in the 1880's and its eventual domination by U.S. copper companies in the early part of this century. No attempt at a comprehensive explanation of why Chile experienced denationalization will be given here. Rather, an attempt will be made to demonstrate that the traditional economic interpretations of this period, which cite factors such as scarcity of capital and lack of industrial organization, do not fit the Chilean case.

Norman Girvan makes an important contribution to our understanding of the denationalization of the Chilean copper industry by placing the denationalization in the context of the changes that were taking place in the size and scale of the copper industry in the United States and the fact that similar changes failed to materialize in Chile. The emergence of the electricity industry in the United States in the 1880's and the resulting rapid growth in demand for copper stimulated a "transformation of small scale industry based on high grade ores and run by a number of small, independent producers, into a large scale industry based on low grade ores and dominated by a small number of producers integrated from copper mining to refining and marketing" (Girvan 1962:9). The changes in the scale of the industrial organization and the huge amounts of capital required for the producing units greatly increased the risks in the industry, with the result that a few large, vertically integrated firms came to dominate the U.S. copper industry. Two of these firms — Anaconda and Kennecott — expanded on the basis of their strong domestic position and purchased Chile's large, low-grade copper deposits.

But this is still only part of the story. The important question that remains is why no similar revolution in demand, production, and organization occurred in the Chilean copper industry. As late as 1876 Chile was producing 62 percent of the world's copper. The same industry was also manufacturing copper utensils for domestic consumption and parts and boilers for distilling apparatus (Rippy and Pfeiffer 1948:297).[3] One writer summarized the situation as follows:

In the second half of the last century [in Chile] an important effort was made in the field of metallurgy. Numerous industries of this type were installed in the region of Santiago and Valparaiso, the majority of them directed by foreigners (but resident in the country and economically Chilean). The projects of these metallurgical industries were ambitious: They manufactured plows, threshing machines, locomotives, railroad freight cars, large bells, etc.; they also constructed four steam locomotives. The initiative developed in the metallurgical industry showed its efficiency by being able to provide the necessary arms and equipment for the Chilean army and navy during the War of the Pacific (1879–83). Nevertheless, this effort, so promisingly begun, was later nullified for the most part by competition from imported production (Nolff 1962).

On purely economic grounds it seems unlikely that Chilean investors could not have supplied the capital and industrial organization necessary to develop their own vertically integrated corporations to withstand the invasion of the U.S. firms. The relatively modest initial cash investments made in what was to become the *Gran Mineria*, or large-scale mining, suggest that scarcity of capital *per se* could not have been a major reason for denationalization. The development expenditures for *Chuquicamata* and *El Teniente*, the Big Two of the *Gran Mineria*, appear to have been about $12 million and $10 million respectively by 1915 (Hiriart 1964; O'Connor (1937:348), whereas Santiago Machiavello estimated the value of Chilean capital invested abroad at 389 million pesos. This figure included Chilean capital invested in beef production in Argentina, nitrate production in the north of Chile, and tin production in Bolivia (Machiavello 1923;110–111).

[3] The reader interested in the advanced state of the development of Chilean industry *before* the period of U.S. capital penetration of Chile is also referred to Pfeiffer 1952:139–144.

An alternative explanation for the denationalization of the Chilean copper industry may be sought in the political realm and in the particular alignment of class forces in the conflict over the role of the state in the Chilean economy. On one side stood President Balmaceda and a section of the industrial bourgeoisie who favored higher taxation for development expenditures and limitations on foreign ownership; on the other side stood, in the words of the Chilean historian Hernan Ramírez Necochea:

a coalition of bankers and landowners, mine-owners and industrialists, opposed to the financial and economic policy of Balmaceda which was rooted in nationalism, opposition to laissez-faire and in favor of the definite intervention of the state in the economic organization of the Republic, who proposed — at the same time as defending the rights of the constitution — to consign these ideas of Balmaceda to oblivion (Ramírez 1951).[4]

The conflict culminated in the Civil War of 1891 and the overthrow of President Balmaceda. The immediately following period saw the arrival of William Braden, a U.S. geological engineer who was instrumental in linking the Chilean copper industry into the vertically integrated operations of Anaconda and Kennecott. By the 1920's Anaconda and Kennecott had secured control over all the important copper reserves in Chile.

THE EMERGENCE OF STATE INTERVENTIONISM IN THE COPPER INDUSTRY

With the passing of ownership and control of the Chilean copper industry into the hands of U.S. capital, the issue of the value of copper that actually remained in Chile — the "returned value" — took on major importance. In this category are included taxes and local expenditures for labor and materials. With the collapse of the world market for natural nitrates at the end of World War I, copper replaced nitrates as Chile's principal export commodity, accounting for approximately 80 percent of Chile's foreign-exchange earning capacity. In addition to supplying the foreign exchange necessary for import financing, copper revenues accounted for 15 to 30 percent of government revenues. The long-term growth prospects for Chilean national development have been integrally related to the fluctuations of the copper-export sector. Chile has thus sought to extract as much returned value as possible from the operation of the copper-export sector.

[4] For an overview of the conflicting interpretations of this period in Chilean history, see Blakemore (1965).

At the same time, Chilean copper has been an important input into the vertically integrated operations of Anaconda and Kennecott in terms of supplying their needs for production, revenues, and profit. Chilean copper also assumed an important role in terms of the long-range profitability and growth of these corporations.[5] It was the differing needs of the vertically integrated corporations and the national economy of Chile that provided the essential context for the emergence of open conflict between the government of Chile and the U.S. copper companies.

In the first years of operation the U.S. copper companies were quite isolated from the rest of the Chilean economy. Their main link to the Chilean economy was the purchase of labor. There were no restrictions on the repatriation of profits, and the vertically integrated companies had little need to purchase capital equipment from Chilean-based industries. The first income tax, amounting to less than 1 percent of the value of production, was levied in 1922. The attitude of the Chilean government toward Anaconda and Kennecott soon began to change in the face of a series of foreign-exchange crises that culminated in the Depression (Grunwald and Musgrove 1970:169). One of the major consequences of being tied to U.S. copper consumption through the vertically integrated corporations was that when U.S. copper consumption was contracted during 1930–1932 the effects were transmitted directly through the U.S. companies to Chilean production. The value of sales plunged from $111 million in 1929 to $31 million in 1931, and prices fell from 17.5 cents to 7.0 cents per ton (Reynolds 1962:54). After 1925 an income tax was established of 6 percent plus an additional tax of 6 percent on profits, resulting in a total rate of taxation of 12 percent. Even with the new taxes, Chile was able to capture only a small share of the total value of its copper exports. In the years 1925–1934, nonreturned value amounted to $306 million, or 62 percent of the value of exports. It was this problem of the low share of returned value that was to preoccupy the Chilean government in its dealings with Anaconda and Kennecott for the next several decades. In 1934 the profits tax was raised from 12 to 18 percent. These early measures of the Chilean government to make the foreign copper companies serve the needs of the Chilean economy culminated in the establishment of the Chilean Development Corporation (CORFO) in 1939 as an agency to ensure that the increased export taxes made a contribution to domestic capital formation. The activities of CORFO were financed by a 15 percent tax on the profits of the copper industry, thus raising the profits tax to 33 percent. More and more taxes were added over the next fifteen years, culminating in state intervention in

---

[5]   Between 1925 and 1968 Chile provided 52 percent of Anaconda's profits. From 1915 through 1968 the companies earned a total of $2.011 billion in net profits and depreciation from Chile, of which $738 million only was used for reinvestment.

pricing and marketing between 1952 and 1955 (Mamalakis and Reynolds 1965; Vera 1961; Mikesell 1970).

CHILEAN "CAPTIVE PRODUCTION" AND THE SALES MONOPOLY OF 1952–1955

With the integration of Chilean copper production into the corporate economies of Anaconda and Kennecott, major decisions about production and pricing were effectively removed from the hands of any Chilean body politic. The consequences of this structural arrangement had serious implications for Chilean national development. In the first place, it meant that Chilean copper production was directly linked to U.S. copper consumption and the fluctuations in the U.S. industrial cycle. In the second place, Chilean sales competed with those of U.S. producers and were vulnerable to U.S. government protectionist policies. The effect of being integrated into the U.S. market took its most serious toll, as has been pointed out earlier, during the Depression of 1930–1932. Following the Depression, the United States imposed a tariff on copper imports that prevented Chile from participating in the recovery of demand in the United States after 1932.[6] This cycle, as we shall see, was repeated in the post–World War II period.

The integration of Chilean copper production into that of the U.S.-owned copper companies also implied the subordination of Chilean national development to the needs of the U.S. *national* economy. Thus when the United States entered World War II, the U.S. government set a price for copper at twelve cents per pound, a price slightly above Depression levels. After the war, with U.S. price controls removed, the copper price rose to twenty-one cents per pound by April 1947. The loss of returned value to Chile as a result of this price freeze has been estimated as high as $500 million (Reynolds 1962:240).

When the war ended, the price of copper kept rising until the 1949 business recession in the United States, at which time copper prices dropped and the U.S. copper companies cut back their production in Chile further than at any of the mines in the United States.[7] The 1949 recession ended with the beginning of the Korean War and the imposition of price controls on Chilean copper without prior consultation with, or

[6] The U.S.-imposed tariff was the equivalent of a 72 percent *ad valorem* duty on the basis of the 1932 average price and has been described as a "practical embargo" on copper imports, U.S. Bureau of Mines (1952).
[7] Most Chilean sources claim that production was being cut back 20 percent in Chile versus 10 percent in the United States. Senator Larrain Vial, of the Conservative Party, later claimed that the U.S. companies planned to cut back production by 30 percent in Chile but were prevailed upon to limit the cutback to 20 percent. See *Historia de la ley* (1955:3909).

approval by, the Chilean government. With the costly experience of World War II behind them and the prospects of a repeat of that experience with the Korean War, the U.S. move provoked a public outcry in Chile that led to the Washington Conference of May 1951 and to an increase in the price of Chilean copper of three cents per pound, which would accrue entirely to the Chilean government. In addition Chile was "given" the right to sell up to 20 percent of its copper on the free market.

But to many groups in Chile the experience of World War II suggested that the entire system of Chile's integration into the corporate economies of Anaconda and Kennecott was fundamentally detrimental to the process of Chilean national economic development. From the Chilean point of view it was the worst possible kind of integration, where Chile was excluded from full participation in the upswings of the industrial cycle while bearing the major brunt of the downswings. Furthermore, this critique began to be elaborated by a broad segment of political groupings within Chile.[8] In a speech before the Senate on April 15, 1952, the conservative Senator Gernan Videla, speaking as chairman of the Senate Mining Committee and president of the National Mining Society, declared: "The time has come for our government to confront the single logical solution for our exports — to get for all our sales a just price" (*Boletín Minero* 1952). The Chilean government subsequently repudiated the Washington agreements as prejudicial to the interests of Chile and, with Congressional approval, established a state monopoly over all copper sales. During the period this monopoly was in force the results were encouraging. In the first year of its operation it produced $100 million[9] in government revenues — an amount that greatly surpassed Anaconda and Kennecott's payments of direct taxes (Vera 1961:63).

But the Chilean sales monopoly had a more far-reaching significance than the extraction of increased revenues by Chile. The government of Chile had successfully asserted, in defiance of the U.S. government during wartime, its right to fix the price of Chilean copper produced by the U.S. companies. The Chilean sales monopoly of 1952–1955 became the first major challenge to the decision-making authority of the vertically integrated MNC's and the U.S. government.

CONFRONTATION AND ACCOMMODATION: THE "NEW DEAL" LEGISLATION OF 1955

The problems that confronted the Chilean sales monopoly were for-

[8] The most comprehensive treatment of the development of economic nationalism in Chile in the postwar period is to be found in Moran 1970:chapter 3.
[9] The figure refers to the period June 1952 to June 1953. Most of the 20 percent was sold on the European "free" market at about fifty-four cents a pound.

midable. First of all, due to the tight monopoly on marketing knowledge held by Anaconda and Kennecott, Chile had very little information on the size of demand in the major U.S. and European industrial markets, and Chile was forbidden to sell to any of the Soviet-bloc nations by the Washington agreement of 1951 (*Panorama Económico* 1952). A second major problem in the marketing of Chilean copper was the fact that Chile's potential customers in the United States and Europe were already integrated, through a series of formal and informal ties, with the major producers of copper. This degree of integration is not only important for the multinational copper companies; it is equally important for the producers and consumers of copper that do not have formal ties of ownership between them. This informal pattern of vertical integration can be established through buyer-seller ties at producers' prices, through long-term contracts, and through joint financing. Rather than face shortages in the world market, producers and consumers prefer to trade in established patterns and are willing to pay a premium or accept a discount, at various stages in the business cycle, in order to preserve that system of vertical integration.[10]

These carefully built-up ties were not about to be suddenly broken by Chile. Both the U.S. government and the U.S. copper companies exerted pressure on European consumers of copper not to make purchases from Chile. Theodore Moran notes that:

After the establishment of the Chilean monopoly in 1952, it appears that the International Materials Conference adopted a practice of deducting purchases from Chile from the quotas granted to the United Nations allies at the lower "ceiling" price. Thus, if France, for example, contracted to buy 10,000 tons from Chile at 54¢ per pound, the French allotment of 27.5¢ copper would be reduced by 10,000 tons by the International Materials Conference (Moran 1970:89).

This would be a major factor in accounting for the low volume of Chilean sales during this period. By 1953 and 1954, with the drop in wartime demand and the aforementioned difficulties, Chilean exports dropped and stocks accumulated.

At the same time, Chile found that the level of production in the *Gran Mineria* was falling. Chile's share in Free World production had been steadily declining since World War II had had not recuperated much even during the Korean War. In 1945 the Chilean share of world production had reached a high of 23 percent, in 1951 16 percent, and in 1954 only 14.9 percent. Despite the rapid growth in world demand, there was no increase in investment by either Anaconda or Kennecott between 1948

---

[10]   John Tilton, for example, has found that most sales in aluminum, bauxite, copper, lead, manganese, tin, and zinc are based on stronger and more dependable ties than mere price considerations. See Tilton (1966).

and 1955. The U.S. companies preferred to expand marginal mines in the United States rather than increase their investment in Chile.

This fall in investment and output has been widely attributed to the measures taken by Chile to maximize the returned value to the industry.[11] In addition to the steadily increasing direct tax Chile levied on the U.S. companies, there was a substantial indirect tax in the form of an artificial exchange rate. From 1932 onward the Chilean government required Anaconda and Kennecott to buy the local currency needed for operations at the fixed rate of 19.35 pesos per dollar, while the import rate averaged about 60 pesos per dollar in 1952. It was from the artificial exchange rate that the greatest increases in returned value came in the 1945–1954 period. In 1952, for example, the effective rate of direct income tax was 32.7 percent while the rate of indirect taxation through exchange controls was 40.4 percent — for a total effective rate of 73.1 percent for the Anaconda and Kennecott mining subsidiaries (Moran 1970:92). While the Chilean share of copper revenues was steadily increasing, the absolute returns to Chile were falling. Throughout the period 1950–1955 the companies were putting pressure on Chile for a drastic change in policy that would permit a higher net profitability as a condition of increased production.

These difficulties, combined with the fact that the United States was unwilling to purchase the Chilean stocks for its strategic stockpile, brought the conflict between Chile and the U.S. companies to crisis proportions. For approximately a year and a half the Chilean Senate debated various options regarding the copper industry — from outright nationalization to a liberalization of their mining laws to encourage investment and increased production by Anaconda and Kennecott. The Senate recommended that the copper be sold to any customer it could find, "free world" or otherwise,[12] and that the Senate would be willing to consider new legislation to stimulate production. The agreement to consider new legislation for the companies, combined with the threat to sell to the Soviet Union, prompted the United States to purchase 100,000 tons of copper for its stockpile at the minimum price set by Chile in March 1954. The following year saw the passage of Law 11.828 — the "New Deal" for the copper companies.

In many ways Chile's "New Deal" legislation was a reaction against the trend of state intervention in the Chilean economy. With the failure of the Chilean sales monopoly, many conservative and business groups were

[11]   For a short history of Chile's taxation of copper profits and the effects on output and investment, see Baklanoff 1966:328–341.

[12]   Dr. Salvador Allende stated that he had talks with Soviet trade representatives in 1955 (*Historia de la ley* 1955:1317) and that the possibilities of opening commercial relations were favorable. After the Korean War, Allende was one of the principal spokesmen for the Marxist left in calling for the total nationalization of the copper industry.

ready to reevaluate their treatment of the American copper companies. The Liberal Senator, Hernan Videla Lira, who had once denounced the subordination of Chilean production to the needs of the vertically integrated corporations (*Boletín Minero* 1952), was now (April 1954) calling for Chile to free itself from the artificiality of state intervention and to rely on free trade and providing a "good investment climate" in which the U.S. copper companies could increase production and contribute to the development of the Chilean economy (*Boletín Minero* 1954).

The 1955 "New Deal" legislation was passed with great conservative support and consisted of the following elements: (1) a fixed rate of 50 percent on net profits of the U.S. copper companies with a variable surtax of 25 percent of profits that declined proportionately as production increased above some basic quota; (2) the elimination of the artificial exchange rate and a return to a free rate of exchange for the companies; (3) deductions on the net taxable income for new investments in electrolytic copper producing installations and other investments; and (4) the creation of a copper department in the Chilean government to control the exports and production of copper.

The "New Deal" legislation embodied a series of concessions to the U.S. copper companies that were made on the assumption that these measures would stimulate production and new capital outlays to build refineries in Chile. By the end of 1959 it was clear to many groups in Chile that Anaconda and Kennecott were not responding to the "good investment climate" in ways that Chilean conservative and business groups had anticipated. It was from this disappointing and frustrating experience that a new phase of conflict emerged between Chile and the vertically integrated multinational copper corporations.

REJECTION OF THE "NEW DEAL" LEGISLATION AND THE MOVE TOWARD CHILEANIZATION

The results of the first five years of the 1955 "New Deal" legislation were considered a failure in terms of Chilean efforts to increase production, refinery capacity, and government revenues. The only major investment project carried out was the Anaconda investment in the *El Salvador* mine to replace its depleted mine at Portrerillos. Production from the Portrerillos mine had been falling since the end of World War II, and it was necessary, from the point of view of maintaining Anaconda's share of production in Chile, to invest in the nearby El Salvador mine.[13] Invest-

---

[13] The *1955 Annual report* for Anaconda noted that "As the Andes Portrerillos ore body has remaining life of less than five years at present rate of production, a four-year programme has been set up for bringing this new mine, which will be known as El Salvador, in order to supplement and eventually to supplant the production from the Portrerillos mine."

ments by Kennecott in Chile were in the nature of replacement and maintenance expenditures only. By the time Chileans began criticizing the "New Deal" in 1959, Chilean production was not significantly different from what it had been at the end of World War II, despite Anaconda's El Salvador mine coming into full production in 1959. Meanwhile, under the generous provisions embodied in the "New Deal," the profits of Anaconda and Kennecott rose to new heights.

Table 2. Average profit rate as a percentage of average book value during the period

Company	Period	Average profit rate
Anaconda	1950 to 1955	9.1 percent per year
	1955 to 1960	13.4 percent per year
Kennecott	1950 to 1955	25.5 percent per year
	1955 to 1960	37.9 percent per year

Source: CODELCO, "Antecedentes economicos y estadisticos relacionados con la Gran Mineria del Cobre." Santiago: June 18, 1969

The other side of the coin, of course, was that government copper revenues fell drastically: in 1955 taxation of the U.S. companies brought in $156 million, while in 1961 it brought in only $68 million. The returned value to Chile from total production fell from 78 percent in 1955 to 56 percent in 1959 (Reynolds 1962:378).

Finally, the "New Deal" was unable to check the trend in the fall of the percentage of copper refined locally, let alone encourage investment in new capacity. In 1951 the percentage of refined copper (electrolytic and fire refined) produced by the U.S. companies in Chile was 89 percent; in 1961 the percentage had declined to 45 percent. The decline was just as serious in absolute terms: in 1951 the American companies refined 319,000 metric tons while in 1961 that figure had dropped to 216,000 metric tons.

A good part of the explanation for the failure of the copper companies to behave according to Chilean expectations lay in the very conception of the "New Deal" legislation. The Chileans were working on the classic liberal economic assumption that a capitalist firm will seek to maximize its returns on each individual operation. Unfortunately, this theory was not complex enough for understanding the behavior of the multinational copper companies. For Anaconda and Kennecott, their primary consideration was to maximize returns for their corporate economies *as a whole* (Girvan 1970:491). In the case of Anaconda and Kennecott this involved pursuing a long-term growth strategy that placed a great deal of emphasis on diversification, by product and by geographical region. In the immediate postwar period Kennecott had made substantial investments in oil exploration, South African gold mining, an iron-titanium project, and a fairly large ($100 million) purchase of the stock of Kaiser Aluminum. Anaconda was also diversifying into aluminum in the 1950's with its Anaconda Aluminum Co. smelter in Montana. In addition, both companies faced demands for investment outside of Chile. Kennecott, for instance, was just breaking off its long-standing relationship with American Smelting and Refining Company in the 1950's and was building facilities for refining its own ores. This move, by the way, accounts for the reduction of exports of refined copper by Kennecott's subsidiary in Chile.[14]

Thus by the early 1950's, before the "New Deal" legislation went into effect, both companies were already committed to long-range growth strategies in which Chile played little or no part. The Chilean operations of Anaconda and Kennecott were simply not part of the companies' planning for long-term growth at the time of the "New Deal" legislation, and little in the way of greater incentives could have induced a more favorable response by Anaconda and Kennecott.

Meanwhile, criticism of the behavior of the multinational copper companies began to be voiced once again by major groupings of the left, right, and center within Chile. Even the conservative President Allesandri (1958–1964) publicly expressed his disappointment that the copper companies, especially Kennecott, did not have more incentive to contribute to the process of national development through private enterprise (Moran 1970:165). The demand by the left for total nationalization of the copper companies received a real boost with the publication of Mario Vera's work (1961), which demonstrated the failure of the "New Deal" from the Chilean point of view. At the same time Chile's need for foreign exchange and public revenues led to the special exchange rate for the companies. During this period (1960–1964) the U.S. companies made it clear that no new major investments would be undertaken unless they were assured that the tax and foreign-exchange provisions of the "New Deal" would remain in force for the next twenty years. It was in this atmosphere of intense antagonism between Chile and the U.S. copper companies that Eduardo Frei won the 1964 elections and began negotiations with the copper companies.

CHILEANIZATION AND NATIONALIZATION

In the period preceding the 1964 presidential election, copper had become the focal point of Chilean domestic politics. Senator Salvador

[14]   For accounts on the corporate history of Anaconda and Kennecott, see Marcosson (1957); O'Connor (1937); O'Hanlon (1966); U.S. Federal Trade Commission (1947); and McDonald (1951).

Allende, who came within 40,000 votes of being elected president of Chile in 1958, and who was now running as head of a leftist coalition in the 1964 election, sponsored a plan for the nationalization of the *Gran Mineria*. Meanwhile, the disaffection of Chilean conservative and business groups over the failure of the U.S. copper companies to contribute to Chilean expansion plans during the period of the "New Deal" legislation was now exacerbated by the intrusion of the Alliance for Progress program into Chilean politics in the early 1960's (Moran 1972:3–24). The Alliance for Progress called for sweeping reforms in Latin America, including a major land reform that posed a significant threat to conservative landholding interests in Chile. The threat posed by the Alliance for Progress only served to heighten the tensions between Chile and the copper companies. As early as 1961 the powerful Conservative Party Senator Francisco Bulnes voiced the growing bitterness about the copper companies in the right-wing newspaper, *El Diario Illustrado*:

There is no need for social change in Chile since the country has many social laws on the books for over 50 years. It would be better if the United States quit stirring up our economic and social problems. . . . What the country does need is huge new investments in copper production. The Nuevo Trato ("New Deal") has been a failure — merely the granting of exaggerated concessions to the companies in return for almost nothing. Therefore, if the companies cannot be made to launch a huge new program and let the proceeds flow to develop Chile as the Alliance envisions, the government should nationalize them! (quoted in Moran 1972:167).

This mounting opposition from left, right, and center groups in Chilean politics provided the context for Kennecott's offer to sell 51 percent of its share in Braden Copper Co., Kennecott's Chilean subsidiary. After only seven weeks in office President Frei was able to announce a $500 million expansion program that contained the following features: (1) the doubling of copper output to more than a million tons by 1970; (2) substantial government participation in copper production and exploration; (3) the tripling of Chilean copper-refining capacities by 1970; (4) considerable state control over sales; and (5) the opening of all world markets (including the Soviet Union) to Chilean copper (Mikesell 1970:375).

The basis of the copper expansion program was the purchase of the 51 percent controlling interest in the Braden Copper Co. and the expansion of its mine, El Teniente, the largest underground mine in the world. As part of the Chileanization agreements, Kennecott retained managerial decision-making authority and Chile reduced the tax rates on the companies as well as providing a twenty-year guarantee on these tax rates. The 1964 agreements did not include Chileanization of Anaconda but rather Anaconda agreed to expand its output by 53 percent between 1965 and 1970.

Kennecott asked for, and received, $81.6 million for the 51 percent of Braden Copper Co., whose book value had been only $65.7 million in 1963. Keith Griffin, in his analysis of the Chileanization agreements, argues that no matter which procedure one uses, "Braden was overvalued. Instead of the $180 million agreed upon, the true value of the enterprise was somewhere between 65.7 million and 119.82 million and the cost to Chile of a controlling interest should have been somewhere between 33.5 and 61.1 million" (Griffin 1969: 154). Moreover, Kennecott's share of the expansion program was financed by the receipts from Chile's payments for 51 percent of the stock of Braden, and the tax rates were cut so drastically (from 86 percent to 44 percent) that Kennecott's share as a 49 percent owner was greater than its share as a 100 percent owner. Since the absolute share of profits rose substantially as a result of the expansion, this meant that Kennecott's earnings from Chile increased for virtually no cash outlay on its part. "The beauty of the deal," according to a New York security analyst for Kennecott, "is that the Chileans are happy, and Kennecott is getting a bigger share of a bigger pie without any big outlay of new money from the states" (*Business Week* 1968).

Under the Chileanization program and the rise in copper prices during the Vietnam War the profits of Anaconda and Kennecott rose to unprecedented heights. Kennecott, which in 1965 made $8 million, withdrew $48 million from Chile in 1969. Anaconda increased its income from $187 million in the triennium 1965–1967 to $239 million in the period 1967–1970. Meanwhile, by 1970, production figures were still at their 1964 level and the refining program had only reached 360,000 tons or about 50 percent of what had been called for (Vaccaro 1971).

"Hanson's American Letter," used by investors in the United States, summed up the results of Chileanization as follows:

No government of the extreme right, in an agreement previously signed, had ever dealt with North American firms with the kind of generosity shown by the Frei government. Its excessively favorable treatment lacked so much balance and justice and was so prejudicial to Chilean interests that it almost provoked hilarity in Washington (quoted in Vaccaro 1971).

With the continuing loss of domestic support for the U.S. copper companies and the increasing Chilean competence in the running of the industry, the Chileanization agreements ended in nationalization. In 1969 Chile bought a 51 percent interest in the two largest Anaconda mines — Chuquicimata and El Salvador. The full nationalization of the mines was completed in July 1971 when Allende proclaimed full national ownership and control over the country's most important industry.

COPPER AS A LEADING SECTOR IN CHILEAN ECONOMIC DEVELOPMENT

The primary importance of Chile's ownership and control of the copper industry lies not only in its income-generating role but even more importantly in its role as a leading factor in the domestic industrialization process. Analyses of Chilean copper policy tend to focus on the returned value to Chile and assume a value of copper that is much lower than its *potential* value to Chile.[15] The potential value is that value of the final product if all its value was added in the Chilean economy. For more than two-thirds of a century the Chilean copper industry has been subjected to the needs of the corporate economies of Anaconda and Kennecott. During this time Chilean copper has supplied an important part of the raw material needs of the fabricating subsidiaries of these companies' plants in the United States. Because of the integration of Chilean production into the operations of Anaconda and Kennecott, Chile has foregone a substantial part of the potential value of copper in the fabricating and marketing stages. According to the U.S. Federal Trade Commission, "Reports of companies which fabricate as well as mine copper show that . . . the greater part of the profits came from the fabrication division of the operation" (U.S. Federal Trade Commission 1947). The price of fabricated copper is almost twice as high as the price of refined copper (Metal Statistics 1969:137), while the copper-refining charges are estimated to be less than ten percent of the price of unrefined copper (Herfindahl 1959:174–175). This amount of potential investible surplus is capable of providing Chile with an important source of investment to raise productivity in other sectors of the economy.

In addition to this potential surplus available to Chile, the copper industry occupies a strategic position in the economy in terms of promoting backward and forward linkages in the rest of the economy. As early as 1923 Santiago Machiavello anticipated the importance that Albert Hirschman was to ascribe to these linkage effects in the process of economic development. Machiavello argued (1923) that copper could serve as a leading factor for other industries on the supply or demand side such as petroleum, coal, iron and steel, sulphuric acid, agriculture, and metallurgy. At the same time that Machiavello was writing, the copper industry was not performing this role due primarily to the denationalization of the industry and the integration of Chilean production into an already vertically integrated industrial structure that received its required capital equipment from U.S. suppliers.

[15] The studies by Reynolds (1962) and Mamalakis, quoted in Mikesell (1970) focus on the returned value to Chile and assume that Chile would have no copper industry if the U.S. companies did not supply capital, technology, etc. An analysis that evaluates Chilean copper policy from the perspective of potential value can be found in Griss (1970).

Since the election of President Salvador Allende in 1970, the Chilean government had been pursuing a program of taking control of vital industries either through nationalization, stock purchase, or government intervention. The objective was to create a state-controlled integrated metallurgical complex. The initial components of such a complex are diagramed in Table 3.

Table 3.   Chile's integrated metallurgical complex

Backward linkages	Copper mines	Forward linkages
ARMCO – leading producer of grinding balls used in the copper-crushing process	Chuquicamata El Teniente	MADECO – largest maker of copper products
E. I. DuPont – explosives and refactory bricks	El Salvador La Exotica	NISBA – major producer of brass fittings and valves
El Melon and Cerro Blanco – the two largest cement producers	Rio Blanco	

Source: "Major interventions and nationalizations in Chile," *New Chile*, Berkeley, Calif.; North American Congress on Latin America, 1972, pp. 24–25.

THE CHILEAN MODEL AND THE INTERNATIONAL CONTEXT

It is possible to identify three major concerns that conditioned the response of the U.S. government and the U.S. copper companies to the Chilean nationalization of copper. The first major concern was the deteriorating position of the U.S. economy in 1971 and especially the chronic balance-of-payments deficit. In testimony before the Senate Subcommittee on International Trade, Kennecott Copper Corporation underscored the case for U.S. government support of multinational mining enterprises when it pointed out that:

In the decade of 1961–70, net capital outflows of the mining and smelting industry ran to about $2 billion. But receipts from abroad, including dividends, interest and branch profits, ran to $4.8 billion. Net contribution of the mining and smelting industry to the balance of payments was therefore close to $3 billion. . . . This contribution is the more impressive when we consider where mining investment is made . . . in the less developed nations of South America, Africa and Australia (Kennecott Copper Corporation 1972:263).

The second major concern of the U.S. government and the U.S. copper companies was the possibility that the Chilean nationalization might encourage other Third World nations seeking greater control over their natural resources to follow the Chilean route. When conflicts between MNC's and host countries arose in the past, it was usually possible for the MNC to threaten to move operations from one country to another and force a settlement of the conflict that would leave the MNC still in control. But at the beginning of the 1970's the situation was changed radically. The drive of economic nationalism was by no means limited to the Marxist government of Chile. At a State Department–sponsored seminar on the "Impact of Economic Nationalism on Key Mineral Resource Industries," a State Department spokesman raised the question as to

whether we are witnessing a basic change in the situation in that competition among host countries tends to be greatly attentuated because of the development of a common attitude, a common political philosophy, and because forums have developed in which they can concert their actions — UNCTAD, the Organization of Oil Exporting Countries, and Andean Pact and so on. More and more we seem to be confronted with a united front of host countries, and the possibilities of playing one against the other are greatly diminished. This may call for a different model, and it may call for a different policy (U.S. Department of State 1972:20–21).

John M. Hennessey, deputy assistant secretary of the Treasury for development finance (a man who helped shape U.S. policy toward Chile), stated the new "hard-line" policy of the government: "I think we assume there is a link between the availability of resources at a reasonable cost and foreign direct investment at this time. . . . At this moment the U.S. has a policy of wanting to promote foreign direct investment, which is why the OPIC (Overseas Private Investment Corporation) exists." Further, he stated, "we assume that the U.S. government *cannot* walk away from any significant expropriation" (U.S. Department of State 1972:119; emphasis added).

The third major concern involved the position of the U.S. copper companies within the international copper industry. Raymond Mikesell, an industry expert, articulated this concern at the State Department-sponsored seminar mentioned above: "Petroleum and mineral firms, regardless of their degree of vertical integration, desire to maintain their position in world markets, and with *control over sources of supply* their position is greatly impaired" (U.S. Department of State 1972:33; emphasis added). Although the international copper industry has long been characterized by a high degree of concentration and control (U.S. Federal Trade Commission 1947:3), there have been important trends undermining the strength of the producers' oligopoly at least since World

War II.[16] It is important to analyze these trends not only because they help us understand the behavior of the U.S. copper companies but because they also specify the conditions under which Chile had to develop its own vertical ties into the large industrial markets of the capitalist and socialist blocs.

Within the United States, the three largest copper producers — Anaconda, Kennecott, and Phelps Dodge — were able to maintain their share of domestic mine production above 80 percent from 1947 to 1954. But by 1960 their share had dropped to 69 percent, and by 1969 it had declined to 61 percent.[17] At the same time, there has been a rise in the number of major U.S. producers from three to eight. These eight include the big three — Anaconda, Kennecott, and Phelps Dodge — in addition to the "newcomers": American Smelting and Refining, Duval, Magma, Copper Range, and Inspiration.

The growth in the number of major oligopoly producers is even more striking at the international level. After World War II the big seven, including the Roan-American Metal group, the Anglo-American group, the Union Minière group, and International Nickel of Canada, as well as Anaconda, Kennecott, and Phelps Dodge, produced about 65 to 70 percent of "free world" copper from 1946 to 1954. By 1960 their share of world production had declined to 60 percent; by 1969 that figure went as low as 54 percent (see Table 4).[18]

Table 4.   Copper production in thousands of short tons

"Big Seven" companies	1948	1960	1969
Kennecott	514	571	699
Anaconda	362	476	597
Phelps Dodge	247	234	284
Roan-AMC group	134	241	368
Anglo-American group	118	392	426
Union Minière	171	331	399
International Nickel	118	155	110
Total	1,664	2,400	2,883
Percent of world production	70	60	54

Source: Elliot (1937)

[16] Theodore Moran (1970) points to five major factors that have accounted for the gradual breakup of the producers' oligopoly: (1) U.S. government intervention during wartime to subsidize small companies; (2) the diversification of companies into copper mining by either forming or buying a mining subsidiary; (3) the preference of companies that have formerly confined their interest almost entirely to smelting or refining to move backwards and develop their own source of supply; (4) the willingness of fabricators and consumers of copper to finance the development of new copper sources and to be paid back in output; and (5) the discovery of large new ore bodies. (See Chapter 1 of Moran).

[17, 18] These computations are based on figures given in the *Yearbook* of the American Bureau of Metal Statistics for the appropriate years (1947, 1948, 1954, 1960, 1969).

The figures above seem to indicate a definite trend in the direction of the dilution of concentration and control that was once exercised by a handful of producers in the international copper industry. The breakup of the producers' oligopoly had important implications for the maneuverability of Chile within this international industry.

One of the factors that has contributed to this dilution of concentration within the industry has been the willingness on the part of fabricators and consumers of copper to finance the development of new copper sources and to be paid back in output. Thus Chile had been able to channel large flows of capital into developing its small- and medium-sized mines because of such an arrangement with three Japanese fabricators, Dowa Mining, Mitsubishi Mining, and Mitsui Mining.

Furthermore, with the growth of many smaller producers since World War II — the "newcomers" — Chile had been able to play off one group against another. Thus one observes that while Kennecott was engaged in a desperate campaign to disrupt sales of Chilean copper (see next section), the Cerro Corporation had signed a contract to act as a purchasing agent for Chilean copper. The Cerro Corporation was a newcomer in Chilean mining and wanted to expand its sources of supply. The actions of Cerro, one of the giants of the U.S. metal industry, came as a blow to Anaconda and Kennecott. "Some people," sneered one copper executive at the time, "will do anything for money" (*Forbes* 1971). But inasmuch as Cerro's only other major copper holdings are in Peru, it could not afford to do otherwise. The Cerro case is just one example of the importance of the "newcomers" to the international copper oligopoly. U.S. Continental Copper and Steel Industries, Inc., concluded an agreement with the Chilean Development Corporation (CORFO) and Chilean private investors in 1969 for a medium-size mine that began operations in 1971. In addition, several Canadian firms including Noranda Mines and Canadian Javelin, Ltd., have also expressed interest in expanding their investments in the Chilean copper industry.

The significance of the newcomers to the copper industry lies not only in their importance for expanding the Chilean copper industry but particularly in their influence on the financial institutions of their respective home countries and in the multilateral financial institutions in which they have representation. Thus at a time when Chile was being denied credit at the Inter-American Development Bank (IDB) and the World Bank, it had no problems with the International Monetary Fund (IMF). In 1971 and 1972 the Allende government received $148 million from the IMF in partial compensation for the fall in the price of copper and from its normal allotment of drawing rights. Part of the explanation for this anomaly may be found in the stronger European influence and weaker U.S. influence in the IMF.

KENNECOTT DECLARES WAR

Since the decision of the Chilean government to deduct an excess-profits tax on the earnings of the U.S. copper companies since 1955 (excess profits were determined by comparing the rate of profit the nationalized companies earned in Chile to the return on capital invested elsewhere), Kennecott has been engaged in a campaign to disrupt the operations of the Chilean copper industry. It should be noted at this point that neither the principle of excess profits nor its retroactive application are novelties in U.S. law. The U.S. government imposed the same tax on the U.S. Steel Corporation after World War I (O'Connor 1939:84). Nevertheless, Kennecott has maintained that Chile acted in violation of international law and announced that it would be Kennecott's policy to "seize El Teniente copper wherever we find it" (*New York Times* 1972).

The immediate objectives of the harassment campaign were to destroy Chile's credibility as a reliable supplier of copper in the international marketplace and to inflict serious financial losses on the Chilean copper industry. It is unlikely that Kennecott ever seriously thought that it could recover its losses in Chile — with only 13 percent of its worldwide investments in Chile, Kennecott earned 21 percent of its total profits from Chile in 1970 (*New York Times* 1971) — by the series of court actions it was undertaking. The first series of suits that Kennecott brought against Chile, for alleged nonpayment of a debt, in New York federal district court resulted in the embargo of Chilean funds in New York bank accounts amounting to no more than $250,000 (*New York Times* 1972). Among the Chilean agencies affected by the embargo was the Chilean Copper Development Corporation (CODELCO), which was the largest single seller of copper in the world.

On October 4, 1972, the Braden Copper Company, a subsidiary of Kennecott, won a preliminary court action in a French court blocking payments to the Chilean government on a cargo of copper from Kennecott's former El Teniente mine. Kennecott sent letters to the usual buyers of Chilean copper warning them of its ability to embargo 49 percent of the metal that they may purchase. Chile's Minister Counsellor in Paris, Jorge Edwards, commented on the timing of the Kennecott move:

This week conversations are being held preparatory to drawing up contracts for the provision of Chilean copper to France and Western Europe in 1973. Kennecott has chosen a critical moment, one when such an embargo is particularly able to arouse anxiety and a sense of insecurity in Chile's regular copper consumers in Europe. It has selected France as the central consumer nation for Chilean copper in Europe (*Chile Economic News* 1972).

The series of court actions taken by Kennecott against Chile is indicative of the strategy of the multinationals to shift the greatest benefits of the industry from the production stage, over which they are losing control, to other stages over which they exercise more influence, such as the marketing and distribution stages of the industry. In terms of inflicting immediate economic damage on Chile, the moves of Kennecott were mildly successful. They resulted in the direct loss of $140,500 for Chile, and CODELCO was forced to reassign 5,000 tons of copper valued at $5 million to other buyers and markets. Kennecott initiated similar suits to obtain injunctions against Chilean ore deliveries across Europe but was rebuffed by courts in Britain, Italy, Sweden, and twice in the Netherlands. Industry opinion was divided on the wisdom of such a strategy. The staff of *Metals Week* noted at the time that ". . . the chances of a large American company winning such a case against a small emerging nation — given the present world climate — seem small, at least outside the U.S." (*Engineering and Mining Journal* 1973). Moreover, at the December 1972 meeting of the Organization of Copper-Exporting Countries (CIPEC, composed of Chile, Peru, Zaire, and Zambia, which together produced 44 percent of the world's copper), the group issued a declaration that they would not deal with Kennecott and that they would refrain from selling copper to markets traditionally serviced by Chilean copper (*Peruvian Times* 1973).

In terms of Kennecott's long-range interests, the risks inherent in pursuing this kind of a strategy were justified. At a time when Kennecott was carrying out delicate negotiations for new copper deposits in Puerto Rico, New Guinea, and Australia, it was imperative that the Chilean model not be seen as one that could be duplicated elsewhere.[19] Even in their summation before the French court, the Kennecott lawyers acknowledged that their actions were an exercise in "teaching Chile the political realities of life."

The timing of the Kennecott offensive in European courts suggests that the actions may have been part of the larger U.S. strategy to wreak havoc with the Chilean economy and provoke a military intervention that would overthrow the Allende government. As Kennecott sought to disrupt sales of Chilean copper in Europe, truck owners in Santiago went on strike for twenty-five days, causing considerable damage in the areas of production and distribution. When a *Forbes* reporter asked a State Department

[19]   In the course of negotiations for a mining permit from the government of Puerto Rico the Episcopal Church sponsored public hearings on copper mining in Puerto Rico. A major concern voiced at the public hearings was that 33⅓ percent of the profits from the mining would go to the government while 72 percent was recently paid by the same company to the government of Chile. (See Council on Economic Priorities 1971). After the government of New Guinea conferred with Peru, Zaire, Zambia, and Chile, it requested major changes in Kennecott's original proposal, particularly in the company's production, taxation, and financing plans. (See *Engineering and Mining Journal* 1973:34).

spokesman whether there was any consultation on Kennecott's problems the reply was: "Sure, we're in touch from time to time. They know our position." The reporter continued, "Which is?" "We're interested in solutions to problems. And you don't get solutions by sitting on your hands" (*Forbes* 1972).

The issue underlying the actions of Kennecott and the U.S. government was only tangentially related to the matter of the value of the uncompensated U.S. copper mines. The larger issues concerned the ability of the large, vertically integrated copper companies to maintain control of copper deposits and reserves on a world scale and the threat that a successful nationalization in Chile would pose for that control. It is only the realization that the Allende government's nationalization of copper provided a *viable alternative* to the domination of the Chilean economy by Kennecott and Anaconda that can explain the unyielding determination on the part of the U.S. government and U.S. corporations to bring the Chilean revolutionary process to a halt.

REFERENCES

ALLENDE, SALVADOR
 1953 Speech before Chilean Senate. January 28. Reprinted in *El Siglo*. January 29.
AMERICAN BUREAU OF METAL STATISTICS
 1947, 1948, 1954, 1960, 1969 *Yearbook*. New York.
AMERICAN METAL MARKET
 1969 *Metal statistics 1969: the purchasing guide to the metal industry*. New York.
ANACONDA CORPORATION
 1955 *Annual report*.
BAKLANOFF, ERIC N.
 1966 International taxation and mineral devélopment: the political economy of Chile's Le Gran Mineria de Cobre. *Proceedings of the 58th National Tax Conference*. Harrisburg, Pa.: National Tax Association.
BLAKEMORE, HAROLD
 1965 The Chilean revolution of 1891 and its historiography. *Hispanic American Historical Review* (45) August.
Business Week
 1968 December 7.
Chile Economic News
 1972 New York: CORFO. November 1.
COUNCIL ON ECONOMIC PRIORITIES
 1971 *Economic priorities report*. Volume two, number two. June–July.
Engineering and Mining Journal
 1972 October
 1973 July.
Forbes
 1971 "Breaking ranks." September 15.
 1972 "A neat job." December 1.

GIRVAN, NORMAN
   1970   Multinational corporations and dependent underdevelopment in mineral export economies. *Social and Economic Studies* 19(4).
   1972   *Copper in Chile.* Jamaica: University of West Indies.
GRIFFIN, KEITH
   1969   *Underdevelopment in Spanish America.* London: George Allen and Unwin.
GRISS, ROBERT
   1970   "The contribution of Chile's highly productive, American owned, export oriented copper industry to the internal development of Chile." Madison: University of Wisconsin, Department of Sociology. Mimeographed.
GRUNWALD, J., P. MUSGROVE
   1970   *Natural resources in Latin American development.* Baltimore: Johns Hopkins.
HERFINDAHL, O.C.
   1959   *Copper costs and prices: 1870–1957.* Baltimore: Johns Hopkins.
HIRIART, LUIS
   1964   *Braden, historia de una mina.* Santiago.
Historia de la ley
   1955   (1) 11.828. Santiago.
KENNECOTT COPPER CORPORATION
   1972   *The case for the multinational mining enterprise.* Testimony. United States Senate Finance Committee, Subcommittee on International Trade. December 29.
MACHIAVELLO, SANTIAGO
   1923   *El problema de la industria del cobre en Chile y sus proyecciones economicas y sociales.* Santiago.
MAMALAKIS, M., C. REYNOLDS
   1965   *Essays on the Chilean economy.* Homewood, Ill.: Richard D. Irwin.
MARCOSSON, ISAAC F.
   1957   *Anaconda.* New York.
MCDONALD, JOHN
   1951   The world of Kennecott. *Fortune.* November.
MIKESELL, RAYMOND, *editor*
   1970   *Foreign investment in the petroleum and mineral industries: case studies in investor-host country relations.* Baltimore: Johns Hopkins.
MORAN, THEODORE H.
   1970   "The multinational corporation and the politics of development: the case of copper in Chile 1945–1970." Unpublished thesis. Harvard University.
   1972   The Alliance for Progress and the foreign copper companies and their local conservative allies in Chile: 1955–1970. *Inter-American Economic Affairs* 25(4) Spring.
New York Times
   1971   January 25.
   1972a   March 10.
   1972b   November 5.
NOLFF, MAX
   1962   Industria manufacturera. *Geografía economica de Chile* (3). Santiago: CORFO.
O'CONNOR, HARVEY
   1937   *The Guggenheims.* New York.

1939 *Steel-Dictator*. New York: John Day.
O'HANLON, THOMAS
1966 The perilous prosperity of Anaconda. *Fortune*. May.
Panorama Economico
1952a May 9.
1952b September 26.
Peruvian Times
1973 "CIPEC committee meeting this month to work out producers' protective mechanisms." January 12.
PETRAS, JAMES
1972 Chile: no. *Foreign Policy*. Summer.
PFEIFFER, JACK B.
1952 Notes on the heavy equipment industry in Chile, 1800–1910. *Hispanic American Historical Review*. February.
PINTO, ANIBAL
1962 *Chile: un caso de desarrollo frustrado*. Santiago: Editorial Universitaria.
RAMÍREZ NECOCHEA, HERNÁN
1951 *La guerra civil de 1891: antecedentes economicos*. Santiago.
REYNOLDS, CLARK W.
1962 "Development problems of an export economy: the historical and developmental relationships of the copper industry to the economy of Chile." Unpublished Ph.D. dissertation, University of California, Berkeley.
RIPPY, J.F., J. PFEIFFER
1948 Notes on the dawn of manufacturing in Chile. *Hispanic American Historical Review*. May.
TILTON, JOHN E.
1966 The choice of trading partners: an analysis of international trade in aluminum, bauxite, copper . . . *Yale Economic Review*. Fall.
U.S. BUREAU OF MINES
1952 *Materials survey: copper*. VI:4. Washington: U.S. Government Printing Office.
U.S. DEPARTMENT OF STATE
1972 *Impact of economic nationalism on key mineral resource industries*. March 20. Washington: U.S. Government Printing Office.
U.S. FEDERAL TRADE COMMISSION
1947 *Report on the copper industry*. Washington: U.S. Government Printing Office.
VACCARO, ALBERTO
1971 Nacionalizacion del cobre en Chile. *Marcha*. October 21.
VERA VALENZUELA, MARIO
1961 *La politica economica del cobre en Chile*. Santiago: Universidad de Chile.
VIDELA LIRA, HERNÁN
1954 Speech in *Boletín Minero,* March–April.

Automobiles: an Obstacle to Socialist Construction

DAVID BARKIN

During the three years of administration under the Popular Unity (UP) government of Salvador Allende in Chile, systematic efforts were considered to ensure that the social and economic structure of Chilean society would be permanently altered. Many policymakers were highly conscious of the need for each new decision to be consistent with the overriding objective of creating the conditions for a future transition to socialism.[1] This was an essential part of the overall plan to gradually incorporate workers into the collective effort and assist in the immediate task of breaking the historical pattern of a government apparatus at the service of an elite. Many government policies were promulgated in the short period of UP administration that effectively redistributed incomes and changed the consciousness of the people with regard to the possibility of constructing a more equitable socioeconomic framework.

This short article discusses some problems that arose in connection with a decision to rationalize automobile production by creating several new companies with governmental and foreign capital to produce a limited number of models efficiently. The decision to produce automobiles not only foreclosed the possibility of further public investments in other key areas and indirectly reduced the pressures from influential sectors for mass transit. It also implied that the government did not feel prepared to eliminate the high concentration of income among the rich in Chile, which was the basis for the pent-up demand for automobiles to which the new policy was responding.

The alternative lines of analysis presented here were not accepted by the government, although they were the subject of a lively debate within

---

[1] For a fuller account of the Popular Government's program see Salvador Allende's first message to Congress (21 May 1971) published in *Allende* (1971).

both governmental and opposition circles. The paper is offered here because it suggests some of the ways in which policies affect peoples' lives in general and the danger of traditional solutions in new settings.

Instead of definitive answers, we suggest lines of analysis and questions about the total impact of the Chilean decision. We raise doubts both of an economic nature, that is, in relation to the allocation of resources; as well as of a political nature, referring to the relationship of the workers to the new productive and distributive structure.

THE AUTOMOTIVE DECISION

In June 1971, bids were solicited from automobile producers around the world. The purpose was to reduce the number of different models of vehicles produced by the Chilean automotive industry and to make production more responsive to the needs of the domestic and export markets. The goals were: (1) to produce commercial and private vehicles for mass consumption; (2) to upgrade the technology of the domestic industry and create a technological infrastructure that would permit the development of new export industries; (3) to create, directly or indirectly, high-productivity jobs; (4) to obtain additional tax revenues and profits for reinvestment by government; (5) to balance the foreign-exchange cost, which the satisfaction of the demand for automobiles requires, with exports; and (6) to achieve levels of efficiency so as to be able to compete successfully in trade with other member states of the Latin American Common Market and the Andean Pact.

Table 1. Bases for automobile bidding

Category	Number of units produced 1973	1980[a]
Small automobile, light truck, van, and related (up to 1,200 cc.)	20,000	45,000
Small automobile, light truck, van, and related (up to 2,000 cc.)	15,000	40,000
Diesel chassis for trucks, buses and other utility vehicles	5,000	15,000

Source: CORFO (1971).
[a] Projected.

To achieve these goals, production was to be limited to three models: a small vehicle with an engine of less than 1,200 cc.; a medium-size vehicle with an engine of less than 2,000 cc.; and a chassis for diesel trucks, buses, and other commercial vehicles. Production would increase from the 20,000 units produced in 1970 to 100,000 units in 1980; the goals were 45,000 small vehicles, 40,000 intermediate vehicles, and 15,000 diesels.

Preliminary proposals were sought from companies willing to enter into a joint venture with the Chilean Development Corporation (CORFO) to produce these vehicles with only a minority participation in the new businesses. Nine proposals were proffered in September 1971 to produce one or more of the vehicles; no North American firm was represented in spite of the fact that both Ford and General Motors had assembly plants in Chile at the time.

RELATION TO THE DISTRIBUTION OF INCOME

The first question posed by many was whether an increase in automotive production was compatible with the sizable redistribution of income promised by the Allende government. Most, if not all, of the answers to this question have been negative. During the past presidential campaign, for example, Radomiro Tomic, the Christian Democratic candidate, declared:

It is a very grave error against the long-term interests of the nation to stimulate the production and sales of automobiles for the internal market . . . the owners of the vehicles will (in 1980) barely represent five per cent of the population (Tomic 1969).

Household expenditure data do indeed show that the wealthiest 5 percent of the population, which earned more than eight times the average annual wage, purchased more than 75 percent of all automobiles sold in Chile in 1969. It is clear, therefore, that the private car was a luxury consumption item in most cases and, therefore, satisfied the demands of only a narrow privileged class.[2]

Table 2. Distribution of personal income and expenditures on individual transportation equipment – 1969[2]

Income	Annual average family income	Percent of families	Percent of family expenditures on transportation equipment	Percent of total consumption of transportation equipment
0–2	8.863	31.2	0.1	0.5
2–4	14–20	35.0	0.1	1.1
4–6	21.309	14.06	1.2	8.1
6–8	30.094	14.3	1.6	14.8
8–more	53.035	4.9	13.2	75.5

Source: CORFO (1971).

[2] Transportation equipment includes bicycles, which explains expenditures in low-income categories.

From an analysis of possible redistributive programs we determined that it would not have been possible to market successfully the planned 1980 production of 85,000 automobiles, even if there had been any sizable transfer of income from the upper classes to the working classes and peasantry. In view of this we must conclude that *the automotive program was incompatible with a progressive program of income redistribution.*

THE AUTOMOBILE AND PUBLIC FUNDS

A second widely discussed question is the effect that an expansion of the number of automobiles would have had on the need for roads and parking facilities, especially in the large metropolitan areas. Here too, the commentators agreed about the injurious effects of such an expansion. Thus, Tomic noted that an even less ambitious program drawn up in 1969 would require a widening of city streets that would cost several times the outlays for the cars themselves. He estimated that one-third of the nation's savings might be needed for such a task (Tomic 1969).

It seems almost unnecessary to detail the impact of an increase in the automotive stock from the approximately 220,000 vehicles now in Chile to the more than 500,000 in 1980 if the plan were fully implemented. With most of the new vehicles concentrated in the capital city, Santiago, it is likely that the number of private cars in Santiago alone would have increased from about 50,000 in 1970 to 250,000 in 1980. To anyone familiar with Santiago such an increase in autos clearly held the promise of interminable traffic delays, air pollution comparable to that of the dirtiest cities in the world, and an expensive and nerve-shattering series of "urban improvements" to permit the private car some minimal movement in the metropolitan area.

Although it would be foolhardy without closer study to attempt to estimate the costs of even the barest minimum of public works (such as new urban streets and highways) that would have been needed to service these vehicles, some comments are in order. Even at present there are enormous deficiencies in the road system for the basic needs of collective (mass) transportation and industrial production. These deficiencies are especially serious where the poorest groups live. The new vehicles were to have been purchased by people living in areas that already have the best road systems and highest incomes. But even these relatively good road systems would have been woefully inadequate for the proposed increase in cars. Their owners would strongly press for further road expenditures in areas where there is relatively the least need for them at present. As in other aspects of the market economy, the tendency would be to exacerbate the existing inequalities rather than to facilitate necessary structural change.

Regardless of the strategy followed, sizable investments were to have been made in the construction, expansion, and maintenance of the road system in the coming years. A doubt arises, however, about the size and design of the new projects. Stress should have been placed on mass transport needs. Expenditures for facilities to satisfy the demands of individuals in the upper classes for more and better roads on which to use their private cars are not consistent with the present stage of Chilean development — even if they were financed out of resources provided by the new-car owners themselves through tolls and taxes.

Our position is based on the obvious scarcity of resources. There are clearly many unsatisfied demands through the country, and a road project would have required that the building of some other vital facility be sacrificed. The government's most important task was to establish priorities for the many demands placed on it; the Popular Government had explicitly expressed its intention to systematically benefit the working classes, in contradistinction to the historical tendency to channel public funds and programs toward the upper-middle and upper classes for their own benefit and that of international capitalists. Roads for private automobiles do not contribute to this new goal.

Increased production of private automobiles was in direct competition with the satisfaction of social (collective) needs. At present mass transport is scarce and is particularly poorly designed for the needs of the working classes. There is no doubt that these services should be expanded. However, the private car competes directly with mass transport not only for space on the city streets but also within the halls of power. A decision to support mass transport probably requires a struggle against those who support automobile production in all but the most affluent of nations.

THE ECONOMICS OF AUTOMOBILES

It is clear that the policymakers' basic assumption when deciding to expand the automotive industry was that it would make a substantial contribution to overall growth, both through direct increases in production as well as through derived demand in other industries. This rationale emerges from the framework of bourgeois economics, in which industrial demand is insufficient to sustain an acceptable rate of economic growth. The auto industry is attractive because of the complex and numerous productive relationships it has with other industries in both manufacturing and services. It was ideal to planners because, once stimulated, it generates a pattern of self-sustained growth without the need for further bureaucratic intervention. Along with advertising and imported cultural patterns, this "demonstration effect" assures auto producers of an adequate pent-up demand as long as some means is found to finance new-car purchases. In this setting, the State creates incentives for industries that will generate self-sustaining growth processes.

The automotive industry seemed to offer an easy route to maintain growth while the Chilean road to socialism was being defined and prepared. The latent demand of elites for more cars could be satisfied with foreign capital anxious to gain a foothold in a potentially profitable auto industry; the foreign partners also would provide the technical assistance and plans necessary for its implementation. A decision to change radically the economic structure and undertake a different development strategy would have required not only the mobilization of new human and material resources in an economy where there were few reserves, especially of qualified people, but also the political power to obtain the understanding and cooperation of those people accustomed rather to the bourgeois pattern of consumption.

Finally, the upper-middle-income groups expected the continued production of private cars, one of their most important prestige symbols. In the charged political environment, restriction of the growth of durable-goods production — like autos — might have been interpreted as an attack on economic freedom. The new automotive industry was the government's way of showing its willingness to take the demands of the more affluent classes into consideration.

Some of these hopes, however, seemed ill-placed, even at the time. The automotive industry does not represent a clear improvement over alternative investments. Its technology, for example, is too specific to have many applications elsewhere. Potential foreign-exchange savings, resulting from making a greater proportion of the parts domestically, would have been more than offset by the increased use of foreign exchange due to the larger volume of production. The employment effect would also probably be less than if the resources were reallocated to investments that utilize less capital and more labor and are more attuned to the immediate needs of the people.

The traditional approach that dictates the production of private autos was a *dangerous* one in spite of the short-run advantages considered above. The expansion of the automotive industry was not a short-run decision whose effects could later be changed. It would reinforce a capitalist pattern of development, one based on a market generated by the existing distribution of income and one that leads to the production and distribution of luxury consumption goods at the expense of the basic needs of the working classes. In the bourgeois scheme, effective demand was the source of productive decisions, and income would have had to remain highly concentrated in capitalist hands to maintain an automobile industry.

SOCIALISM AND ECONOMIC STRATEGY

The transition to socialism offers an alternative more consistent with long-term goals: the re-structuring of production on the basis of social needs rather than private consumer demand, be it actual or potential. That is, the transition to socialism makes possible, or perhaps essential, a change in the industrial structure from one based on consumer demand and under-utilization of productive potential toward one based on needs, defined by a political process, and the full utilization of the nation's human and productive capacity.

In this new context, the political basis for the determination of productive decisions would be mass organizations that participate in the definition of a new policy for consumption. They would encourage workers to exercise political power to ensure that every family receives an adequate quantity of goods for its own welfare and that available luxury goods are not a source of further problems. In such a setting of course, no new luxury goods would be produced. Only in this way can the population actively participate in and help implement a long-term development program that would permit high rates of investment and a proper allocation of scarce resources.

This alternative might be considered complementary to one that accepted the expansion of durable-goods production. Yet, in a poor country like Chile most of these goods must inevitably be luxuries, whose production would require a diversion of resources from mass consumption or investment. Even more important, however, the consumption of these goods would perpetuate the differentiation in personal status, with a consequent heightening of group conflict.[3]

It is precisely for this reason that the decision to expand the automotive industry was most incongruous. Its expansion would have had to depend on a high concentration of income and on differentiated consumption among classes. The government would have had to create propitious conditions for the workers to assume power and improve their living standards while its short-run efforts at stimulating economic activity — building autos — would not have served the workers' needs. The consequence of continuing inequality inherent in this decision is striking and in sharp contrast with a strategy to prepare the way for socialism.

A short parenthetical comment is needed here. The previous comments about the automobile are based on its traditional role and distribution throughout society; I do not wish to totally disregard the important functions that individual vehicles could serve. Rather, I think that present capacity is sufficient to allow individuals freedom of movement in areas where public transport is inadequate or inappropriate. At a

[3] For a further consideration of some of these issues, see Barkin (1973).

later stage of development the possibility of restructuring the distribution system to permit individuals to rent cars for short periods might avoid the stratifying effects of vehicle ownership without eliminating the benefits and flexibility that it offers. For the immediate future, the possibility of restricting vehicular traffic in urban areas would contribute to a fuller use of a well-designed public transport system.

A new economic strategy must clearly define the basic requirements of the population and create the productive capacity to satisfy them. The definition of need itself will determine the structure of the economy. In most capitalist nations real needs are determined by family incomes, materialist culture, and market structures that often channel demands away from socially desirable expenditures; government social-welfare programs only temper the cruelty of market forces — in employment and high prices — for some of the poorest groups. In Chile, on the other hand, people were groping for a way to make fundamental changes in consumption patterns and the basic definition of needs. With a redistribution of wealth and power to the workers there would be greater need for wage goods — principally foodstuffs and nondurable goods — but there would also be a massive expansion of collective services.

The importance of collective services cannot be overstated. It stems from the need to provide a certain minimum to all and to broaden the area in which the workers can control their own lives. Collective services open greater possibilities for local decisions to be taken about production and distribution; these services include education, health care, day-care centers, cultural activities, and public transportation, among others. Their initial organization would be difficult because the private-enterprise system generally is unwilling to divert the necessary resources to these vital areas affecting human welfare; new systems of management and decision-making have to be designed and implemented.

The Popular Government's actions reflected the urgency of providing collective services. They were important in helping eliminate the intergenerational transfer of poverty characteristic of capitalist societies. Equality is not only a function of income and consumption but also of access to culture and schooling, in addition to medical services oriented toward prevention rather than cure. The social position and geographic location of parents should not predetermine the status of their children *if* the immediate goal is a change in the prevailing system of social stratification. A change in the form of ownership of the means of production can only be a first step; it alone cannot guarantee equality of opportunity. The general provision of basic services and the guarantee of minimum levels of consumption is an important facet of a program encouraging equality.

One further area that also requires heavy investments is housing. The capitalist economy is generally unprepared to satisfy the basic needs of its proletariat for housing. Consequently it is one of the most pressing problems facing a revolutionary administration. Its solution cannot be found in the context of a bourgeois economy, where experience has demonstrated an absence of technological innovations to produce inexpensive but serviceable housing.

This general listing of the broad characteristics of a program of mass consumption suggests that the investment program that should have been implemented in Chile would have been very different from that of past decades. The program offers several advantages when compared with a program whose point of departure is the development of the automotive industry. First, it could have a sizable employment effect, since in addition to agriculture, which any government would have to develop, a large part of the improvement in living conditions would come from personal services provided by people for each other. Housing and necessary public works would further contribute to the task of productively incorporating large numbers of people into the labor force. Second, this type of program would require fewer imports than others, since the manpower and materials are available domestically and the country has an ample agricultural potential to develop.

Finally, investment would have to be reemphasized. Only by gradually restraining new demands for consumption would a government be able to divert resources from an economy oriented toward luxury consumption to one responding more to the basic needs of the entire population. This type of restriction on the availability of goods would be all the more difficult if the economy was still producing durable consumption goods in which the increases in production come at the sacrifice of heavy investments and foreign purchases for national development.

CONCLUSIONS

The decision to expand the automotive industry to produce 100,000 vehicles of different types in 1980, with an emphasis on the private car, was a serious error. Not only would it require the maintenance of the existing high concentration of income and divert scarce government funds from other areas with higher social priorities, but it would also further weaken the possibility of improving public transportation and increase air pollution.

But these simple objective criteria are less important for the construction of socialism than the considerations in regard to social relations and stratification. We have seen the difference between a program based on the production of expensive consumer durables and one based on the provision of collective services for all. The short-lived drive to socialism in Chile only permitted short-run improvements in living standards for most of the population. The automobile not only would have been sold to the affluent classes but its continued production would also have called into question the government's ability and willingness to reduce class differences.

REFERENCES

ALLENDE, SALVADOR
    1971   Postscript to *The Chilean revolution: conversations with Allende*. Edited by Regis Debray. New York: Vintage.

BARKIN, DAVID
    1973   "The redistribution of consumption in Cuba," in *Cuba: the logic of the revolution*. Edited by David Barkin. Andover, Mass.: Warner Modular Publications.

CORFO
    1971   *Licitación Publica Internacional, Industria Automotriz*. Chile.

TOMIC, RADOMIRO
    1969   Revolución chilena y Unidad Popular. Speech before National Board, Christian Democratic Party. May.

Biographical Notes

DAVID BARKIN (1942–   ) is Professor of Economics at the Universidad Autonoma Metropolitana in Mexico City and Research Director at the Centro de Ecodesarrollo (National Council of Science and Technology). He has done extensive research on problems of economic strategy and development in Mexico, Chile, and Cuba; he is particularly interested in the problems of developing alternative economic strategies for the transition to socialism. Among his recent publications are *Cuba: Camino abierto* (1978) (in English, *Cuba: The logic of the revolution*); *Desarrollo Regional y Reorganización Campesina* (Regional Development and Peasant Reorganization) (México: Nueva Imagen, 1978), and numerous articles on economic problems in Mexico, Cuba, and the United States.

GEORGE BECKFORD (1934–   ) was born in Jamaica. He received his B.Sc. from McGill University in 1958 and his Ph.D. from Stanford University in 1962. In the late 1960's he was Editor of *New World* quarterly and is now Professor of Political Economy, UWI, Mona, Jamaica.

JOHN H. BODLEY (1942–   ) is Associate Professor of Anthropology at Washington State University where he has taught since 1970. He received his Ph.D. from the University of Oregon in 1970 and has conducted fieldwork among the Campa and Shipibo of eastern Peru. Recent publications include: *Victims of progress* (1975), *Anthropology and contemporary human problems* (1976).

MINA DAVIS CAULFIELD (1931–   ) is a lecturer in Anthropology at San Francisco State University. She received her B.A., M.A., and Ph.D. at the University of California at Berkeley, and conducted her dissertation research in the Caribbean. Her publications include studies of slavery in the Americas, the effects of imperialism on the position of women, and anthropological theory on sex oppression.

SHELTON H. DAVIS (1942–   ) is Visiting Assistant Professor of Anthropology at the Massachusetts Institute of Technology and Director of the Anthropology Resource Center in Cambridge, Massachusetts. He received his Ph.D. in anthropology from Harvard University and has taught at the Federal University of Rio de Janeiro and Harvard University. His recent publications include *The geological imperative* (with Robert O. Mathews, 1976) and *Victims of the miracle: Development and the Indians of Brazil* (1977).

AL GEDICKS (1948–   ) is Director of the Center for Alternative Mining Development Policy and a lecturer in the Department of Sociology at the University of Wisconsin in Madison. He will receive his Ph.D. in sociology from the University of Wisconsin in August of 1978. Since 1971 he has been Research Coordinator for Community Action on Latin America, a Madison-based anti-imperialist research and action collective. He is an advisor to several Indian tribes on mineral resource development and has just completed "Raw materials: The Achilles heel of American imperialism?" which appears in *The Insurgent Sociologist*, Vol. 7 No. 4 (Winter 1978).

GERRIT HUIZER (1929–   ) studied social psychology at Amsterdam University and has been active in community development and peasant organization since 1955. He worked as a volunteer in a village in Central America and later with Danilo Dolci in Sicily. From 1962 to 1971 he worked with different agencies of the United Nations (particularly ILO) in Latin America and Southeast Asia in field projects and action research. He has written numerous articles in literary and professional journals and readers and a book, *The revolutionary potential of peasants in Latin America* (1972, Lexington, Mass.: Heath Lexington Books) which came out also in Spanish and a Dutch version and in an abridged edition (*Peasant rebellion in Latin America*, 1973, Harmondsworth: Penguin). He has been Visiting Professor at the Institute of Social Studies, The Hague, and Fellow of the Institute of Development Research in Copenhagen and has been Director of the Third World Centre, University of Nijmegen, Netherlands, since 1973.

AHAMED IDRIS-SOVEN (1947–   ) is a physician whose research interests are in the field of multinational corporations, social change, and health. He is past director of the Corporate Research Institute, and part of the Deltec Research Project — the work of which appears in this volume.

ELIZABETH IDRIS-SOVEN (1950–   ) studied Anthropology at Vassar College and the University of Chicago, and Sociology at Northwestern University. She is presently a Research Fellow in Public Health at Northwestern University. As an applied anthropologist she has consulted for the American Indian Business Association, the United Steelworkers Union, Corporate Research Institute, and other organizations. She has done extensive lecturing and public education, including film-making, on the social and economic impact of multinational corporations.

STEVEN W. LANGDON (1946–   ) is Assistant Professor of Economics at Carleton University in Ottawa, Canada. He received his B.A. from the University of Toronto, his M.A. from Carleton University, and his D.Phil. in African political economy from the University of Sussex in the United Kingdom. As part of his doctoral research, he spent 1972–1973 in East Africa investigating the impact of multinational corporations on economic and political change in Kenya. His present research concentrates on Canadian and European industrial adjustment to Third World manufacturing expansion, and on the political economy of technology transfer to the Third World. He has also published earlier research on the growth of nineteenth century working-class movements in Canada.

BERNARD MAGUBANE (1930–   ) was educated at the University of Natal (B.A. in sociology and native administration, 1958; M.A., 1960) and at U.C.L.A. (M.A. in Sociology, 1964; Ph.D., 1967). He has been a lecturer at the University of Zambia (1967–1969) and a visiting lecturer at U.C.L.A. (January–June 1970), a Research Fellow of the American Friends Service Committee in Pasadena, California, in a study of the problems of unemployed young Negro males, and a Research Assistant for a U.C.L.A. School of Public Health study of habits associated with heart ailments. His M.A. thesis "Sports and politics in an urban African town" became the basis of a chapter entitled "Politics of football: the urban and district African Football Association" in Leo Kuper's book, *An African bourgeoisie* (1965). Papers by him dealing with social change in Africa have appeared in *African Social Research, Race, East African Journal*, and *The African Political Review*. He is now teaching at the University of Connecticut in Storrs.

GREGORY PALAST is an underpaid economist consultant to U.S. labor unions, including the steel, electrical and other unions. Mr. Palast, a resident of Chicago, teaches at Indiana University. He received his M.B.A. from the University of Chicago Graduate School of Business.

PAUL SHANKMAN (1943–   ) is an Assistant Professor of Anthropology at the University of Colorado. He received his B.A. from the University of

California at Santa Barbara and his Ph.D. from Harvard University. His research in Western Samoa has focused on issues in economic development. Among his recent publications is a monograph, *Migration and underdevelopment: The case of western Samoa* (1976).

BRUCE VANDERVORT (1940–   ) was born in Wisconsin, U.S.A. A holder of B.A. and M.A. degrees in modern European history and modern French history from the Universities of Wisconsin and Cincinnati (U.S.A.), he is currently preparing a Ph.D. dissertation at the University of Wisconsin on pre-1914 French revolutionary syndicalism. From 1972–1976 he worked as an editor and researcher for the International Union of Food and Allied Workers, and the International Federation of Building and Wood Workers in Geneva. Currently a journalist accredited to the United Nations in Geneva, Vandervort writes on trade and development questions for a variety of British and American publications.

MARY KAY VAUGHAN (1942–   ) is Assistant Professor of History and Latin American Studies at the University of Illinois-Chicago Circle. She received her bachelor's degree in modern European history from Cornell University and her M.A. and Ph.D. degrees in Latin American history at the University of Wisconsin-Madison. Her various publications include works on Mexican education, Latin American women, and transnational corporations in Latin America and the United States.

ANTHONY WILDEN (1935–   ) was born in London, studied at the Universities of Victoria and British Columbia, and obtained his Ph.D. degree at Johns Hopkins in 1968. He has taught literature and communications at the University of California, San Diego, and has been a Visiting Professor of Sociology at the Université du Bénin, Togo, West Africa, and the École Pratique des Hautes Études, Sorbonne, Paris, and a Research Associate of the National Science Foundation on the project "Design and Management of Environmental Systems" at Michigan State University. He also served as a consultant to the Research Division of La Radio-Télévision Française. He published three books and fifteen articles on the subjects of communication theory, information theory, epistemology, psychoanalysis, cybernetics and ecosystem and has been a Consulting Editor of *Psychology Today*. Currently he is in the Department of Communication, Simon Fraser University, Burnaby, B.C., Canada.

Index of Names

Index of Subjects